CAMBRIDGE TEXTS IN THE
HISTORY OF POLITICAL THOUGHT

JOHN LOCKE

*Two Treatises of
Government*

CAMBRIDGE TEXTS IN THE
HISTORY OF POLITICAL THOUGHT

Series editors

RAYMOND GEUSS
Professor of Philosophy, University of Cambridge

QUENTIN SKINNER
Professor of the Humanities, Queen Mary, University of London

Cambridge Texts in the History of Political Thought is now firmly established as the major student textbook series in political theory. It aims to make available to students all the most important texts in the history of western political thought, from ancient Greece to the early twentieth century. All the familiar classic texts will be included, but the series seeks at the same time to enlarge the conventional canon by incorporating an extensive range of less well-known works, many of them never before available in a modern English edition. Wherever possible, texts are published in complete and unabridged form, and translations are specially commissioned for the series. Each volume contains a critical introduction together with chronologies, biographical sketches, a guide to further reading and any necessary glossaries and textual apparatus. When completed, the series will aim to offer an outline of the entire evolution of western political thought.

For a list of titles published in the series, please see end of book.

JOHN LOCKE

Two Treatises of Government

EDITED WITH
AN INTRODUCTION
AND NOTES BY

PETER LASLETT

Fellow of Trinity College,
Cambridge

STUDENT EDITION

CAMBRIDGE
UNIVERSITY PRESS

CONTENTS

FOREWORD
(to the Student Edition, 1988)

This is a somewhat reduced version of the scholarly edition originally published in 1960 with a second edition in 1967, latest printing 1988. Much of the scholarly apparatus has been dropped here: the lists of books Locke had in his possession at times relevant to the composition of *Two Treatises*, the List of Printings, the Collation, the successive Forewords to successive printings. All these have been retained in the 1988 printing of the scholarly edition, to which those to whom final detail is important are referred.

Advantage has been taken of the appearance of the book in the Cambridge Texts in the History of Political Thought series to make some alterations not yet present in the scholarly edition. The extremely small number of errors in Locke's own text have been amended, though none of them alters the sense in any respect. The Introduction, its footnotes and the footnotes to Locke's text have been quite extensively corrected, but mainly so as to take account of work done after the second edition of 1971 until the later 1970s. As far as possible, moreover, all contributions made since then which touch on the facts about the writing and publication of Locke's political work have been taken into account. The book cannot, however, claim to cover the whole body of extant scholarship on Locke's *Two Treatises*, and for that reason a list of suggested reading has been added before the Bibliography. One further addition has been made, an Addendum to the Introduction commenting on Professor Richard Ashcraft's recent attempt to amend in detail the account given here of the dates of composition and the order in which the *First* and *Second Treatises* were written.

I should like to record my thanks to Dr Zbigniew Rau for his help with the revisions made to this text. Dr Rau of Lodz University and sometime Visiting Fellow Commoner of Trinity College is the latest of the Cambridge Lockeans, a series which began in the 1950s.

P.L.
TRINITY COLLEGE, CAMBRIDGE
March 1988

The system used for referring to sources and authorities
is described on pp. 132–3.

I

THE BOOK

'Property I have nowhere found more clearly explained, than in a book entitled, Two Treatises of Government.' This remark was made by John Locke in 1703, not much more than a year before he died. It must be a rare thing for an author to recommend one of his own works as a guide to a young gentleman anxious to acquire 'an insight into the constitution of the government, and real interest of his country'. It must be even rarer for a man who was prepared to do this, to range his own book alongside Aristotle's *Politics* and Hooker's *Ecclesiastical Polity*, to write as if the work were written by somebody else, somebody whom he did not know. Perhaps it is unique in a private letter to a relative.* What could possibly be the point of concealing this thing, from a man who probably knew it already?

Odd as it is, this statement of Locke anticipates the judgement of posterity. It was not long before it was universally recognized that Locke on *Government* did belong in the same class as Aristotle's *Politics*, and we still think of it as a book about property, in recent years especially. It has been printed over a hundred times since the 1st edition appeared with the date 1690 on the title-page. It has been translated into French, German, Italian, Russian, Spanish, Swedish, Norwegian, Hebrew, Arabic, Japanese and Hindi: probably into other languages too. It is an established classic of political and social theory, perhaps not in the first flight of them all, but familiar to eight generations of students of politics all over the world, and the subject of a great body of critical literature.

The prime reason for the importance attached to this book of Locke's is its enormous historical influence. We shall not be concerned here with the part which it played in the growth to maturity of English liberalism, or in the development of those movements which had their issue in the American Revolution, the French Revolution and their parallels in southern America, in Ireland, in

---

* The Rev. Richard King. Locke's letter to him of 25 August 1703 is printed in *Works*, 1801, x, 305–9. They had a mutual cousin in Sir Peter, later Lord King.

India—everywhere where government by consent of the governed has made its impact felt. We shall certainly have to decide whether or not the book was worthy of the effect it has had, or perhaps to work out a criterion to make such a decision possible. But our first object must be a modest historian's exercise—to establish Locke's text as he wanted it read, to fix it in its historical context, Locke's own context, and to demonstrate the connection of what he thought and wrote with the Locke of historical influence.

We may begin with Locke's own attitude to his own work on government. Our direct evidence is meagre, for we have only two further references to the book by name from Locke himself. One is an exactly similar recommendation made in the same year in *Some Thoughts Concerning Reading and Study for a Gentleman.** This makes no mention of property, but the tendency is clear enough, and it marks his recognition of the uses which the work would have, the same for *Two Treatises of Government* as for everything else he published. They were to be part of the assimilated atmosphere of the English gentleman, the Member of Parliament, the administrator and politician, at home and overseas, but above all the landowner, the local notable.

In the third and most important reference of all he finally did acknowledge his authorship. He was addressing himself to posterity rather than to his contemporaries, to us who can only read him and not to those who could have known him: it was made in a codicil to his will, signed only a week or two before he died. He was listing his anonymous works for the benefit of the Bodleian Library, and he wrote:

'I do hereby give to the public library of the University of Oxford. . . . *Two Treatises of Government* (whereof Mr Churchill has published several editions, but all very incorrect).'†

Without this final, almost accidental afterthought we should have no direct proof that he wrote the book at all.‡ His anxiety to keep the secret is the more remarkable in that his responsibility was widely suspected from the time of publication. It was talked of in Oxford in 1689, and in 1690 Molyneux was told in London

* *Works*, 1801, III, 272.

† Will, dated 7 April 1704; codicil, 15 September 1704. This clause is printed in *Works*, 1st edition, 1714, as part of the preface. Locke died 28 October 1704.

‡ Though there is conclusive circumstantial evidence. In the former Whitehouse Collection (now MS. Locke b. 8) there are papers of corrections in his hand for the 1694 printing.

that he wrote the work. In 1693 Bayle referred to Locke's authorship as if it were generally known, even on the continent.* Early in 1695 an Englishman wrote casually enough about the second printing, in a private letter. 'Here is a book written by Mr Locke which makes a great noise, called *Two Treatises of Government*, price 3s. 6d. This Locke was expelled from Christ Church College for his Presbyterian principles and was chaplain to the Earl of Shaftesbury.' Inaccurate in detail, but apt in general, this judgement may have been based on special information. Although it would seem that his most hostile critic, John Edwards, was not in the secret in 1697, it was being referred to openly in print in the following year.† Walter Moyle, in his *Essay on the Lacedaemonian Government*, declared: 'I would advise you to read first the answer that has been made to *Filmer* by Mr *Locke*, and his *Essay of the Original, Extent and End of Civil Government*; that piece contains the first Rudiments upon this subject. I know a Gentleman, who calls it the A.B.C. of *Politicks*.'

Molyneux in 1698 was not so frank, but even more complimentary: he called it 'An Incomparable *Treatise*, . . . said to be written by my Excellent Friend, JOHN LOCKE, *Esq*; Whether it be so or not, I know not; This I am sure, whoever is the Author, the greatest Genius in *Christendom* need not disown it.' Leibniz was told in far less enthusiastic terms in the same year of Locke's 'heroic' refutation of Filmer, as if its anonymity was of no account and as a postscript to a notice of Sidney's much more conspicuous volume which had just appeared. In 1701 the most powerful and important of all Locke's friends, John, Lord Somers, cited the book with marked deference to its author: his clear implication was that he knew who wrote it and so did his readers.‡

By then, no doubt, Locke had told the great man by word of mouth that the book indeed was his, as he had told Tyrrell and

* Tyrrell to Locke, 20 December 1689, 30 August 1690 (see below, 52 and 80); Molyneuz to Locke, 27 August 1692 (de Beer, 4, 508), and his *Case of Ireland*, 1698, 1720 ed., 23 and 130 where he refers to *Locke's Treat. Government* (in his reply Clement, 1698, complains of the abuse of 'Mr *Locke*, or whoever was the Author of that Excellent Treatise of Government'); Bayle to Minutoli, 14 September 1693, 1725, IV, 731.

† Historical Manuscript Commission, 12th Report, 1890, Fleming MSS, p. 335, George Fleming to Sir D.F., 29 January 1694-5.

‡ Moyle's *Essay* was printed in his *Works* in 1727 (see p. 58), and the date on the title-page was given as 1698 by the editor, to whom it was dedicated. See Robbins, 1968 pp. 28 ff. For Somers's reference, see note to II, § 138 and for Leibniz, see Jolley 1972, p. 21. Other instances could be found, e.g. Cary, 1698; Leslie (?), 1698.

Molyneux, imploring all of them, everyone who challenged him with the secret, to keep his knowledge to himself and out of print.* And he persisted in all his other exasperating attempts to conceal it, in a way which can only be called abnormal, obsessive. He destroyed all his workings for the book and erased from his papers every recognizable reference to its existence, its composition, its publication, printing and reprinting. All the negotiations with both printer and publisher went on through a third party, who was instructed to refer to the author as 'my friend'. This in spite of the fact that the publisher was a personal acquaintance both of Locke and his agent, and handled nearly all of his other books. In Locke's own library, this book in all its editions was catalogued and placed on the shelves as anonymous, so that even a casual browser should find nothing to compromise the secret.

He showed a similar cautiousness over some of his other works. He was willing to risk a breach with his Dutch friend Limborch for letting it be known that he had written on toleration, since this fact, as well as his responsibility for the *Reasonableness of Christianity*, was also reserved for final revelation in the codicil to his will.† But nothing exceeded his cold fury towards Tyrrell, a lifelong associate, when he had reason to believe that he had betrayed him over *Two Treatises* in 1690. There is no parallel in the papers of this devious man for the labyrinthine methods he used when the book was reprinted in 1694, perhaps no parallel in literature.‡

All this argues a peculiarity in Locke's personality as a man and in his personality as an author, particularly as a controversialist and especially as a commentator on political issues. This we will consider in its due place. The present importance of his anxiety to keep the secret about *Two Treatises* as long as he lived lies in the effect which it has had on the transmission of the text. His state-

* Locke obviously told Tyrrell between August 1691 and August 1692 (see below, 79), and Molyneux when he visited him in England in 1698 (see Molyneux to Locke, 15 March 1698, and Locke to Molyneux, 6 April 1698, *Works*, 1801, IX, 450–4 and compare Bastide, 1907, 286).

† Locke, Limborch letters, April 1690, in King's *Locke*, 1830, II, 305–11. He never put his name on English printings of the *Education*, though it appeared on the French translation.

‡ De Beer, 5, 29–36, and the originals, with some unpublished items, in the Whitehouse Collection (MS. Locke b.8). Rand assumes that the only book referred to in these letters between Locke and Clarke is the *Essay*. But *Two Treatises* is obviously intended in Locke's of 7, 12, 19 (as well as the *Essay*) and 30 March 1694.

ment in his will betrays his vexation that this book had been mangled by the printer, and implies that he was anxious to leave behind him an authoritative text. There is evidence to prove that he went to great pains to ensure that we should read him on politics in the exact words which he used, and we must turn to the history of its printing to see why it is that we do not do so. Our modern reprints of Locke on *Government* represent a debasement of a form of his book which he himself excoriated, and tried his best to obliterate.*

This author lived most of his life amongst books. He was well informed about printing and publishing, and the firm of Awnsham and John Churchill, one of the great houses of his day, came to be a part of his life. Yet he could write in June 1704:

> Books seem to me to be pestilent things, and infect all that trade in them . . . with something very perverse and brutal. Printers, binders, sellers, and others that make a trade and gain out of them have universally so odd a turn and corruption of mind, that they have a way of dealing peculiar to themselves, and not conformed to the good of society, and that general fairness that cements mankind.†

This profound suspicion of book tradesmen, rather than any argued belief in liberty of expression, made John Locke the champion of the freedom of the press. His bitter experience with the publication of his own works was an important reason. It was certainly *Two Treatises of Government* which irritated him most.

We have said that Locke carefully expunged from all his records every overt mention of this book. It is not surprising, then, that no manuscript version of it or any part of it has ever been recovered. This is another indication that his anxiety to conceal it went far beyond what he felt about his writings on toleration, for example, since he preserved draft after draft of his views on that subject. But although it has never been seen we know that the manuscript on *Government* which Locke sent to the press, or perhaps had copied for the printer, in the late summer of 1689, had some interesting peculiarities. It was a remnant: more than half of it had been lost. It was probably written all over with corrections, amendments and extensions: some recent, others going back six years and more. We shall discuss these features of the original

---

* See Laslett, 1952 (iv), 342, note 2, and 1954 (ii), note 1.
† *Works*, 1801, x, 291, Locke to Anthony Collins.

manuscript when we come to the date of composition. The printed text of the first, 1690, edition has the status which comes from being taken from a manuscript original, even though the cunning author may have made sure by using a copyist that his publisher did not recognize the hand.

This is only the beginning of the story which ends with the versions read today. The work of editing is complicated when only printed sources are available, especially when there were several editions in the author's lifetime, and printing difficulties as well. The 1st edition was botched, and no wonder, with such copy and such tortuous communications. We may never know in detail what happened, and the bibliographical problem is for specialists only. Locke certainly interrupted the press, and one of his objects was to change the title of the book and of each treatise, so as to alter the apparent relationship between them. The difficulty is to account for the fact that two sorts, or 'states',* of the finished book were produced. In the earlier state it had no paragraph 21 in the *Second Treatise*, and a few pages before the point where it should have appeared the ordinary print gave way to three pages in the larger type of the Preface. The second state was made to look normal: nothing is obviously missing, there is no large type. Modern editors in a hurry, just well enough informed to seek out the 1st edition to reproduce, have sometimes lighted on one state, sometimes on the other; hence a great deal of confusion and some mixed-up references.†

This 1st printing, our first authority, was completely unsatisfactory to Locke. We have been able to use his personal copy for this edition. Apart from corrections of misprints, it has a few amendments in his hand.

The plot of the story begins to unfold, a story of repeated

---

* Called for reference 1X and 1R, see Laslett, 1952 (iv); Bowers, Gerritsen and Laslett, 1954; Johnston, 1956. Dr Gerritsen has now put forward an explanation which seems to me to make the earlier, more complicated conjectures unnecessary. Though its effects on the text are not important, it implies the following. The passage which is present in 1R and not in 1X was lost at the press and had to be rewritten by Locke. He may have been able to use an earlier copy of his text, or he may have been composing anew. It is therefore very interesting that this passage (see 11, 20–1, and especially paragraph 20, 11–23 and note) should contain statements which refer so definitely to the revolutionary events of 1688. It is hoped that Dr Gerritsen's explanation will finally appear in print.

† See notes on 11, § 16, 1; § 17, 15. And for the extraordinary liberties taken with the text in the *Everyman* edition, see 11, § 20, 2; § 21.

frustration of Locke's attempts to get out a clear text. The book sold, and in 1694 a new printing was wanted. By this time, we may expect, both his manuscript original and all handwritten copies had been destroyed. So Locke sent a corrected copy of the 1st printing on its roundabout way through Edward Clarke, his third party, and Churchill the publisher to the printer. It had over 150 alterations of sense or extensions, but the final text was worse than ever, so bad that Locke felt like abandoning the whole book. On 12 March 1694, he wrote to Clarke:

There is no contesting with everlasting unalterable neglect. If I receive that other paper I sent for I shall go on with it. If not I shall trouble myself no more about it. Its fate is it seems to be the worst printed that ever book was, and it is in vain for anyone to labour against it.*

The chastened Churchill offered to scrap the whole edition. But not before Clarke had been told to 'rub up his carelessness a little' for this second was 'ten times worse than the first edition'. They finally agreed to sell it very cheap, so that it should be 'scattered amongst common readers'. Meantime Locke would correct it more exactly, especially as to punctuation, and then Churchill would print it again with better type and on good paper. This is what seems to have happened, though we have no further correspondence which we can attach to the affair.† The 2nd edition of 1694, and it is in fact a cheap and nasty little book, price sixpence, held the field for four years, when it was sold out in its turn. Then the better quality reprint was issued as Locke had demanded, the 3rd edition, 1698. The modifications in the 2nd edition, and the very minor alterations in the 3rd, have been taken account of in our text.‡

But even this did not satisfy Locke, who seems to have had a standard of perfection above the resources of the printers of his time. This 3rd printing of 1698 had its faults, but it is difficult not

* De Beer, 5, 30. The 'other paper' was a missing page of corrections. The effect of Locke's vain attempts to clear up the worst of the muddle is to be found in the numbers of cancel leaves in this printing, see Johnston, 1956.

† The references to a book printed in 1698 quoted by Bowers, Gerritsen and Laslett, 1954, where the printer left out whole paragraphs 'in the former sheets of this very book' now seems to concern a different work.

‡ It had two cancel leaves. See Editorial Note (127) for the effect of these successive corrections. Where Locke retained them in his 'text for posterity' (see below) they appear in the present text as a matter of course, and occasionally where he omitted to reinsert them there.

to feel the exasperation which he showed in his will over all the printings of this work had an independent source in an inner anxiety about what he had written. As it became obvious to him that no version correct enough to satisfy such meticulousness would ever appear in his lifetime,* he made plans to ensure that it should do so after his death. He corrected a copy of the printed version in minute detail, scrutinizing the word-over, the italics, the punctuation, even the spelling, as well as the general sense. It seems that he intended to carry out this process in duplicate, which is what we might expect in him. It seems also that one of the copies he corrected may have been of the 2nd printing of 1694, rather than the 3rd of 1698, which, though slightly revised, was a page for page reprint of its predecessor. The other copy, the text of the 3rd printing corrected between the lines, in the margins and on the fly leaves, is the one reproduced here. Locke himself did not get further than the first few pages in the laborious correcting process, and the rest is in the hand of his amanuensis, Pierre Coste, though Locke's hand does appear occasionally throughout the book. The indications are that Coste was copying from the other master-copy.

Locke must have left directions behind him for the publication of this text for posterity, just as he did in the case of the *Essay on the Understanding*.† Presumably these directions were left with Churchill, the publisher, though it is a little difficult to understand why nine years were allowed to elapse before the book appeared, for the posthumous *Essay* took only two. It may be that Locke's heir and literary executor, Peter King, later 1st Lord King was given the responsibility, or even Pierre Coste.‡ But whoever it was who made the decision, in 1713 this definitive text appeared over Churchill's imprint as the 4th edition, and in the following year it was included in the 1st edition of Locke's *Collected Works*, published by the same firm. And whatever exactly took place between Locke's death in 1704 and 1713, it is clear that the effect

* Though a new edition was entered in the *Term Catalogues* in 1699.

† The 5th edition, 1706, was obviously a posthumous fulfilment of Locke's own directions, presumably to Churchill: see Yolton's *Everyman* edition, 1961. Introduction.

‡ But see a letter from La Motte to Desmaizeaux of November 1709 (British Museum, Sloane MSS. 4286, f. 91), inquiring for a copy of that edition of *Two Treatises* 'qui a été faite après la mort de l'auteur, où l'on a inséré les corrections dans l'exemplaire laissé à Mr. Coste'. The assumption here is that the text for posterity had already appeared, and it seems to imply rather that someone other than Coste had been charged with it. The context shows that a number of people, including Barbeyrac, knew of the existence of the master-text, and that Coste had a copy of it.

he desired was brought about. A fairly reliable text of the book became established, and the earlier, imperfect printings were left behind.

As the eighteenth century wore on the work was sent to press again and again, about once every five years. Each new printing was usually set up from its immediate predecessor, and so the text inevitably declined in accuracy: it lost its original flavour. But in the 6th edition, 1764, this process was arrested. That fine republican eccentric, Thomas Hollis, had acquired in 'his private walks' the Coste master-copy and he published it. He then presented the volume itself to Christ's College, Cambridge, 'where Milton, the matchless John Milton' was bred.* The present text is a reproduction of this document, made possible by the generosity of the present Master and Fellows of Christ's. But it is not 'the copy from which Mr L hopes that his book will be printed after his death'† to which Coste himself refers. That other volume, the hypothetical second master-copy, has so far escaped a search for recovery begun in 1949. Even now, therefore, editorial work on this book could be overset by the discovery of a yet more authentic version.‡ So end attempts at perfection.

As his gentleman-scholarly habit was, Hollis did some editorial work on the book before he sent the Coste copy to Christ's.¶ Subsequent reprints followed this fresh and better version. It was left to modern scholarship, and in particular to the editors of successive reprints after 1884, to go behind all this to the unsatisfactory printings of Locke's lifetime, and to abate the prevalent confusion over the text. Hence the imperative need for doing Hollis's work over again, in accordance with our own standards of textual accuracy, presenting the book as the author intended us to read it, but registering his successive corrections. These have their own significance, for they show us how Locke's views in 1694, 1698 and in the period from about 1700 to 1704 differed in microscopic detail from those he originally published

* On Hollis, see Robbins, 1950. Professor Robbins has been kind enough to communicate relevant extracts from the full, unpublished diary of Hollis.

† 'L'exemplaire sur lequel il [i.e. Mr L.] souhaite que son livre soit imprimé apres sa mort', note in Coste's hand on the final fly of the Christ's copy: see note on II, § 172.

‡ See Editorial Note (below, p. 127) for a discussion of the second master-copy.

¶ Blackburne's *Memoirs* of Hollis, 1780, I, 224, Hollis collating this copy with the third, the collected and the fifth editions, 'with no little labour'.

in 1689.* Moreover the knowledge that he worked so hard and so often at his text is also important in itself. We must surely suppose that he meant to stand by what he finally approved for us to read. He certainly gave himself every opportunity to see and to revise those points of inconsistency and obscurity which have been seen in his text by so many of his commentators.

So John Locke has not escaped the consequences of the extra-ordinary attitude which he took up to his book on *Government*. There is an appropriate irony in the fact that the scholars of our own day have been confused by it, not the men of the eighteenth century. Though a study of this work must begin with this complicated story of determined anonymity and failure at the press, there is still more to be said. It was a different, a much modified version which entered into the main stream of European political thinking and affected French, even American revolutionism. Ever since it was translated into French, less than eighteen months after publication, the first of his English works to be put into the polite and universal language of that time, *Two Treatises* has led two quite independent lives. They have touched only at one point: in Boston, Massachusetts, in 1773.

In 1691 David Mazel, one of the Huguenot pastors living in Holland, translated the book.† He made an excellent version, which is now highly valued, but the book was transformed as well as translated. Locke's *Preface*, the entire *First Treatise*, the opening chapter of the *Second* connecting it with the *First*, were all left out. An *Advertisement* was prefixed, a fair enough statement of the drift and purpose of the text. The paragraphs were re-numbered under chapters and not consecutively through the book; they were divided slightly differently.‡ A briefer work in an alien language and an altered shape, this essay 'Du Gouvernement Civil' was subtly changed in the direction of the Enlightenment and eighteenth-century Revolutionism. In this form it was re-printed a dozen times in the next century, more often as an independent book in France than in England. In this form it was

---

* Though it bore the date 1690, it was actually printed in 1689 (see below, section III) and was on sale by November of that year. This was normal publishing practice then as it still is for our motor-car makers.

† There seems to be nothing to confirm, but nothing to upset, this traditional attribution.

‡ These divisions are recorded in the footnotes to the text.

read by Montesquieu, Voltaire and Rousseau. From this version and not, until our day, from the English original, the translations into other languages were made. Did Locke know that his book was being altered in this way? Was he himself in any way responsible?

He may have been. He was presumably acquainted with the publisher, Abram Wolfgang, for he also published the periodical *La Bibliothèque Universelle*. During his recent exile in Holland, Locke had contributed to this journal.* Jean Leclerc, the editor, was one of Locke's closest friends in Holland, and he was no doubt acquainted with most of the protestant refugees, perhaps with Mazel himself though we have no evidence of such a connection. *Du Gouvernement Civil* was anonymous both as to author and to translator, but its preface gets very close to Locke's doctrine and object in writing.†

Leclerc published a summary of the whole of *Two Treatises* in his periodical in 1691, from the English original. Nevertheless, the form of the French version may suggest that Locke himself would have approved of the fact that the *Second Treatise*, independent of the *First*, is the form in which it had been read, even by those who have had the *First Treatise* in the volume in hand. We have already seen Locke emphasizing the disconnection between the two treatises when he changed the titles at such a late stage, and we shall present the case for supposing that the *Second Treatise* was the earlier work. I am prepared to believe from these indications that the French, the European and generally appreciated form of this book, was authenticated by Locke. Any overt recognition of the French form would of course have offended his passionate desire for anonymity.

This view has its difficulties, for it makes it necessary to ask why he did not adopt this form for subsequent English editions and in his text for posterity. It leaves open a decision on the extent to which he oversaw the French edition. Nevertheless we may believe that Locke would have been pleased to think that the

---

* See Laslett 1952 (ii). The closer study of Locke's books which has since become possible shows that in this article Locke's contributions were confused with Leclerc's

† The title page to this volume, with Locke's manuscript addition *Pax ac Libertas*, is reproduced from Locke's own copy in H. and L., 1971 (1965), along with Locke's paraph (authenticating sign) on the final page.

French form, the independent *Second Treatise*, was to be received into the canon of classics on political theory.*

Whatever the status of the French version for Locke, it did not affect his corrections to the English versions, and he showed no sign that he realized the growing influence of the work on a readership far wider than his English public. That public, as the eighteenth century wore on, was no longer confined to readers of English in the British Isles, for it included those men, a few of them eminent men, who imported Locke's works into the British colonies in North America in the seventy years after his death. But the book *of Government* was not the most sought after by the colonists, and it is now known that other 'classics of liberal revolutionism' were in greater demand. Sidney, it appears, did more to legitimate the American revolution than ever Locke did, and *Two Treatises* were used in favour of the Royal regime as established in North America as well as against it.† Not until 1773 did the controversy over the rights of Americans call forth a reprint from Boston.

The text of this solitary early American edition was a standard one, following that printed by Hollis in 1764. But it is a singular fact that the form of the book followed the French set of conventions established by Mazel, and not the English: no *First Treatise*, and chapter 1 of the *Second* omitted.† What more intriguing example could be found of the well-known pathway of radical thinking from its origin in England, by way of French Protestants in Holland and French political criticism in France, to the new Englishmen of the New World?.

So much for Locke's book as a book and the plot of its development to a giant of historical importance. The whole story could be told at much greater length. There is a striking illustration of

* Locke's own copy of *Du Gouvernement Civil* has written in in his hand on the title: *Pax ac Libertas*. See Harrison and Laslett, 1965, p. 33 and plate 6. This is the only known example of his adding to the title of one of his own books. On the final page he has also added the personal sign which he used to authenticate his signature on financial documents. This sign is found on a dozen or so of Locke's books, and may have had a meaning to him which has not been recovered.

† See Dunn, 1969 (ii). Further work towards dispelling the myth of Locke's command-ing influence on the American revolution is in progress. Thomas Jefferson may have been a Lockeian, in somewhat the sense that political scientists have used that expression, as is evident from the coincidence of phrases between the *Declaration of Independence* and *Two Treatises* (see the relevant footnotes to the text). But it would seem that not many of his contemporaries went with him.

Locke's attitude to the work, his unwillingness to own it and to take responsibility for its effects, in his failure to take any notice of Molyneux's *Case of Ireland*. Here a close friend was using the book as it was always going to be used, to justify a people in their demand for a voice in their own government. Locke's name appeared in the ensuing controversy. There are signs that Locke felt concern, perhaps even contemplated changing his text, yet he said nothing: his final corrections ignored the whole thing.*

Or we could watch the interplay between editions of Locke and the crises of government and opinion. There was no American edition after 1773 until the twentieth century; a proposal for publication by subscription in 1806 apparently got no response. But during 'L'an III de la République Française' (1795) it appeared in revolutionary Paris in four different sizes, a neat tapering pile. Traditionalists in contemporary Britain were disturbed by the uses being made of the great philosopher of common sense and moderation by revolutionaries at home. In 1798 Bishop Thomas Elrington produced his edition of the book, introduced and annotated with remarks directed against citizen Thomas Paine so as to establish the distinction 'between the system of Locke and the theories of modern democrats'.† The first Spanish edition appeared in 1821, at the outset of the critical decade for the independence of the Spanish-American communities: in 1827 a further reprint was smothered in the press at Madrid.

Meanwhile the political theory of *Two Treatises of Government* had established its place in the mind of Montesquieu and Rousseau, Burke and Jefferson. We must now turn our attention to the personal qualities and the personal experience of the man who brought this system into being, and whose attitude to his own creation was such a singular one.

---

* Information from Prof. John Dunn, of King's College, Cambridge. See references in note ‡, p. 5 above, and compare Laslett, 1957 (i). Molyneux's reproduction of passages from Locke is recorded in the notes to II, §§ 4, 134, 177, 178, etc.

† Elrington was the only editor to notice the peculiarities of the 1st edition: his notes have been incorporated here.

II

LOCKE THE MAN AND LOCKE
THE WRITER

1. LOCKE AND OXFORD

John Locke lived from 1632 to 1704, from the seventh year of the reign of Charles I to the third year of the reign of Queen Anne: 1632 was the year of the birth of Sir Christopher Wren in England, of Pufendorf and Spinoza on the continent. In the course of his seventy-two years Locke saw the worlds in which he spent his life, the intellectual and scientific world, the political and economic world, change farther and faster than any of his forefathers had done, and in England more markedly than anywhere else. He was as much of a mere Englishman as a universal genius could be, though he spent two critical periods of his life abroad, in France from 1675 to 1679 and in Holland from 1683 to 1689. He was as private and ordinary a man as could be expected of an individual who was to help to change the philosophical and political assumptions of Europe, but for two other periods he was a directive political influence in his own right and something of a public personality. This was between about 1667 and 1675 and again in 1679–82 when he was associated with that overpowering political leader, the first earl of Shaftesbury, and between 1694 and 1700 as the confidant of Lord Somers, the chief figure of the government. He died a famous man and he has remained one of the great English names ever since.

That fame was intellectual and literary; it still is. But he was a reluctant author, a professed 'enemy to the scribling of this age'. He was fifty-seven years old before a word of the works which have given him renown was published in print. When he went to France in 1675 he expected to die of what we should call tuberculosis of the lung. He could not have supposed he would live to see his disordered sketches on philosophy become the *Essay on Humane Understanding*, or his notes on religious and political society become

16

the *Letters of Toleration* and *Two Treatises of Government*. He could not have anticipated then, nor at any time before his sixtieth birthday, that what he had noted in private would become famous in public as his *Thoughts on Education* and *Considerations* on money and economics. John Locke wrote and published as an old man, though he was quite confident that he would never live to be old. But like every other man, he thought his important thoughts when he was young. The fascination and difficulty of his career is to recognize the seeds and saplings burgeoning in his early and middle life and to watch them grow and spread into the mature forest trees which he left to posterity.

It could be said of the select group of great Englishmen in the century of our intellectual greatness that only one, John Locke, was a don by choice. Bacon was a lawyer and a politician, Hobbes was a teacher of noblemen, Newton was an academic by necessity until, after a hard struggle, he got into the great world as an administrator. Locke went up to Oxford in 1652 at the age of twenty and he remained a full member of his college, if only nominally resident in later years, paying his fees and receiving his dues until he was ejected, illegally and against his will, in 1684 when he was fifty-two. He did his best to get back his place, and if we are to believe what he tells us himself he would have liked to have lived his whole life at the university. It was his career: for most of his earlier life it was the only thing which he thought he could excel in.

He reached Oxford by the most conventional of paths. He was a scholar, and no very distinguished scholar, of Westminster School under the formidable Doctor Busby. He was there on that awful morning of 30 January 1649 when Charles I was executed, kept in school by his Royalist headmaster but within earshot of the awe-stricken crowd. There was a closed avenue for King's scholars of Westminster either to Trinity College, Cambridge, or to Christ Church, Oxford. John Dryden, of Northamptonshire, went to Trinity but his schoolmate, John Locke of Somerset, a westerner, a member of the Puritan network of families which were intertwined with the Royalist and predominating strands in that loyalist area, went to Christ Church. At the head of his college he found John Owen, the Independent and champion of toleration, all that was best in the Cromwellian attitude to learning and the Church. In his second year of residence Locke made his first appearance in print as an author: it was a salute to the Lord

Protector on his victory over the Dutch in 1653, in a volume of academic poems edited by the admiring Owen.*

There was a great deal to attach this modestly rising academic to the Cromwellian regime and the good old cause of Puritan and Roundhead against King and Cavalier. Down in Somerset his father, John Locke senior, was a late Captain in the parliamentary armies, the second in line of a family recently risen to gentle rank by the exertions and good fortune of its members. Nicholas Locke, the grandfather, had made the money which set the family up as proprietors of some small consequence in the little villages of Chew Magna, and Pensford and Belluton, Belluton which became Locke's family home. Nicholas had succeeded in the familiar way as a clothier, a capitalist middleman, setting on work the cottagers of the countryside round the great port of Bristol and selling the cloth in that flourishing market. But his son, John Locke senior, we are told, was a loser rather than a gainer in the race for wealth and social consequence so typical of his class and time. A Calvinist attorney, Locke's father was, and Clerk to the Justices of Somerset, dependent for patronage on a much more powerful parliamentarian family, the Pophams.

It was the influence of the Pophams which had made it possible for Locke's father to mark out the scholarly calling for him at Westminster and at Christ Church. It was a recognized way up in the world; for the clever boy the most reliable. There were two children only, John and his younger brother who died a youth, and they were authoritatively handled. Although he paid his tribute to parental sternness, much later he was to say that he 'wish'd his Father had design'd rather him for anything else than what he was destined to'.† In 1661 the squire of Belluton died, and left his son a gentleman of Somerset in his own right, the owner of farms and farmhouses and even a small Mendip mine. Academic, unmarried, independent he was to remain, but it is very important that John Locke was always the titular representative of an English landed family.

At Oxford Locke was urbane, idle, unhappy and unremarkable, all these things at the same time and only just successful enough. He passed with fair credit up the steps: scholar; then Student or Fellow as it would be in other colleges; then the holder of the

* Cranston, 1957, 36. Many other men contributed, including clandestine Royalists.
† Lady Masham, 1705, in Colie, 1955, 17.

usual teaching offices. Next in order was ordination in the Church, if he were to stay at the University; but here he hesitated, wavered and refused. He found a way out in medicine, one of the Studentships reserved for doctors. He had played some little part in that remarkable upsurge of interest in 'natural philosophy' at Oxford which was so soon to give rise to the Royal Society, and was associated with Boyle in his laboratory in the High Street. He took up botany, the herbal side of medicine, in a systematic way, and duly proceeded to the bachelor's degree in medicine. Although he finally wriggled his way, as an unsympathetic contemporary put it, into a faculty place or medical Studentship at Christ Church, he never became a full Doctor of Medicine. His academic career was checked by the mid-1660's, and, as it proved, it was checked for ever.

Locke did not begin as a philosopher and at Oxford he was never a philosopher at all. We can now piece together from the mass of papers he has left us what his earliest interests were. Politics was certainly amongst them. His correspondence, reading, notes and sketches show that he was first concerned with the authority of the state in religion, then with the Natural Law which sanctioned that authority, and with the basis of Natural Law in experience. It was only after this, after he had ceased to spend his whole time at Oxford, that he proceeded to philosophy as such, to the problem of knowledge. Apart from his congratulatory poems, his first work written for publication was a polemical tract on the *Civil Magistrate*; it was never printed, but we have his manuscript. His addresses as a college official, and especially as Censor of Moral Philosophy in 1664, have similarly survived, and they are concerned with Natural Law.* The surprising thing is that his attitude to politics then was traditionalist and authoritarian.

Here we would seem to be faced with a clean break with his heritage and a vivid contrast with his final reputation. He firmly proclaims his submission to authority, and his whole position is that in indifferent things, the power of the magistrate is necessarily absolute because the nature of civil society requires it. He insists

---

* Dr Von Leyden has published these writings as Locke's *Essays on the Law of Nature* (1954), with an admirable introduction. The two pieces on the *Magistrate* (MS. e. 7, in English, MS. c. 28, f. 3ff. in Latin with a draft in e. 6) are now published as *John Locke, Two Tracts on Government*, edited by Philip Abrams, Cambridge, 1967. References here are to the version in Dr Abrams's Dissertation of 1961. The English tract was directed against Edward Bagshaw, also of Christ Church.

that each and every individual grants his whole liberty to the supreme legislative power, which is a necessary mark of all civil society, and is the representative of all. Its decisions bind the conscience of everyone, though they may not reach what he defines as his judgement and in case of conflict there is no remedy but passive obedience. Liberty is what is left untouched by regulation. As for the people, this is typical of what he says:

> Nor will the largeness of the governor's power appear dangerous or more than necessary if we consider that as occasion requires it is employed upon the multitude that are as impatient of restraint as the sea, and whose tempests and overflows cannot be too well provided against. . . . To whom are we most likely to be a prey, to those whom the Scripture calls Gods, or those whom knowing men have always found and therefore call beasts?

Kings are called Gods in Scripture, and the people are beasts for the knowledgeable men, of Locke's day and before: no sharper conflict could be found with the doctrine of *Two Treatises of Government*. The uneasy, anarchical months between the death of Oliver Cromwell and the Stuart Restoration had made this slightly sceptical, unselfconfident Oxford don into the determined defender of authority, a man prepared to go to great lengths to secure quiet. But it was legal, not arbitrary authority which he championed, 'a body of laws so well composed' that their preservation 'was the only security of this nation's settlement'. Even in this, to us his earliest, his most authoritarian mood, Locke is revealed as a constitutionalist, and a man convinced of the fundamental distinction between secular and spiritual power, political and religious authority. He was not tempted into that safest and most effective of illiberal positions, the Divine Right of Kings based on patriarchalism, though he does mention it.* Throughout these papers, in fact, he professed indifference as to the origin of political power, 'whether the magistrate's crown drops down on his head immediately from heaven or be placed there by the hands of his subjects', which was to be a main concern of his mature political writings. But searching examination of his manuscript shows that he did assume the popular origin of political power: his references to the possibility of Divine Right were evidently

* See Abrams, 1961, 236–56, and his statement on 255 about 'constitutional' in relation to 'arbitrary' positions. Locke took note of patriarchal theories. There is evidence that he already knew, even respected, Filmer's writings—see below, 33, and Schochet, 1966.

concessions to the outburst of such sentiment which greeted the Restoration.*

These recent recoveries, then, reveal something quite unexpected in the intellectual development which led up to the writing of *Two Treatises*. We do not know why the polemical tract was not printed, but we may assume that its theories were made public to a certain extent, by being developed into a Latin address to members of Christ Church delivered between 1661 and 1664.† It is interesting in itself that Oxford students should have listened to an oration on such a subject, more interesting still to wonder whether they recognized certain elements in it which have a flavour of Hobbes, the arch-authoritarian. No one who set out, as Locke did, to argue from consent to absolute authority, could have avoided arguing to some extent in parallel with the already infamous *Leviathan*. Hobbist notions were in the air: Locke must have absorbed them, more perhaps from the attacks on them than from direct acquaintance. The two men were closer then than at any other time, but beyond this point we should not go: the evidence will not bear it. It is to submit uncritically to the strong tradition which dictates that Locke should always be considered alongside of Hobbes and to go on to claim that he was a conscious Hobbesist at this time, too cautious to reveal himself.‡

But Hobbes is not the only contemporary of Locke's earlier years whose writings are of importance to his development as a political thinker. The resemblance between Locke's final political doctrines and those of the English radicals writing and acting between 1640 and 1660 is most marked. It is so close in some

---

* See e.g. his corrections and overwriting on the first page of his English treatise, on page 4, and the passage deleted on p. 33.

† Von Leyden, 1954. He does not recognize the Latin treatise, undoubtedly the most important writing by Locke on political theory before *Two Treatises*, as one of the *Essays* which he publishes. Dr Abrams (1961, 50–1) also suggests that it was one of the Latin *Essays* or *Lectures*, and stresses (cf. note on English treatise, p. 21) the Oxford context of the politics discussed in both tracts.

‡ This has been the tendency of those who have commented on these writings so far, see Gough, 1950, and Cranston, 1956, and 1957, 61–3: Von Leyden rightly sees certain of Hobbes's arguments absorbed into the discussions of natural law, but it is he who suggests that the influence came from contemporary discussion of them as much as from direct acquaintance. Abrams thinks that the resemblances of the sentence quoted by Cranston (1957, 62, see English treatise, p. 21) with Hobbes's famous description of life in a state is no greater than with many such descriptions of life without government, and quotes one from a book known to have been in Locke's mind (Sanderson, *De Obligatione Conscientiae*, 1660, 1686 ed., 43). On Locke and Hobbes generally, see section IV below.

respects that direct influence would seem obvious, through his personal experience amongst those of the 'honest party' and through his reading. He knew Henry Stubbe, for example, and wrote to him in praise of his *Essay on the Good Old Cause*; through him he could have been in contact with Harrington and the Rota men, and there are many other such possibilities. But we have no indication that he read radical literature at Oxford, or indeed much political literature at all apart from such highly respectable, academic authors as Grotius and Pufendorf, his coeval, whose first work appeared in 1660. Classical and polite learning occupied him, even the French romances. The fact is that as far as we know Locke never read Lilburne or the other Levellers, then or afterwards. He was brought back into the tradition which they began by an unexpected turn in his personal life. Thereafter politics came to mean something very different from scholastic exercises on things indifferent, and on the scope and authority of Natural Law.

He was never to get much further as a Natural Law theorist, and we shall point to this fact as critical to his whole development. Nevertheless these early writings can fairly be called the typical product of a mind capable of enormous expansion, as yet unable to expand at all. Something of the platform for his political theory had been set up, and he could have proceeded either in the authoritarian or in the liberal direction, but to no very important effect. It was not to be a simple question of unfolding the implications of a particular starting point: it never really is for any thinker. As yet he had little sense of political reality, of policy itself. Indeed, a great deal was lacking in this meticulous Oxford bachelor, with his fine conversation, his keen mind and conventional views, lacking that is to *le Sage Locke*, Voltaire's idol, the universal philosopher with an attitude on all things. Something was to happen when his life was nearly half over, something which was to give him that firmness of intellectual tread which accounts for his giant reputation and to transform these early sentiments on authority, political and religious, into the Lockeian liberalism which presses on us still.

Oxford frustrated him, but he was not yet master of himself enough to make his way in the world there or outside. Locke had a name for disputation in the Schools, the established method of instruction and examination: 'Hogshearing' he called it, the laborious clipping of tiny hairs from the skins of vociferating animals, not swine apparently, but yearling lambs. Locke hated it, and he did it badly; his whole life work in one sense was a protest against it. This, he said later, was another reason why he 'pitched upon the study of physic', where he was at one remove from the Schools, and 'as far as might be from any public concerns'.* This second object, to keep away from public affairs, prevented him from pursuing the diplomatic career which opened up in 1665 and 1666.

This was a whiff of Machiavelli's world, and might have convinced him that he had talents and a personality for other things than teaching, the pressing of flowers from the University Botanic Garden and the systematic filling out of a great series of notebooks. He went to Cleves, the capital of Brandenburg, as secretary to a special mission in 1665, and was so successful that he was offered a similar post in Madrid when he returned, and another post after that.† But he preferred to return to his students and his everlasting medical mixtures. His association with Shaftesbury was to change him profoundly, but never quite to convince him that his academic ambition was misplaced.

When that change had taken place, Oxford rejected him. As a traditionalist institution she mistrusted his politics, and the developed originality of his thought menaced her curriculum. All this was to happen twenty years later and more, and his removal from his place was brought about neither by his college nor the university, but by the Crown as a piece of political vindictiveness. But though the inbred little society of clergymen at Christ Church in the 1680's were not actually responsible for expelling the ablest man amongst them, they were not guiltless in the matter. The good and scholarly Dr Fell, head of the house since 1660 and trusted by Locke, wrote thus to the Secretary of State:

Mr Locke being 'a student of this house' . . . and 'suspected to be ill-affected to the Government, I have for divers years had an eye upon him. . . . Very frequently, both in public and in private, discourses have been purposely introduced, to the disparagement of his master, the Earl of Shaftesbury, his party, and designs, he could never be provoked

* Locke to the eighth earl of Pembroke, 3 December 1684, de Beer, 2, 663, see p. 41 below.
† See Cranston, 1957, ch. 7.

to take any notice, or discover in word or look the least concern; so that I believe there is not in the world so great a master of taciturnity and passion'.*

The Royal order to remove Locke from his Studentship in 1684 was the first move made against the universities in the final Stuart bid for personal government, which was to stumble over the obstinacy of the Fellows of Magdalen in 1688. It is ugly to see those who sat with him at table acting as *agents provacateurs*, but typical of the man that not a flicker of an eyelid could be used against him. Half a generation later the teachers of Oxford did greater harm to their university by refusing to acknowledge his books in their teaching.† So little can Oxford and the House justly claim him as their own that he was a power over the whole learned world before they would recognize him. The last days he spent amongst them illustrate his manner of going in a dramatic fashion.

On 21 July 1683 the University of Oxford in Convocation ordered to take place in the Court of the Schools, now the Bodleian Quadrangle, the last burning of books in the history of England. The decree was displayed in the halls and libraries of the colleges, and it anathematized doctrine after doctrine already written into *Two Treatises*. Amongst the authors they condemned to the fire were some of those on the books which then stood on the shelves of Locke's chamber at Christ Church. It seems that he was there himself, to watch the acrid smoke drifting up between the spires, tight lipped as ever and busy packing off his library into the country. Within a few weeks he had certainly left Oxford for the countryside where he was born, and by the autumn he was an exile in Holland. Locke never went to Oxford again in his life.‡

---

* Fell to Sunderland, 8 November 1684, see King, 1830, 1, 279. Prideaux, one of the Students, was passing information to government circles on Locke at this time, see *Letters*, 1875. It is fair to add that the full exchange with Sunderland shows that Fell was doing something to protect Locke, and that he was disturbed by what was forced upon him. See Lady Masham (Colie, 1956, 83).

† See Cranston, 1957, 466–9 and references, for the meeting of heads of houses in 1703 to consider the suppression of the new, Lockeian philosophy.

‡ The *Decree* can best be consulted in *Somers Tracts*, 1812, viii. Locke's movements can be traced in his diary and from the addresses of his letters, though he becomes very elusive in the weeks before he left for Holland, and it is impossible to be certain that he did not pass through Oxford in later life.

2. LOCKE AND THE FIRST EARL
OF SHAFTESBURY

Anthony Ashley Cooper, of Wimborne St Giles in Dorset, later
first Lord Ashley and still later first earl of Shaftesbury, was one
of the ablest and most extraordinary men alive in the England of
Locke's lifetime. He was rich, rich in land and from political
office, rich from investment at home and overseas. He was
powerful, politically powerful both in the regional politics of the
south-west and at Whitehall. It had been done by a series of
swerves of allegiance: first for King, and then for Parliament;
first a minister of Cromwell, then his great opponent, then an
architect of the Restoration. He was one of the small, assertive
men; a phenomenon of shrewdness and penetration, highly intelligent and critical, yet affected with delusions of grandeur and
unscrupulous in his inconsistencies; superb as a leader and
administrator, yet chronically ill, physically not psychologically,
for he had the extraversion of Prime Minister Walpole.

His disease was a hydatid, an affection of the liver, fatal if it
should give rise to an abscess and the abscess not be removed. In
July 1666, Lord Ashley, Chancellor of the Exchequer, con-
valescent after one of his attacks, rumbled down in his great coach
to Oxford to try the waters of Astrop. They were to be brought
to him in bottles, and the man who came into his presence with
the twelve flasks was not the physician he expected, but the
physician's friend, John Locke. This was how the two men first
met, and at that moment a famous friendship began.

It was Locke's conversation which attracted the keen-sighted
politician as well as his skill as a doctor. Courteous and modest,
for Locke always knew his place with the great, he was penetrating
and ironical, immensely well informed. Within a year he had taken
up residence in the Ashley family, with his own apartment at
Exeter House in the Strand, invited there to talk to the great man,
to advise him and to doctor him and those about him. On the body
of his noble patron he brought about one of the medical miracles
of that age. He advised and directed an operation, an operation at
a time when surgery was butchery, to remove the abscess on the
liver and to insert a little pipe through the stomach wall as a drain
to prevent another abscess from forming. Ashley wore the pipe

for the rest of his life: to the satirists of the 1680's it became a great wooden tap to be mocked at, like the tap on a barrel of beer. In fact this pathetic little object was made at first of silver then of gold.*

This operation made Locke famous and it changed the whole course of his life. Ashley was convinced, and he had good reason to be, that he owed his life to Locke. An association which began casually and was continued on a pattern conventional at the time, since it was not unusual for the great to introduce men of Locke's stamp into their families, became a working association for all purposes for both of them. All that political influence could do was directed towards Locke's promotion in his profession of academic medicine, and he was provided for financially, though his obstinate independence evidently made it difficult for Ashley to go as far as he wanted. He was given offices, the secretaryship of the associated proprietors of the colony of Carolina, the secretaryship of Ashley's Board of Trade, the secretaryship for ecclesiastical patronage when Ashley, now earl of Shaftesbury, became Lord Chancellor in November 1672. These were not great offices, and none of them led to the high political career which might well have developed out of this association.

We do not know why this was, though we may believe that it was Locke who held back rather than that Shaftesbury judged him unfitted for the highest promotion. For we do know that he was paid the highest compliment in the gift of a great politician.

My Lord imparted to him from time to time all the secretest affairs then in agitation and by my Lord's frequent discourse of state affairs, religion, toleration and trade, Mr Locke came to have a wonderful knowledge of these things. . . . He writ his book concerning Human Understanding whilst he lived with my Lord.

And again, from a source of the very highest authority, Shaftesbury's grandson and Locke's pupil, the third earl:

Mr Locke grew so much in esteem with my grandfather that, as great a man as he had experienced him in physic, he looked upon this but as his least part. He encouraged him to turn his thoughts another way. . . . He put him upon the study of the religious and civil affairs of the nation with whatsoever related to the business of a minister of state, in which

---

* On the operation, see Osler, 1914: a more recent medical opinion is that the drainage pipe was useless, but that the operation did save Shaftesbury's life and its success was almost miraculous.

he was so successful that my grandfather began soon to use him as a friend and consult with him on all occasions of that kind. . . . When my grandfather quitted the Court and began to be in danger from it, Mr Locke now shared with him in dangers as before in honours and advantages. He entrusted him with his secretest negotiations, and made use of his assistant pen in matters that nearly concerned the state, and were fit to be made public, to raise that spirit in the nation which was necessary against the prevailing Popish party.*

We owe *Two Treatises* to the wonderful knowledge of state affairs which Locke acquired from frequent discourse with the first earl of Shaftesbury; indeed the evidence suggests, as we shall see, that he actually wrote the book for Shaftesbury's purposes. The original meeting may not have been entirely a consulting-room accident. Shaftesbury's grandson tells us that he was recommended by the earl's steward, an important figure in the machinery of local influence.† Local politics, then, the association of families over wide areas and long periods of time, made this meeting no unlikely thing, although no other connection has yet been found between the Lockes of Somerset and the great political family of the neighbouring county of Dorset. But its results were not simply political, nor were they confined to political and social theory. They are to be seen over the whole area of Locke's intellectual activity: without Shaftesbury, Locke would not have been Locke at all.

We have seen that Locke was never a pure philosopher at Oxford, and we have quoted the claim of a witness that his major work on philosophy was written in Shaftesbury's household. It is now known that this was indeed the case, though the actual work of composition took so long, nearly twenty years, that the finished work was never seen by Shaftesbury. Locke began his career as a philosopher in his chamber at Exeter House in the early months of 1671, and by July he had produced a draft of the

* The first extract comes from a document in the Shaftesbury Papers (P.R.O. 30/24, xlvii, 28, 3) endorsed 'F.C.' and copied in what looks like the third earl's hand into a fuller account. The second comes from the third earl's letter written for Jean Leclerc and based on documents like these—dated February 1705, printed by B. Rand in his life and letters of the third earl, 1900, p. 332.

† 'Mr Bennet of the town of Shaftesbury': he and his son were M.P.s for the borough. Even the physician, David Thomas, who commissioned Locke with the water bottles, had a political identity. He was a strong Whig, and when the *Essay on Human Understanding* appeared, would have preferred a life of Shaftesbury. For even stronger emphasis on Locke's association with the Earl, see Viano, 1960; Ashcraft, 1986, 1987.

embryonic *Essay* in one of his own notebooks. Before the end of the year he had rewritten and extended it, but meanwhile he had got someone to copy parts of the original and some of his workings for the information of the earl himself. We know this, and we know that this incomplete manuscript was looked on by Shaftesbury as a personal possession, because it was seized amongst his most private papers from his study when he was arrested in 1681: it has even been suggested that another such paper represented Shaftesbury's own sketched attempt at a theory of knowledge.* Here we have them, the statesman and his medical, scholarly intimate, stimulating each other on the most abstract subject of all. It was not Locke the Oxford don who became a philosopher, but Locke the confidant of an eminent politician, living the political, social and intellectual life of Restoration London.

So it was with Locke the economist, the educationalist, the theorist of toleration, even Locke the scientist and medical reformer. He became a Fellow of the Royal Society in November 1668, from Exeter House and not from Christ Church, sponsored by Sir Paul Neile, a founder of the Royal Society, but also a friend and political associate of Shaftesbury's. In London he met the great Sydenham, joined in his medical practice and helped in his study of smallpox. He helped him also with his writings, leaving most of the relevant papers to join Shaftesbury's. Locke published nothing on medicine as such, but his views on education and economics both appeared in the 1690's in printed treatises, and it is quite clear that they had their origin in the work he did for, and in co-operation with, Shaftesbury. He was entrusted with the delicate and important task of finding a wife for the lumpish heir to the house of Ashley, and making sure that he produced an heir in his turn. What had begun as a medical undertaking, turned itself into an educational experiment, and the third earl tells us that he and his five brothers and sisters were all educated by Locke 'according to his own principles (since published by him)'.†

* See Laslett, 1952 (i): the suggestion is Dr Von Leyden's and cannot be pursued because we have the first few words of the paper only. The subject of the first workings for the *Essay* is complex, see Cranston, 1957, 141-2, Aaron, *Locke*, 2nd ed. 1955, 50-5. Johnston, 1954, rightly corrects my suggestion that the Shaftesbury draft is the earliest still extant. The two other 1671 versions have been edited by Aaron and Gibb, 1936, and Rand, 1931.

† See Axtell, 1968, which discusses the whole question of Locke's educational experience in relation to the house of Ashley. Kelly, 1969, makes the case that Locke was given some oversight of Shaftesbury's heir at Oxford when the two men first met there, and that this furthered their subsequent intimacy.

He had shown no sign of an interest in the upbringing of children at Oxford, nor any trace of the economist's attitude. And yet within two years of his going to London he produced a paper on the rate of interest written for Shaftesbury formulating the position which he consistently maintained for the rest of his life, with results of considerable consequence to the future of the British economy.* In economics he might be called a traditionalist, almost an Aristotelian, but on the subject of toleration his association with the acknowledged champion of religious freedom swiftly transformed the traditionalist and authoritarian views written into the Oxford treatise. In 1667, during the first months of his residence at Exeter House, he composed an *Essay on Toleration*† which turned his earlier arguments into a vigorous defence of the right of dissent, proceeding from analysis of the intellectual problem to positive recommendations about national policy. Advice of this sort was now expected of him, and he seems to have written similar policy documents on many or all of the objects of Shaftesbury's public career. Not the least of these new born interests was colonial administration.‡

Locke the man and Locke the writer make up a complicated personality, very difficult to separate from that of Shaftesbury himself in these truly formative years. Apart from the *Toleration* drafts, there are two published political works which have claims to be the result of literary co-operation between them. The *Fundamental Constitutions of Carolina*, privately and anonymously issued in 1669, and the *Letter from a Person of Quality*, anonymous, 1675, alike appear in an authoritative collection of Locke's works.¶ The manuscript of the *Constitutions* is in Locke's hand in the Shaftesbury papers, and a note of his written during or before composition

---

* See Laslett, 1957 (1), especially footnote 21. The draft, the first of a series, is MS. e.8, dated 1688, compare Viano, 1960, 183 on, and refs.

† Manuscript version in Shaftesbury papers printed by Fox Bourne, 1876, 1, 174–94. There are three other versions, and their relationship is not finally established (see the discussions in Cranston, 1957, 11; Gough, 1950, corrected by Von Leyden, 1954; Johnston, 1956; Brown, 1933). But the evidence implies a close relationship in composition between Locke and Shaftesbury. Further information on Locke, Ashley, economics and toleration is to be found in Abrams, 1967, Haley, 1968, and Kelly, 1969.

‡ See Laslett, 1969 revised by Kelly 1969, who finds Locke to have derived much from his companions and predecessors in Shaftesbury's entourage, especially Benjamin Worsley and Henry Slingsby.

¶ *A Collection of Several Pieces of Mr John Locke* 1720. Desmaizeaux and Collins, who were responsible, were well placed to know what Locke had a hand in. Both pieces are reprinted in collected Lockes from the 4th, 1740.

has been found in one of his books:* in 1679–80 he wrote to his French friends as if he were responsible for the work. No such evidence has come out about the *Letter*, and in 1684 he seemed anxious to repudiate authorship. We shall perhaps never know exactly to what extent the *Constitutions* represented Locke's or Shaftesbury's views of how a society newly set up in the American wilderness should be ideally constituted, or whether it was a compromise between them and the other proprietors. The contrast between its doctrines and those of *Two Treatises* is intriguing. If Locke approved them in 1669, for English as well as colonial society, his views on the people, who they were and how they were related to government, changed profoundly by 1679.

But it may be unprofitable simply to seek for consistency or inconsistency here, just as it is in comparing Locke at Oxford with Locke in Shaftesbury's entourage. These publications indicate one of the ways in which he acted as 'assistant pen' to his master in the first period of their association, before he left for France in 1675. He would also draft official papers, record conversations and negotiations, even prompt his masters from behind his chair, as he is supposed to have done when Lord Chancellor Shaftesbury delivered the famous speech *Delenda est Carthago* against the Dutch enemy in 1673. But his important literary function was to write out for Shaftesbury's use an account of this or that political or social problem, telling him what had been thought or written about it, what arguments were likely to convince intelligent people of the correctness of a certain attitude to it. The successive drafts on toleration, economics, even perhaps on education and philosophy fit into this context, as well as being records of Locke's own intellectual development. They are supplemented by what he wrote in his diaries, his letters and his commonplace books. From these sources a remarkably complete record can be recovered of the story behind nearly all of his final books: the conspicuous exception is the work on *Government*.

In a sense, of course, all this material is relevant to Locke's development as a political theorist, especially the toleration file. We shall see that he began reading and making notes on political authority and the origin of political power as soon as he came under Shaftesbury's influence. It may be true that no draft on

---

* This interesting fragment, in the possession of the present writer, is endorsed 'Carolina, a Draft of some Laws'. It contains two sentences only, highly Harringtonian.

this subject was ever drawn up during this earlier period, to be subsequently destroyed.

For the issue of political obligation as such did not arise in an urgent form until 1679, when Shaftesbury found himself in need of a general, theoretical argument to justify a change in the constitution. There can be little doubt that Locke was summoned back from France early in 1679 to help his master. Shaftesbury was temporarily in office once again, trying to use the national scare over the Popish Plot to force on King Charles II the exclusion from the succession of his brother and heir apparent, the Catholic James, duke of York.* It is certain that Locke knew all about what was going on, and that he took no opportunity to disapprove the forced confessions, the judicial murders, mob oratory and agitation. We do not know whether he 'believed in' the Popish Plot any more than we know if Shaftesbury did, but he never criticized Shaftesbury's actions at any time. He was always his loyal and wholehearted admirer.

He went much further towards revolution and treason than his earlier biographers knew, anxious as they were to present him as a man of unspotted personal and political virtue.† When Parliament was summoned to meet at Oxford early in 1681, at a time when armed resistance seems to have been decided on if the Exclusion Bill failed again, Locke took an active part. He went from house to house finding accommodation for Shaftesbury's entourage, even for Rumsey, the chief of his desperadoes. He was in correspondence with Shaftesbury about influencing elections; he may even have written the famous 'Instructions to the Knights of the County of . . . for their Conduct in Parliament', which has claims to be the first modern party document in history.‡ When

---

* 'In the year 79 the Earl of Shaftesbury being made Lord President of the Council Mr Locke (as it is said) was sent for home', Lady Masham, 1705. Another argument can be based on the fact that, though Locke had been away for four years, he was so busy with Shaftesbury's business directly he arrived in London, that it was seven months before he could get away to Oxford, and a year before he could go down to Somerset to visit his neglected property. There is a list of trials and confessions in MS. b. 2 and Locke sent a collection of literature of this sort to Thomas in Salisbury at his request. On Shaftesbury and the Plot, Haley, 1968; Ashcraft, 1987, 138 ff.

† Prof. Cranston has effectively demolished the belief of Locke's Victorian biographers in his 'political innocence', see especially chs. 14 and 16. Bastide, 1907, still maintained that 'he kept aloof from the struggle' (p. 68), but suspected that he may have helped Monmouth. I am prepared to believe that he was more deeply implicated in Monmouth's rebellion than even Cranston allows: Ashcraft, 1987, makes a strong case for Locke's involvement in radical plots, propaganda and subversion.

‡ P.R.O. 30/24 VIB, Item, 399, endorsed 'The original of this wrote in Mr Locke's own hand'. On all this, see Christie, *Shaftesbury*, 1871, Haley, 1968.

the parliamentary attempt had finally failed and Shaftesbury, after a period of imprisonment, had no other resort than to persuade his associates into consultations verging on treason, Locke went along with him and the others.

With his diary open to us we now know that Locke spent the whole of the summer of 1682 with Shaftesbury while these consultations proceeded. On 15 September he even went with him to Cassiobury, the seat of the earl of Essex, where a meeting of the Whig leaders was scheduled at the height of what is sometimes called the Insurrection Plot. Most significant of all, since it was the action of a man with an independent political personality for the first time, is the fact that he went there again on 24 April 1683, at the very time when preparations are supposed to have been under way for the Assassination, or Rye House, Plot.*

We can assume that he went on this second occasion entirely of his own choosing because Shaftesbury was dead, dead in exile in Holland, his last hours spent, so the tradition goes, in discussing the unorthodox religious doctrines implied in the later part of Locke's *Essay on Human Understanding*. Another frequent visitor to the earl of Essex in those dangerous days was Algernon Sidney, regicide and republican, a man who was to lose his head for his part in the Rye House Plot. Sidney had written at length in support of his views and in refutation of Sir Robert Filmer, the author whose works had become the official exposition of the Royal and Tory view of the basis of governmental power. Sidney's manuscript, later published as his *Discourses Concerning Government*, was an essential part of the case of the Crown at Sidney's trial later in the year.† As we have seen from what happened at Oxford, Locke was already a suspected man, and from the time of the discovery of the Rye House Plot he became a fugitive, quite soon in exile. Nothing specific was ever proved against him, but it was persistently believed that his treasonable activity had been writing against the government, just as Sidney had done.

* There is no reliable evidence of what was discussed on either occasion. Ashcraft (1987, 380) maintains that on the second occasion Locke went 'as a representative of the [revolutionary] Council of Six to summon Essex . . . for an emergency meeting'. Essex was apparently quite unwilling to contemplate tyrannicide, though he died in the Tower when a prisoner for his part in these preparations. Locke preserved a manuscript maintaining the Whig view that Essex did not commit suicide but was murdered, and he was conceivably quite close to Essex.

† See Laslett, 1949, 36 7.

We shall attempt to show that Locke had by this time written a work against the government, and that what was finally published under the title *Two Treatises of Government* was the book in question. The case will have to be presented in full because of the established dogma that it was written in or just after 1688.* We must now turn to such evidence as he has left us of his development as a political theorist whilst he was with Shaftesbury. We may believe if we wish that the train of thought which gave rise to *Two Treatises* departed from the following quotation from one of the works of Sir Robert Filmer, written by Locke into a notebook very early in his days at Exeter House.

Hobs

With noe small content I read Mr Hobs booke De Cive & his Leviathan about the rights of Soveraignty wch noe man yt I know hath soe amply & Judiciously handled. Filmore. Obser. preface:

The list of books on politics, quotations from them and judgments of their value, from which this quotation comes, seems to have been drawn up in Shaftesbury's presence, for a very similar list has been found in Shaftesbury's own papers, in Locke's hand;‡ there are many items common to both. From this evidence we may conclude that the intellectual relationship between Locke and Shaftesbury in the matter of political theory was, as might be expected, much the same as for economics, toleration and so on. The association directed Locke's attention to the works of Milton, Campanella, Guiccardini, Adam Contzen, as well as to such English champions of non-resistance as Heylyn, Dudley Digges and Filmer. Some of these authors were known to him already, and we may believe that he had read, and praised, a work of Filmer's as early as the year 1659, though this was the first time he

---

* See section III.

† MS. f.14, folio 16. The quotation was obviously directly copied from Filmer's *Observations concerning the original of Government, Upon Mr Hobs Leviathan ...*, London, 1652, first words of Preface.

‡ P.R.O. 30/24/47, no. 30, classified book list, section *Politici*. It is a curious fact that in both lists, Sir Robert Filmer, whose tracts had been printed anonymously, is called Sir Thomas Filmore. This is the only occasion known to me when the name 'Filmer' was associated with these tracts before their collected publication in 1679, outside Sir Robert's family and his circle of friends. Locke and Shaftesbury named every one of Filmer's political tracts except his pieces on the *Power of Kings* and his *Freeholder*. Maclean, 1947, recognized that Locke read Filmer as early as 1667, but did not notice the parallel in the Shaftesbury papers.

had been told that Filmer was its author.* It is clear that Shaftesbury's company was bringing him up against the questions he had deliberately left on one side at Oxford. What were the origins of political power, how is it to be analysed, what are its limits and what are the rights of the people?

That these questions were exercising Locke during his first period with Shaftesbury, especially the possibility of a patriarchal origin for political power, is shown by another note made in 1669.† There he made a point which he was to argue at length in *Two Treatises*. In 1672 he schemed something out on *Wisdom*, dividing his observations under the three headings 'Prudence', 'Theology' and 'Politics' (Politia). Politics in its turn is divided into 'Fundamentals', 'The form of the State' and 'Administration', and the two fundamentals are *Jus Paternum* and *Consensus Populi*.‡ This acceptance of patriarchalism alongside of popular consent is also to be found in the final work, here no longer equally fundamental

But though we know that this was the period of his development as a political theorist, the book itself comes as a revelation. The best illustration of this is the important issue of property, for nothing in his literary remains from the years leading up to his writing on *Government* suggests that property would be a major theme. It is mentioned, in a phrase which fits in with his statement about it in his *Essay on the Understanding*, in his Oxford *Essays on Natural Law*; but what he says in his 1667 *Essays on Toleration* seems to imply a general position which is very different from that presented in *Two Treatises*.¶ These are only isolated references. The fact would seem to be, and it can be confirmed for many of the other subjects, that Locke simply had not thought in a systematic way about property before 1679. He had not worked out his justification of ownership in terms of labour.

* There are two references to another set of Filmer's *Observations*, his essay on Philip Hunton which had the title *The Anarchy of a Limited or Mixed Monarchy* (1648) in Locke's notebook entitled *Lemmata Ethica*. Neither reference is dated, and most of the other entries in the book are later, and marked as such. But their position and context suggest that they were made very early in Locke's use of the book. One quotes the definition of absolute monarchy from p. 15 of Filmer's tract and adds appreciatively: 'hujusmodi monarchia optime defenditur'. No author's name is given. It is a curious fact, noted in Kelly, 1969, that Locke's economic writings may well have been affected by Sir Robert Filmer's work on usury, though he never refers to this title.

† MS. c. 29, ff. 7 9, notes on Samuel Parker, *A Discourse of Ecclesiastical Politie*, 1670, printed in full by Cranston, 1957, 131–2.

‡ MS. c. 28, f. 41: 'Sapientia 72.' Compare Abrams, 1961, 311, scheme of? 1661.

¶ See below, 103.

The pre-history of *Two Treatises*, then, is a complex study which cannot be taken further here. Enough has been said to suggest the atmosphere in which its doctrines were formulated, an atmosphere of political decisions and policy itself, with Shaftesbury as the policy-maker and Locke as the confidential co-adjutor, one amongst others but the most important. This is not the atmosphere we associate with philosophy, and too often with political thinking, nevertheless this was also the time of Locke's philosophical maturation. *Two Treatises* and the *Essay* were in gestation at the same time, and the political work reached its almost final form earlier, in spite of the fact that systematic work on it began seven or ten years later.

We shall assign the important part of the work of composition to the years 1679–80. It was then, as we believe, that the book took shape, and took shape suddenly for an author with such slow, deliberate habits. Up till then the train of ideas which had been present in his mind from the beginning had developed in a desultory way, as a subordinate theme to that of toleration. It had been deliberately pushed aside when he wrote on Natural Law at Oxford, and can be seen only in such details as his registration of Filmer's agreement with Hobbes. Since he has left us no sketch, no early form of any part of the book, we cannot tell what his earlier opinions had been on many of the subjects it covers, nor how they developed. He was certainly reflecting on them occasionally in his journeys through France between 1676 and 1679.

In February 1676, when he was at Montpellier, he made a note in his journal on the *Obligation of Penal Laws* which dealt rather obscurely with the problem of resistance. He is quite confident that civil laws do not necessarily oblige the individual conscience, but he maintains that there is a law of God 'which forbids disturbance or dissolution of governments'. Conscience is satisfied if a man 'obeys the magistrate to the degree, as not to endanger or disturb the government, under what form of govenment soever he live'.* Two and a half years later we find an abbreviated sketch of a complete theory, relating man to God, father to son, the individual to society, in familial, patriarchal terms: not Filmer's patriarchalism, but nevertheless closer to the notes of 1669 and 1672 than to *Two Treatises*. The heading he chose was Natural Law, *Lex*

---

* Printed in King, 1830, I, 114 17: compare Lamprecht, 1916, 142 3, who seems slightly to exaggerate Locke's insistence here on passive obedience.

Naturae. Man, he noted, has 'a knowledge of himself, which the beasts have not' and this knowledge was 'given him for some use and end'. It shows men that a son should obey his father (although begot 'only in pursuance of his pleasure, without thinking of his son') and therefore they must obey God as the final 'author of their being'. It is similarly 'reasonable to punish' a child 'that injures another', and from this we may conclude that children, and all men, are expected by God 'to assist and help one another' as a duty. 'If he find that God has made him and all other men in a state wherein they cannot subsist without society, and has given them judgment to discern what is capable of preserving and maintaining that society, can he but conclude that he is obliged, and that God requires him to follow those rules which conduce to the preserving of society?'*

He wrote this when travelling up the Loire in July 1678, a long way from London, Shaftesbury and the dreadful Popish Plot, and he wrote it for himself. We shall claim that his work on *Government* was an exercise on this same theme begun only about a year later, but written for his leader, written also for the public which both men wanted to persuade. Such is the measure of the difference between the Locke who wrote in solitude and the Locke who wrote for Shaftesbury.

But he also wrote for his patron in a way which is much more familiar and typical of his time, to honour and divert him. He presented his little volume on *The Growth of Vines and Olives* to his Lordship on 2 February 1680, and that eminent epicure and cultivator was overjoyed with the exquisite little manuscript volume. To the Countess on the same occasion, it was to celebrate his return from France, he dedicated his translation of the *Essais* of Nicole. In our anxiety to understand the harsh political reality in which these two friends lived their life together, we must not lose sight of its gracefulness, gentility and wit. Locke sat at the Chaplain's table in Lord Chancellor Shaftesbury's meticulously regulated dining hall: he had to trudge through the mud to support that megalomaniac imp when he went out in his coach on state occasions. But he also had a voice in the decoration of his houses, the layout of his gardens: he educated the grandchildren

---

* Journal for 1678, 201–2, modernized: compare I, § 52 and note. In the note to II, § 58, is quoted a further note of importance to politics, written in his journal in Paris in March 1679.

of his master in English gentility, that just and mellow blending of the practical man, with stoic virtue, understatement and a deep respect for learning. The ideal of the English gentleman is with us today, and in part it is Locke's invention. It grew out of his affection for Shaftesbury.

The last thing Locke wrote as literature was a life, a vindication, or an *Éloge* as the French were saying, of his great master. This was as it should be, for it was the final debt which all literary men owed to those who made the life of literature and thought possible for them. His own end came before he could get further than the first few pages, but the Latin epitaph was finished:

> Comitate, acumine, suadela, consilio, animo, constantia, fide,
> Vix parem invenias, superiorem certe nullibi.
> Libertatis civilis, ecclesiasticae,
> Propugnator strenuus, indefessus.

Liberty, then, is the last word we are left with—a tireless, fierce fighter for liberty in religion, liberty in politics, the liberty of Locke's own work on *Government*.

3. LOCKE AND SOMERS

1689 was the year of the great climacteric in the life of Locke. As a result of the Revolution the obscure exile became a man of political influence, with powerful friends in high places. The minor figure in the republic of letters, something of a journalist in the Dutch intellectual community where he had been living, the multiplier of notes and writer of drafts, at last appeared as an author, first of the *Letter on Toleration*, then of *Two Treatises of Government*, both in print by the autumn of that year, but both anonymous. Then in December the John Locke who signed the Preface to *An Essay Concerning Human Understanding* became, by that very act, the John Locke of intellectual history. It turned him into a national institution and an international influence. In the fifteen years left to him he twisted his fingers round the haft of English intellectual life and got so firm a grasp that it pointed at last in the direction which he had chosen.

It was a philosophical reputation which he enjoyed, and it was because of the key position of philosophy that his intellectual domination was possible. Everything else which he wrote was important because he, Locke of the *Human Understanding*, had written it. It was so with his *Thoughts Concerning Education*, 1694, his works on *Money*, 1692 and 1695, and his polemic with Stilling-fleet in defence of his *Essay* in 1697 and 1699. The anonymous works, the three letters on *Toleration* of 1689, 1690 and 1692, the *Reasonableness of Christianity* and its *Vindications* of 1695 and 1697, could not be associated with his philosophy by his contemporaries, or only by very few. It is surely significant that the work on *Government*, the most secret of all, went almost unscathed till its authorship was finally revealed.* But from the time of his death the relation of *Two Treatises* with the *Essay* has been its leading characteristic. Here is an important philosopher, the proposition goes, addressing himself to politics, so what he writes must be important political philosophy.

This way of looking at *Two Treatises of Government* has given rise to a convention of analysis which we shall have to criticize. There is a danger too in the very pattern of Locke's literary career: an apprenticeship of remarkable length leading up to a short final period in which six major works and nine lesser ones were published, most of them in several editions, all by an aging man, busily engaged with other things in his study, and in the world of politics and administration. It makes it look as if he deliberately planned his life in this way, and in the case of political theory this impression is hard to avoid. Here, it would seem, was a mind which trained itself first academically, then at the very seat of political power, and after two important periods of residence abroad, in France and in Holland, finally responded to the Revolution of 1688–9 with a work on *Government*.

The impression of a deliberate plan is of course an illusion, and I believe that he cannot have composed his book after 1683, but there is some value in this commentary on Locke the writer. He felt the need to ripen, particularly as a philosopher, before he appeared in print, and he was also both anxious to publish books and afraid of being criticized. In the final period of his life Locke overcame this fear, and when he found that what he published was a success, he published more. Criticism always disturbed him

---

* Prof. Dunn finds the earliest reply in Leslie, 1703, and what seems to be the second is *An Essay upon Government, wherein the Republican Schemes reviv'd by Mr Locke are Refuted*, London, 1705, author unknown. But it was noticed abroad: *Du Gouvernement Civil* was coolly reviewed by Basnage in his *Histoire des Ouvrages des Sçavans*, Tome VIII, June 1691, 457. 'C'est dommage,' he says on p. 465, 'quel l'Auteur n'a pas toûjours bien dégagé ses pensées, ni bien dévelopé ses sentimens.'

deeply, which must be one of the reasons for his refusing to acknowledge books which he knew would be controversial. The effect of all this was to make him publish late and enter into history only as an older man, but it was not simply a matter of cumulative experience and above all it was not deliberate.

Calculated strategy is to be seen, however, in the way he went about the task of making sure that his ideas and opinions should affect the policy of governments in these years of his intellectual ascendancy. He had never wanted political office of the ordinary kind and once again he found himself refusing diplomatic posts. Hypochondriac as he was, his first need, as he said, was for a place of 'highest convenience for a retired, single life'. He found obstacles in the way of getting back his Studentship at Christ Church, but a far more comfortable and delicate home for an ageing bachelor presented itself. By the middle of 1691 he was established in the household of Sir Francis Masham at his little moated manor house at Otes, in Essex, under the loving care of his lady, Damaris Masham, Locke's closest friend of all. Here twenty miles from London he spent his final, glorious years, his great and growing library around him, his special chair and desk, his cumbrous scientific apparatus, with his own servant and fodder for his own horse, for one guinea a week.* His time went in writing, not simply the works he published in such numbers, but letters, letters to the learned world, to publishers, to stockjobbers, and letters to politicians and to ministers and professional servants of the crown. The political influence he exercised in this way was truly extraordinary, and for the hundred warmest days in the year he exercised it in person from his London address in Lincoln's Inn Fields.

He did hold office of a sort, for from 1689 he was a Commissioner of Appeals and when the Board of Trade was founded in 1696 he was made a paid member. It has been shown, in fact, that Locke himself played a part in the creation of this second body, the architect of the old Colonial System. Though his responsibility for the Great Recoinage of 1695–6† has been misunderstood,

---

* For Locke at Otes, see Laslett, 1954 (i), Harrison and Laslett, 1965. From 1697 Locke had the literary assistance of Pierre Coste, who came to live at Otes as tutor to Lady Masham's son; hence the Christ's master-copy of *Two Treatises*.

† Kelly, 1969, shows that the recoinage was carried out in a way which was against Locke's advice, and that his attempts to influence monetary affairs directly (for instance by obtaining the post at the Mint, which went to Newton) were not very successful.

the expiry of the licensing of the press and other measures too were to some extent his doing.* There was a knot of Lockeian members of parliament, a group cutting across political 'connection' as it is now beginning to be understood, 'the only known example of an association of politicians for the purpose of a set of rationally conceived policies, a programme based not only on common sentiment, but on superior information and abstract thinking'. It was all done by a typically Lockeian foundation called the 'College' whose main function was correspondence, but which met as a club when Locke was in London: its patron was John Somers, later Lord Somers, counsel for the Seven Bishops in 1688, Solicitor-General in 1689, Lord Keeper 1693, Lord Chancellor 1697 and the chief figure in William III's government until 1700.

Somers may well have met Locke in the early 1680's and by 1689 looked to him so much as his mentor that he actually asked his advice on whether he should go on circuit or attend at parliament: in 1690 they exchanged views on the state of the currency. In fact, but with differences, Somers took on Shaftesbury's role for Locke. We need not dwell here on the importance and results of this association for government policy in the 1690's nor list the other noblemen, ministers and members who looked to him for advice and turned that advice into policy. The point of interest for Locke as a writer of political theory lies in the relation between the principles he had published, but not acknowledged, and the practical decisions which he advised so effectively and often helped to carry out. It would almost seem that during these years after the Revolution there was a very distant sense in which liberal or Whig philosophy did in fact inform government and affect politicians in the person of Locke the Whig philosopher.

Such an interpretation cannot be taken too literally. Locke, as we have seen, seemed indifferent to the implications of *Two Treatises*, certainly for communities under English domination. There was a general change towards 'rationalism' over these years, and it is significant that Locke's part in it was not confined to thinking and writing: success and reputation came to him suddenly after 1688 because at that point a secular drift in the atmosphere became a rapid transformation. But historians are

* See Laslett, 1969. The full story is sketched by Kelly, 1969, and will be published at length by him.

40

now careful not to call the events of 1688–9 the triumph of the Whigs, or even a revolution as that word is often used. Nevertheless it was the new general situation, as well as his own skill and good fortune, which enabled Locke to observe something of what we shall call his 'principle for policy' in action. The interesting thing is that he did not feel called upon to revise the text of his political theory in the light of this observation, although he did correct and recorrect its details and he can hardly have been unaware of its difficulties as a guide for ministers and administrators.

Outstanding in Locke's attitude and behaviour was his insistence on the citizen's duties in government: he looked upon himself and his friend Isaac Newton, Warden of the Mint, as contributing what an intellectual owed to government activity. If we are to understand Locke the political writer we must dwell for a little while on his peculiar relationship with the politicians.

In December 1684, he wrote from Holland a defensive letter to his patron at the time, the earl of Pembroke: it is a vindication of himself from the charges which had been used to justify his expulsion from Christ Church, and is an instructive commentary on several of the themes we have discussed. Talking of what he did in Shaftesbury's household, and hinting that as a practising physician he might have done better for himself materially, he continues:

I never did anything undutifully against His Majesty or the government. . . . I have never been of any suspected clubs or cabals. I have made little acquaintance, and kept little company, in an house where so much came. , , , My unmeddling temper . . . always sought quiet, and inspired me with no other desires, no other aims, than to pass silently through this world with the company of a few good friends and books. . . . I have often wondered in the way that I lived, and the make that I knew myself of, how it could come to pass, that I was made the author of so many pamphlets, unless it was because I of all my Lord's family happened to have been bred most among books. . . . I here solemnly protest in the presence of god, that I am not the author, not only of any libel, but not of any pamphlet or treatise whatsoever in print, good, bad or indifferent. The apprehension and backwardness I have ever had to be in print even in matters very remote from anything of libellous or seditious, is so well known to my friends.*

We may raise our eyebrows at Locke's definition of being

---

* Locke to Pembroke, 8 December 1684, de Beer, 2, 663–4; probably not seen by Pembroke, but retained by Edward Clarke, through whom it was to be sent, and who was asked by Locke to destroy it. See his letter to Clarke of 1 January 1685 (de Beer, 2, 671–5), where he also repeats these assertions of his innocence, literary and political.

undutiful to government and feel he was prevaricating over his authorship of political works, but we must welcome this insight into his character as a writer and his attitude to his political patrons. It suggests a delicate and precise portrait of the intellectual in the company of men of action. Obviously fascinated with the consummate effectiveness of all that Shaftesbury thought and wrote, said and did; anxious, perhaps over-anxious, to identify himself with the power he wielded; Locke could not bring himself to share his whole personality with the politicians. There is a hint here of his uneasiness about their lack of scruple and the dusty triviality of political activity day by day. But this was not the inner reason why he held himself back; why he kept up his Oxford career while it lasted, paying token visits there in the summer when the great men were in the country, or insisted on his separate personality as a doctor and a thinker.

He never overcame his inhibitions, although his situation in the 1690's made it possible for him to do what he wanted in spite of them. Locke cannot be described, therefore, simply by the somewhat superficial phrase *intellectuel engagé*: his reticence over his writings relevant to politics and political life makes that impossible in itself. Wonderfully quick and effective as an expository talker and writer, a genius in the calm clarity with which he could see the shape of complicated things, he was not a man who could lose himself in the act of political doing, or even of intellectual creation. His was an effectiveness at one remove, a power to fascinate the men of action, and in his last years he enjoyed to the full the directive influence it gave him.

Locke died on 29 October 1704, in his study at Otes, a room walled in dark oily brown and dull white, the colours of the books which had been so much of his life. He is buried a long way from Oxford and from his ancestors in Somerset, and buried in somewhat strange company, for the Mashams who lie all round him at High Laver were Tories and courtiers of the next generation.* He died a gentleman: 'John Locke, Gent.' is the author's line on the title-pages of the endless reprints of his books which stood on the shelves of eighteenth-century libraries.† This raises the final ques-

* See Laslett, 1954 (i). Abigail Masham is there, the snivelling High Church chambermaid who insinuated Sarah Churchill out of the affections of Queen Anne.

† Locke was so conscious of status, his own in particular, that he actually cancelled the title-page of one of his books because it described him as Esq., and substituted another calling him Gent. See Kelly, 1969, and for these titles in the system of honour, see Laslett, *The World we have lost*, ch. 2.

tion which must be asked about him as the intimate of great politicians and the creator of political principle for the modern world. Can he be called, as so often he is, the spokesman of a rising class, the middle class, the capitalists, the bourgeoisie?

We cannot here pass judgment on the sociological system which regards this question as a critical one. Locke certainly satisfies some of the criteria which it has set up. He was born, as we have said, into the classical atmosphere of early capitalism, into what might well be called a Puritan rising family in the loose way in which the term is used, for he was brought up amongst the lawyers, officials and merchants who had found their way into the Somerset gentry and lived his life as an absentee member. When he joined Shaftesbury, it could be said that he passed from the *petite bourgeoisie* to the *haute bourgeoisie*. He followed his wealthy patron into his investments—the Africa Company, the Lustring Company and finally the Bank of England. He invested in mortgages, lent money all his life to his friends for their convenience and at interest; although he protested that he 'never lov'd stock jobbing' there is in his letters of 1700–1 a clear example of stockmarket profiteering in the shares of the Old and New East India Companies. In his published works he showed himself the determined enemy of beggars and the idle poor, who existed, he thought, because of 'the relaxation of discipline and the corruption of manners'. He even implied that a working family had no right to expect its children to be at leisure after the age of three.*

But at the same time Locke profoundly mistrusted commerce and commercial men. He obviously welcomed the refusal of Somers to permit the control of national economic policy by such men when they attempted to set up a parliamentary Board of Trade in 1695, and though he approved the Bank of England, there is in his hand a curious dialogue expressing deep suspicions of the capitalists who floated it.† Although he was a doctor, it is difficult to make him a representative of the emerging professions which are now taken as symptomatic of the new order, for he despised medical men just to the extent that they were a profession and he shared Shaftesbury's contempt for lawyers. His expulsion

---

* See his report to the Board of Trade on the poor, 1697, for these details: printed by Fox Bourne, 1676, II, 377–90, compare Cranston, 1957, 424–5. Locke's recommendations make it look as if the conditions discovered in the early nineteenth century were not accidents, but the result of deliberate policy.

† See Laslett, 1969.

from Oxford may have been symbolic of the clash of the new view of the world with the old, but the crisis which actually brought it about was a complex conflict of interests and beliefs leading to violent political actions, and his own philosophical and general views were unpublished at the time.

It can be said nevertheless that Locke the individualist was an individual, and this is to claim for him a more exceptional social position than appears at first sight. The remarkable thing about him was his freedom from engagement: family, church, community, locality. To be free in all these directions at that time posed a dilemma to him. This dilemma can be seen in his relations with Oxford and even with the household at Otes. That such a position was possible, for him and a growing number of others, was a development pregnant of the future. Locke was as free as a man could then be from solidarity with the ruling group, and yet he was not one of the ruled; this is the only intelligible definition of 'middle-class' as applied to him and it leaves out many of the things which that expression seems to imply. Ultimately the possibility of living like this did arise as a function of economic change, but Locke can only be made into the spokesman of that change by the use of a whole apparatus of unconscious motivation and rationalization. An order of free individuals is not a concerted group, not a cohesive assemblage actually bringing about change; no simple conception of 'ideology' will relate Locke's thought with social dynamics.

He is perhaps best described as an independent, free-moving intellectual, aware as others were not of the direction of social change. This is evident in the central issue of *Two Treatises*, which is primarily concerned with the structure of the family and its relevance to social and political authority. If ever men dealt with fundamentals, Filmer and Locke did in this polemic. That Locke should have been an innovator in his justification of property may seem even more significant, but in fact it makes a determinist view of his thinking more difficult. For the attempts to make his doctrine into a straight justification of capitalism have to be complex, too complex to be convincing.

So much for Locke's political writing as determined by social structure and his personal situation. We must now turn to our detailed examination of its chronological determination, the actual events which impelled him to write *Two Treatises of Government*.

III

'TWO TREATISES OF GOVERNMENT' AND THE REVOLUTION OF 1688*

Whilst he was waiting at Rotterdam for a ship to take him home after the Revolution, Locke received the following letter from The Hague:

I have been very ill this fortnight. The beginning was what is called disease of one's country, impatience to be there, but it ended yesterday with violence, as all great things do but kings. Ours went out like a farthing candle, and has given us by this Convention an occasion not only of mending the Government but of melting it down and making all new, which makes me wish you were there to give them a right scheme of government, having been infected by that great man Lord Shaftesbury.†

The writer was Lady Mordaunt, wife of his friend who was to become Earl of Monmouth and Earl of Peterborough and who was already in England with William III. The Convention she mentions was the Convention Parliament, then working out the constitutional future of England after James II had sputtered out. By 11 February Locke was in London: on the 12th the Declaration of Right was completed:‡ on the 13th William and Mary were offered the crown.

This letter, except perhaps for its last phrase, aptly expresses the traditional view of the reasons why Locke sat down to write *Two*

---

* This section has been published in a slightly different form in the *Cambridge Historical Journal*, vol. XII, no. 1, March 1956, 40–55 (Laslett, 1956).

† Paraphrased: the original seems to read, e.g.: 'ours whent out: Lyke a farding candle: & has given us by this convension an occasion of mending the government but of melting itt down and make. . . .', Dated 11 January 1689 (de Beer, 3, 528–9), compare p. 77 below.

‡ This date makes it practically impossible that Locke had anything to do with its composition, or with any of the arguments to the Convention, though some of them look not unlike some portions of *Two Treatises* (compare, e.g., the *Proposals Offered to the Present Convention*, printed in *State Tracts*, 1693, with II, §§ 217, 219). Locke's papers contain nothing to suggest that he communicated his views from Holland to such writers or to members of the Convention.

Treatises of Government. What was wanted was an argument, along with a scheme of government, an argument deep in its analysis and theoretical, even philosophical, in its premises, but cogent and convincing in its expression. In its second part, at any rate, *Two Treatises* presents precisely these things. The author's objects and the occasion of his writing are set out just as might be expected in the Preface. He hoped that the book would be:

sufficient to establish the Throne of our Great Restorer, Our present King William; to make good his Title, in the Consent of the People, . . . and to justifie to the World, the People of England, whose love of their Just and Natural Rights, with their Resolution to preserve them, saved the Nation when it was on the very bring of Slavery and Ruine.

The case for supposing that the composition of this work belongs wholly and indissolubly with 1688, the year of the Glorious Revolution, is superficially convincing, therefore. It contains a statement which dates itself in that year.* It did in actual fact justify the Revolution to posterity, as well as to contemporaries. 'It is allowed on all hands,' wrote Josiah Tucker in 1781, 'and it has been a continual belief of the friends and admirers of Mr Locke, that he wrote his Essay on Government with a view to justify the Revolution.'† In the history books and the works on political theory, Locke on the English Revolution is still the supreme example of the way in which political events interplay with political thinking. This belief is far too deeply engrained, far, far too useful, to be easily abandoned. Nevertheless it is quite untrue.

Untrue, that is to say, in its most useful form. What Locke wrote did justify the Glorious Whig Revolution of 1688, if that phrase can be permitted at all. Some of the text undoubtedly was written in 1689 to apply to the situation then and its author must have intended the whole work to be read as a comment on these events. But it cannot be maintained that the original conception of

* 1, § 129, '*Judge Jeffries*, pronounced Sentence of Death in the late Times', the last phrase being in common use in 1689 to refer to James II's reign.

† Tucker, Josiah, *A treatise concerning civil government*, p. 72. In a short paper kept by his parliamentary friend Edward Clarke and probably written in April, 1690, Locke pronounced on the necessity of everyone publicly repudiating divine right doctrines because they divided the nation. Close to the *Preface of Two Treatises* in tone, it is markedly Williamite in tenor: MS Locke c.18 (recovered after being lost for 30 years), printed by Farr and Roberts, 1985.

the book was the justification of a revolution which had been consummated. A detailed examination of the text and the evidence bearing on it goes to show that it cannot have been 1688 which fastened Locke's attention on the nature of society and politics, political personality and property, the rights of the individual and the ethical imperatives on government. The conjunction of events which set his mind at work on these things must be sought at an earlier period. *Two Treatises* in fact turns out to be a demand for a revolution to be brought about, not the rationalization of a revolution in need of defence.

It was suspected as long ago as 1876 that the *First Treatise* was composed several years before 1688, and that the *Second* cannot have been wholly subsequent to the Revolution.* But the evidence available at that time was even more fragmentary and difficult to interpret than it is today, and within a decade or two the dogma that Locke wrote to rationalize the events of 1688–9 became firmly established in the nascent study of political science.† Another reason why this came about was that the reprints of the book which have circulated since that time have been so unsatisfactory.‡ Few of the students who have handled Locke on *Government* in recent generations were to know that he explained himself as he did in his

* Fox Bourne, I, 466, and II, 166: he believed that the *First* was prepared in 1681 or 1682, and that the *Second*, from its tone and method, seemed to have been 'composed before, instead of after, King William's accession . . . It may fairly be assumed that the whole work was substantially completed during the last year or so of Locke's residence in Holland'.

† Sir Leslie and Sir James Fitzjames Stephen, T. H. Green and Sir Frederick Pollock form the very distinguished group who seem to have been responsible, ignoring Fox Bourne and blandly accepting traditional dogma. Writing in 1876 itself, Sir Leslie Stephen merely said (II, 135) that 'Locke expounded the principles of the Revolution of 1688', but in 1879 Green was claiming in his famous *Lectures* that 'Locke wrote with a present political object in view . . . to justify the Revolution' (published 1895, 1931 ed., 76). Fowler was still following Fox Bourne in 1880, but Pollock was much more specific in reading the Revolution into the *Treatises* in his *Introduction to the History of the Science of Politics*, published originally in 1890. Sir James Stephen based his whole critique of the book on the fact that it had this as its occasion: he published this view in his *Horae Sabbaticae*, 2nd series, 1892. In 1904 Pollock developed the case in definitive form in his address to the British Academy, and more recent commentators seem to have followed him uncritically here and in his claim that Locke was really and consciously attacking Hobbes. Bastide, 1907, went farthest in reading the events of 1688–9 into the *Second Treatise*, although he relied heavily on Fox Bourne, and accepted his date for the *First Treatise*—see especially pp. 255–72.

‡ See section 1 and Laslett, 1952 (iv), 1954 (ii).

Preface, or even that the work consists in two treatises, not one, the first breaking off in the middle of a sentence only a quarter of the way through its text. For the *Preface* has not been reprinted in England since 1854, and the *First Treatise* only once since 1884.* When we treat what we are pleased to call our great political classics like this, there can be little wonder that a minor mythology should grow around one of them.

Although Locke makes this statement in his *Preface* of 1689 expressing the hope that what he had written would serve to justify the Revolution, he does not elaborate it. Nothing he says there refers directly to the time at which the work was composed, but he does explain why it would not have been worth his while to rewrite the missing majority of his manuscript. We may take this to imply that the *First Treatise*, described on the title-page as a refutation of Filmer, had been composed some time before, and was not so much a thing of the moment when the *Preface* was being written. It is interesting to recognize that Locke originally wrote such an extensive analysis of the work of a man whom he wanted to regard as an obscure nonentity,† and that the book planned was similar in size and in purpose to Sidney's unmanageable *Discourses*. But it is quite understandable that he should have been unwilling to repeat the performance. Filmer's great vogue had been between 1679 and 1681, and only the lingering attachment to his principles of the passive obedience party in 1689 justified the appearance between the same covers of the *First* and *Second Treatise*.

More recent specialist students of Locke have used this evidence in favour of the view of the date or dates of composition originally proposed in 1876. They have freely granted that the *First Treatise* was written before 1683, before Locke left for Holland, and they explain the fact that it contains the only statement which undoubtedly belongs after 1688 (the reference to 'Judge Jeffries') as an insertion of 1689. But the second book, they seem to agree, must be much later, and can only be dated in the months surround-

---

* Until the appearance of the present work in 1960, that is to say, for the previous English edition with both treatises and the Preface dates from 1824, but they presumably appeared in the last *Collected Locke* in 1854, whose existence has been doubted. They were included in an American reprint of 1947 (Hafner).

† On Filmer, see Laslett, 1948 (i) and (ii), Daly, 1979, Ezell, 1987. The slightly apologetic tone of Locke's remarks about him in the *Preface* may be due to the fact that he knew his family in Kent.

ing the revolutionary events themselves, though they find it difficult to decide which passages came before and which came after William's triumph over James. It has been noticed that the books to which Locke directly refers in his text, though very few in number, were all in print before 1683. But in the absence of any detailed knowledge of the editions and copies he actually used to write any part of his text, this fact has not been taken to point to an earlier date of composition for the whole work. They concede that the drift of Locke's statements makes it look as if the Revolution was yet to come. Nevertheless they see nothing impossible in supposing that the *Second Treatise* was written in its entirety after the event: that is presumably between Locke's return in February 1689 and August of that year, when it must have been complete to receive the Licenser's stamp.*

In view of all the work on this point over the last eighty years it seems extraordinary that the traditional fallacy, that not one but both *Treatises* were written to justify the Revolution of 1688–9, should still survive. But before it is abandoned, it should be pointed out that there is evidence in its favour which has never been brought forward. In some ways it is a better explanation than the one which has just been summarized. If the wording of Locke's *Preface* is considered carefully, it will be seen that he talks of the book as a whole. He cannot be made to imply that it was written in two parts, on two occasions, separated by some years,† though the admission that so much of the manuscript had been lost would seem to invite some such statement. It is a 'Discourse concerning Government', with a beginning, a middle (now missing) and an end, not the two disparate essays which recent commentators seem to have in mind.

His cross-references tend to confirm that this was his view of it.

---

* On 3 August 1689, the limiting date for the completion of the text. Among the Locke scholars referred to here are Gough, 1950, following Maclean, 1947 (i) and (ii), and Barker, 1948. Vaughan, 1925, conjectures from an argument about the inconsistency between the *Essay* and *Two Treatises*, an argument which is quite untenable in view of the history of the *Essay* as it has since become known, that '*Civil Government* . . . was written . . . in or shortly after 1680' (163, cf. 130). Driver, 1928, reaches a similar hypothesis on somewhat similar, though no more reliable grounds. Hinton, 1974, wishes to assign the original work of authorship of the *Second Treatise* to a date even earlier in the 1670s.

† Compare the *Epistle* introducing the *Essay on the Understanding*, explaining that it was 'written by incoherent parcels; and after long intervals . . . resumed again', etc.

They all occur in the first book, which is an interesting point, as we shall see. In § 66 he talks of something he will examine 'in its due place', which turns out to be the second book §§ 52–76: in § 87 he refers to a man's acquiring property, 'which how he . . . could do, shall be shewn in another place', that is in the second book, chapter 5: § 100 contains the words 'for which I refer my Reader to the Second Book'. This second book opens with the phrase 'It having been shewn in the foregoing Discourse', which means the text to be found in the preceding pages, not an earlier and separate discourse, for when unqualified that word refers to the complete work. When Locke wrote these phrases, he must surely have been quite clear about the content of his whole book, and their contexts make it very unlikely that they were later insertions.

We can add to these details Dr Gerritsen's very interesting discovery. Using the exact and subtle methods of analytical bibliography, he has shown that the title-page of the second book was a later insertion, made in the course of printing. The title to the whole, printed even later of course, was presumably brought into line with it.* It follows from this that Locke did not think of his volume originally as in two parts at all, any more than any work presented in two 'books'. The word 'Treatise', the expression 'Two Treatises', the title 'An Essay on Civil Government' applied to the second book were all afterthoughts, appearing finally on the title-pages, but never used in the text at all, not even in the cross-references. What Locke thought he was writing was a whole Discourse, set out in two books for his own literary purposes.

The book, then, was written as a whole. It is permissible to infer from this that it was written within a relatively short time, then an exact chronological argument is possible about the work he put into it, the work of original creation that is to say, as distinct from addition and revision. Given evidence to show that any considerable portion can only belong to the situation of a few particular months, say in 1688–9, then the whole belongs to those months.

But however willing men may have been to read the events of 1688–9 into Locke's text, there are convincing signs that the months of composition cannot have fallen then. The *First Treatise*, as we have seen, was intended as a complete refutation of Filmer,

* See Bowers, Gerritsen and Laslett, 1954.

Patriarcha and all, and in its original form may well have covered all his propositions, except perhaps his specifically historical argument about English institutions. Moreover, the exhaustive contradiction of patriarchalism runs right through the *Second Treatise* too: this is perhaps the most important result of editing it critically. If we believe that the whole book was written at one time, then we are obliged to believe that it was written between 1679 and 1681, or 1683 at the latest, since it is so obviously connected with the controversy of those years over the republication of Filmer. We have already seen that it was this controversy which set Sidney on work at his *Discourses*, which must have been complete by mid-1683 and very probably earlier. It is well known that in republishing Filmer, the Tories, champions of the Monarchy against Shaftesbury and the Whig Exclusionists, scored a notable propaganda victory, and Sidney was only one of a large number who took the risk of writing against it.* If the *First Treatise* belongs to these earlier years and the *Second Treatise* is part and parcel of it, then the whole work was written before 1683, and there is an end of it.

Though a simple proof of this sort carries conviction to its editor, the assumption that the book was composed over a relatively short span of time is open to attack. It could be maintained that it was the result of two separate impulses from historical circumstances, although it was composed as a whole. Granted that it was finished in some form when Filmer's name was on everyone's lips, it could still be supposed that it was rewritten later, and altered so extensively as to be a work of dual or multiple composition. This, as we have seen, was how Locke wrote on the *Understanding*, on *Toleration* and on *Education*. Doubt could even be thrown on the claim that the connection with Filmer must place the work in the early 1680's, for his name was still alive in 1688 and even later. The book, then, was composed as a whole, it might perhaps still be argued, but in the months up to August 1689; an author in a hurry might have started it as late as February of that year.

These possible objections make it necessary to go further into the evidence. Some of it can certainly be used against the position taken up here. There is force in the claim that it was still necessary

* See Laslett, 1948 (ii) and 1949: on the Whig Exclusionists, Furley, 1957; Pocock, 1957; Ashcraft, 1986, 1987.

for a Whig writer to go to some trouble to refute Filmer as late as 1689. His works were reissued in 1696, and any acquaintance with English political literature up to 1714 will show that Locke was not wasting his publisher's money by including the *First Treatise*. Locke's own correspondence makes this clear. James Tyrrell, who knew him best as a political writer, published *Patriarcha non Monarcha* against Filmer in 1681, but he found it necessary to return to the attack in 1691.*. When he first saw *Two Treatises* in December 1689, he thought of it as an attack on patriarchalism, 'a very solid and rational treatise called of Government in which Sr R Filmers Principles are very well confuted'. In the previous June, Furly the English Quaker who had been Locke's host in Rotterdam and was then in England, wrote thus to him: 'I met with a scrupulous Cambridge scholar that thought nothing could discharge him of the Oath of Allegiance that he had taken to James II and his successors. I had pleasant sport with him upon Sir R Filmers maggot.'† The letter which Leibniz received in 1698 telling him of Locke's book was also quite unequivocal on the point.

'Le livre de Monsy. Lock sur le gouvernement repond par tout son traité à celui de Chevalier Filmer'.‡

But all this goes to show why it was that Locke published what he had written against Filmer in 1689, rather than to demonstrate that he actually composed his refutation then. It is just possible that a man could find time to do all that Locke is known to have done between February and August and also to begin and complete a work at such length against the patriarchal extremists. The tracts he acquired make it plain that he interested himself in all that was coming out for and against the new order of things at that critical time.¶ But it is very difficult indeed to believe that he allowed himself to be rushed into print in this way. If he did, he

---

* *Bibliotheca Politica*, 1st dialogue and *passim*.

† Tyrrell to Locke, *c*.19 December 1689: Benjamin Furly to Locke, 10 June 1689, compare his letter of 26 October 1690, which confirms that he knew of the authorship of *Two Treatises* (de Beer 3, 638 39, 763 64; 4, 144 45). The book was in circulation a little before Tyrrell saw it. It was advertised in the *London Gazette* for 14 18 November.

‡ Gerhardt, *Leibniz*, vol. 3, 1887, p. 243.

¶ Locke bought political pamphlets only sporadically. Quite a number in his library catalogue date from 1679 82, though it it clear that at that time he was using some of Shaftesbury's copies of such works. A superficial survey shows that he bought for himself as much in 1689 as in all other years together. Ashcraft, 1987, 294 5, takes a different view of Locke's interest in and purchase of political pamphlets.

must have lost over half his manuscript immediately after he had finished writing, and this is almost inconceivable.

For we must never lose sight of his personality. 'Reader, Thou hast here the Beginning and End of a Discourse concerning Government; what Fate has otherwise disposed of the Papers that should have filled up the middle, and were more than all the rest, 'tis not worth while to tell thee' are the exact words he uses to explain the fragmentary nature of his text. Whatever this mysterious fate was, it cannot have been that Locke the precisionist had simply mislaid a whole sheaf of his own papers within the previous week or two, and he was not the man to allow an agent, a printer or a publisher to do such a thing.* Nor was he a man to do things in a hurry: we have seen how long and complicated was the process through which all his other books had to go before they appeared in print. To think of him as a man who would write for publication a rationalization of events which had just taken place is to misunderstand his character completely. This makes against the traditional interpretation in all its possible forms.

Did he compose the work, or at least the second book, in the leisurely, Lockeian manner during his Dutch exile, bringing it home with him for final revision and publication? This is the tendency of recent Locke scholarship, at least as to the *Second Treatise*, and there is evidence for it. It accounts for the fact that his political comment reads for the most part as if it were made before and not after William's accession.† It allows for a much earlier date of germination. His connection with such architects of the Revolution as Mordaunt naturally gave rise to the expectation that he might write about it. He was pressed as early as 1687 to publish on *Toleration*,‡ and if he could go into print on this

---

* This obvious point can be illustrated by his behaviour when a paper of his corrections was said to be mislaid in 1694, see above, 8–9 and note* on page 9.

† It will be seen from the passage in the Preface quoted on p. 46 that Locke writes of William alone, and not his co-sovereign Mary. This may mark him as a supporter of William's sole sovereignty, an attitude typical of the Whigs who had been in exile, but one which ceased to be held by the latest date at which the Preface can have been written—October 1689.

‡ Tyrrell to Locke, 6 May 1687: 'your Discourse about Liberty of Conscience would not do amiss now to dispose people's minds to pass it when the Parliament sits'. This 'Discourse' was not the final *Epistola*, which was composed in Holland in 1684–5 and was unknown to Tyrrell, and to everyone except Limborch, see Fox Bourne, 1876, II, 34. In Laslett, 1956, evidence is cited about a work which Locke was trying to get printed in 1687. Prof. Cranston has since convinced me that it cannot have been *Two Treatises*.

subject, why should he not be writing on politics? Any sign that he was actually engaged on *Two Treatises* in Holland in or just before 1688 would make this view formidable.

There is an entry in his journal in February 1687 which seems at first sight to provide just the detail to sanction such an interpretation. It is an extract from Garcilaso de la Vega which is also to be found in the *Second Treatise*, § 14.* But even this turns out to be quite inconclusive. For it so happens that the passage is present in the second state of the first edition only, and therefore could easily have been added when he made the modifications which turned the first into the second state in October 1689.† Nevertheless the possible implication of this one item and the necessity of finding positive confirmatory evidence of the view put forward here makes it very important that there should be a whole class of sources which has yet to be used. In Locke's notes on his reading, in his lists of books, in the books themselves and their whereabouts at the dates under discussion, we have indications of a much more specific and reliable kind than those so far cited.

But before we turn to this material we may refer to some obvious features of the text of the book. Quite apart from its unmistakable connections with the Filmer controversy of 1679–81, there are political references which make sense for those years and those years alone. In 1689 the phrase 'King James' with no number following could mean King James II and nobody else. Yet in the text printed in that year Locke twice refers to 'King James' when he meant James I, surely a very significant anachronism and one which he corrected in later printings.‡ It seems strange that this should not have been noticed before, but even stranger that the parliamentary issues of the Exclusion Controversy have not been noticed in the constitutional discussion of the *Second Treatise*.

---

* See II, § 14, 12–17 and note, and Locke's diary for 2 February 1687.

† See Laslett, 1952 (iv) and 1954 (ii), for the two states. The item was either a MS. addition to author's copy, misunderstood by the compositor of the first state, or an alteration between the two states. Even if it were the former, it could have been done in 1689, when he modified his MS. in so many other respects. In fact this detail may confirm the view that Locke did not have his MS. with him in 1687 when he made the diary entry, but copied that entry into it two years later.

‡ *Second Treatise*, §§ 133 and 200, corrected in 1694 and 1698 respectively—see Collation. This perhaps should not be pressed too far. James I was also a literary figure and the omission of the number would not confuse the reader in obviously literary contexts.

Except perhaps in the last chapter, Locke's chief concern there was the summoning and dissolution of Parliament. This was for him the crucial relationship between Legislative and Executive. It was this which could lead to '*a state of War*' (that is with the people) when the 'Executive Power shall make use of . . . force to hinder the *meeting* and *acting of the Legislative*' (II, § 155). Now this was not the major issue of 1688, nor of James II's reign. But it was typical of the years between 1678 (or even 1675) and 1681, when Shaftesbury with Locke so often at his side had made attempt after attempt to force Charles II either to dissolve a parliament long out of date, or to summon it after an intolerable series of prorogations. The 'long train of Abuses, Prevarications and Artifices' of § 225 became a phrase in the American Declaration of Independence. It included underhand favouring of Catholicism '(though publickly proclaimed against)' (§ 210). These abuses were those of Charles II, not James II. He did not find it necessary either to be underhand in favouring Catholicism, or to proclaim against it.

We can go no further into the results of reducing Locke's theories to their revised historical context. Let us begin our consideration of the evidence now open to us in Locke's books and reading by taking a straightforward example. His diary tells us that he was in London in August 1681, in Shaftesbury's house, though Shaftesbury was away, in the Tower. On the 29th he bought 'Knox, R' Historical Relation of Ceylon, fol. London 81' for eight shillings (that is, Robert Knox on Ceylon, 1681). In § 92 of the *Second Treatise* he refers to 'the late Relation of Ceylon', and the word *late* here means, presumably, just published. Now we know that Locke kept this book in London, and that he lost sight of it in 1683 when he went to Holland. There is no sign that it was ever amongst the separate collection which he kept at Oxford, and which was transported to Tyrrell's house in 1684 when he was expelled from Christ Church. Knox does not appear in any document from the period of his exile; journal, book bill, book list or notebook. We have no evidence that he ever saw this copy, or any other copy, until the title appears in the catalogue he made of his London books in the summer of 1689.* His Oxford books were not delivered to him by Tyrrell until 1691. It is, therefore, very unlikely that he wrote this phrase in the

---

* The complicated story of the disposition of his books whilst he was in Holland, and of Tyrrell's actions over them, is told in Harrison and Laslett, 1965, Part I, Chapter II.

Second Treatise between 1683 and 1689, and very likely that he wrote it between 1681 and 1683.

'Very likely' could become 'certainly' only if we could exclude the possibility of access to another copy later, and if we had cumulative evidence. It is in the nature of things that later access cannot be entirely excluded,* though in this and many other cases it is highly improbable. But cumulative evidence is just what we do possess. Although he refers to so few books directly in his text, we can work out a sizeable list of those he may have consulted and compare it with three other lists. One is the census of the books in his rooms at Christ Church which he wrote out in his diary under July 1681, another is the London list of 1689, and the third is Tyrrell's catalogue of the books returned in 1691. It appears that Locke's library of the early 1680's, divided between Shaftesbury's house and Christ Church, contained nearly all the works which he used for the writing of *Two Treatises*.

This can be supplemented from his records of his reading and purchases over the relevant years. They show that between 1679 and 1682 Locke was more interested in publications on political theory and natural law than ever before or after. One or two of the critical titles, as we shall see, are to be found amongst those which Shaftesbury drew to his attention in 1679, and which were lent to him, or made available in London. It was only in the period before 1683 that Locke had convenient access to the particular books which he needed for writing on *Government*. Any other suggested date of composition implies that he went painfully from friend to friend and library to library consulting them one by one.

We may take a further particular example in confirmation, a book of much greater importance to his political thinking than Knox—Hooker's *Ecclesiastical Polity*. He had read Hooker before, we know, though perhaps not far into that tall folio.† But it was not until 13 June 1681 that he bought in London 'Hooker

---

* Maclean, 1947 (ii), ingeniously argues that a book which he believes is vital to *Two Treatises* (Lawson, 1657, see below) could have been used by Locke in Furly's house in Rotterdam. But though it has this Lawson and some other relevant items, the catalogue of Furly's library (*Bibliotheca Furleina*, 1714) does not contain enough of the right titles to make it likely that the reading for the book was done there. On these topics, see Ashcraft, 1969 (ii), 1987, and Addendum, pp. 123–6 below.

† In his early essay on the *Civil Magistrate* he states that he had only read the Preface, see Abrams, 1961, p. 32, though within a few months he had read at least the first book, and Hooker appears occasionally in his notebooks up to 1681.

Ecclesiasticall Politie fol Lond. 66'. He read in the book during the rest of the month, making lengthy extracts from it into his journal, some of them important for his philosophizing. Now, there are sixteen passages from Hooker quoted in the *Second Treatise*,* and in § 239 Locke explains why he had used the work. When the quotations in his diary are set alongside those in the *Second Treatise*, they are seen to alternate, never overlapping. The conclusion must be that in June 1681 Locke was working on the *Second Treatise*, incorporating extracts from Hooker into it, and at the same time copying into his diary other passages of philosophical interest.† These details are interesting not only for the implication that the Hooker quotations were added to the text after it had been begun, but also because they reveal Locke at work on *Two Treatises* and the *Essay on the Understanding* at the same time.

We have chosen these examples from books quoted in the *Second Treatise* only, and enough has been said to establish a presumption against assuming that only the *First Treatise* could have been in existence in 1681. For closer indications that the composition of the whole book can plausibly be supposed to belong to a particular series of months we may turn to the copies Locke used of the works of Filmer, which enter into both treatises.

These tracts had originally been published separately in 1648, 1652 and 1653, but Filmer's original writing, the famous *Patriarcha*, from which they finally derive, had never been printed.‡ About the middle of 1679 the printed tracts were hurriedly republished as a collection under the title *The Freeholders Grand Inquest*, each tract being individually paginated. In January 1680 this collection was printed again, with continuous pagination. At about the same time *Patriarcha* was first published. Locke bought this 1680 collection with *Patriarcha* bound up with it for 4*s*. 6*d*. on 22 January 1680,¶ and in his Preface to *Two Treatises* he tells us

---

* Four in the text (§§ 15, 60, 61), eleven in Locke's notes (see §§ 74, 90, 91, 94 (two), 111, 134 (two passages quoted together), 135, 136 (same passage as in 134)).

† A 1666 edition of Hooker appears in the London list and in a slightly puzzling entry in his final catalogue (Harrison and Laslett, 1491), which also contains the 1676 edition (Harrison and Laslett, 1490) still among his books. These volumes therefore may not be distinct. He had yet another Hooker dated 1632 in Oxford (Harrison and Laslett, 1492), though it is interesting that he did not use it to finish this work when he visited his rooms during July. He continued when he got back to London.

‡ See Laslett, 1949, especially 47-8, *Concise Bibliography of Filmer's Works*.

¶ This volume is in front of the present writer. Some of the leaves are folded up to indicate passages, but there are no marginal notes.

that these were the editions he used. He explains his references to Filmer thus: 'O for his *Observations on Hobbs, Milton* etc. . . . a bare Quotation of Pages always means Pages of his *Patriarcha*. Edit. 1680.'* This was presumably the volume short-titled 'Filmer' which was standing in his rooms in July 1681, for it was certainly the one which Tyrrell took charge of whilst Locke was in exile, and returned in 1691.

As we should expect with the meticulous Locke, these conventions are consistently respected. In the 200 or so references to Filmer in the *First Treatise*, a passage marked 'O 245' is always found on p. 245 of the 1680 Collection, and one marked '13' is always found on p. 13 of *Patriarcha*. But on the single occasion on which he cites this author by page number in the *Second Treatise*, he breaks his convention.

He is discussing liberty as being 'for every one to do what he lists' in § 22, and he refers to 'what Sir R.F. tells us *O.A.* 55'. Now this will not work for the 1680 Collection. Nothing resembling what he quotes is to be seen on p. 55 of that volume. But it does work for a p. 55 of the 1679 Collection, p. 55 of the *Observations on Aristotle* which becomes p. 143 in the 1680 reprint, where Filmer does make this particular statement about liberty. It looks as if Locke must have been using the 1679 volume when he wrote § 22 of the *Second Treatise*, and so observing a different convention of reference. And it looks as if he had reached that paragraph before even reading *Patriarcha*: indeed the text of the *Second Treatise*, although written against patriarchalism, could have been originally composed without his having seen *Patriarcha* at all.

We have independent evidence that Locke was in fact reading the 1679 Collection in the year of its appearance, and that he was making extracts from the book in almost precisely the form found in the *Second Treatise*. A 'Tablet', or note pad, of his has survived from this period, used for notes and references, some taken into Shaftesbury. On p. 119 he wrote under '79' (for 1679): 'Filmer to resolve the conscience O p. 59.'† On p. 59 of Filmer's *Observations on Aristotle* in the 1679 Collection, resolving the conscience is discussed, discussed along with the consent of the people to

* 'Observations on Hobbs', etc. refers collectively to the tracts in the volume, with the exception of the *Freeholder*, printed first; Locke never refers to the *Freeholder* in *Two Treatises* as we now know it.

† Resolving the conscience was a crucial issue in the Exclusion years. Ashcraft objects that this note was not necessarily made in 1679 because it was the first entry on the page: see below p. 124.

government, a major theme of the *Second Treatise*. Good evidence this, as such circumstantial evidence goes, that Locke may have been engaged on the early part of that essay in 1679.*

I am prepared to venture a general assertion on the basis of this discussion. As early as 1679 Locke had begun a work on government, and a work with the immediate object of refuting Filmer. He had begun it, it would seem, with Shaftesbury's connivance, perhaps at his request and with his assistance in the matter of sources. But the work he had begun was not the *First Treatise*, but the *Second*. He seems to have reached paragraph number 22 of that *Treatise*, possibly number 57 and even number 236, almost the very end, when he changed his mind sometime in 1680, and decided to write the *First Treatise* too.† We need not look far for the reason why he did this. It was the appearance of *Patriarcha* in January 1680, together with the enormous growth of Filmer's influence which went on during the rest of that year. The reply he had originally planned was insufficient because it left out of account the most important work of the man he was criticizing and did not contain the phrase-by-phrase refutation which he recognized was now needed. It is possible moreover that a somewhat similar path was taken by his friend James Tyrrell during the writing of his own independent essay in refutation of Filmer, *Patriarcha non Monarcha*, published in 1681.

Locke and Tyrrell had been friends from their Oxford days, and mutually interested in primitive peoples, Natural Law and toleration as well as politics; they exchanged books, corresponded and from time to time discussed.‡ It was no even, undisturbed friendship for Tyrrell, as will be seen, was not the most tactful of

---

* The 'Tablet' is MS. f. 28. On p. 40 he notes, also under 1679, 'Shaftesbury: Lawson's book of the English Government', an entry later crossed through, showing, it is clear, that Shaftesbury made Locke a loan of this book, who crossed out the entry when he returned it (or it may have been Locke who lent, and Shaftesbury who returned). The two men were presumably reading Lawson then, and so Maclean's supposition that Locke read him in 1687 in Holland is otiose. If Shaftesbury was the lender, it may be that he lent Locke the 1679 collection of Filmer too. Locke had Lawson, 1660, in Holland, and finally bought the 1689 reprint. Ashcraft rejects this use of Locke's 'Tablet'.

† See notes on these paragraphs. In § 57 he repeats, without reference, the phrase from Filmer used in § 22, and in § 236 inserts another quotation noted in his 'Tablet', this time under 1680. In the *First Treatise*, § 14, there is a phrase which might possibly imply that he read *Patriarcha* first, and the other tracts later, but statements in I §§ 6, 11 confirm the view taken here.

‡ On Locke and Tyrrell, see J. W. Gough, 1976.

men. 'He never polished himself out of his sincerity', as his epitaph admits.

In the crisis years of 1680–3 Locke spent much of his time at Tyrrell's house at Shotover, some miles away from his suspicious college, and they engaged in collaborative writing: a critical commentary on Stillingfleet's *Unreasonableness of Separation* (1681).* But each may have been at work at another literary task as well. In January 1680 Tyrrell wrote a letter to an eminent Whig historian which remarked 'There is lately come to this town a new treatise of Sir Robert Filmer's called *Patriarcha*'.† This suggests that he was already at work on *Patriarcha non Monarcha* using Filmer's previously republished tracts, in the 1679 edition.‡ He may have had to take the new publication into account by modifying his text. The published book begins with a page by page refutation of *Patriarcha* in rather the same way as Locke's work in its final form begins with the *First Treatise* also specifically directed against *Patriarcha*.

Locke and Tyrrell, then, were in close communication when, as I am prepared to believe, both were engaged in refuting Filmer, and their writing plans followed a remarkably similar pattern. So close were they, indeed, that some sort of collaboration would seem possible, or even likely. But the remarkable thing is that the evidence we have goes to show that Locke most certainly did not let Tyrrell see his manuscript, or even know of its existence, and that Tyrrell seems to have been almost as guarded about his too.¶ This is of some interest, since so many of Tyrrell's positions against Filmer were also those of Locke, more particularly the account of the right of property.‖ But whatever the exact relationship of the two men

* MS. c. 34: Locke's, Tyrrell's and another hand (? an amanuensis) interspersed. Tyrrell actually made notes, on subjects of importance to political theory, in Locke's journal for 1680, see note on II, § 108, 6.

† Inner Temple MS. 583 (17), f. 302, Tyrrell to Petyt 'Jan. 12th', obviously 1680. See Pocock, 1957, 187–8: Mr Pocock helped with this reference.

‡ This book was divided between compositors in such a way as to give rise to three inconsistent paginations. In earlier editions my *Introduction* suggested that the discontinuities arose because Tyrrell sent added copy dealing with *Patriarcha*. This does not seem to have been so and the facts are as set out in a letter to me of January, 1972 by Mr J. Attig, and as printed in 1978 by J. W. Gough.

¶ Locke bought a copy of *Patriarcha non Monarcha* 'for Mr Tyrrell' soon after its appearance in June, 1981. No man buys a book to give it to its anonymous author, if he knows who wrote it. Tyrrell later sent Locke a copy amended in manuscript (H. and L. 2999, see note on II, 74, 14–37).

‖ See footnotes to text throughout, especially note on II, § 27. *Patriarcha non*

over their two books, it is clear that when Locke decided to deal as he did with Filmer's *Patriarcha* he did as Tyrrell did and what circumstances demanded.

Only in *Patriarcha*, and after January 1680, was the authoritarian, patriarchal, Tory case at work on the minds of the politically important as one influential whole. In his tracts Filmer had commented on the constitution and on the origin of government in separate contexts, so much so that it has been widely believed that the *Freeholders Grand Inquest*, his specifically constitutional work, was by a different author.* Locke may have modified, rearranged, perhaps extensively rewritten the *Second Treatise* when he knew that the *First* would be added: we have seen him working at it in this way in 1681 when he added the Hooker passages. As Ashcraft insists, the Oxford parliament where the Exclusion Bill finally failed gave great urgency to the issues and may well have had a considerable effect on Locke's text. Moreover he certainly made further additions and presumably modifications in 1689, and the decision to print the treatises in their final order could have been taken then. But much of it was left as originally written, including the reference in § 22 which survived all his repeated correction. From the point of view of our discussion, the book as a response to political and literary circumstances, its origin belongs to the autumn and winter of 1679–80, exactly a decade earlier than it is traditionally supposed to have been written. *Two Treatises* is an Exclusion Tract, not a Revolution Pamphlet.

As it stands, Locke's book is cumbersome and uninviting: two hundred unreadable pages introducing an essay which is lively and convincing if a little laboured and repetitive. We can see why he arranged it thus, though we may feel aggrieved at his insensitivity. But there is no good reason for supposing that he thought his thoughts in such an unlikely order, or wrote them down like this.

Every one of his positions is assumed in the *First Treatise*, but when he refers to them there he has to send us forward to the

---

Monarcha is referred to appreciatively, by title if not by author, in I, § 124. It can be argued from the facts presented here that Tyrrell, not Locke, must be regarded as the initiator of the 'labour theory of value', unless these two claims are accepted. One is that Locke had written, or worked out, the substance of his text by 1679, and the other is that he had communicated his conceptions to his friend. It is quite possible to accept the first of these claims, but the second is not so clearly established, and any assessment of the 'originality' of any part of *Two Treatises* must take these facts into account.

* See Allen, 1928, a view forcibly restated by C. C. Weston in 1980.

Second. Who would deliberately choose to begin the exposition of a complicated theme by the refutation of another man's system without laying down his own premises? It would seem undeniable that the *Second Treatise* is logically prior to the *First* because its author never had occasion to cite the *First* in composing the *Second.* I believe that a satisfactory account of the writing of the book must assume that the *Second Treatise*, the positive statement, was already in existence in some form or other when the *First*, the negative commentary, was begun.

This is as much as may be safely inferred from what is certainly known about the date and manner of composing *Two Treatises*. It leaves a great deal open to conjecture, and this interlude will be given up to conjecture. Only one guess will be made, but if it is a lucky guess it explains a great deal.

There is a document referred to in the papers of both Locke and Shaftesbury which had a history corresponding quite exactly with the history of the manuscript or manuscripts of *Two Treatises* as it has been worked out here. It had a cover name, *de Morbo Gallico*, a cant expression for syphilis, the French disease. This may seem vulgar, but Locke's medical identity must not be forgotten, and cover names are common in these papers, especially for secret, dangerous or embarrassing documents. Moreover Locke and Shaftesbury did think of despotism as a French disease, and when he wrote in 1679 Locke had just returned from France, from studying the French disease as a political system.

When Shaftesbury was arrested in July 1681, Locke was presumably in the house. But by the time lists had been drawn up of the papers which had been seized, Locke was in Oxford, making the catalogue of his books there. Amongst his folios, standing close to Hooker and to the big bound notebook containing his first draft on the *Understanding*, he entered *Tractatus de Morbo Gallico*.* Meanwhile in London the government men were searching amongst Shaftesbury's papers, and they had come across several Locke items. There was the Shaftesbury copy of the draft on the *Understanding*, the letter on the Oxford Parliament, 'Mr Locke's book of fruit trees'. 'Notes out of Mors Gallicus in my

---

* This must be distinct from his old material book with the title *Morbus Gallicus. Omnia quae extant de eo*, Venice, 1566 (Harrison and Laslett, 2041), which was a folio too.

lord's hand' was another document registered by them.* Shaftesbury must have had some reason to go to the trouble of making
these notes: he may conceivably have been a syphilitic, but this
has never been suspected before. Anyway Locke took his document with this title over to Tyrrell's house on 17 July, and when
he left for London on the 18th wrote in shorthand in his diary
'Left with him De Morbo Gallico'.

A year later Dr Thomas of Salisbury, his medical and political
friend, wrote and told him that 'You may send your Observations
de Morbo Gallico' and named a messenger.† If this was the same
thing, it must have been something Locke had himself written.
It next appears in November 1683, in a letter written to Clarke
from Holland soon after he had arrived, full of cryptic allusions to
possessions left behind.

Honest Adrian writes me word that the chest that is now in Mrs . . .
custody was not opened, though he had the key and directions to do it.
Neither do I ask whether anything else was in her custody was opened,
only give me leave to tell you that I either think or dreamt you enquired
of me concerning the title of a treatise, part whereof is in Mr Smith's
hands, and it is *Tractatus de Morbo Gallico*. If there were another copy of
it I should be glad to have that at any reasonable rate, for I have heard
it commended and shall apply myself close to the study of physic by the
fireside this winter. But of this I shall write to your more hereafter,
when I hear there are more copies than one, for else it will not be
reasonable to desire it. I desire also to know whether Dr Sydenham
hath published anything this year.‡

Locke seems to say that he wants another copy of a treatise which
exists in part in the keeping of someone he names, perhaps
Mrs Smithsby his London landlady. But he is evidently afraid
that the cautious Clarke may have destroyed the full copy. Well
he might have, if this was the manuscript we are after, for in that
very month Sidney was up at the Old Bailey for writing against

---

* P.R.O. Shaftesbury Papers, 30/24 Bundle VIA, item 349, paper 3.

† Thomas to Locke, 25 July 1682; on 5 August he acknowledged arrival of the man
who was to bring 'your opinion *de Morbo Gallico*' (de Beer, 2, 535, 537).

‡ Locke to Clarke, 21 November (1683), de Beer, 2, 606. The 'Mrs' whose name has
perished may be Mrs Smithsby, and the same with the later 'Mr Smith':'Adrian' is Dr
Thomas: the medical references look like a blind. Unfortunately this and the next letter are
missing from the collection (now in the Locke papers in the Bodleian Library) as Rand knew
it, and his unreliable transcription cannot be checked.

Filmer: in his previous letter Locke had asked for 'what news the Old Bailey affords'.

The last context is mutilated but clearer. In a much later letter to Clarke of 18 February 1687, Locke writes: 'I beg also that the half . . .*de Morbo Gallico*, which I left with R. Smith sealed up in a little [box] about the length of a hand and about [half a] hand in breadth, may be sent into. . . .' And a little further on in the letter: 'You may easily [perceive] why I would have that tract *de Morbo Gallico*. . . .'* It would seem that the full copy of the work had not been available, for it had evidently not been sent to him in Holland. It is tempting to suppose that the reason why he wanted the other half-copy was political, and only recently Locke had complained of hearing little about politics.† Nothing with this title, or on a subject which would fit these references, has survived in Locke's voluminous papers, although other writings he found at Mrs Smithsby's when he returned to London in 1689 are still to be seen amongst them.

If this exercise in conjecture could be substantiated it would imply all these things. The first form of *Two Treatises*, under the name *De Morbo Gallico*, was originally written into a folio note-book, in the same way as Locke's first sketch of his *Essay*. Shaftesbury had seen and noted it before his arrest in July 1681, when it had already been placed on Locke's shelves at Christ Church amongst the books he used to write it. Tyrrell had charge of it for a while a little after this, though he did not know its identity: Thomas, who read it in 1682, and Clarke were let into the secret. It existed in two copies by 1683, but before Locke went to Holland, one of the copies had been halved and then left with Mrs Smithsby: Clarke had orders to destroy the other copy completely if it should seem advisable, with an eye to what was happening at the trial of Sidney.‡

Clarke did dispose of the full copy, and Locke did not regain any

---

* De Beer, 3, 132. The dots represent passages which had perished when Rand saw the letter, and the square brackets his suggested readings.

† Locke to Limborch, 14 February 1687, de Beer, 3, 128.

‡ Locke was in a high state of anxiety at this time and destroyed a great deal: it was probably then that he effaced the references to the writing of the book from his papers. Campbell (*The Chancellors*, 1845, III, 374) states that Locke had Shaftesbury's autobiography destroyed because of Sidney's fate. In the 1950's Locke's letters to Clarke contained a sheet numbered 185 containing cyphers to be used, which Clarke seems to have received in Feb. 1684-5 (de Beer, 2, 685). This document has not subsequently been referred to.

part of this writing, as far as we know, before 1689, certainly not before 1687. We may identify the half of his manuscript which he left with Mrs Smithsby with the whole work as we now have it. His motive for destroying the remainder can easily be inferred. Presumably this area was the dangerous one. It came, it will be remembered, at the end, not in the middle, of the manuscript, since it was a continuation of the *First Treatise*. It contained those passages which he and his friends were afraid might be of use to a counsel for the Crown in persuading a court of justice that in writing this book John Locke had been as much of a traitor as Algernon Sidney. Such, then, in the words of the Preface was the 'Fate' which 'otherwise disposed of the Papers that should have filled up the middle'.

Quite apart from conjecture, the evidence presented here and further analysed in the footnotes to Locke's text* makes possible the following tentative reconstruction of the stages of composition. In the winter of 1679–80 the *Second Treatise* was written, perhaps only partially, perhaps as a completed work. Early in 1680 the *First Treatise* was added to it, and if Shaftesbury did read the book, he probably read it at this stage. Perhaps he or someone else suggested revisions to Locke, for he went at it again in the summer of 1681, adding the Hooker references and excerpts, and probably chapters XVI, XVII, XVIII and part of chapter VIII in the *Second Treatise*, in all some fifty paragraphs. The process of revision and extensions went on into 1682, it may be, and there are parts of chapter XVIII which seem to belong to 1683, with perhaps some or most of the final chapter. From February to August 1689 further revision and extension went on, as we have seen, throughout the volume, and continued until the very last possible printer's moment. In all, however, only the Preface, the titles and some twenty-five new paragraphs seem to have been written then, including the whole of chapters I, IX and XV in the *Second Treatise*. In these passages only, together with the considerable number of much briefer additions and modifications, can the book be said to belong to the year of the Glorious Revolution.

The writing of *Two Treatises of Government* as it has been reconstructed here can only belong to the association of Locke with

---

* An attempt has been made to assign each chapter of the *Second Treatise* to one of the conjectured periods of composition: see the notes on the first paragraph of each chapter. Where any particular paragraph or passage seems to be of different date from the surrounding text, this has been commented upon.

Shaftesbury, and that association ended in trauma. The necessity of going into exile, the loss of his position at Christ Church, the threat of trial and perhaps even execution were all connected in the mind of this careful, introverted, timid man with his having written on politics. When he returned in 1689 and made up his mind to publish what he had written, it was not to a country whose political future seemed stable. The return of James II was a possibility throughout the 1690's: if he had returned, it would have meant exile for Locke, and perhaps, he must have argued, a harder fate for the known writer of this book. His own experience and the treatment of his friends and associates made it clear to him that a Catholic Stuart monarch would not hesitate to use anything found in his private papers against him. This begins to explain his extraordinary furtiveness about the writing of *Two Treatises*, and his persistent refusal to admit that he had written it.

But there may be another reason, much more interesting for political thinking and for its relation with philosophy. It is possible that Locke was unwilling to let it be known that the same man who wrote the *Essay concerning Humane Understanding* also wrote *Two Treatises of Government* because he was quite well aware that it was no simple matter to reconcile their doctrines. We have described a man who disliked criticism and shrank from controversy. There can be no doubt that he would have had to face both of these things if his contemporaries had been invited to compare the assumptions of his theory of knowledge with the assumptions of his political principles. The critical issue was his view of the Natural Law. The reputation of Thomas Hobbes had been blasted beyond recovery, and one of the reasons was that he had laid himself open in this way. It is time to examine the relationship of Hobbes and Locke as a subject in itself.

IV
LOCKE AND HOBBES

1. FILMER, LOCKE AND HOBBES.
'TWO TREATISES' AND CONTEMPORARY
POLITICAL WRITING

If Locke wrote his book as a refutation of Sir Robert Filmer, then he cannot have written it as a refutation of Thomas Hobbes. It is almost as mistaken to suppose that he was arguing deliberately against *Leviathan* as to believe that he wrote to rationalize the Revolution. There would have been no point whatsoever for the intellectual champion of the Whig exclusionists to produce one more criticism of Hobbes. Professor Skinner* has demonstrated that Hobbes did have an intellectual context and a following: he did not spring from nowhere and exist without effect, except on his opponents. But he was politically the least important of all the absolutist writers. Filmer, on the other hand, was the man of the moment, a formidable and growing force with those whose political opinions mattered, and representing in himself the *ipsissima verba* of the established order. Therefore Locke found himself impelled to write on this subject, and for that reason Filmer's thinking lies directly behind his political doctrines. Moreover, his controversy with patriarchalism has a fundamental significance in the history of political and social thinking, for the development of the structure of modern society.†

Locke rejected Hobbesian absolutism along with Filmer's, of course: the word 'Leviathan' occurs in his *Second Treatise*, and there are phrases and whole arguments which recall the Hobbesian position, and must have been intended in some sense as comments upon them.‡ Moreover, the thinking of Hobbes was of systematic

---

* See his three very interesting and convincing articles, 1965 (ii), 1966 (i) and (ii).

† See Laslett, *The World we have lost*, especially chapter 9. Bastide, 1907, particularly 208–9, takes the view that Hobbes was an important political influence because of his purchase over Charles II's Court. Pollock again seems to have done most to establish the view that Locke was really writing against Hobbes: see 1904, 238, and also Vaughan, 1925; Gough, 1950. The most interesting assessment of Locke's relationship with Hobbes, and of the reasons why *Two Treatises* was not directed against *Leviathan*, is in Dunn, 1969 (i), chapter 7.

‡ See footnotes to II, § 19, 21, 98, 133, 211, 212.

importance to Locke and enters into his doctrines in a way which goes much deeper than a difference in political opinion. But this cannot alter the fact that Filmer's tracts occupy for the *Second Treatise* the position which has traditionally been reserved for the works of Hobbes. This has had some effects which have previously gone unnoticed.

Filmer influenced Locke, in the way all men influence those who choose to refute them. It was he, and not Locke himself, and decidedly not Hobbes, who set the terms of the argument. No doubt Locke would have found some opportunity to declare his belief in the freedom and equality of all men, but as it happened he was forced to do so at the very outset of his work on government, because Filmer had directly denied it, against Hobbes amongst others. It may well be that some of Locke's arguments would never have been developed at all if it had not been for Filmer. We have seen that he showed no sign of an interest in the theory of property before he sat down to this polemic, and found himself faced with an argument in favour of primitive communism which was very difficult to refute unless a new justification of ownership was devised.* Patriarchalism influenced him in a more straightforward way, and in his concessions to it we may see in his thinking some signs that he recognized the limitations of his own intellectualistic rationalism.†

If in fact *Two Treatises* had been directed against Hobbes and not Filmer it would have been a far less interesting, far less influential work. To say this is not to claim that Locke did succeed in annihilating Filmer as completely as he himself believed, and as subsequent history seems to confirm. As a piece of formal dialectic what he wrote is less complete and in some ways less convincing, to his own contemporaries anyway, than the identical work of his friend Tyrrell.‡ It is true that Locke completely outclassed his chosen opponent in intellect and in scholarship. After he had added the detailed argumentation of the *First Treatise* to the

---

* See above, p. 34 and note to II, § 25, 16–19. Tyrrell similarly developed many of his arguments only because of Filmer. Viano, 1960, esp. pp. 209 on, also insists on the importance of Filmer and patriarchalism to the understanding of both *Treatises*.

† See note to II, § 74, 14–37 and references, and compare Schochet, 1969, 1975.

‡ *Patriarcha non Monarcha* is fairer to the opposing case and considers it within its whole literary context, which *Two Treatises* does not. It is much more difficult to read, of course, and contains nothing comparable as a positive political theory, but I should like to retract the statement in Laslett, 1949, 38–9.

Second, we may feel that nobody could any longer believe that the texts of the Old Testament which Filmer had used to justify patriarchal kingship could possibly apply to contemporary monarchs. But what was the conscientious reader to believe about the content of Revelation and its relationship with the political world in which he lived, and about the origin of government? For Locke was assuming that in some way Old Testament history joined on, so to speak, with his account of what happened, but unlike Filmer he was never prepared to say quite how it did so.* 'We must not deny the truth of the history of the creation', urged Filmer against Hobbes. Locke would not admit he was doing this, when in reality he was making use of rationalist arguments which simply could not be contained in Filmer's world of Biblical politics.

Not only did Locke refuse to meet Filmer on his own ground, and fail to recognize the full strength, antiquity and importance of the patriarchal tradition,† he persistently ignored the searching counter-criticisms which are the strength of Filmer's case. How could Locke's bland assertion of the historicity of a state of nature, of an agreement or compact behind all established government, of the justifiability of assuming universal concept to political institutions, be defended against Filmer's sceptical commentary? It was Tyrrell, not Locke, who recognized Filmer's needling effectiveness, and admitted that there was really no stopping place between the ground he and Locke occupied and logical individualism, final democracy, the sharing of political power with women, children and servants.‡ All this is quite apart from Locke's failure to share Filmer's vision of the emotional togetherness implied by all political relationships, the physically, physiologically natural element which, as has been argued elsewhere, political thinking since Locke has misunderstood to the danger of us all.¶

* See notes on 1, § 130 and 1, § 136.

† See e.g. note on 1, § 64, 11–16.

‡ Tyrrell, 1681, 83–4; his only comment is that such a form of government had never existed. Locke's silence on this point laid him open to the extremist interpretations of the English supporters of the French Revolution; see the footnotes made by Elrington to the *Second Treatise*. It was this obtuseness, or inadvertence, or prudence, which makes it legitimate to describe him in colourful terms as a 'father of democracy', our sort of democracy. Compare Laslett, *The World we Have Lost*, 221–2.

¶ Laslett, 1949, 42–3, Dunn, 1969 pp. 113–14 rejects this view of Locke's inferiority to Filmer in such directions. I now feel disposed to agree with his statement, that Locke and Filmer were at one on the 'banal truths' about family and society: compare Schochet, 1969 (i).

Locke certainly absorbed something from patriarchalism. It has been shown above that there had been a time when he went a very long way with this traditional argument. But he did not learn enough, not enough to understand such institutions as the family, the nation, the community of a neighbourhood, as we think they should be understood. And Hobbes could do nothing with the patriarchal attitude. To him patriarchal societies were those 'the concord whereof dependeth on natural lust', and that was all. He was unwilling to distinguish the authority of a father from the naked exercise of force. In all these respects, then, Hobbes, Locke, Tyrrell, Sidney and the others were on the one side, with Filmer and the tradition he stood for on the other. Leibniz apparently classed *Two Treatises* with *Leviathan* in contrast with *Patriarcha*, and Leibniz was in no doubt that Filmer was Locke's target throughout the book. A controversy between Locke and Hobbes would have been within one party only, and could never have given rise to the characteristic political attitude of the modern world. A clash between two such men as Locke and Filmer was a symbolic, a necessary occurrence: it changed men's minds.*

Nevertheless Hobbes and Filmer shared nearly every one of the attributes of absolutism as it was rejected by English parliamentarians—will as the source of all law and the form of all authority, the necessity of perpetual and absolute submission to the arbitrary dictates of an indivisible sovereign, the impossibility of mixed government. In so far as Locke's writing was directed against these things, it would not seem to have mattered whether it was Hobbes or Filmer he had in mind. But when his statements are examined closely it appears that the form of the absolutist propositions he was rejecting was almost always Filmer's.† If it had been the precise content and force of Hobbes's statements which he wished to examine, he would have quoted them verbatim.

We can say this with some confidence, for Locke was a meticulous and practised controversialist. We have seen that he had known of Filmer's agreement with Hobbes for over a decade when he wrote *Two Treatises*.‡ When in the earliest work he wrote he

---

*The whole content of patriarchal political argument in England, and of the significance for liberalism of its rejection, is set out by Schochet, 1966. For Leibniz, Locke and Filmer, see Jolley, 1975.

† See e.g. notes on ii, § 92, 7; ii, § 95, 9.

‡ See above, p. 33. The sentence from Filmer quoted there continues: 'I consent with him [Hobbes] about the rights of exercising government, but I cannot agree to his means of acquiring it.'

commented on Bagshaw, and when he defended himself against Stillingfleet and Proast much later on, Locke carefully cited paragraph and sentence of the book he was discussing. He did so, with exasperating tediousness, in the *First Treatise*, out of Filmer. There is no reason why we should expect him to behave differently in the *Second Treatise* if Hobbes had been his critical target there.

Locke's habits in controversy, and the facts we have cited about the importance of patriarchalism at this time, make it impossible to argue that Filmer was simply Locke's whipping boy, his opportunity for attacking Hobbes by proxy. No doubt there was something faintly ridiculous about Filmer even by the year 1679. But we have seen that both Locke and Shaftesbury seemed to take him quite seriously not very long before. It is even more wrong-headed to suppose that the point of this public flagellation was to humiliate the Hobbesists among the spectators, a lash or two being aimed at them directly. Locke never called Filmer a Hobbesist, nor said anything to link the two names together, though Sidney did not hesitate to do so, and Tyrrell also commented on Hobbesian positions whilst engaged with Filmer's.*

Indeed it cannot be shown that when he wrote Locke had had any recent contact with *Leviathan* or with any other work of Hobbes at first hand.† If it were not for the passages in the *Second Treatise* which are Hobbesian in flavour or seem to have been directed particularly at him, we should not know that Locke was concerned in any way with Hobbes as a thinker at that time, for his notes, his diaries, his letters, his book lists and purchases show no sign of such an interest. His one overt mention of the word *Leviathan*, in paragraph 98 of the *Second Treatise*, is very far from specific: indeed if it were taken literally it would seem to imply a serious misunderstanding, or misremembrance, of Hobbes's doctrine.‡

---

* See, e.g. Sidney, 1772, 5 and Tyrrell, 1681, 138–41, 2nd pagination. On p. 209 he accuses Filmer of directly borrowing from Hobbes, which is historically almost impossible.

† He lent his *Leviathan* in 1674, and did not get it back till 1691. He possessed no other political or philosophical work of Hobbes.

‡ 'Such a Constitution as this would make the mighty *Leviathan* of a shorter duration, than the feeblest Creatures.' The 'constitution' at issue would require universal consent to all the acts of a political body, though Hobbes accepted decision by a majority in assemblies. The passage is clearly ironic and general, not a comment on a passage in Hobbes, see note there.

There is an interesting parallel to this in Locke's *Essay on the Understanding*. Again, he mentions *Leviathan* only once in the course of that lengthy work, which covers a great deal of the same ground as Hobbes had done, and which many commentators have also supposed was written with Hobbes in mind. And again he mistakes the Hobbesian case in a passage which was clearly also meant to be sarcastic and general.* Nevertheless his *Essay* shows clear signs of proximity to Hobbes, even on the critical subject of property and justice. ' "Where there is no property there is no injustice" is a proposition as certain as any demonstration in Euclid', says Locke in his *Essay*.† 'Where there is no *Own*, that is no Propriety, there is no Injustice', says *Leviathan*,‡ and Hobbes goes on to a conclusion that Locke decisively rejected, not in the *Essay*, but in *Two Treatises*, that property cannot exist before and apart from government. Did Locke when he wrote this striking re-echo of a phrase of Hobbes consciously recollect its source? All these examples suggest that he did not. He seems to have been in the curious position of having absorbed Hobbesian sentiments, Hobbesian phraseology in such a way that he did not know where they came from: his early reading, never repeated, perhaps; or other men's books and the general discussion of Hobbes; or both.

The exact literary relationship between the two men, then, is an interesting and intricate study. Locke never escaped the shadow of *Leviathan*. As we shall see, there were men in Oxford who suspected him of leaning in a Hobbesian direction in the early 1690's, and in 1693 Isaac Newton himself asked Locke to pardon him for having done the same. Newton was in a neurotic, or even a

* I, iii, 5 (Nidditch, ed., 68), where he claims that a Hobbesist kept his promise because the public required it and because of the fear of punishment by Leviathan. In fact, of course, the keeping of covenants was the third of the laws of nature, as Hobbes understood them. Some commentators on Hobbes might say that Locke was ultimately right in this reflection, but he surely would not have formulated this fundamental criticism in such an offhand way if it had been seriously intended.

† IV, iii, 18 (Nidditch, ed., 549). Locke had made a very similar statement many years before: 'Quid enim justitia ubi nulla proprietas aut dominium', eighth *Essay on the Law of Nature*, Von Leyden, 1954, p. 212, and he developed it in his *Education*, § 110: 'Children cannot well comprehend what injustice is, till they understand property' (*Works*, 1801, IX, 101, passage added in later editions). In the *Essay* Locke even hints at his justification of ownership in terms of industry: 'Just the same is it in moral knowledge: let a man have the idea of taking from others, without their consent, what their honest industry has possessed them of, and call this *justice* if he please' (Nidditch, ed., 567).

‡ Chapter 15, 1904, 97–8. It is probable that both Locke and Hobbes were here using 'property' in the wider sense, of which material possessions is only one part. See below, p. 101.

psychotic state at the relevant time, but during the controversy over his views on Christianity which grew so violent in the late 1690's Locke found himself directly accused of reproducing Hobbesian positions by other eminent intellectuals. In 1697, Richard Willis, later Bishop of Winchester, claimed that the thesis of Locke's *Reasonableness of Christianity* (1695) was 'consonant to the words of the Leviathan, whence his doctrine is borrowed, Part IV Ch. 43',* and the more forthright John Edwards henceforth described his theological writings as written all over with Hobbesism. When the two passages are compared, the resemblance is surprisingly close: there is little verbal similarity, and the common use of some texts of scripture is to be expected, but the doctrine is almost identical. Locke replied to his critic at the very end of *A Second Vindication of the Reasonableness of Christianity*, 1697: 'I tell him, I . . . did not know those words, he quoted out of the Leviathan, were there, or any thing like them. Nor do I know yet, any farther than as I believe to be there, from his quotation.'†

This may insinuate that he had never read *Leviathan*, as it certainly declares his unwillingness to do so much as open the book and check a reference when the challenge arose. Indeed the resemblance in this case could have been coincidence, a result of that rationalist attitude which the two men had in common, applied here to the Christian Revelation. Or it may likewise be a case of a man having read something many years before, having read it and forgotten it, which he then reproduced as a notion of his own. This view, the more sympathetic one, seems to me to be the more likely. When Locke wrote philosophy he 'utterly refused to read any books upon that subject' so as to keep other men's notions out of his head.‡ He said of politics 'This subject . . . requires more meditation than reading',¶ and when he wrote on political theory he may also have made a conscious effort to spin everything out of his own mind, to take nothing from the thoughts

---

* *Occasional Paper No. 1*, 1697. On Newton's accusation, see Dunn, 1969 (i) p. 81, where he also reproduces from one of Locke's notebooks of the 1680s an extract from an interesting judgement of Hobbes and from Cranston, 1957, 133, a mention of 'Mr. Hobbes's doctrine'.

† *Works*, 1801, VII, 420. Locke may be prevaricating here, for in the same tract he denied all knowledge of Socinian literature which he certainly possessed and had almost certainly read: a year or two later he was citing it in his Biblical annotations.

‡ This is independent testimony. Tyrrell to Locke, 18 March 1690 (de Beer 4, 36).

¶ *Works*, 1801, X, 308.

of other men. The result was that he reproduced some ideas from books which he had read, even books he had read to reject.

'I am not so well read in Hobbes or Spinosa', he said in 1698, and made an ironical comment about 'those justly decried names'.* He did read Hobbes nevertheless, although it is so difficult to say when, or how much. The cumulative body of Locke's notebooks is very considerable, and it consists to a very large extent of citations of the books of other men, referenced and arranged with monumental carefulness. It is a most remarkable fact that it has not been possible to find a single referenced extract from the works of Hobbes in the whole Lockeian corpus. Only one citation has so far come to light, and that is not found in a notebook, but on the flyleaf of a volume in his library, published in 1668: even then the famous passage from *Leviathan* written there is given without its source, and might appear to the unwary reader to have been a sentiment written by Locke himself.† We have seen that when he was young, when his tendency was authoritarian and his analysis at its closest to Hobbes, his acquaintance with him was as much, perhaps, through literature about him as through direct reading.‡

The young Locke may well have gone through an experience which must have been common after 1651, when *Leviathan* appeared, and was much in demand, as Pepys tells us, in spite of its ugly reputation. Hobbes fascinated him, then and for the rest of his life. He found it an effort to reject his doctrine, though he did reject it very early. When he wrote *Two Treatises*, then, *Leviathan* was an influence, a gravitational constant exercised by a large body though at a great distance. But an influence nevertheless, positive in its effects, and quite unlike the influence of Filmer, which, though

---

* *Works*, 1801, IV, 477; compare Strauss, 1953, p. 211.

† It is in Locke's copy of Velschius, *Sylloge Observationum Medicanalium*, Ulm, 1668 (H. and L. 3062): 'In wrong or noe definitions, lyes and first abuse of speech, from wch. proceeds all false and uselesse Tenets; wch. make those men who take their instruction from the authority of books, not from their owne meditation to be as much below the condition of ignorant men, as men indued with true science are above it. For between true science and erroneous doctrines Ignorance is in the middle.' [*Leviathan*, chapter IV (1 ed. 1651, 15).] Arthur Wainwright, working on the Scriptural commentaries which engaged Locke in the final years of his life, has discovered similarities between the theology of the two thinkers (Wainwright, 1987). Otherwise the intensive research on Locke's papers which has proceeded over the last twenty years has failed to produce any further evidence of close literary relationship between the two men.

‡ See above, p. 21. Cox, 1960, lists several derivative references. There are other surprises in Locke's reading: e.g. his failure to get much further with Hooker than the first book (above, p. 56), his statement that he never read Sidney (*Works*, 1801, III, 272).

negative in its direction, was a close up, documentary affair.

Under these circumstances it is idle to look for a direct source, or the source, of Locke's political thinking in Hobbes or anyone else. But of the writers he consulted when engaged on his book, Samuel Pufendorf was perhaps of the greatest use to him, in spite of the fact that their views on constitutional matters were in such contrast. He took advantage of Pufendorf's arguments, he reproduced his positions, and he described his major work as 'the best book of that kind', better than the great Grotius on *War and Peace*.* Now this book of Pufendorf's, the *De Jure Naturae* (1672), had much to say about Hobbes. Here, and in his *Elementa* of 1660, Pufendorf criticized Hobbesian doctrine, but he accepted and appreciated something of the Hobbesian analysis. Locke possessed other critiques of Hobbes.† It is perhaps in this direction that we should look for the documentary connection between Hobbes and Locke in the *Two Treatises*.

This account can only be tentative, and it may seem unsatisfactory to those who expect such a literary relationship to fit a framework neatly fashioned from 'influence' and 'rejection', expect it to be a wholly conscious and independent affair. It never is. Hobbes and Locke were caught up within the living tissue, the innumerable threads and fibres growing together, which connects one intellectual generation with its successor in the same country, in the same small society. We have seen that it was from this source, from conversation and casual contact, not from documentary acquaintance, that Locke inherited the fruit of the radical writings of the Civil War.‡ With his interests and with his experience, he could never have escaped the Hobbesian impact.

We must describe *Two Treatises*, then, as a deliberate and

---

* *Works*, 1801, III, 272, *Thoughts Concerning Reading and Study*. He also recommended Pufendorf in his other list (x, 308). On Pufendorf as used by Locke, see notes on II, 58, 65, 74 (Pufendorf and Tyrrell), 105 etc. In 1702 Barbeyrac began a correspondence with Locke, asking his advice, and telling him of his intention to translate Pufendorf.

† Clarendon, 1676 (bought December 1681); Tenison, 1670; Lawson, 1657. Locke also had a positively Hobbesist work in Matthew Wren's *Monarchy Asserted*, which had been known to him from the time of its publication in 1659, and was on his shelves in 1681. Von Leyden (1954, p. 39) states that Locke had read Pufendorf's *Elementa* as early as 1660.

‡ See above, p. 22. Mr Abrams draws attention to the close personal link between Hobbes, Henry Stubbe and perhaps other students of Christ Church in the late 1650s, and cites Stubbe's letters to Hobbes; British Museum Add. MSS. 32553.

polemically effective refutation of the writings of Sir Robert
Filmer, intellectually and historically important because of that
fact and not in spite of it, related only in the indirect way we have
discussed with the work of Hobbes, though antithetical in its
political and constitutional doctrine. It was other things as well,
of course, and it is as an independent treatise on politics that it has
had its influence, although its connection with Hobbes has so
often been distorted and exaggerated. It was intended to affect,
and it most decidedly did affect, the political and constitutional
beliefs of the Englishmen who created the constitution and the
political habits under which we still live. But there was one thing
it did not contain which every similar treatise included as a matter
of course: there was one set of interests passionately pursued by
the men who read it and accepted its doctrines, which it made no
play upon; there was one 'Whig', or 'liberal', or anti-absolutist
intellectual tradition about which it had nothing whatsoever to
say. This tradition, these interests, this argument, made up the
historical case for English liberty, for the Common Law, for the
House of Commons, for the 'ancient constitution', a case which
had exercised all Locke's like-minded predecessors since the days
of Sir Edward Coke and which had suffered a severe reverse at the
hands of Sir Robert Filmer himself.

In *Two Treatises* as we now have it Filmer's constitutional
position is never mentioned at all. No reference is made by Locke
to the later part of *Patriarcha* and to the *Freeholders Grand Inquest*
where the argument is presented, in spite of the fact that the
Freeholder stood first in order of the works of Filmer as Locke
considered them. When he set out his method of referring to
Filmer's tracts,* he blandly ignored the existence of the *Freeholder*.
In so far as Locke touched at all on the historical case which he,
Shaftesbury and the Exclusionists were all fighting for, it seems to
have been in a chapter inserted later in order to overset the antithetical case based on conquest. But Filmer had not used that
argument, and here Hobbes may conceivably have been his target,
for Hobbes unlike Locke did attempt to demonstrate his case in

---

* See above, p. 58: Locke once cites the part of *Patriarcha* which deals with the
constitution (Laslett's edition, 106–26: the citation is in I, § 8, 30–2 and quotes a
passage from p. 133), but he does not comment on it. It is interesting that 60 per cent
of all Locke's references to Filmer in the book as we now have it intend pp. 53–64 of
Patriarcha, and 80 per cent this and four other passages only.

terms of English historical fact.* As far as Locke was concerned, Filmer might never have made the statements which maintained that the House of Commons was not originally a part of Parliament, that it was first summoned in the forty-ninth year of Henry III and owed its existence, as did all English law, even the Common Law, to the Royal will.† To the constitutionalists of Locke's day and ours arguments of this sort mattered a very great deal: to Locke, apparently, they mattered not at all.

We must say 'apparently' because it should never be forgotten that more than half of Locke's text is lost. It may be that in the missing portion he did develop a case against Filmer's constitutional position and a direct commentary on the legal issues raised by the Exclusion controversy. If it is justifiable to suppose that he destroyed this very part of the text because it contained statements which might have cost him his head, then it would seem likely that it did concern matters much closer to the law of treason than did the rest of the *First Treatise*.‡ But in the brief sentence which Locke gave to constitutional and legal history in the *Second Treatise* he merely 'sent his readers' to a group of writers, whose works he did not own and evidently had never read. He repeated these titles in his lists of recommended books in 1703 and named one or two 'ancient lawyers', all Whig-tainted source books. He added the writings of some of the authors who had engaged in the controversy on the Whig side. He even used this phrase of them: 'wherein he will find the antient constitution of the government of England'.¶

* See note on II, § 175 (chapter XVI) and on § 175 itself. There is no evidence whatsoever that Locke had read the lesser works of Hobbes listed there. Skinner, 1966 (ii) presents a convincing case for conquest being a commoner argument than is allowed above: compare Goldie, 1977.

† See *Patriarcha*, pp. 106–26, especially p. 117, and the *Freeholder, passim*. It is Mr Pocock in his important book *The Ancient Constitution and the Feudal Law*, 1957, who has demonstrated how far-reaching were the effects of these statements and how difficult Filmer's opponents found it to answer them. Seliger, 1968, 233ff, submits that Locke's disregard of history was due to his polemical purposes, rather than to indifference; literal historical argumentation was no longer effective.

‡ See above, p. 64.

¶ See II, 239, 42–3 and note: *Works*, 1801, III, 272–3, and X, 308. Of the titles in these lists, Locke possessed the works of Tyrrell, seven of those of Atwood, the worst of the Whig constitutional writers; Sadler's *Rights of the Kingdom*, 1682; the 1689 *State Tracts*; Chamberlayn's *Anglia Notitia*, 1700. (See Harrison and Laslett, 1965; he had no relevant title by Coke, Spelman, Bracton, Petyt or Brady, nor the *Mirror*, *Fleta*, the *Modus Tenendi*.)

Though it would be very difficult to argue convincingly that the complete *Two Treatises* contained a lengthy constitutional argument, now lost, the Constitution was undoubtedly in Locke's mind in 1689. Just before he left Holland, when he must have been considering whether to publish his work on *Government*, he wrote thus to Clarke: 'The settlement of the nation upon sure ground of peace and security . . . can no way so well be done as by restoring our ancient government; the best possible that ever was, if taken and put together all of a piece in its original constitution. If this has not been invaded men have done very ill to complain. . . . Now they have an opportunity offered to find remedies, and set up a constitution, that may be lasting, for the security of civil rights and the liberty and property of all the subjects of the nation.'*

The absence of specifically constitutional discussion from his text, therefore, is not only extraordinary in view of what had been previously written and in view of the attitude and expectations of the men who first read it. It makes the book unique. It was at once a response to a particular political situation and a statement of universal principle, made as such and still read as such. This work, the authoritative statement of Anglo-Saxon political assumptions, often regarded as one of the testaments to English historical and constitutional development, refers to England as 'a neighbour kingdom', and the Common Law as 'the municipal law of some countries'.† Neither Machiavelli, nor Hobbes, nor Rousseau succeeded in making the discussion of politics so completely independent of historical example, so entirely autonomous an area of discourse, yet Locke has affected the everyday activity of practising politicians more perhaps than any of them.

This is a tribute both to the effectiveness of the political theorist's technique in general and to Locke's particular exercise of it. Only a man of such endowment as an abstract thinker could have transformed the issues of a predominantly historical, highly parochial political controversy of this sort into a general political theory. That it should have been done in a sense in anticipation of events, so that from hindsight it has always looked as if it were a rationalization of something which had not yet occurred when it was written, emphasizes this quality still further, marks it perhaps

* Letter to Clarke, 8 February 1689: de Beer, 3, 545.
† See I, § 90, 29–31; II, § 205, 11.

with the distinctive sign of this particular discipline of the mind and the imagination. Locke's instinct in leaving the whole legal, historical and constitutional controversy on one side, in deciding, when something of this sort had to be undertaken, to place it apart from his analytic argument, was eminently correct and in this character. This is why his book is with us, and Tyrrell, Petyt, Brady, even Filmer and Sidney, have sunk beneath the surface of our intellectual and literary tradition. We should expect that a man capable of this would be a philosopher, even if he turned out to be a philosopher unwilling to admit that he had written out a political theory.

But in what sense should we expect his philosophy to be related to his political theory? If we ask ourselves this question we can discover an exquisite contrast between the Civil Philosophy of Hobbes and Locke's Political Principle.

2. LOCKE THE PHILOSOPHER AND LOCKE THE POLITICAL THEORIST

In August 1692 Tyrrell sent to Locke a copy of his newly published book on natural law, with this comment:

> I hope that this treatise may give the world sufficient satisfaction, or at least may excite your self, or some other thinking person, to give the world a better account of the Law of Nature and its obligation, than what hath been already performed, as also to confute with better reasons the Epicurean principles of Mr Hobbes. For the doing of which I know no man more capable than yourself if you please to undertake it, and shall no more resent it than the publishing of the *Two Treatises of Government* after *Patriarcha Non Monarcha*. Since, if truth can be better represented and improved by a greater hand, I shall not value my small performances [the less if they] serve for a foil to set it off.*

This letter hints at much of the relationship between a great literary figure and his less distinguished, less successful friend, as it shows that Tyrrell by this time was one of the few who certainly knew

---

* Tyrrell to Locke, 9 August 1692 (de Beer 4, 79), spelling and punctuation modernized, and words within square brackets supplied. The work was *A Brief Disquisition of the Law of Nature*, 1692, a paraphrase of Richard Cumberland's *De Legibus Naturae Disquisitio Philosophica*, 1672, with special emphasis on his polemic against Hobbes.

that Locke had written *Two Treatises*. But it also makes it clear that Tyrrell was not satisfied with what had been said on natural law in that work or in the *Essay on Humane Understanding*, and felt that Hobbes had still to be confounded, by Locke himself. And it comes at the end of an exchange between the two men which almost severed the friendship of a lifetime.

Between December 1689 and April 1690 Tyrrell wrote six times from Oxford to Locke in London, telling him how his *Essay* was being received, and reporting criticisms of it. In three of his letters he also asked the name of the author of *Two Treatises*, and though Locke seems to have replied four times, defending himself against the criticisms, he refused to answer that question. When Tyrrell told him that 'the people in Oxford had now found out a better author than I for it, viz. yourself, your answer was to this effect, that since they would not have you to be the author of a book that you owned' (this was the *Essay*, which his critics were saying was lifted from Descartes) 'you did not think it worth while to give them any satisfaction in those that you did not own at all'. In April Tyrrell came to London and faced him with his suspicions about the work on government, but Locke 'declined the discourse' and was told he must 'thank your own reservedness' if the results were unfortunate.* On his return in June, Tyrrell read the *Essay* again and discussed it 'with some thinking men at Oxford'; he found them 'dissatisfied with what you have said concerning the law of nature (or reason) whereby we distinguish moral good, from evil and virtue from vice'.

The coincidence of these two things, the suspicion that he had written *Two Treatises* and that he was unsound on natural law, seems to have infuriated Locke, but the explosion was delayed a little while. He saw Tyrrell again in July, and gave him a paper of explanation which seems to have maintained that natural law 'since it did not proceed from God as a lawgiver . . . could not properly be called a law, and the not taking God into this hypothesis has been the great reason of Mr Hobbeses mistake that the laws of nature are not properly laws nor do oblige mankind to their observation when out of a civil state or commonwealth'.† In August Locke seems to have found reason to suppose that Tyrrell had been spreading the report about his authorship of *Two*

* Leibniz was apparently informed by a London correspondent that Locke wrote *Patriarcha non Monarcha*.

† Tyrrell to Locke 30 June, 27 July, 30 August 1690 (de Beer, 4, 108, 118).

Treatises and he lost his temper: he sent him an icy letter repudiating the attack on the *Essay* and enclosed another one, now destroyed, demanding an explanation about *Two Treatises.*

The letter in defence of the *Essay* has always been regarded as the most important source for Locke's attitude to his critics,* but its context has been previously unknown. If the statements on natural law in *Two Treatises* are set alongside those references in the *Essay* which are discussed in this correspondence, it will be seen why he had reason to be annoyed with Tyrrell at this time. Throughout the political work the expression natural law is used with suave assurance, as if there could be no doubt of its existence, of its meaning, of its content in the minds of author and reader. It is 'plain and intelligible to all rational Creatures' (II, § 124), it is so much a positive code that it governs the state of nature (II, § 6), but its obligations 'cease not in Society'; all men everywhere must be 'conformable to the Law of Nature, *i.e.* to the will of God' (II, § 135). In the *Essay* it is allowed, in parenthesis, that natural law does not depend on the existence of innate ideas: nevertheless men should not deny 'that there is a law knowable by the light of nature' (I, ii, 13). But when it comes (II, xxviii, 7–) to the description of the law or rules which men actually refer their actions to, no natural law is mentioned. In this exchange of letters Locke fails to convince Tyrrell that natural law can be equated with or made part of divine law, civil law (the law of the law-courts) or the 'philosophic law' (in later editions the 'law of opinion or reputation') which he maintains are as a matter of fact the standards which men use to judge of right and wrong. The *Essay* has no room for natural law.

So sharp here is the contrast between two almost contemporaneous works by the same man that in one passage in *Two Treatises*, perhaps in a second passage also, Locke uses language on the subject of natural law which seems inconsistent with his own statements about innate ideas in the *Essay.*† Questioning on this point cannot be pressed too far, for we are told that 'it would be besides my present purpose, to enter here into the particulars of

---

* It was printed by King (1930, 366–73), from a copy preserved by Locke, his only extant letter to Tyrrell, and now in Bodley, dated 4 August 1690 (de Beer, 4, 110–13). It may, indeed, have never been received by Tyrrell in this form: perhaps a milder version was actually sent. Aarsleff, 1969, takes a different view of this letter.

† See note on II, § 11, 30–1 ('so plain was it writ in the Hearts of all Mankind'). I, § 86, 20–1 and references, where it is recorded that neither Yolton nor Kemp is willing to accept that Locke was literally contradicting himself.

the Law of nature, or its *measure of punishment*; yet, it is certain there is such a Law, and that too, as intelligible and plain to a rational Creature, and a Studier of that Law, as the positive Laws of Commonwealths, nay possibly plainer' (II, § 12). It seems that it was always 'beside his present purpose' for Locke to demonstrate the existence and content of natural law. He did not do so in his *Essay*, even in the 2nd edition where the passage in the second book which Tyrrell had complained of was rewritten. He would not do so by bringing out his early *Essays on the Law of Nature*, which Tyrrell asked him to do in the course of their exchange.* As Dr Von Leyden has shown, these earlier essays would not have provided a doctrine of natural law capable of reconciling the theory of knowledge in Locke's *Essay* with the ethical doctrine of that work and of *Two Treatises*. This, it is suggested, may have been one of the reasons why Locke was unwilling to be known as the author of both books.

Locke is, perhaps, the least consistent of all the great philosophers, and pointing out the contradictions either within any of his works or between them is no difficult task. Sometimes it seems quite clear that he was unconscious of his inconsistency; at other times, and this appears to be one of them, he himself realized his dilemma, but was unable to find a solution. The objective existence of a body of natural law is an essential presupposition of his political theory and when we find him using the phrase we should perhaps think of him as taking up what might be called a stance to a series of possible explanations. Natural law, in his system in *Two Treatises*, was at one and the same time a command of God, a rule of reason, and a law in the very nature of things as they are, by which they work and we work too. This conception of adopting a more or less conscious stand-pat attitude could perhaps be used as a general sympathetic approach towards the problem created by Locke's ethical statements, which point in many directions at the same time and which have been much discussed.† It invites us to

* Tyrrell to Locke, 27 July 1690, compare Von Leyden, 1954, 9–10. Aarsleff, 1969, pp. 128–9, takes a view of this letter quite contrary to my own, and goes to some lengths to disprove the claim that Locke's *Essay* contained no natural law doctrine.

† See, e.g. Leslie Stephen, 1876; James Stephen, 1892; Lamprecht, 1918; Vaughan, 1925; Kendall, 1941; Von Leyden, 1954 and 1956; Strauss, 1953; Simon, 1951; Yolton, 1955; Brogan, 1958; Polin, 1960; Singh, 1961; Abrams, 1961; Aarsleff, 1969; Ashcraft, 1969, 1987. The trouble was that Locke based right and wrong on God's commands and punishments, but also adopted a hedonistic ethic as well, an ethic of the Hobbesian sort. Meanwhile he passionately believed in the possibility of demonstrating ethics mathematically, though he was perpetually complicating everything with his anthropological relativism, noting the variety of ethical values among the world's peoples and hinting that virtue and vice were simply customary.

look upon *Two Treatises* as something very different from an extension into the political field of the general philosophy of the *Essay*, and reminds us that Locke differed in the character of his thinking from Hobbes. He did not reply to *Leviathan* because it was irrelevant to his purposes as a writer of political principle.

It is natural that posterity should have chosen to look upon the philosophical and the political work as complementary. But Locke himself, as we have shown, was perfectly willing, indeed very anxious, that they should be seen apart. There is interesting evidence that even the truly theoretically minded of those who acquainted themselves with both books saw no continuity between them, or perhaps found *Two Treatises* so lacking in philosophical interest that it never struck them as appropriate to consider it in the same context as the *Essay*. Mr Jolley says of Leibniz that 'he never connected *Two Treatises* with the *Essay*, although . . . he considered it as a serious work of political philosophy, worthy of being set alongside Aristotle and Hobbes. One might infer that the idea of examining the consistency of the two books never occurred to Leibniz.'* It is easily demonstrated that the literary continuity between them was about as slight as it possibly could be under such circumstances.

The close analysis of his text has revealed only one example of this author using identical material in both works,† and then in a passage probably inserted later. The style, the type of argument, the atmosphere are all recognizable as from the same writer, but in every other respect they differ remarkably. *Two Treatises* is not written on the 'plain, historic method' of the *Essay*. If it were, we might expect in the first place that it would insist on the limitations of our social and political understanding, for that is Locke's chief enterprise in the *Essay*, to portray the character of our knowledge by showing up its limits. Then the situations, the rights, the duties discussed, would have been presented recognizably as the 'complex ideas' or 'mixed modes' of Locke's system of knowledge, the product of ratiocination and therefore fixed and definite, capable of entering into a mathematically demonstrable morality.

---

* See Jolley, 1972. He goes on to consider why it was that Leibniz, by no means averse to discovering incoherencies in Locke's thought, never took note of those inconsistencies between *Two Treaties* and the *Essay* which would seem, from what he wrote on the relevant topics, to have been patent to him. Perhaps Locke's fear of being taken to task for the disjunction between the works was indeed unnecessary because even in his day political theory had its autonomy as an arena of discourse and works belonging to it were not readily seen as philosophical, in intent or in their implications.

† See note on 1, § 57.

Just such a discussion is implied by, or even begun in, the statement about property we have quoted, and there are many other examples.*

Some such construction as this might be made by a modern scholar attempting to create a theory of politics out of Locke's *Essay*, if, as so nearly happened, it had never become certainly known that *Two Treatises* was also Locke's.† Such an exercise might have illuminating results, though it cannot be our subject here, for the implications of Locke's theory of knowledge for politics and political thinking were very considerable and acted quite independently of the influence of *Two Treatises*. The famous doctrine of the *tabula rasa*, for example, the blank sheet of the mind on which experience and experience alone can write, made men begin to feel that the whole world is new for everyone and we are all absolutely free of what has gone before.

The political results of such an attitude have been enormous. It was, perhaps, the most effective solvent of the natural-law attitude. In a sense these results were intended. For though Locke wrote the *Essay* about how men know things, his final object, the object he had in mind when he started, was to help men to know what to do. 'Our business here is not to know all things', his classic statement goes, 'but those which concern our conduct.' He keeps on slipping into this mood throughout the book, but the only work he actually produced on how men should behave was *Two Treatises*. And it cannot be said to represent his account of the implications for conduct, for politics, of the doctrines of the *Essay*. It was written for an entirely different purpose and in an entirely different state of mind.

None of the connecting links is present. It is extraordinary, for example, how little definition there is in the political work, though the *Essay*, is, as it should be, much concerned with definition and though he reproaches Filmer for failing to define. *Two Treatises*

---

* See p. 72 above, and an even better illustration in the note to II, § 22, 8–9, citing a passage from Locke's *Essay* on the ideas of absolute liberty and of government. Chapter 8 of Yolton, 1970, is entitled *Property: an example of mixed-mode analysis* and he examines Locke's notions exhaustively on this model. He does not claim, however, that all of the subjects of Locke's book could be thus explicated. For a different view of *Two Treatises* and the *Essay*, see Polin, 1960, and compare Dunn, 1967; Edwards, 1969.

† In 1983 Neal Wood published just such an attempt on neo-Marxist lines; *The politics of Locke's philosophy*, an impressive and important reinterpretation.

relies heavily upon natural law, but the term, as we have seen, is never analysed there. It is all about freedom and consent, but they are nowhere discussed as subjects in themselves. It is the same with law, with reason, with will, with government itself. Political power is defined, and so is property (though used in two meanings, alternated without warning), but not in philosophic terms, on nothing like the principles laid down in his *Essay* and insisted upon from his earliest writings.* Prof. Dunn has shown that justice was a Lockeian theme, but it is largely absent from *Two Treatises*. The issue about justice and property is never raised, though there is a reference to it in the *Education*. Even more singular, perhaps, is the way in which Locke brushes aside the question of conscience and political obligation, which had worried him as a young man as it had worried all his predecessors and contemporaries.†

If we try to pass from one work to another and use the definitions offered in the *Essay* for the political discussion, we find that they do not fit very well: at least one important term, consent, is not defined even there. The political argument is not presented as a part of a general philosophy, and does not seem to be intended to be read as such. There is a note in Locke's journal which was written at the time when, as we suppose, he was working over *Two Treatises*, and adding the Hooker quotations. It reads almost as a conscious commentary on the relationship between philosophy, ethics and politics. He had just expressed his belief in the possibility of demonstrating ethics, and his scepticism about the potentialities of natural science. He goes on:

The well management of public or private affairs depending upon the various and unknown humours, interests and capacities of men we have to do with in the world, and not upon any settled ideas of things physical, polity and prudence are not capable of demonstration. But a man is principally helped in them by the history of matter of fact, and a sagacity of finding out an analogy in their operations and effects.

[The truths of mathematics are certain.] But whether this course in public or private affairs will succeed well, whether rhubarb will purge or quinquina cure an ague, is only known by experience, and there is

---

* On Filmer, and definition, see note on 1, § 23, 22–5, and references: on meanings of property, p. 101 below.

† See above, p. 72 note † on property in the *Education,* and note on 1, § 105, for Locke's slight reference to conscience. On justice, see Dunn, 1967 (ii).

but probability grounded upon experience, or analogical reasoning, but no certain knowledge or demonstration.*

Empirical medicine, rather than philosophy, seems to be the model for the man who sets out to comment on political matters. Locke the doctor rather than Locke the epistemologist is the man we should have in mind when we read his work on *Government*. To call it 'political philosophy', to think of him as a 'political philosopher', is inappropriate.† He was, rather, the writer of a work of intuition, insight and imagination, if not of profound originality, who was also a theorist of knowledge.

He was also a writer on economics, toleration and education, active in many areas where political generalization had to be made. When the text of *Two Treatises* is put alongside these other works, the literary relationship is found to be somewhat closer than in the case of the *Essay*.‡ Religious freedom was a fundamental to Locke and the assumptions on which he based it are common to the writings in defence of it and to the writing on politics, yet it is not mentioned in *Two Treatises*.¶ His economic theory has some points in common with his political principle, and his educational theory has even more: there are details from the political text which can be seen developing in his later writings, especially the successive editions of the *Education*. But the inconsistencies are even more conspicuous. It would indeed be difficult to show that they entail one another, or that they all arise with a logical necessity from his theory of knowledge. Even between the *Essay* and the work on education, where the barrier of anonymity is absent

* Journal, 1681, under 26 June, modernized: printed in full by Aaron and Gibb, 1936, 116–18. Dugald Stewart seems first to have stressed the importance of Locke's medical experience and attitude for his ethical and political thought.

† Compare Strauss, 1953, 220–1. I am unable to follow him, however, when he claims that the *Treatises* are the 'civil' presentation of a political doctrine which could have been presented 'philosophically'. The passage which he cites from the *Essay* (III, ix, 3) seems to state quite clearly that the civil use of words in ordinary affairs can only be discussed by the philosophic use of words, and so *Two Treatises*, if it is not 'political philosophy', can only be philosophical in this sense. The passage which Strauss cites from II, § 52, 1–3 appears to me to repeat this assertion, though he evidently believes that it marks off the book as in 'civil' language. Like the other statements which Locke makes (see note on I, § 23, 22–5 and references) it insists that the language of the discussion of politics must be consistent and of clear definition, 'philosophic' in fact. Locke may have contradicted his own rules in practice, but there can be no doubt what those rules were and how they defined this book.

‡ On toleration see notes on II, § 3, 87, 108, 134, 135. On economics see II, §§ 45–7.

¶ Freedom of expression is not mentioned either. Locke seems to have helped to bring about the freedom of the press without ever considering it as a political right.

on both sides and the connection is intimate, Locke makes no cross-references. It is pointless to look upon his work as an integrated body of speculation and generalization, with a general philosophy at its centre and as its architectural framework.

This marks Locke off very sharply from the other political theorists of his generation, indeed from the traditional attitude which dominated political thinking before and after him. It separates him even more definitely from Thomas Hobbes. The heavy books of Grotius, Pufendorf, Hooker and the others, standing on Locke's shelves and dominating intellectual activity in this field, were all presentations of a single, synthetic system, a view of the world which proceeded from an account of reality to an account of knowledge, and so to an ethic and to politics. They varied in completeness and in the extent to which they relied on Christian revelation to fill out the great chain of being, or in the use which they made of historical examples and concrete political situations. But natural law was their common assumption, and in its terms they endeavoured to discover a closed system, a system which ideally would be complete and entirely consistent. We should be disposed to give the title 'philosopher' to very few of them, but the task they set themselves was a philosophical one. And in the mind of the ablest of them all philosophy was civil philosophy: Hobbes created a general determinist system, where political obligation, even the form and function of the state, was made to follow from a new definition of natural law. Locke was a philosopher too, but to him the system was an open one.

We cannot explore the various directions which this position lays open to view. It gives to Locke's thinking a somewhat un-expected precedent, for in Machiavelli and the writers of political advice, the reminiscent statesmen themselves, there did exist a counter-tradition to natural law, a convention of discussing politics and its theory outside the area of philosophy. Here the relationship between Shaftesbury the statesman and Locke the thinker comes very close to the surface, and it is recalled by a sentence in Locke's *Essay*. He is discussing the medieval scholarly doctors and he says: 'Notwithstanding these learned disputants, these all knowing doctors, it was to the unscholastic statesmen that the governments of the world owed their peace, defence, and liberties.'*

* III, x, 9: Nidditch, ed., 495.

This opens out an inquiry of a different sort, the extent to which the actual doctrine of Locke's *Essay* allowed for the peculiar relationship of political theory with general philosophical inquiry by its very incompleteness, suggesting that beyond its chosen limits the system was indeed an open matter. In this sense, its anti-synthetic quality, Locke's philosophy could be said to inform the whole of his thinking, but in quite the antithetical way from Hobbes and the natural-law theorists. He, and not Hobbes, could perhaps be looked upon as Machiavelli's philosopher, but most certainly not because the content of his philosophy entailed the content of Machiavellian political doctrine.

A great deal more could be said, then, of Locke the philosopher and Locke the political theorist to illuminate his position in the history of thought as well as the logic of the problem of philosophy and politics. The conventional description of Locke's thought as a peculiar and fertile admixture of empiricism and rationalism suggests the terms of the discussion. In his attitude these two elements were, so to speak, held in solution, only to be precipitated by the men who followed him, Berkeley and Hume in particular. If, then, there was not a Lockeian philosophy in the Hobbesian sense, there was a Lockeian attitude and this can be traced in all that he wrote. Natural law was, in this analysis, a part of his rationalism, his conviction that the universe is to be understood rationally, even the workings of the deity, even the relations of human beings, but at all points it must be compared with, made to fit into, the observed, the empirical facts about the created world and human behaviour.

This position is no easy one to occupy, even if it is taken up as a stance towards the problem in the way which has been suggested.* It led Locke later into his attempt to supplement his rationalism and empiricism with revelation. Although the laws of the rational heathens had enough of natural virtue to 'hold societies together', the holy scriptures, rationally interpreted, were to be used almost as sources of empirically verified facts for moral and political purposes. This was necessary because of the patent insufficiency of reason: 'It is plain, in fact, that human reason,

---

* Von Leyden suggests that the difficulty arises from the ambiguity of natural law, but, like Polin, takes an opposite view to mine of Locke's attitude to it: compare Edwards, 1969. Dunn, 1969 (i) rejects the distinction between 'attitude' and 'philosophy' (p. 199) and thinks it unlikely that *Two Treatises* could have been intended as a work of 'policy'.

unassisted failed men in its great and proper business of morality. It never from unquestionable principles, by clear deductions, made out an entire body of the "law of nature".'* This scepticism about natural law and about reason itself contrasts strangely once again with the easy confidence of *Two Treatises*. In this mood Locke doubted the efficacy of reason not simply because it had failed to demonstrate morality, but also because men obeyed it so little. In this particular, then, the Lockeian attitude led to the doubt and self-searching of which we now have so much evidence. But elsewhere it led to the comfortable certainties of eighteenth-century thought.

If a distinction between the philosophy and the attitude of Locke is legitimate, we could fill out the picture of him as a thinker; we could account, for example, for his unwillingness to push any argument to its extreme. But to do this is not to transfer parts of the content of his philosophy into his political theory: to claim, for instance, that there is more than accidental symmetry, an aesthetic coherence, between his atomic view of matter and his atomic view of society, or to imply that there is a relationship of cause and effect between his conceptualism (or nominalism, some would say) and his belief in toleration.† This is to assume that his political thinking was related to his philosophy as the part to the whole. It implies that a formal consistency, a purely logical interrelationship between parts, is always to be looked for in a thinker, who must be judged accordingly: where it is found wanting some more remote and unrealistic principle of reconciliation must be found to defend a great reputation. It is to lose sight of the possibility that the more successful a man is as a political thinker, the more difficult he will find it to come to terms with his view of the world as a whole. In fact it may be taken to lay it down that all political thought is meta-political thought, formal analysis of the way men discuss politics and never also intuitive explorations of what they do. If this is done the distinction between Locke and Hobbes is made somewhat obscure and

---

* *Reasonableness of Christianity*, 1697, *Works*, 1801, VII, 139–40: compare Strauss, 1953, 205, where Locke's proviso about heathen societies is ignored, as is his implied (though perhaps confused) distinction between natural law and moral law.

† See Simon, 1951: even more extraordinary seems to be the question raised there as to why Locke's optimism survived his conversion to the Copernican hypothesis, as if it were literally true that the conception men have of the stars cannot help but be a directive influence on their beliefs.

Locke may even turn out to be a Hobbesian, a muddle-headed one.* To complete our examination of the relationship between these two men, we must examine these terms more closely.

But before we do this we may look at what has already been said in the light, Locke's own unfailing light, of common sense. A great deal, perhaps too much, has been made of Locke's inconsistencies. But it must be remembered that all thinkers are inconsistent, and a notably ingenious exponent of Hobbes himself has no more than this to say on the question of consistency: 'He is not obviously more contradictory than Locke.'† We have chosen to expound the case in these terms because it arises more easily out of the documentary evidence, and because inconsistency, doubt, hesitation seem to be crucial to the position as it can be more positively examined in the *Essay* and *Two Treatises* themselves, in their sources and in the circumstances of their composition and publication. Then we have emphasized, perhaps over-emphasized, the distinction between Locke the philosopher and Locke the political theorist. But it is not true to say that to understand his political writing as philosophy is necessarily to misapprehend him. His influence as a political writer, as we have said,‡ probably arose because of his philosophical fame. Nevertheless it is of importance to see in Locke, the recognized point of departure for liberalism, the liberal dilemma already present, the dilemma of maintaining a political faith without subscribing to a total, holistic view of the world.

Hobbes's view of the world might have had its logical difficulties, but there can be no doubt that it was wholly Hobbesian. He was the greatest of all the meta-political writers, those who refine and analyse political language and elaborate axioms into axiologies. For this reason his influence on thought about politics

* Polin, 1960, claims in opposition that Locke's doctrine is a coherent whole, and that only an extreme empiricist, an historian, could argue as above.

† Warrender, 1957, *Preface*. The subject of this book, the great difficulty of finding ethical continuity between Hobbes's state of nature and his state of society, shows Hobbes in an incoherency much more serious than any of Locke's.

‡ Above, p. 38. In his later years, Locke obviously looked on politics as related to philosophy in the traditional way. This comes out in his various letters of advice about reading for young men. 'True politics I look on as a part of moral philosophy, which is nothing but the art of conducting men right in society and supporting a community amongst its neighbours', he wrote in 1697 to Lady Mordaunt, now the Countess of Peterborough. 'A young man should begin with Aristotle and then read the moderns if he please.'

has been enormous, but his purchase over what men do politically has been negligible. After he had written, this discipline became entirely different, but the political habits of his countrymen were changed not one little bit, except in so far as clarity of thinking in some men can modify the attitude of a whole society, and on Hobbes's own submission this is very little. The reason for his historical ineffectiveness is not very far to seek. A man who can say, as he did, that 'The skill of making, and maintaining Commonwealths, consisteth in certain rules, as doth Arithmetique and Geometry; not (as Tennis-play) on Practise only'* lacks what might be called a sense of policy. The skill, the consistency, the imagination and the insight with which he sets about discovering what those rules are and how they are related to each other and to knowledge in general must attract his readers, but they will read him as literature only, not literature which is also advice. His work is condemned to be rationalization, and the paradox of the relationship between Locke and Hobbes is that *Leviathan* is much more dated than *Two Treatises*; it is rationalization even of a historical situation. The complete failure of Hobbes as a political, as distinct from a literary and philosophical, realist, is shown up by the fact that he seems to have thought that *Leviathan* would be adopted as a political programme.

The secret of his success in transforming the way men study and write about politics lies in the fact that all political theory must be rationalization, must aspire to the status of philosophy, to some extent. A work of policy exclusively, a work which would deny *in toto* the aphorism which we have quoted from *Leviathan*, could never be written. When, therefore, John Locke set out in 1679 to convince his readers about 'the true original extent and end of civil government' he produced a book which was in some respects like *Leviathan*, although it was not a refutation of it.

It was quite unlike it in doctrine, and for two reasons. He had rejected Hobbes's psychological assumptions and also his entirely rationalistic, unempirical view of natural law, which was widely felt to be a sophistry in any case.† With his instinct against synthetic thinking, therefore, Locke was under no logical necessity of considering the authoritarian conclusions of the Hobbesian

---

* *Leviathan*, chapter 20, last sentence.
† See Tyrrell's letter quoted on p. 80 above.

system and we have shown that there was no possible political motive for doing so. *Two Treatises* differed very considerably from *Leviathan* in the form of its argument, because of these things, because of Filmer, and because of the Lockeian attitude we have discussed, so completely in contrast with the Hobbesian attitude. It contained just that ingredient which *Leviathan* lacked—policy; statement of guidance of what men will accept, respond to and pursue, allowance for the limits of their loyalty and for the limits on possible generalization about their behaviour. But Locke *on Government* was also the presentation of a cogitated case, a piece of intellectual persuasion, from a mind with a great deal in common with that of Hobbes, fully aware of the change which Hobbes had wrought.

It may not, we have seen, have been a matter of direct derivation, since it is quite possible that Locke made his own way along the same road trodden by Hobbes before him, aided only by derivative acquaintance with what Hobbes had said. Locke was a post-Hobbesian, in spite of the fact that so great a part of Hobbesian belief was so much an irrelevance to his purpose in writing on politics that he did not have to refute it. It is right to think of *Two Treatises* as a work of greater importance than *Leviathan* because of the pregnant difference in its relationship with philosophy; it was for this reason that its text could become a part of political habit, and incidentally create the paradox that in so far as Hobbes has done that at all, it is through Locke that he has done it.

In the political doctrines we shall now examine, Locke presented a set of principles more effective and persuasive than any before written in the English language.

V

THE SOCIAL AND POLITICAL
THEORY OF 'TWO TREATISES
OF GOVERNMENT'

When men think of themselves as organized with each other they must remember who they are. They do not make themselves, they do not own themselves, they do not dispose of themselves, they are the workmanship of God. They are his servants, sent into the world on his business, they are even his property (II, § 6). To John Locke this was a proposition of common sense, the initial proposition of a work which appeals to common sense throughout. It is an existentialist proposition, which men have not thought it worth while to question seriously until our own day, and it relies not so much on the proved existence of a Deity as upon the possibility of taking what might be called a synoptic view of the world, more vulgarly a God's-eye view of what happens among men here on earth. If you admit that it is possible to look down on men from above, then you may be said to grant to Locke this initial position.

From this common-sense starting-point he proceeds to two inferences, that we are all free and we are all equal; free of each other, that is to say, and equal to each other, for we are not free of God's superiority and not equal to him. If God could be shown to have given any man, or any order of men, superiority over other men, then these inferences could not be drawn. It was because Sir Robert Filmer had claimed that there was to be found in Revelation a proof that God had set some men above other men, fathers above sons and men above women, the older above the younger and kings above all others that his doctrine was so dangerous and had to be refuted. It became necessary to show in minute detail, analysing text after text of the Scriptures, that this interpretation was quite wrong.

This is the logical function of the *First Treatise* in Locke's work on government, but he says nothing there which is not laid down in the *Second Treatise*. The polemic against Filmer had to be in the form of a Scriptural argument, but it is necessarily an argument from observation and reason as well, for the Scripture does not interpret itself.* Observation shows, says Locke the empiricist, that the superiority of fathers is temporary only, and observation combined with reason shows us why: such superiority is necessary for the preservation of mankind and its duration is determined by the zoological facts (II, §§ 80, 81). Filmer, following Grotius, had interpreted those facts to show that procreation, one individual creating another individual by begetting him, gave a right of superiority, subjection of will to will, even ownership. This is not only bad observation, but it is utterly unreasonable and moreover it offends against the first principle that man is the workmanship and property of God, not of himself. Quite simply and quite literally, then, men were born free in Locke's view, as quite simply and quite literally they had been born unfree in Filmer's system, and in the patriarchal tradition.

No, Locke says; 'the Lord and Master of them all' has not 'by any manifest Declaration of his Will set one above another' (II, § 4), and we all have the same faculties, the same natural advantages; power and jurisdiction is and must be reciprocal amongst us. Again, you do not have to accept a theology to agree that this is all a matter of common sense. All that happens if you wish to disagree is that you find the task of proving something different uncomfortably thrust upon you.

But if it is true that God leaves us free, that nothing in the natural order can be shown to subject one man to another even apart from the revealed will of God, it may still be relevant to ask what positively makes us free, in what does this freedom consist. For absolute freedom has no meaning, it must be defined—'*Where there is no Law, there is no freedom*' (II, § 57). It is the law of nature which sets the bounds to natural freedom (II, § 4) and since the law of nature is an expression of God's will, God's omnipotence can be reconciled with human freedom.† Moreover, God's posi-

---

* This is an important general position of Locke's, best known perhaps from his rejection of 'enthusiasm'. The *First Treatise* repeatedly argues from scripture on the one hand, and reason on the other—see e.g. §§ 4, 60 (Reason and Revelation), 112.

† Quite how, is never shown. Locke is famous for his confession that this problem was beyond him, and it is typical that he should never have raised it in his work on political theory.

tive direction is known to all of us through our reason, since reason, as the Platonists were saying in Locke's day, is *'the Voice of God'* in man (i, § 86, see note there). But in the stance, as we have called it, which Locke took up towards natural law, 'the Law of Nature . . . is the Law of Reason' (i, § 101). It is our reason, therefore, which promulgates to us the law of nature and it is our reason which makes us free. 'We are *born Free*, as we are born Rational' (ii, § 61), and the liberty of acting according to our own will, never from compulsion by the will of others, is grounded on the possession of reason (ii, § 63).

But reason means even more than this and has further consequences for natural liberty and equality. Conceived of as a law (the law of nature), or almost as a power, it is sovereign over all human action. It can dictate to a man as conscience does (ii, § 8) and to more than one man in the social situation, since it is given by God to be the rule betwixt man and man (ii, § 172). It is a quality too, in fact it is the human quality which places man above the brutes, and when it is present to the full almost brings him up to the level of the angels (i, § 58). This language is traditional and the distinction between man and beasts based on the presence or absence of the quality of reason goes back beyond Christianity to the Stoics and Aristotle, but it was of peculiar significance to Locke's generation, as witness the curious debate as to whether brutes, which can work in the world although not being human they do not have the quality, must therefore be machines. And Locke makes full and peculiar use of it in his account of state and society.

It justifies in the first place the subordinate position of children, who though they are born to the full of equality are not born in it (ii, § 55). They only attain freedom when they reach what we still call the age of reason. All this is obvious enough, and only has to be stated at the length Locke gives to it because of Filmer, but it should be noticed that even children under age are not subject to the will of their parents so much as without will, their parents will for them: reason is still sovereign over parent and child. This is one of the very few ways in which age, process or development is relevant to human relationships, though Locke admits that age, virtue, intelligence and blood (none of which seems easily described as a difference in rationality) in some way unimportant to his purpose can infringe natural equality (ii, § 54). But the next consequence is more startling. When we look upon ourselves as God's workmanship, we recognize that we all possess reason because he gave it to us, and therefore any man who behaves unreasonably is to that extent an animal, and may be treated as such. Specifically, any man who seeks to get anyone else into his power, under his will, denying that this other person is as free as he is because he too possesses reason, refusing to recognize that reason is the rule between men, that man 'becomes liable to be destroied by the injured person and the rest of mankind, as any other wild beast, or noxious brute that is destructive to their being' (II, § 172).

This is a drastic argument, and we may think it somewhat crude. It serves to spell out in thick, black letters Locke's quite literal belief that reason is the mode of co-operation between men; reason, he had just said, is 'the common bond whereby humane kind is united into one fellowship and societie'. It is not an isolated statement, but a recurrent repetitive theme, perhaps developed in detail as a later insertion (see note on II, § 172), but essential to Locke's account of the maintenance of justice inside and outside organized society. It may be looked upon as his final judgment on the consequences to the actual relationships between men of the synthetic civil philosophy of Hobbes, for *Leviathan*, like the royal patriarch, did subordinate all human wills to one will, it made law and government a matter of will, therefore it did treat men as beasts and anyone pretending to its rights and powers could be treated as a beast. But the actual object which he had in mind seems to have been much more personal and political. When the passages presenting this argument are examined closely, Charles and James Stuart fit easily enough into the role of those 'wild Savage Beasts, with whom Men can have no Society nor Security',* for they had tried to rule England as despots, if not of the Hobbesian, then certainly of the patriarchal type.

In perfect freedom, equal to each other, capable of rational behaviour and so able to understand and co-operate with each other, that is how we are born. It must be emphasized that we are all born this way, bond or free, savage or civilized, inside or outside society or the state, for it is a truly universal doctrine in

---

* II, § 11, 25 6. This is a reference to an aggressor in the state of nature, but the last phrase also appeared in the final text of II, § 172, 16. The subject of II, §§ 171 and 172 is clearly the established government of a country, Locke's country, and these are the words applied to it when it claims the right to 'Absolute, Arbitrary Power' ('Having quitted Reason' to do so).

Locke and he does not, for example, go on to argue from this dogmatic rationalist position that the basis of political life is the rule of the rational man over his irrational fellows.* There can be no arbitrary source of power of one man over another, not even a source in Revelation, for Divine right has already been disposed of as not proven. How then does it come about that there is such a thing as rulership in the world? How is government possible at all?

Locke answers this fundamental question, and it is significant of his radical individualism that it should ever arise in such an urgent form, by introducing what he calls a 'Strange Doctrine'. By this he may intend to warn us that he is innovating,† but what he says comes as no great surprise: '*every one*', he declares, '*has the Executive Power* of the Law of Nature' (II, §§ 6, 7, 8, 9, 13). If anyone offends against the law of nature, everyone else has the right to punish him for it and exact retribution, not simply for his own damage but to vindicate the rule 'of *reason* and common Equity, which is that measure God has set to the actions of Men, for their mutual security' (II, § 8). We may do so individually, but we may and must co-operate with other individuals against this 'trespass against the whole Species'. On this natural right, which arises out of humanity itself, is based not simply the right of governing, but its power as well, for it is a collective power which is used against an offender even if only one man wields it. The right of governing, and power to govern, is a fundamental, individual, natural right and power, set alongside that of preserving oneself and the rest of mankind (II, §§ 128–30). It is judicial in its nature, for it is the pronouncing and enforcing of a law, the law of nature which is the law of reason.

The whole of Locke's political theory is already in view, even

---

* Though he concedes wide inequality in capacity, reasoning capacity, see note on II, § 4, 11 and references. Locke took a sober, almost a gloomy view of the powers of most of the human race to follow an argument, to take part in 'rational society' at all in its sophisticated definition, and texts to illustrate this can be found throughout his works, the *Essay* especially: the title of 'optimistic rationalist' sits oddly upon him. Nevertheless it does not seem to me justifiable to read into his statements, certainly the statements of *Two Treatises*, any doctrine of differential rationality as has sometimes been done. Strictly the non-rational man was not a man at all and Locke never denies that any individual can be rational according to his capacity, he only insists that he is blameworthy if he is not. He may not be a consistent optimist, but he is no cynic: see Polin, 1961, 40n.

† Strauss, 1953, lays some stress on Locke's use of this phrase, but it seems to me to be not much more than a literary device to him. As Strauss points out, Locke's doctrine on the point differs only by a twist of emphasis from that of Pufendorf and Cumberland.

the concept of trust and the separation of powers. We shall make general the implications of this position on the executive power of the law of nature under the title of a doctrine, the Lockeian doctrine of natural political virtue. Dogmatically presented as a 'strange doctrine', no demonstration of its truth is offered but it is implied in a particular provision of the law of nature as distinct from the law of nature generally. This is the right and duty of every man to preserve himself and everybody else as much as possible, which is the only law of nature used in such a way.* Government, when first viewed from this position, is simply a 'Magistrate, who by being Magistrate, hath the common right of punishing put into his hands' (II, § 11). But we have not yet reached the stage of established government. All the characteristics of men, and the relationship between them, which we have discussed so far belong to the state of nature.

The state of nature is simply the condition in which the executive power of the law of nature remains exclusively in the hands of individuals and has not been made communal. It can be inferred that it was the original condition of all humanity, because wherever established and permanent collective authority is found, it is always discovered to be the result of men taking thought, making deliberate arrangements to secure and establish the rule of rationality and the provisions of natural law. It is not an adequate reply to this to say that men are all observed in fact to live under government, because 'Government is everywhere antecedent to Records' (II, § 101, compare I, §§ 144, 145) and because primitive tribes are known to be living now without government, or very nearly so. But although these historical and anthropological facts are important, demonstrating as they do that individual men have lived and do live with each other in the state of nature, it is much more significant that states themselves, and heads of states, can be related to each other in no other way, now or at any time. The King of France and the King of England can collaborate to maintain the peace of the world, so as to preserve mankind. For the most part they do, but each is individually executing the law of

* Because of the particular attitude to the law of nature which we have described, Locke never lists the laws themselves and he never relates one law of nature with another, though this law of preservation is called 'fundamental'; see note on II, § 16, 9–10 and references, including a passage in his *Education*. In all these respects he is a very unconventional natural-law writer, much more so than Hobbes.

nature: there is no institution or authority for the purpose. This fact, and the persistence of areas of the earth in the state of nature, may also put private individuals into this state with each other even now. Such are the Swiss and the Indian bargaining for truck in the woods of America (II, § 14).*

The state of nature, therefore, has obvious disadvantages; it is to be expected that men will do their best to replace it, and we have seen that they are constituted in such a way that they are perfectly well able to do so. For the state of nature leaves every man judge in his own case (II, § 13). He has the law of nature to guide him, but this law is unwritten, 'no where to be found but in the minds of Men', so that 'they who through Passion or Interest shall mis-cite, or mis-apply it, cannot so easily be convinced of their mistake where there is no establish'd Judge' (II, § 136). But this does not mean that the state of nature is a state of war, 'however some Men', meaning Hobbes, 'have confounded' them (II, § 19). War, in fact, is not a state but an incident, although a 'sedate setled Design' on life makes it permissible to use 'state' in describing it (II, § 16). War is indeed an incident apparently inseparable from human life, because it is the appeal to God in cases where men cannot settle things reasonably, and we have to recognize that such a final appeal is always a possibility even within highly developed political society, a possibility which has important consequences. It is to be expected that war should be much closer to the surface in a state of nature, as witness the frequency and importance of war in the international state of nature, but this cannot mean that war describes the state of nature, or that it is otherwise relevant to the distinction between the state of nature and the state of society.

'In the beginning all the World was *America*' (II, § 49) and a complete account of human development would show us that in the primitive, patriarchal, Old Testament stage in Europe we once lived as the American Indians now do (see notes on I, § 130 and 144,

---

* The scattered references to primitive societies in *Two Treatises*, with the more extensive discussion in the *Essay*, cover an enormous amount of reading, a perpetual preoccupation and an intellectual dilemma. (See Laslett, 1965 (ii).) Locke may be said to have done more than anyone else to found the study of comparative anthropology, and he was well aware that the evidence did not demonstrate a 'state of nature' of the sort he described in his political theory. Once more, then, he had to take up a stance towards the problem. We may believe that this was his position: natural men cannot be proved to have lived universally in comparative peace, in immanent sociability, but the evidence does not make such an assumption impossible, and it certainly does not make it necessary to assume that he lives in a state of war.

27–34). In fact this condition of living together according to reason without a common superior on earth, in mutual assistance, peace, goodwill and preservation (II, § 19), is the universal background against which government should be understood. It tells us what government is and what it does by showing us what it is not and what it does not do.* It even makes it possible to distinguish proper forms of government from improper ones. '*Absolute Monarchy*', for example, is '*inconsistent with Civil Society*, and so can be no Form of Civil Government at all' (II, § 90). It must be so, because an absolute monarch is judging in his own case, as all men must in the state of nature. Therefore in respect of him the whole society he rules is itself in a state of nature; moreover he is substituting the rule of force and will, his force and will, for the rule of reason clothed in natural law. But this does not mean that there is no peace, no justice, no means of social and political co-operation within the society he rules, any more than the international state of nature precludes international peace and co-operation. For men are not like that. The state of nature is already social and political. The state of society never completely transcends the state of nature: the contrast is never complete.

These considerations undoubtedly complicate Locke's view of the state of nature, but the complication demonstrates his superior realism and allows room in his system for elements often supposed to be absent from him and from the individualist attitude generally.† At the point we have now reached, however, where the question arises why it should be that men ever do proceed from a state of nature to a state of society, he suddenly departs from all his predecessors, classical and medieval. Although his state of nature is inconvenient, and although his individual is perfectly capable of transcending it and we can already see why he and his fellows should wish to do so, Locke introduces here a motive for the

* This is the analytic function of this concept in the political theory of early modern times, and can be criticized as the error of supposing that what is logically prior is historically previous and institutionally basic. That Locke was uneasy about its implications is shown by his unwillingness to do more than hint at the assimilation between Old Testament history and the condition of America in his day, and in any case the incompleteness of the contrast which he draws between the two states makes him somewhat less vulnerable than his predecessors.

† Locke's state of nature, with its immanent sociability and its acceptance of man's dependence on his fellows, does in a sense incorporate the Aristotelian attitude. See Polin, 1961, 174, for the *theoretical* as distinct from the *actual* state of nature and compare Jenkins, 1967 (who cannot accept its sociability); Seliger, 1968, pp. 108, 122, etc.; Ashcraft, 1968, 1969. Rau, 1987, makes ingenious use of Locke's position for contemporary political purposes.

establishment of political society which few had considered in the context of political origins, and none had given much prominence. He abruptly injects into the discussion the concept of property.

Property generally is justified ethically in Locke's system by arguments not unlike those of the other thinkers of the time. Mankind's right to the goods of nature derives from God's grant in the Scriptures, from man's rationality, from the fundamental natural law of self-preservation (II, § 25 on, I, §§ 86, 87). But on these grounds it is man as a species which has a right to own things, not an individual man. This means that the goods of nature were originally common, both because the Bible says so, and because universal freedom and equality must mean original communism. Locke and his fellows were in some difficulty in accounting for the fact that this original communism had given way to private property. They could and did argue from occupancy, 'findings is keepings', but in the end this must imply consent. In fact, as Filmer had argued with ingenuity and force, the only way out of original communism was to assume that in some way or other every individual in the world had consented to every act of property acquisition.

Locke's solution to the problem was to lay it down that 'every Man has a *Property* in his own *Person*' so that 'the *labour* of his Body, and the *Work* of his Hands' are his. Therefore whatsoever 'he removes out of the State that Nature hath provided, and left it in, he hath mixed his *Labour* with . . . and thereby makes it his *Property*' (II, § 27). This famous passage, which almost contradicts his first principle that men belong to God, not themselves, together with the general claim that ''tis *Labour* indeed that *puts the difference of value* on every thing' (II, § 40) are perhaps the most influential statements he ever made.* Property so acquired was not unlimited, for it was confined originally to what a man and his family could consume or use, and must not be wasted (II, § 36). It extended to the land as well as to the fruits of it (II, §§ 32–40), but even in this form it must never be used as an instrument of oppression, as a means of getting others to submit to your will (I, §§ 42–3). The whole argument is intended to show that individual property did not arise from the common consent of all

* See note on II, § 27 for Tyrrell's very similar passage, possibly however suggested to him by Locke, and note on II, § 28 for a further discussion of Locke as an innovator in this matter. It cannot be proved to have been entirely original to Locke, and is close to the traditional dogma that a labourer had an inalienable right to his tools. Polin, 1960, 255, prints a further reference to property and justice, and Olivecrona, 1974 (i) (ii), places Locke's theory in its natural law context.

mankind, though in the end the actual distribution of it is held to be due to money, which is a matter of consent, perhaps even worldwide consent.* In the state of nature, then, the exertions of men and above all their invention of money had brought them all into relationships with each other which were not those of rational and conscious co-operation but sprang from their differing contact, almost physical contact, with the world of material things —from their property as thus defined.

In fact men were led to leave the state of nature and to set up a source of power 'for the Regulating and Preserving of Property' (II, § 3). As the *Second Treatise* goes on, more and more emphasis is laid on the 'great and *chief end* . . . of Mens uniting into Common-wealths, and putting of themselves under Government, *is the Preservation of their Property*. To which in the state of Nature there are many things wanting.'† Meanwhile it has become obvious that Locke's account of the origin of property cannot be intended to cover all meanings of the word. For it is not defined as material possessions, nor in units of the conveniences or necessities of life but much more generally as 'Lives, Liberties and Estates, which I call by the general name, *Property*' (II, § 123).‡ Except in the chapter on property, and in other cases where it is clear that material possessions are meant, the word 'property' in the *Second Treatise* is usually to be read in this sense. It is the sense in which Locke's contemporaries could talk of the protestant religion established by law as their 'property', and Richard Baxter maintain that 'men's *lives* and *Liberties* are the chief parts of their propriety' though he, like Locke, sought the origin of 'propriety in a man's industry'.¶

Property, moreover, seems to give the political quality to personality. A slave lacks all political rights because he is in-

---

* II, § 45, see especially ll. 20–2 and note, II, § 50, etc.

† II, § 124: compare II, § 94, 22–3 and note there on Tyrrell's similar statement: also II, §§ 127, 134, 138, etc.

‡ The occurrences of this wider definition are listed in the note to II, § 87, 5: it may be noteworthy that at least two of the contexts (those in §§ 123 and 173) were possibly additions of 1689.

¶ See Baxter, 1680, passage noted under II, § 27. 'Propriety' and 'property' seem to have the same meaning, or combination of meanings, in Locke and in Baxter, though Locke occasionally substituted the second for the first in correcting his book (e.g. in title to 1st *Treatise*, chapter VII). The extended meaning of property has been noticed occasionally (Gough, 1950; Brogan, 1959) but I owe to the late Professor Viner of

capable of property: despotical power, not properly political at all, can only be exercised over the propertyless (II, § 174). We well may complain that Locke does not make it sufficiently clear which definition of property he is using in which context. But the fact that he was prepared to allow material property, labour-mixed-with-natural-objects property, to stand for many or all the abstract rights of the individual does help us to understand why the concept as a whole enters into his account of the foundation of civil society.

For property to Locke seems to symbolize rights in their con-crete form, or perhaps rather to provide the tangible subject of an individual's powers and attitudes. It is because they can be symbolized as property, something a man can conceive of as distinguishable from himself though a part of himself, that a man's attributes, such as his freedom, his equality, his power to execute the law of nature, can become the subject of his consent, the sub-ject of any negotiation with his fellows. We cannot alienate any part of our personalities, but we can alienate that with which we have chosen to mix our personalities.* Whether Locke's mind was working quite in this way or not, it is clear from what he says elsewhere about civil as opposed to spiritual society that it can only concern itself with 'civil concernments', which on examina-tion seem to be identical with 'property' in its extended meaning in the *Second Treatise*.† In some way, then, it is through the theory of property that men can proceed from the abstract world of liberty and equality based on their relationship with God and natural law, to the concrete world of political liberty guaranteed by political arrangements.

To see a symbolic system in a writer so down-to-earth as Locke,

Princeton the demonstration that the extended meaning is to be taken as a normal usage both for Locke and his contemporaries. Professor Viner communicated an unpublished paper on the subject, which was printed in part, but not in full, in Viner, 1963. Locke's extraordinary vagueness about the use of this term is well illustrated by the phrase used at II, 131, 6.

* The conventional judgment of Locke's view of property, that it described a natural, inalienable right, seems on this view to be exactly wrong. Property is precisely that part of our attributes (or, perhaps to be pedantic, that attribute of our attributes) which we can alienate, but only of course by our own consent. I differ here from Olivecrona who takes property to be an extension of the personality.

† See passages cited in note on II, § 3 from Locke on *Toleration*. His whole argument on that subject is intended to prove that the subjective world of religious conviction is completely inaccessible to the objective world of 'civil concernments', of property in fact.

however, may be to read more than should be read into an expedient forced upon him by the necessity of replying to Sir Robert Filmer. Property, both in the narrow and in the extended sense, is insufficiently protected and inadequately regulated in the state of nature and this is the critical inconvenience which induces men to 'enter into Society to make one People, one Body Politick under one Supreme Government . . . by setting up a Judge on Earth with Authority to determine all Controversies' (II, § 89). It is critical only in the cumulative sense, for it is to be added to the love and want of society (II, § 101) and to the danger of aggression from abroad (II, § 3) as well as to all the other inconveniences which arise from men being judges in their own cases, and which are so considerable that it can be said that 'God hath certainly appointed Government to restrain the partiality and violence of Men' (II, § 13). Once this stage is reached, Locke's political principle can be written out in full. But before this is done, we should perhaps review Locke's theory of property a little further since it has been the subject of so much criticism and misunderstanding.*

'God gave the World . . . to the use of the Industrious and Rational', says he (II, § 34), gave it to them in the state of nature that is, and appointed government also as a remedy for the inconveniences of that state. For by their very industriousness and rationality these people created inconveniences for themselves and the rest of mankind, setting up relationships between men through their ever-more-complicated contact with material things which defeated the control of individuals acting as lone executors of the law of nature. Conscious, co-operative control was set up, therefore, under governments where 'the Laws regulate the right of property, and the possession of land is determined by positive constructions' (II, § 50).

This regulation of property and determination of landowner-ship by political authority is not easy to interpret from Locke's text. His object seems to be to guarantee secure and quiet possession, however large the estate and whatever it contained. In spite of the statements presenting the 'labour theory of value', it would be extremely difficult to argue that he had any sort of doctrine in mind which we should call socialist. Nevertheless he never contra-

---

* Locke's doctrine of property has been extensively discussed: see, e.g. Larkin, 1930: Czajkowski, 1941; Kendall, 1941 (the first to criticize the 'individualist' interpretation); Gough, 1950; Strauss, 1953; Cherno, 1957; Pietranea, 1957; Monson, 1958; Polin, 1960; Viano, 1961 (Locke's theory and Shaftesbury's policy); Macpherson 1951 and 1962; Dunn, 1967 (ii) and 1969; Milam, 1967; Olivecrona, 1974 (i), (ii) and 1975; Tully, 1980; Wood, 1984.

dicts the assertion he made in 1667, that the magistrate can appoint ways of transferring properties from one man to another, and make what property laws he likes, provided they are equitable.* In § 90 of the *First Treatise* he clearly implies that the community always had a residual interest in property and even an original right to it, for the possessions of an intestate without kin revert to the community (line 34).

Even the minutest control of property by political authority can be reconciled with the doctrine of *Two Treatises*. The property he defends is never confined to substantial possessions, or looked on as what we (not Locke) call capital. He hints that even the poorest has enough to need society's protection for it (II, § 94 and note). If not complete communism, certainly redistributive taxation, perhaps nationalization could be justified on the principles we have discussed: all that would be necessary is the consent of the majority of the society, regularly and constitutionally expressed, and such a law would hold even if all the property-owners were in the minority.

On the other hand the whole tenor of his argument is in favour of those with a great deal to lose. It may be felt that his anxiety to make property rights independent of the universal consent of all mankind, even though property distribution through money is subject to it,† represents an interest more cogent than the necessity of answering Filmer. The same preoccupation with the absolute security of material property may be seen in the confusion left by his dual definition of the concept. If he was prepared to allow all his references to be taken in the sense of material possessions, then his whole position looks very like an uncompromising defence of wealth and its power. If it is permissible to look on his use of the concept 'property' as symbolic, as has been suggested, then the symbolic system seems to express all human rights as market commodities. He is perfectly willing to contemplate the continuous or permanent appropriation of the product of one man's labour by another, a servant's by a master.‡ Slave labour in no

---

* The 1667 *Essay on Toleration*: see note on II, § 120. Dunn, 1960 (i) p. 36, dissents from this use of Locke's writing of 1667.

† See note * on p. 101 above.

‡ Macpherson, 1951, 560. It seems, however, to be an over-interpretation to say that a man can sell his labour in the sense of the propensity to work, and I cannot follow the statement (p. 564) that 'Locke has separated life and labor'. When Locke writes on the wage relationship in II, § 85, he uses the word 'service' not 'labour', and though he seems specific enough in II, § 28, 16–26 in making the master own his servant's labour, it is not clearly a matter of a wage relationship: see Laslett, 1964.

way perturbs him: a reading of § 130 of the *First Treatise* leaves a modern believer in the enormity of personal servitude very uncomfortable, if not indignant. He fails to make any specific provision against the obvious consequences of allowing unlimited accumulation of precious stones, metals and money in all its forms, once consent had given them value.

Nevertheless it is gratuitous to turn Locke's doctrine of property into the classic doctrine of the 'spirit of capitalism', whatever that may be. It can only be done by explaining away all the statements which he makes about the origin and limitations of property as obstacles to his true meaning. All that he says about 'regulating' property, even though this is the first word he uses about it when it is introduced into the *Second Treatise* (II, § 3), has to be ignored. Half-conscious traditionalism or plain hypocrisy must be held to account for Locke's description of unlimited acquisitiveness as '*amor sceleratus habendi*, evil Concupiscence' (II, § 111). Above all it has to be done by denying point blank that Locke's consistent claim, 'The Obligations of the Law of Nature, cease not in Society, but only in many Cases are drawn closer' (II, § 135), can apply to property.* If we are prepared to treat historical texts in such a way we can prove just what we like from them.

In fact, of course, Locke was neither a 'socialist' nor a 'capitalist', though it is fascinating to find elements of both attitudes of ours in his property doctrine—more, perhaps, in what he left out or just failed to say than in the statements themselves. He was not even an advocate of land and landownership as the basis of political power, to be 'represented' in a nation's counsels. For all the intellectual and political influence which he wielded in the eighteenth century he was in these respects a barren field for anyone who wished to justify what once was called the Whig

---

* Strauss, 1953, 240: see p. 246 for his reference to the spirit of capitalism. The case for Locke as a crypto-capitalist is presented with far greater exactness and subtlety by Macpherson, 1962, from a point of view which scorns 'petty bourgeois socialism'. Interesting as it is, Strauss's view seems to be based on so arbitrary a textual reading, one so much concerned to discover a 'real' meaning (generally a Hobbesist or a capitalist one), that it is quite unacceptable to an editor of *Two Treatises*; for a critique, see Yolton, 1958. Macpherson's close and revealing analysis clarified the issues remarkably, but it would seem that he could only have come to his thoroughly unrealistic and occasionally unhistorical conclusions because he set out to demonstrate that Locke's object could only have been to 'provide the ideological support for capitalist appropriation'. Ryan, 1965, analyses Macpherson's position with great acuteness, and Dunn, 1967 (ii), prints new evidence on Locke's view of the just price.

oligarchy. But he did use his property doctrine to give continuity to a political society, to join generation to generation.

Locke's doctrine of property was incomplete, not a little confused and inadequate to the problem as it has been analysed since his day, lacking the humanity and the sense of social co-operation to be found in the canonists who had preceded him.

We should not in fact expect it to be wholly developed and coherent, a doctrine of property at large, because close working of his text seems to confirm what several commentators have suggested. This is that Locke's primary and overriding interest was in taxation, arbitrary taxation and its iniquities, not in property as a subject in itself. He is naturally led to discuss the nature of property, but a general theory of ownership was not his intellectual object. This in spite of the remark cited at the outset of this *Introduction*. We must surely recognize nevertheless that the doctrine of property he did sketch out was an original doctrine, particularly important in its bearing on the way men analysed social and political origins, and his own judgment on it must stand—no man has ever quite done this before or since.

We are now in a position to follow Locke's political principle through to its conclusion. Men may enter into society quite suddenly, and it is perhaps best to assume that any given company actually decided at some point in time to change their condition to this new state. But there can be degrees of 'community', a variety of ways in which political authority can be founded, and even apparently permanent conditions which cannot be called one or the other state. The most usual development is in fact patriarchal, where a large family grows into a political society and its hereditary head gives rise to a royal lineage. But this must not lead us into the mistake of supposing that patriarchal is political power, or to confuse the relation of man and wife, parent and child, master and servant, with the political relation. However political power comes into being, it can only be looked on as the formation of a community by a band of rational creatures, all with the power to punish transgression of the law of nature and offences against their property. Any number of them can exercise the power collectively, and they can replace their patriarchs or make their generals into elective kings as and when they please. The unmistakable sign of civil society having come into being is when every individual has resigned up to the society or the public his individual power to exercise the law of nature and protect his property. This is the social compact and it is fair to everybody, since everybody makes the same sacrifice for the same benefits. It sets up a judge on earth, with authority to determine all the controversies and redress the injuries that may happen to any member of the commonwealth, as it is now called.

All this will be done by consent, the consent of every individual concerned. The judge thus established will be a legislative power, able to pronounce on offences because it can promulgate settled, standing rules in accordance with the law of nature; rules, or laws, which are indifferent, and so fair to everybody, guaranteeing, defining and giving substance to everybody's freedom. To sanction those laws and judgments, this 'legislative', as we may call it, will have at its disposal the mingled force of all the members of society—and 'executive' power in fact. It will have a third power in virtue of the condition in which the community finds itself, a power of protection from foreign enemies and of communication with other such communities and with individuals in a state of nature. This is the 'federative' power. It will not need a separate judicial power, because, we have seen, the pronouncing of judgment is its general function. These three powers are distinct in themselves, and the executive and legislative are best kept in separate hands, except that the head of the executive may be a part of the legislative, with power of summons and prorogation. But there can be no doubt of the ultimate superiority of the legislative in the constitution.

Its establishment, and the form of government generally, are 'the fundamental Appointment of the Society', the Constitution as we should say (II, § 214). The original compact which set it up will imply majority rule, for the state is not simply a rightful power, it is a collective body, and a body which can only move on the side of the greater mass. Its gravitational logic requires that those who are a part of it shall not resist its final direction. Political power, now that it has arrived, will not be special in the sense that it is different from the power all men continue to exercise in preserving the law of nature where their governors cannot, or by agreement must not, intervene. It will be special only in the sense that it is collective, and so cannot be an attribute, least of all the property, of a single man or family. Every effort must be made to ensure that those who wield it shall never develop an interest separate from that of the community, the people. Any individual born outside the community is free to join it, or born inside can decide to leave for another community, or even to live in some part of the world still in a state of nature. When he is within the community he must accept the rulership of its governors and obey its laws.

But the governors are only entrusted with the power they have. Government comes into being at the same time and perhaps by the same act as that which established civil society, but its power is given for attaining an end and limited to it. If that end should be neglected, the government is dissolved and the power devolves to the people, or to the community which is all one. Now this does not restore a state of nature, or it does not necessarily do so. The people under these circumstances may themselves act as a 'legislative', and so maintain government, but it is likely that after a very short while they will set up new trustees for government, or change the form and conditions of governing. It is for the people only to decide whether or when their governmental trustees have acted contrary to their trust, or their legislative has been changed, and for the people as a whole to act as umpire in any dispute between the governors and a part of their body. If the governors resist such judgment, or behave in any way which threatens that the people will cease to be a community and become a confused multitude, then the state of nature is at hand, with all its disadvantages. This will seldom, perhaps never, happen for the people can be relied upon to be patient and long-suffering. If such an extreme situation does come about, and the question arises of who is to be the final judge, the answer brings us back to where Locke began. There is no final judge of these things on earth, the ultimate appeal can only be to God.

This is the major theme of Locke on *Government*,* and it is extended into a discussion of conquest, tyranny and other related subjects. It will be seen that the theme as a whole does develop out of the assertion that each individual possesses the executive power of the law of nature. We may look on his intention as being to lay down a doctrine in this way, a doctrine which we shall call that of natural political virtue. This would seem to be the most probable and sympathetic reading of the book, though not all that is said is quite consistent with it.

* It has had to be interpreted somewhat for purposes of straight exposition; see below for trust, dissolution of government, etc.

This doctrine lays it down that all individuals, whether grouped together formally or informally, or even when alone, will have some tendency* to allow for the existence, the desires, actions and needs of other men: this is what is to be expected if each is to be trusted with the means of maintaining the humanity of all. It accounts for the quasi-social character of the state of nature, and makes it possible to talk of 'all the Priviledges' of that 'ill condition' (ii, § 127). It permits any number of men to set up a political society: 'when any number of Men have, by the consent of every individual, made a *Community*' (ii, § 96); this 'any number of Men may do, because it injures not the Freedom of the rest' (ii, § 95). This is important because it denies that there has to be a special shape for a body of men before they can take on ethical unity, as Filmer had claimed when he insisted that they must be a family under patriarchal will.

The doctrine of natural political virtue goes some way to justify in ethical terms Locke's rather perfunctory defence of majority rule in mechanical terms. For a majority, which is simply a random sample of those who voted, will under this doctrine tend to act with some responsibility towards those in the minority.† It can be seen most clearly in Locke's insistence that 'in well order'd Commonwealths' the men who wield the legislative power should be ordinary citizens, drawn from the main body of those for whom they legislate and reverting to that status when out of office (ii, § 143, with note and references). Applied in this way the doctrine becomes an essential presupposition of representative government as it developed after Locke had written, essential to such things as virtual representation, which he implies at all points, and the rule of parties, which he never contemplated. It sanctions the right of a group of leaders to take revolutionary action, and it is always behind an individual acting alone in a political situation, a judge, a king, or a Speaker.‡

It may be noted that in expounding this doctrine Locke is once more occupying a position which looks two ways at once, rather than selecting a unitary definition and pursuing its implications.

* Almost the Aristotelian *nisus*, though Locke did not mean to make society natural in quite the Aristotelian way.

† Kendall, 1941, seems unable to concede such a doctrine to Locke, and interprets his statements in such a way as to make him a 'majority-rule authoritarian', though see his final chapter, 'The Latent Premise', as expounded against Laslett in 1966.

‡ Safeguarded in all cases, of course, by the concept of trust—see below.

We all possess natural political virtue, both because we are disposed favourably towards each other in our very make-up, our nature, and because, when we co-operate, when we discuss things together, the tendency of what we do and what we say will inevitably be towards the politically efficacious, that which will work out for all of us. We might distinguish the two facets of the phrase as 'naturalistic' and 'intellectualistic' respectively, and we must insist that Locke recognized both of them. In this he found himself very close to Hooker, and he was thus able to make very effective use of that respected name, so authoritative with his opponents.* But he does not base social life on love and sociability to any extent, for his rejection of patriarchalism made it difficult, though he does make concessions even over this. We have natural political virtue, he seems to say, primarily because of a symmetry in reason between all of us.

Locke's theories of political obligation and political freedom, in so far as he worked them out in any detail, can be looked on as developments of natural political virtue. The virtue which we all possess is outward-facing: we might use a later, utilitarian expression and call it 'other regarding'. We must stress the point that in Locke's system it is the power which men have over others, not the power which they have over themselves, which gives rise to political authority. Organized government is not to be regarded as a form of self-government. We do not dispose of ourselves, and so we have no right to give ourselves up to anybody or anything else. All that rational co-operation enables us to do is to give up our other-regarding powers to found political authority. We do this by an act of consent and it can even be said that 'the Judgments of the Commonwealth' are our own judgments, they being made by ourselves or our 'Representative' (II, § 88).

We cannot, then, be obliged by any government to which we have not given some sign of consent—walking on a road is enough (II, § 119), but owning property under its jurisdiction is much more tangible. And only this can give a man permanent membership of a society (II, § 122), where there has been no express declaration of allegiance. Nevertheless it is a little misleading to say that we are actually governed exclusively by our own consent. We come under the jurisdiction of the other-regarding

* See footnotes to *Second Treatise*, especially to § 5, see Polin, 1961, 105 etc.

powers of our fellow citizens when we cease to act rationally and socially, and in society this means that we must submit to the common executive power, the power of the state sanctioning natural law and those settled standing rules which it has established. We have consented to the establishment of that executive power, and through its character as a legislative we may be said to have had a voice in the codifying of those rules, more especially where the legislating body is a representative one. But we should be under the executive power of the law of nature in any case, as exercised by others over us. If this were not so, how could any government punish the crimes of aliens within its jurisdiction (II, § 9)?*

Property, on the other hand, is of such a nature that '*without a Man's own consent* it *cannot be taken away from him*' (II, § 193). In all matters of property, then, the warrant of a government's action must always be consent. Since Locke lays so much emphasis on the preservation of property as the reason for establishing the state, as the end of government, and since he assigns so many social and political functions to property ownership, it may seem that consent is the sole basis of obligation in his system. He has been read almost exclusively in this sense, but obligation does have an independent source in his doctrine of natural political virtue.

We may look on this position in another way and say that the passage from the state of nature to the state of society and government makes possible rule by consent, which is not possible in a state of nature. This is important because it lays stress on the fact that in Locke's theory freedom is not merely absence of restraint, it is positive. It is something which is enlarged by the creation of society and government, which is given substance by the existence of laws, the laws of the law courts. It can be negatively defined, therefore, as being under no other legislative power but that established by consent in the commonwealth (II, § 22), and positively as the progressive elimination of the arbitrary from political and social regulation. He is very insistent on this positive point, resting it originally on the right to preservation, and on the individual's inability to dispose of himself (II, §§ 22–3). He develops it into the denial that government can be a personal matter, a matter of will: it must always be

---

* See Lewis, 1940 and, for criticism of Locke, see Plamenatz, 1936, Gough, 1950 and especially the very interesting discussion in Dunn, 1967 (ii) and 1969 (i). It is odd that Locke does not insist on the necessity of a representative legislature for a government to be legitimate, though he seems to assume it and in II, § 176 talks of the 'native Right' of a people to have a legislative approved by a majority.

an institutional matter, a matter of law. Law makes men free in the political arena, just as reason makes men free in the universe as a whole. It is progressively codified by a legislative brought into being by consent, it is expressive of and in harmony with the law of nature, which continues of course in society (II, § 135). For 'Law ... is ... *the direction of a free and intelligent Agent* to his proper Interest', and its end is '*to preserve and enlarge Freedom*' (II, § 57) Locke is much closer here than was once recognized to Rousseau's position that men can be compelled to be free, compelled by the law of the legislative which they have consented to set up.*

Men cannot, however, be compelled by will, the individual will of a ruler or the general will of a society. Locke's insistence that government is defined and limited by the end for which political society is established, that it can never be arbitrary or a matter of will, can never be owned, is expressed in a particular and exact application of his doctrine of natural political virtue—the concept of trust. He tends to use the language of trust whenever he talks of the power of one man over another, even for fathers and children (II, § 59). 'Some Trust one in another' is an assumption of all who join to make up society (II, § 107). This must be so if the tendency of men is to be responsible, if governors and governed are interchangeable; we can and must trust each other if natural political virtue is a reality. But there is an easily discovered limit to the trust which can be accorded or assumed, and this limit is implied in the concept of trust itself. Trust is both the corollary and the safeguard of natural political virtue.

The concept of trust is very specific to Locke, though it is not original with him.† His actual words must be looked at if we are to see its function clearly, and yet not make him more precise than he intended to be. We may notice that the word 'contract' does not occur more than about ten times in his book, and it is hardly ever applied to political matters at all.‡ It is 'compact' or often mere 'agreement' which creates a society, a community (II, §§ 14, 8; 97, 5; 99, 6; etc.), or political power (I, §§ 94, 5; 113, 7 and 9: II, §§ 97,

---

* See Gough, 1950, 32, commenting on Kendall, 1941; Abrams, 1961 (government *is* a matter of will), and Seliger, 1963 (ii) (consent and natural law).

† See the valuable discussion of the concept in Gough, 1950, chapter VII.

‡ But to legal and quasi-legal agreements, such as marriage (I, §§ 47, 10; 98, 17 and 19; II, §§ 81, 10: 82, 8; 11, 16; 83, 17: but he calls marriage a *compact* in II, §§ 78, 1; 84, 4) or to property arrangements, e.g. in II, 194, 16. In I, § 96, 13 there is, however, a reference to political 'power founded on *Contract*'.

5 *original Compact*; 102, 22; 171, 24; 173, 6; etc.), even law (II, § 35, 5). Now compact and agreement are more general than contract: they are further removed from the language of the law. Vague as Locke is, we seem to have here a deliberate attempt to avoid being specific and to leave legal models on one side. It may imply that the transmutation into the social and political condition must not be looked on in a legal way; it is a variable thing and a pretty loose one too.

The word 'trust' is much more frequent than either contract or compact, and it is a legal word.* But although Locke used it with legal overtones, and was as always quite willing to take advantage of all the suggestions it contained for his readers, we need not assume, as is often done, that he was trying to describe a formal trust deed for government. In applying the word trust to the various political powers in the state, the constitution, Locke draws an important distinction for us, perhaps two of them. He divides off the process of compact, which creates a community, from the further process by which the community entrusts political power to a government; although they may take place at the same time, these two are distinct. This puts his system amongst those which distinguish the 'contract of society' from the 'contract of government', though in Locke this second process is not a contract at all. And this may be his second point; to underline the fact that the relation between government and governed is not contractual, for a trust is not a contract.

If a contract is to be set up, or understood, it is necessary that the parties to it should each get something out of it, and applied to politics this would mean that the government got something out of governing which the subjects are bound to give. Now this is what Locke was most anxious to avoid. Although contractually related to each other, the people are not contractually obliged to government, and governors benefit from governing only as fellow members of the 'Politick Body' (I, § 93, 11–12). They are merely deputies for the people, trustees who can be discarded if they fail in their trust (II, § 240, 8). The property trusts which his landowning readers were so accustomed to were a little like this, but they contained no provisions about trustees being deputies, liable to be discarded by those for whose benefit the trust is established. This

---

* The technical term for a lawyer's instrument much in use, we may note, in Chancery when Locke was himself a Chancery secretary—see above, p. 26.

should convince us that Locke did not intend to go further in his references to trust than to make suggestive use of legal language.* He does not describe *a* trust at all; the phrase itself is absent. It is always 'this', 'that' or 'their trust'—'the trust of prerogative', 'this express or tacit trust', even 'double trust'. The stress is solely on the fiduciary nature of all political power ('a Fiduciary Power' (II, § 149, 6), 'a Fiduciary Trust' (II, § 156, 3)). He could even talk elsewhere of bishops as trustees, trustees of religion on behalf of all the Christians of the nation. The concept is obviously intended to make it clear that all actions of governors are limited to the end of government, which is the good of the governed, and to demonstrate by contrast that there is no contract in it—a fiduciary relationship, that is all.†

When trust is substituted in this way for contract, constitutional change is sanctioned, even revolution; it secures the sovereignty of the people, though that phrase must be used with care, a perpetual residual power to cashier their governors and remodel their government. '*Governments are dissolved* . . . when the Legislative, or the Prince, either of them act contrary to their Trust' (II, § 221, 2–5), power reverts to the people, who may then establish a new legislative and executive (II, § 222, 23–4). It is the people (the community, the public) who decide when a breach of trust has occurred, for only the man who deputes power can tell when it is abused (II, § 240, 5–7), and in case of dispute the final appeal is to God—revolution. The people are able to do all these things because their ability to act as a community survives the dissolution of government, which does not itself bring back the state of nature.

The trend of Locke's statements about the ultimate right of the people to revolt is quite unmistakable. But close examination shows that it was not formulated with much precision, and its connection with the concept of trust has to be filled in for him. In the chapter *Of the Dissolution of Government* (II, ch. XIX) he is not at all explicit about what actually happens when people find

---

* Gough, 1950, and Sir Ernest Barker, 1948, among others (compare Vaughan, 1925), see a formal trust in Locke's theory, with the people as both trustor and beneficiary, acting as defrauded beneficiaries when the government breaches its trust. Locke does talk of breach of trust (II, § 222), but more often and more vaguely of acting contrary to their trust (II, § 149, 8; 155, 6; 221, 3; 226, 3; 240, 2–3). When governors do this it is the government, not the trust, which is dissolved, and, though he does once refer to forfeit of the trust itself (II, § 149), it is very difficult to make sense of his text by interpreting the actions of a people on breach of trust as those of defrauded beneficiaries under a formal trust.

† Dunn, 1984, is the best recent discussion of Locke's concept of trust.

themselves at liberty to entrust new hands with the government. Although we are expressly told (II, § 211, 3–4) to distinguish between the dissolution of government and the dissolution of society, and informed that overwhelming force from abroad is almost the only thing which can dissolve political society itself, he often seems to talk as if the dissolution of government brings about a state of nature. James II, for it can only be he, is condemned for 'actually putting himself into a State of War with his People', dissolving the government and leaving them 'to that defence', 'which belongs to every one in the State of Nature' (II, § 205, 8–9). This state of nature, moreover, sometimes looks less like the Lockeian than the Hobbesian condition, that miserable condition of war of all against all, where no such thing as an organized community could possibly exist, since 'the People become a confused Multitude, without Order or Connexion' (II, § 219, 10).*

This is not so inconsistent as it may appear, for we have seen that Locke drew no very rigid distinction between the natural and the political condition, and his doctrine of natural political virtue could be manipulated so as to cover these cases. His intention in the rather confused argument of this chapter may have been to insist on the efficacy of a threat to return to the state of nature— a present sanction, we are to believe, both when government exists and when it does not, and particularly at that point of crisis when no one is quite sure, which is as far as what we call anarchy ever really goes. But this interpretation is suggested by the whole tenor of his doctrine, rather than demonstrated by his statements.

And it does not help us to understand quite how, or quite when, the trust relationship between the people and their government is brought into being. An original agreement undoubtedly made it a matter of trust that a specified form of government should be preserved, but we are not told whether this agreement is always part of the social compact.† He seems content, in fact, to suggest a

---

* It may be significant that both these passages, and others pointing in this direction, were very probably additions of 1689. Compare the discussion in Vaughan, 1925, and Strauss, 1953, 234 note 100. On the people, see Polin, 1961, 157–61, and, on their function as judges, 272 on (also Seliger, 1963 (i), 1968).

† See e.g. II, §§ 239, 10 and 227; compare I, § 96, 13–14 (where power *is* based on contract). Elsewhere (II, §§ 134, 1–8; II, 136, 21; 142; 171, 1–4; 242, 9) he seems to suppose an entrusting action, which took place in past time, taken by the 'first Framers of Government' (II, § 156, 6). In his *Second Letter concerning Toleration* (1690) he talks of God as the final arbiter of the Magistrates' trust (*Works*, 1801, VI, 133). For the most part, however, he talks of trust as a continuing relationship between governor and governed in the way described above.

continuing understanding between governed and governors. It is to be referred in its origin to the compact of society, because that was what gave the governed an identity, but it is continuously maintained because the governed go on existing and go on entrusting. It is a matter of suggestion rather than demonstration, relying for its plausibility on the language of trust, on trust as a concept.

This is not untypical of Locke as a political writer, and though it makes exact analysis difficult, it helps to give him his strength. Locke's impreciseness over the dissolution of government has not led to any misunderstanding of his principles, and no more has his metaphor of trust. No man, no nation, no exasperated colony about to throw off the insensitive rule of men who had no acceptable policy for them, could ever have sat down to ask whether the state of nature had returned, and if so what it was like. But they have responded to the statements which Locke made with that hypothetical, but vaguely conceived, situation in mind. And they have been influenced by the trust image. This certificate of responsibility still hangs above the desks of administrators, especially of international political and welfare administrators; held there—to some extent anyway—by the influence of British legal and constitutional precedent, and by Locke's own reputation. Once more it is a question of the ethics of common sense in politics. If you trust people, they will trust you, and you and they will get things done together, but especially if all your actions proceed on the recognition that your power is not yours but a trust from them to you.

We have tried to show that the main theme of Locke's book was the development of the implications of this doctrine of natural political virtue, defined, checked and safeguarded by the concept of trust. From time to time, and especially in discussing majorities, we have found ourselves referring to a different strand of argument, an argument in terms of power, even of will. It might be incorrect to claim that these strains are distinct in his thinking, or that Locke himself saw them apart: what he says about power is in the way of an adjunct to his other statements, not a different and parallel explanation. Nevertheless it is useful to look on this part of what he said as independent, for its most important consequence, the association of Locke with the historic doctrine of the separation of powers, could not possibly have arisen out of the theories which we have discussed so far.

Locke's initial definition is in terms of power (II, § 3) and throughout his book he seems to be consciously discussing a power system. It might be suggested that the reason for this was his recognition that there were in his attitude recognizable anarchist elements, a disposition found in all individualists to regard state, society and government as unnecessary, or accidental, or just unfortunate. It is to be seen in his aside declaring that it was only corruption, viciousness, degeneracy in some men which made it necessary for humanity to set up communities 'separate from this great and natural Community' of all mankind (II, § 128, 7–10). The doctrine of natural political virtue is anarchistic in its implications generally, and we have seen that Locke had to answer in a somewhat urgent form the question of why men set up states at all. His contemporaries, certainly Sir Robert Filmer, would have looked on the most important of all his claims as obviously anarchical, the claim that there is no final appeal in ultimate political questions, only God—which means combat, revolution.

But, Locke is anxious to convince us, this does not mean that the state which we set up and obey, which guarantees our property in all its forms and under all its definitions, lacks unity, direction, power. When we meet together to set up artificially that final judge which is lacking to us in the state of nature we create a rightful legislative authority, the nature of which is ethical and which we are bound to obey however weak its sanctions. But we create something else as well, we create a principle of unity, a 'living Body', out of our separate selves. In this paragraph (II, § 212) Locke goes on, in language we may think strange in him, to talk of the legislative as the '*Soul that gives Form, Life, and Unity* to the Commonwealth', and of 'the *Essence and Union of the Society* consisting in having one Will, the Legislative', which, when once it is broken, leaves every one 'at the disposure of his own Will' because 'the publick Will' is at a stand.* Here it may be thought he comes near to denying his own principle that government is not a matter of will, or even to concepts belonging to a quite different political system, a general will analysis. In fact, however, he seems to be doing no more than insist that when men come together politically they create power, which is available to them in institutional form for the purposes of their association, and

* Compare the 'will' language used in II, § 151.

which will find its first and highest expression in the making of law.

When, therefore, Locke talks of the various powers of the commonwealth, the supremacy of one and the derivative nature of the others, he should be taken in the simple sense of force, at least initially. The supreme power, the legislative, is supreme because it literally represents the united force of the commonwealth, and the commonwealth to remain one body can have only one supreme power. The executive power is thus inevitably inferior. It is distinguished from the legislative in that it cannot make law, and has for the most part only a delegated power. The legislative, being preferably a representative body, need not, should not be in continuous existence (II, § 153). Now this does not exclude the possibility that both powers can be exercised by the same body or person. It supposes, in fact, that the executive will have a part to play in the legislative, as is the case in the constitution of England, which Locke so obviously had in mind.*

That he was looking on these powers in this straightforward sense is illustrated by the very nature of the third power, the federative. This was simply the power of the community directed outwards, towards other such communities in amicable relationship, or in protection against aggression. It is a distinct power, no doubt, but this outward direction is its only characteristic. It is almost essential, therefore, that it be in the same hands as that of the executive and be given the freest possible play for quick, arbitrary decision. It must have the greatest possible freedom from everyday control by the legislative or its laws—to which it is of course finally responsible.†

It is surely already obvious from this that Locke cannot be said to have had a doctrine in mind. There is here no theory of the importance and desirability of the perpetual residence of these powers in separate hands in order to preserve liberty, guarantee

---

* All this is insisted on at length (especially the points about the summoning of the legislature by the executive, the conditions which the constitution may lay down about the intervals at which it shall meet, and so on) because, as is suggested above, Locke was writing with Charles II and his parliaments in mind.

† On the federative power, see Laslett, 1957 (i), 396, and the discussion in Cox, 1960, where he makes exaggerated claims for the primacy of foreign policy in Locke. Dunn calls in question Laslett's interpretation of the issue of Virginian government in the 1690s in relation to Locke's doctrine, and presents a different view.

rights, or keep the constitution in harmony, unison and health. This is confirmed by two further considerations. One is that the judiciary, that separate power whose independence is recognized as an essential to constitutional government both by Locke's predecessors and by all his successors, whether they have expounded the separation of the powers or not, is never mentioned by Locke along with the other three. As we have said, the judiciary was no separate power, it was the general attribute of the state. It would not make sense to put it alongside the executive and legislative. Locke recognized that the judiciary should be indifferent and upright (II, § 131, 16), known and authorized (II, § 136, 4), or else nothing he wanted would come about: that is all. Finally, the proper functioning and just exercise of these powers is provided for by Locke, but not by any doctrine of necessary separation. It is done by the concept of trust, which applies to the legislative in its fullest force, but also to the executive and federative.

Locke shared the traditional opinion about balancing the power of government by placing several parts of it in different hands (II, § 107, 19–20). He seems to have attached some importance to the distinct natures of legislative, executive and federative, for they are introduced, by function if not all by name, immediately after he gives his first formal account of how the state comes into being (II, § 88). One of the reasons why an absolute monarchy cannot be a properly constituted political authority is because it institutes a ruler who has 'all, both Legislative and Executive Power in himself alone', so that 'there is no Judge' (II, § 91, 1–2). This is as far as he goes.

It may be historically interesting that Montesquieu and later the American founders took him up in a sense which he cannot be said to have contemplated, just as it is interesting to find that Locke conspicuously ignored the clearest issue over the separation of powers which arose in our constitutional history, even though it involved him personally.* It is one example of the extraordinary fashion in which the thinking of Locke and the constitutional practice of Englishmen so soon began to coalesce in the minds of a posterity determined to benefit from both. The result was a mingled misunderstanding of the greatest possible historical consequence.

---

* Laslett, 1969: this was the issue of whether the Crown or the Commons should appoint the Board of Trade of 1696, of which Locke was a member.

We cannot dwell on this subject, nor on Locke as an exponent of the English constitution of his day. In his analysis of politics in terms of force as well as in terms of rightful authority Locke is closer to the thought of our own day on the subject of sovereignty than he was to the assumptions of his own time. Behind the superior power of the legislative in his system there is always to be seen the finally supreme, all-important power of the people themselves, again conceived of as a force, though justified in its interferences once more by the concept of trust. It was a power which would only rarely display itself, and, as we have tried to show, there is considerable obscurity about the actual circumstances in which it could come into action and more about what it might achieve. Nevertheless this residual power must be called Locke's idea of what we now think of as popular sovereignty.

Locke reads as if his reflections on the true original, extent and end of civil government were directed towards political universals, instead of directed towards the highly specific situation of his own party, at a particular time and within the highly individual context of English politics. We have described this as an achievement, the achievement of a philosophic mind writing, in a sense, against its philosophic bent. It has inevitably led to his being criticized for raising expectations which he did not fulfil, for propounding theories, whose final implications he never contemplated. Some of these criticisms have been considered here, but one still remains. It is often said that Locke is the supreme representative of those individualist thinkers who stress rights instead of duties. As early as 1798 Bishop Elrington reproached him for not declaring that man had a duty to set up the state and to leave the condition of mere nature. But if his system as we have analysed it is sympathetically considered, this appears, perhaps, as the greatest of all the misapprehensions about him. Natural political virtue can only work if we obey the tendency within all of us, for it is a tendency, it is not the full description of ourselves. Trust is a matter of conscience, which may have its final and unlikely sanctions but which operates because of the sense of duty which Locke dogmatically, unthinkingly assumes in every man he contemplates.

Locke's psychological insight may be imperfect, his logic often odd, his general standpoint ungrateful to our generation and not easily understood even within his own personal historical context. His rationalist sociology may seem fantastic, even in comparison with the uncritical traditionalism of a man like Filmer. But after he had written and what he had written had had its enormous impact on the European mind, it was no longer possible to believe that politics went forward in a moral sphere in which the good man was the good citizen. Citizenship was now a specific duty, a personal challenge in a world where every individual either recognized his responsibility for every other, or disobeyed his conscience. Political duties have not changed since then.

ADDENDUM TO INTRODUCTION,

1987

*The dating of the composition of Two Treatises and the question of
whether the* Second *was composed before the* First

Professor Richard Ashcraft in his recent book, Locke's *Two
Treatises of Government*, 1987, has decisively rejected the version of
the composition and dating of Locke's book set out in this
Introduction. In his view the *First* was written in 1680–1 and the
Second in 1681–2, neither as early as 1679, in whole or in part.

Neither in this book, nor in his extremely detailed analysis of
Revolutionary Politics and Locke's Two Treatises of Government,
1986, does Professor Ashcraft produce any new references in
materials previously unknown to underwrite his new interpretation. I had hoped that in the exhaustive analysis, interesting and
valuable as it is in so many ways, which he has undertaken on the
books and papers of the radicals who surrounded Shaftesbury in
the 1680s, who plotted against James II after Shaftesbury's death
and who involved themselves in Monmouth's attempt to
overthrow him, some allusion to the text of *Two Treatises* might
appear. It was perhaps unlikely, considering Locke's cautious
habits and his attitude to what he had written, that any such allusion
would be in plain language. But one or other of those who
associated with Locke might well have known and written about
the manuscript *de Morbo Gallico* (see above, pp. 62–5). This would have
made the hypothesis that *de Morbo Gallico* was indeed the unpublished
manuscript form of the book less hazardous than it seemed to
me to be when I suggested it in the early 1950s, and so have given a
large number of statements in the original Introduction greater
security than they had when they were written, and still have.

Ashcraft apparently has no difficulty with *de Morbo Gallico* (1986,
p. 536), and it is the circumstantial evidence used by me to tie the
writing of the *Second Treatise* to the year 1679 which he disbelieves.
On one point let it be admitted, a point previously raised by two
others (Gough, 1976 and Menake, 1982), Ashcraft is quite right. I
made an error in stating that Locke bought Tyrrell's *Patriarcha non
Monarcha* on 2 June 1680: the year should have been 1681 (1st and

2nd editions, p. 61). This confusion—for in other places in my edition the date was given correctly—certainly affects the argument that Locke and Tyrrell were engaged in writing against Filmer at the same time, and that each found it necessary to compose a '1st Treatise' after *Patriarcha* appeared in January 1680. But though the original case for my suggestions of the dates and order of the *Two Treatises* may be a little less persuasive for this reason, it certainly does not fail. And the other considerations which Ashcraft puts forward do not seem strong enough to require me to withdraw my own hypothesis.

A full statement of the reasons why I am not convinced that Ashcraft is right would soon become complicated, lengthy and tedious. Let it be said here, however, that his arguments about the little notebook of Locke (MS. f. 28) seem no stronger, indeed rather weaker, than my own. This notebook may have been a confidential one and intended by Locke for other purposes, but it is evident that he did use it for noting the titles of books, for the exchange and borrowing of books, and for extracts from books. The entry which Ashcraft makes into an issue is not the only one relevant to the case; see the note on IIT, 236. I cannot comprehend how Ashcraft knows that the date at the head of a page in that notebook 'generally' refers only to the first entry on that page and to that entry only, a point which he uses in order to dispose of the possibility that Locke was engaged in 1679 on § 22 of the *Second Treatise*. If 'generally', how are we to know of the exceptions?

When Locke writes the address of Furly under the heading 79, there seems to be no justification for Ashcraft to assert that Locke must have been in Holland at the time he made the entry, and therefore cannot have written it in the year 1679 but later. If indeed the notebook was intended to be used for addresses, as Ashcraft supposes, is it not more probable that he wrote out Furly's name and city for his future use? When Ashcraft protests that Locke could not have composed the *Second Treatise* in response to the 1679 collection of Filmer's tracts because he did not own the book he seems to me to be mistaken on two counts. One is that Shaftesbury may well have lent him the book, which he returned when he acquired the 1680 volume, or subsequently disposed of without making any known recording. The other is that it cannot possibly be known by its absence from the record that a particular title was not in an author's possession or in his keeping at any time. The *Tablet* shows that Shaftesbury did lend Locke books used in composing *Two Treatises* and the study of his library confirms what must be expected, that he must have bought, borrowed, destroyed, lost many, many titles without leaving evidence known to us.

I used Locke's *Tablet*, his own description of MS. f. 28, to guess about the time at which he wrote the *Second Treatise*, just as I guessed that he and Shaftesbury called the manuscript *de Morbo Gallico*. The object being aimed at in the 1950s and 1960s was to remove the date of composition of the book from its hitherto revered position as one written and published in 1690, and any inference from a document external to the work itself which might locate it up to ten years earlier was important. The inferences which I made from Locke's diaries, his *Tablet* and so on as to his order of writing were all subsidiary to the internal, literary argument about the relationship of the two sections of his book, an argument to which Ashcraft never refers, but which still convinces me. One sentence may be repeated here: 'It would seem undeniable that the *Second Treatise* was logically prior to the *First Treatise* because the author had never had occasion to cite the *First* when composing the *Second*.'

The rest of Ashcraft's submission turns on a point on which we agree, that Locke may well have written in some sense for Shaftesbury's purposes. For him, however, these purposes were exclusively political, apparently entirely propagandist. This is how he interprets Locke's function as Shaftesbury's 'assistant pen'. He cannot have written any justification of rebellion unless his master Shaftesbury had reached the point when rebellion was the proper next political expedient.

Important as it is to see works of political theory in their context, interesting and significant as it is to recognise that *Two Treatises* was to an extent a *pièce d'occasion*, Ashcraft's account of the influence of these things on Locke leaves me unpersuaded. No doubt he did write to inform Shaftesbury, to provide arguments for him, and so on. But this does not make him Shaftesbury's ghost-writer. In any case, the possibility, indeed the probability, of a variety of periods of composition and of subsequent insertion is too slippery for such definite assertions. Professor Ashcraft pronounces on the question of the dating of *Two Treatises* with an assurance which surprises me, considering the nature of the evidence and the frailty of his case, indeed of any case based on such materials. Accordingly, I have toned down my original statements on this subject in this printing, based on inference and guesswork as they had to be. I have corrected the errors of fact mentioned, and I have left the reader to make his choice between the arguments. The arguments of Professor Olivecrona presented in the *Locke Newsletter* for 1976 (no. VII) I find mildly persuasive but not convincing enough for me to give up the view that Locke wrote his book as a whole, the *Second Treatise* as well as the *First* against Filmer. In general, then, I retain my view, that the proper conclusion from such evidence as we have is that Locke wrote the two parts of his book at the times and in the order propounded here.

EDITORIAL NOTE

1. THE TEXT

General. The attempt here is to present Locke's 'text for posterity' (see above, pp. 9–11) from the Christ's corrected copy. It has been set up in type from a photograph of that document. The compositors have in fact worked from printer's copy prepared for the press between 1698 and 1704 by Locke himself and by Coste. Locke's hand appears only occasionally after the first few pages, and Coste seems to have been copying rather than taking his dictation: it seems possible that he may have been copying from another, very similar exemplar, the hypothetical second master-copy which is discussed below.

The decision to reproduce the Christ's copy, modified only in such particulars as were absolutely necessary, was the simplest, most consistent solution to an intricate editorial problem. The reader has before him the version which would have satisfied Locke at the time of his death, or something as close to that version as the editor can make it. He has also a record, complete in all essentials, but not absolutely exhaustive, of all the variants from that final version which were seen by Locke, and then rejected by him at one correcting stage or other.

Documents used. In order to appreciate why the editor has ventured to alter the Christ's copy in any way whatsoever, it is necessary to record the documents from which he has worked. They are:

(i) Locke's own copy of the 1st printing of 1689–90. This is in the 2nd state (1R, see above, p. 8 and references), complete with errata slip. Locke has entered the errata, and made a few further modifications of his own.

(ii) The 2nd printing, 1694, with its errata list.

(iii) The Christ's copy of the 3rd printing, 1698, with its errata list and the very extensive corrections in Locke's hand and in Coste's.

(iv) The 4th printing, 1713, reproducing Locke's text for posterity, possibly from the hypothetical second master-copy: it could, of course, have been the result of comparison between the Christ's copy and that copy, or with other, unknown authoritative sources.

(v) The printing in the 1st Collected edition, 1714, apparently a reprint of (iv), but conceivably also influenced by other, unknown authoritative sources (see below).

(vi) The 5th edition, 1727, reprinting the 4th, showing minor editorial clarification and important for (vii).

(vii) The 6th edition, 1764, Hollis's attempt to reproduce the Christ's copy, collating it (so he claimed) with (i), (ii) and (iii), but not apparently with (iv) or (v). The basic text is that of (vi).

(viii) Locke's own copy of the first French edition, 1691, not, however, marked in any way by him in the text.

Obscurities in (iii), the copy text, have been elucidated by comparison with all of the seven other documents, though some of them (especially (i), (ii), (iv), (v)) are obviously much more important than the others. In some cases the editor has been led to prefer a reading of his own to all of these. These obscurities are such as must arise in a text of this date and history, and, though they are fairly numerous, it must be stressed that they affect Locke's meaning only in very minor matters. Their main sources are as follows:

1. Faults in Locke's original manuscript appearing in the printings of 1689–90, 1694, 1698 and not corrected in the Christ's copy.

2. Faults in these printings not corrected in the Christ's copy.

3. Faults, of incompleteness, illegibility, etc., in the manuscript corrections in the Christ's copy.

Emendation. In emending these details in the Christ's copy the editor has been guided by an obvious principle. He has assumed that they only appear there because Locke failed to notice them in his final correction and he has corrected them as he supposed Locke would have done. Comparison with the first three printings has disposed of most of the obscurities, and a proper deference has been shown to the first printing, as being the closest to the original manuscript—especially in the form of the particular copy owned and corrected by the author. But since Locke corrected the book so extensively again in 1694 and 1698, a later reading has always been preferred to an earlier one, except where it seemed clear that it was due to a compositor's blunder. Such blunders were common in both later printings and often went uncorrected in the Christ's copy.

In tackling the remaining textual obscurities the editor has turned for guidance to the 4th, Collected and 6th editions, since they were all alike attempts to do what he has tried to do, to reproduce Locke's 'text for posterity'. The status of these versions depends to a large extent on the possibility that one, some, or all of them derive (wholly or partially) from a source different from the Christ's copy, and even closer to Locke's textual intentions. The particular question to be answered is this. Does the 4th edition, on which all these versions seem to be based, represent the hypothetical second master-copy whose existence seems clearly to be implied by Coste's note on the final fly of the Christ's copy? There are subsidiary questions about the possible existence of other authoritative sources (and conceivable links between them and editions later than the 4th), but we have no evidence on these points and only this crucial question can be discussed here.

Second master-copy. The evidence suggesting that the 4th edition was not necessarily (or exclusively) based on the Christ's copy is as follows. In the first place Coste makes it quite clear that this particular document was *not* the one which Locke wanted to be used for posthumous publication. An editor in 1713, therefore, anxious to carry out Locke's directions, would have done his best to get hold of the other copy which Coste seems to have in mind and print from that.* Secondly, comparison shows that there are small particulars in which the 4th edition, and those based on it, differ from the Christ's copy (and sometimes from each other).

---

* The letter of La Motte quoted in footnote‡ to p. 10 above presumably implies that a second, more authentic copy did exist, otherwise Coste would surely never have had the Christ's copy bequeathed to him. Mr John Biddle, sometime of Trinity College, Cambridge, is undertaking an edition of Locke's *Reasonableness of Christianity*, and finds grounds for suspecting that Locke left behind him two corrected copies of that work also.

All these variant details are recorded in the Second edition (repr. 1988), but some may be cited here. I, § 154 shows variations from the Christ's copy which seem to derive from a different document. A correction to II, § 50 seems impossible to recover from the Christ's copy. A correction to II, § 13, present in the Christ's copy and so in the 6th edition, is omitted from the 4th edition and derived texts. On the other hand a word occurs in II, § 230 in the 4th edition, etc., which is not in the Christ's copy, but seems to be a genuine Locke insertion nevertheless. There are further details which suggest that the alternative source of all these variations, if it existed, was a corrected exemplar of the 2nd, not the 3rd printing: a mis-spelling, for example, in II, § 16, and a passage in II, § 36.

On this evidence there is a possible case for supposing that the 4th edition was indeed a printing of the other 'exemplaire' referred to by Coste, that this was a copy of the 1694 printing more authoritatively corrected, and that a critical edition should be based on this text, corrected by comparison with the other authoritative documents, and not on the Christ's copy. But the difficulties of such a case are so formidable that it has been found impossible to accept it. For if the 4th edition and its derived texts do in fact represent Coste's other master-copy, then they should contain the very passage which he writes out from that other copy as a variant from his own version in his note on II, § 172. Neither the 4th edition, the Collected edition nor any derived text does print the passage in this way.* Then, though the detailed evidence may seem convincing when cited alone, there is simply not enough of it. The number of variants to be expected between printings of this date is so great that the resemblances, omissions, additions on which the case rests could be coincidental. Finally, even if the 4th and derived texts were based on another authoritative source, we cannot say what that source (or sources) was. We

---

* The statement about the texts used, made at the end of the message To the Reader in the first collected edition, 1714, seems to imply a separate and a more authoritative source than that used for the 4th edition of the previous year. 'I have this to advertise the reader; that most of them are printed from copies corrected and enlarged under Mr Locke's own hand, and in particular that the Two Treatises of Government were never till now published from a copy corrected by himself.' The author of this statement (whose identity is still unknown, though it may well have been Peter King, Locke's heir and literary executor) confirms that Locke did in fact leave 'texts for posterity' behind him. But the version he prints differs so little from the 4th edition that it would seem not to be distinct from it. Perhaps this 4th edition (1713) was issued separately by John Churchill without preface or explanation, and happened to appear earlier than the collection (1714).

have nothing but unconfirmed inference to persuade us that it was the authentic second master-copy.

For these reasons, therefore, the question has had to be left open here.* The editor is satisfied that a text presented on the basis of the hypothesis just discussed would not differ in any very important respects from the one given here. The Christ's master-copy is of unimpeachable authenticity; it has not been printed from the original since 1764 and never comparatively; it clearly represents for us now the most obvious, authentic source for Locke's 'text for posterity'. There are even signs that some of its amendments were later than those in its hypothetical source. It has been taken as the copy text, therefore, and these other authoritative sources have been used for its elucidation.†

Other modifications of copy text. Inevitably there have been problems which have had to be solved without reference to these other authoritative documents, some of them presumably arising from obscurities in what Locke originally wrote down. Wherever the editor has ventured a reading of his own, or supplied a word, square brackets have been used, and the fact noted in the Collation. Moreover, Locke's citations from the classics, the Bible, the works of Filmer and so on have been checked and amended. Only two further liberties have been taken with Locke's 'text for posterity'. After his citations of Filmer's page numbers, and whenever he quotes or refers to Filmer in a way which might require a modern reader to look up the original, the corresponding page number in the modern reprint of Filmer‡ has been inserted in square brackets. Locke's quotations from Hooker have been removed from the side and lower margins, where they appear in all three early printings without exact reference signs in the body of the text. They have been printed at the bottom of the page, with

---

* I have not gone so far as to undertake the minute, statistical analysis which might yield further evidence.

† Professor Bowers has pointed out that the perfect text, or super text, might have been brought about by taking the 1st printing as the copy, and modifying it by the corrections of 1694, 1698, of the Christ's copy and of the 4th edition and derived texts. This would be nearer to the manuscript of 1689, but it could hardly be said to represent Locke's 'text for posterity'. The printing style, for example, would be for the most part of 1690, and it is clear that in the years up to 1698 spelling and printing style altered, in ways which seem to inform some of Locke's corrections.

‡ *Patriarcha, and other Political Writings of Sir Robert Filmer, edited from the Original Sources*, by Peter Laslett. Blackwell's Political Texts, Oxford, 1949.

reference signs inserted where the editor believes Locke intended them to be.

Apart from these things, and it must be repeated that they are mostly of the smallest importance to Locke's meaning, the type of the 3rd printing has been followed as exactly as possible, up to the point where it might become a burden to the twentieth-century reader. Its free use of capitals, its very extensive use of italics, its characteristic spelling, have all been retained, but the long 's' has been eliminated. The manuscript amendments have been reproduced precisely as they were intended to be, as an integral part of a running text.

2. THE FOOTNOTES

The editorial footnotes elucidate the text and draw attention to variations, sometimes reproducing them when they are significant of changes of meaning. They explain Locke's allusions,* draw attention to his sources, provide cross-references, and contain much of the evidence for the views expressed in the Introduction, especially about the history and dates of composition of the book.†
They are not intended as a commentary on Locke's social and political ideas. The editor has spared himself many observations of this sort, except perhaps in Locke's treatment of Filmer and his relationship with Hobbes. A determined effort has been made to keep down the number and length of the footnotes, so as to make reading and consultation as convenient as possible.

3. REFERENCES TO SOURCES
AND AUTHORITIES

Much of the complication of footnote references arises from such expressions as *op. cit.*, *ibid.*, *loc. cit.* and so on. They have been

---

* Even to translating simple Latin phrases, and describing the familiar figures of ancient mythology. The editor's apology must be that he has tried to bear in mind the student reader, all over the English-speaking world.

† Little reference is made to the use of Locke's book by his successors: his influence has been so extensive that an attempt to represent it would obviously be impossible. The one exception is in the citation of Elrington's notes of 1798, the only previous English edition annotated on any scale.

eliminated here as far as possible. Internal references are mostly by page number throughout the book, except for the text itself, where they are by the paragraph number (ɪ for the *First Treatise*, ɪɪ for the *Second Treatise*) and sometimes line number. References to other works are made on a system more usual in scientific books and papers; that is, by author and date only, followed by a Roman figure in brackets if the author published in that year more than one work used here. A full description of each book or article appears in the Bibliography on pp. 433–450. Locke's journal, letters referred to by the date only and manuscript sources prefixed simply by 'MS.' are all in the Lovelace Collection, Bodleian Library, Oxford. This collection is described in detail and the pressmarks given for all documents, in Long, P., 1959. The letters H. and L. coming after a book title and preceding a number refer to John Harrison and Peter Laslett, *The Library of John Locke*, Oxford (1965), 1971, and the reference de Beer followed by a number between ɪ and 7 indicates the volumes of Esmond de Beer, *The Correspondence of John Locke*, Oxford, 1976–82.

TWO
TREATISES
OF
Government:

In the Former,

The False Principles and Foundation

OF

Sir *Robert* *Filmer* ,

And His FOLLOWERS,
ARE

Detected and Overthrown.

The Latter is an

ESSAY

CONCERNING

The True Original, Extent, and End
OF

Civil-Government.

LONDON: Printed for *Awnsham* and *John Churchill*, at the *Black Swan* in *Pater-Noster-Row.* 1 6 9 8.

An Englishman, a Lover of Liberty, Citizen of the World, is desirous of having the honor to deposite this Book in the Library of Christ College Cambridge.

To Dr Thomas
Master of Christ College Cambridge
April 20, 1764.

Letter of Thomas Hollis. The original is now pasted into the binding of the volume in Christ's College Library. It is typical of Hollis to describe himself in this way, without giving his name; see above, p. 11 and note *. He presented a copy of his edition printed from this text to William Pitt, the elder, on 26 May, and the British Museum on 8 June 1764. Hugh Thomas was Master of Christ's from 1764 to 1780.

Quod si nihil cum potentiore juris humani relinquitur inopi, at ego ad Deos vindices humanae superbiae confugiam: et precabor ut iras suas vertant in eos, quibus non suae res, non alienae satis sint quorum saevitiam non mors noxiorum exatiet: placari nequeant, nisi hauriendum sanguinem laniandaque viscera nostra praebuerimus.   Liv. Lib. ix. c. i.

Note on title-page. This is reproduced from the Christ's copy, i.e. the 1698 printing. An additional phrase *Pax ac Libertas* appears on the title-page of Locke's copy of the first French printing, where it is written in his hand (see above, p. 13 and note). The above quotation from Livy is written on the fly-leaf facing the title in the Christ's volume, and appears (in a rather more accurate version) on the title of the 4th edition, 1713, and the 5th edition, 1728, but not elsewhere (see Loeb edition, IV, 164, showing considerable variation). Its general meaning is as follows: 'But if, in dealing with the mighty, the weak are left no human rights, yet will I seek protection in the gods, who visit retribution on human pride. And I will beseech them that they turn their anger against those who are not content with their own, or with that of others, who will not be sated with the death of the guilty. They are not to be placated unless we yield to them our blood to drink and our entrails to tear out.' The surprising ferociousness of these sentiments may well be another expression of Locke's savagery against despotism in general and against Charles II and James II in particular, compare note on II, § 172 and references.

The PREFACE.

Reader,

THOU *haſt here the Beginning and End of a Discourse concerning Government; what Fate has otherwise disposed of the Papers that should have filled up the middle, and were more than all the reſt, 'tis not worth while to tell thee. These, which remain, I hope are sufficient to eſtablish the Throne of our Great Reſtorer, Our present King* William; *to make good his Title, in the Consent of the People, which being the only one of all lawful Governments, he has more fully and clearly than any Prince in* Chriſtendom: *And to juſtifie to the World, the People of* England, *whose love of their Juſt and Natural Rights, with their Resolution to preserve them, saved the Nation when it was on the very brink of Slavery and Ruine. If these Papers have that evidence, I flatter my self is to be found in them, there will be no great miss of those which are loſt, and my Reader may be satisfied without them. For I imagine I shall have neither the time, nor inclination to repeat my Pains, and fill up the wanting part .of my Answer, by tracing Sir* Robert *again, through all the Windings and Obscurities which are to be met with in the several Branches of his wonderful Syſtem. The King, and Body of the Nation, have since so thoroughly confuted his* Hypothesis, *that, I suppose, no Body hereafter will have either the Confidence to appear againſt our Common Safety, and he again an Advocate for Slavery; or the Weakness to be deceived with Contradictions dressed up in a Popular Stile, and well turned Periods. For if any one will be at the Pains himself, in those Parts which are here untouched, to ſtrip Sir* Robert's *Discourses of the Flourish of doubtful Expressions, and endeavour to reduce his Words to direct, positive, intelligible Propositions, and then compare them one with another, he will quickly be satisfied there was never so much glib Nonsense*

5

10

15

20

25

The Preface. (Compare MS Locke c.18 written for Clarke; above, 46.n.) Presumably written in 1689, about the month of August, after the preparation of the text for the press, but before the revision of the titles—see notes on titles and Introduction, section III. From line 31, however, it resembles the Preface to Tyrrell's *Patriarcha non Monarcha,* 1681, so closely that the final passages may have been written earlier.

1 *Discourse*—perhaps the original word for the book—see Introduction, 50, and II, § 15, 16; II, § 52, 2. Compare Olivecrona, 1976, a diametrically opposite interpretation.

5 *Great Restorer*—in a letter to Mordaunt dated 21 February 1689, refusing the King's offer of an ambassadorship, Locke called William 'our great deliverer'.

6 Compare I, § 95, 15 and note.

put together in well sounding English. *If he think it not worth while to examine his Works all through, let him make an Experiment in that part where he Treats of Usurpation; and let him try whether he can, with*
30 *all his Skill, make Sir* Robert *intelligible, and consistent with himself, or common sense. I should not speak so plainly of a Gentleman, long since past answering, had not the Pulpit, of late Years, publickly owned his Doctrine, and made it the Currant Divinity of the Times. 'Tis necessary those Men, who taking on them to be Teachers, have so dan-*
35 *gerously misled others, should be openly shewed of what Authority this their Patriarch is, whom they have so blindly followed, that so they may either retract what upon so ill Grounds they have vented, and cannot be maintained, or else justifie those Principles which they Preachd up for Gospel; though they had no better an Author than an* English Courtier.
40 *For I should not have Writ against Sir* Robert, *or taken the pains to shew his mistakes, Inconsistencies, and want of (what he so much boasts of, and pretends wholly to build on) Scripture-proofs, were there not Men amongst us, who, by crying up his Books, and espousing his Doctrine, save me from the Reproach of Writing against a dead Adversary. They have*
45 *been so zealous in this Point, that if I have done him any wrong; I cannot hope they should spare me. I wish, where they have done the Truth and the Publick wrong, they would be as ready to Redress it and allow its just Weight to this Reflection, viz. That, there cannot be done a greater Mischief to Prince and People, than the Propagating wrong Notions*
50 *concerning Government, that so at last all times might not have reason to complain of the* Drum Ecclesiastick. *If any one, concerned really for Truth, undertake the Confutation of my* Hypothesis, *I promise him either to recant my mistake, upon fair Conviction; or to answer his Difficulties. But he must remember two Things;*
55 *First, That Cavilling here and there, at some Expression, or little incident of my Discourse, is not an answer to my Book.*

Secondly, That I shall not take railing for Arguments, nor think

---

27 Compare I, §§ 20, 110, etc. and Tyrrell's reference to Filmer's 'gentile stile'. These compliments to Filmer as a stylist puzzle the modern reader; for though he has his merits as a phrasemaker, as a writer of continuous, controversial prose Filmer is no more attractive than any of his contemporaries.

32–3 Compare II, § 112, 8–12.

36–40 Modified and extended in 1698, and the reference to 'courtier' inserted. Filmer himself was never at court; see note on I § 5, 7–8.

44 Filmer had died in 1653; see note on Introduction 57 and reference, and compare Tyrrell's very similar apology.

51 *Drum Ecclesiastick*—the pulpit: Tyrrell talks of the 'wind blown theologue'.

either of these worth my notice: Though I shall always look on my self as bound to give satisfaction to any one who shall appear to be conscienciously scrupulous in the point, and shall shew any just Grounds for his Scruples. 60

I have nothing more, but to advertise the Reader, that A *stands for our Author.* O *for his Observations on* Hobbs, Milton, *&c. And that a bare* Quotation *of Pages always means Pages of his* Patriarcha. Edit. 1680.

The CONTENTS of BOOK I.

The CONTENTS of BOOK II.

61–4 See Introduction, 58, for Locke's method of referring to Filmer. The words 'Edit. 1680' were added in 1698.

The End of the Contents.

BOOK I.

CHAP. I.

§ 1. SLavery is so vile and miserable an Estate of Man, and so directly opposite to the generous Temper and Courage of our Nation; that 'tis hardly to be conceived, that an *Englishman*, much less a *Gentleman*, should plead for't. And truly, I should have taken Sr. Rt: Filmer's *Patriarcha* as any other 5 Treatise, which would perswade all Men, that they are Slaves, and ought to be so, for such another exercise of Wit, as was his who writ the Encomium of *Nero*, rather than for a serious Discourse meant in earnest, had not the Gravity of the Title and Epistle, the Picture in the Front of the Book, and the Applause 10 that followed it, required me to believe, that the Author and Publisher were both in earnest. I therefore took it into my hands with all the expectation, and read it through with all the attention due to a Treatise, that made such a noise at its coming abroad, and cannot but confess my self mightily surprised, that in a Book, 15 which was to provide Chains for all Mankind, I should find nothing but a Rope of Sand, useful perhaps to such, whose Skill and Business it is to raise a Dust, and would blind the People, the better to mislead them, but in truth is not of any force to draw those into Bondage, who have their Eyes open, and so much 20 Sense about them as to consider, that Chains are but an ill wearing, how much Care soever hath been taken to file and polish them.

§ 2. If any one think I take too much liberty in speaking so freely of a Man, who is the great Champion of absolute Power,

---

§ 1 8 'the Encomium of *Nero*', *Encomium Neronis* by Jerome Cardan, 1546. Locke owned Cardan's *Opera*, Leyden, 1663 (H. and L. 587).

9 The title of Filmer's book was *Patriarcha: or the Natural Power of Kings*, and was prefixed by an epistle from his friend Peter Heylyn, the Royalist Divine. Van Hove's engraved portrait of Charles II was the frontispiece, marking the connection of its publication with the Royal Court. Compare 1, § 14, 5 and 1, § 129, 1, and on Heylyn see Laslett, 1948, 1949: on the publication of *Patriarcha*, and Locke's personal copy, see Introduction, 57 and note.

Locke is disingenuous in implying that this was his first encounter with Filmer's works, see Introduction, 34.

and the Idol of those who Worship it; I beseech him to make this small allowance for once, to one, who, even after the reading
5 of Sir *Robert*'s Book, cannot but think himself, as the Laws allow him, a Freeman: And I know no fault it is to do so, unless any one better skill'd in the Fate of it, than I, should have it revealed to him, that this Treatise, which has lain dormant so long, was, when it appeared in the World, to carry by strength of its Argu-
10 ments, all Liberty out of it; and that from thenceforth our Author's short Model was to be the Pattern in the Mount, and the perfect Standard of Politics for the future. His System lies in a little compass, 'tis no more but this,

That all Government is absolute Monarchy.

15 And the Ground he builds on, is this,

That no Man is Born free.

3. In this last age a generation of men has sprung up among us, who would flatter princes with an Opinion, that they have a Divine Right to absolute Power, let the Laws by which they are constituted, and are to govern, and the Conditions under which
5 they enter upon their Authority, be what they will, and their Engagements to observe them never so well ratified by solemn Oaths and Promises. To make way for this doctrine they have denied Mankind a Right to natural Freedom, whereby they have not only, as much as in them lies, exposed all Subjects to the
10 utmost Misery of Tyranny and Oppression, but have also un-settled the Titles, and shaken the Thrones of Princes: (For they too, by these Mens systeme, except only one, are all born Slaves, and by Divine Right, are Subjects to *Adam*'s right Heir); As if they had design'd to make War upon all Government, and subvert the very
15 Foundations of Human Society, to serve their present turn.

4. However we must believe them upon their own bare Words, when they tell us, we are all born Slaves, and we must continue so; there is no remedy for it: Life and Thraldom we enter'd into together, and can never be quit of the one, till we part with the

---

§ 2   8   *Patriarcha* was written *c.* 1637-8, not published till 1680: see Introduction, 57, and Laslett, 1949.
    11   'Pattern in the Mount', Heb. viii. 5, itself a reference to God's Commandments on Sinai.
    12-16   Filmer's system, summarized by him on p. 229 of Laslett's edition.

other. Scripture or Reason I am sure doe not any where say so ₅ notwithstanding the noise of divine right, as if Divine Authority hath subjected us to the unlimited Will of another. An admirable State of Mankind, and that which they have not had Wit enough to find out till this latter Age. For however Sir *Robert Filmer* seems to condemn the Novelty of the contrary Opinion, *Patr.* 10 *p.* 3 [53]. yet I believe it will be hard for him to find any other Age or Country of the World, but this which has asserted Monarchy to be *Jure Divino.* And he confesses, *Patr. p.* 4 [54]. That *Heyward, Blackwood, Barclay, and others, that have bravely vindi-cated the Right of Kings in most Points,* never thought of this, *but* 15 *with one Consent admitted the Natural Liberty and Equality of Mankind.*

5. By whom this Doctrine came at first to be broach'd, and brought in fashion amongst us, and what sad Effects it gave rise to, I leave to *Historians* to relate, or to the Memory of those who were Contemporaries with *Sibthorp* and *Manwering* to recollect. My business at present is only to consider what Sir *R. F.* who is ₅ allowed to have carried this Argument farthest, and is supposed to have brought it to perfection, has said in it; for from him every one, who would be as fashionable as *French* was at Court, has learned, and runs away with this short System of Politics, *viz. Men are not born free,* and *therefore could never have the liberty to choose* 10 *either Governors, or Forms of Government. Princes have their Power Absolute, and by Divine Right, for Slaves could never have a Right to Compact or Consent. Adam was an absolute Monarch, and so are all Princes ever since.*

---

§ 4   14   For these authors see *Patriarcha* (Laslett, 1949), p. 54, and compare 1, § 67, 28–30. Barclay is quoted in 11, §§ 232, 6; 235–9: Locke listed in 1681 Barclay's *De Potestate Papae* and his *De Regno et Regali Potestate*—see notes on 11, §§ 232, 239.
§ 5   1   Paragraph number omitted in 1st edition, both states.
4   Refers to the famous sermons exalting the Royal Prerogative preached and published in 1627 by Robert Sybthorpe (*Of Apostolique Obedience*) and Roger Manwaring (*Religion and Allegiance*), see Allen, 1938, 176–80. They are also named by Sidney in somewhat the same way: 1772, 5.
7–8   Compare Preface 39 (added in 1698): Sir Robert Filmer's brother Edward was at the Court of Charles I and a francophile, a friend of Henrietta Maria's, and his son Edward was Gentleman of the Privy Chamber to Charles I and Charles II (see Laslett, 1948 (ii)), but he himself was never a courtier. In this sentence 'was' seems to have been changed from 'is' in 1689.

Chap. II.

Of Paternal and Regal Power.

6. SIR R. F.'s great Position is, that *Men are not naturally free.* This is the Foundation on which his absolute Monarchy ſtands, and from which it erects it self to an height, that its Power is above every Power, *Caput inter nubila,* so high above all Earthly
5 and Human Things, that Thought can scarce reach it; that Promises and Oaths, which tye the infinite Deity, cannot confine it. But if this Foundation fails, all his Fabric falls with it, and Governments muſt be left again to the old way of being made by contrivance, and the consent of Men ('Ανθρωπίνη κτίσις) making
10 use of their Reason to unite together into Society. To prove this grand Position of his, he tells us, *p. 12 [57]. Men are born in subjection to their Parents,* and therefore cannot be free. And this Authority of Parents, he calls *Royal Authority,* p. 12, 14 [57, 58]. *Fatherly Authority, Right of Fatherhood,* p. 12, 20 [57, 61]. One
15 would have thought he would in the beginning of such a Work as this, on which was to depend the Authority of Princes, and the Obedience of Subjects, have told us expressly what that Fatherly Authority is, have defined it, though not limited it, because in some other Treatises of his he tells us, 'tis Unlimited, and Un-
20 limitable;* he should at leaſt have given us such an account of it, that we might have had an entire Notion of this *Fatherhood,* or *Fatherly Authority,* whenever it came in our way in his Writings. This I expected to have found in the firſt Chapter of his *Patriarcha.* But inſtead thereof, having, 1. *En Passant,* Made his Obeysance

---

* *In Grants and Gifts that have their Original from God or Nature, as the Power of the Father hath, no inferior Power of Man can limit, nor make any Law of Prescription againſt them,* O. 158 [233].
   The Scripture teaches, that supreme Power was Originally in the Father without any Limitation, O. 245 [234].

---

§ 6 4 *Caput inter nubila*—head in the clouds.
   6 Compare ii, § 195, 5–7.
   8–10 1 Peter ii. 13, 'submit yourselves to every ordinance of men' (ἀνθρωπίνη κτίσει). Compare the second *Letter on Toleration* (*Works,* 1801, VI, 121).
   11–23 Implying that Locke had dealt with the 'Other Treatises' when he decided to analyse *Patriarcha,* see above, p. 59, note † and references.

to the *Arcana Imperii*, p. 5 [54]. 2. Made his Compliment to the 25
Rights and Liberties of this, or any other Nation, p. 6. [55] which he
is going presently to null and destroy; And, 3. Made his Leg to
those Learned Men, who did not see so far into the Matter as
himself, *p. 7* [55]. He comes to fall on *Bellarmine*, p. 8. [56] and,
by a Victory over him, Establishes his *Fatherly Authority* beyond 30
any question. *Bellarmine* being routed by his own Confession,
p. 11. [57] the day is clear got, and there is no more need of any
Forces: For having done that, I observe not that he states the
Question, or rallies up any Arguments to make good his Opinion,
but rather tells us the Story, as he thinks fit, of this strange kind 35
of domineering Phantom, called the *Fatherhood*, which whoever
could catch, presently got Empire, and unlimited absolute Power.
He assures us how this *Fatherhood* began in *Adam*, continued its
course, and kept the World in order all the time of the *Patriarchs*
till the Flood, got out of the Ark with *Noah* and his Sons, made 40
and supported all the Kings of the Earth till the Captivity of the
Israelites in *Egypt*, and then the poor *Fatherhood* was under hatches,
till *God by giving the Israelites Kings, Re-established the ancient and
prime Right of the Lineal Succession in Paternal Government*. This is
his business from *p.* 12. to 19 [57–60]. And then obviating an 45
Objection, and clearing a Difficulty or two with one half Reason,
p. 23. [62] *to confirm the Natural Right of Regal Power*, he ends the
first Chapter. I hope 'tis no Injury to call an half Quotation an
half Reason, for God says, *Honour thy Father and Mother*; but our
Author contents himself with half, leaves out *thy Mother* quite, as 50
little serviceable to his purpose. But of that more in another place.

7. I do not think our Author so little skill'd in the way of
writing Discourses of this nature, nor so careless of the Point
in hand, that he by oversight commits the fault that he himself,
in his *Anarchy of a mix'd Monarchy*, p. 239. [280] objects to

---

29   Bellarmine. Filmer directed much of his argument against Cardinal Bellarmine's subordinating secular power to the papacy in his *De Potestate Summi Pontifici*,
1610—see Laslett, 1949; McIlwain, 1918.
   43–4   Not a quotation, but a summary of *Patriarcha*, 57–8.
   48   'first Chapter', i.e. paragraphs i–viii of *Patriarcha* in Laslett's edition, where
there are no chapters since it reproduces Filmer's manuscript which lacks them.
   51   'in another place'; see I, § 11, 31 note and references.
§ 7   4   Filmer's *Observations upon Mr Hunton's Treatise of Monarchy, or, the Anarchy of
a Limited or Mixed Monarchy* (Laslett, 1949, 277–313). On Hunton's *Treatise of
Monarchie* (1643) and Locke, see note on II, § 168, 1–2.

5 Mr. *Hunton* in these words: *Where first I charge the A. that he hath not given us any Definition, or Description of Monarchy in general; for by the Rules of Method, he should have first defin'd.* And by the like **Rule** of Method Sir *Robert* should have told us, what his *Fatherhood* or *Fatherly Authority* is, before he had told us, in whom it was to 10 be found, and talked so much of it. But perhaps Sir *Robert* found, that this *Fatherly Authority*, this Power of Fathers, and of Kings, for he makes them both the same, *p.* 24. [63] would make a very odd and frightful Figure, and very disagreeing, with what either Children imagine of their Parents, or Subjects of their Kings, if 15 he should have given us the whole Draught together in that Gigantic Form, he had painted it in his own Phancy: and therefore like a wary Physician, when he would have his Patient swallow some harsh or *Corrosive Liquor*, he mingles it with a large quantity of that, which may dilute it; that the scatter'd Parts may go down 20 with less feeling, and cause less Aversion.

8. Let us then endeavour to find what account he gives us of this *Fatherly Authority*, as it lies scatter'd in the several Parts of his Writings. And first, as it was vested in *Adam*, he says, *Not only* Adam, *but the succeeding Patriarchs, had by Right of Fatherhood Royal* 5 *Authority over their Children, p.* 12 [57]. *This Lordship which* Adam *by Command had over the whole World, and by Right descending from him the Patriarchs did enjoy, was as large and ample as the Absolute Dominion of any Monarch which hath been since the Creation, p.* 13 [58]. *Dominion of Life and Death, making War, and concluding Peace,* ·10 *p.* 13 [58]. Adam *and the Patriarchs had absolute Power of Life and Death, p.* 35 [76]. *Kings, in the Right of Parents, succeed to the Exercise of Supreme Jurisdiction, p.* 19 [61]. *As Kingly Power is by the Law of God, so it hath no Inferior Law to Limit it,* Adam *was Lord of all, p.* 40 [78]. *The Father of a Family governs by no other Law, than by* 15 *his own Will, p.* 78 [96]. *The Superiority of Princes is above Laws, p.* 79 [96]. *The unlimited Jurisdiction of Kings is so amply described by* Samuel, *p.* 80 [96]. *Kings are above the Laws, p.* 93 [103]. And to this purpose, see a great deal more which our A—— delivers in

---

17–18 This has the professional touch of Locke the physician.
§ 8 7 '*Absolute*', 'absolutest' in original; these quotations are mainly accurate, though two passages are conflated.
19–22 Filmer's works are studded with quotations from Bodin's *République*. Locke does not seem to have possessed any of Bodin's works, though he shows acquaintance with him—compare note on 1, § 56, 3.

Bodin's words: *It is certain, that all Laws, Priviledges, and Grants of Princes, have no Force, but during their Life; if they be not ratified by* 20 *the express Consent, or by Sufferance of the Prince following, especially Priviledges*, O. p. 279 [304]. *The reason why Laws have been also made by Kings, was this; When Kings were either busied with Wars, or distracted with public Cares, so that every private Man could not have Access to their Persons, to learn their Wills and Pleasure, then were Laws of* 5 *Necessity invented, that so every particular Subject might find his prince's Pleasure decypher'd unto him in the Tables of his Laws*, p. 92 [102]. *In a Monarchy, the King must by necessity be above the Laws*, p. 100 [105]. *A perfect Kingdom is that, wherein the King rules all things according to his own Will*, p. 100 [105]. *Neither Common nor Statute Laws are,* 30 *or can be, any Diminution of that General Power, which Kings have over their People by right of Fatherhood*, p. 115 [113]. *Adam was the Father, King, and Lord over his Family; a Son, a Subject, and a Servant or Slave, were one and the same thing at first. The Father had Power to dispose or sell his Children or Servants; whence we find, that at the first* 35 *reckoning up of Goods in Scripture, the Man-servant, and the Maid-servant, are numbred among the Possessions and Substance of the Owner, as other Goods were*, O. Præf. [188]. *God also hath given to the Father a Right or Liberty, to alien his Power over his Children to any other; whence we find the Sale and Gift of Children to have been much in use* 40 *in the Beginning of the World, when Men had their Servants for a Possession and an Inheritance, as well as other Goods, whereupon we find the Power of Castrating and making Eunuchs much in use in Old Times,* O. p. 155 [231]. *Law is nothing else but the Will of him that hath the Power of the Supream Father,* O. p. 223 [72]. *It was God's Ordinance* 45 *that the Supremacy should be unlimited in* Adam, *and as large as all the Acts of his Will; and as in him, so in all others that have Supream Power*, O. p. 245 [284].

9. I have been fain to trouble my Reader with these several Quotations in our A——'s own Words, that in them might be seen his own Description of his *Fatherly Authority*, as it lies scatter'd up and down in his Writings, which he supposes was first vested in *Adam*, and by Right belongs to all Princes ever 5 since. This *Fatherly Authority* then, or *Right of Fatherhood*, in our

---

30-2   Locke's only citation of a passage from Filmer having to do with the constitution, see Introduction 76.

38   'Praef.'—indicates the Preface to Filmer's 'Forms'.

A——'s sence is a Divine unalterable Right of Sovereignty, whereby a Father or a Prince hath an Absolute, Arbitrary, Unlimited, and Unlimitable Power, over the Lives, Liberties, and Estates of his Children and Subjects; so that he may take or
10 alienate their Estates, sell, castrate, or use their Persons as he pleases, they being all his Slaves, and he Lord or Proprietor of every Thing, and his unbounded Will their Law.

10. Our A—— having placed such a mighty Power in *Adam*, and upon that supposition, founded all Government, and all Power of Princes, it is reasonable to expect, that he should have proved this with Arguments clear and evident, suitable to the
5 weightiness of the Cause. That since Men had nothing else left them, they might in Slavery have such undeniable Proofs of its Necessity, that their Consciences might be convinced, and oblige them to submit peaceably to that Absolute Dominion, which their Governors had a Right to exercise over them. Without this,
10 What Good could our A—— do, or pretend to do, by erecting such an unlimited Power, but flatter the Natural Vanity and Ambition of Men, too apt of it self to grow and encrease with the Possession of any Power? And by perswading those, who, by the consent of their Fellow-Men, are advanced to great, but
15 limited degrees of it, that by that part which is given them, they have a Right to all, that was not so; and therefore may do what they please, because they have Authority to do more then others, and so tempt them to do what is neither for their own, nor the good of those under their Care, whereby great Mischiefs cannot
20 but follow.

11. The Sovereignty of *Adam*, being that on which, as a sure Basis, our A—— builds his mighty Absolute Monarchy, I expected, that, in his *Patriarcha*, this his main Supposition would have been proved and established with all that Evidence of
5 Arguments, that such a Fundamental Tenet required; and that this, on which the great stress of the Business depends, would have been made out with Reasons sufficient to justifie the Confidence with which it was assumed. But in all that Treatise, I could find very little tending that way; the Thing is there so taken for

---

§ 11   3, etc.   References to *Patriarcha*—see Introduction, 59–61. Locke had found that Filmer did not demonstrate the sovereignty of Adam in his tracts, discussed in the *Second Treatise*, and he now finds that *Patriarcha* evades the issue.

granted without Proof, that I could scarce believe my self, when 10
upon attentive reading that Treatise, I found there so mighty
a Structure rais'd upon the bare supposition of this Foundation.
For it is scarce credible, that in a Discourse where he pretends
to confute the *Erroneous Principle* of Man's *Natural Freedom*, he
should doe it by a bare supposition of *Adam's Authority*, without 15
offering any Proof for that Authority. Indeed he confidently
says, that *Adam had Royal Authority*, p. 12 [56], and 13 [57].
Absolute Lordship and Dominion of Life and Death, p. 13 [58]. *An
Universal Monarchy*, p. 33 [75]. *Absolute Power of Life and Death*,
p. 35 [76]. He is very frequent in such Assertions, but what 20
is strange in all his whole *Patriarcha*, I find not one Pretence of
a Reason to establish this his great Foundation of Government;
not any thing that looks like an Argument, but these words:
*To confirm this Natural Right of Regal Power, we find in the Decalogue,
that the Law which injoyns Obedience to Kings, is delivered in the Terms,* 25
Honour thy Father, as if all Power were Originally in the Father [62].
And why may I not add as well, That in the *Decalogue*, the Law that
enjoyns Obedience to Queens, is delivered in the Terms of *Honour
thy Mother*, as if all Power were originally in the Mother? The
Argument, as Sir *Robert* puts it, will hold as well for one as 30
t'other. But of this, more in its due place.

   12. All that I take notice of here, is, that this is all our A——
says in this first, or any of the following Chapters, to prove the
Absolute Power of Adam, which is his great Principle; and yet, as
if he had there settled it upon sure Demonstration, he begins his
2d Chapter with these words, *By conferring these Proofs and Reasons,* 5
drawn from the Authority of the Scripture [63]. Where those *Proofs
and Reasons* for *Adam's* Sovereignty are, bating that of *Honour thy
Father* above mentioned, I confess, I cannot find, unless what he
says, *p.* 11 [57]. *In these words we have an evident Confession, viz. of
Bellarmine, that Creation made Man Prince of his Posterity,* must be 10
taken for Proofs and Reasons drawn from Scripture, or for any
sort of Proof at all: though from thence by a new way of inference
in the Words, immediately following, he concludes *the Royal
Authority of Adam*, sufficiently settled in him.

---

31   'in its due place'—compare 1, §6, 51: see 1, §52, 10–14, §55, 8–19, §60 on and 11, §64
on.
§ 12   2, 5   'Chapters', '2d Chapter'—see note on 1, § 6, 48.

13. If he has in that Chapter, or any where in the whole Treatise, given any other Proofs of *Adam's Royal Authority*, other than by often repeating it, which, among some Men, goes for Argument, I desire any body for him to shew me the Place and Page, that I may be convinced of my mistake, and acknowledge my oversight. If no such Arguments are to be found, I beseech those Men, who have so much cryed up this Book, to consider whether they do not give the World cause to suspect, that it's not the Force of Reason and Argument, that makes them for Absolute Monarchy, but some other by Interest, and therefore are resolved to applaud any Author, that writes in favour of this Doctrine, whether he support it with Reason or no. But I hope they do not expect that rational and indifferent Men should be brought over to their Opinion, because this their great Dr. of it, in a Discourse made on purpose, to set up the *Absolute Monarchical Power of Adam*, in opposition to the *Natural Freedom* of Mankind, has said so little to prove it, from whence it is rather naturally to be concluded, that there is little to be said.

14. But, that I might omit no care to inform my self in our A——'s full Sense, I consulted his *Observations on Aristotle, Hobs, &c.* to see whether in disputing with others he made use of any Arguments, for this his darling Tenet of *Adam's Sovereignty*, since in his Treatise of the *Natural Power of Kings*, he hath been so sparing of them. In his Observations on Mr. *Hob's Leviathan*, I think he has put, in short, all those Arguments for it together, which in his Writings I find him any where to make use of; his Words are these. *If God Created only* Adam, *and of a piece of him made the Woman, and if by Generation from them two, as parts of them all Mankind be propagated: If also God gave to* Adam *not only the Dominion over the Woman and the Children that should Issue from them, but also over the whole Earth to subdue it, and over all the Creatures on it, so that as long as* Adam *lived, no Man could claim or enjoy any thing but by Donation, Assignation, or Permission from him, I wonder,* &c. O. 165 [241]. Here we have the Sum of all his Arguments, for *Adam's Sovereignty*, and against *Natural Freedom*, which I find

---

§ 14 2 '*Observations...*'—a collective reference to Filmer's works other than *Patriarcha* and the *Freeholder*; that is, Laslett's edition, 185–326. This phrase might be used against the view of the purpose and order of writing of the *Two Treatises* adopted here; compare note on 1, § 11, 3 and reference.

5 '*Natural Power of Kings*'—sub-title of *Patriarcha*.

up and down in his other Treatises; and they are these following;
God's Creation of *Adam*, the *Dominion* he gave him *over Eve:*
And the *Dominion* he had as *Father over his Children*, all which I shall   20
particularly consider.

CHAP. III.

Of Adam's *Title to Sovereignty by Creation.*

15. SIR *Robert* in his Preface to his Observations on *Aristotle's*
Politicks, tells us, *A Natural Freedom of Mankind cannot be
supposed without the denial of the Creation of* Adam [188]: But how
Adam's being Created, which was nothing but his receiving a
Being immediately from Omnipotency, and the hand of God, gave   5
Adam a *Sovereignty* over any thing, I cannot see, nor consequently
understand, how a *Supposition of Natural Freedom is a denial of*
Adam's *Creation*, and would be glad any body else (since our
A—— did not vouchsafe us the favour) would make it out for
him. For I find no difficulty to suppose the *Freedom of Mankind*,   10
though I have always believed the *Creation of Adam*; He was
Created, or began to exist, by God's immediate Power, without
the Intervention of Parents or the pre-existence of any of the
same Species to beget him, when it pleased God he should; and
so did the Lion, the King of Beasts before him, by the same   15
Creating Power of God: and if bare existence by that Power, and
in that way, will give Dominion, without any more ado, our
A——, by this Argument, will make the Lion have as good a Title
to it as he, and certainly the Ancienter. No! for *Adam* had his
Title *by the Appointment of God*, says our A—— in another   20
place [289]. Then bare *Creation* gave him not Dominion, and one
might have *supposed Mankind Free* without *denying the Creation of
Adam* since 'twas God's *Appointment* made him Monarch.

16. But let us see, how he puts his *Creation* and this *Appointment*
together. *By the Appointment of God*, says Sir *Robert, as soon as*

---

§ 14   20–1   Locke deals with these three points in chapters 3, 5 and 6 of this
treatise.

Adam *was Created he was Monarch of the World, though he had no Subjects, for though there could not be actual Government till there were* 5 *Subjects, yet by the Right of Nature it was due to* Adam *to be Governor of his Posterity: though not in act, yet at least in habit,* Adam *was a King from his Creation* [289]. I wish he had told us here what he meant *by God's Appointment.* For whatsoever Providence orders, or the Law of Nature directs, or positive Revelation declares, may be 10 said to be *by God's Appointment,* but I suppose it cannot be meant here in the first Sense, *i.e.* by Providence; because that would be to say no more, but that *as soon as Adam was Created* he was *de facto* Monarch, because *by Right of Nature it was due to* Adam, *to be Governor of his Posterity.* But he could not *de facto* be by Providence 15 Constituted the Governor of the World at a time, when there was actually no Government, no Subjects to be governed, which our *A——* here confesses. *Monarch of the world* is also differently used by our Author, for sometimes he means by it a Proprietor of all the World exclusive of the rest of Mankind, and thus he 20 does in the same page of his Preface before cited, *Adam,* says he, *being Commanded to Multiply and People the Earth and to subdue it, and having Dominion given him over all Creatures, was thereby the Monarch of the whole World, none of his Posterity had any Right to possess any thing but by his Grant or Permission, or by Succession from him* [187–8]. 25   2. Let us understand then by *Monarch* Proprietor *of the World,* and by *Appointment* God's actual Donation, and revealed positive Grant made to *Adam,* 1 Gen. 28. as we see Sir *Robert* himself does in this parallel place, and then his Argument will stand thus, *by the positive Grant of God; As soon as* Adam was *Created, he was* 30 *Proprietor of the World, because by the Right of Nature it was due to Adam to be Governor of his Posterity.* In which way of arguing there are two manifest Falshoods. *First,* It is false that God made that Grant to *Adam,* as soon as he was Created, since though it stands in the Text immediately after his Creation, yet it is plain it could 35 not be spoken to *Adam* till after *Eve* was made and brought to him, and how then could he be *Monarch by Appointment as soon as Created,* especially since he calls, if I mistake not, that which

---

§ 16 25 '2.'—presumably indicates the second part of the argument of this paragraph, although there is no '1.'

34 Compare 1, § 29, 11–12. Tyrrell makes exactly this point in *Patriarcha non Monarcha,* 1681, 101 (second pagination).

37 'if I mistake not'—Hunton, not Filmer, used this text for this purpose, though the phrase quoted in line 38 occurs on p. 283 of Filmer.

God says to *Eve*, 3 *Gen.* 16: *The original Grant of Government*, which not being till after the Fall, when *Adam* was somewhat, at leaſt in time, and very much, diſtant in condition from his 40 *Creation*, I cannot see, how our *A*—— can say in this Sense, that *by God's Appointment, as soon as* Adam *was Created he was Monarch of the World. Secondly*, Were it true that God's actual Donation *appointed* Adam *Monarch of the World as soon as he was Created*, yet the Reason here given for it would not prove it, but it would 45 always be a false Inference, that God, by a positive Donation *appointed* Adam *Monarch of the World, because by Right of Nature it was due to* Adam *to be Governor of his Poſterity*: for having given him the Right of Government by Nature, there was no need of a positive Donation, at leaſt it will never be a proof of such 50 a Donation.

17. On the other side the Matter will not be much mended, if we underſtand by *God's appointment* the Law of Nature, (though it be a pretty harsh Expression for it in this place) and by *Monarch of the World*, Sovereign Ruler of Mankind; for then the Sentence under Consideration muſt run thus: *By the Law of Nature, as soon* 5 *as* Adam *was Created he was Governor of Mankind, for by Right of Nature it was due to* Adam *to be Governor of his Poſterity*, which amounts to this, He was *Governor by Right of Nature*, because he was *Governor by Right of Nature*. But ſuppoſing we should grant, that a Man is *by Nature Governor* of his Children, *Adam* could not 10 hereby *be Monarch as soon as Created*; for this Right of Nature being founded in his being their Father, how *Adam* could have a *Natural Right* to be *Governor* before he was a Father, when by being a father only he had that *Right*, is, methinks, hard to conceive, unless he will have him to be a Father before he was 15 a Father, and to have a Title before he had it.

18. To this foreseen Objection, our *A*—— answers very Logically, *He was Governor in Habit, and not in Act*; A very pretty way of being a Governour without Government, a Father without Children, and a King without Subjects. And thus Sir *Robert* was

---

§§ **18–20**   These paragraphs are typical of the least attractive features of Locke on Filmer: he has the grace to apologize. Some parts of this passage, especially in paragraph 20, are reminiscent of the *Preface*, and may have been written in 1689. In the 1st edition § 19 is almoſt incomprehensible because of errors in the printing, corrected by Locke in his copy.

5 an Author before he writ his Book, not *in Act* 'tis true, but *in Habit*, for when he had once Publish'd it, it was due to him *by the Right of Nature*, to be an Author, as much as it was *to Adam to be Governor of his Children* when he had begot them; And if to be such a *Monarch of the World*, an absolute Monarch *in Habit*,

10 *but not in Act*, will serve the turn, I should not much envy it to any of Sir *Robert's* Friends that he thought fit graciously to bestow it upon, tho' even this of *Act* and *Habit*, if it signified any thing but our A——'s skill in distinctions, be not to his purpose in this place. For the Question is not here about *Adam's* actual

15 Exercise of Government, but actually having a Title to be Governor: Government, says our A——, was *due to* Adam *by the Right of Nature.* What is this Right of Nature? A Right Fathers have over their Children by begetting them; *Generatione jus acquiritur parentibus in liberos*, says our A—— out of *Grotius, O.* 223 [71].

20 The Right then follows the begetting as arising from it, so that according to this way of reasoning or distinguishing of our A——, *Adam*, as soon as he was Created, had a Title *only in Habit, and not in Act*, which in plain *English* is, He had actually no Title at all.

19. To speak less Learnedly, and more Intelligibly, one may say of *Adam*, he was in a possibility of being *Governor*, since it was possible he might beget Children, and thereby acquire that Right of Nature, be it what it will, to Govern them, that accrues

5 from thence, but what Connection has this with *Adam's Creation*, to make him say, That *as soon as he was Created, he was Monarch of the World?* For it may be as well said of *Noah*, that as soon as he was born, he was Monarch of the World, since he was in possibility (which in our A——'s Sense is enough to make

10 a Monarch, *a Monarch in Habit*,) to outlive all Mankind but his own Posterity. What such necessary Connection there is betwixt *Adam's Creation* and his *Right to Government*, so that a *Natural Freedom of Mankind cannot be supposed without the denial of the Creation of* Adam, I confess for my part I do not see; Nor how those words,

15 *by the Appointment, &c. O.* 254. [289] how ever explain'd, can be put together to make any tolerable Sense, at least to establish this Position, with which they end, *viz. Adam was a King from his Creation*; A King, says our A——, *not in Act, but in Habit, i.e.* actually no King at all.

20. I fear I have tired my Reader's Patience, by dwelling longer on this Passage than the weightiness of any Argument in it, seems to require: but I have unavoidably been engaged in it by our A——'s way of writing, who hudling several Suppositions together, and that in doubtful and general terms makes such a medly and confusion, that it is impossible to shew his Mistakes, without examining the several Senses, wherein his Words may be taken, and without seeing how, in any of these various Meanings, they will consist together, and have any Truth in them; for in this present Passage before us, how can any one argue against this Position of his, that *Adam was a King from his Creation*, unless one examine, whether the Words, *from his Creation*, be to be taken, as they may, for the time of the Commencement of his Government, as the foregoing words import, *as soon as he was Created he was Monarch*, or, for the cause of it, as he says, p. 11 [57]. *Creation made Man Prince of his Posterity?* How farther can one judge of the truth of his being thus King, till one has examined whether King be to be taken, as the words in the beginning of this Passage would perswade, on supposition of his *Private Dominion*, which was by God's positive Grant, *Monarch of the World by Appointment*; or *King* on supposition of his *Fatherly Power* over his Off-spring which was by Nature, *due by the Right of Nature*, whether, I say, King be to be taken in both, or one only of these two Senses, or in neither of them, but only this, that Creation made him Prince, in a way different from both the other? For though this assertion, that *Adam was King from his Creation*, be true in no Sense, yet it stands here as an evident Conclusion· drawn from the preceding words, though in truth it be but a bare assertion joyn'd to other assertions of the same kind, which confidently put together in words of undetermined and dubious meaning, look like a sort of arguing, when there is indeed neither Proof nor Connection: A way very familiar with our A——, of which having given the Reader a taste here, I shall, as much as the Argument will permit me, avoid touching on hereafter, and should not have done it here, were it not to let the World see, how Incoherencies in Matter, and Suppositions without Proofs put handsomly together in good Words and a plausible Style, are apt to pass for strong Reason and good Sense, till they come to be look'd into with Attention.

CHAP. IV.

Of Adam's *Title to Sovereignty by Donation,* Gen. 1. 28.

21. HAving at last got through the foregoing Passage, where we have been so long detain'd, not by the Force of Arguments and Opposition, but the Intricacy of the Words, and the Doubtfulness of the Meaning; Let us go on to his next Argu-
5 ment, for *Adam*'s Sovereignty. Our A—— tells us in the Words of Mr. *Selden,* that *Adam by Donation from God,* Gen. 1. 28. *was made the General Lord of all Things, not without such a private Dominion to himself, as without his Grant did exclude his Children. This Determination of Mr.* Selden, says our A——, *is consonant to the History of the Bible,*
10 *and natural Reason,* O. 210 [63, 64]. And in his Pref. to his Obs: on *Arist.* he says thus; *The first Government in the World was Monarchical in the Father of all Flesh,* Adam *being commanded to Multiply and People the Earth, and to subdue it, and having Dominion given him over all Creatures, was thereby the Monarch of the whole*
15 *World, none of his Posterity had any Right to possess any thing, but by his Grant or Permission, or by Succession from him; The Earth, saith the Psalmist, hath he given to the Children of Men, which shews the Title comes from Fatherhood* [187, 188].

22. Before I examine this Argument, and the Text on which it is founded, it is necessary to desire the Reader to observe, that our A——, according to his usual Method, begins in one Sense, and concludes in another; he begins here with *Adam*'s
5 propriety, or *Private Dominion, by Donation*; and his conclusion is, *which shews the Title comes from Fatherhood.*

23. But let us see the Argument. The words of the Text are these; *And God Blessed them, and God said unto them, be Fruitful and Multiply and Replenish the Earth and subdue it, and have Dominion over the Fish of the Sea, and over the Fowl of the Air, and over every*
5 *living thing that moveth upon the Earth,* 1 Gen. 28. From whence our

---

§ 21 6 'Selden'—on Filmer and Selden see Laslett, 1949. Filmer's quotations come from *Mare Clausum,* translated by M. Nedham, 1635, not owned by Locke, though he had several of the other works of Selden.

A—— concludes, *that Adam, having here Dominion given him over all Creatures, was thereby the Monarch of the whole World.* Whereby must be meant, that either this Grant of God gave *Adam* Property, or as our A—— calls it, *Private Dominion* over the Earth, and all inferior or irrational Creatures, and so consequently that he was thereby *Monarch*; or 2°, that it gave him Rule and Dominion over all Earthly Creatures whatsoever, and thereby over his Children, and so he was *Monarch*: for, as Mr. *Selden* has properly worded it, *Adam was made General Lord of all Things,* one may very clearly understand him, that he means nothing to be granted to *Adam* here but Property, and therefore he says not one word of *Adam's Monarchy.* But our A—— says, *Adam was hereby Monarch of the World,* which properly speaking, signifies Sovereign Ruler of all the Men in the World, and so *Adam,* by this Grant, must be constituted such a Ruler. If our A—— means otherwise, he might, with much more clearness have said, that *Adam was hereby Proprietor of the whole World.* But he begs your Pardon in that point, clear distinct Speaking not serving every where to his purpose, you must not expect it in him, as in Mr. *Selden,* or other such Writers.

24. In opposition therefore to our A——'s Doctrine, that *Adam was Monarch of the whole World,* founded on this Place, I shall shew.

1°. That by this Grant, 1 *Gen.* 28. God gave no immediate Power to *Adam* over Men, over his Children, over those of his own Species, and so he was not made Ruler, or *Monarch* by this Charter.

2°. That by this Grant God gave him not *Private Dominion* over the Inferior Creatures, but right in common with all Mankind; so neither was he *Monarch,* upon the account of the Property here given him.

---

§ 23 13 For Selden's wording, see *Mare Clausum,* translated by Nedham, 1635, 20: Locke does not seem to have gone back to the original. Tyrrell uses very similar arguments against Filmer, 1681, 98–116 (second pagination).

22–5 The clearest connection of this polemic against Filmer with Locke's philosophical writing is this insistence on fixed definitions and distinct terms. Compare the *Essay,* III, ix, 10 (1894, II, 110), referring to writers of their own opinions: 'if they do not use their words with a due clearness and perspicuity, we may lay them aside, and without any injury done them, resolve thus with ourselves, *Si non vis intelligi, debes negligi'.* Compare I, § 108, I, § 109; II, § 52 and for Locke's own neglect of definition in this very work, see Introduction, p. 84.

25. 1. That this Donation, 1 *Gen.* 28. gave *Adam* no power over Men, will appear if we consider the words of it. For since all Positive Grants convey no more than the express words they are made in will carry, let us see which of them here will compre-
5 hend Mankind, or *Adam's* Posterity; and those, I imagin, if any, must be these, *every living thing that moveth*, the words in *Hebrew* are, חיה הרמשת *i.e. Bestiam Reptantem*, of which words the Scripture it self is the best interpreter. God having Created the Fishes and Fowles the 5*th* day, the beginning of the 6*th*, he creates
10 the Irrational Inhabitants of the dry Land, which, *v.* 24. are described in these words, *let the Earth bring forth the living Creature after his kind; Cattle and creeping things, and beasts of the Earth, after his kind, and v.2. and God made the Beasts of the Earth after his kind, and Cattle after their kind, and every thing that creepeth on the Earth*
15 *after his kind;* Here in the Creation of the brute Inhabitants of the Earth, he first speaks of them all under one General Name, of *Living Creatures*, and then afterwards divides them into three ranks, 1. *Cattle*, or such Creatures as were or might be tame, and so be the Private possession of Particular Men; 2. חיה which
20 *ver.* 24 and 25 in our Bible, is Translated Beasts, and by the *Septuagint* θηρία, *Wild beasts*, and is the same word, that here in our Text, *ver.* 28. where we have this great Charter to *Adam*, is Translated *Living thing*, and is also the same Word used, *Gen.* 9. 2. where this Grant is renewed to *Noah*, and there likewise
25 Translated *Beast*, 3. The third Rank were the Creeping Animals, which *ver.* 24 and 25 are comprised under the word, הרמשת, the same that is used here *ver.* 28. and is Translated *moving*, but in the former Verses *Creeping*, and by the *Septuagint* in all these places, ἑρπετὰ, or Reptils; from whence it appears that the words
30 which we Translate here in God's Donation, *ver.* 28. *Living Creatures moving*, are the same which in the History of the Creation, *ver.* 24, 25. signify two Ranks of terrestrial Creatures, *viz. Wild Beasts* and *Reptils*, and are so understood by the *Septuagint*.

---

§ 25 Mr D. W. Thomas, Regius Professor of Hebrew in the University of Cambridge, states that Locke's Hebrew as displayed here and in paragraphs 26 and 27 is adequate to his purpose. But it adds very little to the argument. It is printed correctly in the 1st edition only. For a detailed examination, see Pareyson's Italian critical edition, 1948.
1 '1'—the '2' is on line 1 of paragraph 29.

26. When God had made the Irrational Animals of the World, divided into three kinds, from the places of their Habitation, *viz. Fishes of the Sea, Fowls of the Air*, and *Living Creatures of the Earth*, and these again into *Cattle, Wild Beasts*, and *Reptils*, he considers of making Man, and the Dominion he should have over the Terrestrial World, *ver.* 26. and then he reckons up the Inhabitants of these three Kingdoms, but in the Terrestrial, leaves out the second Rank חיה, or wild Beasts: But here, *ver.* 28. where he actually executes this design, and gives him this Dominion, the Text mentions *the Fishes of the Sea, and Fowls of the Air*, and the *Terrestrial Creatures* in the words, that signifie the *Wild Beasts* and *Reptils*, though Translated *Living thing that moveth*, leaving out Cattle. In both which places, though the Word that signifies *Wild Beasts* be omitted in one, and that which signifies *Cattle* in the other, yet, since God certainly executed in one place, what he declares he designed in the other, we cannot but understand the same in both places, and have here only an account, how the Terrestrial irrational Animals, which were already created and reckon'd up at their Creation, in three distinct Ranks *of Cattle, Wild Beasts*, and *Reptils* were here, *ver.* 28. actually put under the Dominion of Man, as they were designed *ver.* 26. nor do these words contain in them the least appearance of any thing, that can be wrested, to signifie God's giving to one Man Dominion over another, *Adam* over his Posterity.

27. And this further appears from *Gen.* 9. 2. where God renewing this Charter to *Noah* and his Sons, he gives them Dominion over *the Fowls of the Air*, and *the Fishes of the Sea*, and *the Terrestrial Creatures*, expressed by חיה and הרמש Wild Beasts and Reptils, the same words that in the Text before us 1 *Gen.* 28. are Translated *every moving thing, that moveth upon the Earth*, which by no means can comprehend Man, the Grant being made to *Noah* and his Sons, all the Men then living, and not to one part of Men over another: Which is yet more evident from the very next words *ver.* 3. where God gives every רמש, *every moving thing*, the very words used *Ch.* 1. 28. to them for Food. By all which it is plain, that God's Donation to *Adam, Ch.* 1. 28. and his designation, *v.* 26. and his Grant again to *Noah* and his Sons, refer to, and contain in them, neither more nor less, than the Works of the Creation the 5*th* day, and the Beginning of the 6*th*, as they are

set down from the 20*th*, to the 26*th ver.* inclusively of the 1*st Chap.*
and so comprehend all the Species of irrational Animals of the
Terraqueous Globe, though all the words whereby they are expressed
in the History of their Creation, are no where used in any of the
20 following Grants, but some of them omitted in one, and some in
another. From whence I think it is past all doubt, that Man
cannot be comprehended in this Grant, nor any Dominion over
those of his own Species be convey'd to *Adam*. All the Terrestrial
irrational Creatures are enumerated at their Creation, *ver.* 25.
25 under the Names, *Beasts of the Earth, Cattle and creeping things*, but
Man being not then Created, was not contained under any of
those Names, and therefore, whether we understand the *Hebrew*
words right or no, they cannot be supposed to comprehend Man
in the very same History, and the very next Verses following,
30 especially since that *Hebrew* word רמש which if any in this
Donation to *Adam, Ch.* 1. 28. must comprehend Man, is so plainly
used in contradistinction to him, as *Gen.* 6. 20; 7. 14. 21. 23;
Gen. 8. 17, 19. And if God made all Mankind slaves to *Adam*
and his Heirs, by giving *Adam* Dominion over *every living thing*
35 *that moveth on the Earth, Chap.* 1. 28. as our *A——* would have it,
methinks Sir *Robert* should have carried his Monarchical Power
one step higher, and satisfied the World, that Princes might eat
their Subjects too, since God gave as full Power to *Noah* and his
Heirs, *Chap.* 9. 2. to eat *every Living thing that moveth*, as he did to
40 *Adam* to have Dominion over them, the *Hebrew* words in both
places being the same.

28. *David*, who might be supposed to understand the Donation
of God in this Text, and the Right of Kings too, as well as our
A——, in his Comment on this place, as the Learned and Judicious *Ainsworth* calls it, in the 8*th Psalm*, finds here no such
5 Charter of Monarchical Power, his words are, *Thou hast made him,*
i.e. Man the Son of Man, *a little lower than the Angels, thou mad'st
him to have Dominion over the works of thy hands, thou hast put all
things under his Feet, all Sheep and Oxen and the Beasts of the Field,
and the Fowl of the Air, and Fish of the Sea, and whatsoever passeth*

§ 28   4 '*Ainsworth*'—see Henry Ainsworth, *Annotations upon the Five Books of
Moses, the books of the Psalmes* ... 1622 (1639). Locke bought this book at Cooper's auction in
December 1681: it was an edition of a collection of commentaries originally published
separately. On Gen. i. 28, Ainsworth says 'For this state of Man ... David laudeth the Lord in
Psal. 8'.

through the paths of the Sea. In which words, if any one can find 10
out that there is meant any Monarchical Power of one Man over
another, but only the Dominion of the whole Species of Mankind,
over the inferior Species of Creatures, he may, for ought I know,
deserve to be one of Sir *Robert's Monarchs in habit,* for the rareness
of the discovery. And by this time, I hope it is evident, that he 15
that gave *Dominion over every Living thing that moveth on the Earth,*
gave *Adam* no Monarchical Power over those of his own Species,
which will yet appear more fully in the next thing I am to shew.

29. 2. Whatever God gave by the words of this Grant, 1 *Gen.* 28.
it was not to *Adam* in particular, exclusive of all other Men:
whatever *Dominion* he had thereby, it was not a *Private Dominion,*
but a Dominion in common with the rest of Mankind. That this
Donation was not made in particular to *Adam,* appears evidently 5
from the words of the Text, it being made to more than one, for
it was spoken in the Plural Number, God blessed *them,* and said
unto *them,* Have Dominion. God says unto *Adam* and *Eve,* Have
Dominion; *thereby,* says our *A., Adam was Monarch of the World:*
But the Grant being to them, *i.e.* spoke to *Eve* also, as many 10
Interpreters think with reason, that these words were not spoken
till *Adam* had his Wife, must not she thereby be Lady, as well as
he Lord of the World? If it be said that *Eve* was subjected to
Adam, it seems she was not so subjected to him, as to hinder her
Dominion over the Creatures, or *Property* in them: for shall we say 15
that God ever made a joint Grant to two, and one only was to
have the benefit of it?

30. But perhaps 'twill be said, *Eve* was not made till afterward:
Grant it so, What advantage will our *A.* get by it? The Text will
be only the more directly against him, and shew that God in this
Donation, gave the World to Mankind in common, and not to
Adam in particular. The word *Them* in the Text must include the 5
Species of Man, for 'tis certain *Them* can by no means signifie
Adam alone. In the 26*th* Verse, where God declares his intention
to give this Dominion, it is plain he meant, that he would make
a Species of Creatures, that should have Dominion over the other
Species of this Terrestrial Globe: The words are, *And God said,* 10
Let us make Man in our Image, after our likeness, and let them have

---

§ 29   1   '2.'—refers back to '1' on line 1 of paragraph 25.
12   Compare 1, § 16, 34.

Dominion over the Fish, &c. *They* then were to have Dominion. Who? even those who were to have the *Image* of God, the Individuals of that Species of *Man* that he was going to make, for that

15 *Them* should signifie *Adam* singly, exclusive of the rest, that should be in the World with him, is against both Scripture and all Reason: And it cannot possibly be made Sense, if *Man* in the former part of the *Verse* do not signifie the same with *Them* in the latter, only *Man* there, as is usual, is taken for the Species, and

20 *them* the individuals of that Species: and we have a Reason in the very Text. God makes him *in his own Image after his own Likeness,* makes him an intellectual Creature, and so capable of *Dominion.* For wherein soever else the *Image of God* consisted, the intellectual Nature was certainly a part of it, and belong'd to the whole

25 Species, and enabled them to have *Dominion* over the inferiour Creatures; and therefore *David* says in the 8*th Psalm* above cited, *Thou hast made him little lower than the Angels, thou hast made him to have Dominion.* 'Tis not of *Adam* King *David* speaks here, for *Verse* 4. 'tis plain, 'tis of *Man, and the Son of Man,* of the Species

30 of Mankind.

31. And that this Grant spoken to *Adam* was made to him, and the whole Species of Man, is clear from our *A*'s own Proof out of the *Psalmist. The Earth,* saith the Psalmist, *hath he given to the Children of Men; which shews the Title comes from Fatherhood:* These

5 are Sir *Robert*'s words in the Preface before cited, and a strange Inference it is he makes, *God hath given the Earth to the Children of Men,* ergo *the Title comes from Fatherhood.* 'Tis pity the Propriety of the *Hebrew* Tongue had not used *Fathers of Men* instead of *Children of Men,* to express Mankind: then indeed our *A.* might

10 have had the countenance of the sound of the words, to have placed the *Title* in the *Fatherhood.* But to conclude, that the *Fatherhood* had the Right to the Earth, because God gave it *to the Children of Men,* is a way of arguing peculiar to our *A.* And a Man must have a great mind to go contrary to the Sound as

15 well as Sense of the Words, before he could light on it. But the Sense is yet harder, and more remote from our *A*'s purpose:

---

§ 30   17–20   Pareyson comments that Locke is right and the patriarchalists wrong here, because in Hebrew, which the Authorized Version follows very closely, and in English a singular can be a collective.

26   'above cited'—1, § 28, 5–10.

§ 31   5   'Preface...'—the Preface to Filmer's 'Forms', last cited 1, § 21, 10.

For as it ſtands in his Preface [187–188], it is to prove *Adam's* being Monarch, and his reasoning is thus, *God gave the Earth to the Children of Men*, ergo *Adam was Monarch of the World*. I defie any Man to make a more pleaſant Conclusion than this, which cannot be excused from the moſt obvious Absurdity, till it can be shewn, that by *Children of Men*, he who had no Father, *Adam*, alone is signified; but whatever our *A.* does, the Scripture speaks not Nonsense.

32. To maintain this *Property and Private Dominion of* Adam, our *A.* labours in the following Page [64] to deſtroy the Community granted to *Noah* and his Sons, in that parallel place, 9 *Gen.* 1, 2, 3. and he endeavours to do it two ways.

1°. Sir *Robert* would perswade us againſt the express words of the Scripture, that what was here granted to *Noah*, was not granted to his Sons in common with him. His words are; *As for the general Community between* Noah *and his Sons, which Mr.* Selden *will have to be granted to them*, 9. Gen. 2. *the Text doth not warrant it* [64]. What *Warrant* our *A.* would have, when the plain express words of Scripture, not capable of another meaning, will not satisfie him, who pretends to build wholly on Scripture, is not easie to imagine. The Text says, *God blessed* Noah *and his Sons, and said unto them*, i.e. as our *A.* would have it, *unto him: For*, saith he, *although the Sons are there mentioned with* Noah *in the Blessing, yet it may beſt be underſtood, with a Subordination or Benediction in Succession*, O. 211 [64]. That indeed is *beſt*, for our *A.* to be under-ſtood, which beſt serves to his purpose, but that truly *may beſt be underſtood* by any body else, which beſt agrees with the plain conſtruction of the words, and arises from the obvious meaning of the place, and then *with Subordination* and *in Succession*, will not *be beſt underſtood*, in a Grant of God, where he himself put them not, nor mentions any such Limitation. But yet, our *A.* has reasons, why it *may beſt be underſtood so. The Blessing*, says he in the following words, *might truly be fulfilled, if the Sons either under or after their Father, enjoy'd a private Dominion*, O. 211. [64] which is to say, that a Grant, whose express words give a joynt Title in present (for the Text says, into your hands they are delivered) *may beſt be underſtood with a Subordination* or in *Succession:* because 'tis possible, that in *Subordination*, or *Succession* it may be enjoy'd. Which is all one as to say, that a Grant of any thing in present

possession, *may best be understood* of reversion: because 'tis possible one may live to enjoy it in reversion. If the Grant be indeed to a Father, and to his Sons after him, who is so kind as to let his
35 Children enjoy it presently in common with him, one may truly say, as to the event one will be as good as the other: but it can never be true, that what the express words grant in possession, and in common, *may best be understood*, to be in reversion. The sum of all his reasoning amounts to this: God did not give to the
40 Sons of *Noah* the World in common with their Father, because 'twas possible they might enjoy it under, or after him. A very good sort of Argument, against an express Text of Scripture: but God must not be believed, though he speaks it himself, when he says he does any thing, which will not consist with Sir *Robert's*
45 Hypothesis.

33. For 'tis plain, however he would exclude them, That part of this *Benediction*, as he would have it in *Succession*, must needs be meant to the Sons, and not to *Noah* himself at all. *Be Fruitful, and Multiply, and Replenish the Earth*, says God, in this Blessing.
5 This part of the Benediction, as appears by the sequel, concerned not *Noah* himself at all: for we read not of any Children he had after the Flood, and in the following Chapter, where his Posterity is reckon'd up, there is no mention of any, and so this *Benediction in Succession*, was not to take place till 350 Years after, and to save
10 our *A*'s imaginary *Monarchy*, the Peopling of the World must be deferr'd 350 Years; for this part of the *Benediction* cannot be understood with *Subordination*, unless our *A*. will say, that they must ask leave of their Father *Noah* to lie with their Wives. But in this one point our *A*. is constant to himself in all his Discourses,
15 he takes great care there should be Monarchs in the World, but very little that there should be People: and indeed his way of Government is not the way to People the World. For how much Absolute Monarchy helps to fulfil this great and primary Blessing of God Almighty, *Be fruitful, and multiply, and replenish the Earth*,
20 which contains in it the improvement too of Arts and Sciences,

---

§ 33 7 'following Chapter'—Gen. x.
    9 and 11 '350 Years'—the time Noah lived after the Flood.
    13–27 The point about absolute monarchy and depopulation is taken up again in I, § 41, and in II, § 42, 21–8—an addition made in the late 1690's. This passage may itself be an addition of 1689. Increase of population was an important aim of policy for Locke, insisted upon in his economic writings.

and the conveniences of Life, may be seen in those large and rich Countries, which are happy under the *Turkish* Government, where are not now to be found ⅓, nay in many, if not most parts of them 1/30, perhaps I might say not 1/100 of the People, that were formerly, as will easily appear to any one, who will compare the 25 Accounts we have of it at this time, with Antient History. But this by the by.

34. The other Parts of this *Benediction* or Grant are so expressed, that they must needs be understood to belong to *Noah* and his Sons, to them as much as to him, and not to his Sons *with a subordination or in Succession. The fear of you, and the dread of you,* says God, *shall be upon every Beast,* &c. Will any Body but our *A.* 5 say, that the Creatures feared and stood in awe of *Noah* only, and not of his Sons without his leave, or till after his death? And the following words, *into your hands they are delivered,* are they to be understood as our *A.* says, if your Father please, or they shall be deliver'd into your hands hereafter. If this be to argue from 10 Scripture, I know not what may not be proved by it, and I can scarce see how much this differs from that *Fiction and Phansie,* or how much a surer Foundation it will prove than the opinions of *Philosophers and Poets,* which our *A.* so much condemns in his Preface. 15

35. But our *A——* goes on to prove, that *it may best be understood with a Subordination or a Benediction in Succession,* for, says he, *it is not probable, that the private Dominion which God gave to* Adam, *and by his Donation, Assignation or Cession to his Children, was Abrogated, and a Community of all things instituted between* Noah *and his* 5 *Sons.* —— Noah *was left the sole Heir of the World, why should it be thought that God would disinherit him of his Birthright, and make him of all Men in the World the only Tenant in Common with his Children,* O. 211 [64].

36. The Prejudices of our own ill grounded Opinions, however by us called *Probable,* cannot Authorize us to understand Scripture contrary to the direct and plain meaning of the Words.

---

§ 34   12-14   In his Preface to the *Forms,* Filmer says (188) 'there never was any such thing as an independent multitude, who at first had a natural right to a community: this is but a fiction, or fancy of too many in these days, who please themselves in running after the opinions of philosophers and poets'. See I, § 154.

I grant, 'tis not probable that *Adams private Dominion was* here
5 *Abrogated*; because it is more than improbable (for it will never
be proved) that ever *Adam* had any such *Private Dominion:* And
since parallel places of Scripture are moſt probable to make us
know, how they *may be beſt underſtood*, there needs but the comparing this Blessing here to *Noah* and his Sons after the Flood,
10 with that to *Adam* after the Creation, 1 *Gen.* 28. to assure any one
that God gave *Adam* no such *Private Dominion.* 'Tis *Probable*,
I confess, that *Noah* should have the same Title, the same Property
and Dominion after the Flood, that *Adam* had before it. But
since *Private Dominion* cannot consiſt with the Blessing and Grant
15 God gave to him and his Sons in Common, 'tis a sufficient
Reason to conclude that *Adam* had none, especially since in the
Donation made to him, there is no words that express it, or do
in the leaſt favour it; And then let my Reader judge whether
it may beſt be underſtood, when in the one place there is not one
20 word for it, not to say, what has been above proved, that the
Text it self proves the contrary, and in the other, the Words and
Sense are directly againſt it.

37. But our *A.* says, *Noah was the sole Heir of the World, why
should it be thought that God would disinherit him of his Birth-right?*
Heir, indeed, in *England*, signifies the Eldeſt Son, who is by the
Law of *England* to have all his Fathers Land, but where God ever
5 appointed any such *Heir of the World*, our *A.* would have done
well to have shewed us, and how *God disinherited him of his Birth-
right*, or what harm was done him if God gave his Sons a Right
to make use of a part of the Earth for the support of themselves
and Families, when the whole was not only more then *Noah*
10 himself, but infinitely more than they all could make use of, and
the Possessions of one could not at all Prejudice, or as to any
use ſtreighten that of the other.

38. Our *A.* probably foreseeing he might not be very successful in persuading People out of their Senses, and, say what he
could, Men would be apt to believe the plain words of Scripture,
and think, as they saw, that the Grant was spoken to *Noah* and
5 his Sons jointly. He endeavours to insinuate, as if this Grant to
Noah, conveyed no Property, no Dominion; because, *Subduing
the Earth and Dominion over the Creatures are therein omitted, nor the
Earth once named.* And therefore, says he, *there is a considerable*

difference between these two Texts, the first Blessing gave Adam *a Do-minion over the Earth and all Creatures, the latter allows* Noah Liberty 10 *to use the Living Creatures for Food, here is no alteration or diminishing of his Title, to a Property of all Things, but an Enlargement only of his Commons,* O. 211 [64]. So that in our *A's* Sense, all that was said here to *Noah* and his Sons, gave them no Dominion, no Property, but only *Enlarged* the *Commons;* Their *Commons,* I should 15 say since, God says, *to you are they given,* though our *A.* says *his,* for as for *Noah's* Sons, they it seems by Sir *Robert's* appointment during their Fathers Life time, were to keep Fasting days.

39. Any one but our *A.* would be mightily suspected, to be blinded with Prejudice, that in all this Blessing to *Noah* and his Sons, could see nothing but *only* an Enlargement of Commons. For as to *Dominion* which our *A.* thinks omitted, *the fear of you, and the dread of you,* says God, *shall be upon every Beast,* which 5 I suppose, expresses the *Dominion,* or Superiority was designed Man over the living Creatures, as fully as may be, for in that fear and dread, seems chiefly to consist what was given to *Adam,* over the inferiour Animals; who as absolute a Monarch as he was, could not make bold with a Lark or a Rabbet to satisfie his 10 hunger, and had the Herbs but in common with the Beasts, as is plain from 1 *Gen.* 29. and 30. In the next place, 'tis manifest that in this Blessing to *Noah* and his Sons, Property is not only given in clear words, but in a larger extent than it was to *Adam. Into your hands they are given,* says God, to *Noah* and his Sons, 15 which Words, if they give not Property, nay, Property in Pos-session, 'twill be hard to find Words that can, since there is not a way to express a Man's being possessed of any thing more Natural, nor more certain, than to say, *it is delivered into his Hands.* And, *Verse* 3*d,* to shew, that they had then given them the utmost 20 Property Man is capable of, which is to have a right to destroy any thing by using it; *Every moving thing that Liveth,* saith God, *shall be Meat for you,* which was not allowed to *Adam* in his Charter. This our *A.* calls, *a Liberty of using them for Food, and only an Enlargement of Commons,* but *no alteration of Property,* O. 211 [64]. 25 What other Property Man can have in the Creatures, but the *Liberty of using them,* is hard to be understood: So that, if the first Blessing, as our *A.* says, gave *Adam Dominion over the Creatures,* and the Blessing to *Noah* and his Sons, gave them *such a Liberty*

30 *to use them*, as *Adam* had not; it must needs give them something
that *Adam* with all his Soveraignty wanted, something that one
would be apt to take for a greater Property; for certainly he has
no absolute Dominion over even the Brutal Part of the Creatures,
and the Property he has in them is very narrow and scanty, who
35 cannot make that use of them, which is permitted to another.
Should any one, who is Absolute Lord of a Country, have bidden
our *A. Subdue the Earth*, and given him Dominion over the
Creatures in it, but not have permitted him to have taken a Kid
or a Lamb out of the Flock, to satisfie his hunger, I guess he
40 would scarce have thought himself Lord or Proprietor of that
Land, or the Cattel on it: But would have found the difference
between *having Dominion*, which a Shepherd may have, and having
full Property as an Owner. So that, had it been his own *Case*,
Sir *Robert* I believe, would have thought here was an *Alteration*,
45 nay, an enlarging of *Property*, and that *Noah* and his Children had
by this Grant, not only Property given them, but such a property
given them in the Creatures, as *Adam* had not; for however, in
respect of one another, Men may be allowed to have propriety
in their distinct Portions of the Creatures; yet in respect of God
50 the Maker of Heaven and Earth, who is sole Lord and Proprietor
of the whole World, Mans Propriety in the Creatures is nothing
but that *Liberty to use them*, which God has permitted, and so
Man's property may be altered and enlarged, as we see it was
here, after the Flood, when other uses of them are allowed, which
55 before were not. From all which I suppose, it is clear, that
neither *Adam* nor *Noah*, had any *Private Dominion*, any Property
in the Creatures, exclusive of his Posterity, as they should successively grow up into need of them, and come to be able to make
use of them.

40. Thus we have Examined our *A*'s Argument for *Adam*'s
Monarchy, founded on the Blessing pronounced, 1 *Gen.* 28. Wherein
I think 'tis impossible for any sober Reader, to find any other
but the setting of Mankind above the other kinds of Creatures,
5 in this habitable Earth of ours. 'Tis nothing but the giving to
Man, the whole Species of Man, as the chief Inhabitant, who is
the Image of his Maker, the Dominion over the other Creatures.
This lies so obvious in the plain words, that any one but our
A. would have thought it necessary to have shewn, how these

words that seem'd to say the quite contrary, gave *Adam Mon-* 10
archical Absolute Power over other Men, or the *Sole Property* in all
the Creatures, and methinks in a business of this moment, and
that whereon he Builds all that follows, he should have done
something more than barely cite words which apparently make
against him; for I confess, I cannot see any thing in them, tending 15
to *Adam's Monarchy*, or *Private Dominion*, but quite the contrary.
And I the less deplore the dulness of my apprehension herein,
since I find the Apostle seems to have as little notion of any such
Private Dominion of Adam as I, when he says, God *gives us all
things richly to enjoy*, which he could not do, if it were all given 20
away already, to Monarch *Adam*, and the Monarchs his Heirs and
Successors. To conclude, this Text is so far from proving *Adam*
Sole Proprietor, that on the contrary, it is a Confirmation of the
Original Community of all things amongst the Sons of Men,
which appearing from this Donation of God, as well as other 25
places of Scripture; the Soveraignty of *Adam*, built upon his
Private Dominion, must fall, not having any Foundation to support it.

41. But yet, if after all, any one will needs have it so, that by
this Donation of God, *Adam* was made sole Proprietor of the
whole Earth, what will this be to his Soveraignty? And how will
it appear, that *Property* in Land gives a Man Power over the Life
of another? Or how will the Possession even of the whole Earth, 5
give any one a Soveraign Arbitrary Authority over the Persons
of Men? The most specious thing to be said, is, that he that is
Proprietor of the whole World, may deny all the rest of Mankind
Food, and so at his pleasure starve them, if they will not acknowledge his Soveraignty, and Obey his Will. If this were true, it 10
would be a good Argument to prove, that there was never any
such *Property*, that God never gave any such *Private Dominion*;
since it is more reasonable to think, that God who bid Mankind
increase and multiply, should rather himself give them all a Right,
to make use of the Food and Rayment, and other Conveniencies 15
of Life, the Materials whereof he had so plentifully provided
for them; than to make them depend upon the Will of a Man

§ 40   14   'apparently'—means 'obviously' here.
   19–20   'God, who giveth richly all things to enjoy', I Tim. vi. 17, also quoted in
II, § 31, 6. Locke nowhere cites biblical texts *proving* original communism.

for their Subsistence, who should have Power to destroy them all
when he pleased, and who being no better then other Men, was
20 in Succession likelier by want and the dependance of a scanty
Fortune, to tye them to hard Service, than by liberal Allowance
of the Conveniencies of Life, to promote the great Design of God,
Increase and *Multiply*: He that doubts this, let him look into the
Absolute Monarchies of the World, and see what becomes of the
25 Conveniencies of Life, and the Multitudes of People.

42. But we know God hath not left one Man so to the Mercy
of another, that he may starve him if he please: God the Lord and
Father of all, has given no one of his Children such a Property,
in his peculiar Portion of the things of this World, but that he
5 has given his needy Brother a Right to the Surplusage of his
Goods; so that it cannot justly be denied him, when his pressing
Wants call for it. And therefore no Man could ever have a just
Power over the Life of another, by Right of property in Land or
Possessions; since 'twould always be a Sin in any Man of Estate,
10 to let his Brother perish for want of affording him Relief out of
his Plenty. As *Justice* gives every Man a Title to the product of
his honest Industry, and the fair Acquisitions of his Ancestors
descended to him; so *Charity* gives every Man a Title to so much
out of another's Plenty, as will keep him from extream want,
15 where he has no means to subsist otherwise; and a Man can no
more justly make use of another's necessity, to force him to become
his Vassal, by with-holding that Relief, God requires him to
afford to the wants of his Brother, than he that has more strength
can seize upon a weaker, master him to his Obedience, and with
20 a Dagger at his Throat offer him Death or Slavery.

43. Should any one make so perverse an use of God's Blessings
poured on him with a liberal Hand; should any one be Cruel and
Uncharitable to that extremity, yet all this would not prove that
Propriety in Land, even in this Case, gave any Authority over
5 the Persons of Men, but only that Compact might; since the

---

§ 41 23–5 Compare I, § 33, 13–27, note and references: this may be an addition
of 1689. Paragraphs 41–3 mark an important limitation on men's rights in property,
see Introduction, 100–1, and compare Polin, 1960, 195 on.
§ 42 5 Locke may here have in mind the injunction in Luke xi. 41.
  11–15 On Justice and Charity, see II, § 5. This passage hints at the labour theory
of property, stated at length in *Second Treatise*, ch. v, paragraph 27 on: 'honest
industry' is mentioned in II, § 42, 26.

Authority of the Rich Proprietor, and the Subjection of the Needy Beggar began not from the Possession of the Lord, but the Consent of the poor Man, who preferr'd being his Subject to starving. And the Man he thus submits to, can pretend to no more Power over him, than he has consented to, upon Compact. Upon this Ground a Man's having his Stores filled in a time of Scarcity, having Money in his Pocket, being in a Vessel at Sea, being able to Swim, &c. may as well be the Foundation of Rule and Dominion, as being Possessor of all the Land in the World, any of these being sufficient to enable me to save a Mans Life who would perish if such Assistance were denied him; and any thing by this Rule that may be an occasion of working upon anothers necessity, to save his Life, or any thing dear to him, at the rate of his Freedom, may be made a Foundation of Sovereignty, as well as Property. From all which it is clear, that tho' God should have given *Adam Private Dominion*, yet that *Private Dominion* could give him no *Sovereignty*; But we have already sufficiently proved, that God gave him no *Private Dominion*.

Chap. V.

Of Adam's *Title to Sovereignty by the Subjection of* Eve.

44. THE next place of Scripture we find our *A.* Builds his Monarchy of *Adam* on, is 3. *Gen.* 16. *And thy desire shall be to thy Husband, and he shall rule over thee.* Here we have (says he) *the Original Grant of Government*, from whence he concludes, in the following part of the Page *O.* 244 [283]. *That the Supream Power is settled in the Fatherhood, and limited to one kind of Government, that is to Monarchy:* For let his premises be what they will, this is always the conclusion, let *Rule* in any Text, be but once named, and presently *Absolute Monarchy* is by Divine Right Establish'd. If any one will but carefully Read our *A*'s own reasoning from these Words, *O.* 244. [283] and consider among other things,

---

§ 44   5-7   Quotation not quite literal: Locke has turned up this page of his Filmer.

the Line and Posterity of Adam, as he there brings them in, he will find some difficulty, to make Sense of what he says; but we will allow this at present, to his peculiar way of Writing, and consider
15 the Force of the Text in hand. The Words are the Curse of God upon the Woman, for having been the first and forwardest in the Disobedience, and if we will consider the occasion of what God says here to our first Parents, that he was Denouncing Judgment, and declaring his Wrath against them both, for their
20 Disobedience, we cannot suppose that this was the time, wherein God was granting *Adam* Prerogatives and Priviledges, investing him with Dignity and Authority, Elevating him to Dominion and Monarchy: For though as a helper in the Temptation, as well as a Partner in the Transgression, *Eve* was laid below him, and
25 so he had accidentally a Superiority over her, for her greater Punishment, yet he too had his share in the fall, as well as the sin, and was laid lower, as may be seen in the following Verses, and 'twould be hard to imagine, that God, in the same Breath, should make him Universal *Monarch* over all Mankind, and a day
30 labourer for his Life; turn him out of *Paradice, to till the Ground, ver.* 23. and at the same time, advance him to a Throne, and all the Priviledges and Ease of Absolute Power.

45. This was not a time, when *Adam* could expect any Favours, any grant of Priviledges, from his offended Maker. If this be *the Original Grant of Government,* as our *A——* tells us, and *Adam* was now made Monarch, whatever Sir *Robert* would have him,
5 'tis plain, God made him but a very poor Monarch, such an one, as our *A——* himself would have counted it no great Priviledge to be. God sets him to work for his living, and seems rather to give him a Spade into his hand, to subdue the Earth, than a Scepter to Rule over its Inhabitants. *In the Sweat of thy Face thou shalt eat*
10 *thy Bread,* says God to him, *ver.* 19. This was unavoidable, may it perhaps be answered, because he was yet without Subjects, and had no body to work for him, but afterwards living as he did above 900 Years, he might have People enough, whom he might command, to work for him; no, says God, not only whilst
15 thou art without other help, save thy Wife, but as long as thou livest, shalt thou live by thy Labour. *In the Sweat of thy Face, shalt thou eat thy Bread, till thou return unto the Ground, for out of it wast thou taken, for dust thou art, and unto dust shalt thou return, v.* 19.

It will perhaps be answered again, in Favour of our *A*——, that these words are not spoken Personally to *Adam*, but in him, as their Representative, to all Mankind, this being a Curse upon Mankind, because of the fall.

46. God, I believe, speaks differently from Men, because he speaks with more Truth, more Certainty: but when he vouchsafes to speak to Men, I do not think, he speaks differently from them, in crossing the Rules of language in use amongst them. This would not be to condescend to their Capacities, when he humbles himself to speak to them, but to lose his design in speaking, what thus spoken, they could not understand. And yet thus must we think of God, if the Interpretations of Scripture, necessary to maintain our *A*——s Doctrine, must be received for good. For by the ordinary Rules of Language, it will be very hard to understand, what God says; If what he speaks here, in the Singular Number to *Adam*, must be understood to be spoken to all Mankind, and what he says in the Plural Number, 1 *Gen.* 26. and 28. must be understood of *Adam* alone, exclusive of all others, and what he says to *Noah* and his Sons Joyntly, must be understood to be meant to *Noah* alone, *Gen.* 9.

47. Farther it is to be noted, that these words here of 3 *Gen.* 16. which our *A.* calls *the Original Grant of Government* were not spoken to *Adam*, neither indeed was there any Grant in them made to *Adam*, but a Punishment laid upon *Eve:* and if we will take them as they were directed in particular to her, or in her, as their representative to all other Women, they will at most concern the Female Sex only, and import no more but that Subjection they should ordinarily be in to their Husbands: But there is here no more Law to oblige a Woman to such a Subjection, if the Circumstances either of her Condition or Contract with her Husband should exempt her from it, then there is, that she should bring forth her Children in Sorrow and Pain, if there could be found a Remedy for it, which is also a part of the same Curse upon her: for the whole Verse runs thus, *Unto the Woman he said, I will greatly multiply thy sorrow and thy conception; In sorrow thou shalt bring forth Children, and thy desire shall be to thy Husband, and he shall rule over thee.* 'Twould, I think, have been a hard matter for any Body, but our *A.* to have found out a Grant of *Monarchical Government*

to Adam in these Words, which were neither spoke to, nor of
20 him: neither will any one, I suppose, by these Words, think the
weaker Sex, as by a Law so subjected to the Curse contained in
them, that 'tis their duty not to endeavour to avoid it. And will
any one say, that *Eve*, or any other Woman, sinn'd, if she were
brought to Bed without those multiplied Pains God threatens
25 her here with? Or that either of our Queens *Mary* or *Elizabeth*,
had they Married any of their Subjects, had been by this Text
put into a Political Subjection to him? or that he thereby should
have had *Monarchical Rule* over her? God, in this Text, gives not,
that I see, any Authority to *Adam* over *Eve*, or to Men over their
30 Wives, but only foretels what should be the Womans Lot, how
by his Providence he would order it so, that she should be subject
to her husband, as we see that generally the Laws of Mankind
and customs of Nations have ordered it so; and there is, I grant,
a Foundation in Nature for it.

48. Thus when God says of *Jacob* and *Esau*, That *the Elder
should serve the Younger*, 25 *Gen.* 23. no body supposes that God
hereby made *Jacob Esau*'s Sovereign, but foretold what should
de facto come to pass.

5 But if these words here spoke to *Eve* must needs be understood
as a Law to bind her and all other Women to Subjection, it can
be no other Subjection than what every Wife owes her Husband,
and then if this be the *Original Grant of Government* and the *Foundation of Monarchical Power*, there will be as many Monarchs as there
10 are Husbands. If therefore these words give any Power to *Adam*,
it can be only a Conjugal Power, not Political, the Power that
every Husband hath to order the things of private Concernment
in his Family, as Proprietor of the Goods and Land there, and
to have his Will take place before that of his wife in all things
15 of their common Concernment; but not a Political Power of
Life and Death over her, much less over any body else.

49. This I am sure: If our *A.* will have this Text to be a *Grant*,
the Original Grant of Government, Political Government, he ought

---

§ **47** 25 Mary and Elizabeth Tudor are clearly meant, and it seems unlikely that
Locke would have written like this after April 1689, when Mary Stuart was crowned
joint sovereign with William III: compare references to James II, II, § 133, 10;
II, § 200, 3, and Introduction, 54. Locke's attitude towards the curse on women in
childbearing is typical of his progressive, humanitarian rationalism.

to have proved it by some better Arguments than by barely saying,
That *thy desire shall be unto thy Husband,* was a Law whereby *Eve*
and *all that should come of her,* were subjected to the absolute 5
Monarchical Power of *Adam* and his Heirs. *Thy desire shall be to
thy Husband,* is too doubtful an expression, of whose signification
Interpreters are not agreed, to build so confidently on, and in
a Matter of such moment, and so great and general Concernment:
But our *A.* according to his way of Writing, having once named 10
the Text, concludes presently without any more ado, that the
meaning is, as he would have it. Let the words *Rule* and *Subject*
be but found in the Text or Margent, and it immediately signifies
the Duty of a Subject to his Prince, the Relation is changed, and
though God says *Husband,* Sir *Robert* will have it *King; Adam* 15
has presently *Absolute Monarchical Power* over *Eve,* and not only
over *Eve,* but *all that should come of her,* though the Scripture says
not a word of it, nor our *A.* a word to prove it. But *Adam* must
for all that be an Absolute Monarch, and so down to the end of
the Chapter. And here I leave my Reader to consider, whether 20
my bare saying, without offering any Reasons to evince it, that
this Text gave not *Adam* that *Absolute Monarchical Power,* our *A.*
supposes, be not as sufficient to destroy that Power, as his bare
Assertion is to Establish it, since the Text mentions neither *Prince*
nor *People,* speaks nothing of *Absolute* or *Monarchical Power,* but 25
the Subjection of *Eve* to *Adam,* a Wife to her Husband. And he
that would trace our *A.* so all through, would make a short and
sufficient answer to the greatest part of the Grounds he proceeds
on, and abundantly confute them by barely denying; It being
a sufficient answer to Assertions without Proof, to deny them 30
without giving a Reason. And therefore should I have said
nothing but barely deny'd that by this Text *the Supreme Power
was setled and founded by God himself, in the Fatherhood, Limited to
Monarchy, and that to* Adam's *Person and Heirs,* all which our *A.*
notably concludes from these words, as may be seen in the same 35
Page, *O.* 244. [283] it had been a sufficient answer; should I have
desired any sober Man only to have read the Text, and considered
to whom, and on what occasion it was spoken, he would no doubt

---

§ 49   13   'Margent'— presumably refers to the margins of the Authorized Version,
with its references and sub-headings; compare I, § 66, 19–20 and note.

19–20   'down to the end of the Chapter', that is the first chapter of *Patriarcha*; see
note on I, § 6, 48. It ends in the middle of section VII (p. 63).

have wondered how our *A.* found out *Monarchical absolute Power*
40 in it, had he not had an exceeding good Faculty to find it himself,
where he could not shew it others. And thus we have examined
the two places of Scripture, all that I remember our *A.* brings to
prove *Adam*'s *Sovereignty*, that *Supremacy*, which he says, *it was*
Gods Ordinance should be unlimited in Adam, *and as large as all the*
45 *Acts of his Will*, O. 245. [284] viz. 1 *Gen.* 28. and 3. *Gen.* 16. one
whereof signifies only the Subjection of the Inferior Ranks of
Creatures to Mankind, and the other the Subjection that is due
from a Wife to her Husband, both far enough from that which
Subjects owe the Governours of Political Societies.

Chap. VI.

Of Adam*'s Title to Sovereignty by Fatherhood.*

50. THere is one thing more, and then I think I have given you
all that our *A.* brings for proof of *Adam*'s Sovereignty,
and that is a Supposition of a natural Right of Dominion over
his Children, by being their Father, and this Title of *Fatherhood*
5 he is so pleased with, that you will find it brought in almost in
every Page, particularly, he says, *Not only* Adam, *but the succeeding*
Patriarchs had by Right of Fatherhood Royal Authority over their
Children, p. 12 [57]. And in the same page, *This Subjection of Children*
being the Fountain of all Regal Authority, &c. This being, as one
10 would think by his so frequent mentioning it, the main Basis
of all his Frame, we may well expect clear and evident Reason for
it, since he lays it down as a Position necessary to his purpose,
That every Man that is born is so far from being free, that by his very
Birth he becomes a Subject of him that begets him, O. 156 [232]. So that
15 *Adam* being the only Man Created, and all ever since Being
Begotten, no body has been born free. If we ask how *Adam*
comes by this Power over his Children, he tells us here 'tis by

§ 50   8   '*Subjection*'—Subordination in Filmer.
   13   '*free*'—free-born in Filmer.

176

begetting them: And so again, *O.* 223 [71]. *This Natural Dominion of* Adam, says he, *may be proved out of* Grotius *himself, who teacheth, That* generatione jus acquiritur parentibus in liberos. And indeed 20 the Act of begetting being that which makes a Man a Father, his Right of Father over his Children can naturally arise from nothing else.

51. *Grotius* tells us not here how far this *jus in liberos*, this Power of Parents over their Children extends; but our *A.* always very clear in the point, assures us, 'tis *Supreme Power*, and like that of Absolute Monarchs over their Slaves, Absolute Power of Life and Death. He that should demand of him, How, or for what 5 Reason it is, that begetting a Child gives the Father such an Absolute Power over him, will find him answer nothing: we are to take his word for this as well as several other things, and by that the Laws of Nature and the Constitutions of Government must stand or fall. Had he been an Absolute Monarch, this way 10 of talking might have suited well enough; *pro ratione voluntas*, might have been of force in his mouth, but in the way of proof or argument is very unbecoming and will little advantage his plea for Absolute Monarchy. Sir Robert has to much lessen'd a Subjects authority to leave himself the hopes of establishing 15 any thing by his bare saying it. One Slave's Opinion without proof is not of weight enough to dispose of the Liberty and fortunes of all Mankind: If all Men are not, as I think they are, naturally equal, I'm sure all Slaves are; and then I may without presumption oppose my single Opinion to his, and be confident 20 that my Saying, *That Begetting of Children makes them not Slaves to their Fathers*, as certainly sets all Mankind Free; as his affirming the contrary makes them all Slaves. But that this Position, which is the Foundation of all their Doctrine, who would have Monarchy

---

19 'Grotius'—'by generation a right over children is acquired by the parents' is quoted by Filmer from Grotius in that part of his *Original* which he devotes to Grotius, and in that passage of this tract which was taken from the original *Patriarcha* manuscript as printed by Laslett, see pp. 71–2.

18–23 Compare II, § 52, 11, note and references.

§ 51 1 Grotius analyses the rights of parents over their children in *De Jure Belli ac Pacis*, II, v (1712 ed. 234–): the phrase under discussion occurs in section 1. But his concern here is with the three periods into which the relationship of parent and child should be divided, and it is quite clear that Locke was justified in accusing Filmer of making what he wanted stand in the place of argument (*pro ratione voluntas*, line 11) in the use he made of Grotius.

to be *Jure Divino,* may have all fair play, let us hear what Reasons others give for it, since our *A.* offers none.

52. The Argument, I have heard others make use of, to prove that Fathers, by begetting them, come by an Absolute Power over their Children, is this; That *Fathers have a Power over the Lives of their Children, because they give them Life and Being,* which is the
5 only proof it is capable of, since there can be no reason, why naturally one Man should have any claim or pretence of Right over that in another, which was never his, which he bestowed not, but was received from the bounty of another. 1°. I answer, That every one who gives another any thing, has not always thereby
10 a Right to take it away again. But, 2°. They who say the *Father* gives Life to his Children, are so dazled with the thoughts of Monarchy, that they do not, as they ought, remember God, who is *the Author and Giver of Life: 'Tis in him alone we live, move, and have our Being.* How can he be thought to give Life to another,
15 that knows not wherein his own Life consists? Philosophers are at a loss about it after their most diligent enquiries; And Anatomists, after their whole Lives and Studies spent in Dissections, and diligent examining the Bodies of Men, confess their Ignorance in the Structure and Use of many parts of Mans Body, and in
20 that Operation wherein Life consists in the whole. And doth the Rude Plough-Man, or the more ignorant Voluptuary, frame or fashion such an admirable Engine as this is, and then put Life and Sense into it? Can any Man say, He formed the parts that are necessary to the Life of his Child? Or can he suppose himself
25 to give the Life, and yet not know what Subject is fit to receive it, nor what Actions or Organs are necessary for its Reception or Preservation?

---

§ **52** In this paragraph and down to number 55 there are evident traces of Locke's medical studies and of his scientific scepticism, attaching here to embryology as it does to the constitution of matter in his *Essay.* His answer to Filmer has an impressiveness here that it lacks elsewhere, though it is not strictly relevant as refutation, and is in contrast with Tyrrell's comments on the same point, for he merely denies that procreation gives absolute power to fathers because the mother would get a greater right from it. Man as the workmanship of God occurs again in the *First Treatise* (see §86, 7) and is a major theme of the *Second Treatise,* see II, §§ 6, 56, etc., and Introduction, 93. Pufendorf (1672, VI, ii, 4) contradicts Grotius, and insists as Locke does (see also note in 1678 journal, Introduction, 36 and I, § 54, 3–5) that in procreation parents usually seek merely their own pleasure, and therefore it is the occasion not the foundation of parental power. Nozick, 1974, claims Locke is explaining in these paragraphs, though not very satisfactorily, why parents do not own their children, whom they have made, and whom, on the theory laid down in the *Second Treatise,* they should accordingly own.

53. To give Life to that which has yet no being, is to frame and make a living Creature, fashion the parts, and mould and suit them to their uses, and having proportion'd and fitted them together, to put into them a living Soul. He that could do this, might indeed have some pretence to destroy his own Workman- 5 ship. But is there any one so bold, that dares thus far Arrogate to himself the Incomprehensible Works of the Almighty? Who alone did at first, and continues still to make a living Soul, He alone can breathe in the Breath of Life. If any one thinks himself an Artist at this, let him number up the parts of his Childs 10 Body which he hath made, tell me their Uses and Operations, and when the living and rational Soul began to inhabit this curious Structure, when Sense began, and how this Engine which he has framed Thinks and Reasons: If he made it, let him, when it is out of order, mend it, at least tell wherein the defects lie. *Shall he* 15 *that made the Eye not see?* says the Psalmist, *Psalm* 94. 9. See these Mens Vanities: The Structure of that one part is sufficient to convince us of an All-wise Contriver, and he has so visible a claim to us as his Workmanship, that one of the ordinary Appellations of God in Scripture is, *God our Maker*, and *the Lord our Maker*. 20 And therefore though our *A.* for the magnifying his *Fatherhood*, be pleased to say, O 159. [233] *That even the Power which God himself exerciseth over Mankind is by Right of Fatherhood*, yet this Fatherhood is such an one as utterly excludes all pretence of Title in Earthly Parents; for he is *King* because he is indeed Maker of 25 us all, which no Parents can pretend to be of their Children.

54. But had Men Skill and Power to make their Children, 'tis not so slight a piece of Workmanship, that it can be imagined they could make them without designing it. What Father of a Thousand, when he begets a Child, thinks farther then the satisfying his present Appetite? God in his infinite Wisdom has 5 put strong desires of Copulation into the Constitution of Men, thereby to continue the race of Mankind, which he doth most commonly without the intention, and often against the Consent and Will of the Begetter. And indeed those who desire and design Children, are but the occasions of their being, and when 10 they design and wish to beget them, do little more towards their

---

§ 54   3-5   Compare I, § 52, note and references.
       5-7   Compare II, § 66, 8-9.

making, than *Ducalion* and his Wife in the Fable did towards the making of Mankind, by throwing Pebbles over their Heads.

55. But grant that the Parents made their Children, gave them Life and Being, and that hence there followed an Absolute Power. This would give the *Father* but a joynt Dominion with the Mother over them. For no body can deny but that the Woman hath an
5 equal share, if not the greater, as nourishing the Child a long time in her own Body out of her own Subſtance. There it is fashion'd, and from her it receives the Materials and Principles of its Conſtitution; And it is so hard to imagine the rational Soul should presently Inhabit the yet unformed Embrio, as soon as the Father
10 has done his part in the Aĉt of Generation, that if it muſt be supposed to derive any thing from the Parents, it muſt certainly owe moſt to the Mother: But be that as it will, the Mother cannot be denied an equal share in begetting of the Child, and so the Absolute Authority of the Father will not arise from hence. Our
15 *A——* indeed is of another mind; for he says, *We know that God at the Creation gave the Sovereignty to the Man over the Woman, as being the Nobler and Principal Agent in Generation,* O. 172 [245]. I remember not this in my Bible, and when the place is brought where God at the *Creation* gave the Sovereignty to Man over the
20 Woman, and that for this Reason, because *he is the Nobler and Principal Agent in Generation,* it will be time enough to consider and answer it: But it is no new thing for our *A——* to tell us his own Fancies for certain and Divine Truths, though there be often a great deal of difference between his and Divine Revela-
25 tions: for God in the Scripture says, *his Father and his Mother that begot him.*

56. They who alledge the Praĉtice of Mankind, for *exposing or selling* their Children, as a Proof of their Power over them, are with Sir *Rob.* happy Arguers, and cannot but recommend their

---

12 Deucalion's story corresponds in Greek mythology to Noah's. He and his wife made an ark to survive the deluge, and afterwards were told by the oracle to throw stones behind them. Those thrown by Deucalion became men, those thrown by his wife became women, and so the world was repopulated.

§ 55 25–6 '*his Father and Mother that begot him*', from Zech. xiii. 3, where parents punish their children with death for prophesying.

§ 56 3 'happy Arguers'—in *Patriarcha* (77–8) Filmer shows, with an example from Roman history, that fathers could punish their children with death, and in the

Opinion by founding it on the most shameful Action, and most unnatural Murder, humane Nature is capable of. The Dens of Lions and Nurseries of Wolves know no such Cruelty as this: These Savage Inhabitants of the Desert obey God and Nature in being tender and careful of their Off-spring: They will Hunt, Watch, Fight, and almost Starve for the Preservation of their Young, never part with them, never forsake them till they are able to shift for themselves; And is it the Priviledge of Man alone to act more contrary to Nature than the Wild and most Untamed part of the Creation? Doth God forbid us under the severest Penalty, that of Death, to take away the Life of any Man, a Stranger, and upon Provocation? and does he permit us to destroy those he has given us the Charge and Care of, and by the dictates of Nature and Reason, as well as his Reveal'd Command, requires us to preserve? He has in all the parts of the Creation taken a peculiar care to propagate and continue the several Species of Creatures, and makes the Individuals act so strongly to this end, that they sometimes neglect their own private good for it, and seem to forget that general Rule which Nature teaches all things of self Preservation, and the Preservation of their Young, as the strongest Principle in them over rules the Constitution of their particular Natures. Thus we see when their Young stand in need of it, the timorous become Valiant, the Fierce and Savage Kind, and the Ravenous Tender and Liberal.

57. But if the Example of what hath been done, be the Rule of what ought to be, History would have furnish'd our A—— with

---

Directions (231) he says: 'God also hath given to the Father a right...to alien his power over his children...whence we find the sale and gift of children...much in use in the beginning of the world...the power of castrating...much in use.' These statements come unaltered from Bodin's *République*, where it is said that it is 'needful to restore unto parents...their power of life and death over their children' (Knolles's translation, p. 22). Bodin must have been among the 'happy Arguers', but there were others perhaps even as late as Montesquieu (see *Esprit des Lois*, v, 7). Tyrrell is more straightforward than Locke over this, and tackles Bodin direct, as does Sidney. It is notable that only Locke in answering Filmer failed to go behind him to his source, for Bodin is of the very greatest importance to all that Filmer wrote—see Laslett, 1949.

18–27 There is an echo of the medieval bestiary in this paragraph: on natural love for children compare II, § 60, 16–20; II, § 63; II, § 67, 16–21 and II, § 170. On preservation of self or offspring compare I, § 88, 14–18, and Strauss, 1953, 227, where Locke's slight vacillation here is made into a Hobbesian insistence on the primacy of self.

instances of this *Absolute Fatherly Power* in its heighth and perfection, and he might have shew'd us in *Peru*, People that begot
5 Children on purpose to Fatten and Eat them. The Story is so
remarkable, that I cannot but set it down in the A——'s Words.
'In some Provinces, *says he*, they were so liquorish after Mans
'Flesh, that they wou'd not have the patience to ſtay till the
'Breath was out of the Body, but would suck the Blood as it
10 'ran from the Wounds of the dying Man; they had publick
'Shambles of Man's Flesh, and their Madness herein was to that
'degree, that they spared not their own Children which they had
'Begot on Strangers taken in War: For they made their Captives
'their Miſtresses and choisly nourished the Children they had
15 'by them, till about thirteen Years Old they Butcher'd and Eat
'them, and they served the Mothers after the same fashion, when
'they grew paſt Child bearing, and ceased to bring them any
'more Roaſters, *Garcilasso de la vega hiſt. des yncas de* Peru, I. 1. c. 12.'

58. Thus far can the busie mind of Man carry him to a Brutality
below the level of Beaſts, when he quits his reason, which places
him almoſt equal to Angels. Nor can it be otherwise in a Creature,
whose thoughts are more than the Sands, and wider than the
5 Ocean, where fancy and passion muſt needs run him into ſtrange
courses, if reason, which is his only Star and compass, be not
that he ſteers by. The imagination is always reſtless and suggeſts
variety of thoughts, and the will, reason being laid aside, is
ready for every extravagant projeft; and in this State, he that
10 goes fartheſt out of the way, is thought fitteſt to lead, and is sure

§ 57   18   The French translation of the *Commentarios Reales* of Garcilaso de la Vega,
published in 1633, seems to have been a favourite book, and it was in Locke's Oxford
study in 1681. It is frequently quoted in his diaries and published works: indeed the very
passage used here is also to be found, somewhat differently differently translated, in his *Essay on
the Understanding*, 1, iii, 9 (1894, 1, 73). It was probably added to both works in 1689: here it has
no particular relevance and seems to have been dragged in to make a sensation. But
see Introduction, 54, and compare 1, § 153, 19–20 and note.
§ 58   This paragraph forms an important declaration of the essential rightness of
'Natural Man' and reads almost like Rousseau, the Rousseau of the *Discours sur
l'Inégalité*; compare 11, § 6. In talking here of the strength of fashion, Locke touches
on a determinist strain which runs through his thought about society: compare the
Essay, 11, xxviii, especially section 12, 'the greatest part of mankind govern themselves chiefly, if not solely, by this *law of fashion*', which in section 10 was 'the *law of
opinion or reputation*', in the earlier editions of the *Essay* even the '*philosophical law*'
(Nidditch, ed., 357, compare Introduction, 81).

of most followers: And when Fashion hath once Established, what Folly or craft began, Custom makes it Sacred, and 'twill be thought impudence or madness, to contradict or question it. He that will impartially survey the Nations of the World, will find so much of their Governments, Religions, and Manners brought in and continued amongst them by these means, that he will have but little Reverence for the Practices which are in use and credit amongst Men, and will have Reason to think, that the Woods and Forests, where the irrational untaught Inhabitants keep right by following Nature, are fitter to give us Rules, than Cities and Palaces, where those that call themselves Civil and Rational, go out of their way, by the Authority of Example. If precedents are sufficient to establish a rule in the case, our A—— might have found in holy writ Children sacrificed by their parents and this amongst the people of God themselves. The Psalmist tells us *Psalm.* cvi. 38. *They shed innocent bloud even the bloud of their sons and of their daughters whom they sacrificed unto the Idols of Canaan.* But God judgd not of this by our A——s rule, nor allowd of the authoritie of practise against his righteous Law, but as it follows there, *The Land was polluted with bloud, therefore was the wrath of the Lord kindled against his people in so much that he abhorred his own inheritance.* The killing of their Children, though it were fashionable, was charged on them as *innocent bloud*, and so had, in the account of God, the guilt of murder, as the offering them to Idols had the guilt of Idolatry.

59. Be it then as Sir *Robert* says, that *Anciently*, it was *usual for Men to sell and Castrate their Children*, O. 155 [231]. Let it be, that they exposed them; Add to it, if you please, for this is still greater Power, that they begat them for their Tables to fat and eat them: If this proves a right to do so, we may, by the same Argument, justifie Adultery, Incest and Sodomy, for there are examples of these too, both Ancient and Modern; Sins, which I suppose, have their Principal Aggravation from this, that they cross the main intention of Nature, which willeth the increase of Mankind, and the continuation of the Species in the highest perfection, and the distinction of Families, with the Security of the Marriage Bed, as necessary thereunto.

60. In confirmation of this Natural Authority of the Father, our *A.* brings a lame Proof, from the positive Command of God

in Scripture; His words are, *to confirm the Natural Right of Regal Power, we find in the Decalogue, that the Law which injoyns Obedience* 5 *to Kings, is delivered in the Terms, Honour thy Father,* p. 23 [62]. *Whereas many confess, that Government only in the Abſtract, is the Ordinance of God, they are not able to prove any such Ordinance in the Scripture, but only in the Fatherly Power, and therefore we find the Commandment, that injoyns Obedience to Superiors, given in the Terms,* 10 *Honour thy Father; so that not only the Power and Right of Government, but the Form of the Power Governing, and the Person having the Power, are all the Ordinances of God. The firſt Father had not only simply Power, but Power Monarchical, as he was Father immediately from God,* O. 254 [289]. To the same purpose, the same Law is cited by our 15 *A.* in several other places, and juſt after the same Fashion, that is, *and Mother,* as Apocriphal Words, are always left out; a great Argument of our *A*'s ingenuity, and the goodness of his Cause, which required in its Defender Zeal to a degree of warmth, able to warp the Sacred Rule of the Word of God, to make it comply 20 with his present occasion; a way of proceeding, not unusual to those, who imbrace not Truths, because Reason and Revelation offer them; but espouse Tenets and Parties, for ends different from Truth, and then resolve at any rate to defend them; and so do with the Words and Sense of Authors, they would fit to their 25 purpose, juſt as *Procruſtes* did with his gueſts, lop or ſtretch them, as may beſt fit them to the size of their Notions: And they always prove like those, so served, Deformed, Lame, and useless.

61. For had our *A.* set down this Command without Garbling, as God gave it, and joyned *Mother* to Father, every Reader would have seen that it had made directly againſt him, and that it was so far from Eſtablishing the *Monarchical Power of the Father,* that 5 it set up the *Mother* equal with him, and injoyn'd nothing but

§ **60** 3–13 These quotations differ in detail from Filmer's text: 'several other places' in line 15 presumably refers to 188, 283.

16 '*and Mother*'—this discussion of Filmer's omission of 'Mother' in his use of the Fifth Commandment occupies Locke until paragraph 66 and fulfils the promise of I, §§ 6 and 11. The argument is stated in II, §§ 52, 53. Sidney and Tyrrell do not make such use of this obvious equivocation, indeed Sidney implies that Filmer omitted 'Mother' by accident (1772, 57).

25 'Procrustes'—the legendary brigand of Eleusis who trimmed or stretched his victims to the length of a bed.

§61 Four of the texts cited here are quoted less exactly in II, § 52, 15–19, see note there.

what was due in common, to both Father and Mother: for that
is the constant Tenor of the Scripture, *Honour thy Father and thy
Mother*, Exod. 20. *He that smiteth his Father or Mother, shall surely
be put to Death*, 21. 15. *He that Curseth his Father or Mother, shall
surely be put to Death*, Ver. 17. Repeated *Lev*. 20. 9. and by our 10
Saviour, *Matth*. 15. 4. *Ye shall fear every Man his Mother and his
Father*, Lev. 19. 3. *If a Man have a Rebellious Son, which will not
Obey the Voice of his Father, or the Voice of his Mother; then shall his
Father and his Mother, lay hold on him, and say, this our Son is Stubborn
and Rebellious, he will not Obey our Voice*, Deut. 21. 18, 19, 20, 21. 15
Cursed be he that setteth Light by his Father or his Mother, 27. 16.
*My Son, hear the Instructions of thy Father, and forsake not the Law of
thy Mother*, are the Words of *Solomon* a King, who was not ignorant
of what belonged to him, as a Father or a King, and yet he joyns
Father and *Mother* together, in all the Instructions he gives Children 20
quite through his Book of *Proverbs, Wo unto him, that sayeth unto
his Father, what begettest thou, or to the Woman, what hast thou brought
forth*, Isa. 45. ver. 10. *In thee have they set Light by Father or Mother*,
Ezek. 22. 7. *And it shall come to pass, that when any shall yet Prophesie,
then his Father and his Mother that begat him, shall say unto him, thou* 25
*shalt not live, and his Father and his Mother that begat him, shall thrust
him through when he Prophesieth*, Zech. 13. 3. Here not the Father
only, but Father and Mother joyntly, had Power in this Case of
Life and Death. Thus ran the Law of the Old Testament, and in
the New they are likewise joyn'd, in the Obedience of their 30
Children, *Eph*. 6. 1. The Rule is, *Children Obey your Parents*, and
I do not remember, that I any where read, *Children Obey your
Father* and no more. The Scripture joyns *Mother* too in that
Homage, which is due from Children, and had there been any
Text, where the Honour or Obedience of Children had been 35
directed to the *Father* alone, 'tis not likely that our *A.*, who pretends to Build all upon Scripture, would have omitted it. Nay,
the Scripture makes the Authority of *Father and Mother*, in respect
of those they have begot, so equal, that in some places it neglects,
even the Priority of Order, which is thought due to the Father, 40
and the *Mother* is put first, as *Lev*. 19. 3. From which so constantly
joyning Father and Mother together, as is found quite through the
Scripture, we may conclude that the Honour they have a Title

---

41 '*Lev*. 19. 3'.—'Ye shall fear every man his mother and his father', cited
II, § 52, 17.

to from their Children, is one common Right belonging so equally to them both, that neither can claim it wholly, neither can be excluded.

62. One would wonder then how our *A*. infers from the 5th Commandment, that all *Power was originally in the Father*. How he finds *Monarchical Power of Government, settled and fixed by the Commandment, Honour thy Father* and thy Mother. If all the Honour due by the Commandment, be it what it will, be the only right of the *Father*, because he, as our *A*—— says, *has the Soveraignty over the Woman, as being the Nobler and Principal Agent in Generation* [245], why did God afterwards all along joyn the *Mother* with him, to share in this Honour? Can the Father, by this Sovereignty of his, discharge the Child from paying this *Honour* to his *Mother?* The Scripture gave no such License to the Jews, and yet there were often Breaches wide enough betwixt Husband and Wife, even to Divorce and Separation, and, I think, no Body will say a Child may withhold Honour from his Mother, or, as the Scripture terms it, *set light by her*, though his Father should command him to do so, no more than the Mother could dispense with him, for neglecting to *Honour* his Father, whereby 'tis plain, that this Command of God, gives the Father no Sovereignty, no Supremacy.

63. I agree with our *A*——, that the Title to this *Honour* is vested in the Parents by Nature, and is a right which accrews to them, by their having begotten their Children, and God by many positive Declarations has confirm'd it to them: I also allow our *A*——s Rule, *that in Grants and Gifts, that have their Original from God and Nature, as the Power of the Father* (let me add *and Mother*, for whom God hath joyned together, let no Man put asunder) *no inferior Power of Men can limit, nor make any Law of Prescription against them*, O. 158. [233] so that the Mother having by this Law of God, a right to Honour from her Children, which is not Subject to the Will of her Husband, we see this *Absolute Monarchical Power of the Father*, can neither be founded on it, nor consist with it; And he has a Power very far from *Monarchical*, very far from that Absoluteness our *A*—— contends for, when another has over his Subjects the same Power he hath, and by the same Title:

---

§ 62   13–19   This point is made in II, § 69, 9–12.

And therefore he cannot forbear saying himself that *he cannot see how any Mans Children can be free from Subjection to their Parents, p.* 12. [57] which, in common Speech, I think, signifies *Mother* as well as *Father*, or if *Parents* here signifies only *Father*, 'tis the first time I ever yet knew it to do so, and by such an use of Words, one may say any thing.

64. By our *A⸻s* Doctrine, the Father having Absolute Jurisdiction over his Children, has also the same over their Issue, and the consequence is good, were it true, that the Father had such a Power: And yet I ask our *A⸻* whether the Grandfather, by his Sovereignty, could discharge the Grand-child from paying to his Father the Honour due to him by the *5th* Commandment. If the Grandfather hath by *right of Fatherhood*, sole Sovereign Power in him, and that Obedience which is due to the Supreme Magistrate, be Commanded in these Words, *Honour thy Father*, 'tis certain the Grandfather might dispense with the Grand-sons Honouring his Father, which, since 'tis evident in common Sense, he cannot, it follows from hence that, *Honour thy Father and Mother*, cannot mean an absolute Subjection to a Sovereign Power, but something else. The right therefore which Parents have by Nature, and which is confirmed to them by the *5th* Commandment, cannot be that political Dominion, which our *A⸻* would derive from it: For that being in every Civil Society Supreme somewhere, can discharge any Subject from any Political Obedience to any one of his fellow Subjects. But what Law of the Magistrate, can give a Child liberty, not to *Honour his Father and Mother?* 'Tis an Eternal Law annex'd purely to the relation of Parents and Children, and so contains nothing of the Magistrates Power in it, nor is subjected to it.

65. Our *A⸻* says, *God hath given to a Father, a Right or Liberty to alien his Power over his Children to any other*, O. 155 [231].

---

§ 64 3–6 This argument was used against Filmer by both Sidney (chapter 1, section 15) and by Tyrrell (1681, 3), though not so pointedly.

11–16. In denying, as he seems to do here, that the Fifth Commandment has anything to do with political obedience, Locke was repudiating far more than the principles of Filmer. He was attacking a tradition of Christianity, and particularly of Protestant Christianity. Luther, for example, develops his whole doctrine of political and social authority as a commentary on the Fifth Commandment (*Von den Guten Werken*, 1520(1888)), and Tyndale argues in a precisely similar manner in his *Obedience of a Christian Man*, 1528 (1848). See the discussion in Laslett, 1949, 20–33, and especially Schochet, 1969 (ii).

I doubt whether he can *Alien* wholly the right of *Honour* that is due from them; But be that as it will, this I am sure, he cannot
5 *Alien,* and retain the same Power, if therefore the Magistrates Sovereignty be as our *A——* would have it, *nothing but the Authority of a Supreme Father, p.* 23. [62] 'tis unavoidable, that if the Magistrate hath all this Paternal Right as he must have if *Fatherhood* be the Fountain of all Authority, then the Subjects
10 though Fathers, can have no Power over their Children, no right to Honour from them: for it cannot be all in anothers hands, and a part remain with the Parents. So that according to our *A——*s own Doctrine, *Honour thy Father and Mother* cannot possibly be understood of Political Subjection and Obedience; since the Laws
15 both in the Old and New Testament, that Commanded Children to *Honour and obey their Parents,* were given to such, whose Fathers were under civil Government, and fellow Subjects with them in Political Societies; and to have bid them *Honour and obey their Parents* in our *A——*s Sense, had been to bid them be Subjects
20 to those who had no Title to it, the right to Obedience from Subjects, being all vested in another: and instead of teaching Obedience, this had been to foment Sedition, by setting up Powers that were not. If therefore this Command, *Honour thy Father and Mother,* concern Political Dominion, it directly over-
25 throws our *A——*s Monarchy; since it being to be paid by every Child to his Father, even in Society, every Father must necessarily have Political Dominion, and there will be as many Sovereigns as there are Fathers: besides that the Mother too hath her Title, which destroys the Sovereignty of one Supream Monarch. But
30 if *Honour thy Father and Mother* mean something distinct from Political Power, as necessarily it must, it is besides our *A——*s business, and serves nothing to his purpose.

66. *The Law that enjoyns Obedience to Kings is delivered,* says our *A——, in the Terms, Honour thy Father, as if all Power were Originally in the Father, p.* 23 [62]. And that Law is also delivered, say I, in the Terms, *Honour thy Mother,* as if all Power were Originally

---

§ 65   3–12   Compare II, § 71, 1–7.
    26–8   Compare Sidney, 1772, 21: 'This paternal power must necessarily accrue to every father: he is a king by the same right as the sons of Noah.' See also Tyrrell, 1681, for example, 38.
§ 66   3   'p. 23'—Locke wrote 'O. 254', assimilating it with the next reference, line 8. His quotations and references are careless in this part of the text.

in the Mother. I appeal whether the Argument be not as good
on one side as the other, *Father and Mother* being joyned all along
in the Old and New Testament where ever Honour or Obedience
is injoyn'd Children. Again our *A——* tells us, O. 254. [289]
*that this Command, Honour thy Father gives the right to govern,
and makes the Form of Government, Monarchical.* To which I answer,
that, if by *Honour thy Father* be meant Obedience to the Political
Power of the Magistrate, it concerns not any duty we owe to our
natural Fathers who are Subjects: because they, by our *A——s*
Doctrine, are divested of all that Power, it being placed wholly
in the Prince, and so being equally Subjects and Slaves with their
Children, can have no right by that Title, to any such *Honour or
Obedience,* as contains in it Political Subjection: If *Honour thy Father
and Mother* signifies the duty we owe our Natural Parents, as by
our Saviour's Interpretation, *Matth.* 15. 4. and all the other mentioned places, 'tis plain it does, then it cannot concern Political
Obedience, but a duty that is owing to Persons, who have no
Title to Sovereignty, nor any Political Authority as Magistrates
over Subjects. For the Person of a private Father, and a Title to
Obedience, due to the Supreme Magistrate, are things inconsistent;
and therefore this Command, which must necessarily comprehend
the Persons of our Natural Fathers, must mean a duty we owe them
distinct from our Obedience to the Magistrate, and from which
the most Absolute Power of Princes cannot absolve us: What this
Duty is, we shall in its due place examine.

67. And thus we have at last got through all that in our *A.*
looks like an Argument for that *Absolute Unlimited Sovereignty*
described, Sect. 8. which he supposes in *Adam,* so that Mankind
ever since have been all born *Slaves,* without any Title to Freedom.
But if *Creation* which gave nothing but a Being, made not *Adam
Prince of his Posterity:* If *Adam,* Gen. 1. 28. was not constituted
Lord of Mankind, nor had a *Private Dominion* given him exclusive
of his Children, but only a Right and Power over the Earth, and

---

19-20   See Matt. xv. 4: 'For God commanded, saying, Honour thy father and
mother: and He that curseth father or mother, let him die the death', compare
I, § 49, 13. The Authorized Version has eleven 'mentioned places' in the margin, all
in the Old Testament.

29   The 'due place' is evidently the *Second Treatise,* chapter VI (§§ 52–76), see
Introduction, 50.

§ 67   3   'Sect. 8.'—that is, section V (60–1) of *Patriarcha* in Laslett's edition.

inferiour Creatures in common with the Children of Men: If also
10 *Gen.* 3. 16. God gave not any Political Power to *Adam* over his
Wife and Children, but only subjected *Eve* to *Adam*, as a punishment, or foretold the Subjection of the weaker Sex, in the ordering
the common Concernments of their Families, but gave not thereby
to *Adam*, as to the Husband, Power of Life and Death, which
15 necessarily belongs to the Magistrate: If Fathers by begetting
their Children acquire no such Power over them: And if the
Command, *Honour thy Father and Mother*, give it not, but only
enjoyns a Duty owing to Parents equally, whether Subjects or
not, and to the *Mother* as well as the *Father*; If all this be so,
20 as I think, by what has been said, is very evident, then Man
has a *Natural Freedom*, notwithstanding all our *A.* confidently
says to the contrary, since all that share in the same common
Nature, Faculties and Powers, are in Nature equal, and ought
to partake in the same common Rights and Priviledges, till the
25 manifest appointment of God, who is *Lord over all, Blessed for
ever*, can be produced to shew any particular Persons Supremacy,
or a Mans own consent subjects him to a Superior. This is so
plain, that our *A.* confesses, that Sir *John Hayward, Blackwood*
and *Barclay, the great Vindicators of the Right of Kings*, could not
30 deny it, but *admit with one consent the Natural Liberty and Equality
of Mankind*, for a Truth unquestionable. And our *A.* hath been
so far from producing any thing, that may make good his great
Position, That *Adam was Absolute Monarch*, and so *Men are not
Naturally Free*, that even his own Proofs make against him; so
35 that to use his own way of Arguing, *This first erroneous Principle
failing, the whole Fabrick of this vast Engine* of Absolute Power
and Tyranny, *drops down of it self*, and there needs no more to
be said in answer to all that he builds upon so false and frail
a Foundation.

22–6   A striking re-echo of the language of 11, § 4, setting forth the basis of
human equality, see Introduction, 54.

25   Rom. ix. 5: 'Christ...who is over all, God blessed for ever.'

28–30   *Patriarcha*, 54: on these authors see the previous citation in 1, § 4, note and
references.

35–7   Locke is refuting Filmer in his own words, substituting 'Absolute Power
and Tyranny' for 'Popular Sedition'. The phrase as Locke modifies it occurs
on p. 4 of the 1680 printing, but in the manuscript Filmer had written 'the
main foundation of popular sedition would be taken away', Laslett's edition,
p. 54.

68. But to save others the Pains, were there any need, he is not sparing himself to shew, by his own Contradictions, the weakness of his own Doctrine. *Adam*'s Absolute and Sole Dominion is that which he is every where full of, and all along builds on, and yet he tells us, *pag.* 12. [57] *That as Adam was Lord of his Children, so his Children under him had a Command and Power over their own Children.* The unlimited and undivided Sovereignty of *Adam's Fatherhood*, by our *A*'s Computation, stood but a little while, only during the first Generation, but as soon as he had Grand-Children, Sir *Rob.* could give but a very ill account of it. *Adam, as Father of his Children*, saith he, *hath an Absolute, Unlimited Royal Power over them, and by virtue thereof over those that they begot, and so to all Generations* [57]; and yet *his Children*, viz. *Cain* and *Seth*, have a Paternal Power over their Children at the same time: so that they are at the same time *Absolute Lords*, and yet *Vassals and Slaves*: *Adam* has all the Authority, as *Grand-Father of the People*, and they have a part of it as Fathers of a part of them: He is Absolute over them and their Posterity, by having begotten them, and yet they are Absolute over their Children by the same Title. *No*, says our *A.*, *Adam's Children under him, had Power over their own Children, but still with Subordination to the first Parent* [57]. A good distinction that sounds well, and 'tis pity it signifies nothing, nor can be reconciled with our *A*'s Words. I readily grant, that supposing *Adam's Absolute Power* over his Posterity, any of his Children might have from him a delegated, and so a *Subordinate* Power over a part, or all the rest: But that cannot be the Power our *A.* speaks of here, it is not a Power by Grant and Commission, but the Natural Paternal Power he supposes a Father to have over his Children. For 1°, he says, *As* Adam *was Lord of his Children, so his Children under him had a Power over their own Children:* They were then Lords over their own Children after the same manner, and by the same Title, that *Adam* was, *i.e.* by right of Generation, by right of *Fatherhood*. 2°. 'Tis plain he means the Natural Power of Fathers, because he limits it to be only *over their own Children*; a delegated Power has no such limitation, as only over their own Children, it might be over others, as well as their own Children. 3°. If it were a delegated Power, it must appear in Scripture: but there is no ground in Scripture to affirm, that *Adam*'s Children had any other Power over theirs, than what they Naturally had as Fathers.

69. But that he means here Paternal Power, and no other, is past doubt from the Inference he makes in these words immediately following, *I see not then how the Children of* Adam, *or of any Man else can be free from Subjection to their Parents* [57]: whereby it appears, that the *Power* on one side, and the *Subjection* on the other, our *A.* here speaks of, is that *Natural Power* and *Subjection* between Parents and Children. For that which every Mans Children owed, could be no other: and that our *A.* always affirms to be Absolute and Unlimited. This Natural *Power* of Parents over their Children, *Adam* had over his Posterity, says our *A.*, and this *Power* of Parents over their Children, his Children had over theirs in his Life-time, says our *A.* also: so that *Adam*, by a Natural Right of Father, had an Absolute, Unlimited Power over all his Posterity, and at the same time his Children had by the same Right Absolute Unlimited Power over theirs. Here then are two Absolute Unlimited Powers existing together, which I would have any body reconcile one to another, or to common Sense. For the *Salvo* he has put in of *Subordination*, makes it more absurd: To have one *Absolute, Unlimited,* nay *Unlimitable Power* in Subordination to another, is so manifest a Contradiction, that nothing can be more. Adam *is Absolute Prince with the Unlimited Authority of Fatherhood over all his Posterity*; All his Posterity are then absolutely his Subjects, and, as our *A.* says, his *Slaves*, Children and Grand-Children, are equally in this State of Subjection and Slavery, and yet, says our *A. the Children of* Adam *have Paternal*, i.e. Absolute, Unlimited *Power over their own Children*: which in plain *English* is, they are Slaves and Absolute Princes at the same time, and in the same Government, and one part of the Subjects have an Absolute Unlimited Power over the other by the Natural Right of Parentage.

70. If any one will suppose in favour of our *A.* that he here meant, that Parents, who are in Subjection themselves to the Absolute Authority of their Father, have yet some Power over their Children: I confess he is something nearer the Truth: But he will not at all hereby help our *A.* For he no where speaking of the Paternal Power, but as an Absolute Unlimited Authority, cannot be suppos'd to understand any thing else here, unless he himself had limited it, and shewed how far it reach'd. And that he means here Paternal Authority in that large Extent, is plain

from the immediate following words; *This Subjection of Children* 10
being, says he, *the Fountain of all Regal Authority*, p. 12 [57]. *The*
Subjection, then that in the former Line he says, *every Man is in*
to his Parents, and consequently what *Adam*'s Grand-Children
were in to their Parents, was that which was the Fountain of all
Regal Authority, *i.e.* According to our *A.*, *Absolute*, *Unlimitable* 15
Authority. And thus *Adam*'s Children had *Regal Authority* over
their Children, whilst they themselves were Subjects to their
Father, and Fellow-Subjects with their Children. But let him
mean as he pleases, 'tis plain he allows *Adam's Children to have*
Paternal Power, p. 12. [57] as also all other Fathers to have *Paternal* 20
Power over their Children, O. 156 [232]. From whence one of these
two things will necessarily follow, that either *Adam*'s Children,
even in his lifetime, had, and so all other Fathers have, as he
phrases it, *p. 12* [57]. *By Right of Fatherhood Royal Authority over*
their Children, or else, that *Adam*, *by Right of Fatherhood*, *had not* 25
Royal Authority: For it cannot be but that *Paternal Power* does,
or does not, give *Royal Authority* to them that have it: If it does
not, then *Adam* could not be Sovereign by this Title, nor any
body else, and then there is an end of all our *A*'s Politics at once;
If it does give *Royal Authority*, then every one that has *Paternal* 30
Power has *Royal Authority*, and then by our *A*'s Patriarchal Government, there will be as many Kings as there are Fathers.

71. And thus what a Monarchy he hath set up, let him and his
Disciples consider. Princes certainly will have great Reason to
thank him for these new Politics, which set up as many Absolute
Kings in every Country as there are Fathers of Children. And
yet who can blame our *A.* for it, it lying unavoidably in the way 5
of one discoursing upon our *A*'s Principles? For having placed
an *Absolute Power* in *Fathers by Right of Begetting*, he could not
easily resolve how much of this Power belong'd to a Son over
the Children he had begotten; And so it fell out to be a very hard
matter to give all the Power, as he does, to *Adam*, and yet allow 10
a part in his Lifetime to his Children, when they were Parents,
and which he knew not well how to deny them. This makes him
so doubtful in his Expressions, and so uncertain where to place
this Absolute Natural Power, which he calls *Fatherhood*; sometimes *Adam* alone has it all, as *p. 13.* [58] O. 244, 245 [282/3]. 15
& Pref. [188].

Sometimes *Parents* have it, which word scarce signifies the Father alone, *p.* 12. [57] 19 [61].

Sometimes *Children* during their Fathers Lifetime, as *p.* 12 [57].

20 Sometimes *Fathers* of *Families*, as *p.* 78 [96], and 79 [96].

Sometimes *Fathers* indefinitely, *O.* 155 [231].

Sometimes the *Heir to Adam*, *O.* 253 [289].

Sometimes *the Posterity of Adam*, 244 [283], 246 [284].

Sometimes *prime Fathers, all Sons or Grand-Children of* Noah,

25 *O.* 244 [283].

Sometimes *the eldest Parents*, *p.* 12 [57].

Sometimes all Kings, *p.* 19 [60].

Sometimes all that have Supreme Power, *O.* 245 [281].

Sometimes *Heirs to those first Progenitors, who were at first the*

30 *Natural Parents of the whole People*, *p.* 19 [61].

Sometimes an Elective King, *p.* 23 [62].

Sometimes those whether a few or a multitude that Govern the *Commonwealth*, *p.* 23 [62].

Sometimes he that can catch it, an Usurper, *p.* 23. [62] *O.* 155

35 [232].

72. Thus this *New Nothing*, that is to carry with it all Power, Authority, and Government; This *Fatherhood* which is to design the Person, and Establish the Throne of Monarchs, whom the People are to obey, may, according to Sir *Robert*, come into any 5 Hands, any how, and so by his Politicks give to Democracy Royal Authority, and make an Usurper a Lawful Prince. And if it will do all these fine Feats, much good do our Author and all his Followers with their Omnipotent *Fatherhood*, which can serve for nothing but to unsettle and destroy all the Lawful Govern- 10 ments in the World, and to Establish in their room Disorder, Tyranny, and Usurpation.

---

§ 72 1 '*New Nothing*'—a conventional phrase for an empty novelty: in Victorian Oxford they used the expression 'A silver new nothing and a tantadling tart'.

Chap. VII.

Of Fatherhood and Property Considered together as Fountains of Sovereignty.

73. IN the foregoing Chapters we have seen what *Adam*'s Monarchy was, in our *A*'s Opinion, and upon what Titles he founded it. The Foundations which he lays the chief stress on, as those from which he thinks he may best derive Monarchical Power to future Princes, are two, *viz*. *Fatherhood and Property*, 5 and therefore the way he proposes to *remove the Absurdities and Inconveniences of the Doctrine of Natural Freedom*, is, *to maintain the Natural and Private Dominion of Adam*, O. 222 [71]. Conformable hereunto, he tells us, the *Grounds and Principles of Government necessarily depend upon the Original of Property*, O. 108 [204]. *The* 10 *Subjection of Children to their Parents is the Fountain of all Regal Authority*, p. 12 [57]. And *all Power on Earth is either derived or usurped from the Fatherly Power, there being no other Original to be found of any Power whatsoever*, O. 158 [233]. I will not stand here to examine how it can be said without a Contradiction, that the 15 *first Grounds and Principles of Government necessarily depend upon the Original of Property*, and yet, *that there is no other Original of any Power whatsoever, but that of the Father:* It being hard to understand how there can be *no other Original* but *Fatherhood*, and yet that the *Grounds and Principles of Government depend upon the Original of* 20 *Property; Property and Fatherhood* being as far different as Lord of a Mannor and Father of Children. Nor do I see how they will either of them agree with what our *A*. says, O. 244. [283] of God's Sentence against *Eve*, Gen. 3. 16. *That it is the Original Grant of Government:* so that if that were the *Original*, Government had not 25 its *Original* by our *A*'s own Confession, either from *Property* or *Fatherhood*; and this Text which he brings as a proof of *Adam*'s Power over *Eve*, necessarily contradicts what he says of the *Fatherhood*, that it is the *Sole Fountain of all Power*. For if *Adam*

---

§ 73   Title to chapter VII—'*Property*' substituted for '*Propriety*' by Locke after 1698, a correction frequently made elsewhere, though it is difficult to see why, unless the language had changed between 1680 and 1700.

had any such Regal Power over *Eve*, as our *A.* contends for, it must be by some other Title than that of begetting.

74. But I leave him to reconcile these Contradictions as well as many others, which may plentifully be found in him by any one, who will but read him with a little Attention, and shall come now to consider how these two Originals of Government, *Adam*'s
5 *Natural* and *Private Dominion*, will consist, and serve to make out and Establish the Titles of succeeding Monarchs, who, as our *A.* obliges them, must all derive their Power from these *Fountains*. Let us then suppose *Adam* made *by God's Donation* Lord and Sole Proprietor of the whole Earth, in as large and ample a manner
10 as Sir *Robert* could wish; let us suppose him also *by Right of Fatherhood* Absolute Ruler over his Children with an unlimited Supremacy, I ask then upon *Adam*'s Death what becomes of both his *Natural* and *Private Dominion*, and I doubt not 'twill be answered, that they descended to his next Heir, as our *A.* tells
15 us in several places; But this way 'tis plain, cannot possibly convey both his *Natural* and *Private Dominion* to the same Person. For should we allow that all the Property, all the Estate of the Father ought to descend to the Eldest Son, (which will need some proof to Establish it) and so he has by that Title all the *Private Dominion*
20 of the Father, yet the Father's *Natural Dominion*, the Paternal Power cannot descend to him by Inheritance. For it being a Right that accrews to a Man only by *begetting*, no Man can have this Natural Dominion over any one he does not *beget*: unless it can be suppos'd, that a Man can have a Right to any thing, without
25 doing that upon which that Right is solely founded. For if a Father by *begetting*, and no other Title, has *Natural Dominion* over his Children, he that does not beget them, cannot have this *Natural Dominion* over them: and therefore be it true or false that our *A.* says, *O.* 156. [232] That *every Man that is born, by his very Birth*
30 *becomes a Subject to him that begets him*, this necessarily follows, *viz*. That a Man by his Birth cannot become a Subject to his Brother, who did not beget him: unless it can be suppos'd that a Man by the very same Title can come to be under the *Natural and Absolute Dominion* of two different Men at once, or it be Sense to say, that
35 a Man by Birth is under the *Natural Dominion* of his Father, only because he begat him, and a Man by Birth also is under the *Natural Dominion* of his Eldest Brother, though he did not beget him.

75. If then the *Private Dominion* of *Adam*, i.e. his Property in the Creatures, descended at his Death all entirely to his Eldest Son, his Heir; (for if it did not, there is presently an end of all Sir *Robert*'s Monarchy) and his *Natural Dominion*, the Dominion a Father has over his Children by begetting them, belong'd 5 immediately upon *Adam*'s decease equally to all his Sons who had Children, by the same Title their Father had it, the Sovereignty founded upon *Property*, and the Sovereignty founded upon *Fatherhood*, come to be divided: since *Cain* as Heir had that of *Property* alone, *Seth* and the other Sons that of *Fatherhood* equally with him. 10 This is the best can be made of our *A*'s Doctrine, and of the two Titles of Sovereignty he sets up in *Adam*, one of them will either signifie nothing, or if they both must stand, they can serve only to confound the Rights of Princes, and disorder Government in his Posterity. For by building upon two Titles to Dominion, 15 which cannot descend together, and which he allows may be separated (for he yields that *Adam*'s *Children had their distinct Territories by Right of Private Dominion*, O. 210. [54] *p*. 40 [78]) he makes it perpetually a doubt upon his Principles where the Sovereignty is, or to whom we owe our Obedience, since *Father-* 20 *hood* and *Property* are distinct Titles, and began presently upon *Adam*'s Death to be in distinct Persons. And which then was to give way to the other?

76. Let us take the account of it, as he himself gives it us. He tells us out of *Grotius*, That *Adam*'s *Children by Donation, Assignation, or some kind of Cession before he was dead, had their distinct Territories by Right of private Dominion*; Abel *had his Flocks and Pastures for them*; Cain *had his Fields for Corn, and the Land of* Nod 5 *where he built him a City*, O. 210 [63/64]. Here 'tis obvious to demand which of these two after *Adam*'s Death, was Sovereign? *Cain*, says our *A*. *p*. 19 [61]. By what Title? *As Heir; for Heirs to Progenitors, who were Natural Parents of their People, are not only Lords of their own Children, but also of their Brethren*, says our *A*. 10

---

§ **76** 2 '*Grotius*' a mistake. In the passage quoted, Filmer was using Selden's *Mare Clausum* to contradict Grotius. Tyrrell gets it right, 1681, 101 (second pagination).

4–6 See Gen. iv. 16–17. This argument is used in II, § 38, and this part of the text has some importance for Locke's own account of the relation of property to government. Filmer's inconsistency on the subject is grosser than Locke's, but Locke's offhand superiority is hardly justifiable.

p. 19 [61]. What was *Cain* Heir to? Not the entire Possessions, not all that which *Adam* had *Private Dominion* in, for our *A.* allows that *Abel* by a Title derived from his Father, *had his diſtinct Territory for Paſture by Right of Private Dominion.* What then *Abel* had by *Private Dominion* [64], was exempt from *Cain's* Dominion. For he could not have *Private Dominion* over that, which was under the Private Dominion of another, and therefore his Sovereignty over his Brother is gone with this *Private Dominion,* and so there are presently two Sovereigns, and his imaginary Title of *Fatherhood* is out of doors, and *Cain* is no Prince over his Brother: Or else if *Cain* retain his Sovereignty over *Abel,* notwithſtanding his *Private Dominion,* it will follow that the *firſt Grounds and Principles of Government* have nothing to do with *Property,* whatever our *A.* says to the contrary. 'Tis true, *Abel* did not out-live his Father *Adam,* but that makes nothing to the Argument, which will hold good againſt Sir *Robert* in *Abel's* Issue, or in *Seth,* or any of the Poſterity of *Adam,* not descended from *Cain.*

77. The same inconvenience he runs into about *the three Sons of Noah,* who, as he says, *p.* 13. [58] *had the whole World divided amongſt them by their Father.* I ask then in which of the three shall we find *the Eſtabliſhment of Regal Power* after *Noah's* Death? If in all three, as our *A.* there seems to say; then it will follow, that Regal Power is founded in Property of Land, and follows *Private Dominion,* and not in *Paternal Power* or *Natural Dominion,* and so there is an end of Paternal Power as the Fountain of Regal Authority, and the so much magnified *Fatherhood* quite vanishes. If the *Regal Power* descended to *Shem* as Eldeſt, and Heir to his Father, then *Noah's Division of the World by Lot to his Sons, or his Ten Years Sailing about the Mediterranean to appoint each Son his part,* which our *A.* tells of, *p.* 15. [59] was labour loſt, his Division of the World to them, was to ill, or to no purpose. For his Grant to *Cham* and *Japhet* was little worth if *Shem,* notwithſtanding this Grant, as soon as *Noah* was dead, was to be Lord over them. Or, if this Grant of *Private Dominion* to them over their assigned Territories, were good, here were set up two diſtinct sorts of Power, not Subordinate one to the other, with all those Inconveniences which he muſters up againſt the *Power of the People,* O. 158. [233] which I shall set down in his own words, only

changing *Property* for *People. All Power on Earth is either derived or usurped from the Fatherly Power, there being no other Original to be found of any Power whatsoever: For if there should be granted two sorts of Power, without any Subordination of one to the other, they would* 25 *be in perpetual strife which should be Supreme, for two Supremes cannot agree: If the Fatherly Power be Supreme, then the Power* grounded on Private Dominion *must be subordinate, and depend on it; and if the Power* grounded on Property *be Supreme, then the Fatherly Power must submit to it, and cannot be exercised without the License of the* 30 *Proprietors, which must quite destroy the Frame and Course of Nature.* This is his own arguing against two distinct Independent Powers, which I have set down in his own words, only putting Power rising from Property, for *Power of the People*; and when he has answered what he himself has urged here against two distinct 35 Powers, we shall be better able to see how, with any tolerable Sense, he can derive all Regal Authority *from the Natural and Private Dominion of* Adam, from *Fatherhood* and *Property* together, which are distinct Titles that do not always meet in the same Person; and 'tis plain, by his own Confession, presently separated 40 as soon both as *Adam*'s and *Noah*'s Death made way for Succession: Though our *A.* frequently in his Writings jumbles them together, and omits not to make use of either, where he thinks it will sound best to his purpose. But the Absurdities of this will more fully appear in the next Chapter, where we shall examine 45 the ways of conveyance of the Sovereignty of *Adam*, to Princes that were to Reign after him.

Chap. VIII.

Of the Conveyance of Adam's *Sovereign Monarchical Power.*

78. SIR *Robert*, having not been very happy in any Proof he brings for the Sovereignty of *Adam*, is not much more fortunate in conveying it to future Princes, who, if his Politicks be true, must all derive their Titles from that first Monarch. The

5 ways he has assigned, as they lie scatter'd up and down in his Writings, I will set down in his own Words: In his Preface he tells us [188], That *Adam being Monarch of the whole World, none of his Posterity had any right to possess any thing, but by his Grant or Permission, or by Succession from him:* Here he makes two ways of

10 conveyance of any thing *Adam* ſtood possessed of, and those are *Grant* or *Succession.* Again he says *All Kings either are, or are to be reputed, the next Heirs to those firſt Progenitors, who were at firſt the Natural Parents of the whole People,* p. 19 [60, 61]. *There cannot be any Multitude of Men whatsoever, but that in it, consider'd by it self,*

15 *there is one Man amongſt them, that in Nature hath a Right to be the King of all the reſt, as being the next Heir to* Adam, O. 253 [288, 289]. Here in these places *Inheritance* is the only way he allows of conveying Monarchical Power to Princes. In other places he tells us O. 155. [232] *All Power on Earth is either derived or usurped from*

20 *the Fatherly Power,* O. 158. [233] *All Kings that now are, or ever were, are or were either Fathers of their People, or the Heirs of such Fathers or Uſurpers of the Right of such Fathers,* O. 253 [288]. And here he makes *Inheritance* or *Uſurpation* the only ways whereby Kings come by this Original Power: But yet he tells us, *This Fatherly*

25 *Empire, as it was of it self Hereditary, so it was alienable by Patent, and seizable by an Uſurper,* O. 190 [256]. So then here Inheritance, Grant or Usurpation will convey it. And laſt of all, which is moſt admirable, he tells us, *p.* 100. [106] *It skills not which way Kings come by their Power, whether by Election, Donation, Succession,*

30 *or by any other means, for it is ſtill the Manner of the Government by Supreme Power, that makes them properly Kings, and not the Means of obtaining their Crowns.* Which I think is a full answer to all his whole *Hypothesis,* and Discourse about *Adam*'s Royal Authority, as the Fountain from which all Princes were to derive theirs: And he

35 might have spared the trouble of speaking so much, as he does, up and down of Heirs and Inheritance, if to make any one *properly a King,* needs no more but *Governing by Supreme Power, and it matters not by what Means he came by it.*

---

§ 78   19   'O. 155'—redundant reference. The preceding words are an insertion of Locke's in the Christ's copy, but he did not strike out this reference. It is clear from such things as this that he did not make his final revision, after 1698, with Filmer's book in his hand.

25   'by Patent'—Filmer wrote 'by the Parent' in his manuscript (1949 ed., p. 256).

34–7   This gives Filmer's whole case away: cf. Salmon, 1959, 111 n.

79. By this notable way, our *A.* may make *Oliver* as *properly King*, as any one else he could think of: And had he had the Happiness to live under *Massanello's* Government, he could not by this his own Rule have forborn to have done Homage to him, with O *King live for ever*, since the Manner of his Government by 5 Supreme Power, made him *properly* King, who was but the Day before *properly* a Fisherman. And if *Don Quixot* had taught his Squire to Govern with Supreme Authority, our *A.* no doubt could have made a most Loyal Subject in *Sancho Pancha's Island*: and he must needs have deserved some Preferment in such 10 Governments, since I think he is the first Politician, who, pretending to settle Government upon its true Basis, and to establish the Thrones of lawful Princes, ever told the World, That he was *properly a King, whose Manner of Government was by Supreme Power, by what Means soever he obtained it*; which in plain *English* is to say, 15 that Regal and Supreme Power is properly and truly his, who can by any Means seize upon it: and if this be, to be *properly a King*, I wonder how he came to think of, or where he will find, an *Usurper*.

80. This is so strange a Doctrine, that the surprize of it hath made me pass by, without their due Reflection, the Contradictions he runs into, by making sometimes *Inheritance* alone, sometimes only *Grant* or *Inheritance*, sometimes only *Inheritance* or *Usurpation*, sometimes all these three, and at last *Election*, or *any other means*, 5 added to them, the ways whereby *Adam's* Royal *Authority*, that is, his right to Supreme Rule, could be convey'd down to future Kings and Governors, so as to give them a Title to the Obedience and Subjection of the People. But these Contradictions lie so open, that the very reading of our *A*'s own Words, will discover 10

---

§ 79 1 '*Oliver*'—Oliver Cromwell. It may be worth noting that Filmer actually wrote his justification for obedience to usurpers under Cromwell, in particular his *Directions* (231–5). It is a little unsympathetic of Locke to reproach him perpetually with statements made under such necessity, especially since the only work he himself had actually published at this time was his poetic eulogy of Cromwell—see Introduction, 18; compare I, § 121, 12.

3 See *Cambridge Modern History* (1906), IV, 656–7. The revolt of Tommaso Aniello (Masaniello) in 1647 in Naples against the Spanish government became a symbol for mob rule all over Europe for the next few generations. In the Hilary Term 1682/3, for example, a poem was published in London entitled *Massinello, or a Satyr against the Association* (Wing, M 1043).

9 See Cervantes, *Don Quixote*, Part II, chapters 37, 38, 42, 45, etc. Locke possessed four editions, two in French and two in English.

them to any ordinary Underſtanding: and though what I have quoted out of him (with abundance more of the same Strain and Coherence which might be found in him) might well excuse me from any farther trouble in this Argument, yet having proposed
15 to my self, to examine the main parts of his Doctrine, I shall a little more particularly consider how *Inheritance*, *Grant*, *Usurpation* or *Election*, can any way make out Government in the World upon his Principles; or derive to any one a right of Empire, from this Regal Authority of *Adam*, had it been never so well proved,
20 that he had been Absolute Monarch, and Lord of the whole World.

Chap. IX.

Of Monarchy, by Inheritance from Adam.

81. THough it be never so plain that there ought to be Government in the World, nay should all Men be of our *A*——s mind, that Divine appointment had ordained it to be *Monarchical*, yet since Men cannot obey any thing, that cannot command, and
5 Ideas of Government in the Fancy, though never so perfect, though never so right, cannot give Laws, nor prescribe Rules to the Actions of Men; it would be of no behoof for the setling of Order, and Eſtablishment of Government in its Exercise and Use amongſt Men, unless there were a way also taught how to
10 know the Person, to whom it belonged to have this Power, and Exercise this Dominion over others. 'Tis in vain then to talk of Subjection and Obedience, without telling us whom we are to obey. For were I never so fully perswaded, that there ought to be Magiſtracy and Rule in the World, yet I am nevertheless at
15 Liberty ſtill, till it appears who is the Person that hath Right to my Obedience: since if there be no Marks to know him by, and diſtinguish him, that hath Right to Rule from other Men, it may be my self, as well as any other. And therefore though Submission to Government be every ones duty, yet since that signifies nothing
20 but submitting to the Direction and Laws of such Men, as have

Authority to Command, 'tis not enough to make a Man a Subject, to convince him that there is *Regal Power* in the World, but there must be ways of designing, and knowing the Person to whom this *Regal Power* of Right belongs, and a Man can never be oblig'd in Conscience to submit to any Power, unless he can be satisfied 25 who is the Person, who has a Right to Exercise that Power over him. If this were not so, there would be no distinction between Pirates and Lawful Princes, he that has Force is without any more ado to be obey'd, and Crowns and Scepters would become the Inheritance only of Violence and Rapine. Men too might as often 30 and as innocently change their Governours, as they do their Physicians, if the Person cannot be known, who has a right to direct me, and whose Prescriptions I am bound to follow. To settle therefore Mens Consciences under an Obligation to Obedience, 'tis necessary that they know not only that there is a Power 35 somewhere in the World, but the Person who by Right is vested with this Power over them.

82. How successful our *A——* has been in his attempts, to set up a *Monarchical Absolute Power* in *Adam*, the Reader may judge by what has been already said: but were that *Absolute Monarchy* as clear as our *A——* would desire it, as I presume it is the contrary, yet it could be of no use to the Government of 5 Mankind now in the World, unless he also make out these two things.

First, That this *Power of Adam* was not to end with him, but was upon his Decease conveyed intire to some other Person, and so on to Posterity.   10

Secondly, That the Princes and Rulers now on Earth, are possessed of this *Power of Adam*, by a right way of conveyance derived to them.

83. If the first of these fail, the *Power of Adam*, were it never so great, never so certain, will signifie nothing to the present Governments and Societies in the World, but we must seek out some other Original of Power for the Government of Politys then this of *Adam*, or else there will be none at all in the World. If the 5 latter fail, it will destroy the Authority of the present Governours, and absolve the People from Subjection to them, since they having no better a Claim then others to that Power, which is alone the Fountain of all Authority, can have no Title to Rule over them.

84. Our *A*—— having Fansied an Absolute Sovereignty in *Adam*, mentions several ways of its conveyance to Princes, that were to be his Successors, but that which he chiefly insiſts on, is, that of *Inheritance*, which occurs so often in his several Discourses, and I having in the foregoing Chapter quoted several of these passages, I shall not need here again to repeat them. This Sovereignty he erects, as has been said upon a double Foundation, *viz*. that of *Property*, and that of *Fatherhood*. One was the right he was supposed to have in all Creatures, a right to possess the Earth with the Beaſts, and other inferior Ranks of things in it for his Private use, exclusive of all other Men. The other was the Right he was supposed to have, to Rule and Govern Men, all the reſt of Mankind.

85. In both these Rights, there being supposed an exclusion of all other Men, it muſt be upon some Reason peculiar to *Adam*, that they muſt both be founded.

That of his *property* our *A.* supposes to arise from God's immediate *Donation*, *Gen*. 1. 28. and that of *Fatherhood* from the Act of *Begetting*: Now in all Inheritance, if the Heir succeed not to the reason, upon which his Father's Right was founded, he cannot succeed to the Right which followeth from it: For Example, *Adam* had a Right of Property in the Creatures, upon the *Donation* and *Grant* of God Almighty, who was Lord and Proprietor of them all, let this be so as our *A*—— tells us, yet upon his Death his Heir can have no Title to them, no such right of Property in them, unless the same reason, *viz*. God's *Donation*, veſted a right in the *Heir* too. For if *Adam* could have had no Property in, nor use of, the Creatures without this positive *Donation* from God, and this *Donation*, were only personally to *Adam*, his *Heir* could have no right by it, but upon his death, it muſt revert to God the Lord and Owner again: for positive Grants give no Title farther than the express words convey it, and by which only it is held. And thus, if as our *A*—— himself contends, that *Donation*, *Gen*. 1. 28. were made only to *Adam* personally his Heir could not suceed to his property in the Creatures; and if it were a Donation to any but *Adam*, let it be shewn, that it was to his Heir in our *A*'s Sense, *i.e.* to one of his Children exclusive of all the reſt.

86. But not to follow our *A*—— too far out of the way, the plain of the Case is this. God having made Man, and planted in

him, as in all other Animals, a strong desire of Self-preservation,
and furnished the World with things fit for Food and Rayment and
other Necessaries of Life, Subservient to his design, that Man   5
should live and abide for some time upon the Face of the Earth,
and not that so curious and wonderful a piece of Workmanship
by its own Negligence, or want of Necessaries, should perish
again, presently after a few moments continuance: God, I say,
having made Man and the World thus, spoke to him, (that is)   10
directed him by his Senses and Reason, as he did the inferior
Animals by their Sense, and Instinct, which he had placed in
them to that purpose, to the use of those things, which were
serviceable for his Subsistence, and given him as means of his
Preservation. And therefore I doubt not, but before these words   15
were pronounced, 1 *Gen.* 28, 29. (if they must be understood
Literally to have been spoken) and without any such Verbal
Donation, Man had a right to a use of the Creatures, by the Will
and Grant of God. For the desire, strong desire of Preserving
his Life and Being having been Planted in him, as a Principle of   20
Action by God himself, Reason, *which was the Voice of God in him,*
could not but teach him and assure him, that pursuing that natural
Inclination he had to preserve his Being, he followed the Will
of his Maker, and therefore had a right to make use of those
Creatures, which by his Reason or Senses he could discover would   25
be serviceable thereunto. And thus Man's *Property* in the Creatures,
was founded upon the right he had, to make use of those things,
that were necessary or useful to his Being.

---

§ **86**   7   'Workmanship'—see note on 1, § 52, and references.

19–21   These lines raise a number of important problems in Locke's political
theory in relation to his philosophy (see Introduction, section IV, 2). Preservation,
of oneself and all mankind, is a natural law for Locke, perhaps the natural law, here
presented as 'a Principle of Action' planted by God in man. This would seem to
contradict chapter III of Book I of his *Essay,* headed 'No Innate Practical Principles',
but the language here is very close to the exception he makes (Nidditch, ed., 1975, 67) for the
'desire for happiness' an 'innate practical principle', see Yolton, 1956. 'Reason' as '*the voice of
God*' is a famous neoplatonism, see II, § 56, 5 and Locke's *Reasonableness* (1695) where reason is
called 'a spark of the divine nature', 'the candle of the Lord' (*Works,* 1801, VII, 133), and on
reason generally, see Polin, 1960, 25 etc.

19–28   This, and the following paragraph, state Locke's ultimate justification of
property, here typified by property in animals; see Introduction, 101. Compare
II, § 30, 1–4, where the labour theory is called the 'Law of reason', and compare and
contrast his eighth *Essay on the Law of Nature* where possession of private property
(*res sua, res privata*) is said to be protected by the law of nature (Von Leyden, 1954,
206–7).

87. This being the Reason and Foundation of *Adams Property* gave the same Title, on the same Ground, to all his Children, not only after his death, but in his life time: So that here was no Priviledge of his *Heir* above his other Children, which could exclude them from an equal Right to the use of the inferior Creatures, for the comfortable preservation of their Beings, which is all the *Property* Man hath in them: and so *Adams* Sovereignty built on *property*, or as our *A.* calls it, *Private Dominion* comes to nothing. Every Man had a right to the Creatures, by the same Title *Adam* had, *viz.* by the right every one had to take care of, and provide for their Subsistence: and thus Men had a right in common, *Adams* Children in common with him. But if any one had began, and made himself a Property in any particular thing, (which how he, or any one else, could do, shall be shewn in another place) that thing, that possession, if he dispos'd not otherwise of it by his positive Grant, descended Naturally to his Children, and they had a right to succeed to it, and possess it.

88. It might reasonably be asked here, how come Children by this right of possessing, before any other, the properties of their Parents upon their Decease. For it being Personally the Parents, when they dye, without actually Transferring their Right to another, why does it not return again to the common stock of Mankind? 'Twill perhaps be answered, that common consent hath disposed of it, to the Children. Common Practice, we see indeed does so dispose of it but we cannot say, that it is the common consent of Mankind; for that hath never been asked, nor actually given: and if common tacit Consent hath establish'd it, it would make but a positive and not Natural Right of Children to Inherit the Goods of their Parents: But where the Practice is Universal, 'tis reasonable to think the Cause is Natural. The ground then, I think, to be this. The first and strongest desire God Planted in Men, and wrought into the very Principles of their Nature being that of Self-preservation, that is the Foundation of a right to the Creatures, for the particular support and use of each individual Person himself. But next to this, God Planted in Men a strong desire also of propagating their Kind, and continuing themselves in their Posterity, and this gives Children

---

§ 87 14–15 A clear cross-reference to the fifth chapter of the *Second Treatise*, see Introduction, 50, 61–2.

a Title, to share in the *Property* of their Parents, and a Right to Inherit their Possessions. Men are not Proprietors of what they have meerly for themselves, their Children have a Title to part of it, and have their Kind of Right joyn'd with their Parents, in the Possession which comes to be wholly theirs, when death having put an end to their Parents use of it, hath taken them from their Possessions, and this we call Inheritance. Men being by a like Obligation bound to preserve what they have begotten, as to preserve themselves, their issue come to have a Right in the Goods they are possessed of. That Children have such a Right is plain from the Laws of God, and that Men are convinced, that Children have such a Right, is evident from the Law of the Land, both which Laws require Parents to provide for their Children.

89. For Children being by the course of Nature, born weak, and unable to provide for themselves, they have by the appointment of God himself, who hath thus ordered the course of nature, a Right to be nourish'd and maintained by their Parents, nay a right not only to a bare Subsistance but to the conveniences and comforts of Life, as far as the conditions of their Parents can afford it. Hence it comes, that when their Parents leave the World, and so the care due to their Children ceases, the effects of it are to extend as far as possibly they can, and the Provisions they have made in their Life time, are understood to be intended as nature requires they should, for their Children, whom after themselves, they are bound to provide for, though the dying Parents, by express Words, declare nothing about them, nature appoints the descent of their Property to their Children, who thus come to have a Title, and natural Right of Inheritance to their Fathers Goods, which the rest of Mankind cannot pretend to.

90. Were it not for this Right of being Nourished, and Maintained by their Parents, which God and Nature has given to

---

§ 90   Interesting as a statement of Locke's view of the ethical relationships between generations: compare Laslett, 1977. Viner, 1963, cites it for Locke's distinction between property as a general category, which could include 'Reverence, . . . Respect and Honour' and property specifically defined as 'Possessions and commodities of Life valuable by Money'. Contrast II, § 87, 5, note and references.

29–31   Locke seems clearly to have in mind the 'Municipal Laws' of his own country (compare II, § 205, 1), which direct that land ('Estate') cannot be inherited by a man's father, or anyone in the ascending line, though this is not true of goods.

Children, and obliged Parents to, as a Duty, it would be reasonable, that the Father should Inherit the Estate of his Son, and be
5 preferr'd in the Inheritance before his Grand Child. For to the Grand Father, there is due a long Score of Care and Expences laid out upon the Breeding and Education of his Son, which one would think in Justice ought to be paid. But that having been done in Obedience to the same Law, whereby he received Nourish-
10 ment and Education from his own Parents, this Score of Education received from a Man's Father, is paid by taking care, and providing for his own Children; is paid, I say, as much as is requir'd of Payment by Alteration of Property, unless present necessity of the Parents require a return of Goods for their necessary
15 Support and Subsistence. For we are not now speaking of that Reverence, Acknowledgment, Respect and Honour that is always due from Children to their Parents, but of Possessions and Commodities of Life valuable by Money. But tho' it be incumbent on parents to bring up and provide for their children, yet this
20 Debt to the Children does not quite cancel the Score due to the Parents, but only is made by Nature preferable to it. For the Debt a Man owes his Father, takes place, and gives the Father a Right to Inherit the Sons Goods, where for want of Issue, the Right of Children doth not exclude that Title. And therefore
25 a Man having a Right to be maintain'd by his Children where he needs it, and to enjoy also the comforts of Life from them, when the necessary Provision due to them, and their Children will afford it, if his Son dye without Issue, the Father has a Right in Nature to possess his Goods, and Inherit his Estate (whatever
30 the Municipal Laws of some Countries, may absurdly direct otherwise,) and so again his Children and their Issue from him, or for want of such, his Father and his Issue. But where no such are to be found, *i.e.* no Kindred, there we see the Possessions of a Private Man revert to the Community, and so in Politic Societies
35 come into the Hands of the Public Magistrate: but in the State of Nature become again perfectly common, no body having a right to Inherit them: nor can any one have a Property in them, otherwise then in other things common by Nature, of which I shall speak in its due place.

See Holdsworth, *History of English Law*, 1923, II, 171–85, especially p. 175, and compare I, § 123, 11–12, and II, § 12, 16. In this discussion, and in I, § 89 also, Locke may have in mind Grotius, 1625, III, iii.

38–9   A cross-reference to chapter v of the *Second Treatise*, see I, § 87, 14–15 and reference.

91. I have been the larger in shewing upon what ground Children have a Right to succeed to the Possession of their Fathers Properties, not only because by it, it will appear, that if *Adam* had a Property (a Titular insignificant useless Property; for it could be no better, for he was bound to Nourish and Maintain 5 his Children and Posterity out of it) in the whole Earth and its Product, yet all his Children coming to have by the Law of Nature and Right of Inheritance a joynt Title, and Right of Property in it after his Death, it could convey no Right of Sovereignty to any one of his Posterity over the rest: Since every 10 one having a Right of Inheritance to his Portion, they might enjoy their Inheritance, or any part of it in common, or share it, or some parts of it by Division, as it best liked them. But no one could pretend to the whole Inheritance, or any Sovereignty supposed to accompany it, since a Right of Inheritance gave every 15 one of the rest, as well as any one, a Title to share in the Goods of his Father. Not only upon this Account, I say, have I been so particular in examining the Reason of Childrens inheriting the Property of their Fathers, but also because it will give us farther Light in the Inheritance of *Rule* and *Power*, which in Countries 20 where their particular Municipal Laws give the whole Possession of Land entirely to the First Born, and Descent of Power has gone so to Men by this Custom, some have been apt to be deceived into an Opinion, that there was a Natural or Divine Right of Primogeniture, to both *Estate* and *Power*; and that the Inheritance 25 of both *Rule* over Men and *Property* in things, sprang from the same Original, and were to descend by the same Rules.

92. Property, whose Original is from the Right a Man has to use any of the Inferior Creatures, for the Subsistence and Comfort of his Life, is for the benefit and sole Advantage of the Proprietor, so that he may even destroy the thing, that he has Property in by his use of it, where need requires: but Government being for 5 the Preservation of every Mans Right and Property, by preserving him from the Violence or Injury of others, is for the good of the

---

§ **91**   21   Locke obviously has the English Common Law in mind here also; compare 1, § 90, 29–31 and note, 1, § 37, 3.
§ **92**   1–3   Here Locke assimilates all property to rights over animals, justified in 1, § 86: see lines 9–18 of that paragraph, and 11, § 6, 18–19 and note.
   5–6   A major theme of the *Second Treatise*; see, for example, 11, § 124, 1–3.

Governed. For the Magistrates Sword being for a *Terror to Evil Doers*, and by that Terror to inforce Men to observe the positive
10 Laws of the Society, made conformable to the Laws of Nature, for the public good, *i.e.* the good of every particular Member of that Society, as far as by common Rules, it can be provided for; the Sword is not given the Magistrate for his own good alone.

93. Children therefore, as has been shew'd, by the dependance they have on their Parents for Subsistence, have a Right of Inheritance to their Fathers Property, as that which belongs to them for their proper good and behoof, and therefore are fitly
5 termed Goods, wherein the First Born has not a sole or peculiar Right by any Law of God and Nature, the younger Children having an equal Title with him founded on that Right they all have to maintenance, support and comfort from their Parents, and nothing else. But Government being for the benefit of the
10 Governed, and not the sole advantage of the Governors (but only for theirs with the rest, as they make a part of that Politick Body, each of whose parts and Members are taken care of, and directed in its peculiar Functions for the good of the whole, by the Laws of the Society) cannot be inherited by the same Title
15 that Children have to the Goods of their Father. The Right a Son has to be maintained and provided with the necessaries and conveniences of Life out of his Fathers Stock, gives him a Right to succeed to his Fathers *Property* for his own good, but this can give him no Right to succeed also to the *Rule*, which his Father
20 had over other Men. All that a Child has Right to claim from his Father is Nourishment and Education, and the things nature furnishes for the support of Life: But he has no Right to demand *Rule* or *Dominion* from him: He can subsist and receive from him the Portion of good things, and advantages of Education naturally
25 due to him, without *Empire* and *Dominion*. That (if his Father hath any) was vested in him, for the good and behoof of others, and therefore the Son cannot Claim or Inherit it by a Title, which is founded wholly on his own private good and advantage.

---

§ **92** 8–9, 13 Phrases from the famous thirteenth chapter of Romans, verses 3–4: 'For rulers are not a terror to good works, but to evil...for he beareth not the sword in vain.'

94. We must know how the first Ruler, from whom any one claims, came by his Authority, upon what ground any one has *Empire*, what his Title is to it, before we can know who has a right to succeed him in it, and inherit it from him. If the Agreement and consent of Men first gave a Scepter into any ones 5 hand, or put a Crown on his Head, that also must direct its descent and conveyance. For the same Authority, that made the first a Lawful *Ruler*, must make the Second too, and so give Right of Succession: in this Case Inheritance or Primogeniture, can in its self have no Right, no pretence to it, any farther then that 10 Consent, which Established the Form of the Government, hath so settled the Succession. And thus we see the Succession of Crowns, in several Countries places it on different Heads, and he comes by Right of Succession, to be a Prince in one place, who would be a Subject in another. 15

95. If God by his positive Grant and revealed Declaration, first gave *Rule* and *Dominion* to any man, he that will Claim by that Title, must have the same positive Grant of God for his Succession. For if that has not directed the Course of its descent and conveyance down to others, no body can succeed to this 5 Title of the first Ruler; Children have no Right of Inheritance to this; and Primogeniture can lay no Claim to it, unless God the Author of this Constitution hath so ordained it. Thus we see the pretensions of *Sauls* Family, who received his Crown from the immediate Appointment of God, ended with his Reign; and 10 *David* by the same Title that *Saul* Reigned, *viz.* Gods Appointment, succeeded in his Throne, to the exclusion of *Jonathan*, and all pretentions of Paternal Inheritance. And if *Salomon* had a Right to Succeed his Father, it must be by some other Title, then that of Primogeniture. A *Cadet*, or Sisters Son, must have the Preference 15 in Succession, if he has the same Title the first Lawful Prince had: and in Dominion that has its Foundation only in the positive appointment of God himself, *Benjamin* the youngest, must have the Inheritance of the Crown, if God so direct as well as one of that Tribe had the first possession. 20

---

§ 95 15–20 This passage may mark §§ 93, 94, 95 (wholly or partially) as an insertion of 1689. William was a 'Cadet, or Sister's Son' with respect to the English Royal line, his mother being a sister of Charles II and James II. If this is the intention, William's claim is upheld as on a level with that of 'the first Lawful Prince'. Compare the Preface, line 6 and Lamprecht, 1918, 140.

96. *If Paternal Right*, the Act of *Begetting*, give a Man *Rule* and *Dominion*, Inheritance or Primogeniture can give no Title. For he that cannot succeed to his Fathers Title, which was *Begetting*, cannot succeed to that Power over his Brethren, which his Father had by Paternal Right over them. But of this I shall have occasion to say more in another place. This is plain in the mean time, that any Government, whether supposed to be at first founded in *Paternal Right, Consent of the People*, or the *positive Appointment of God himself*, which can supersede either of the other, and so begin a new Government upon a new Foundation, I say, any Government began upon either of these, can by Right of Succession come to those only, who have the Title of him, they succeed to. Power founded on *Contract*, can descend only to him, who has Right by that Contract: Power founded on *Begetting*, he only can have that *Begets*: And Power founded on the positive *Grant* or Donation of God, he only can have by Right of Succession, to whom that Grant directs it.

97. From what I have said, I think this is clear, that a Right to the use of the Creatures, being founded Originally in the Right a Man has to subsist and enjoy the conveniences of Life, and the natural Right Children have to inherit the Goods of their Parents, being founded in the Right they have to the same Subsistence and Commodities of Life, out of the Stock of their Parents, who are therefore taught by Natural Love and Tenderness to provide for them, as a part of themselves: and all this being only for the good of the Proprietor, or Heir; it can be no Reason for Childrens Inheriting of *Rule* and *Dominion*, which has another Original and a different end. Nor can Primogeniture have any Pretence to a Right of solely Inheriting either *Property* or *Power*, as we shall, in its due place, see more fully. 'Tis enough to have shew'd here, that *Adam*'s *Property*, or *Private Dominion*, could not convey any Sovereignty or Rule to his Heir, who not having a Right to inherit

---

§ 96   6   'in another place'—this reads 'bye and bye' in the 1st edition. It seems to refer, then, to a later part of the *First Treatise*, and not to the *Second*, for chapter VI there, 'Of Paternal Power', contains no specific discussion of the political rights of an eldest brother. The most likely area of the text is 1, §§ 110–19, though it is just conceivable that Locke intended some part of the lost portion.
§ 97   1–3   See 1, § 92, 1–3, note and references.
   12–13   Compare note on 1, § 96, 6, though here the reference seems probably to be to 1, § 111 on.

all his Fathers Possessions, could not thereby come to have any Sovereignty over his Brethren: and therefore if any Sovereignty on account of his *Property*, had been veſted in *Adam*, which in Truth there was not; yet it would have Died with him.

98. As *Adam*'s Sovereignty, if by vertue of being Proprietor of the whole World, he had any Authority over Men, could not have been inherited by any of his Children over the reſt, because they had the same Title to divide the Inheritance, and every one had a Right to a Portion of his Fathers Possessions: So neither 5 could *Adam*'s Sovereignty by Right of *Fatherhood*, if any such he had, descend to any one of his Children. For it being in our *A*'s Account, a Right acquired by *Begetting* to Rule over those he had begotten, it was not a Power Possible to be Inherited, because the Right being consequent to, and built on, an Aƈ perfeƈly Personal, 10 made that Power ſo too, and impossible to be Inherited. For Paternal Power, being a Natural Right rising only from the relation of Father and Son, is as impossible to be Inherited as the Relation itself, and a Man may pretend as well to Inherit the Conjugal Power the Husband, whose Heir he is, had over his 15 Wife, as he can to Inherit the Paternal Power of a Father over his Children. For the Power of the Husband being founded on Contraƈ, and the Power of the Father on *Begetting*, he may as well Inherit the Power obtained by the conjugal contraƈ, which was only Personal, as he may the Power obtained by Begetting, 20 which could reach no farther then the Person of the Begetter, unless Begetting can be a Title to Power in him, that does not beget.

99. Which makes it a reasonable queſtion to ask, Whether *Adam*, dying before *Eve*, his Heir (suppose *Cain* or *Seth*) should have had, by Right of Inheriting *Adam's Fatherhood*, Sovereign Power over *Eve* his Mother. For *Adam's Fatherhood* being nothing but a Right he had to Govern his Children, because he begot them, 5 he that inherits *Adam's Fatherhood*, inherits nothing, even in our *A*'s Sense, but the Right *Adam* had to Govern his Children, because he begot them: So that the Monarchy of the Heir would not have taken in *Eve*, or if it did, it being nothing but the *Fatherhood of Adam* descended by inheritance, the Heir muſt have 10 Right to Govern *Eve*, because *Adam* begot her; for *Fatherhood* is nothing else.

100. Perhaps it will be said with our *A*—— [231], that a Man can alien his Power over his Child, and what may be transfer'd by compact, may be possessed by Inheritance. I answer, a Father cannot alien the Power he has over his Child, he may perhaps to some degrees forfeit it, but cannot transfer it: and if any other Man acquire it, 'tis not by the Fathers Grant, but by some Act of his own. For Example, a Father, unnaturally careless of his Child, sells or gives him to another Man; and he again exposes him: a third Man finding him, breeds up, cherishes and provides for him as his own. I think in this Case, no body will doubt but that the greatest part of filial Duty and Subjection was here owing, and to be paid to this Foster-Father: and if any thing could be demanded from the Child, by either of the other, it could be only due to his Natural Father: who perhaps might have forfeited his Right to much of that Duty comprehended in the Command, *Honour your Parents*, but could transfer none of it to another. He that purchased, and neglected, the Child, got by his Purchase and Grant of the Father, no Title to Duty or Honour from the Child, but only he acquired it, who by his own Authority, performing the Office and Care of a Father, to the forlorn and Perishing Infant, made himself by Paternal Care, a Title to proportionable Degrees of Paternal Power. This will be more easily admitted upon Consideration of the Nature of Paternal Power, for which I refer my Reader to the Second Book.

101. To return to the Argument in hand: This is evident, That Paternal Power arising only from *Begetting*, for in that our *A.* places it alone, can neither be *transfer'd*, nor *inherited*: And he that does not beget, can no more have Paternal Power which arises from thence, than he can have a Right to any thing who performs not the Condition, to which only it is annexed. If one should ask, By what Law has a Father Power over his Children? It will be answered, no doubt, by the Law of Nature, which gives such a Power over them, to him that begets them. If one should

---

§ 100   7–10   Compare II, § 65, 5–7 and Tyrrell, 1681, 16. The whole discussion of the rights of fathers, foster-fathers and so on springing from their duty of *educating* children is very similar in Locke and Tyrrell, and may have a common source in Grotius, who denies that the *jus paternum* can be entirely alienated (1625, II, v, 26), though in section 5 he admits that under certain conditions a child can be pledged or sold.

23–4   This is the only reference in the *First Treatise* to the *Second Treatise* by name and it is very significant that it is called the second *Book*, not *Treatise*. See the Introduction, 50.

ask likewise, By what Law does our *A*'s Heir come by a Right   10
to Inherit? I think it would be answered, By the Law of Nature
too. For I find not that our *A*. brings one word of Scripture to
prove the Right of such an Heir he speaks of: Why then the Law
of Nature gives Fathers Paternal Power over their Children,
because they did *beget* them, and the same Law of Nature gives the   15
same Paternal Power to the Heir over his Brethren, who did not
beget them: whence it follows, that either the Father has not his
Paternal Power by begetting, or else that the Heir has it not at all:
For 'tis hard to underſtand how the Law of Nature, which is the
Law of Reason, can give the Paternal Power to the Father over   20
his Children, for the only Reason of *Begetting*, and to the firſt-born
over his Brethren without this only Reason, *i.e.* for no Reason
at all: and if the Eldeſt, by the Law of Nature, can inherit this
Paternal Power, without the only Reason that gives a Title to it,
so may the Youngeſt as well as he, and a Stranger as well as   25
either; for where there is no Reason for any one, as there is not,
but for him that begets, all have an equal Title. I am sure our *A*.
offers no Reason, and when any body does, we shall see whether
it will hold or no.

102. In the mean time 'tis as good Sense to say, that by the
Law of Nature a Man has Right to inherit the Property of another,
because he is of Kin to him, and is known to be of his Blood,
and therefore by the same Law of Nature, an utter Stranger to
his Blood, has Right to inherit his Eſtate: As to say that by the   5
Law of Nature he that begets them, has Paternal Power over his
Children, and therefore by the Law of Nature the Heir that
begets them not, has this Paternal Power over them: or supposing
the Law of the Land gave Absolute Power over their Children,
to such only who nursed them, and fed their Children themselves,   10
could any body pretend that this Law gave any one, who did no
such thing, Absolute Power over those, who were not his Children?

103. When therefore it can be shew'd, that conjugal Power
can belong to him that is not an Husband, it will also I believe be
proved, that our A——'s Paternal Power acquired by begetting,
may be inherited by a Son, and that a Brother as Heir to his
Fathers Power, may have Paternal Power over his Brethren, and   5
by the same Rule conjugal Power too, but till then, I think we
may reſt satisfied, that the Paternal Power of *Adam*, this Sovereign

Authority of *Fatherhood*, were there any such, could not descend to, nor be inherited by, his next Heir. *Fatherly Power* I easily grant our A—— if it will do him any good, can never be lost, because it will be as long in the World as there are Fathers: but none of them will have *Adam*'s Paternal Power, or derive theirs from him, but every one will have his own, by the same Title *Adam* had his, *viz.* by *Begetting*, but not by Inheritance or Succession, no more then Husbands have their conjugal Power by Inheritance from *Adam*. And thus we see as *Adam* had no such *Property*, no such *Paternal Power*, as gave him *Sovereign* Jurisdiction over Mankind; so likewise his Sovereignty built upon either of these Titles, if he had any such, could not have descended to his Heir, but must have ended with him. *Adam* therefore, as has been proved, being neither Monarch, nor his imaginary Monarchy hereditable, the Power which is now in the World, is not that which was *Adam*'s, since all that *Adam* could have upon our *A*'s grounds, either of *Property* or *Fatherhood*, necessarily Died with him, and could not be convey'd to Posterity by Inheritance. In the next place we will consider whether *Adam* had any such Heir, to inherit his Power, as our *A*. talks of.

CHAP. X.

Of the Heir to Adam's *Monarchical Power.*

104. OUR *A*. tells us, *O*. 253. [288, 289] *That it is a truth undeniable, that there cannot be any Multitude of Men whatsoever, either great or small, tho' gathered together from the several corners and remotest Regions of the World, but that in the same Multitude considered by its self, there is one Man amongst them, that in Nature hath a Right to be King of all the rest, as being the next Heir to* Adam, *and all the other Subject to him, every Man by Nature is a King or a Subject.* And again, p. 20. [61] *If* Adam *himself were still living, and now ready to die, it is certain that there is one Man, and but one in the World who is next Heir.* Let this *Multitude of Men* be, if our *A*. pleases, all the Princes upon the Earth, there will then be by our

A's Rule, *one amongst them, that in Nature hath a Right to be King of all the rest, as being the Right Heir to* Adam; an excellent way to Establish the Thrones of Princes, and settle the Obedience of their Subjects, by setting up an Hundred, or perhaps a Thousand 15 Titles (if there be so many Princes in the World) against any King now Reigning, each as good upon our *A*'s Grounds, as his who wears the Crown. If this Right of *Heir* carry any weight with it, if it be the *Ordinance of God,* as our *A.* seems to tell us, O. 244. [283] must not all be subject to it, from the highest to the lowest? Can 20 those who wear the Name of Princes, without having the Right of being *Heirs to* Adam, demand Obedience from their Subjects by this Title, and not be bound to pay it by the same Law? Either Governments in the World are not to be claim'd and held by this Title of *Adam*'s Heir, and then the starting of it is to no 25 purpose, the being or not being *Adam*'s Heir signifies nothing as to the Title of Dominion; or if it really be, as our *A.* says, the true Title to Government and Sovereignty, the first thing to be done, is to find out this true Heir of *Adam,* seat him in his Throne, and then all the Kings and Princes of the World ought to come 30 and resign up their Crowns and Scepters to him, as things that belong no more to them, than to any of their Subjects.

105. For either this Right in Nature, of *Adam*'s Heir, to be King over all the race of Men, (for altogether they make one *Multitude*) is a Right not necessary to the making of a Lawful King, and so there may be Lawful Kings without it, and then Kings Titles and Power depend not on it, or else all the Kings 5 in the World but one are not Lawful Kings, and so have no Right to Obedience: Either this Title of Heir to *Adam* is that whereby Kings hold their Crowns, and have a Right to Subjection from

---

§ 105   On the argument of this paragraph, compare Sidney, *Discourses,* I, 12, 24–5. Compare *First Treatise,* § 81, 24–7; § 110, 11; § 119, 32; § 120, 2; § 122. 2; § 125, 10; § 126, 28. In all these contexts the issue of conscience and government is confined to the straightforward question of recognizing who it is that the citizen must obey, and all the more complex and difficult discussion, so important to Locke's predecessors and his own generation, is left on one side. This is in marked contrast with such writers as Pufendorf, even with the younger Locke himself, for in his Latin essay on the civil magistrate he had put forward quite complicated arguments about conscience and obligation. Even in the notes he made on Filmer in 1679 (see Introduction, 58) 'resolving the conscience' was a point he picked upon. There are three further references in the *Second Treatise* (§ 8, 5; § 21, 23; § 209, 5) but little is added by them: conscience is neither defined nor discussed in this book, compare Introduction, 84.

their Subjects, and then one only can have it, and the rest being
10 Subjects can require no Obedience from other Men, who are but
their fellow Subjects, or else it is not the Title whereby Kings
Rule, and have a Right to Obedience from their Subjects, and
then Kings are Kings without it, and this Dream of the Natural
Sovereignty of *Adam*'s Heir is of no use to Obedience and
15 Government. For if Kings have a Right to Dominion, and the
Obedience of their Subjects, who are not, nor can possibly be,
Heirs to *Adam*, what use is there of such a Title, when we are
obliged to Obey without it? If Kings, who are not Heirs to *Adam*,
have no Right to Sovereignty, we are all free till our *A.* or any
20 body for him, will shew us *Adam*'s right Heir. If there be but
one Heir of *Adam*, there can be but one Lawful King in the
World, and no body in Conscience can be obliged to Obedience
till it be resolved who that is; for it may be any one who is not
known to be of a Younger House, and all others have equal
25 Titles. If there be more than one Heir of *Adam*, every one is
his Heir, and so every one has Regal Power. For if two Sons can
be Heirs together, then all the Sons are equally Heirs, and so
all are Heirs, being all Sons, or Sons Sons of *Adam*. Betwixt
these two the Right of Heir cannot stand: for by it either but one
30 only Man, or all Men are Kings. Take which you please, it
dissolves the Bonds of Government and Obedience: since if all
Men are Heirs, they can owe Obedience to no body; if only one,
no body can be obliged to pay Obedience to him, till he be known
and his Title made out.

Chap. XI.

Who HEIR?

106. THE great Question which in all Ages has disturbed
Mankind, and brought on them the greatest part of those
Mischiefs which have ruin'd Cities, depopulated Countries, and
disordered the Peace of the World, has been, Not whether there
5 be Power in the World, nor whence it came, but who should

have it. The settling of this point being of no smaller moment than the security of Princes, and the peace and welfare of their Estates and Kingdoms, a Reformer of Politicks, one would think, should lay this sure, and be very clear in it. For if this remain disputable, all the rest will be to very little purpose; and the skill 10 used in dressing up Power with all the Splendor and Temptation Absoluteness can add to it, without shewing who has a Right to have it, will serve only to give a greater edge to Man's Natural Ambition, which of it self is but too keen. What can this do but set Men on the more eagerly to scramble, and so lay a sure and 15 lasting Foundation of endless Contention and Disorder, instead of that Peace and Tranquility, which is the business of Government, and the end of Humane Society?

107. This Designation of the person our *A.* is more than ordinarily obliged to take care of, because he, affirming that *the Assignment of Civil Power is by Divine Institution*, hath made the Conveyance as well as the Power it self Sacred: so that no Consideration, no Act or Art of Man can divert it from that Person, 5 to whom by this Divine Right, it is assigned, no Necessity or Contrivance can substitute another Person in his room. For if the *Assignment of Civil Power be by Divine Institution*; and *Adam's Heir* be he, to whom it is thus Assigned, as in the foregoing Chapter our *A.* tells us, it would be as much Sacriledge for any 10 one to be King, who was not *Adam's* Heir, as it would have been amongst the *Jews*, for any one to have been *Priest*, who had not been of *Aarons* Posterity: For *not only* the Priesthood *in general being by Divine Institution, but the Assignment of it* to the Sole Line and Posterity of *Aaron*, made it impossible to be enjoy'd or exercised 15 by any one, but those Persons, who are the Off-spring of *Aaron*: whose Succession therefore was carefully observed, and by that the Persons who had a Right to the Priesthood certainly known.

108. Let us see then what care our *A.* has taken, to make us know who is this *Heir*, who *by Divine Institution, has a right to be*

---

§ **107**   8   At this point ends a passage covering five pages in the 1st edition (133–7 of its pages, beginning at § 104) minutely corrected by Locke for the 2nd.

9–10   This cannot refer to a foregoing chapter of *Patriarcha*, since Locke has only discussed the first chapter, and in his text as we have it he never goes further. It must then intend Locke's own previous chapter, chapter x. This reference is the result of a correction for the 2nd edition, 1694.

King over all Men. The firſt account of him we meet with is
p. 12. [57] in these words: *This Subjection of Children, being the*
Fountain of all Regal Authority, by the Ordination of God himself;
it follows, that Civil Power not only in general, is by Divine Inſtitution,
but even the Assignment of it specifically to the Eldeſt Parents. Matters
of such Consequence as this is, should be in plain words, as little
liable as might be to Doubt or Equivocation; and I think if
Language be capable of expressing any thing diſtinctly and clearly,
that of Kindred, and the several Degrees of nearness of Blood, is
one. It were therefore to be wish'd, that our *A.* had used a little
more intelligible Expressions here, that we might have better
known who it is, to whom the *Assignment of Civil Power* is made
by *Divine Inſtitution,* or at leaſt would have told us what he meant
by *Eldeſt Parents.* For I believe if Land had been Assigned or
Granted to him, and the *Eldeſt Parents* of his Family, he would
have thought it had needed an Interpreter, and 'twould scarce
have been known to whom next it belong'd.

109. In propriety of Speech, and certainly Propriety of Speech
is necessary in a Discourse of this Nature, *Eldeſt Parents* signifies
either the Eldeſt Men and Women that have had Children, or
those who have longeſt had Issue: and then our *A*'s Assertion
will be, That those Fathers and Mothers who have been longeſt
in the World, or longeſt Fruitful, have by *Divine Inſtitution* a Right
to *Civil Power.* If there be any Absurdity in this, our *A.* muſt
answer for it: and if his Meaning be different from my Explication,
he is to be blam'd, that he would not speak it plainly. This I am
sure, *Parents* cannot signifie Heirs Male, nor *Eldeſt Parents* an
Infant Child: who yet may sometimes be the true Heir, if there
can be but one. And we are hereby ſtill as much at a loss, who
Civil Power belongs to, notwithſtanding this *Assignment by Divine*
Inſtitution, as if there had been no such *Assignment* at all, or our
A. had said nothing of it. This of *Eldeſt Parents* leaving us more
in the dark, who by *Divine Inſtitution* has a Right to *Civil Power,*
than those who never heard any thing at all of *Heir,* or descent,
of which our *A.* is so full. And though the chief matter of his
Writings be to teach Obedience to those who have a Right to it,
which he tells us is conveyed by descent, yet who those are to

---

§ **109** 1–2 On this and`1, § 108 compare 1, § 23, 22–5 and note.

whom this Right by descent belongs, he leaves like the Philosophers Stone in Politicks, out of the reach of any one to discover from his Writings.

110. This obscurity cannot be imputed to want of Language in so great a Master of Style as Sir *Robert* is, when he is resolved with himself what he would say: and therefore, I fear, finding how hard it would be to settle Rules of descent by Divine Institution, and how little it would be to his purpose, or conduce to ₅ the clearing and establishing the Titles of Princes, if such Rules of descent were settled, he chose rather to content himself with doubtful and general terms, which might make no ill sound in Mens Ears, who were willing to be pleas'd with them, rather than offer any clear Rules of descent of this *Fatherhood* of *Adam*, by 10 which Mens Consciences might be satisfied to whom it descended, and know the Persons who had a Right to Regal Power, and with it to their Obedience.

111. How else is it possible, that laying so much stress as he does upon *descent*, and *Adam*'s *Heir, next Heir, true Heir*, he should never tell us what *Heir* means, nor the way to know who the *next* or *true Heir* is. This I do not remember he does any where expresly handle, but where it comes in his way very warily ₅ and doubtfully touches: though it be so necessary that without it all Discourses of Government and Obedience upon his Principles would be to no purpose, and *Fatherly Power*, never so well made out, will be of no use to any body. Hence he tells us, *O.* 244. [283] *That not only the Constitution of Power in general, but* 10 *the limitation of it to one kind,* (i.e.) *Monarchy and the Determination of it to the individual Person and Line of* Adam, *are all three Ordinances of God, neither* Eve *nor her Children could either limit* Adam's *Power, or joyn others with him*; *and what was given unto* Adam *was given in his Person to his Posterity.* Here again our *A.* informs us, that the 15 *Divine Ordinance* hath limited the descent of *Adam*'s Monarchical Power. To whom? *To* Adam's *Line and Posterity*, says our *A.*

---

§ 109   21–2   'the Philosophers Stone', the substance capable of changing baser material into gold or silver, the supreme object of alchemy. For all his rationalistic contempt of Filmer, Locke was interested in alchemy, and it is a remarkable fact that Robert Boyle left to Locke and Newton a recipe for increasing gold, which Locke seems to have worked at. See Cranston, 1957.

A notable *Limitation*, a *Limitation* to all Mankind. For if our *A.* can find any one amongst Mankind that is not of the *Line* and 20 *Posterity* of *Adam*, he may perhaps tell him who this next Heir of *Adam* is: But for us, I despair how this *Limitation* of *Adam*'s Empire to his *Line* and *Posterity* will help us to find out *one Heir*. This *Limitation* indeed of our *A.* will save those the labour who would look for him amongst the Race of Bruits, if any such there 25 were; but will very little contribute to the discovery of *one next Heir* amongst Men, though it make a short and easie determination of the Question about the descent of *Adam*'s Regal Power, by telling us, that the *Line* and *Posterity* of *Adam* is to have it, that is in plain *English*, any one may have it, since there is no Person 30 living that hath not the Title of being of the *Line* and *Posterity* of *Adam*, and while it keeps there, it keeps within our *A*'s Limitation by God's Ordinance. Indeed, *p.* 19. [61] he tells us, that *such Heirs are not only Lords of their own Children, but of their Brethren*, whereby, and by the words following, which we shall 35 consider anon, he seems to insinuate that the Eldest Son is *Heir*: but he no where, that I know, says it in direct words, but by the instances of *Cain* and *Jacob* that there follow, we may allow this to be so far his Opinion concerning Heirs, that where there are divers Children, the Eldest Son has the Right to be *Heir*. That 40 Primogeniture cannot give any Title to Paternal Power we have already shew'd. That a Father may have a Natural Right to some kind of Power over his Children, is easily granted, but that an Elder Brother has so over his Brethren remains to be proved. God or Nature has not any where, that I know, placed such 45 Jurisdiction in the First-born, nor can Reason find any such Natural Superiority amongst Brethren. The Law of *Moses* gave a double Portion of the Goods and Possessions to the Eldest, but we find not any where that naturally, or by *God's Institution*, Superiority or Dominion belong'd to him, and the Instances there 50 brought by our *A.* are but slender Proofs of a Right to Civil Power and Dominion in the First-born, and do rather shew the contrary.

112. His words are in the forecited place [61]: *And therefore we find God told* Cain *of his Brother* Abel; *his desire shall be Subject unto thee, and thou shalt Rule over him.* To which I answer,

1. These words of God to *Cain*, are by many Interpreters with

great Reason, understood in a quite different Sense than what 5
our *A.* uses them in.

2. Whatever was meant by them, it could not be, that *Cain*
as Elder, had a natural Dominion over *Abel*; for the words are
conditional: *If thou dost well* and so personal to *Cain*, and whatever
was signified by them, did depend on his Carriage and not follow 10
his Birth-right, and therefore could by no means be an Establishment of Dominion in the First-born in general. For before this
Abel had his *distinct Territories by Right of Private Dominion*, as our
A. himself confesses, *O.* 210. [64] which he could not have had
to the prejudice of the Heirs Title, *If by Divine Institution, Cain* 15
as Heir were to inherit all his Father's Dominion.

3. If this were intended by God as the Charter of Primogeniture, and the Grant of Dominion to Elder Brothers in general
as such, by Right of Inheritance, we might expect it should have
included all his Brethren. For we may well suppose, *Adam*, from 20
whom the World was to be peopled, had by this time, that these
were grown up to be Men, more Sons than these two: whereas
Abel himself is not so much as named; and the words in the
Original, can scarce, with any good Construction, be applied to him.

4. It is too much to build a Doctrine of so mighty consequence 25
upon so doubtful and obscure a place of Scripture, which may
be well, nay better, understood in a quite different Sense, and
so can be but an ill Proof, being as doubtful as the thing to be
proved by it, especially when there is nothing else in Scripture
or Reason to be found, that favours or supports it.   30

113. It follows, *p.* 19. [61] *Accordingly when Jacob bought his*
Brothers Birth-right, Isaac blessed him thus; be Lord over thy Brethren,
and let the Sons of thy Mother bow before thee. Another instance
I take it, brought by our *A.* to evince Dominion due to Birth-
right, and an admirable one it is. For it must be no ordinary way 5
of reasoning in a Man, that is pleading for the natural Power
of Kings, and against all compact to bring for Proof of it, an
example where his own account of it founds all the right upon
compact, and settles Empire in the Younger Brother, unless
buying and selling be no compact; for he tells us, *when Jacob* 10
bought his Brothers Birth-right. But passing by that, let us consider
the History it self, with what use our *A.* makes of it, and we shall
find these following Mistakes about it.

1°. That our *A.* reports this, as if *Isaac* had given *Jacob* this
15 Blessing, immediately upon his Purchasing the *Birth-right*; for
he says, *when Jacob bought Isaac blessed him*, which is plainly otherwise in the Scripture. For it appears there was a distance of time
between, and if we will take the Story in the order it lies, it must
be no small distance; all *Isaac's* Sojourning in *Gerar*, and Trans-
20 actions with *Abimelech, Gen.* 26. coming between, *Rebeka* being
then Beautiful and consequently young, but *Isaac* when he Blessed
Jacob, was old and decrepit; And *Esau* also complains of *Jacob,
Gen.* 27. 36. that *two times* he had Supplanted him, *he took away
my Birth-right*, says he, *and behold now he hath taken away my Blessing*;
25 words, that I think signifie distance of time and difference of
Action.

2°. Another mistake of our *A's*, is, that he supposes *Isaac* gave
Jacob the *Blessing*, and bid him be *Lord over his Brethren*, because
he had the *Birth-right*: for our *A.* brings this Example to prove,
30 that he, that has the *Birth-right*, has thereby a right to *be Lord over
his Brethren*. But it is also manifest by the Text, that *Isaac* had no
consideration of *Jacobs* having bought the Birth-right, for when
he blessed him, he considered him not as *Jacob*, but took him for
Esau. Nor did *Esau* understand any such connection between
35 *Birth-right* and the *Blessing*, for he says, *he hath Supplanted me these
two times, he took away my Birth-right, and behold now he hath taken
away my Blessing*: whereas had the *Blessing*, which was to be *Lord
over his Brethren*, belong'd to the *Birth-right, Esau* could not have
complain'd of this second as a Cheat, *Jacob* having got nothing
40 but what *Esau* had sold him, when he sold him his *Birth-right*:
so that it is plain, Dominion, if these words signifie it, was not
understood to belong to the *Birth-right*.

114. And that in those days of the Patriarchs, Dominion was
not understood to be Right of the Heir, but only a greater Portion
of Goods, is plain from *Gen.* 21. 10. for *Sarah* taking *Isaac* to be
Heir, says, *Cast out this Bond-woman and her Son, for the Son of this
5 Bond-woman shall not be Heir with my Son*: whereby could be meant
nothing, but that he should not have a pretence to an equal share
of his Fathers Estate after his death, but should have his Portion
presently and be gone. Accordingly we read, *Gen.* 25. 5, 6.
That *Abraham gave all that he had unto Isaac, but unto the Sons of the
10 Concubines which Abraham had, Abraham gave Gifts and sent them*

away from Isaac his Son, while he yet lived: That is, *Abraham* having given Portions to all his other Sons, and sent them away, that which he had reserved, being the greatest part of his Substance, *Isaac* as Heir Possessed after his Death, but by being Heir, he had no Right to be *Lord over his Brethren*; for if he had, why should 15 *Sarah* endeavour to Rob him of one of his *Subjects*, or lessen the number of his *Slaves*, by desiring to have Ishmael sent away.

115. Thus, as under the Law, the Priviledge of *Birth-right* was nothing but a double Portion, so we see that before *Moses* in the Patriarchs time, from whence our *A.* pretends to take his Model, there was no knowledge, no thought, that Birth-right gave Rule or Empire, Paternal or Kingly Authority, to any one over his 5 Brethren. If this be not plain enough in the Story of *Isaac* and *Ishmael*, he that will look into 1 *Chron.* 5.12. may there read these words, *Ruben was the first Born, but forasmuch as he defiled his Fathers Bed, his Birth-right was given unto the Sons of Joseph, the Son of Israel, and the Genealogy is not to be reckon'd after the Birth-right; for Judah* 10 *prevailed above his Brethren, and of him came the chief Ruler, but the Birth-right was Joseph's*: what this Birth-right was, *Jacob* Blessing *Joseph*, *Gen.* 48. 22. telleth us in these words, *Moreover I have given thee one Portion above thy Brethren, which I took out of the Hand of the Amorite, with my Sword and with my Bow.* Whereby it is not only 15 plain, that the Birth-right was nothing but a double Portion, but the Text in *Chron.* is express against our *A's* Doctrine, and shews that Dominion was no part of the Birth-right. For it tells us that *Joseph* had the Birth-right, but *Judah* the Dominion. One would think our *A.* were very fond of the very name of *Birth-right* 20 when he brings this Instance of *Jacob* and *Esau*, to prove that Dominion belongs to the Heir over his Brethren.

116. 1°. Because it will be but an ill example to prove, that Dominion by God's Ordination belonged to the Eldest Son, because *Jacob* the Youngest here had it, let him come by it how he would. For if it prove any thing, it can only prove against our *A.* that the *Assignment of Dominion to the Eldest, is not by Divine* 5 *Institution*, which would then be unalterable. For if by the Law of God, or Nature, Absolute Power and Empire belongs to the Eldest Son and his Heirs, so that they are Supream Monarchs, and all the rest of their Brethren Slaves, our *A.* gives us reason to doubt whether the Eldest Son has a Power to part with it, to 10

the Prejudice of his Posterity, since he tells us, *O.* 158. [233] That *in Grants and Gifts that have their Original from God or Nature, no inferior Power of Man can limit, or make any Law of Prescription against them.*

117. 2°. Because this place, *Gen.* 27. 29. brought by our *A.* concerns not at all the Dominion of one Brother over the other, nor the Subjection of *Esau* to *Jacob.* For 'tis plain in the History, that *Esau* was never Subject to *Jacob*, but lived a part in Mount
5 *Seir*, where he founded a distinct People and Government, and was himself Prince over them, as much as *Jacob* was in his own Family. This Text if considered, can never be understood of *Esau* himself, or the Personal Dominion of *Jacob* over him: For the words *Brethren* and *Sons of thy Mother*, could not be used literally
10 by *Isaac*, who knew *Jacob* had only one Brother; and these words are so far from being true in a literal Sense, or Establishing any Dominion in *Jacob* over *Esau*, that in the Story we find the quite contrary, for *Gen.* 32. *Jacob* several times calls *Esau* Lord and himself his Servant, and *Gen.* 33. *he bowed himself seven times to the*
15 *ground to* Esau. Whether *Esau* then were a Subject and Vassal, nay (as our *A.* tells us, all Subjects are) Slave to *Jacob*, and *Jacob* his Sovereign Prince by Birth-right, I leave the Reader to Judge; and to believe if he can, that these words of *Isaac*, *be Lord over thy Brethren, and let thy Mothers Sons bow down to thee*, confirm'd
20 *Jacob* in a Sovereignty over *Esau*, upon the account of the *Birthright* he had got from him.

118. He that reads the Story of *Jacob* and *Esau*, will find there was never any Jurisdiction or Authority, that either of them had over the other after their Father's Death: they lived with the Friendship and Equality of Brethren, neither *Lord*, neither *Slave*
5 to his Brother, but independent each of other, were both heads of their distinct Families, where they received no Laws from one another, but lived separately, and were the Roots out of which sprang two distinct Peoples, under two distinct Governments. This Blessing then of *Isaac*, whereon our *A.* would Build the
10 Dominion of the Elder Brother, signifies no more but what

---

§ **117** 4–5 'Mount *Seir*'—compare II, § 38, 30–2. The foundation of a 'distinct People and Government' by one man and his family is described at length in chapter VIII of the *Second Treatise*, 'Of the Beginning of Political Societies'; see especially § 105 on.

Rebecca had been told from God, Gen. 25. 23. *Two Nations are in thy Womb, and two manner of People, shall be separated from thy Bowels, and the one People shall be stronger than the other People, and the Elder shall serve the Younger*; And so *Jacob* Blessed *Judah, Gen.* 49. and gave him the Scepter and Dominion, from whence our *A.* might have argued as well, that Jurisdiction and Dominion belongs to the third Son over his Brethren, as well as from this Blessing of *Isaac*, that it belonged to *Jacob*: Both these places contain only Predictions of what should long after happen to their Posterities, and not any declaration of the Right of Inheritance to Dominion in either. And thus we have our *A's* two great and only Arguments to prove, that *Heirs are Lords over their Brethren.*

1°. Because God tells *Cain, Gen.* 4. That however sin might set upon him, he ought or might be Master of it: For the most Learned Interpreters understand the words of sin, and not of *Abel*, and give so strong Reasons for it, that nothing can convincingly be inferr'd from so doubtful a Text, to our *A*'s purpose.

2°. Because in this of *Gen. 27. Isaac* foretels that the *Israelites*, the Posterity of *Jacob*, should have Dominion over the *Edomites*, the Posterity of *Esau*; therefore says our *A. Heirs are Lords of their Brethren*: I leave any one to judge of the Conclusion.

119. And now we see how our *A.* has provided for the descending and conveyance down of *Adam's* Monarchical Power, or Paternal Dominion to Posterity, by the Inheritance of his *Heir*, succeeding to all his Father's Authority, and becoming upon his Death as much Lord as his Father was, *not only over his own Children, but over his Brethren*, and all descended from his Father, and so *in infinitum.* But yet who this Heir is, he does not once tell us; and all the light we have from him in this so Fundamental a Point, is only that in his instance of *Jacob*, by using the word *Birth-right*, as that which passed from *Esau* to *Jacob*, he leaves us to guess, that by Heir, he means the Eldest Son, though I do not remember he any where mentions expresly the Title of the First-born, but all along keeps himself under the shelter of the indefinite Term *Heir.* But taking it to be his meaning, that the Eldest Son is Heir, (for if the Eldest be not, there will be no pretence why the Sons should not be all Heirs alike) and so by Right of Primogeniture has Dominion over his Brethren; this is but one step towards the Settlement of Succession, and the difficulties remain still as

much as ever, till he can shew us who is meant by Right Heir,
20 in all those cases which may happen where the present Possessor
hath no Son. This he silently passes over, and perhaps wisely too:
For what can be wiser after one has affirm'd, That *the Person having*
that Power, as well as the Power and Form of Government, is the Ordinance
of God, and *by Divine Institution,* vid. O. 254. [289] *p.* 12. [57] than
25 to be careful, not to Start any Question concerning the Person,
the resolution whereof will certainly lead him into a Confession,
that God and Nature hath determined nothing about him. And
if our A. cannot shew who by Right of Nature, or a clear positive
Law of God, has the next Right to inherit the Dominion of this
30 Natural Monarch, he has been at such pains about, when he died
without a Son, he might have spared his pains in all the rest,
it being more necessary for the setling Mens Consciences, and
determining their Subjection and Allegiance, to shew them who
by Original Right, Superior and Antecedent to the Will, or any
35 Act of Men, hath a Title to this *Paternal Jurisdiction,* than it is to
shew that by Nature there was such a *Jurisdiction*: it being to no
purpose for me to know there is such a *Paternal Power,* which
I ought, and am disposed to obey, unless where there are many
Pretenders, I also know the Person that is rightly invested and
40 endow'd with it.

120. For the main matter in question being concerning the
Duty of my Obedience, and the Obligation of Conscience I am
under to pay it to him that is of right my Lord and Ruler, I must
know the Person that this Right of Paternal Power resides in,
5 and so impowers him to claim Obedience from me. For let it
be true what he says, *p.* 12. [57] That *Civil Power not only in general*
is by Divine Institution, but even the assignment of it specifically to the
Eldest Parents; and O. 254. [289] *That not only the Power or Right of*

---

§ 119   21   'This he silently passes over'—Pareyson comments here that Filmer
does in fact provide for such a case in his section on the *Escheating of Kingdoms* (61–2),
where 'heads of families and Princes of provinces...have power to consent in the
uniting or conferring of their fatherly right'. Sidney comments on this in *Discourses,*
1, 19, and Tyrrell (1681), 54, but Locke does not in the text we now have, although it
raises the whole issue between natural and conventional in the origin of political
power. It seems not unlikely that Locke did comment, and at length, on Filmer's
concession to election and consent in this case, but in the lost part of his work. Here
he is merely registering Filmer's unwillingness to be specific about the rules of
inheritance, which Tyrrell also notices: 'he nowhere positively answers this important Question' (1681, 45).

Government, but the Form of the Power of Governing, and the person *having that power, are all the Ordinance of God*; yet unless he shew 10 us in all Cases who is this Person, *Ordain'd* by God, who is this *Eldeſt Parent*, all his Abſtraƈt Notions of Monarchical Power will signifie juſt nothing, when they are to be reduced to Praƈtice, and Men are conscientiously to pay their Obedience. For *Paternal Jurisdiƈtion* being not the thing to be obeyed, because it cannot 15 command, but is only that which gives one Man a Right, which another hath not, and if it come by Inheritance, another Man cannot have, to command and be Obey'd; it is ridiculous to say, I pay Obedience to the *Paternal Power*, when I obey him, to whom Paternal Power gives no Right to my Obedience; for he can 20 have no Divine Right to my Obedience, who cannot shew his Divine Right to the Power of ruling over me, as well as that by Divine Right, there is such a Power in the World.

121. And hence not being able to make out any Princes Title to Government, as Heir to *Adam*, which therefore is of no use, and had been better let alone, he is faln to resolve all into present Poſseſsion, and makes Civil Obedience as due to an *Usurper* as to a lawful King; and thereby the *Usurper's* Title as good. His 5 words are, *O.* 253. [289] And they deserve to be remembered: *If an Usurper dispossess the true Heir, the Subjeƈts Obedience to the Fatherly Power muſt go along and wait upon God's Providence.* But I shall leave his Title of Usurpers to be examin'd in its due place, and desire my ſober Reader to consider what thanks Princes owe 10 such Politicks as this, which can suppose *Paternal Power* (*i.e.*) a Right to Government in the Hands of a *Cade*, or a *Cromwel*, and so all Obedience being due to Paternal Power, the Obedience of Subjeƈts will be due to them by the same Right, and upon as good Grounds as it is to lawful Princes; and yet this, as dangerous 15 a Doƈtrine as it is, muſt necessarily follow from making all Political

---

§ 121   9   The 'due place' was almost certainly a part of the lost continuation of the *First Treatise*; see the referencé to usurpation in Locke's Preface, where he implies that this subject was discussed there, lines 29–30. In his two-paragraph chapter XVII of the *Second Treatise*, 'Of Usurpation', Locke does not discuss 'his', that is, Filmer's, 'Title of Usurpers'.

12   'Cromwel' is discussed in the note to 1, § 79, 1: Jack Cade was the leader of the Kentish uprising of 1450, which had also become a symbol for popular revolt, compare the note on Masaniello, 1, § 79, 3. In 1680 John Crowne published a play about Cade, *The Misery of Civil War*, acted in 1681.

Power to be nothing else but *Adam*'s Paternal Power by Right and *Divine Institution*, descending from him, without being able to shew to whom it descended, or who is Heir to it.

122. To settle Government in the World, and to lay Obligations to Obedience on any Mans Conscience, it is as necessary (supposing with our *A.* that all Power be nothing but the being possessed of *Adam's Fatherhood*) to satisfie him, who has a Right
5 to this Power, this *Fatherhood*, when the Possessor dies without Sons to succeed immediately to it, as it was to tell him that upon the death of the Father, the Eldest Son had a Right to it: For it is still to be remember'd, that the great Question is, (and that which our *A.* would be thought to contend for, if he did not
10 sometimes forget it) what Persons have a Right to be obeyed, and not whether there be a Power in the World, which is to be called *Paternal*, without knowing in whom it resides: for so it be a Power, *i.e.* Right to Govern, it matters not, whether it be termed *Paternal*, or *Regal*; *Natural*, or *acquired*; whether you call it *Supreme*
15 *Fatherhood*, or *Supreme Brotherhood*, will be all one provided we know who has it.

123. I go on then to ask whether in the inheriting of this *Paternal Power*, this *Supreme Fatherhood*, The Grand-Son by a Daughter, hath a Right before a Nephew by a Brother? Whether the Grand-Son by the Eldest Son, being an Infant, before the
5 Younger Son a Man and able? Whether the Daughter before the Uncle? or any other Man, descended by a Male Line? Whether

---

§ 123 The objections in the paragraph look a little far-fetched, since Filmer and his supporters had assumed the validity of the rules which in fact governed the succession of the English Crown. The important point is hinted at in lines 11–12, where Locke implies that on Filmer's premises such rules cannot merely be the 'Municipal or Positive Laws' of one country (compare note on 1, § 90, 29–31), but must be a part of natural law: Tyrrell (1681, 54 on) spends a great deal of time showing that 'there is nothing but custom in the case' and Sidney (*Discourses*, I, 18) takes Filmer up on it. Such issues were a standard subject of the natural-law theorists, and these questions of Locke's could almost have been translated from the section headings xxx–xxxvii of chapter vii of the Second Book of Grotius, *De Jure Belli*. It must be remembered that the issues of 'the Elder Son by a Concubine' (8) and 'the difference between a Wife and a Concubine' (11) were crucial to Locke when he wrote this, because the claimant to the throne adopted by Shaftesbury against the future James II was the Duke of Monmouth, Charles II's eldest son by a concubine. To establish the precedency of Monmouth over all other claimants, William Lawrence was enabled by Shaftesbury in 1681 to publish the second part of his *Marriage by the Morall Law of God* (see Furley, 1957, 21, note 11). Locke owned this book. (H. and L. 1693).

a Grand-Son by a Younger Daughter, before a Grand-Daughter
by an Elder Daughter? Whether the Elder Son by a Concubine,
before a Younger Son by a Wife? From whence also will arise
many Questions of Legitimation, and what in Nature is the 10
difference betwixt a Wife and a Concubine? For as to the Municipal or Positive Laws of Men, they can signifie nothing here.
It may farther be asked, Whether the Eldest Son being a Fool,
shall inherit this *Paternal Power*, before the Younger a wise Man?
And what Degree of Folly it must be, that shall exclude him? 15
And who shall be judge of it? Whether the Son of a Fool excluded
for his Folly, before the Son of his wise Brother who Reign'd?
Who has the *Paternal Power*, whilst the Widow-Queen is with
Child by the deceased King, and no body knows whether it will
be a Son or a Daughter? Which shall be Heir of two Male-Twins, 20
who by the Dissection of the Mother, were laid open to the
World? Whether a Sister by the half Blood, before a Brothers
Daughter by the whole Blood?

124. These, and many more such Doubts, might be proposed
about the Titles of Succession, and the Right of Inheritance;
and that not as idle Speculations, but such as in History we shall
find, have concerned the Inheritance of Crowns and Kingdoms;
and if ours want them, we need not go farther for famous 5
Examples of it, than the other Kingdom in this very Island, which
having been fully related by the Ingenious and Learned Author
of *Patriarcha non Monarcha*, I need say no more of. Till our *A.*
hath resolved all the Doubts that may arise about the next Heir,

---

§ 124   6 and 7–8   James Tyrrell was of course the author of *Patriarcha non Monarcha*
(1681), published in the middle of 1681 and acquired by Locke on 2 June; see Introduction,
57–61, for this book and for the relationship between Locke and Tyrrell when it was being
written. This is the only specific acknowledgement to the work, but the parallel passages
between it and Locke's noted in this edition show how close the two men were. In Tyrrell's
letter of 20 December 1689 referring to *Two Treatises* (see Introduction, 52) he says, evidently
with this reference in mind, that the writer concerned 'speaks of the author of *Patriarcha non
Monarcha* more respectful than he deserves', and writing to Locke on 30 August 1690 he adds
that the author of *Two Treatises* 'agreed perfectly with my conceptions in *Patriarcha non
Monarcha* (which he had quoted)'.
   Locke presumably intended here pp. 54–60 of Tyrrell's book, dealing with the
succession of uncle or nephew, son or grandson, bastard or legitimate in Navarre,
Castile, Portugal, among the Moguls of India and especially, and at length, in
Scotland—'the other Kingdom of this very Island', which was also Lawrence's
favourite source of illustration—see note on 1, § 123.

10 and shewed that they are plainly determin'd by the Law of Nature,
or the revealed Law of God, all his Suppositions of a *Monarchical,*
Absolute, Supreme, Paternal Power in *Adam,* and the descent of
that Power to his Heirs, would not be of the least use to Establish
the Authority, or make out the Title of any one Prince now on
15 Earth, but would rather unsettle and bring all into question:
For let our *A.* tell us as long as he please, and let all Men believe
it too, that *Adam* had a *Paternal,* and thereby *a Monarchical Power*;
That this (the only Power in the World) *descended to his Heirs,* and
that there is no other Power in the World but this: let this be all
20 as clear Demonstration, as it is manifest Error, yet if it be not
past doubt, to whom this *Paternal Power descends,* and whose now
it is, no body can be under any Obligation of Obedience, unless
any one will say, that I am bound to pay Obedience to *Paternal*
Power in a Man, who has no more *Paternal Power* than I my self;
25 which is all one as to say, I obey a Man, because he has a Right
to Govern, and if I be asked, How I know he has a Right to
Govern, I should answer, It cannot be known, that he has any
at all. For that cannot be the reason of my Obedience, which
I know not to be so; much less can that be a reason of my
30 Obedience, which no body at all can know to be so.

125. And therefore all this ado about *Adam*'s *Fatherhood,* the
greatness of its Power, and the necessity of its supposal, helps
nothing to Establish the Power of those that Govern, or to determine the Obedience of Subjects, who are to obey, if they cannot
5 tell whom they are to obey, or it cannot be known who are to
Govern, and who to Obey. In the State the world now is,
irrecoverably ignorant who is *Adam*'s heir, this *Fatherhood,* this
Monarchical Power of Adam descending to his Heirs, would be of
no more Use to the Government of Mankind, than it would be
10 to the quieting of Mens Consciences, or securing their Healths,
if our *A.* had assured them, that *Adam* had a *Power* to forgive
Sins or cure Diseases, which by Divine Institution descended to
his *Heir,* whilst this Heir is impossible to be known. And should
not he do as rationally, who upon this assurance of our *A.* went
15 and confessed his Sins, and expected a good Absolution, or took
Physick with expectation of Health from any one who had taken
on himself the Name of Priest or Physician, or thrust himself
into those Employments, saying, I acquiesce in the Absolving

Power descending from *Adam*, or I shall be cured by the Medicinal
Power descending from *Adam*; as he who says, I submit to, and   20
obey the *Paternal Power* descending from *Adam*, when 'tis confessed all these Powers descend only to his single Heir, and that
Heir is unknown.

126. 'Tis true, the Civil Lawyers have pretended to determine
some of these Cases concerning the Succession of Princes; but
by our *A*'s Principles, they have medled in a matter that belongs
not to them: For if all Political Power be derived only from
Adam, and be to descend only to his Successive Heirs, by the   5
Ordinance of God and *Divine Institution*, this is a Right Antecedent
and Paramount to all Government; and therefore the positive
Laws of Men, cannot determine that which is it self the Foundation
of all Law and Government, and is to receive its Rule only from
the Law of God and Nature. And that being silent in the Case,   10
I am apt to think there is no such Right to be conveyed this way:
I am sure it would be to no purpose if there were, and Men would
be more at a loss concerning Government and Obedience to
Governours, then if there were no such Right: since by positive
Laws and Compact, which *Divine Institution* (if there be any) shuts   15
out, all these endless inextricable Doubts, can be safely provided
against; but it can never be understood, how a Divine Natural
Right, and that of such moment as is all Order and Peace in the
World, should be convey'd down to Posterity, without any Plain
Natural or Divine Rule concerning it. And there would be an   20
end of all Civil Government, if the *Assignment* of Civil Power were
by *Divine Institution* to the Heir, and yet *by that Divine Institution*,
the Person of the Heir could not be known. This *Paternal Regal
Power*, being by Divine Right only his, it leaves no room for
humane prudence, or consent to place it any where else: for if   25
only one Man hath a Divine Right to the Obedience of Mankind,
no body can claim that Obedience, but he that can shew that
Right; nor can Mens Consciences by any other pretence be obliged
to it. And thus this Doctrine cuts up all Government by the Roots.

---

§ 126   1   'Civil Lawyers', the professors of the Civil or Roman Law of Locke's
day, and right back to the age of Justinian: writers such as Grotius and Pufendorf
are probably intended to be included here. Filmer quotes the Civil Law frequently,
but not on the point of succession, but Locke was indifferent to Roman Law as such,
though he possessed his *Institutes* and *Corpus Juris Civilis*. (H. and L. 1598 and 1599). On this
paragraph compare Tyrrell (1681), 54, and Sidney, 1, § 18.

127. Thus we see how our *A.* laying it for a sure Foundation, that the very *Person* that is to Rule, is *the Ordinance* of God, and by *Divine Inſtitution*, tells us at large, only that this Person is the *Heir*, but who this Heir is, he leaves us to guess; and so this 5 *Divine Inſtitution* which Assigns it to a Person, whom we have no Rule to know, is juſt as good as an Assignment to no body at·all. But whatever our *A.* does, *Divine Inſtitution* makes no such ridiculous Assignments: nor can God be supposed to make it a Sacred Law, that one certain Person should have a Right to 10 something, and yet not to give Rules to mark out, and know that Person by, or give an *Heir* a Divine Right to Power, and yet not point out who that *Heir* is. 'Tis rather to be thought, that an *Heir*, had no such Right by *Divine Inſtitution*, than that God should give such a Right to the *Heir*, but yet leave it doubtful, and undeter- 15 minable who such Heir is.

128. If God had given the Land of *Canaan* to *Abraham*, and in general Terms to some body after him, without naming his Seed, whereby it might be known, who that some body was, it would have been as good and useful an Assignment, to determine 5 the Right to the Land of *Canaan*, as it would to the determining the Right of Crowns, to give Empire to *Adam* and his Successive Heirs after him, without telling who his Heir is: For the word *Heir*, without a Rule to know who it is, signifies no more than somebody, I know not whom. God making it a *Divine Inſtitution*, 10 that Men should not marry those who were *near of Kin*, thinks it not enough to say, *none of you shall approach to any that is near of Kin to him, to uncover their Nakedness*: But Moreover, gives Rules to know who are those *near of Kin*, forbidden by *Divine Inſtitution*, or else that Law would have been of no use: it being to no 15 purpose to lay reſtraint, or give Privileges, to Men, in such general Terms, as the Particular Person concern'd cannot be known by. But God not having any where said, the next Heir shall Inherit all his Fathers Eſtate or Dominion, we are not to wonder that he hath no where appointed who that Heir should be, for never 20 having intended any such thing, never designed any Heir in that Sense, we cannot expeɗ he should any where nominate, or appoint any Person to it, as we might, had it been otherwise. And there-

---

§ **128** 11–14 See Lev. xviii: the text quoted comes from verse 6, and the specified incestuous relationships in the rest of the chapter.

fore in Scripture, though the word *Heir* occur, yet there is no such thing as Heir in our *A*'s Sense, one that was by Right of Nature to Inherit all that his Father had, exclusive of his Brethren. Hence 25 *Sarah* supposes, that if *Ishmael* ſtaid in the House, to share in *Abrahams* Eſtate after his Death, this Son of a bond woman might be Heir with *Isaac*: and therefore, says she, *caſt out this Bond-woman and her Son, for the Son of this Bond-woman shall not be Heir with my Son*; But this cannot excuse our *A*——, who telling 30 us there is in every Number of Men, one who is *Right* and next *Heir* to *Adam* [288–9], ought to have told us what the Laws of descent are. He having been so sparing to inſtruct us by Rules, how to know who is *Heir*, let us see in the next place, what his Hiſtory out of Scripture, on which he pretends wholly to build 35 his Government, gives us in this necessary and Fundamental point.

129. Our *A*. to make good the Title of his Book, *p*. 13. [58] begins the Hiſtory of the descent of *Adams* Regal Power, *p*. 13. in these words: *This Lordship which* Adam *by command had over the whole World, and by Right descending from him, the Patriarchs did enjoy was as large*, &c. How does he prove that the Patriarchs by 5 descent did enjoy it? for *Dominion of Life and Death*, says he, *we find* Judah *the Father pronounced Sentence of Death againſt* Thamar *his Daughter-in-Law for playing the Harlot, p*. 13 [58]. How does this prove that *Judah* had Absolute and Sovereign Authority, *He pronounced Sentence of Death*? The pronouncing of Sentence of Death 10

28–30   See Gen. xxi. 10, noted previously in i, § 114.
§ 129   1   This can only be intended to refer to the title *Patriarcha, or the Natural Power of Kings*, and is one of the indications that the *First Treatise*, as distinct from the *Second*, was directed at *Patriarcha* particularly—see Introduction, 61 and compare, i, § 1, 9 and note.
3   '*by command*'—thus in the 1680 printing of *Patriarcha*: the manuscript reads '*by creation*' (58).
10–15   Filmer in claiming that the power to pronounce on life and death was a certain mark of sovereignty was following Bodin's classic definition: in his *Methodus*, probably behind the references to sovereignty in the Latin Tract of 1664 (see p. 6 and note in Abrams' edition, compare Von Leyden, 1954. p. 20). 'The power of life and death when the law itself leaves no room for extenuating' was the fifth and final mark of sovereignty. Comparison with such passages as i, § 131, ii, § 3, ii, § 11, 6–8 (see note there) and ii, § 65 shows that Locke did argue about 'marks of sovereignty' in somewhat Bodin's way. It seems quite unjustifiable to maintain as Green did that Locke never used the term sovereignty in the way his contemporaries did (1931, 75) or that he avoided it because of the use Hobbes had made of the word (see Gough, 1950, 41).

is not a certain mark of Sovereignty, but usually the Office of Inferior Magiſtrates. The Power of making Laws of Life and Death, is indeed a Mark of Sovereignty, but pronouncing the Sentence according to those Laws may be done by others, and therefore this will but ill prove that he had Sovereign Authority: As if one should say, *Judge Jefferies*, pronounced Sentence of Death in the late Times, therefore *Judge Jefferies*, had Sovereign Authority: But it will be said, *Judah* did it not by Commission from another, and therefore did it in his own Right. Who knows whether he had any Right at all? heat of Passion might carry him to do that which he had no Authority to do. *Judah had Dominion of Life and Death*, how does that appear? he exercised it, he *pronounced Sentence of Death againſt* Thamar, our *A——* thinks it is very good Proof, that because he did it, therefore he had a Right to do it; He lay with her also: By the same way of Proof, he had a Right to do that too: If the consequence be good from doing to a Right of doing. *Absalon* too may be reckon'd amongſt our *A-s* Sovereigns, for he pronounced such a Sentence of Death againſt his Brother *Amnon*, and much upon a like occasion, and had it executed too; if that be sufficient to prove a Dominion of Life and Death.

But allowing this all to be clear Demonſtration of Sovereign Power, who was it that had this *Lordship by Right descending to him from* Adam, *as large and ample as the Abſoluteſt Dominion of any Monarch* [58]? Judah, says our *A——*, *Judah* a younger Son of *Jacob*, his Father and Elder Brethren living: so that if our *A——s* own Proof be to be taken, a younger Brother may in the Life of his Father and Elder Brothers, *by Right of descent, enjoy Adams* Monarchical Power; and if one so qualified may be Monarch by descent, why may not every man? if *Judah*, his Father and Elder Brother living were one of *Adams* Heirs, I know not who can be excluded from this Inheritance; all Men by Inheritance may be Monarchs as well as *Judah*.

130. *Touching War, we see that* Abraham *Commanded an Army of* 318 *Souldiers of his own Family, and* Esau *met his Brother* Jacob

---

15–17 The reference to Judge Jeffreys 'in the late Times' must have been inserted after the end of James II's reign and is the only sentence in *Two Treatises* which dates itself, in 1689. See Introduction, 46.

27–9 For Absalon and Amnon see II Sam. xiii.

with 400 *Men at Arms*; *For matter of Peace*; Abraham *made a League with* Abimilech, &c. *p.* 13 [58]. Is it not possible for a Man to have 318 Men in his Family, without being Heir to *Adam*? 5 A Planter in the *West Indies* has more, and might, if he pleased (who doubts) Muster them up and lead them out against the *Indians*, to seek Reparation upon any Injury received from them, and all this without the *Absolute Dominion of a Monarch, descending to him from Adam*. Would it not be an admirable Argument to 10 prove, that all Power by Gods Institution descended from *Adam* by Inheritance, and that the very Person and Power of this Planter were the *Ordinance of God*, because he had Power in his Family over Servants, born in his House, and bought with his Money? For this was just *Abrahams* Case: Those who were rich in the 15 *Patriarchs* Days, as in the *West-Indies* now, bought Men and Maid Servants, and by their increase as well as purchasing of new, came to have large and numerous Families, which though they made use of in War or Peace, can it be thought the Power they had over them was an Inheritance descended from *Adam*, when 20 'twas the Purchase of their Money? A Mans Riding in an expedition against an Enemy, his Horse bought in a Fair, would be as good a Proof that the owner *enjoyed the Lordship which* Adam *by command had over the whole World, by Right descending to him*, as *Abrahams* leading out the Servants of his Family is, that the 25 Patriarchs enjoy'd this Lordship by descent from *Adam*: since the Title to the Power, the Master had in both Cases, whether over Slaves or Horses, was only from his purchase; and the getting a Dominion over any thing by Bargain and Money, is a new way of proving one had it by Descent and Inheritance. 30

---

§ 130   6   'A Planter in the *West Indies*'—compare 1, § 131, 2–10. Locke speaks here from his personal knowledge as secretary to the proprietors of Carolina, which was regarded as an extension of the West Indies (compare 1, § 144, 23 and note), and as Secretary to Shaftesbury's Board of Trade and Plantations, see Introduction, 26. It is interesting that both Locke and Filmer, whose brother was a planter in Virginia, accepted the political character of the family under such circumstances, as did Tyrrell who talks much as Locke does, but his planter is in the Barbadoes (1681, 105). All of them to varying degrees imply in this way that the position of the colonial planter can be assimilated to that of the Biblical patriarch. It may be permissible to guess that the planters themselves, although they acquired their subjects (slaves and indentured servants) by purchase, as Locke says, would have regarded their power as patriarchal as Filmer claimed, rather than as resting finally on consent, and that Filmer's Biblical arguments would have appealed to them more than Locke allowed.

131. *But making War and Peace are marks of Sovereignty* [58]. Let it be so in Politick Societies. May not therefore a Man in the *West-Indies*, who hath with him Sons of his own, Friends, or Companions, Soldiers under Pay, or Slaves bought with Money, or perhaps a Band made up of all these, make War and Peace, if there should be occasion, and *ratifie the Articles too with an Oath* [58], without being a Sovereign, an Absolute King over those who went with him? he that says he cannot, must then allow many Masters of Ships, many private Planters to be Absolute Monarchs, for as much as this they have done. War and Peace cannot be made for Politick Societies, but by the Supream Power of such Societies; because War and Peace, giving a different Motion to the force of such a Politick Body, none can make War or Peace, but that which has the direction of the force of the whole Body, and that in Politick Societies is only the Supream Power. In voluntary Societies for the time, he that has such a Power by consent, may make War and Peace, and so may a single Man for himself, the State of War not consisting in the number of *Partysans*, but the enmity of the Parties, where they have no Superiour to appeal to.

132. The actual making of War or Peace is no proof of any other Power, but only of disposing those to exercise or cease Acts of enmity for whom he makes it, and this Power in many Cases any one may have without any Politick Supremacy: And therefore the making of War or Peace will not prove that every one that does so is a Politick Ruler, much less a King; for then Common-wealths must be Kings too, for they do as certainly make War and Peace as Monarchical Government.

133. But granting this *a mark of Sovereignty* in *Abraham*, Is it a proof of the Descent to him, of *Adam's Sovereignty* over the whole World? If it be, it will surely be as good a proof of the *descent of Adam's Lordship* to others too. And then Common-wealths, as well as *Abraham*, will be *Heirs of Adam*, for they make *War and Peace*, as well as he. If you say, that the *Lordship*

---

§ **131** 1 Declaring war and peace was Bodin's third mark of sovereignty, *Methodus*, 1945, 172, compare I, § 129, 10–15 and note.

19 The lack of a common superior as characterizing the state of nature is discussed at length in the *Second Treatise*, chapter II, 'Of the State of Nature', and references in this paragraph to war supplement the following chapter there, 'Of the State of War', see especially §§ 20–1. In the relationships within and between planters' families in America, we have a model for the origin and nature of the Lockeian state, and its contrast with the state of nature—see Introduction.

of Adam doth not by Right descend to Common-wealths, though they make War and Peace, the same say I of *Abraham*, and then there is an end of your Argument; if you stand to your Argument, and say those that do make War and Peace, as Common- 10 wealths do without doubt, do *inherit Adam's Lordship*, there is an end of your Monarchy, unless you will say, that Common-wealths *by descent enjoying Adam's Lordship* are Monarchies, and that indeed would be a new way of making all the Governments in the World Monarchical.   15

134. To give our *A.* the honour of this new invention, for I confess it is not I have first found it out by tracing his Principles, and so charged it on him, 'tis fit my Readers know that (as absurd as it may seem) he teaches it himself, *p.* 23. [62] where he ingeniously says, *In all Kingdoms and Common-wealths in the World,* 5 *whether the Prince be the Supream Father of the People, or but the true Heir to such a Father, or come to the Crown by Usurpation or Election, or whether some few or a Multitude Govern the Common-wealth: yet still the Authority that is in any one, or in many, or in all these is the only Right, and natural Authority of a Supream Father,* which Right 10 of *Fatherhood* he often tells us, is *Regal and Royal Authority;* as particularly, *p.* 12. [57] the page immediately preceding this Instance of *Abraham.* This Regal Authority, he says, those that Govern Common-wealths have: and if it be true, that Regal and Royal Authority be in those that govern Common-wealths, it is 15 as true, that Common-wealths are govern'd by Kings: for if Regal Authority be in him that Governs, he that Governs must needs be a King, and so all Common-wealths are nothing but down right Monarchies, and then what need any more ado about the matter? the Governments of the World are as they should 0 be, there is nothing but Monarchy in it. This without doubt, was the surest way our *A.* could have found, to turn all other Governments, but Monarchical, out of the World.

135. But all this scarce proves *Abraham,* to have been a King as Heir to *Adam.* If by Inheritance he had been King, *Lot,* who was of the same Family, must needs have been his Subject, by that Title before the Servants in his Family: but we see they liv'd as Friends and Equals, and when their Herdsmen 5 could not agree, there was no pretence of Jurisdiction or

---

§ 133   7   The word 'Common-wealths' here means republics, all non-monarchical forms of government.

239

Superiority between them, but they parted by consent, *Gen.* 13. hence he is called both by *Abraham*, and by the Text *Abraham's Brother*, the Name of Friendship and Equality, and not of Juris-
10 diction and Authority, though he were really but his Nephew. And if our *A.* knows that *Abraham* was *Adam*'s Heir, and a King, 'twas more it seems then *Abraham* himself knew, or his Servant whom he sent a wooing for his Son; for when he sets out the advantages of the Match, 24 *Gen.* 35. thereby to prevail with the
15 Young-woman and her Friends, he says, *I am Abrahams Servant, and the Lord hath Blessed my Master greatly, and he is become great, and he hath given him Flocks and Herds and Silver and Gold, and Men-Servants and Maid-servants, and Camels and Asses, and Sarah my Masters Wife, bare a Son to my Master when she was old, and unto*
20 *him he hath given all he hath.* Can one think that a discreet Servant, that was thus particular to set out his Master's Greatness, would have omitted the Crown *Isaac* was to have, if he had known of any such? Can it be imagin'd he should have neglected to have told them on such an occasion as this that *Abraham* was a King,
25 a Name well known at that time, for he had nine of them his Neighbours, if he or his Master had thought any such thing, the likeliest matter of all the rest, to make his Errand Successful?

136. But this discovery it seems was reserved for our *A.* to make 2 or 3000 Years after, and let him injoy the Credit of it, only he should have taken care that some of *Adam*'s Land should have descended to this his *Heir*, as well as all *Adam*'s Lordship,
5 for though this Lordship which *Abraham*, (if we may believe our *A.*) as well as the other Patriarchs, *by Right descending to him did enjoy, was as large and ample as the Absolutest Dominion of any Monarch which hath been since the Creation* [58]. Yet his Estate, his Territories, his Dominions were very narrow and scanty, for he had not the
10 Possession of a Foot of Land, till he bought a Field and a Cave of the Sons of *Heth* to bury *Sarah* in.

---

§ **135**   7   'they parted by consent'—II, § 38, 28–9 'they, by consent, as Abraham and Lot did,...separated': see note there.
  15   The young woman was Rebecca.
  25   These nine kings are listed in Gen. xiv. 1–2, and cited by Filmer, 59.
§ **136**   11   Gen. xxiii for the burial of Sarah. Compare II, § 36, 9–25 and note. Sidney makes the same point about the restricted territory of Abraham and the other patriarchs in *Discourses*, 1, 8. According to Ussher's chronology, in the margins of the Authorized Version, it took place in 1872 B.C., about 2500 years before Locke and

137. The Instance of *Esau* joyn'd with this of *Abraham*, to prove that the *Lordship which* Adam *had over the whole World, by Right descending from him, the Patriarchs did enjoy*, is yet more pleasant then the former: *Esau met his Brother Jacob with* 400 *Men at Arms* [58]; He therefore was a King by Right of Heir to *Adam*. 400 Arm'd   5
Men then however got together are enough to prove him that leads them to be a King and *Adam*'s Heir. There have been Tories in *Ireland*, (whatever there are in other Countries) who would have thankt our *A*. for so honourable an Opinion of them, especially if there had been no body near with a better Title of   10
500 Armed Men, to question their Royal Authority of 400. 'Tis a shame for Men to trifle so, to say no worse of it, in so serious an Argument. Here *Esau* is brought as a Proof that *Adam*'s Lordship, *Adam's absolute Dominion, as large as that of any Monarch descended by Right to the Patriarchs*, and in this very *Chap. p*. 19. [61]   15
Jacob is brought as an instance of one, that by *Birth-right was Lord over his Brethren*. So we have here two Brothers Absolute Monarchs by the same Title, and at the same time Heirs to *Adam*: The Eldest Heir to *Adam*, because he met his Brother with 400 Men, and the youngest Heir to *Adam* by *Birth-right*: Esau *injoy'd the Lordship*   20
which Adam *had over the whole World by Right descending to him, in as large and ample manner, as the absolutest Dominion of any Monarch,* and at the same time, *Jacob Lord over him, by the Right Heirs have to be Lords over their Brethren*. *Risum teneatis?* I never, I confess, met with any Man of Parts so Dexterous as Sir *Robert* at this way   25

Filmer, and the reference in line 2 shows that Locke was accepting this chronology: compare, 1, § 147, 53, 1, § 150, 9 and notes. This he did in general, though both he and Newton found it so difficult to reconcile with their cosmology, and in Locke's case, with his comparative anthropology. MS. c. 27 shows that he was working at the chronology of the Old Testament in the year 1680.

§ **137** 7–8   This would seem to be the only direct reference to Locke's political opponents, the Royalists, traditionalists or tories, in his book, and it is tempting to look on it as a jibe at the opponents of the Revolution of 1688–9. But though it is just possible that the phrase in brackets, where 'other Countries' means England of course, was added in 1689, the sentence itself can only have been written in 1679–81, when 'tory' was still an opprobrious nickname for Irish bog-trotters, and had not become irrevocably attached to a body of English political opinion.

15   'this very *Chap*.'—Chapter 1 of *Patriarcha* (53–63), see note on 1, § 6, 48. The form of this reference implies that Locke, in the lost continuation of the *First Treatise*, may have commented on the second and third chapters of Filmer's *Patriarcha*, as printed in 1680; see Introduction, Section III.

24   '*Risum teneatis?*'—'can you help laughing', Horace, *Ars Poetica*, 5, though probably a conventional phrase in academic disputation.

of Arguing: But 'twas his Misfortune to light upon an hypothesis that could not be accommodated to the Nature of things, and Human Affairs, his principles could not be made to agree with that Conſtitution and Order which God had settled in the World,
30 and therefore muſt needs often clash with common Sense and Experience.

138. In the next Seƈtion, he tells us [58], *This Patriarchal Power continued not only till the Flood, but after it, as the name Patriarchs doth in part prove.* The word Patriarch doth more then *in part prove*, that *Patriarchal Power* continued in the World as long as
5 there were Patriarchs, for 'tis necessary that Patriarchal Power should be whilſt there are Patriarchs, as it is necessary there should be Paternal or Conjugal Power whilſt there are Fathers or Husbands: but this is but playing with Names. That which he would fallaciously insinuate is the thing in queſtion to be
10 proved, viz. that the *Lordship which* Adam *had over the World*, the supposed Absolute Universal Dominion of *Adam* by *Right descending from him the Patriarchs did enjoy.* If he affirms such an Absolute Monarchy continued to the Flood, in the World, I would be glad to know what Records he has it from; for I confess
15 I cannot find a word of it in my Bible: If by *Patriarchal Power*, he means any thing else, it is nothing to the matter in hand: And how the name *Patriarch* in *some part proves*, that those, who are called by that name, had Absolute Monarchical Power, I confess, I do not see, and therefore I think needs no answer, till
20 the Argument from it be made out a little clearer.

139. *The three Sons of Noah had the World*, says our *A.*, *divided amongſt them by their Father, for of them was the whole World overspread*, p. 14 [58]. The World might be overspread by the Offspring of *Noah*'s Sons, though he never divided the World
5 amongſt them; For the *Earth* might be *Repleniſhed* without being divided, so that all our *A*——'s Argument here, proves no such Division. However I allow it to him, and then ask, the World being divided amongſt them, which of the three was *Adam*'s Heir? If *Adam*'s *Lordship*, *Adam*'s *Monarchy*, by Right descended
10 only to the Eldeſt, then the other two could be but his *Subjeƈts*,

---

§ 138　1　'next Section'—section 5 of the 1680 printing, section III and part of section IV (58–60) in Laslett's edition.

his *Slaves*; If by Right it descended to all three Brothers, by the same Right, it will descend to all Mankind, and then it will be impossible what he says, *p.* 19. [61] that *Heirs are Lords of their Brethren*, should be true, but all Brothers, and consequently all Men will be equal and independent, all Heirs to *Adam*'s Monarchy, 15 and consequently all Monarchs too, one as much as another. But 'twill be said *Noah* their Father divided the World amongst them, so that our *A.* will allow more to *Noah*, than he will to God Almighty, for *O.* 211. [64] he thought it hard, that God himself should give the World to *Noah* and his Sons, to the 20 prejudice of *Noah*'s Birth-right, his words are, *Noah was left Sole Heir to the World, why should it be thought that God would disinherit him of his Birth-right, and make him of all Men in the World, the only Tenant in common with his Children?* and yet here he thinks it fit, that *Noah* should disinherit *Shem* of his Birth-right, and divide 25 the World betwixt him and his Brethren, so that this *Birth-right*, when our *A.* pleases, must, and when he pleases, must not, be sacred and inviolable.

140. If *Noah* did divide the World between his Sons, and his Assignment of Dominions to them were good, there is an end of Divine Institution; all our *A*'s Discourse of *Adam*'s Heir, with whatsoever he builds on it, is quite out of doors; and the Natural Power of Kings falls to the ground; and then *the form of* 5 *the Power Governing, and the Person having that Power*, will not be (as he says they are *O.* 254 [289]) *the ordinance of God*, but they will be *Ordinances* of man. For if the right of the Heir be the Ordinance of God, a Divine Right, no Man, Father, or not Father, can alter it: If it be not a Divine right, it is only Human depending 10 on the Will of Man: and so where Human Institution gives it not, the First-born has no right at all above his Brethren; and Men may put Government into what hands, and under what form, they please.

141. He goes on, *Most of the civillest Nations of the Earth, labour to fetch their Original from some of the Sons or Nephews of* Noah, *p.* 14 [58]. How many do most of the civillest Nations amount to? and who are they? I fear the *Chineses*, a very great and civil People, as well as several other People of the *East*, *West*, 5 *North* and *South*; trouble not themselves much about this matter. All that believe the Bible, which I believe are our *A*'s *most of the*

civillest Nations, must necessarily derive themselves from *Noah*,
but for the rest of the World, they think little of his Sons or
10 Nephews. But if the Heralds and Antiquaries of all Nations, for
'tis these Men generally that labour to find out the Originals of
Nations, or all the Nations themselves should *labour to fetch their*
Original from some of the Sons or Nephews of Noah, what would this
be to prove, that the *Lordship which* Adam *had over the whole World,*
15 *by right descended to the Patriarchs?* Whoever, Nations, or Races
of Men, *labour to fetch their Original from,* may be concluded to be
thought by them, Men of Renown, famous to Posterity for the
Greatness of their Virtues and Actions; but beyond these they
look not, nor consider who they were Heirs to, but look on them
20 as such as raised themselves by their own Virtue to a Degree that
would give a Lustre to those, who in future Ages could pretend
to derive themselves from them. But if it were *Ogygis, Hercules,*
Brama, Tamberlain, Pharamond; nay, if *Jupiter* and *Saturn* were the
Names, from whence divers Races of Man, both Ancient and
25 Modern, have labour'd to derive their Original; will that prove
that those Men *enjoyed the Lordship of Adam, by right descending to*
them? If not, this is but a flourish of our *A*'s to mislead his Reader,
that in it self signifies nothing.

142. To as much purpose, is, what he tells us, *p.* 15. [59]
concerning this Division of the World, *That some say it was by*
lot, and others that Noah *sail'd round the* Mediterranean *in Ten Years,*
and divided the World into Asia, Afric *and* Europe, Portions for his
5 three Sons. *America* then, it seems, was left to be his that could
catch it. Why our *A.* takes such pains to prove the Division of
the World by *Noah* to his Sons, and will not leave out an Imagination, though no better than a Dream, that he can find any where
to favour it, is hard to guess, since such a *Division,* if it prove any
10 thing, must necessarily take away the Title of *Adam*'s Heir: unless
three Brothers can altogether be Heirs of *Adam*; And therefore

---

§ 141 22–3 Ogygis, first king of Thebes, reigning at the time of the flood, and so
connected with a new race of Greeks: Hercules, Heracles, from whom the Dorians
of Ancient Greece thought themselves descended: Brama, Brahma, from whom the
Brahmans—the dominant caste of India—claimed divine descent: Tamberlain,
Timur, the Mongol leader, from whom Locke perhaps supposes that the Mongols
or even the Russians claimed descent: Pharamond, the Merovingian legendary king,
may be included as a fabulous father of the French, and Jupiter and Saturn as
originators of the Romans.

the following Words, *Howsoever the manner of this Division be uncertain, yet it is most certain the Division it self was by Families from* Noah *and his Children, over which the Parents were Heads and Princes,* p. 15. [59] if allow'd him to be true, and of any force to prove,   15
that all the Power in the World is nothing but the Lordship *of* Adam's *descending by Right*, they will only prove that the Fathers of the Children are all Heirs to this Lordship of *Adam*. For if in those days *Cham* and *Japhet*, and other Parents besides the Eldest Son were Heads and Princes over their Families, and had   20
a right to divide the Earth by Families, what hinders Younger Brothers, being Fathers of Families, from having the same Right? If *Cham* and *Japhet* were Princes by Right descending to them, notwithstanding any Title of Heir in their Eldest Brother, Younger Brothers by the same Right descending to them are Princes now,   25
and so all our *A*'s Natural Power of Kings will reach no farther than their own Children, and no Kingdom by this Natural Right, can be bigger than a Family. For either this *Lordship of Adam over the whole World*, by Right descends only to the Eldest Son, and then there can be but one Heir, as our *A*. says, p. 19 [60/61].   30
Or else, it by Right descends to all the Sons equally, and then every Father of a Family will have it, as well as the three Sons of *Noah:* Take which you will, it destroys the present Governments and Kingdoms, that are now in the World, since whoever has this *Natural Power of a King*, by Right descending to him, must   35
have it either, as our A. tells us, *Cain* had it, and be Lord over his Brethren, and so be alone King of the whole World, or else as he tells us here, *Shem, Cham* and *Japhet* had it, three Brothers, and so be only Prince of his own Family, and all Families independent one of another; All the World must be only one Empire   40
by the right of the next Heir, or else every Family be a distinct Government of it self, by the *Lordship of Adam's descending to Parents of Families*. And to this only tends all the Proofs he here gives us of the descent of *Adam*'s Lordship: For continuing his Story of this descent he says;   45

143. *In the dispersion of* Babel, *we must certainly find the Establishment of* Royal Power, *throughout the Kingdoms of the World*, p. 14 [58]. If you must find it, pray do, and you will help us to a new piece of History: But you must shew it us before we shall be bound to believe, that Regal Power was Established in the World upon   5

your Principles. For, that Regal Power was Established *in the Kingdoms of the World*, I think no body will dispute, but that there should be Kingdoms in the World, whose several Kings enjoy'd their Crowns, *by right descending to them from Adam*, that we think not only *Apocrypha*, but also utterly impossible. If our A. has no better Foundation for his Monarchy than a supposition of what was done at the dispersion of *Babel*, the Monarchy he erects thereon, whose top is to reach to Heaven to unite Mankind, will serve only to divide and scatter them as that Tower did; and instead of establishing civil government and order in the World will produce nothing but confusion.

144. For he tells us, the *Nations* they were divided into, *were distinct Families, which had Fathers for Rulers over them*; *whereby it appears, that even in the confusion, God was careful to preserve the Fatherly Authority, by distributing the Diversity of Languages, according to the Diversity of Families*, p. 14 [58]. It would have been a hard matter for any one but our *A.* to have found out so plainly in the Text, he here brings, that all the Nations in that dispersion were governed by *Fathers*, and that *God was careful to preserve the Fatherly Authority*. The words of the Text are; *These are the Sons of* Shem *after their Families, after their Tongues in their Lands, after their Nations*; and the same thing is said of *Cham* and *Japhet*, after an Enumeration of their Posterities: in all which there is not one word said of their Governors, or Forms of Government; of *Fathers*, or *Fatherly Authority*. But our *A.* who is very quick sighted, to spy out *Fatherhood*, where no body else could see any the least glimpses of it, tells us positively their *Rulers were Fathers, and God was careful to preserve the Fatherly Authority*; and why? Because those of the same Family spoke the same Language, and so of necessity in the Division kept together. Just as if one should argue thus; *Hanibal* in his Army, consisting of divers Nations, kept those of the same Language together, therefore Fathers were Captains of each Band, and *Hanibal* was careful of the *Fatherly Authority*. Or in Peopling of *Carolina*, the *English, French, Scotch*, and *Welch* that are there, Plant themselves together, and by them

---

§144   9   The text is Gen. x. 31.
    23   'Peopling of Carolina'—compare 1, § 130, 6 and note. The *Fundamental Constitutions of Carolina* makes no provision for, nor reference to, the peopling of individual 'counties' or 'manors' in this way, but, as was natural, English, French, Welsh and Scots did tend to settle the area of the colony so.

the Country is divided *in their Lands after their Tongues, after their* 25
Families, after their Nations; therefore care was taken of the *Fatherly
Authority*. Or because in many parts of *America*, every little
Tribe was a distinct People, with a different Language, one should
infer, that therefore *God was careful to preserve the Fatherly Authority*,
or that therefore their Rulers *enjoy'd Adam's Lordship by right* 30
descending to them, though we know not who were their Governors,
nor what their Form of Government, but only that they were
divided into little Independent Societies, speaking different
Languages.

145. The Scripture says not a word of their Rulers or Forms
of Government, but only gives an account, how Mankind came
to be divided into distinct Languages and Nations; and therefore
'tis not to argue from the Authority of Scripture, to tell us
positively, *Fathers* were their *Rulers*, when the Scripture says no 5
such thing, but to set up Fancies of ones own Brain, when we
confidently aver Matter of Fact, where Records are utterly silent.
Upon a like ground, *i.e.* none at all he says, *That they were not
confused Multitudes without Heads and Governors, and at liberty to
choose what Governors or Governments they pleased* [58]. 10

146. For I demand, when Mankind were all yet of one Language,
all Congregated in the Plain of *Shinar*, were they then all under one
Monarch, *who enjoy'd the Lordship of Adam by Right descending to
him?* If they were not, there was then no thoughts, 'tis plain,
of *Adam's Heir*, no Right to Government known then upon that 5
Title, no Care taken by God or Man, of *Adam's Fatherly Authority*.
If when Mankind were but one People, dwelt altogether, and
were of one Language, and were upon Building a City together;
and when 'twas plain, they could not but know the Right Heir,
for *Shem* lived till *Isaac's* time, a long while after the Division at 10
Babel; If then, I say, they were not under the Monarchical Government of *Adam's* Fatherhood, by Right descending to the Heir,
'tis plain there was no regard had to the *Fatherhood*, no Monarchy
acknowledg'd due to *Adam's* Heir, no Empire of *Shem's* in *Asia*,
and consequently no such Division of the World by *Noah*, as our 15

27-34   This amplifies Locke's view of a state of nature as described in his *Second
Treatise* in an interesting way. If he was right, primitive America should be just like
this. Compare I, § 153, 19 and Introduction, 98.
§ 145   7   Compare I, § 144, 31-2; II, § 101, 11-12.

A. has talked of. As far as we can conclude any thing from Scripture in this matter, it seems from this place, that if they had any Government, it was rather a Commonwealth than an Absolute Monarchy: For the Scripture tells us, *Gen.* 11. *They said.* 'Twas
20 not a Prince commanded the Building of this City and Tower, 'twas not by the Command of one *Monarch*, but by the Consultation of many, a Free People, *Let us build us a City*; They built it for themselves as Free-men, not as Slaves for their Lord and Master: *That we be not scattered abroad*; having a City once built,
25 and fixed Habitations to settle our Abodes and Families. This was the Consultation and Design of a People, that were at liberty to part asunder, but desired to keep in one Body, and could not have been either necessary or likely in Men tyed together under the Government of one Monarch, who if they had been, as our
30 *A.* tells us, all *Slaves* under the Absolute Dominion of a Monarch, needed not have taken such care to hinder themselves from wandering out of the reach of his Dominion. I demand whether this be not plainer in Scripture than any thing of *Adam's Heir* or *Fatherly Authority?*

147. But if being, as God says, *Gen.* 11. 6. one People, they had one Ruler, one King by Natural Right, Absolute and Supreme over them, *what care had God to preserve the Paternal Authority of the Supreme Fatherhood* [58], if on a suddain he suffers 72 (for so
5 many our A. talks of [58]) *distinct Nations*, to be erected out of it, under distinct Governors, and at once to withdraw themselves from the Obedience of their Sovereign. This is to entitle God's care how, and to what we please. Can it be Sense to say, that God was careful to preserve the *Fatherly Authority* in those who
10 had it not? For if these were Subjects under a Supreme Prince, what Authority had they? Was it an instance of God's care to preserve the *Fatherly Authority*, when he took away the true *Supreme Fatherhood* of the Natural Monarch? Can it be reason to

§ 146 17–19 In the 1st Edition, 1, § 147, 36–7 is more explicit than this: 'God himself says they were a Commonwealth'—cf. 11, § 133, 2–3. In his early *Essay on the Civil Magistrate* Locke denied that God laid down in Scripture any rules of government or bounds to political power, except only the government of the Jews which he had himself constituted (English treatise, f.33). There had been controversy over the constitution of the Israelites since the mid-sixteenth century—compare for example the *Vindiciae*. Locke may have discussed the point further in the missing section, together with Filmer's use of Old Testament monarchical history. Compare 1, § 165, 2–3 and note.

say, That God, for the Preservation of *Fatherly Authority*, lets
several new Governments with their Governors ſtart up, who 15
could not all have *Fatherly Authority?* and is it not as much reason
to say, That God is careful to deſtroy *Fatherly Authority*, when
he suffers one who is in Possession of it, to have his Government
torn in pieces, and shared by several of his Subjects? Would
it not be an Argument juſt like this, for Monarchical Government, 20
to say, when any Monarchy was shatter'd to pieces, and divided
amongſt revolted Subjects, that God was careful to preserve
Monarchical Power, by rending a settled Empire into a Multitude
of little Governments? If any one will say, that what happens in
Providence to be preserved, God is careful to preserve as a thing 25
therefore to be eſteemed by Men as necessary or useful, 'tis
a peculiar Propriety of Speech, which every one will not think
fit to imitate: but this I am sure is impossible to be either proper,
or true speaking, that *Shem*, for example (for he was then alive)
should have *Fatherly Authority*, or Sovereignty by Right of *Father-* 30
hood over that one People at *Babel*, and that the next moment
Shem yet living, 72 others should have *Fatherly Authority*, or
Sovereignty by Right of Fatherhood over the same People,
divided into so many diſtinct Governments; either these 72
Fathers actually were Rulers, juſt before the Confusion, and then 35
they were not one People, but that God himself says they were;
or else they were a Common-wealth, and then where was
Monarchy? or else these 72 Fathers had *Fatherly Authority*, but
knew it not. Strange! that *Fatherly Authority* should be the only
Original of Government amongſt Men, and yet all Mankind not 40
know it; and ſtranger yet, that the confusion of Tongues should
reveal it to them all of a sudden, that in an inſtant these 72 should
know that they had *Fatherly Power*, and all others know that they
were to obey it in them, and every one know that particular
Fatherly Authority to which he was a Subject. He that can think 45
this Arguing from Scripture, may from thence make out what
Model of an *Eutopia* will beſt suit with his Fancy or Intereſt, and
this *Fatherhood* thus disposed of, will juſtifie both a Prince who
claims an Universal Monarchy, and his Subjects, who being

---

§ 147   36–7   See note on 1, § 146, 17–34.

47   'Eutopia'—a reference to the *Utopia* of Sir Thomas More (1516), already
current as a collective name for all fanciful political models. *Utopia* was the only
work of More's which Locke possessed in two Latin editions (H. and L. 2048, 2049).

50 Fathers of Families, shall quit all Subjection to him, and *Canton*
his Empire into less Governments for themselves: For it will
always remain a doubt in which of these the Fatherly Authority
resided, till our *A.* resolves us, whether *Shem*, who was then alive,
or these 72 new Princes, beginning so many new Empires in his
55 Dominions, and over his Subjects, had right to govern, since our
A. tells us, that both one and t'other had *Fatherly*, which is
Supreme, Authority, and are brought in by him as Instances of
those, who did *enjoy the Lordship of Adam by right descending to*
them, which was as large and ample as the Absolutest Dominion of any
60 *Monarch* [58]. This at least is unavoidable, that if *God was careful*
to preserve the Fatherly Authority, in the 72 New erected Nations [58],
it necessarily follows, that he was as careful to destroy all pretences
of *Adams* Heir; since he took care, and therefore did preserve the
Fatherly Authority in so many, at least 71, that could not possibly
65 be *Adams* Heirs, when the right Heir (if God had ever ordained
any such Inheritance) could not but be known, *Shem* then living,
and they being all one People.

148. *Nimrod* is his next instance of enjoying this Patriarchal
Power, *p.* 16. [59] but I know not for what Reason our *A.* seems
a little unkind to him, and says, that he *against Right enlarged his*
Empire, by seizing violently on the Rights of other Lords of Families:
5 These *Lords of Families* here were called *Fathers of Families*, in
his account of the dispersion at *Babel*: but it matters not how they
were called, so we know who they are; for this Fatherly Authority
must be in them, either as Heirs to *Adam*, and so there could not
be 72, nor above one at once, or else as natural Parents over their
10 Children, and so every Father will have *Paternal Authority* over

---

50 '*Canton*'—to split up into independent political units, or cantons.
53 Shem, Noah's eldest son and so, as Filmer would say, the natural heir to his
power and possessions, lived for 600 years, and so would have seen all these events—
see Gen. xi. 11–12. This is another example of Locke's accepting Biblical chronology,
see 1, § 136, 11 and note.
§ 148 1 '*Nimrod*'—the story of Nimrod (Gen. x. 1–10), Noah's grandson but not
in the elder line, was commonly used by those who founded political power,
particularly monarchy, on force or conquest. Filmer deals with this interpretation
in the paragraph which Locke is criticizing here, admitting in 'his conclusion of that
paragraph' (see line 24 of this one) that Nimrod was a usurper. Sidney follows the sixteenth-
and early seventeenth-century interpreters whom Filmer had in mind, using their case to
insinuate, of course, that all kings were usurpers by violence of the rights of the people: see
Discourses, 1, 8, headed 'Nimrod was the first King'.

his Children by the same Right, and in as large extent as those 72 had, and so be Independent Princes over their own Off-spring. Taking his *Lords of Families*, in this latter sense (as 'tis hard to give those words any other sense in this place) he gives us a very pretty account of the Original of Monarchy in these following 15 words, *p.* 16. [59] *And in this Sense he may be said to be the Author and Founder of Monarchy*, viz. As against Right seizing violently on the Rights of Fathers over their Children, which Paternal Authority, if it be in them by right of Nature; (for else how could those 72 come by it) no body can take from them without their 20 own consents, and then I desire our *A.* and his Friends to consider how far this will concern other Princes, and whether it will not according to his conclusion of that Paragraph, resolve all Regal Power of those, whose Dominions extend beyond their Families, either into Tyranny and Usurpation, or Election and 25 Consent of Fathers of Families, which will differ very little from Consent of the People.

149. All his Instances, in the next *Section, p.* 17. [59] of the 12. Dukes of *Edom*, the 9. Kings in a little corner of *Asia* in *Abrahams* days, the 31 Kings in *Canaan* destroyed by *Joshua*, and the care he takes to prove that these were all Sovereign Princes, and that every Town in those days had a King, are so many direct Proofs 5 against him, that it was not the *Lordship of* Adam *by Right descending* to them that made Kings: For if they had held their Royalties by that Title, either there must have been but one Sovereign over them all, or else every Father of a Family had been as good a Prince, and had as good a claim to Royalty as these: For if all the Sons of 10 *Esau*, had each of them, the Younger as well as the Eldest, the right of *Fatherhood*, and so were Sovereign Princes after their Fathers Death, the same Right had their Sons after them, and so on to all Posterity, which will limit all the natural Power of Fatherhood, only to be over the Issue of their own Bodies, and 15 their descendants, which Power of Fatherhood dies with the head

---

16 '*p.* 16'.—omitted in the 1st edition. This may imply that Locke had his Filmer beside him when he corrected the 1st edition for the 2nd in 1694, although he did not when he made the final corrections which appear in the Christ's copy. Compare notes on 1, § 157, 2 and 1, § 78, 19.

§ 149 1 'in the next *Section*'—see note on 1, § 138, 1: Section 7 of the 1680 printing begins on p. 17. Locke seems to have felt that he had got through two sections, 5 and 6, of *Patriarcha* in paragraphs 138–48.

of each Family, and makes way for the like power of Fatherhood to take place, in each of his Sons, over their respective Posterities, whereby the Power of Fatherhood will be preserv'd indeed, and
20 is intelligible, but will not be at all to our *A*——s purpose: None of the instances he brings, are proofs of any Power they had, as Heirs of *Adam*'s Paternal Authority, by the title of his fatherhood descending to them, no—nor of any power they had by Vertue of their own: For *Adams Fatherhood* being over all
25 Mankind, it could descend but to one at once, and from him to his right Heir only, and so there could by that Title be but one King in the World at a time; And by Right of Fatherhood, not descending from *Adam*, it must be only as they themselves were Fathers, and so could be over none but their own Posterity:
30 So that if those 12 Dukes of *Edom*; If *Abraham* and the 9 Kings his Neighbours; If *Jacob* and *Esau* and the 31 Kings in *Canaan*, the 72 Kings mutilated by *Adonibeseck*, the 32 Kings that came to *Benhadad*, the 70 Kings of *Greece* making War at *Troy*, were as our *A*. contends [60], all of them Sovereign Princes; 'tis evident that
35 Kings deriv'd their Power from some other Original *then Father-hood*, since some of these had Power over more than their own Posterity, and 'tis Demonstration, they could not be all Heirs to *Adam*: For I challenge any Man to make any pretence to Power by right of *Fatherhood*, either intelligible or possible in any one,
40 otherwise, than either as *Adams* Heir, or as Progenitor over his own Descendants, naturally sprung from him. And if our *A*. could shew that any one of these Princes, of which he gives us here so large a Catalogue, had his Authority by either of these Titles, I think I might yield him the cause: though 'tis manifest
45 they are all impertinent and directly contrary to what he brings them to prove, *viz*. That the *Lordship which* Adam *had over the World by Right descended to the Patriarchs.*

150. Having told us, *p.* 16. [59, 60] That *the Patriarchal Govern-ment continued in* Abraham, Isaac, *and* Jacob, *until the* Egyptian Bondage, p. 17. [60] he tells us, *By manifest Footsteps we may trace this Paternal Government unto the* Israelites *coming into* Egypt, *where*
5 *the exercise of Supream Patriarchal Government was intermitted, because they were in Subjection to a stronger Prince.* What these Footsteps are of paternal Government, in our *A*'s Sense, *i.e.* of Absolute Monarchical Power descending from *Adam*, and exercised by

Right of *Fatherhood* we have seen, that is for 2290 Years no Footsteps at all: since in all that time he cannot produce any one 10
Example of any Person who claim'd or Exercised Regal Authority
by right of *Fatherhood*; or shew any one who being a King was
Adams Heir. All that his Proofs amount to, is only this, that
there were Fathers, Patriarchs and Kings in that Age of the
World; but that the Fathers and Patriarchs had any Absolute 15
Arbitrary Power, or by what Title those Kings had theirs, and
of what extent it was, the Scripture is wholly silent; 'tis manifest
by Right of *Fatherhood* they neither did, nor could claim any
Title to Dominion and Empire.

151. To say, *that the Exercise of Supream Patriarchal Government
was intermitted, because they were in Subjection to a stronger Prince,*
proves nothing but what I before suspected, *viz.* That *Patriarchal
Jurisdiction or Government* is a fallacious expression, and does not
in our *A.* signifie (what he would yet insinuate by it) *Paternal* 5
and *Regal Power*; such an Absolute Sovereignty, as he supposes
was in *Adam.*

152. For how can he say that *Patriarchal Jurisdiction was intermitted in Egypt,* where there was a King, under whose Regal
Government the *Israelites* were, if *Patriarchal* were *Absolute
Monarchical Jurisdiction?* And if it were not, but something else,
why does he make such ado about a Power not in question, and 5
nothing to the purpose? The Exercise of *Patriarchal* Jurisdiction,
if *Patriarchal* be *Regal,* was not intermitted whilst the *Israelites*
were in *Egypt.* 'Tis true, the Exercise of *Regal* Power was not
then in the hands of any of the promised Seed of *Abraham,* nor
before neither that I know, but what is that to the intermission 10
of *Regal Authority, as descending from Adam,* unless our *A.* will
have it, that this chosen Line of *Abraham,* had the Right of
Inheritance to *Adams* Lordship? And then to what purpose are
his instances of the 72 Rulers, in whom the Fatherly Authority
was preserv'd in the Confusion at *Babel?* Why does he bring the 15

§ 150   9   '2290 Years'—from the Creation (4004 B.C.) to the Exile in Egypt
(706 B.C.) according to Ussher's chronology in the Authorized Version. Compare
note on 1, § 136, 11, though here Locke follows the chronology with startling
exactness.
§ 152   This paragraph was extensively modified in 1694 by Locke: the page is a
cancel in the 2nd edition of that year, but it is further corrected in the Errata, and
again in the Christ's copy.

12 Princes Sons of *Ismael*; and the Dukes of *Edom*, and joyn them
with *Abraham, Isaac,* and *Jacob,* as examples of the exercise of
true *Patriarchal Government,* if the exercise of *Patriarchal Jurisdiction* were intermitted in the World, whenever the Heirs of
20 *Jacob* had not Supream Power? I fear *Supream Patriarchal Jurisdiction* was not only *intermitted,* but from the time of the Egyptian
Bondage quite loſt in the World, since 'twill be hard to find from
that time downwards, any one who exercised it as an Inheritance
descending to him from the Patriarchs *Abraham, Isaac,* and *Jacob.*
25 I imagined Monarchical Government would have served his turn
in the hands of *Pharaoh* or any Body. But one cannot easily discover in all places what his discourse tends to, as particularly in
this place, it is not obvious to guess what he drives at, when he
says, *the exercise of Supream Patriarchal Jurisdiction* in *Egypt,* or how
30 this serves to make out the descent of *Adams* Lordship to the
Patriarchs or any Body else.

153. For I thought he had been giving us out of Scripture,
Proofs and Examples of Monarchical Government, founded on
Paternal Authority, descending from *Adam;* and not an Hiſtory
of the *Jews:* amongſt whom yet we find no Kings, till many Years
5 after they were a People: and when Kings were their Rulers,
there is not the leaſt mention or room for a pretence that they
were Heirs to *Adam* or Kings by Paternal Authority. I expeƈted,
talking so much as he does of Scripture, that he would have
produced thence a Series of Monarchs, whose Titles were clear
10 to *Adams Fatherhood,* and who, as Heirs to him, own'd and exercised Paternal Jurisdiƈtion over their Subjeƈts, and that this was
the true Patriarchical Government: whereas he neither proves,
that the Patriarchs were Kings, nor that either Kings or Patriarchs
were Heirs to *Adam,* or so much as pretended to it: and one may
15 as well prove, that the Patriarchs were all Absolute Monarchs;
that the Power both of Patriarchs and Kings was only Paternal;
and that this Power descended to them from *Adam;* I say all these
Propositions may be as well proved by a confused account of
a multitude of little Kings in the *Weſt-Indies,* out of *Ferdinando*

§ 153   19   'multitude of little Kings'—compare 1, § 144, 27–34 and note.
19–20   'Ferdinando Soto', 'Histories of Northern America'. The reference to Soto
could apply to any of the three accounts of that famous explorer published in French,
Spanish or Portuguese in various editions. The most likely book is another work of

254

Soto, or any of our late Histories of the *Northern America*, or by 20
our *A*-s 70 Kings of *Greece*, out of *Homer*, as by any thing he brings
out of Scripture, in that Multitude of Kings he has reckon'd up.

154. And Methinks he should have let *Homer* and his Wars of
Troy alone, since his great Zeal to Truth or Monarchy carried
him to such a pitch of transport against *Philosophers and Poets*, that
he tells us in his Preface [188], that there *are too many in these days,*
who please themselves in running after the Opinions of Philosophers and 5
Poets, to find out such an Original of Government, as might promise
them some Title to Liberty, to the great Scandal of Christianity, and
bringing in of Atheism. And yet these Heathens, Philosopher
Aristotle, and Poet *Homer*, are not rejected by our zealous Christian
Politician, whenever they offer any thing that seems to serve his 10
turn, whether to the great Scandal of Christianity, and bringing in of
Atheisme; let him looke. This I cannot but observe in Authors who
('tis visible) write not for truth, how ready zeale for interest and
party is to entitle *Christianity* to their design, and to charge
Atheisme on those who will not without examining, submit to 15
their Doctrines, and blindly swallow their nonsense.

But to return to his Scripture History, our *A*. farther tells us,
p. 18. [60] that *after the return of the* Israelites *out of* Bondage, *God*
out of a special care of them, chose Moses *and* Joshua *Successively to*
Govern as Princes in the place and stead of the Supream Fathers. If it 20
be true, that they *returned out of Bondage*, it must be into a State of
Freedom, and must imply, that both before and after this *Bondage*
they were free, unless our *A*. will say, that changing of Masters,
is returning *out of Bondage*, or that a Slave *returns out of Bondage*,
when he is removed from one Gally to another. If then they 25

Garcilaso (see note on 1, § 57, 18), Richelet's French translation of his *La Florida del*
Inca, 1605, *Histoire de la Floride, ou Rélation...de Ferdinand de Soto*, 1670, which
Locke owned. The American histories might be Sagard's *Canada*, 1636, or his *Voyage des*
Hurons, 1632—even John Smith's *Description of New England*, 1616, all of which Locke is
known to have read when working at this book. His final library included many other likely
titles.
§ 154 4, 27 'his Preface'—the Preface to Filmer's *Forms*; see note on 1, § 8, 38.
11–16 Passage in Christ's copy. The rather biting tone may betray his resentment of the
attacks being made on him in his last years as an enemy of Christianity—Filmer is here classed
with men like John Edwards (see Introduction, 73) though his sentiment recalls that of his
earliest political writing.
21–2 Locke seems to be playing on the ambiguity of the word 'freedom',
freedom as national independence and as government by consent.

returned out of Bondage, 'tis plain that in those days, whatever our *A.* in his Preface [188] says to the contrary, there was difference between a *Son,* a *Subject,* and a *Slave;* and that neither the *Patriarchs* before, nor their Rulers after this *Egyptian Bondage, numbered their* 30 *Sons or Subjects amongst their Possessions,* and disposed of them with as Absolute a Dominion, as they did *their other Goods.*

155. This is evident in *Jacob,* to whom *Reuben* offered his two Sons as Pledges, and *Judah* was at last surety for *Benjamin's* safe return out of *Egypt:* Which all had been vain, superfluous, and but a sort of mockery, if *Jacob* had had the same Power over 5 every one of his Family as he had over his Ox or his Ass, as an *Owner* over his *Substance;* and the offers that *Reuben* or *Judah* made had been such a Security for returning of *Benjamin,* as if a Man should take two Lambs out of his Lords flock, and offer one as security, that he will safely restore the other.

156. When they were out of this *Bondage,* what then? *God out of a special care of them, the Israelites* [60]. 'Tis well that once in his Book, he will allow God to have any care of the People, for in other places he speaks of Mankind, as if God had no care of 5 any part of them, but only of their Monarchs, and that the rest of the People, the Societies of Men, were made as so many Herds of Cattle, only for the Service, Use, and Pleasure of their Princes.

157. *Chose* Moses *and* Joshua *Successively to Govern as Princes* [60]; A shreud Argument our *A.* has found out to prove Gods care of the Fatherly Authority, and *Adams* Heirs, that here as an expression of his care of his own People, he chooses those for 5 Princes over them, that had not the least pretence to either. The Persons chosen were, *Moses* of the Tribe of *Levy,* and *Joshua* of the Tribe of *Ephraim,* neither of which had any Title of *Fatherhood:* But says our *A.* they were in the place and stead of the Supream Fathers: If God had any where, as plainly declared his choise

§ 155 See Gen. xlii–xliii.
§ 156 Locke compares the subjects of absolute monarchies to herds of animals in II, § 93, 7–15: compare also II, § 163, 19–23 and note on II, § 172, 10–19.
§ 157 2 In the Christ's copy 'p. 18' is deleted, a reference to Filmer which came after 'out' and which was inserted at the 2nd printing. The passage indicated (Laslett's edition, 60) begins in the first line of I, § 156, and is completed here. This perhaps implies that the whole of I, § 156 after '*Israelites*' in line 2 is an insertion of 1689: compare I, §§ 159, 160 and note.

of such *Fathers* to be Rulers, as he did of *Moses* and *Joshuah*, we   10
might believe *Moses* and *Joshuah* were in *their place and stead*, but
that being the question in debate, till that be better proved, *Moses*
being chosen by God to be Ruler of his People, will no more
prove that Government belong'd to *Adam*'s *Heir* or to the *Fatherhood*, than God's choosing *Aaron* of the Tribe of *Levy* to be   15
Priest, will prove that the Priesthood belong'd to *Adam*'s Heir
or the *Prime-fathers*, since God could choose *Aaron* to be Priest,
and *Moses* Ruler in *Israel*, though neither of those Offices, were
settled on *Adam*'s *Heir* or the *Fatherhood*.

158. Our *A*. goes on. *And after them likewise for a time he raised
up Judges, to defend his People in time of peril*, p. 18 [60]. This proves
Fatherly Authority to be the original of Government, and that
it descended from *Adam* to his Heirs, just as well as what went
before: only here our *A*. seems to confess, that these Judges,   5
who were all the Governours, they then had, were only Men
of valour, whom they made their Generals to defend them in
time of peril; and cannot God raise up such Men, unless Fatherhood have a Title to Government?

159. But says our *A*. *When God gave the* Israelites *Kings, he
re-established the ancient and prime Right of Lineal Succession to Paternal
Government*, p. 18 [60].

160. How did God *re-establish* it? By a Law, a positive command? We find no such thing. Our *A*. means then, that when

---

§ **158**   5–7   The view that the first monarchs, like the Judges of the Israelites, were
military leaders is put forward at length in the *Second Treatise*, §§ 105–10, especially
109.
§§ **159, 160**   The paragraph number '159' was omitted from the 2nd and 3rd
printings and not restored in Locke's final correction—159 was printed as if it
continued 158. In fact, of course, 159 is simply the quotation from Filmer on which
160 is a commentary, just as 156 was originally a quotation criticized in 157—see
note on 157. It seems possible that these two quotations were made to stand alone
as paragraphs in order to keep numeration continuous in an area of extensive
correction, deletion and perhaps even losses. The paragraphs from 160 to 169,
especially 161, 162, were recorrected for punctuation in 1694, 1698 and after 1698. All this
betrays confusion in Locke's manuscript, and may be connected with the imminent breaking
off of the *First Treatise*, or even with the peculiarities of the first printing of the early part of
the *Second*. Moreover, the text hereabouts seems to consist simply in comments on Filmer's
sentences, prolonging the chapter to twice the size of its predecessors, and wandering far
from its title 'Who Heir?' It may represent a stringing together of surviving fragments of the
lost portion of Locke's original manuscript.

God gave them a King, in giving them a King, he *re-eſtabliſhed the Right, &c.* To re-eſtablish *de faſto* the Right of Lineal Succession
5 to Paternal Government, is to put a Man in Possession of that Government which his Fathers did enjoy, and he by Lineal Succession had a Right to. For, firſt, if it were another Government, than what his Anceſtors had, it was not succeeding to an *Ancient Right*, but beginning a new one. For if a Prince should give
10 a Man, besides his Ancient Patrimony, which for some Ages his Family had been disseiz'd of, an additional Eſtate, never before in the Possession of his Anceſtors, he could not be said to *re-eſtabliſh the Right of Lineal Succession* to any more, than what had been formerly enjoy'd by his Anceſtors. If therefore the Power
15 the Kings of *Israel* had, were any thing more than *Isaac* or *Jacob* had, it was not the *re-eſtabliſhing* in them the Right of Succession to a Power, but giving them a new Power, however you please to call it *Paternal* or not: and whether *Isaac* and *Jacob* had the same Power, that the Kings of *Israel* had, I desire any one, by what has
20 been abovesaid, to consider, and I do not think they will find that either *Abraham, Isaac,* or *Jacob* had any Regal Power at all.

161. Next, there can be no *Re-eſtabliſhment of the Prime and Ancient Right of Lineal Succession* to any thing, unless he, that is put in Possession of it has the right to succeed, and be the true and next Heir to him he succeeds to. Can that be a Re-eſtablish-
5 ment, which begins in a new Family? or that the *Re-eſtabliſhment of an Ancient Right of Lineal Succession,* when a Crown is given to one, who has no Right of Succession to it, and who, if the Lineal Succession had gone on, had been out of all possibility of pretence to it? *Saul* the firſt King that God gave the *Israelites,* was of the
10 Tribe of *Benjamin.* Was the *Ancient and Prime Right of Lineal Succession Re-eſtabliſhed* in him? The next was *David* the Youngeſt Son of *Jesse,* of the Poſterity of *Judah, Jacob's third* Son. Was the *Ancient and Prime Right of Lineal Succession to Paternal Government Re-eſtabliſhed* in him? Or in *Solomon* his younger Son and Suc-
15 cessor in the Throne? Or in *Jeroboam* over the ten *Tribes*? Or in *Athaliah* a Woman, who Reigned six Years an utter Stranger to the Royal Blood? *If the Ancient and Prime Right of Lineal Succession to Paternal Government,* were *Re-eſtabliſhed* in any of these or their Poſterity, *the Ancient and Prime Right of Lineal Succession to Paternal*
20 *Government* belongs to Younger Brothers as well as Elder, and

may be Re-established in any Man living: For whatever Younger
Brothers, by *Ancient and Prime Right of Lineal Succession*, may have
as well as the Elder, that every Man living may have a Right to,
by Lineal Succession, and Sir *Robert* as well as any other. And
so what a brave Right of Lineal Succession, to his *Paternal* or 25
Regal Government, our *A.* has *Re-establish'd* for the securing the
Rights and Inheritance of Crowns, where every one may have it,
let the World consider.

162. But says our *A.* however, *p.* 19. [60] *Whensoever God made
choice of any special Person to be King, he intended that the Issue also
should have benefit thereof, as being comprehended sufficiently in the Person
of the Father, although the Father was only named in the Grant.* This
yet will not help out Succession; for if, as our *A.* says, the benefit 5
of the Grant be intended to the *Issue* of the Grantee, this will
not direct the Succession; Since if God give any thing to a Man
and his *Issue* in general, the Claim cannot be to any one of that
Issue in particular, every one that is of his Race will have an equal
Right. If it be said, our *A.* meant *Heir*, I believe our *A.* was as 10
willing as any Body to have used that word, if it would have
served his turn; but *Solomon* who succeeded *David* in the Throne,
being no more his Heir than *Jeroboam*, who succeeded him in
the Government of the Ten Tribes, was his Issue; our *A.* had
reason to avoid saying, that God intended it to the *Heirs*, when that 15
would not hold in a Succession, which our *A.* could not except
against, and so he has left his Succession as undetermined, as if
he had said nothing about it. For if the Regal Power be given
by God to a Man and his *Issue*, as the Land of *Canaan* was to
Abraham and his Seed, must they not all have a Title to it, all 20
share in it? And one may as well say, that by God's Grant to
Abraham and his Seed, the Land of *Canaan* was to belong only
to one of his Seed exclusive of all others, as by God's Grant of
Dominion to a man and his *Issue*, this Dominion was to belong
in peculiar to one of his *Issue* exclusive of all others. 25

163. But how will our *A.* prove, that whensoever God made
choice of any special Person to be a King, he intended that *the*
(I suppose he means *his*) *Issue also should have benefit thereof.* Has
he so soon forgot *Moses* and *Joshua* whom in this very *Section* [60],

---

§ 163   4   '*Section*'—section v of the 1680 printing; see note on 1, § 138, 1.

5 he says, *God out of a special care chose to govern as Princes,* and the Judges that God raised up? Had not these Princes, having the Authority of the *Supream Fatherhood,* the same Power that the Kings had, and being specially chosen by God himself, should not their Issue have the benefit of that choice, as well as *David's* or
10 *Solomon's?* If these had the Paternal Authority put into their hands immediately by God, why had not their *Issue* the benefit of this Grant in a Succession to this Power? Or if they had it as *Adam's* Heirs, why did not their Heirs enjoy it after them by Right descending to them? For they could not be Heirs to one another.
15 Was the Power the same, and from the same Original in *Moses, Joshua* and the *Judges,* as it was in *David* and the *Kings,* and was it inheritable in one and not in the other? If it was not *Paternal Authority,* then God's own People were govern'd by those that had not *Paternal Authority,* and those Governours did well enough
20 without it: If it were *Paternal Authority* and God chose the Persons that were to exercise it, our *A's* Rule fails, that *whensoever God makes choice of any Person to be Supream* Ruler (for I suppose the name King has no Spell in it, 'tis not the Title, but the Power makes the difference) *he intends that the Issue also should have the*
25 *benefit of it,* since from their coming out of *Egypt* to *David's* time, 400 Years, the *Issue* was never *so sufficiently comprehended in the Person of the Father* [60], as that any Son after the Death of his Father, succeeded to the Government amongst all those Judges that judged *Israel.* If to avoid this, it be said, God always chose
30 the Person of the Successor, and so transferring the *Fatherly Authority* to him, excluded his Issue from succeeding to it, that is manifestly not so in the Story of *Jephtha,* where he Articled with the People, and they made him Judge over them, as is plain, *Judg.* 11.

164. 'Tis in vain then to say [60], that *whensoever God chooses any special Person* to have the exercise of *Paternal Authority* (for if that be not to be King, I desire to know the difference between a King and one having the exercise of *Paternal Authority,*) *he*
5 *intends the Issue also should have the benefit of it,* since we find the

26 '400 years'—that is, 1491 B.C. to c. 1050 B.C. in Ussher's chronology; see note on I, § 136, 11.
32 On the story of Jephthah, critical to Locke's use of Scripture to sanction his political theory, see II, § 21, 10 and 17, note and references.

Authority, the Judges had, ended with them, and descended not to their *Issue*, and if the Judges had not *Paternal Authority*, I fear it will trouble our *A.* or any of the Friends to his Principles, to tell who had then the *Paternal Authority*, that is, the Government and Supream Power amongst the *Israelites*; and I suspect they 10 muft confess that the chosen People of God continued a People several hundreds of Years, without any Knowledge or Thought of this *Paternal Authority*, or any appearance of Monarchical Government at all.

165. To be satisfied of this, he need but read the Story of the *Levite*, and the War thereupon with the *Benjamites*, in the 3 laft *Chapt.* of *Jud.*: and when he finds, that the *Levite* appeals to the People for Juftice; that it was the Tribes and the Congregation, that debated, resolved, and directed all that was done on that 5 occasion, he muft conclude, either that *God* was not *careful to preserve the Fatherly Authority* amongst his own chosen People; or else that the *Fatherly Authority* may be preserved, where there is no Monarchical Government; If the latter, then it will follow that though *Fatherly Authority* be never so well proved, yet it 10 will not infer a necessity of Monarchical Government; If the former, it will seem very ftrange and improbable that God should ordain *Fatherly Authority* to be so Sacred amongst the Sons of Men, that there could be no Power or Government without it, and yet that amongft his own People, even whilft he is providing 15 a Government for them, and therein prescribes Rules to the several States and Relations of Men, this Great and Fundamental one, this moft material and necessary of all the reft should be concealed, and lye neglected for 400 Years after.

166. Before I leave this, I muft ask how our *A.* knows that *whensoever God makes choice of any special Person to be King, he intends that the Issue should have the benefit thereof?* [60] does God by the

---

§ **165**   2–3   These chapters, Judg. xix, xx, xxi, were much relied upon by that body of seventeenth-century opinion which held that the Israelites had a representative form of government; see the *Vindiciae Contra Tyrannos*, Selden's *Mare Clausum* and Sidney's *Discourses*, chapter 11, section 9, headed 'The Government instituted by God over the Israelites was Aristocratical', especially 1772, 105. Locke hints at this argument in 1, § 146. The appeal of the Levite to the people for justice occurs in Judg. xx. 7.

19   The 400 years were from the events under the Judges to the anointing of Saul, 1406–1095 B.C. in Ussher's chronology; see note on 1, § 136, 11.

Law of Nature or Revelation say so? By the same Law also he
5 must say, which of his *Issue* must enjoy the Crown in Succession,
and so point out the Heir, or else leave his *Issue* to divide or
scramble for the Government: both alike absurd, and such as
will destroy the benefit of such Grant to the *Issue*. When any such
Declaration of God's Intention is produced, it will be our Duty
10 to believe God intends it so, but till that be done, our *A*. must
shew us some better Warrant, before we shall be obliged to receive
him as the Authentick Revealer of God's Intentions.

167. *The Issue*, says our *A*. *is comprehended sufficiently in the Person
of the Father, although the Father only was named in the Grant* [60]:
And yet God, when he gave the Land of *Canaan* to *Abraham*,
Gen. 13. 15. thought fit to put *his Seed* into the Grant too. So the
5 Priesthood was given to *Aaron and his Seed*; And the Crown God
gave not only to *David*, but *his Seed* also: And however our *A*.
assures us that *God intends, that the Issue should have the benefit of it,
when he chooses any Person to be King*, yet we see that the Kingdom
which he gave to *Saul*, without mentioning his Seed after him,
10 never came to any of his *Issue*; and why when God chose a Person
to be King, he should intend that his *Issue* should have the benefit
of it, more than when he chose one to be Judge in *Israel*, I would
fain know a reason; or why does a Grant of *Fatherly Authority*
to a King more comprehend the *Issue*, than when a like Grant is
15 made to a Judge? Is *Paternal Authority* by Right to descend to
the *Issue*, of one and not of the other? There will need some
Reason to be shewn of this difference, more than the name, when
the thing given is the same *Fatherly Authority*, and the manner of
giving it, God's choice of the Person the same too; for I suppose
20 our *A*., when he says, *God raised up Judges*, will by no means allow,
they were chosen by the People.

168. But since our *A*. has so confidently assured us of the care
of God to preserve the *Fatherhood*, and pretends to build all, he
says, upon the Authority of the Scripture, we may well expect

§ 167   10   'chose'—at this word sheet P begins in the first printing, 1689. This
sheet contained the text up to II, § 8, line 6; see note there: Locke's interference in
the course of printing in 1689 could conceivably have affected the text at any point
from here to the end of Sheet S; see note on II, § 51.
§§ 168, 169   Here the chronological argument becomes the main theme, see I, § 136,
11: it presumably occupied the early part of the missing portion.
It will be seen that the *First Treatise* breaks off abruptly in the middle of a phrase,

262

that the People whose Law, Constitution and History is chiefly
contained in the Scripture, should furnish him with the clearest 5
Instances of God's care of preserving of the Fatherly Authority,
in that People who 'tis agreed he had a most peculiar care of.
Let us see then what State this *Paternal Authority* or Government
was in amongst the *Jews*, from their beginning to be a People.
It was omitted by our *A*'s confession, from their coming into 10
Egypt, till their return out of that Bondage, above 200 Years.
From thence till God gave the *Israelites* a King about 400 Years
more, our *A*. gives but a very slender account of it, nor indeed
all that time are there the least Footsteps of Paternal or Regal
Government amongst them. But then says our *A*. [60] *God* 15
Re-established the Ancient and Prime Right of Lineal Succession to
Paternal Government.

169. What a *Lineal Succession to Paternal Government* was then
Established, we have already seen. I only now consider how long
this lasted, and that was to their Captivity about 500 Years: From
thence to their Destruction by the *Romans*, above 650 Years after,
the *Ancient and Prime Right of lineal Succession to Paternal Govern-* 5
ment was again lost, and they continued a People in the promised
Land without it. So that of 1150 Years that they were God's
peculiar People, they had Hereditary Kingly Government amongst
them, not one third of the time, and of that time there is not the
least Footstep of one moment of *Paternal Government, nor the* 10
Re-establishment of the Ancient and Prime Right of Lineal Succession
to it, whether we suppose it to be derived, as from its Fountain,
from *David, Saul, Abraham*, or, which upon our *A*'s Principles
is the only true; From *Adam*. ****

obviously where Locke's manuscript reached the foot of a page. In the later
eighteenth-century editions and on, the stars were omitted and, although it made
nonsense, the final phrase seemed to end a sentence. Tarlton, 1978, disagrees that these final
phrases make nonsense, and allots a considerably greater significance to the whole *Treatise*
than is usual, or has been done here.

THE SECOND TREATISE
OF GOVERNMENT

A N

E S S A Y

Concerning the

True Original, Extent, and End

O F

Civil Government

Title. The title-page was an insertion in the course of printing, as subtly demonstrated by Gerritsen, 1954. The original title, not allotted a page to itself in the printing as first planned, was presumably simply the 'Book II' at the head of the first page of its text, the *First Treatise* having 'Book I'. The title to the whole volume seems to have been altered to take account of this new title to the second book. See Introduction, 50.

The correct title to this second book, then, is either 'The Second Treatise of Government', to conform with that of the whole volume, or the full title given here, abbreviated 'Of Civil Government' (or alternatively 'An Essay Concerning Civil Government'). It was entitled thus in the French translation, the first appearance of the *Second Treatise* independently, perhaps with Locke's approval (see Introduction, 12)—'Du Gouvernement Civil'. The title in common use is a solecism: 'The Second Treatise on (or of) Civil Government.' It may have arisen because the collected editions from the first (1714) on, and the individual editions from the 6th (1764) on, had the running title 'Of Government' for the *First Treatise* and 'Of Civil Government' for the *Second*—a distinction without meaning or usefulness.

BOOK II.

CHAP. I.

1. IT having been shewn in the foregoing Discourse,

1°. That *Adam* had not either by natural Right of Fatherhood, or by positive Donation from God, any such Authority
over his Children, or Dominion over the World as is pretended.

2°. That if he had, his Heirs, yet, had no Right to it.   5

3°. That if his Heirs had, there being no Law of Nature nor
positive Law of God that determines, which is the Right Heir
in all Cases that may arise, the Right of Succession, and consequently of bearing Rule, could not have been certainly determined.

4°. That if even that had been determined, yet the knowledge 10
of which is the Eldest Line of *Adam*'s Posterity, being so long
since utterly lost, that in the Races of Mankind and Families of the
World, there remains not to one above another, the least pretence
to be the Eldest House, and to have the Right of Inheritance.

All these premises having, as I think, been clearly made out, 15
it is impossible that the Rulers now on Earth, should make any
benefit, or derive any the least shadow of Authority from that,
which is held to be the Fountain of all Power, *Adam's Private
Dominion and Paternal Jurisdiction*, so that, he that will not give just
occasion, to think that all Government in the World is the product 20

---

§ 1 *Chapter* 1.—obviously written by Locke to bridge the gap between the fragmentary *First Treatise* and the *Second*, presumably in 1689. As originally composed,
this book must have started at § 4 (chapter II), or perhaps at an introductory paragraph to this one, now cancelled—see note on II, § 54, 1. Locke may, of course,
have modified this area of the text considerably in 1689.

This chapter is omitted from the French version of 1691, and so from all editions
in languages other than English until recent years. It was also left out of the early American
edition, Boston, 1773—see Introduction, 14.

20–2 This has been taken as a covert reference to Hobbes, and in fact may be a
reminiscence of Filmer's attack on the Hobbesian state of nature: 'It is not to be

267

only of Force and Violence, and that Men live together by no other Rules but that of Beasts, where the strongest carries it, and so lay a Foundation for perpetual Disorder and Mischief, Tumult, Sedition and Rebellion, (things that the followers of that Hypo-
25 thesis so loudly cry out against) must of necessity find out another rise of Government, another Original of Political Power, and another way of designing and knowing the Persons that have it, then what Sir *Robert F.* hath taught us.

2. To this purpose, I think it may not be amiss, to set down what I take to be Political Power. That the Power of a *Magistrate* over a Subject, may be distinguished from that of a *Father* over his Children, a *Master* over his Servant, a *Husband* over his Wife,
5 and a *Lord* over his Slave. All which distinct Powers happening sometimes together in the same Man, if he be considered under these different Relations, it may help us to distinguish these Powers one from another, and shew the difference betwixt a Ruler of a Common-wealth, a Father of a Family, and a Captain of a Galley.

3. *Political Power* then I take to be *a Right* of making Laws with Penalties of Death, and consequently all less Penalties, for the Regulating and Preserving of Property, and of employing the force of the Community, in the Execution of such Laws, and in
5 the defence of the Common-wealth from Foreign Injury, and all this only for the Publick Good.

---

thought that God would create man in a condition worse than any beast, as if he had made men to no other end by nature but to destroy one another' (Laslett's edition, 241). Filmer was Hobbes's first critic, and Locke had read and noted this work of his at least as early as 1667—see Introduction, 33. Compare II, § 93, 30-2.

23-4 Compare I, §§ 3; 83; 106, 15-16; § 143.

§ 3 Compare the definition of *respublica* in Locke's *Epistola de Tolerantia* (1689, that is, closer to this chapter than to the text as a whole): 'The commonwealth seems to me to be a society of men constituted only for procuring and preserving their own *civil interests* (bona civilia)...therefore is the magistrate armed with the force and strength of all his subjects (toto scilicet subditorum robore) in order to the punishment of those that violate any other man's rights' (Klibansky and Gough, ed., 1968, 66-7, slightly differently translated). Here external security is omitted and property is replaced by *bona civilia*, defined as 'life, liberty, health and indolency of body; and the possession of outward things, such as money, lands, houses, furniture and the like (vitam, libertatem, corporis integritatem, et indolentiam, et rerum externarum possessiones, ut sunt latifundia, pecunia, supellex etc.)'. See Introduction, 102; and on capital laws, see I, § 129, 10-15 and note, II, §§ 87-9, 171. Elrington (1798) remarks on the distinction between power and right in this paragraph, implying that Locke confuses them.

CHAP. II.

Of the State of Nature.

4. TO understand Political Power right, and derive it from its Original, we must consider what State all Men are naturally in, and that is, a *State of perfect Freedom* to order their Actions, and dispose of their Possessions, and Persons as they think fit, within the bounds of the Law of Nature, without asking leave, 5 or depending upon the Will of any other Man.

A *State* also *of Equality*, wherein all the Power and Jurisdiction is reciprocal, no one having more than another: there being nothing more evident, than that Creatures of the same species and rank promiscuously born to all the same advantages of Nature, 10 and the use of the same faculties, should also be equal one amongst another without Subordination or Subjection, unless the Lord and Master of them all, should by any manifest Declaration of his Will set one above another, and confer on him by an evident and clear appointment an undoubted Right to Dominion and 15 Sovereignty.

§ 4   *Chapter* II   The French and other versions begin with this chapter, and in Locke's original text there may have been only one paragraph before this point, introducing the whole work; see note on II, § 54, 1. Although it was extended when Locke added his Hooker material (see §§ 5 and 15) and certainly corrected to some extent, perhaps a great deal, in 1689—see, for example, § 14, 12–17—there is no reason to suppose that it was not substantially completed in 1679.

2   'are'—Seliger points out that this means that the state of nature was *not* past history.

9–10   A reference to the Creation, compare 1, §§ 25–7, etc.

9–11   Quoted verbatim by Molyneux, *Case of Ireland*, 1698 (1720 ed., 127).

11   'should'—to be read as imperative in feeling, for Locke recognized inequality in capacity. See II, § 54, and *The Conduct of the Understanding*: 'there is, it is visible, a great variety in men's understandings, and their natural constitutions...the woods of America, as well as the schools of Athens, produce men of several abilities in the same kind'. In the same work, however, he is prepared to use the example of the natural equality of men for the purpose of illustrating the necessity of bottoming, that is discovering a 'truth well settled in the understanding' (*Works*, 1801, III, 189 and 259). Compare Hobbes, *Elements of Law* (16, 4 (1928, p. 54): 'men considered in mere nature ought to admit amongst themselves equality', and the similar statements in *Leviathan* (chapter 13) and *De Cive*, though the context and grounds of this statement of Locke's are very different.

5. This *equality* of Men by Nature, the Judicious *Hooker* looks upon as so evident in it self, and beyond all queſtion, that he makes it the Foundation of that Obligation to mutual Love amongſt Men, on which he Builds the Duties they owe one another, and 5 from whence he derives the great Maxims *of Juſtice* and *Charity*. His words are;

The like natural inducement, hath brought Men to know that it is no less their Duty, to Love others than themselves, for seeing those things which are equal, muſt needs all have one measure; If I cannot but wish to 10 *receive good, even as much at every Man's hands, as any Man can wish unto his own Soul, how should I look to have any part of my desire herein satisfied, unless my self be careful to satisfie the like desire, which is undoubtedly in other Men, being of one and the same nature? to have any thing offered them repugnant to this desire, muſt needs in all respeĉts* 15 *grieve them as much as me, so that if I do harm, I muſt look to suffer, there being no reason that others should shew greater measure of love to me, than they have by me, shewed unto them; my desire therefore to be lov'd of my ₴quals in nature, as much as possible may be, imposeth upon me a natural Duty of bearing to themward, fully the like affeĉtion; From* 20 *which relation of equality between our selves and them, that are as our selves, what several Rules and Canons, natural reason hath drawn for direĉtion of Life, no Man is ignorant.* Eccl. Pol. Lib. 1.

6. But though this be a *State of Liberty*, yet it is *not a State of Licence*, though Man in that State have an uncontroleable Liberty,

---

§ 5 1 It was probably Locke, slavishly followed by his friend Molyneux, who did most to give currency to the title 'judicious' to Richard Hooker. He was genuinely indebted to Hooker both in his philosophy and his political theory, and in his lists of recommended reading for young men he talks of the *Ecclesiastical Polity* as one of 'the most talked of' books on politics, and requires thorough study of 'the judicious Hooker's first book' (*Works*, 1801, III, 272; X, 308). But the reference to him here and throughout the *Second Treatise* was also intended to lend respectability to his position and to turn the flank of his opponents, especially the good churchmen amongst them.

7-23 *Ecclesiastical Polity*, Book I, ch. VIII, § 7 (Keble ed. 1836, I, 288-9), not quite exactly quoted. Compare I, § 42 on Justice and Charity.

Like the other quotations from Hooker, this, and the rest of the paragraph with it, was probably added after the body of the text had been written (see Introduction, 57 and note, 11, § 239, 45 and note), probably on 28 June 1681, on which date Locke copied into his diary extracts from just before and just after this one (Ashcraft, 1987, 286 rejects this interpretation). All the extracts came from pp. 80-2 of the *Ecclesiastical Polity* which he had bought on 13 June. This was probably the 1676 edition, and it is referred to as such in these footnotes, but it could have been that of 1666, see Introduction, 57.

to dispose of his Person or Possessions, yet he has not Liberty to destroy himself, or so much as any Creature in his Possession, but where some nobler use, than its bare Preservation calls for it. 5 The *State of Nature* has a Law of Nature to govern it, which obliges every one: And Reason, which is that Law, teaches all Mankind, who will but consult it, that being all equal and independent, no one ought to harm another in his Life, Health, Liberty, or Possessions. For Men being all the Workmanship 10 of one Omnipotent, and infinitely wise Maker; All the Servants of one Sovereign Master, sent into the World by his order and about his business, they are his Property, whose Workmanship they are, made to last during his, not one anothers Pleasure. And being furnished with like Faculties, sharing all in one Community 15 of Nature, there cannot be supposed any such *Subordination* among us, that may Authorize us to destroy one another, as if we were made for one anothers uses, as the inferior ranks of Creatures are for ours. Every one as he is *bound to preserve himself*, and not to quit his Station wilfully; so by the like reason when his own 20 Preservation comes not in competition, ought he, as much as he can, *to preserve the rest of Mankind*, and may not unless it be to do Justice on an Offender, take away, or impair the life, or what tends to the Preservation of the Life, the Liberty, Health, Limb or Goods of another. 25

7. And that all Men may be restrained from invading others Rights, and from doing hurt to one another, and the Law of Nature be observed, which willeth the Peace and *Preservation of all Mankind*, the *Execution* of the Law of Nature is in that State, put into every Mans hands, whereby every one has a right to 5 punish the transgressors of that Law to such a Degree, as may hinder its Violation. For the *Law of Nature* would, as all other Laws that concern Men in this World, be in vain, if there were no body that in the State of Nature, had a *Power to Execute* that Law, and thereby preserve the innocent and restrain offenders, and if 10

---

§ 6   10–14   On man as God's workmanship see I, §§ 30, 52–4; 86; II § 56, 12–14; and as God's property I, § 85, 10–11; compare II, § 56, 12–14, and English Tract of 1660, II.

14–19   Compare I, §§ 86; 87; 92, 1–3 and note; II, § 135, 13–17. These statements are generally taken as directed against Hobbes, especially the thirteenth chapter of *Leviathan*, but there is no verbal resemblance.

18   'made for another's use'—Brogan, 1958, suggests a Kantian parallel.

any one in the State of Nature may punish another, for any evil he has done, every one may do so. For in that *State of perfect Equality*, where naturally there is no superiority or jurisdiction of one, over another, what any may do in Prosecution of that Law, 15 every one must needs have a Right to do.

8. And thus in the State of Nature, *one Man comes by a Power over another*; but yet no Absolute or Arbitrary Power, to use a Criminal when he has got him in his hands, according to the passionate heats, or boundless extravagancy of his own Will, but 5 only to retribute to him, so far as calm reason and conscience dictates, what is proportionate to his Transgression, which is so much as may serve for *Reparation* and *Restraint*. For these two are the only reasons, why one Man may lawfully do harm to another, which is that we call *punishment*. In transgressing the 10 Law of Nature, the Offender declares himself to live by another Rule, than that of *reason* and common Equity, which is that measure God has set to the actions of Men, for their mutual security: and so he becomes dangerous to Mankind, the tye, which is to secure them from injury and violence, being slighted 15 and broken by him. Which being a trespass against the whole Species, and the Peace and Safety of it, provided for by the Law of Nature, every man upon this score, by the Right he hath to preserve Mankind in general, may restrain, or where it is necessary, destroy things noxious to them, and so may bring such evil on 20 any one, who hath transgressed that Law, as may make him repent the doing of it, and thereby deter him, and by his Example others, from doing the like mischief. And in this case, and upon this ground, *every Man hath a Right to punish the Offender, and be Executioner of the Law of Nature.*

9. I doubt not but this will seem a very strange Doctrine to some Men: but before they condemn it, I desire them to resolve

---

§ 8 6 'proportionate'—at this word sheet P ends and sheet Q begins in the first printing. This sheet exists in variant states (see Laslett, 1952 (iv), and Bowers, Gerritsen and Laslett, 1954 (ii)). Even more than in the case of the later part of sheet P (see 1, § 167, 10 and note), any part of it may be the result of Locke's last-minute modifications. It ends with the last word of § 21.

§ 9 1 'strange Doctrine'—this seems to be Locke's way of announcing that his doctrine of punishment was, or was intended by him to be, a novelty; compare 11, § 13, 1; 11, § 180, 6 and Introduction, 97. It is certainly in subtle contrast with Hobbes's doctrine in chapter 28 of *Leviathan*, with which it is often compared. The

me, by what Right any Prince or State can put to death, or *punish an Alien*, for any Crime he commits in their Country. 'Tis certain their Laws by vertue of any Sanction they receive from 5 the promulgated Will of the Legislative, reach not a Stranger. They speak not to him, nor if they did, is he bound to hearken to them. The Legislative Authority, by which they are in Force over the Subjects of that Common-wealth, hath no Power over him. Those who have the Supream Power of making Laws in 10 *England*, *France* or *Holland*, are to an *Indian*, but like the rest of the World, Men without Authority: And therefore if by the Law of Nature, every Man hath not a Power to punish Offences against it, as he soberly judges the Case to require, I see not how the Magistrates of any Community, can *punish an Alien* of another 15 Country, since in reference to him, they can have no more Power, than what every Man naturally may have over another.

10. Besides the Crime which consists in violating the Law, and varying from the right Rule of Reason, whereby a Man so far becomes degenerate, and declares himself to quit the Principles of Human Nature, and to be a noxious Creature, there is commonly *injury* done to some Person or other, and some other Man receives 5 damage by his Transgression, in which Case he who hath received any damage, has besides the right of punishment common to him with other Men, a particular Right to seek *Reparation* from him that has done it. And any other Person who finds it just, may also joyn with him that is injur'd, and assist him in recovering 10 from the Offender, so much as may make satisfaction for the harm he has suffer'd.

11. From thence *two distinct Rights*, the one of *Punishing* the Crime *for restraint*, and preventing the like Offence, which right of punishing is in every body; the other of taking *reparation*, which belongs only to the injured party, comes it to pass that the Magistrate, who by being Magistrate, hath the common right of 5

---

whole of Locke's *Second Letter on Toleration* (1690) is concerned with punishment as a means of '*Reparation* and *Restraint*'.

10–12   That is to say the Indian, presumably the American Indian, is in a state of nature with respect to all established political power, which implies there is no international law (see Cox, 1960, 138).

§ 10   On this paragraph, Elrington comments (1798) that throughout the whole of this treatise Locke's 'zeal for liberty has very frequently led him to speak of men's *duties* as *rights* which they may exercise or renounce at pleasure'.

4   'noxious Creature'—compare 11, § 172, 9–19, note and references.

punishing put into his hands, can often, where the publick good demands not the execution of the Law, *remit* the punishment of Criminal Offences by his own Authority, but yet cannot *remit* the satisfaction due to any private Man, for the damage he has received. That, he who has suffered the damage has a Right to demand in his own name, and he alone can *remit*: The damnified Person has this Power of appropriating to himself, the Goods or Service of the Offender, by *Right of Self-preservation*, as every Man has a Power to punish the Crime, to prevent its being committed again, *by the Right he has of Preserving all Mankind*, and doing all reasonable things he can in order to that end: And thus it is, that every Man in the State of Nature, has a Power to kill a Murderer, both to deter others from doing the like Injury, which no Reparation can compensate, by the Example of the punishment that attends it from every body, and also *to secure* Men from the attempts of a Criminal, who having renounced Reason, the common Rule and Measure, God hath given to Mankind, hath by the unjust Violence and Slaughter he hath committed upon one, declared War against all Mankind, and therefore may be destroyed as a *Lyon* or a *Tyger*, one of those wild Savage Beasts, with whom Men can have no Society nor Security: And upon this is grounded the great Law of Nature, *Who so sheddeth Mans Blood, by Man shall his Blood be shed*. And *Cain* was so fully convinced, that every one had a Right to destroy such a Criminal, that after the Murther of his Brother, he cries out, *Every one that findeth me, shall slay me*; so plain was it writ in the Hearts of all Mankind.

12. By the same reason, may a Man in the State of Nature *punish the lesser breaches* of that Law. It will perhaps be demanded,

---

§ **11** 6–8 Compare II, § 159, 24–6. The power of pardon was the fourth mark of sovereignty (Bodin, *Methodus*, 1945, 173, see I, § 129, 10–15, note and references, II, § 88, 4–6) and Locke may be following the traditional argument here.

24–6 Compare II, § 172, 18–19 (verbal parallel), note and references.

27–8 Genesis ix. 6: a divine command is equated here with a law of nature.

30–1 Genesis iv. 14. The final phrase is the most conspicuous instance in the whole book of Locke's willingness here to take advantage of the belief in innate ideas and innate practical principles, excoriated in Book 1 of his *Essay concerning Humane Understanding*. The words 'writ in the Hearts' are typical of what Yolton (1956, section II) calls the naïve form of the belief, and the principle at issue cannot well be explained as an exception, as in the case of a similar passage in I, § 86, 19–21—see note and references there. He would seem to imply here that his whole 'strange doctrine' about punishment was part of innate knowledge, a possibility he had rejected as early as 1659–64, see Von Leyden, 1954.

with death? I answer, Each Transgression may be *punished* to that *degree*, and with so much *Severity* as will suffice to make it an ill bargain to the Offender, give him cause to repent, and terrifie others from doing the like. Every Offence that can be committed in the State of Nature, may in the State of Nature be also punished, equally, and as far forth as it may, in a Common-wealth; for though it would be besides my present purpose, to enter here into the particulars of the Law of Nature, or its *measures of punishment*; yet, it is certain there is such a Law, and that too, as intelligible and plain to a rational Creature, and a Studier of that Law, as the positive Laws of Common-wealths, nay possibly plainer; As much as Reason is easier to be understood, than the Phansies and intricate Contrivances of Men, following contrary and hidden interests put into Words; For so truly are a great part of the *Municipal Laws* of Countries, which are only so far right, as they are founded on the Law of Nature, by which they are to be regulated and interpreted.

13. To this strange Doctrine, *viz.* That *in the State of Nature, every one has the Executive Power* of the Law of Nature, I doubt not but it will be objected, That it is unreasonable for Men to be Judges in their own Cases, that Self-love will make Men partial to themselves and their Friends. And on the other side, that Ill Nature, Passion and Revenge will carry them too far in punishing others. And hence nothing but Confusion and Disorder will follow, and that therefore God hath certainly appointed

---

§ 12   9-10   For Locke's attitude to the law of nature and the claim that it was always beside his present purpose to give its particulars, see Introduction, 82.

10-12   Compare II, § 124, 8-9, verbal parallel.

13-19   This passage is indicative of Locke's hostility to those who would multiply laws, indeed to the law, law-courts and lawyers, especially the Common Lawyers, in general (compare I, § 90, 29-31, note and references). This he shared with the 1st Earl of Shaftesbury: see the 79th and 80th *Fundamental Constitutions of Carolina*, which provide that all statute laws should be null after a century, and that no comments upon the *Constitutions* should be permitted. Elrington (1798) comments that this criterion of a nation's law in terms of natural law, and not the will of a majority, 'points out the true principles of civil government'.

16-19   Compare II, § 135, 23-6, and the striking parallels pointed out by Von Leyden in the *Essays on the Laws of Nature*, 118-19, 188-9, of his 1954 edition.

§ 13   1-2   See II, § 9, 1, note and references. Pollock, 1904, 241-2, comments on a 'strange verbal parallel in that strangest of medieval vagaries the *Mirror of Justices* ... "Ordinary jurisdiction has every one who is not deprived of it by sin, for every one may judge his neighbour according to the holy rules of right", Book IV, chap II.' On the *Mirror* see II § 239, 42-3 and note.

Government to restrain the partiality and violence of Men. I easily
10 grant, that *Civil Government* is the proper Remedy for the Inconveniences of the State of Nature, which must certainly be Great,
where Men may be Judges in their own Case, since 'tis easily to
be imagined, that he who was so unjust as to do his Brother an
Injury, will scarce be so just as to condemn himself for it: But
15 I shall desire those who make this Objection, to remember that
Absolute Monarchs are but Men, and if Government is to be the
Remedy of those Evils, which necessarily follow from Mens
being Judges in their own Cases, and the State of Nature is therefore not to be endured, I desire to know what kind of Government
20 that is, and how much better it is than the State of Nature, where
one Man commanding a multitude, has the Liberty to be Judge
in his own Case, and may do to all his Subjects whatever he
pleases, without the least liberty to any one to question or controle
those who Execute his Pleasure? And in whatsoever he doth,
25 whether led by Reason, Mistake or Passion, must be submitted
to? Much better it is in the State of Nature wherein Men are not
bound to submit to the unjust will of another: And if he that
judges, judges amiss in his own, or any other Case, he is answerable
for it to the rest of Mankind.

14. 'Tis often asked as a mighty Objection, *Where are*, or ever
were, there any *Men in such a State of Nature*? To which it may
suffice as an answer at present; That since all *Princes* and Rulers
of *Independent* Governments all through the World, are in a State
5 of Nature, 'tis plain the World never was, nor ever will be, without Numbers of Men in that State. I have named all Governors
of *Independent* Communities, whether they are, or are not, in
League with others: For 'tis not every Compact that puts an end
to the State of Nature between Men, but only this one of agreeing

---

22–7 Modified by Locke in his final corrections.
§ 14   1–3 Compare II, § 101, where the full answer is given, perhaps as a later
extension—see note there.
1–8 Governments in a state of nature with each other: compare II, § 183, 7–8,
II, § 184, 31–2 (an aside in both cases). It is often assumed that Locke was following
Hobbes here, perhaps consciously: compare *Leviathan*, chapter 13 (1904, 85), where
the sequence of thought is much the same. But Gierke insists that this conception
was a commonplace with the natural-law theorists of the time (1934, i, 97): he cites
ten authorities on the point (ii, 288), including Pufendorf's *Elementa* and *De Jure
Naturae*. If Locke had any writer specifically in mind, it seems most likely that it was
Pufendorf. See Introduction, 73.

together mutually to enter into one Community, and make one 10
Body Politick; other Promises and Compacts, Men may make
one with another, and yet still be in the State of Nature. The
Promises and Bargains for Truck, &c. between the two Men in
the Desert Island, mentioned by *Garcilasso De la vega*, in his
History of *Peru*, or between a *Swiss* and an *Indian*, in the Woods 15
of *America*, are binding to them, though they are perfectly in
a State of Nature, in reference to one another. For Truth and
keeping of Faith belongs to Men, as Men, and not as Members
of Society.

15. To those that say, There were never any Men in the State
of Nature; I will not only oppose the Authority of the Judicious
Hooker, Eccl. Pol. Lib. 1. *Sect.* 10. where he says, *The Laws which
have been hitherto mentioned,* i.e. the Laws of Nature, *do bind Men
absolutely, even as they are Men, although they have never any settled* 5
*fellowship, never any Solemn Agreement amongst themselves what to
do or not to do, but for as much as we are not by our selves sufficient to
furnish our selves with competent store of things, needful for such a Life,
as our Nature doth desire, a Life, fit for the Dignity of Man; therefore*

12–17   In the first state of the 1st edition this passage reads differently, and is the
most important variation between the two states. The bargains for truck there are
'Between the two Men in *Soldania*, in or between, a *Swiss* and an *Indian*' and Garcilaso's
desert island is not mentioned. It is clear that Locke did not simply add, in the second state, a
phrase omitted in the first, because Soldania (Saldanha Bay in South Africa) is not mentioned
by Garcilaso, who is concerned with America. Locke seems to have decided to omit this
imperfect reference to Soldania altogether, and to substitute for it this incident from Book 1,
chapter 8 of Garcilaso's *Commentarios Reales* (34–43, of his French translation of 1633; see
note on 1, § 57, 18 and compare 1, § 153, 19–20 and note). He made the following note in his
diary on 8 February 1687: 'Pedro Serrano that lived three years in a desolate island alone and
after that time another shipwrecked man came to him and being but two they could not agree.
Garcilasso de la Vega, Histoire des Incas 1. 1. c. 8.' This correction, therefore, raises the
possibility that Locke wrote this passage in 1687, which is considered in the Introduction,
54. The original reference to the Hottentots of Soldania was genuine enough, for Locke
frequently cited the example of this people as having no belief in God: these references (in the
Essay and elsewhere) are listed in Von Leyden, 1954, 65, 81, for Locke cited this region
along with Brazil as early as his fifth *Essay on the Law of Nature* (early 1660's, *op. cit.* 174). His
information probably came from Terry's *Voyage to East India*, 1655, which was on his shelves
in 1681.
18–19   Compared by Von Leyden with the first and seventh *Essays on the Law of Nature*
(1954, 81).
§ 15   3–13   Hooker, ed. Keble, 1836, Volume 1, pages 298–9, fairly accurately quoted,
with alterations of punctuation. It comes from p. 85 of Locke's 1676 edition, a little after a
passage copied into his diary on 2 June 1681; see note on 11, § 5, 7–23.

10 *to supply those Defetts and Imperfettions which are in us, as living singly and solely by our selves, we are naturally induced to seek Communion and Fellowship with others, this was the Cause of Mens uniting themselves, at first in Politick Societies.* But I moreover affirm, That all Men are naturally in that State, and remain so, till by their own Consents 15 they make themselves Members of some Politick Society; And I doubt not in the Sequel of this Discourse, to make it very clear.

CHAP. III.

Of the State of War.

16. THE *State of War* is a State of Enmity and Destruction; And therefore declaring by Word or Action, not a passionate and hasty, but a sedate setled Design, upon another Mans Life, *puts him in a State of War* with him against whom he has 5 declared such an Intention, and so has exposed his Life to the others Power to be taken away by him, or any one that joyns with him in his Defence, and espouses his Quarrel: it being reasonable and just I should have a Right to destroy that which threatens me with Destruction. For *by the Fundamental Law of*

§ 16   *Chapter* III   In the same way as chapter II (see note on § 4) this was presumably substantially written in 1679, but certainly amended and extended in 1689 (see, for example, § 17, 18–21 and note) and its text was the subject of the printing confusion in that year.

1   The large type, which is the most conspicuous feature distinguishing the first from the second state of the 1st edition, begins at this point and continues until line 15 of § 17. It may well be the result of the cutting out of part of the text by Locke during the course of printing, but this cannot be confirmed bibliographically, and even if it happened the passage excised need not have come from this area of large type—see Introduction, 8, Laslett, 1952 (iv), and Bowers, Gerritsen and Laslett, 1954. In the second state of the 1st edition the type of this area is of normal size, but it has two variant readings in this paragraph.

9–10   Compare II, § 6, 22; § 7, 3–4; § 128, 3–4; § 129, 1–2; § 135, 31; § 149, 24–5; § 159, 17–18; § 171, 12, etc., and Tyrrell, 1681, 15. On Locke's tendency to regard this law of universal preservation as the fundamental natural law, see footnote to the Introduction, 97. In his *Education* (1695) he says, 'And truly, if the preservation of all mankind, as much as in him lies, were every one's persuasion, as indeed it is every one's duty, and the true principle to regulate our religion, politics and morality by, the world would be much quieter, and better-natured, than it is' (*Works*, 1801, IX, 113).

Nature, Man being to be preserved, as much as possible, when all 10
cannot be preserv'd, the safety of the Innocent is to be preferred:
And one may deſtroy a Man who makes War upon him, or has
discovered an Enmity to his being, for the same Reason, that he
may kill a *Wolf* or a *Lyon*; because such Men are not under the
ties of the Common Law of Reason, have no other Rule, but 15
that of Force and Violence, and so may be treated as Beaſts of
Prey, those dangerous and noxious Creatures, that will be sure
to deſtroy him, whenever he falls into their Power.

17. And hence it is, that he who attempts to get another Man
into his Absolute Power, does thereby *put himself into a State of
War* with him; It being to be underſtood as a Declaration of
a Design upon his Life. For I have reason to conclude, that he
who would get me into his Power without my consent, would 5
use me as he pleased, when he had got me there, and deſtroy me
too when he had a fancy to it: for no body can desire to *have me
in his Absolute Power*, unless it be to compel me by force to that,
which is againſt the Right of my Freedom, *i.e.* make me a Slave.
To be free from such force is the only security of my Preservation: 10
and reason bids me look on him, as an Enemy to my Preſervation,
who would take away that *Freedom*, which is the Fence to it:
so that he who makes an *attempt to enslave* me, thereby puts himself
into a State of War with me. He that in the State of Nature,
would take away the Freedom, that belongs to any one in that State, 15
muſt necessarily be supposed to have a design to take away every
thing else, that *Freedom* being the Foundation of all the reſt:
As he that in the State of Society, would take away the *Freedom*
belonging to those of that Society or Common-wealth, muſt be
supposed to design to take away from them every thing else, 20
and so be looked on as *in a State of War*.

18. This makes it Lawful for a Man to *kill a Thief*, who has
not in the leaſt hurt him, nor declared any design upon his Life,
any farther then by the use of Force, so to get him in his Power,

---

16–17 'Beasts of Prey...noxious Creatures'—compare II, § 172, 18–19, note and
references: 'and so' to the end of the paragraph may be an addition of 1689.
§ 17   15 'State'—end of large type in first state of 1st edition, see II, § 16, 1.
18–21 This last sentence may be an interpolation of 1689, an implication that
James II was 'in a State of War' with Englishmen. Indeed § 18 follows more
naturally on to § 16, and the whole paragraph may have been inserted.
§ 18   1 Compare II, § 207, 12–13.

as to take away his Money, or what he pleases from him: because
5 using force, where he has no Right, to get me into his Power,
let his pretence be what it will, I have no reason to suppose,
that he, who would *take away my Liberty*, would not when he had
me in his Power, take away every thing else. And therefore it is
Lawful for me to treat him, as one who has put *himself into a State*
10 *of War* with me, *i.e.* kill him if I can; for to that hazard does he
juſtly expose himself, whoever introduces a State of War, and
is *aggressor* in it.

19. And here we have the plain *difference between the State of
Nature, and the State of War*, which however some Men have
confounded, are as far diſtant, as a State of Peace, Good Will,
Mutual Assiſtance, and Preservation, and a State of Enmity,
5 Malice, Violence, and Mutual Deſtruction are one from another.
Men living together according to reason, without a common
Superior on Earth, with Authority to judge between them, is
properly the State of Nature. But force, or a declared design of
force upon the Person of another, where there is no common
10 Superior on Earth to appeal to for relief, *is the State of War*: And
'tis the want of such an appeal gives a Man the Right of War
even againſt an *aggressor*, though he be in Society and a fellow
Subject. Thus a *Thief*, whom I cannot harm but by appeal to the
Law, for having ſtolen all that I am worth, I may kill, when he
15 sets on me to rob me, but of my Horse or Coat: because the Law,
which was made for my Preservation, where it cannot interpose
to secure my Life from present force, which if loſt, is capable
of no reparation, permits me my own Defence, and the Right of
War, a liberty to kill the aggressor, because the aggressor allows
20 not time to appeal to our common Judge, nor the decision of

---

§ 19 1–5 A comma should be understood after 'which'. Locke altered the last
phrase of this sentence, but then restored the previous reading. The 'some men' can only be
the Hobbesists. Compare ii, §§6 and 7 for the general position and Locke's *Essays on the Law
of Nature, c.* 1661. In his fifth *Essay* he leaves it as a possibility that 'there is in the state of nature
a general war and a perpetual and deadly hatred among men' as is maintained by some (quod
aliqui volunt)—Von Leyden's edition, 1954, 162–3. But in his eighth *Essay* he pronounces
against those 'some'. For if by the law of nature men are in a state of war, 'all society is
abolished, and all faith, which is the bond of society' (tollitur omnis societas et societatis
vinculum fides); see ii, § 212, 9–13, and the Introduction. The peaceful condition of the state
of nature should be compared with the dangers etc. talked of in ii, §§ 13, 92, 101, 123–4,
etc.
31–21 Compare ii, § 182, 22–3.

the Law, for remedy in a Case, where the mischief may be irreparable. *Want of a common Judge with Authority, puts all Men in a State of Nature: Force without Right, upon a Man's Person, makes a State of War*, both where there is, and is not, a common Judge.

20. But when the actual force is over, the *State of War ceases* between those that are in Society, and are equally on both sides Subjected to the fair determination of the Law; because then there lies open the remedy of appeal for the past injury, and to prevent future harm: but where no such appeal is, as in the State 5 of Nature, for want of positive Laws, and Judges with Authority to appeal to, *the State of War once begun, continues*, with a right to the innocent Party, to destroy the other whenever he can, until the aggressor offers Peace, and desires reconciliation on such Terms, as may repair any wrongs he has already done, and secure 10 the innocent for the future: nay where an appeal to the Law, and constituted Judges lies open, but the remedy is deny'd by a manifest perverting of Justice, and a barefaced wresting of the Laws, to protect or indemnifie the violence or injuries of some Men, or Party of Men, *there* it *is* hard to imagine any thing but *a State* 15 *of War*. For wherever violence is used, and injury done, though by hands appointed to administer Justice, it is still violence and injury, however colour'd with the Name, Pretences, or Forms of Law, the end whereof being to protect and redress the innocent,

---

§ **20**   2   'sides'—at this point begins the passage which is present in the second state of the 1st edition, but absent in the first state, see Introduction, 8, Laslett, 1952 (iv) and Bowers, Gerritsen and Laslett, 1954. In the first state the text goes straight on to 'And therefore in such Controversies,..,' at the beginning of line 15 in § 21, thus: '20. But when the actual force is over, the State of War ceases between those that are in Society, and are equally on both sides Subject to the Judge: And therefore in such controversies...' (and so on, identically with the text in the second state to the end of the paragraph, starting the next as § 22. No sign for a § 21 is present). This anomaly has been variously dealt with by editors of the text; see footnote 2 to p. 342 of Laslett, 1952 (iv) and footnote 1 to p. 83 of Laslett, 1954 (iv). W.S. Carpenter, the editor of the *Everyman* text (c. 1924, with many subsequent printings) misnumbered all the paragraphs from this point to 11, §§ 36, 37; see note on line 14 of 11, § 36. Elrington (1798) first noticed this peculiarity, and has a note here on it.

11–23   This passage may, well be an addition of 1689, directly referring to the events of the Revolution: the final 'appeal to Heaven' being most significant. It contains (line 15) the phrase which inspired Elrington to the following protest against Locke's theory of resistance, or perhaps the interpretation put on it by Thomas Paine and others.

'But what shall we say of a theory which thus invests an individual with a right of throwing a whole society in confusion for the purpose of redressing his own particular grievance?'

20 by an unbiassed application of it, to all who are under it; wherever that is not *bona fide* done, *War is made* upon the Sufferers, who having no appeal on Earth to right them, they are left to the only remedy in such Cases, an appeal to Heaven.

21. To avoid this State of War (wherein there is no appeal but to Heaven, and wherein every the least difference is apt to end, where there is no Authority to decide between the Contenders) is one great *reason of Mens putting themselves into Society*, 5 and quitting the State of Nature. For where there is an Authority, a Power on Earth, from which relief can be had by *appeal*, there the continuance of the State of War is excluded, and the Controversie is decided by that Power. Had there been any such Court, any superior Jurisdiction on Earth, to determine the right 10 between *Jephtha* and the *Ammonites*, they had never come to a State of War, but we see he was forced to appeal to *Heaven. The Lord the Judge* (says he) *be Judge this day between the Children of* Israel, *and the Children of* Ammon, *Judg.* 11. 27. and then Prosecuting, and relying on his *appeal*, he leads out his Army to Battle: 15 And therefore in such Controversies, where the question is put, *who shall be Judge?* It cannot be meant, who shall decide the Controversie; every one knows what *Jephtha* here tells us, that *the Lord the Judge*, shall judge. Where there is no Judge on Earth, the *Appeal* lies to God in Heaven. That Question then cannot 20 mean, who shall judge? whether another hath put himself in a State of War with me, and whether I may as *Jephtha* did, appeal to Heaven in it? Of that I my self can only be Judge in my own Conscience, as I will answer it at the great Day, to the Supream Judge of all Men.

---

§ 21   1–5 Hobbes had also made the social state a remedy for the state of war, and this sentence might be called Locke's closest formal approach to him in his political theory. It is interesting that it occurs in a passage omitted from one state of the 1st edition (see Laslett, 1952 (iv)), but it cannot be shown that the two facts are connected.

15 'And'—end of missing passage; see II, § 20, 2, note.

17 '*Jephtha*'—Locke evidently regarded the story of Jephthah as crucial to the scriptural foundations of his case about civil society and justice. See I, § 163, 32; II, § 109, 1–11; II, § 176, 28 and compare note on II, § 168, and references. Grotius and St Augustine before him had used the Jephthah story for political analysis, and Locke may have in mind the Calvinist position expressed by Jurieu (1689, 365) that the Judges, Jephthah among them, represented a stage between the anarchy of primeval innocence and established sovereignty, a stage which inevitably passed because of the effects of the Fall.

CHAP. IV.

Of SLAVERY.

22. THE *Natural Liberty* of Man is to be free from any Superior
Power on Earth, and not to be under the Will or Legislative Authority of Man, but to have only the Law of Nature for
his Rule. The *Liberty of Man, in Society*, is to be under no other
Legislative Power, but that established, by consent, in the   5
Common-wealth, nor under the Dominion of any Will, or Restraint of any Law, but what the Legislative shall enact, according
to the Trust put in it. *Freedom* then is not what Sir R. F. tells us,

---

§ 22 *Chapter* IV There is positive evidence for this chapter, as distinct from
presumption in the case of chapters II and III, of composition in 1679 (see note on
lines 8–9 below) and of revision in 1689.

1   At this point sheet R begins in the 1st edition; compare notes on II, § 8, 6:
there are no further obvious printing peculiarities after this point in the 1st edition.

8–9 'what Sir R. F. tells us, *O.A.* 55'. The only reference to Filmer's works in
the *Second Treatise*, though his name is mentioned at II, § 1, 28 and II, § 61, 14. The
statement is repeated in II, § 57, 21–2; see note there and on II, § 236. It is one of the
many signs that this work, as well as the *First Treatise*, was written with the object
of refuting Filmer, in particular against his tracts, whilst the *First* was written against
Patriarcha. In the Introduction, 58–61 this anomalous form of reference to Filmer—
for it will be seen to be quite different from that used in the *First Treatise*—is taken as one of
the indications that the *Second Treatise* was written in 1679–80 in some form, and as the clue to
the priority in writing of the *Second* to the *First* though Ashcraft disagrees. The entry in
Locke's *Tablet* which makes it possible to guess the time of writing of this paragraph is
relevant. It refers to a passage in Filmer's *Forms* (Laslett's edition, 2:6): 'amongst all them
that plead the necessity of the consent of the people, none hath ever touched upon these so
necessary doctrines [that is, of the manner of obtaining it]; it is a task it seems too difficult,
otherwise surely it would not have been neglected, considering how necessary it is to resolve
the conscience, touching the manner of the peoples passing their consent'.

Such, then, was the statement which Locke had in mind when he wrote in his
Tablet 'Filmer to resolve the conscience' and went on to compose this part of the
Second Treatise. The same point about law and freedom appears also in his *Essay
concerning Humane Understanding*, IV, iii, 18: '"No government allows absolute
liberty." The idea of government being the establishment of society upon certain
rules or laws which require conformity to them; and the idea of absolute liberty
being for any one to do whatever he pleases; I am as capable of being certain of the
truth of this proposition as of any in mathematics' (Nidditch, ed., 550)—see Introduction, 83. Elrington (1798) is disturbed by the implications of this paragraph
and finds it contradictory. He concludes that the great *desideratum* is an agreed
definition of liberty: 'Whether Locke has given such a definition the reader will
judge.'

O.A. 55 [224]. *A Liberty for every one to do what he lists, to live as he*
10 *pleases, and not to be tyed by any Laws:* But *Freedom of Men under
Government,* is, to have a standing Rule to live by, common to
every one of that Society, and made by the Legislative Power
erected in it; A Liberty to follow my own Will in all things, where
the Rule prescribes not; and not to be subject to the inconstant,
15 uncertain, unknown, Arbitrary Will of another Man. As *Freedom
of Nature* is to be under no other restraint but the Law of Nature.

23. This *Freedom* from Absolute, Arbitrary Power, is so necessary to, and closely joyned with a Man's Preservation, that he
cannot part with it, but by what forfeits his Preservation and Life
together. For a Man, not having the Power of his own Life,
5 *cannot,* by Compact, or his own Consent, *enslave himself* to any one,
nor put himself under the Absolute, Arbitrary Power of another,
to take away his Life, when he pleases. No body can give more
Power than he has himself; and he that cannot take away his own
Life, cannot give another power over it. Indeed having, by his
10 fault, forfeited his own Life, by some Act that deserves Death; he, to
whom he has forfeited it, may (when he has him in his Power) delay
to take it, and make use of him to his own Service, and he does him
no injury by it. For, whenever he finds the hardship of his Slavery
out-weigh the value of his Life, 'tis in his Power, by resisting the
15 Will of his Master, to draw on himself the Death he desires.

24. This is the perfect condition of *Slavery,* which *is* nothing
else, but *the State of War continued, between a lawful Conquerour, and
a Captive.* For, if once *Compact* enter between them, and make an
agreement for a limited Power on the one side, and Obedience

---

§ 23 This paragraph invites comparison and contrast with Hobbes's *Leviathan,*
chapter 20, especially pp. 142–3 (1904 edition). Hobbes did maintain that a man can
enslave himself by compact and consent, because he can bargain away the power over
his own life. Locke, however, seems to contradict himself in his last sentence by
justifying indirect suicide; compare also II, § 6, 3–4; § 135, 9–12 (a parallel passage);
and § 178, 5–6, note and reference. Elrington (1798) urges this against him, and also
objects to 'the indefinite continuance of a right to take away the life of another'. Dunn, 1969(i)
(see especially footnote 2 on p. 108 and references) insists that Locke always respected the
suicide taboo.

§ 24 1–8 See § 23 and compare § 85, 8–16. In gauging Locke's attitude to slavery it is
worth bearing in mind that, as Leslie Stephen pointed out (1902, II, 139), the *Fundamental
Constitutions of Carolina* provide that every freeman 'shall have absolute power and authority
over his negro slaves' (ex); compare notes on I, § 130, 6, and I, § 144, 23. The Instructions to
Governor Nicholson of Virginia, which Locke did so much to draft in 1698 (see Laslett, 1957
(i)), regard negro slaves as justifiably enslaved because they were captives taken in a just war,

on the other, the State of War and *Slavery* ceases, as long as the ₅
Compact endures. For, as has been said, no Man can, by agreement, pass over to another that which he hath not in himself,
a Power over his own Life.

I confess, we find among the *Jews*, as well as other Nations, that
Men did sell themselves; but, 'tis plain, this was only to *Drudgery*, ₁₀
not to Slavery. For, it is evident, the Person sold was not under
an Absolute, Arbitrary, Despotical Power. For the Master could
not have power to kill him, at any time, whom, at a certain time,
he was obliged to let go free out of his Service: and the Master
of such a Servant was so far from having an Arbitrary Power over ₁₅
his Life, that he could not, at pleasure, so much as maim him, but
the loss of an Eye, or Tooth, set him free, *Exod.* XXI.

Chap. V.

Of PROPERTY.

25.   **W**Hether we consider natural *Reason*, which tells us, that
Men, being once born, have a right to their Preservation,
and consequently to Meat and Drink, and such other things, as
Nature affords for their Subsistence: Or *Revelation*, which gives

who had forfeited their lives 'by some Act that deserves Death' (§ 23, 10; compare Tyrrell,
1681, 62). Locke seems satisfied that the forays of the Royal Africa Company were just wars
of this sort, and that the negroes captured had committed such acts. Locke on slavery is
discussed by Polin, 1960, 277–81, and Dunn, 1969; 175 etc.

9–16   In Exod. xxi the Mosaic law regulates the treatment of bought servants;
they are to be freed in the seventh, Jubilee, year, not to be killed, to be freed if
maimed by their masters. Hobbes notices this and Grotius calls it 'imperfecta
servitus', II, v, 30 (1712, 264).

§ 25   *Chapter* v   This important chapter is obviously integral to Locke's argument,
and it is also obviously part of his polemic against Filmer—see notes on lines 9–16 and 16–19
below, and on II, § 38, 9–11, etc. Olivecrona takes a different view of 9–16 and the date of the
chapter. There is nothing, however, to indicate that it was written in 1689, or at any time later
than the first form of the book, though it was perhaps subsequently amended, and it will be
remembered that it falls within that part of the 1st edition which could have been modified in
the course of printing. Apart from this, it seems right to me to suppose that the chapter is to be
dated between 1679 and 1681.

1–3   This discussion of property is referred to in I, § 87, 14–15, and I, § 86, 1–4
echoes the language used here. Kendall, 1941, 77, notes the illogical transition from
'men' here, meaning individuals, to 'mankind' in line 8.

L

5 us an account of those Grants God made of the World to *Adam*,
and to *Noah*, and his Sons, 'tis very clear, that God, as King
David says, *Psal.* CXV. xvj. *has given the Earth to the Children of
Men*, given it to Mankind in common. But this being supposed,
it seems to some a very great difficulty, how any one should ever
10 come to have a *Property* in any thing: I will not content my self
to answer, That if it be difficult to make out *Property*, upon a supposition, that God gave the World to *Adam* and his Posterity in
common; it is impossible that any Man, but one universal Monarch,
should have any *Property*, upon a supposition, that God gave the
15 World to *Adam*, and his Heirs in Succession, exclusive of all the
rest of his Posterity. But I shall endeavour to shew, how Men
might come to have a *property* in several parts of that which God
gave to Mankind in common, and that without any express Compact of all the Commoners.

26. God, who hath given the World to Men in common,
hath also given them reason to make use of it to the best advantage
of Life, and convenience. The Earth, and all that is therein, is
given to Men for the Support and Comfort of their being. And
5 though all the Fruits it naturally produces, and Beasts it feeds,
belong to Mankind in common, as they are produced by the
spontaneous hand of Nature; and no body has originally a private
Dominion, exclusive of the rest of Mankind, in any of them, as
they are thus in their natural state: yet being given for the use of
10 Men, there must of necessity be a means *to appropriate* them some
way or other before they can be of any use, or at all beneficial

6–8 The biblical evidence for original communism, or rather against the primacy
of private property, is discussed at length in the *First Treatise*; see 1, § 21 and on: the
text from Psalm cxv is cited in 1, § 31 as part of a reference to Filmer's case.

9–16 Compare the *First Treatise*. Olivecrona, 1975, argues that the lines were put in later
and the paragraph and chapter were written in ignorance of Filmer's position, a view which I
cannot share: see next note.

16–19 This sentence confirms that this paragraph, and the whole chapter on
property which follows, were written with Filmer's works in mind, and as a direct
refutation of them. For it was Filmer who has raised the difficulty that original
communism could not give way to private property without the universal consent
of mankind. The discussions in Hobbes (the *Epistola Dedicatoria* of *De Cive*, 1647,
presents the issue most clearly), Grotius (1625, ii, ii, 2) and Pufendorf (1672, iv, 3)
do not discuss this crux as Filmer does.

§ 26 Compare and contrast the discussion of the goods of nature in this paragraph
with Pufendorf, *De Jure Naturae*, 1672, iv, iv, 13, and Locke's own earlier sentiments
in his eighth *Essay on the Law of Nature*, which are markedly different: Von Leyden,
1954, 210–11.

12–16 Compare ii, § 28, 16–26, note and references.

to any particular Man. The Fruit, or Venison, which nourishes
the wild *Indian*, who knows no Inclosure, and is still a Tenant
in common, must be his, and so his, *i.e.* a part of him, that another
can no longer have any right to it, before it can do him any good   15
for the support of his Life.

27. Though the Earth, and all inferior Creatures be common
to all Men, yet every Man has a *Property* in his own *Person*. This
no Body has any Right to but himself. The *Labour* of his Body,

---

§ 27 Compare Locke's introduction of the proposition about labour and property
in this paragraph, its predecessor and those following, with that of Tyrrell: 'Supposing the Earth and the fruits thereof to have been at first bestowed in Common on
all its inhabitants; yet since God's first command to man was, encrease and multiply,
if he hath a right to perform the end, he hath certainly a right to the means of his
preservation, and the propagation of his species, so that though the fruits of the
earth, or beasts, for food, were all in common, yet when once any man had by his own
labour acquired such a proportion of either as would serve the necessities of himself
and Family, they became so much his own as that no man could without manifest
injustice rob him of those necessities' (1681, 99–100, second pagination). Tyrrell
goes on to talk of 'this sort of community' being retained among the Americans,
the wild beast the Indian kills (compare II, § 30, 1–2), the fish he takes up (*ibid.* 8),
the fruit of his trees and his venison (II, § 26, 12). But he talks in this parallel way in
a different context. Following Grotius, he refers to the Stoic axiom about seats in the
theatre, and cites many other arguments about property, ignored by Locke: for him
the labour proposition is not the one rational method of making use of the earth's
produce, but rather a ground for retaining property acquired, and he does not talk
of a man owning himself (compare note on II, § 32, 1–7). These points, and the known
relationship between them (see above, §9–61), it may imply that Locke suggested
this line of thinking to Tyrrell, who followed it without quite realizing what it
meant to Locke. It is not impossible that they arrived at this position independently,
for in a work published in 1680 but described on the title as 'Mostly written many
years past' Richard Baxter writes in vaguer but in similar terms 'Propriety is
naturally antecedent to *Government*, which doth not *Give it*, but *regulate it* to the *Common
good*; Every man is born with a propriety in his *own members*, and nature giveth him a
propriety in *his Children*, and his *food* and other just *acquisitions* of his industry.
Therefore no Ruler can justly deprive men of their *propriety*, unless it be by some
Law of God (as in execution of justice on such as forfeit it) or by their *own consent*, by
themselves or their Delegates or *Progenitors*; And men's *lives* and *Liberties* are the chief
parts of their propriety. That is the peoples just *reserved Property*, and *Liberty*, which
neither *God taketh from them*, by the power which his own Laws give the Ruler, nor
is *given away* by their *own* foresaid consent' (Baxter, 1680, 54–5; see Schlatter, 1957,
39, and compare passage from Baxter's *Holy Commonwealth*, cited by Gough, 1950, 80).
    What Baxter says here about life, liberty and property shows that he had the same
combined definition of property as Locke, both an extended and a specific definition;
see Introduction, 101 and note on II, § 87, 5. It is possible to find many much vaguer
hints at what is too loosely called the labour theory of value (in Petty, 1662, for example, of which Locke had the 1667 printing (H. and L. 2839), or even in Hobbes; see
Gough, 1950, 81) but these are the only passages in books he may have read known to me
which seem to show a systematic resemblance. See also the hint in I, § 42, 11–15.
    2 Repeated in II, § 173, 5, cf. Walwyn, the Leveller quoted Macpherson, 1962, 140.

and the *Work* of his Hands, we may say, are properly his. What-
5 soever then he removes out of the State that Nature hath provided,
and left it in, he hath mixed his *Labour* with, and joyned to it
something that is his own, and thereby makes it his *Property*.
It being by him removed from the common ſtate Nature placed
it in, it hath by this *labour* something annexed to it, that excludes
10 the common right of other Men. For this *Labour* being the
unqueſtionable Property of the Labourer, no Man but he can
have a right to what that is once joyned to, at leaſt where there
is enough, and as good left in common for others.

28. He that is nourished by the Acorns he pickt up under
an Oak, or the Apples he gathered from the Trees in the Wood,
has certainly appropriated them to himself. No Body can deny
but the nourishment is his. I ask then, When did they begin to
5 be his? When he digeſted? Or when he eat? Or when he boiled?
Or when he brought them home? Or when he pickt them up?
And 'tis plain, if the firſt gathering made them not his, nothing
else could. That *labour* put a diſtinction between them and
common. That added something to them more than Nature, the
10 common Mother of all, had done; and so they became his private
right. And will any one say he had no right to those Acorns
or Apples he thus appropriated, because he had not the consent
of all Mankind to make them his? Was it a Robbery thus to
assume to himself what belonged to all in Common? If such
15 a consent as that was necessary, Man had ſtarved, notwithſtanding
the Plenty God had given him. We see in *Commons*, which remain

---

§ 28   1–4   Compare Pufendorf, *De Jure Naturae*, 1672, IV, iv, 13, 'Quercus erat
nullius: quae deciderant glandes ejus fiebant, qui legisset'. Gough, 1950, draws
attention to this parallel, and to Blackstone's account of the clash between Locke on
the one hand and both Pufendorf and Grotius on the other in their views on the
origin of property. For in spite of the above coincidence about acorns, Pufendorf
follows Grotius in assigning the origin of property to universal agreement, not
labour. Barbeyrac, in his edition of Pufendorf's *De Jure Naturae*, registers his
agreement with Locke's views on this matter, and maintains that Locke was the first
to formulate it, earlier than the only other author he quotes, C. G. Titius of Leipzig
(1661–1714). He also notes that Locke's discussion grew out of his refutation of
Filmer: Barbeyrac, 1734, I, 576–7. Barbeyrac corresponded with Locke (see
Introduction, 75n), and no man in the early eighteenth century was in a generally
better position than he to know about the relationship of his writings with the
natural-law jurists and with the whole tradition of social and political theory.

16–26   Locke is using here the language of agrarian enclosure, the parcelling out
of the common fields of the traditional manor as private property, which was so
marked a feature of English economic history in the sixteenth century, in his own

so by Compact, that 'tis the taking any part of what is common, and removing it out of the State Nature leaves it in, which *begins the Property*; without which the Common is of no use. And the taking of this or that part, does not depend on the express consent 20 of all the Commoners. Thus the Grass my Horse has bit; the Turfs my Servant has cut; and the Ore I have digg'd in any place where I have a right to them in common with others, become my *Property*, without the assignation or consent of any body. The *labour* that was mine, removing them out of that common State 25 they were in, hath *fixed* my *Property* in them.

29. By making an explicit consent of every Commoner, necessary to any ones appropriating to himself any part of what is given in common, Children or Servants could not cut the Meat which their Father or Master had provided for them in common, without assigning to every one his peculiar part. Though the 5 Water running in the Fountain be every ones, yet who can doubt, but that in the Pitcher is his only who drew it out? His *labour* hath taken it out of the hands of Nature, where it was common, and belong'd equally to all her Children, and *hath* thereby *appropriated* it to himself.   10

30. Thus this Law of reason makes the Deer, that *Indian's* who hath killed it; 'tis allowed to be his goods who hath bestowed his labour upon it, though before, it was the common right of every one. And amongst those who are counted the Civiliz'd part of Mankind, who have made and multiplied positive Laws to deter- 5 mine Property, this original Law of Nature for the *beginning of Property*, in what was before common, still takes place; and by vertue thereof, what Fish any one catches in the Ocean, that great and still remaining Common of Mankind; or what Ambergriese any one takes up here, is *by the Labour* that removes it out 10

---

time to some extent, and even more in the eighteenth century; see also II, § 32, 7–10; § 35; § 42, 17–20; § 37, 10–29. It is not quite consistent with his statement about enclosure and the Indians in II, § 26, 12–16, for the Indian lived in a state of nature, before compact had taken place. Here '*Commons*' must mean the common land of the traditional manorial system, remaining so 'by Compact'. As Locke makes clear in II, § 35, only the men of the manor, and not just anyone, could usually graze, turf and mine on the common land, and then only if the custom of the manor allowed. It is a bad example of communism. Lines 24–6 contain the only example of Locke transferring labour from one man to another. See the discussion in Macpherson, 1962, Laslett, 1964.
§ 30 1–4 Compare I, § 86, 19–28, Tully, 1980, Wood, 1984.

of that common State Nature left it in, *made* his *Property* who takes that pains about it. And even amongst us the Hare that any one is Hunting, is thought his who pursues her during the Chase. For being a Beast that is still looked upon as common, and no Man's private Possession; whoever has imploy'd so much *labour* about any of that kind, as to find and pursue her, has thereby removed her from the State of Nature, wherein she was common, and hath *begun a Property*.

31. It will perhaps be objected to this, That if gathering the Acorns, or other Fruits of the Earth, *&c.* makes a right to them, then any one may *ingross* as much as he will. To which I Answer, Not so. The same Law of Nature, that does by this means give us Property, does also *bound* that *Property* too. *God has given us all things richly*, 1 Tim. vi. 17. is the Voice of Reason confirmed by Inspiration. But how far has he given it us? *To enjoy*. As much as any one can make use of to any advantage of life before it spoils; so much he may by his labour fix a Property in. Whatever is beyond this, is more than his share, and belongs to others. Nothing was made by God for Man to spoil or destroy. And thus considering the plenty of natural Provisions there was a long time in the World, and the few spenders, and to how small a part of that provision the industry of one Man could extend it self, and ingross it to the prejudice of others; especially keeping within the *bounds*, set by reason of what might serve for his *use*; there could be then little room for Quarrels or Contentions about Property so establish'd.

32. But the *chief matter of Property* being now not the Fruits of the Earth, and the Beasts that subsist on it, but the *Earth it self*; as that which takes in and carries with it all the rest: I think it is plain, that *Property* in that too is acquired as the former. *As much Land* as a Man Tills, Plants, Improves, Cultivates, and can use the Product of, so much is his *Property*. He by his Labour does,

---

§ 31   6   Compare 1, § 40, 19–20.
§ 32   1–7   Tyrrell extends the labour theory to the possession of land in the same way as Locke, but with the same difference. Labour confirms a man's property in what he rightfully possesses, 'since the owner hath possessed himself of this land, and bestowed his Labour and Industry upon it' no man can take it away (1681, 112, 2nd pagination). See note on 11, § 27.
7–10   The language of agrarian enclosure, see 11, § 28, 16–26, and references.

as it were, inclose it from the Common. Nor will it invalidate his right to say, Every body else has an equal Title to it; and therefore he cannot appropriate, he cannot inclose, without the Consent of all his Fellow-Commoners, all Mankind. God, when he gave the World in common to all Mankind, commanded Man also to labour, and the penury of his Condition required it of him. God and his Reason commanded him to subdue the Earth, *i.e.* improve it for the benefit of Life, and therein lay out something upon it that was his own, his labour. He that in Obedience to this Command of God, subdued, tilled and sowed any part of it, thereby annexed to it something that was his *Property*, which another had no Title to, nor could without injury take from him.

33. Nor was this *appropriation* of any parcel of *Land*, by improving it, any prejudice to any other Man, since there was still enough, and as good left; and more than the yet unprovided could use. So that in effect, there was never the less left for others because of his inclosure for himself. For he that leaves as much as another can make use of, does as good as take nothing at all. No Body could think himself injur'd by the drinking of another Man, though he took a good Draught, who had a whole River of the same Water left him to quench his thirst. And the Case of Land and Water, where there is enough of both, is perfectly the same.

34. God gave the World to Men in Common; but since he gave it them for their benefit, and the greatest Conveniencies of Life they were capable to draw from it, it cannot be supposed he meant it should always remain common and uncultivated. He gave it to the use of the Industrious and Rational, (and *Labour* was to be *his Title* to it;) not to the Fancy or Covetousness of the Quarrelsom and Contentious. He that had as good left for his Improvement, as was already taken up, needed not complain, ought not to meddle with what was already improved by another's Labour: If he did, 'tis plain he desired the benefit of another's Pains, which he had no right to, and not the Ground which God had given him in common with others to labour on, and whereof there was as good left, as that already possessed, and more than he knew what to do with, or his Industry could reach to.

35. 'Tis true, in *Land* that is *common* in *England*, or any other Country, where there is Plenty of People under Government, who have Money and Commerce, no one can inclose or appropriate any part, without the consent of all his Fellow-Commoners:
5 Because this is left common by Compact, *i.e.* by the Law of the Land, which is not to be violated. And though it be Common, in respect of some Men, it is not so to all Mankind; but is the joint property of this Country, or this Parish. Besides, the remainder, after such inclosure, would not be as good to the rest
10 of the Commoners as the whole was, when they could all make use of the whole: whereas in the beginning and first peopling of the great Common of the World, it was quite otherwise. The Law Man was under, was rather for *appropriating*. God Commanded, and his Wants forced him to *labour*. That was his *Property*
15 which could not be taken from him where-ever he had fixed it. And hence subduing or cultivating the Earth, and having Dominion, we see are joyned together. The one gave Title to the other. So that God, by commanding to subdue, gave Authority so far to *appropriate*. And the Condition of Humane Life, which
20 requires Labour and Materials to work on, necessarily introduces *private Possessions*.

36. The measure of Property, Nature has well set, by the Extent of Mens *Labour, and the Conveniency of Life*: No Mans Labour could subdue, or appropriate all: nor could his Enjoyment consume more than a small part; so that it was impossible
5 for any Man, this way, to intrench upon the right of another, or acquire, to himself, a Property, to the Prejudice of his Neighbour, who would still have room, for as good, and as large a Possession (after the other had taken out his) as before it was appropriated. This *measure* did confine every Man's *Possession*, to a very moderate
10 Proportion, and such as he might appropriate to himself, without

§ 35 Here Locke seems to recognize the inappropriateness of agrarian enclosure to his argument (see note on II, § 28, 16–26), but he persists. His statements are accurate, but vague, and it is interesting that the words 'Country' (presumably in its older meaning of 'locality') and 'Parish' are used where 'Manor' might be expected (line 8).
  8 'property'—altered by Locke from 'propriety' in 1698; compare title to chapter VII of the *First Treatise*.
§ 36 9–25 The smallness of men's possessions in early Biblical times is commented on in I, § 136, 11. This passage is a direct statement of Locke's assumption that the state of nature in contemporary America can be assimilated to the conditions of patriarchal times, compare note on I, § 130.

Injury to any Body in the first Ages of the World, when Men
were more in danger to be lost, by wandering from their Company, in the then vast Wilderness of the Earth, than to be straitned
for want of room to plant in. And the same *measure* may be allowed
still, without prejudice to any Body, as full as the World seems.   15
For supposing a Man, or Family, in the state they were, at first
peopling of the World by the Children of *Adam*, or *Noah*; let
him plant in some in land, vacant places of *America*, we shall
find that the *Possessions* he could make himself upon the *measures*
we have given, would not be very large, nor, even to this day,   20
prejudice the rest of Mankind, or give them reason to complain,
or think themselves injured by this Man's Incroachment, though
the Race of Men have now spread themselves to all the corners
of the World, and do infinitely exceed the small number [which]
was at the beginning. Nay, the extent of *Ground* is of so little   25
value, *without labour*, that I have heard it affirmed, that in *Spain*
it self, a Man may be permitted to plough, sow, and reap, without
being disturbed, upon Land he has no other Title to, but only his
making use of it. But, on the contrary, the Inhabitants think
themselves beholden to him, who, by his Industry on neglected,   30
and consequently waste Land, has increased the stock of Corn,
which they wanted. But be this as it will, which I lay no stress
on; This I dare boldly affirm, That the same *Rule of Propriety*,
(*viz.*) that every Man should have as much as he could make
use of, would hold still in the World, without straitning any body,   35
since there is Land enough in the World to suffice double the
Inhabitants had not the *Invention of Money*, and the tacit Agreement
of Men to put a value on it, introduced (by Consent) larger
Possessions, and a Right to them; which, how it has done, I shall,
by and by, shew more at large.   40

---

14   The *Everyman* text, having misnumbered its paragraphs since II, § 20, starts a
new paragraph (§ 36) after 'plant in.', omitting the 'And'—see note on II, § 20, 2.
   26–34   Private appropriation of waste land in this way was possible all over
Spain in Locke's day, and is apparently still the custom in Andalusia. In Aragon the
land, in the mountain area, had to be cleared within sixty days to become the
property of the cultivator: in Catalonia such ownership became absolute once the
plot had been worked, but lapsed if it was left uncultivated for three years: in Castile
the labourer could only take enough for himself and his family. See Costa, 1898,
250–63. I owe this reference and information to Dr J. H. Elliott. Compare II,
§ 184, 27–9.
   39–40   See II, § 45 and note: II, § 46 on.

37. This is certain, That in the beginning, before the desire of having more than Men needed, had altered the intrinsick value of things, which depends only on their usefulness to the Life of Man; or [Men] had *agreed, that a little piece of yellow Metal,* which 5 would keep without wasting or decay, should be worth a great piece of Flesh, or a whole heap of Corn; though Men had a Right to appropriate, by their Labour, each one to himself, as much of the things of Nature, as he could use: Yet this could not be much, nor to the Prejudice of others, where the same plenty was still 10 left, to those who would use the same Industry. To which let me add, that he who appropriates land to himself by his labour, does not lessen but increase the common stock of mankind. For the provisions serving to the support of humane life, produced by one acre of inclosed and cultivated land, are (to speak much 15 within compasse) ten times more, than those, which are yielded by an acre of Land, of an equal richnesse, lyeing wast in common. And therefor he, that incloses Land and has a greater plenty of the conveniencys of life from ten acres, than he could have from an hundred left to Nature, may truly be said, to give ninety acres 20 to Mankind. For his labour now supplys him with provisions out of ten acres, which were but the product of an hundred lying in common. I have here rated the improved land very low in making its product but as ten to one, when it is much nearer an hundred to one. For I aske whether in the wild woods and 25 uncultivated wast of America left to Nature, without any improvement, tillage or husbandry, a thousand acres will yield the needy and wretched inhabitants as many conveniencies of life as ten acres of equally fertile land doe in Devonshire where they are well cultivated?

30 Before the Appropriation of Land, he who gathered as much of the wild Fruit, killed, caught, or tamed, as many of the Beasts as he could; he that so employed his Pains about any of the

---

§ 37   4   'Men'—added by editor.
  10–29   Passage added in two parts in the Christ's copy, also recalling English agrarian enclosure, or even justifying it; see note on 11, § 28, 16–26. It is taken by Macpherson (1951, 559 and 1962, 212 on) to have been inserted by Locke to remove the 'sufficiency limitation' on the acquisition of property, which obtained before money was introduced.
  32–41   Cited by Kendall, 1941, 72, as a conspicuous example of 'the "public" right to interfere with the liberty and property of private persons', making against the individualist interpretation of Locke's theory of property; see Introduction, 105.

spontaneous Products of Nature, as any way to alter them, from
the State which Nature put them in, *by* placing any of his *Labour*
on them, did thereby *acquire a Propriety in them*: But if they 35
perished, in his Possession, without their due use; if the Fruits
rotted, or the Venison putrified, before he could spend it, he
offended against the common Law of Nature, and was liable to
be punished; he invaded his Neighbour's share, for he had *no*
Right, farther than his Use called for any of them, and they might 40
serve to afford him Conveniencies of Life.

38. The same *measures* governed the *Possession of Land* too:
Whatsoever he tilled and reaped, laid up and made use of, before
it spoiled, that was his peculiar Right; whatsoever he enclosed,
and could feed, and make use of, the Cattle and Product was also
his. But if either the Grass of his Inclosure rotted on the Ground, 5
or the Fruit of his planting perished without gathering, and laying
up, this part of the Earth, notwithstanding his Inclosure, was
still to be looked on as Waste, and might be the Possession of any
other. Thus, at the beginning, *Cain* might take as much Ground
as he could till, and make it his own Land, and yet leave enough 10
to *Abel*'s Sheep to feed on; a few Acres would serve for both their
Possessions. But as Families increased, and Industry inlarged their
Stocks, their *Possessions inlarged* with the need of them; but yet
it was commonly *without any fixed property in the ground* they made
use of, till they incorporated, settled themselves together, and 15
built Cities, and then, by consent, they came in time, to set out
the *bounds of their distinct Territories*, and agree on limits between
them and their Neighbours, and by Laws within themselves,
settled the *Properties* of those of the same Society. For we see,
that in that part of the World which was first inhabited, and 20
therefore like to be best peopled, even as low down as *Abraham*'s
time, they wandred with their Flocks, and their Herds, which
was their substance, freely up and down; and this *Abraham* did,
in a Country where he was a Stranger. Whence it is plain, that
at least, a great part of the *Land lay in common*; that the Inhabitants 25
valued it not, nor claimed Property in any more than they made
use of. But when there was not room enough in the same place,

---

§ 38   9–11   These three lines are a paraphrase of a quotation by Filmer from
Selden's *Mare Clausum*; see Laslett's edition, 63–4. The passage is given in full in
I, § 76 and commented upon, see note there.

for their Herds to feed together, they, by consent, as *Abraham* and *Lot* did, *Gen.* xiii. 5. separated and inlarged their pasture, 30 where it best liked them. And for the same Reason *Esau* went from his Father, and his Brother, and planted in *Mount Seir*, Gen. xxxvi. 6.

39. And thus, without supposing any private Dominion, and property in *Adam*, over all the World, exclusive of all other Men, which can no way be proved, nor any ones Property be made out from it; but supposing the *World* given as it was to the 5 Children of Men *in common*, we see how *labour* could make Men distinct titles to several parcels of it, for their private uses; wherein there could be no doubt of Right, no room for quarrel.

40. Nor is it so strange, as perhaps before consideration it may appear, that the *Property of labour* should be able to over-ballance the Community of Land. For 'tis *Labour* indeed that *puts the difference of value* on every thing; and let any one consider, what 5 the difference is between an Acre of Land planted with Tobacco, or Sugar, sown with Wheat or Barley; and an Acre of the same Land lying in common, without any Husbandry upon it, and he will find, that the improvement of *labour makes* the far greater part of *the value*. I think it will be but a very modest Computation 10 to say, that of the *Products* of the Earth useful to the Life of Man $\frac{9}{10}$ are the *effects of labour*: nay, if we will rightly estimate things as they come to our use, and cast up the several Expences about them, what in them is purely owing to *Nature*, and what to *labour*, we shall find, that in most of them $\frac{99}{100}$ are wholly to be put on the 15 account of *labour*.

41. . There cannot be a clearer demonstration of any thing, than several Nations of the *Americans* are of this, who are rich in Land, and poor in all the Comforts of Life; whom Nature having furnished as liberally as any other people, with the materials of

---

28–9 See 1, § 135, 7, verbal parallel.
31 See 1, § 117, 4–5. It is obvious from these parallels that this paragraph was written with Filmer's argument and Filmer's text in mind. Locke is sketching his account of the passage from a state of nature to a state of society in terms of biblical history.
§ 39 Also clearly directed against Filmer: its argument occupies a great deal of the *First Treatise*, which surely would have been referred to here if it had been written at the time.

Plenty, *i.e.* a fruitful Soil, apt to produce in abundance, what ₅
might serve for food, rayment, and delight; yet for want of
improving it by labour, have not one hundreth part of the Conveniencies we enjoy: And a King of a large and fruitful Territory
there feeds, lodges, and is clad worse than a day Labourer in
England.   10

42. To make this a little clearer, let us but trace some of the
ordinary provisions of Life, through their several progresses,
before they come to our use, and see how much they receive of
their *value from Humane Industry*. Bread, Wine and Cloth, are
things of daily use, and great plenty, yet notwithstanding, Acorns, ₅
Water, and Leaves, or Skins, must be our Bread, Drink and
Clothing, did not *labour* furnish us with these more useful Commodities. For whatever *Bread* is more worth than Acorns, *Wine*
than Water, and *Cloth* or *Silk* than Leaves, Skins, or Moss, that
is wholly *owing to labour* and industry. The one of these being the 10
Food and Rayment which unassisted Nature furnishes us with;
the other provisions which our industry and pains prepare for us,
which how much they exceed the other in value, when any one
hath computed, he will then see, how much *labour makes the far
greatest part of the value* of things, we enjoy in this World: And 15
the ground which produces the materials, is scarce to be reckon'd
in, as any, or at most, but a very small part of it; So little, that
even amongst us, Land that is left wholly to Nature, that hath no
improvement of Pasturage, Tillage, or Planting, is called, as indeed
it is, *wast*; and we shall find the benefit of it amount to little more 20
than nothing. This shews, how much numbers of men are to be
preferd to largenesse of dominions, and that the increase of lands

---

§ 42   17–21   A further reference to open-field tillage in England; see II, § 28,
16–26, note and references. The '*wast*' (waste) of line 20 was the manorial land outside
the fields, often a grazing area of some value, and Locke's implied criticism of the
system is once more a little out of place in this context, though it is interesting that he
should have made it.

21–8   A marginal addition in the Christ's copy, dating from the later 1690's
(probably after 1698) and belonging therefore to the period of Locke's activities at
the Board of Trade—see Laslett, 1957 (i). It is very significant of his attitude to that
institution and his policy for it, and for King William III's government in its struggle
with France, particularly the insistence on increased population (compare I, § 33,
13–27 and note) as against territory as a source of power, and the criticism of the
'narrownesse of Party'. The reference to a 'wise and godlike' Prince (compare II,
§ 166, 1), reveals the sense in which Locke, the enemy of divine-kingship, accepted
the metaphor of divinity for the ruler as he thought of him.

and the right imploying of them is the great art of government. And that Prince who shall be so wise and godlike as by established
25 laws of liberty to secure protection and incouragement to the honest industry of Mankind against the oppression of power and narrownesse of Party will quickly be too hard for his neighbours. But this bye the bye. To return to the argument in hand.

43. An Acre of Land that bears here Twenty Bushels of Wheat, and another in *America*, which, with the same Husbandry, would do the like, are, without doubt, of the same natural, intrinsick Value. But yet the Benefit Mankind receives from the one, in
5 a Year, is worth 5 *l.* and from the other possibly not worth a Penny, if all the Profit an *Indian* received from it were to be valued, and sold here; at least, I may truly say, not $\frac{1}{1000}$. 'Tis *Labour* then which *puts the greatest part of Value upon Land*, without which it would scarcely be worth any thing: 'tis to that we owe
10 the greatest part of all its useful Products: for all that the Straw, Bran, Bread, of that Acre of Wheat, is more worth than the Product of an Acre of as good Land, which lies wast, is all the Effect of Labour. For 'tis not barely the Plough-man's Pains, the Reaper's and Thresher's Toil, and the Bakers Sweat, is to be
15 counted into the *Bread* we eat; the Labour of those who broke the Oxen, who digged and wrought the Iron and Stones, who felled and framed the Timber imployed about the Plough, Mill, Oven, or any other Utensils, which are a vast Number, requisite to this Corn, from its being seed to be sown to its being made
20 Bread, must all be *charged on* the account of *Labour*, and received as an effect of that: Nature and the Earth furnished only the almost worthless Materials, as in themselves. 'Twould be a strange *Catalogue of things, that Industry provided and made use of, about every Loaf of Bread*, before it came to our use, if we could trace them;
25 Iron, Wood, Leather, Bark, Timber, Stone, Bricks, Coals, Lime, Cloth, Dying-Drugs, Pitch, Tar, Masts, Ropes, and all the Materials made use of in the Ship, that brought any of the Commodities made use of by any of the Workmen, to any part of the Work, all which, 'twould be almost impossible, at least too long, to reckon up.

44. From all which it is evident, that though the things of Nature are given in common, yet Man (by being Master of himself, and *Proprietor of his own Person*, and the Actions or *Labour* of it) had still in himself *the great Foundation of Property*; and that which

made up the great part of what he applyed to the Support or   5
Comfort of his being, when Invention and Arts had improved
the conveniencies of Life, was perfectly his own, and did not
belong in common to others.

45. Thus *Labour*, in the Beginning, *gave a Right of Property*,
where-ever any one was pleased to imploy it, upon what was
common, which remained, a long while, the far greater part, and
is yet more than Mankind makes use of. Men, at first, for the
most part, contented themselves with what un-assisted Nature   5
offered to their Necessities: and though afterwards, in some parts
of the World, (where the Increase of People and Stock, with the
Use of Money) had made Land scarce, and so of some Value, the
several *Communities* settled the Bounds of their distinct Territories,
and by Laws within themselves, regulated the Properties of the   10
private Men of their Society, and so, *by Compact* and Agreement,
settled the Property which Labour and Industry began; and the
Leagues that have been made between several States and Kingdoms, either expressly or tacitly disowning all Claim and Right
to the Land in the others Possession, have, by common Consent,   15
given up their Pretences to their natural common Right, which
originally they had to those Countries, and so have, by *positive
agreement, settled a Property* amongst themselves, in distinct Parts
and parcels of the Earth: yet there are still *great Tracts of Ground*
to be found, which (the Inhabitants thereof not having joyned with   20
the rest of Mankind, in the consent of the Use of their common
Money) *lie waste*, and are more than the People, who dwell on it,
do, or can make use of, and so still lie in common. Tho' this can
scarce happen amongst that part of Mankind, that have consented
to the Use of Money.   25

46. The greatest part of *things really useful* to the Life of Man, and
such as the necessity of subsisting made the first Commoners of

---

§ 45   Beginning of the argument promised in II, § 36, 39–40, continued until § 51;
compare II, § 184.

20–2   It is all mankind, not a particular collection or society, which consents to
the use of money, that is precious metals. Locke had stated this in his first writing
on money (see note on § 46, 5–7), but this fact is used somewhat obscurely in this
paragraph to relate the origin of the property of individuals in objects and the land
with the ownership of areas of the earth by nations or states. It was traditional to
consider these two forms of ownership side by side, for example, in Grotius and
Pufendorf.

the World look after, as it doth the *Americans* now, *are* generally
things *of short duration*; such as, if they are not consumed by use,
5 will decay and perish of themselves: Gold, Silver, and Diamonds,
are things, that Fancy or Agreement hath put the Value on, more
then real Use, and the necessary Support of Life. Now of those
good things which Nature hath provided in common, every one
had a Right (as hath been said) to as much as he could use, and
10 had a Property in all that he could affect with his Labour: all that
his Industry could extend to, to alter from the State Nature had
put it in, was his. He that *gathered* a Hundred Bushels of Acorns
or Apples, had thereby a *Property* in them; they were his Goods
as soon as gathered. He was only to look that he used them
15 before they spoiled; else he took more then his share, and robb'd
others. And indeed it was a foolish thing, as well as dishonest, to
hoard up more than he could make use of. If he gave away a part
to any body else, so that it perished not uselesly in his Possession,
these he also made use of. And if he also bartered away Plumbs
20 that would have rotted in a Week, for Nuts that would last good
for his eating a whole Year, he did no injury; he wasted not the
common Stock; destroyed no part of the portion of Goods that
belonged to others, so long as nothing perished uselesly in his
hands. Again, if he would give his Nuts for a piece of Metal,
25 pleased with its colour; or exchange his Sheep for Shells, or Wool
for a sparkling Pebble or a Diamond, and keep those by him all
his Life, he invaded not the Right of others, he might heap up
as much of these durable things as he pleased; the *exceeding of
the bounds of his* just *Property* not lying in the largeness of his
30 Possession, but the perishing of any thing uselesly in it.

47. And thus *came in the use of Money*, some lasting thing that
Men might keep without spoiling, and that by mutual consent

---

§ 46 5–7 Compare II 184, 15–18 and note, and Locke's *Considerations of Interest and
Money*, drafted about 1668, published in 1692 (see Introduction, 29 and note). 'For
mankind, having consented to put an imaginary value upon gold and silver, by reason of
their durableness, scarcity, and not being very liable to be counterfeited, have made them,
by general consent, the common pledges.' It is universal consent, world-wide, for
foreigners are insisted on (*Works*, 1801, v, 22). There is some resemblance between Locke's
account of the origin and functions of money and that of Matthew Wren, *Monarchy
Asserted*, 1660, see p. 22 on. Locke owned this book (H. and L. 3188).
§47 Compare *Considerations:* Money has a value, as it is capable, by exchange, to procure
us the necessaries, or conveniences of life, and in this it has the nature of a commodity'
(1801, 5, 34).

Men would take in exchange for the truly useful, but perishable Supports of Life.

48. And as different degrees of Industry were apt to give Men Possessions in different Proportions, so this *Invention of Money* gave them the opportunity to continue and enlarge them. For supposing an Island, separate from all possible Commerce with the rest of the World, wherein there were but a hundred 5 Families, but there were Sheep, Horses and Cows, with other useful Animals, wholsome Fruits, and Land enough for Corn for a hundred thousand times as many, but nothing in the Island, either because of its Commonness, or Perishableness, fit to supply the place of *Money*: What reason could any one have there to 10 enlarge his Possessions beyond the use of his Family, and a plentiful supply to its Consumption, either in what their own Industry produced, or they could barter for like perishable, useful Commodities, with others? Where there is not something both lasting and scarce, and so valuable to be hoarded up, there Men will 15 not be apt to enlarge their *Possessions of Land*, were it never so rich, never so free for them to take. For I ask, What would a Man value Ten Thousand, or an Hundred Thousand Acres of excellent *Land*, ready cultivated, and well stocked too with Cattle, in the middle of the in-land Parts of *America*, where he had no 20 hopes of Commerce with other Parts of the World, to draw *Money* to him by the Sale of the Product? It would not be worth the inclosing, and we should see him give up again to the wild Common of Nature, whatever was more than would supply the Conveniencies of Life to be had there for him and his 25 Family.

49. Thus in the beginning all the World was *America*, and more so than that is now; for no such thing as *Money* was any where known. Find out something that hath the *Use and Value of Money* amongst his Neighbours, you shall see the same Man will begin presently to *enlarge* his *Possessions*. 5

50. But since Gold and Silver, being little useful to the Life of Man in proportion to Food, Rayment, and Carriage, has its *value* only from the consent of Men, whereof Labour yet makes,

---

§ 49   1   Compare II, § 108, 1–2.

in great part, *the measure*, it is plain, that Men have agreed to
5 disproportionate and unequal Possession of the Earth, they
having by a tacit and voluntary consent found out a way, how
a man may fairly possess more land than he himself can use the
product of, by receiving in exchange for the overplus, Gold and
Silver, which may be hoarded up without injury to any one, these
10 metalls not spoileing or decaying in the hands of the possessor.
This partage of things, in an inequality of private possessions,
men have made practicable out of the bounds of Societie, and
without compact, only by putting a value on gold and silver and
tacitly agreeing in the use of Money. For in Governments the
15 Laws regulate the right of property, and the possession of land
is determined by positive constitutions.

51. And thus, I think, it is very easie to conceive without any
difficulty, *how Labour could at first begin a title of Property* in the
common things of Nature, and how the spending it upon our uses
bounded it. So that there could then be no reason of quarrelling
5 about Title, nor any doubt about the largeness of Possession it
gave. Right and conveniency went together; for as a Man had
a Right to all he could imploy his Labour upon, so he had no
temptation to labour for more than he could make use of. This
left no room for Controversie about the Title, nor for Incroach-
10 ment on the Right of others; what Portion a Man carved to
himself, was easily seen; and it was useless as well as dishonest to
carve himself too much, or take more than he needed.

---

§ **50** 4–16 Passage extensively corrected in the Christ's copy, in such a way as to
make parts of text in lines 5–9 unintelligible except by comparison with text in
1st Collected edition, 1714, and 4th edition, 1713. The original printed version reads very
oddly, containing such phrases as 'the consent of Men have agreed', which has been the
subject of some learned commentary—for example, Kendall, 1941, 84. Macpherson, 1962,
has some trenchant things to say on this passage as an implied, or overt, justification of
capitalist accumulation, see 209–10.

§ **51** Von Leyden compares this paragraph and §§ 31 and 36 with the statements
about property in Locke's eighth *Essay on the Law of Nature* (1954, 204–15).

1–2 This curiously repetitive phrase may also be a result of confusion in Locke's
manuscript, here uncorrected.

12 With the end of this paragraph and chapter also ends the section of the
1st edition which could have been involved in the printing difficulties of 1689;
compare note on 1, § 167, 10, and Laslett 1952 (iv), 1954 (ii).

CHAP. VI.
Of Paternal Power.

52. IT may perhaps be censured as an impertinent Criticism in a discourse of this nature, to find fault with words and names that have obtained in the World: And yet possibly it may not be amiss to offer new ones when the old are apt to lead Men into mistakes, as this of *Paternal Power* probably has done, which 5 seems so to place the Power of Parents over their Children wholly in the *Father*, as if the *Mother* had no share in it, whereas if we consult Reason or Revelation, we shall find she hath an equal Title. This may give one reason to ask, Whether this might not be more properly called *Parental Power*. For whatever obligation 10 Nature and the right of Generation lays on Children, it must certainly bind them equal to both the concurrent Causes of it. And accordingly we see the positive Law of God every where joyns them together, without distinction, when it commands the Obedience of Children, *Honour thy Father and thy Mother*, Exod. 15 20. 12. *Whosoever curseth his Father or his Mother*, Lev. 20. 9. *Ye shall fear every Man his Mother and his Father*, Lev. 19. 3. *Children obey your Parents*, &c. Eph. 6. 1. is the stile of the Old and New Testament.

53. Had but this one thing been well consider'd without looking any deeper into the matter, it might perhaps have kept

§ 52   *Chapter* vi. This chapter is obviously directed against Filmer, who is mentioned by name in § 61, and so seems clearly to belong to the original writing of 1679. Its argument is presented at greater length in the *First Treatise*: there are repetitions of phrases and of biblical citations. It is remarkable how evasive Locke is about the 5th Commandment throughout this chapter. There can be no doubt that this commandment provided the secure biblical basis for traditional patriarchalism, and for social subjection generally. See Laslett, 1965, chap. 8; Schochet, 1969; Dunn, 1969 (i), especially pp. 74–6.

1–3   Compare 1, §23, 22–5, note and references: Strauss, 1953, 221, sees in this a hint by Locke at the status of this 'discourse'; see Introduction, 86, note †.

8–19   The argument that the mother's authority is equal with that of the father is developed extensively in the *First Treatise*, and a cross-reference is given in 1, § 6, 51, again in 1, § 11, 31—see, in general, chapter vi of that treatise (§§ 50–73). The appeal to reason is made in 1, § 55, and to revelation in 1, § 61, where these four texts are cited.

10   '*Parental*'—see 11, § 69, 1 and note.

11   'right of Generation'—particularly attacked in 1, § 52: in 1, § 18, 18 and 1, § 50, 20, Grotius is attacked by implication, since Filmer uses him, but there is no reason to suppose that Locke had anyone but Filmer in mind. Hobbes's similar argument in *Leviathan*, chapter 20, looks coincidental: it was attacked by Filmer, 245.

Men from running into those gross mistakes, they have made, about this Power of Parents: which however it might, without
5 any great harshness, bear the name of Absolute Dominion, and Regal Authority, when under the Title of *Paternal Power* it seem'd appropriated to the Father, would yet have sounded but odly, and in the very name shewn the Absurdity, if this supposed Absolute Power over Children had been called *Parental*, and
10 thereby have discover'd, that it belong'd to the *Mother* too; for it will but very ill serve the turn of those Men who contend so much for the Absolute Power and Authority of the *Fatherhood*, as they call it, that the *Mother* should have any share in it. And it would have but ill supported the *Monarchy* they contend for,
15 when by the very name it appeared that that Fundamental Authority from whence they would derive their Government of a single Person only, was not plac'd in one, but two Persons joyntly. But to let this of Names pass.

54. Though I have said above, Chap. II, *That all Men by Nature are equal*, I cannot be supposed to understand all sorts of *Equality*: *Age* or *Virtue* may give Men a just Precedency: *Excellency of Parts and Merit* may place others above the Common Level: *Birth* may
5 subject some, and *Alliance* or *Benefits* others, to pay an Observance to those to whom Nature, Gratitude or other Respects may have made it due; and yet all this consists with the *Equality*, which all Men are in, in respect of Jurisdiction or Dominion one over another, which was the *Equality* I there spoke of, as proper to the
10 Business in hand, being that *equal Right* that every Man hath, *to his Natural Freedom*, without being subjected to the Will or Authority of any other Man.

55. *Children*, I confess are not born in this full State of *Equality*, though they are born to it. Their Parents have a sort of Rule and Jurisdiction over them when they come into the World, and for some time after, but 'tis but a temporary one. The Bonds of this
5 Subjection are like the Swadling Cloths they are wrapt up in, and supported by, in the weakness of their Infancy. Age and Reason as they grow up, loosen them till at length they drop quite off, and leave a Man at his own free Disposal.

---

§ 54 1 'Chap. II'—a late correction from '(2)'. Originally, perhaps, a paragraph rather than a chapter reference, to what is now II, § 4; see note there. On the statements about equality, compare II, § 4, 6–16.

56. *Adam* was created a perfect Man, his Body and Mind in full possession of their Strength and Reason, and so was capable from the first Instant of his being to provide for his own Support and Preservation, and govern his Actions according to the Dictates of the Law of Reason which God had implanted in him. From 5 him the World is peopled with his Descendants, who are all born Infants, weak and helpless, without Knowledge or Understanding. But to supply the Defects of this imperfect State, till the Improvement of Growth and Age hath removed them, *Adam* and *Eve*, and after them all *Parents* were, by the Law of Nature, *under an obligation to* 10 *preserve, nourish, and educate the Children*, they had begotten, not as their own Workmanship, but the Workmanship of their own Maker, the Almighty, to whom they were to be accountable for them.

57. The Law that was to govern *Adam*, was the same that was to govern all his Posterity, the *Law of Reason*. But his Off-spring having another way of entrance into the World, different from him, by a natural Birth, that produced them ignorant and without the use of *Reason*, they were not presently *under that Law*: for no 5 Body can be under a Law, which is not promulgated to him; and this Law being promulgated or made known by *Reason* only, he that is not come to the Use of his *Reason*, cannot be said to be *under this Law*; and *Adam*'s Children being not presently as soon as born, *under this Law of Reason* were not presently *free*. For *Law*, 10 in its true Notion, is not so much the Limitation as *the direction of a free and intelligent Agent* to his proper Interest, and prescribes no farther than is for the general Good of those under that Law. Could they be happier without it, the *Law*, as an useless thing would of it self vanish; and that ill deserves the Name of Confine- 15 ment which hedges us in only from Bogs and Precipices. So that,

---

§ 56 4–5 Compare 1, § 86, 19–20 and note.
  12–13 Compare 11, § 6, 10–14, note and references.
§ 57 This famous paragraph was apparently directed against Filmer, rather than Hobbes, in spite of the verbal resemblance noted under line 16. This is shown by the other details recorded here. Locke made niggling corrections to it, but none alters the sense.
  1–10 The references to Adam and his posterity criticize Filmer, who had made all Adam's children subject to his will, and all children subject to the will of their fathers, reason or no reason. Compare 11, § 60, and the seventh *Essay on the Law of Nature* (Von Leyden, 1954, 202–3).
  16 Compare *Leviathan*, chapter 30: 'For the use of Lawes is...to direct and keep [the People] in such a motion, as not to hurt themselves...as Hedges are set, not to

however it may be mistaken, *the end of Law* is not to abolish or restrain, but *to preserve and enlarge Freedom*: For in all the States of created beings capable of Laws, *where there is no Law, there is no*
20 *Freedom*. For *Liberty* is to be free from restraint and violence from others which cannot be, where there is no Law: But Freedom is not, as we are told, *A Liberty for every Man to do what he lists*: (For who could be free, when every other Man's Humour might domineer over him?) But a *Liberty* to dispose, and order, as he
25 lists, his Person, Actions, Possessions, and his whole Property, within the Allowance of those Laws under which he is; and therein not to be subject to the arbitrary Will of another, but freely follow his own.

58. The *Power*, then, *that Parents have* over their Children, arises from that Duty which is incumbent on them, to take care of their Off-spring, during the imperfect State of Childhood. To inform the Mind, and govern the Actions of their yet ignorant Nonage,
5 till Reason shall take its place, and ease them of that Trouble, is what the Children want, and the Parents are bound to. For God having given Man an Understanding to direct his Actions, has allowed him a freedom of Will, and liberty of Acting, as properly belonging thereunto, within the bounds of that Law he is under.
10 But whilst he is in an Estate, wherein he has not *Understanding* of his own to direct his *Will*, he is not to have any Will of his own to follow: He that *understands* for him, must *will* for him too;

---

stop Travellers, but to keep them in the way.' Presumably a verbal coincidence or an unconscious re-echo, though see Gough, 1950, 32.

16–28 Elrington, 1798, uses the statement about law and freedom to claim that men are free if governed by just laws, even if they were not consulted in their framing, and quotes Plato against the 'unsettled fancies of modern theorists'.

22 'as we are told'—that is, by Filmer, who makes the statement quoted, which is also quoted in II, § 22, 8–10; see note there and references.

§ 58 Tyrrell's account of the origin and nature of parental power is very similar to Locke's; see 1681, 15 and on. Both writers stress the parental duty of education, though Tyrrell is much more specific than Locke. In his diary for 1679 Locke made a note on the point from Sagard's *Canada* (1636), under the title '*Pietas*': education, not generation, gave the obligation, he wrote, and compared the Hurons with the Janissaries, initialling the note as his (compare II, § 106, 16–18 and note). The classical discussion is in Grotius (*De Jure Belli*, II, v), rejected by Filmer but characteristically close to the surface in Tyrrell: Pufendorf's commentary on the position of Grotius may well have been in Locke's mind—see especially *De Jure Naturae* (1672), VI, ii, De Potestate Patria.

10–11 Elrington (1798) uses this phrase about the understanding and will to justify the political inferiority of adults who lack intellectual attainments.

he mu&t prescribe to his Will, and regulate his Actions; but when
he comes to the E&tate that made his *Father a Freeman*, the *Son
is a Freeman* too.   15

59. This holds in all the Laws a Man is under, whether Natural
or Civil. Is a Man under the Law of Nature? *What made him free*
of that Law? What gave him a free disposing of his Property
according to his own Will, within the compass of that Law?
I answer; State of Maturity wherein he might be suppos'd capable 5
to know that Law, that so he might keep his Actions within the
Bounds of it. When he has acquired that &tate, he is presumed to
know how far that Law is to be his Guide, and how far he may
make use of his *Freedom*, and so comes to have it; till then, some
Body else mu&t guide him, who is presumed to know how far 10
the Law allows a Liberty. If such a &tate of Reason, such an Age
of Discretion *made him free*, the same shall make his Son free too.
Is a Man under the Law of *England*? *What made him free* of that
Law? That is, to have the Liberty to dispose of his Actions and
Possessions according to his own Will, within the Permission of 15
that Law? A capacity of knowing that Law. Which is supposed
by that Law, at the Age of one and twenty years, and in some
cases sooner. If this *made* the Father *free*, it shall *make* the Son
free too. Till then we see the Law allows the Son to have no Will,
but he is to be guided by the Will of his Father or Guardian, who 20
is to under&tand for him. And if the Father die, and fail to
sub&titute a Deputy in this Tru&t, if he hath not provided a Tutor
to govern his Son during his Minority, during his want of Under-
&tanding, the Law takes care to do it; some other mu&t govern
him, and be a Will to him, till he hath *attained to a &tate of Freedom*, 25
and his Under&tanding be fit to take the Government of his Will.
But after that, the Father and Son are equally *free* as much as
Tutor and Pupil after Nonage; equally Subjects of the same Law
together, without any Dominion left in the Father over the Life,
Liberty, or E&tate of his Son, whether they be only in the State 30
and under the Law of Nature, or under the positive Laws of an
E&tablish'd Government.

60. But if through defects that may happen out of the ordinary
course of Nature, any one comes not to such a degree of Reason,
wherein he might be supposed capable of knowing the Law, and
so living within the Rules of it, he is *never capable of being a Free*

5 *Man*, he is never let loose to the disposure of his own Will (because he knows no bounds to it, has not Understanding, its proper Guide) but is continued under the Tuition and Government of others, all the time his own Understanding is uncapable of that Charge. And so *Lunaticks* and *Ideots* are never set free from the
10 Government of their Parents; *Children, who are not as yet come unto those years whereat they may have; and Innocents which are excluded by a natural defect from ever having;* Thirdly, *Madmen, which for the present cannot possibly have the use of right Reason to guide themselves, have for their Guide, the Reason that guideth other Men which are Tutors*
15 *over them, to seek and procure their good for them, says* Hooker, Eccl. Pol. Lib. 1. Sect. 7. All which seems no more than that Duty, which God and Nature has laid on Man as well as other Creatures, to preserve their Off-spring, till they can be able to shift for themselves, and will scarce amount to an instance or
20 proof of *Parents* Regal Authority.

61. Thus we are *born Free*, as we are born Rational; not that we have actually the Exercise of either: Age that brings one, brings with it the other too. And thus we see how *natural Freedom and Subjection to Parents* may consist together, and are both founded
5 on the same Principle. A *Child* is *Free* by his Father's Title, by his Father's Understanding, which is to govern him, till he hath it of his own. The *Freedom of a Man at years of discretion*, and the *Subjection* of a Child *to* his *Parents*, whilst yet short of that Age, are so consistent, and so distinguishable, that the most blinded
10 Contenders for Monarchy, *by Right of Fatherhood*, cannot miss this *difference*, the most obstinate cannot but allow their consistency. For were their Doctrine all true, were the right Heir of *Adam* now known, and by that Title settled a Monarch in his Throne, invested with all the Absolute, Unlimited Power Sir *R.F.* talks of;
15 if he should die as soon as his Heir was born, must not the *Child*, notwithstanding he were never so free, never so much Sovereign, be in subjection to his Mother and Nurse, to Tutors and Governors,

§ 60 10–16 Keble's *Hooker*, 1836, 1, 276–7: 1676, 78, some lines after a passage copied into Locke's diary on 26 June 1681. Probably added after composition of the paragraph; see note on 11, § 5, 7–23.
16–20 Compare 1, § 56, 18–27.
§ 61 14 'Sir R.F.'—Sir Robert Filmer, an overt indication that Locke is here writing specifically against him; see note on 11, § 52 (chapter VI) and 11, § 22, 8–9 and note. This passage reads very like much of the *First Treatise*.

till Age and Education brought him Reason and Ability to govern himself, and others? The Necessities of his Life, the Health of his Body, and the Information of his Mind would require him to 20 be directed by the Will of others and not his own: and yet will any one think, that this Restraint and Subjection were inconsistent with, or spoiled him of that Liberty or Sovereignty he had a Right to, or gave away his Empire to those who had the Government of his Nonage? This Government over him only prepared him 25 the better and sooner for it. If any body should ask me, When my Son is *of Age to be free?* I shall answer, Just when his Monarch is of Age to govern. *But at what time,* says the judicious *Hooker,* Eccl. Pol. Lib. 1. Sect. 6. *a Man may be said to have attain'd so far forth the use of Reason, as sufficeth to make him capable of those Laws* 30 *whereby he is then bound to guide his Actions; this is a great deal more easie for sense to discern, than for any one by Skill and Learning to determine.*

62. Common-wealths themselves take notice of, and allow that there is *a time when Men* are to *begin to act like Free Men,* and therefore till that time require not Oaths of Fealty, or Allegiance, or other publick owning of, or Submission to the Government of their Countreys.   5

63. The *Freedom* then of Man and Liberty of acting according to his own Will, is *grounded on* his having *Reason,* which is able to instruct him in that Law he is to govern himself by, and make him know how far he is left to the freedom of his own will. To turn him loose to an unrestrain'd Liberty, before he has Reason 5 to guide him, is not the allowing him the priviledge of his Nature, to be free; but to thrust him out amongst Brutes, and abandon him to a State as wretched, and as much beneath that of a Man, as theirs. This is that which puts the *Authority* into the *Parents* hands to govern the *Minority* of their Children. God hath made 10 it their business to imploy this Care on their Off-spring, and hath placed in them suitable Inclinations of Tenderness and Concern to temper this power, to apply it as his Wisdom designed it, to the Childrens good, as long as they should need to be under it.

28–33   Keble's *Hooker,* 1836, 1, 273. Hooker's original has 'common sense', and 'for any man . . . to determine'. See 1676, 77 a few lines after a passage quoted in the *Essay concerning Humane Understanding* (1894, 1, 402–3). Evidently inserted after the composition of the paragraph; see note on II, § 5, 7–23 (and on II, § 5, 1 for 'judicious').

64. But what reason can hence advance this Care of the *Parents* due to their Off-spring into an *Absolute Arbitrary Dominion* of the Father, whose power reaches no farther, than by such a Discipline as he finds moſt effeᶜtual to give such ſtrength and health to their Bodies, such vigour and reᶜtitude to their Minds, as may beſt fit his Children to be moſt useful to themselves and others; and, if it be necessary to his Condition, to make them work when they are able for their own Subsiſtence. But in this power the *Mother* too has her share with the *Father*.

65. Nay, this *power* so little belongs to the *Father* by any peculiar right of Nature, but only as he is Guardian of his Children, that when he quits his Care of them, he loses his power over them, which goes along with their Nourishment and Education, to which it is inseparably annexed, and it belongs as much to the *Foſter-Father* of an exposed Child, as to the Natural Father of another: So little power does the bare *aᶜt of begetting* give a Man over his Issue, if all his Care ends there, and this be all the Title he hath to the Name and Authority of a Father. And what will become of this *Paternal Power* in that part of the World where one Woman hath more than one Husband at a time? Or in those parts of *America* where when the Husband and Wife part, which happens frequently, the Children are all left to the Mother, follow her, and are wholly under her Care and Provision? If the Father die whilſt the Children are young, do they not naturally every where owe the same Obedience to their *Mother*, during their Minority, as to their Father were he alive? And will any one say, that the *Mother* hath a Legislative Power over her Children? that she can make ſtanding Rules, which shall be of perpetual Obligation, by which they ought to regulate all the Concerns of

---

§ 64 4–9 These sentiments recall Locke on *Education* (already formulated though not written when this was composed, see Introduction, 28), and even his insistence in his paper for the Board of Trade that the children of the poor must work (Introduction, 43): compare Tyrrell, 1681, 19.

§ 65 5–7 Compare I, § 100, 7–10 and Tyrrell, 1681, 16: in lines 23–4 of I, § 100 Locke makes a cross-reference to the *Second Treatise*, evidently with such passages in this chapter in mind.

17–24 Locke's references here imply denials of the marks of political sovereignty which Filmer found in fatherly power; see I, § 129, 10–15 and note, II, § 3 and note. On the right of children to their property, compare Grotius, 1625, II, v, 2 and Pufendorf, 1672, VI, ii, 8: Locke's whole argument here and in II, § 69 (q.v.) is close to Pufendorf's.

their Property, and bound their Liberty all the course of their Lives? Or can she inforce the observation of them with Capital Punishments? For this is the proper *power of the Magistrate*, of which the Father hath not so much as the shadow. His Command over his Children is but temporary, and reaches not their Life 25 or Property. It is but a help to the weakness and imperfection of their Nonage, a Discipline necessary to their Education: And though a *Father* may dispose of his own Possessions as he pleases, when his Children are out of danger of perishing for want, yet *his power* extends not to the Lives or Goods, which either their 30 own industry, or anothers bounty has made theirs; nor to their Liberty neither, when they are once arrived to the infranchisement of the years of discretion. The *Father's Empire* then ceases, and he can from thence forwards no more dispose of the liberty of his Son, than that of any other Man: And it must be far from an 35 absolute or perpetual Jurisdiction, from which a Man may withdraw himself, having Licence from Divine Authority to *leave Father and Mother and cleave to his Wife.*

66. But though there be a time when a *Child* comes to be as *free* from subjection to the Will and Command of his Father, as the father himself is free from subjection to the Will of any body else, and they are each under no other restraint but that which is common to them both, whether it be the Law of Nature, or 5 municipal Law of their Country: yet this freedom exempts not a Son from that *honour* which he ought, by the Law of God and Nature, *to pay* his *Parents.* God having made the Parents Instruments in his great design of continuing the Race of Mankind, and the occasions of Life to their Children, as he hath laid on them an 10 obligation to nourish, preserve, and bring up their Off-spring; So he has laid on the Children a perpetual Obligation of *honouring their Parents,* which containing in it an inward esteem and reverence to be shewn by all outward Expressions, ties up the Child from any thing that may ever injure or affront, disturb, or endanger 15 the Happiness or Life of those, from whom he received his; and engages him in all actions of defence, relief, assistance and comfort

23–24 Compare I, § 129, 10–15, and note.
37–8 Gen. ii. 24, quoted in Matt. xix. 5, etc., and used by Tyrrell, 1681, 31.
§ 66 6–8 Compare I, § 63, 1–2; I, § 66, 19–20 and Tyrrell, 1681, 19, etc., following Grotius and Pufendorf.
8–9 Compare I, § 54, 5–7, verbal parallel.

of those, by whose means he entred into being, and has been made capable of any enjoyments of life. From this Obligation no State, no Freedom, can absolve Children. But this is very far from giving Parents a power of command over their Children, or an Authority to make Laws and dispose as they please, of their Lives or Liberties. 'Tis one thing to owe honour, respeét, gratitude and assiſtance; another to require an absolute obedience and submission. The *honour due to Parents*, a Monarch in his Throne owes his Mother, and yet this lessens not his Authority, nor subjeéts him to her Government.

67. The subjeétion of a Minor places in the Father a temporary Government, which terminates with the minority of the Child: and the *honour due from a Child*, places in the Parents a perpetual right to respeét, reverence, support and compliance too, more or less, as the Father's care, coſt and kindness in his Education, has been more or less. This ends not with minority, but holds in all parts and conditions of a Man's Life. The want of diſtinguishing these two powers; viz. that which the Father hath in the right of *Tuition*, during Minority, and the right of *Honour* all his Life, may perhaps have caused a great part of the miſtakes about this matter. For to speak properly of them, the firſt of these is rather the Priviledge of Children, and Duty of Parents, than any Prerogative of Paternal Power. The Nourishment and Education of their Children, is a Charge so incumbent on Parents for their Childrens good, that nothing can absolve them from taking care of it. And though the *power of commanding and chaſtising* them go along with it, yet God hath woven into the Principles of Humane Nature such a tenderness for their Off-spring, that there is little fear that Parents should use their power with too much rigour; the excess is seldom on the severe side, the ſtrong byass of Nature drawing the other way. And therefore God Almighty when he would express his gentle dealing with the *Israelites*, he tells them, that tho' he chaſten'd them, *he chaſten'd them as a Man chaſtens his Son*, Deut. 8. 5. *i.e.* with tenderness and affeétion, and kept them under no severer Discipline than what was absolutely beſt for them, and had been less kindness to have slacken'd. This is that power to which *Children* are commanded *Obedience*, that the pains and care of their Parents may not be increased, or ill rewarded.

§ 67   16–21   Compare 1, § 56, 18–27.

68. On the other side, *honour* and support, all that which Gratitude requires to return for the Benefits received by and from them is the indispensible Duty of the Child, and the proper Priviledge of the Parents. This is intended for the Parents advantage, as the other is for the Childs; though Education, the 5 Parents Duty, seems to have most power, because the ignorance and infirmities of Childhood stand in need of restraint and correction; which is a visible exercise of Rule, and a kind of Dominion. And that Duty which is comprehended in the word *honour*, requires less Obedience, though the Obligation be stronger on grown 10 than younger Children. For who can think the Command, *Children obey your Parents*, requires in a Man that has Children of his own the same submission to his Father, as it does in his yet young Children to him; and that by this Precept he were bound to obey all his Father's Commands, if out of a conceit of Authority 15 he should have the indiscretion to treat him still as a Boy?

69. The first part then of *Paternal* Power, or rather Duty, which is *Education*, belongs so to the Father that it terminates at a certain season; when the business of Education is over it ceases of it self, and is also alienable before. For a Man may put the Tuition of his Son in other hands; and he that has made 5 his Son an *Apprentice* to another, has discharged him, during that time, of a great part of his Obedience both to himself and to his Mother. But all the *Duty of Honour*, the other part, remains never the less entire to them; nothing can cancel that. It is so inseparable from them both, that the Father's Authority cannot dispossess 10 the Mother of this right, nor can any Man discharge his Son from honouring her that bore him. But both these are very far from a power to make Laws, and inforcing them with Penalties that may reach Estate, Liberty, Limbs and Life. The power of Commanding ends with Nonage; and though after that, *honour* and 15 respect, support and defence, and whatsoever Gratitude can oblige a Man to for the highest benefits he is naturally capable of, be

---

§ **69**   1   '*Paternal* Power'—Locke seems already to have forgotten his determination in II, § 52, 10 to call it '*Parental*'; compare II, § 170, 1.

6   '*Apprentice*'—this association of the filial relationship with apprenticeship is very significant for the social structure of seventeenth-century England; compare II, § 85, 8–16, and Laslett, 1965.

9–12   Compare I, § 62, 13–19.

14–24   Compare II, § 65, 17–24, and references, especially Pufendorf.

always due from a Son to his Parents; yet all this puts no Scepter
into the Father's hand, no Sovereign Power of Commanding.
20 He has no Dominion over his Sons Property or Actions, nor
any right, that his Will should prescribe to his Sons in all things;
however it may become his Son in many things, not very inconvenient to him and his Family, to pay a Deference to it.

70. A Man may owe *honour* and respect to an ancient, or wise
Man; defence to his Child or Friend; relief and support to the
Distressed; and gratitude to a Benefactor, to such a degree, that
all he has, all he can do, cannot sufficiently pay it: But all these
5 give no Authority, no right to any one of making Laws over
him from whom they are owing. And 'tis plain, all this is due not
to the bare Title of Father; not only because, as has been said, it
is owing to the Mother too; but because these Obligations to
Parents, and the degrees of what is required of Children, may be
10 varied, by the different care and kindness, trouble and expence,
which is often imployed upon one Child, more than another.

71. This shews the reason how it comes to pass, that *Parents
in Societies*, where they themselves are Subjects, retain a *power over
their Children*, and have as much right to their Subjection, as
those who are in the State of Nature, which could not possibly
5 be, if all Political Power were only Paternal, and that in truth
they were one and the same thing: For then, all Paternal Power
being in the Prince, the Subject could naturally have none of it.
But these two *Powers*, *Political* and *Paternal*, *are so perfectly distinct*
and separate; are built upon so different Foundations, and given
10 to so different Ends, that every Subject that is a Father, has as
much a *Paternal Power* over his Children, as the Prince has over
his; And every Prince that has Parents owes them as much filial
Duty and Obedience as the meanest of his Subjects do to theirs;
and can therefore contain not any part or degree of that kind of
15 Dominion, which a Prince, or Magistrate has over his Subject.

72. Though the Obligation on the Parents to *bring up* their
Children, and the Obligation on Children to *honour* their Parents,
contain all the Power on the one hand, and Submission on the
other, which are proper to this Relation; yet there is *another Power*
5 ordinarily *in the Father*, whereby he has a tie on the Obedience of

§ 71   1–7   Compare 1, § 65, 3–12.

his Children: which though it be common to him with other Men, yet the occasions of shewing it, almost constantly happening to Fathers in their private Families, and the Instances of it elsewhere being rare, and less taken notice of, it passes in the World for a part of *Paternal Jurisdiction*. And this is the Power Men 10 generally have to *bestow their Estates* on those, who please them best. The Possession of the Father being the Expectation and Inheritance of the Children ordinarily in certain proportions, according to the Law and Custom of each Country; yet it is commonly in the Father's Power to bestow it with a more sparing 15 or liberal hand, according as the Behaviour of this or that Child hath comported with his Will and Humour.

73. This is no small Tye on the Obedience of Children: And there being always annexed to the Enjoyment of Land, a Submission to the Government of the Country, of which that Land is a part; It has been commonly suppos'd, That a *Father* could *oblige his Posterity to that Government*, of which he himself was 5 a Subject, and that his Compact held them; whereas, it being only a necessary Condition annex'd to the Land, and the inheritance of an Estate which is under that Government, reaches only those who will take it on that Condition, and so is no natural Tye or Engagement, but a voluntary Submission. For *every Man's* 10 *Children* being by Nature as *free* as himself, or any of his Ancestors ever were, may, whilst they are in that Freedom, choose what Society they will join themselves to, what Common-wealth they will put themselves under. But if they will enjoy the *Inheritance* of their Ancestors, they must take it on the same terms their 15 Ancestors had it, and submit to all the Conditions annex'd to such a Possession. By this Power indeed Fathers oblige their Children to Obedience to themselves, even when they are past Minority, and most commonly too subject them to this or that Political Power. But neither of these by any peculiar right of 20 *Fatherhood*, but by the Reward they have in their hands to inforce

---

§ 73　This paragraph represents perhaps the weakest point of Locke's argument against Filmer. Elrington, 1798, seizes on Locke's denial of a 'natural Tye' (lines 9–10) to maintain that 'it cannot be concluded that no degree of obligation whatsoever is imposed on a man by the acts of his ancestors', and this is the burden of Burke's criticism of Lockeian politics, especially as they were interpreted in Revolutionary France.

and recompence such a Compliance; and is no more Power than
what a *French-man* has over an *English-man*, who by the hopes of
an Estate he will leave him, will certainly have a strong Tye on
25 his Obedience: And if when it is left him, he will enjoy it, he must
certainly take it upon the Conditions annex'd to the *Possession of Land*
in that Country where it lies, whether it be *France* or *England*.

74. To conclude then, though the *Father's Power* of commanding
extends no farther than the Minority of his Children, and to
a degree only fit for the Discipline and Government of that Age:
And though that *Honour* and Respect, and all that which the *Latins*
5 called *Piety*, which they indispensibly owe to their Parents all
their Life times, and in all Estates, with all that Support and
Defence [which] is due to them, gives the Father no Power of
Governing, *i.e.* making Laws and enacting Penalties on his
Children; Though by all this he has no Dominion over the
10 Property or Actions of his Son: yet 'tis obvious to conceive how
easie it was in the first Ages of the World, and in places still,
where the thinness of People gives Families leave to separate into
unpossessed Quarters, and they have room to remove and plant
themselves in yet vacant Habitations, for the *Father of the Family*
15 to become the Prince of it;† he had been a Ruler from the
beginning of the Infancy of his Children: and since without some

† *It is no improbable Opinion, therefore, which the* Arch-Philosopher *was of, That the
chief Person in every Houshold was always, as it were, a King: So when Numbers of Housholds
joyn'd themselves in Civil Societies together, Kings were the first kind of Governours amongst
them, which is also, as it seemeth, the reason why the name of Fathers continued still in them,
who, of Fathers, were made Rulers; as also the ancient Custom of Governours to do as
Melchizedec, and being Kings, to exercise the Office of Priests, which Fathers did, at the first,
grew perhaps by the same Occasion. Howbeit, this is not the only kind of Regiment that has
been received in the World. The Inconveniences of one kind have caused sundry other to be
devised; so that in a word, all publick Regiment of what kind soever, seemeth evidently to
have risen from the deliberate Advice, Consultation and Composition between Men, judging
it convenient, and behoveful; there being no impossibility in Nature, considered by it self, but
that Man might have lived without any publick Regiment.* Hooker's Eccl. P. l. 1. Sect. 10.

§ 74 7 'which'—inserted by editor to make sense.
14–37 This passage, and the two succeeding paragraphs (compare II, §§ 105–12, § 162),
make considerable concessions to patriarchalism, and represent the direct influence on
Locke of Filmer and traditional attitudes. But not only is Locke's argument very close to
Tyrrell's (1681, 35–9), but also to that of Pufendorf, *De Jure Naturae* (1672), VII, iii, *De
Generatione Summi Imperii Civilis*, see especially § 7 (904–5). Tyrrell cites 'Mr Pufendorf a late
judicious writer of great judgment and learning' at this point (p. 37, words added in the copy
Tyrrell corrected for Locke, see above p. 60, note ¶), and also Sir William Temple's *Essay of
Government* (published in *Miscellanea*, 1680), for Temple was the great exponent of

Government it would be hard for them to live together, it was likeliest it should, by the express or tacit Consent of the Children, when they were grown up, be in the Father, where it seemed without any change barely to continue; when indeed nothing 20 more was required to it, than the permitting the *Father* to exercise alone in his Family that executive Power of the Law of Nature, which every Free-man naturally hath, and by that permission resigning up to him a Monarchical Power, whilst they remained in it. But that this was not by any *Paternal Right*, but only by 25 the Consent of his Children, is evident from hence, That no Body doubts but if a Stranger, whom Chance or Business had brought to his Family, had there kill'd any of his Children, or committed any other Fact, he might Condemn and put him to Death, or otherwise have punished him as well as any of his Children: 30 which it was impossible he should do by virtue of any Paternal Authority over one, who was not his Child, but by virtue of that Executive Power of the Law of Nature, which, as a Man he had a right to: And he alone could punish him in his Family, where the respect of his Children had laid by the Exercise of such 35 a Power, to give way to the Dignity and Authority, they were willing should remain in him, above the rest of his Family.

75. Thus 'twas easie, and almost natural for Children by a tacit, and scarce avoidable consent to make way for the *Father's Authority and Government*. They had been accustomed in their Childhood to follow his Direction, and to refer their little differences to him, and when they were Men, who fitter to rule them? Their little 5 Properties, and less Covetousness seldom afforded greater Controversies; and when any should arise, where could they have

---

patriarchalism tempered with consent and apart from Divine Right. Locke does not seem to have read or possessed Temple's book, and these sentiments seem to be the result of his consideration of Filmer, and perhaps his acquaintance with Pufendorf.

§ **74**   15   The reference sign is inserted by the editor at this point to show where it seems most likely that Locke wished to draw the attention of his reader to the passage in Hooker, printed without reference sign in the margins of the 1st and later editions. All subsequent citations from Hooker appear in the margins in this way, which marks them even more obviously as later additions, made perhaps about June 1681 after the original text was complete (see note on II, § 5, 7-23 and references). The passage is found on pp. 303-4 of Keble's *Hooker*, 1836, vol. 1 and on p. 86 of Locke's 1676 Hooker. The 'Arch-Philosopher' is of course Aristotle; see the passages in *Politics*, 1, especially 1252b, which Filmer had made use of.

   22   'executive Power of the Law of Nature'—see II, § 9, 1, note and references.

a fitter Umpire than he, by whose Care they had every one been sustain'd, and brought up, and who had a tenderness for them
10 all? 'Tis no wonder, that they made no distinction betwixt Minority, and full Age; nor looked after one and Twenty, or any other Age, that might make them the free Disposers of themselves and Fortunes, when they could have no desire to be out of their Pupilage. The Government they had been under, during
15 it, continued still to be more their Protection than restraint: And they could no where find a greater security to their Peace, Liberties, and Fortunes, than in the *Rule of a Father*.

76. Thus the natural *Fathers of Families*, by an insensible change, became the *politick Monarchs* of them too: And as they chanced to live long, and leave able, and worthy Heirs, for several Successions, or otherwise; So they laid the Foundations of
5 Hereditary, or Elective Kingdoms, under several Constitutions, and Manners, according as Chance, Contrivance, or Occasions happen'd to mould them. But if Princes have their Titles in the Fathers Right, and it be a sufficient proof of the natural *Right of Fathers* to Political Authority, because they commonly were those,
10 in whose hands we find, *de facto*, the Exercise of Government: I say, if this Argument be good, it will as strongly prove that all Princes, nay Princes only, ought to be Priests, since 'tis as certain, that in the Beginning, *The Father of the Family was Priest, as that he was Ruler in his own Houshold.*

Chap. VII.

Of Political or Civil Society.

77. G OD having made Man such a Creature, that, in his own Judgment, it was not good for him to be alone, put him under strong Obligations of Necessity, Convenience, and Inclination to drive him into *Society*, as well as fitted him with Under-

---

§ 77 *Chapter* VII   All the evidence goes to show that this chapter formed a part of the original critique of Filmer; compare note on chapter VI, 11, § 52. There are references to men who can only be Filmer and his followers (§ 90) and arguments

standing and Language to continue and enjoy it. The *first Society* 5 was between Man and Wife, which gave beginning to that between Parents and Children; to which, in time, that between Master and Servant came to be added: And though all these might, and commonly did meet together, and make up but one Family, wherein the Master or Mistress of it had some sort of Rule proper 10 to a Family; each of these, or all together came short of *Political Society*, as we shall see, if we consider the different Ends, Tyes, and Bounds of each of these.

78. *Conjugal Society* is made by a voluntary Compact between Man and Woman: and tho' it consist chiefly in such a Communion and Right in one anothers Bodies, as is necessary to its chief End, Procreation; yet it draws with it mutual Support, and Assistance, and a Communion of Interest too, as necessary not only to unite 5 their Care, and Affection, but also necessary to their common Off-spring, who have a Right to be nourished and maintained by them, till they are able to provide for themselves.

79. For the end of *conjunction between Male and Female*, being not barely Procreation, but the continuation of the Species, this conjunction betwixt Male and Female ought to last, even after Procreation, so long as is necessary to the nourishment and support of the young Ones, who are to be sustained by those that 5 got them, till they are able to shift and provide for themselves. This Rule, which the infinite wise Maker hath set to the Works of his hands, we find the inferiour Creatures steadily obey. In those viviparous Animals which feed on Grass, the *conjunction*

directly pointed at Filmer's text (§§ 92, 93): it is closely parallel to Tyrrell's discussion which was overtly directed against Filmer. There is no positive indication of insertions or revision in 1689, though the cross-reference in § 84, 3, may imply some revision at an earlier date.

§ 77   1–4   Compare the fourth *Essay on the Law of Nature*. Man 'feels himself . . . urged to enter into society by a certain propensity of nature, and to be prepared for the maintenance of society by the gift of speech and through the intercourse of language' (Von Leyden, 1954, 156–7).

2   Gen. ii. 18: 'God said, it is not good that the man should be alone.'

5–13   Compare II, § 2, and also Aristotle's *Politics*, I, especially 1252a and b.

§ 78   Compare Tyrrell, 1681, 14: 'Marriage, which is a mutual Compact between a Man and a Woman for their Cohabitation, the generation of Children, and their joint care and provision for them.'

§ 79   Natural history of this sort was a persistent pre-occupation of Locke's, and he possessed many of the standard works. The pre-Linnaean, pre-Darwinian system of classification comes out clearly here, as it does in the *First Treatise*.

10 *between Male and Female* lasts no longer than the very Act of
Copulation: because the Teat of the Dam being sufficient to
nourish the Young, till it be able to feed on Grass, the Male only
begets, but concerns not himself for the Female or Young, to
whose Sustenance he can contribute nothing. But in Beasts of
15 Prey the *conjunction* lasts longer: because the Dam not being able
well to subsist her self, and nourish her numerous Off-spring by
her own Prey alone, a more laborious, as well as more dangerous
way of living, than by feeding on Grass, the Assistance of the
Male is necessary to the Maintenance of their common Family,
20 which cannot subsist till they are able to prey for themselves,
but by the joynt Care of Male and Female. The same is to be
observed in all Birds (except some domestick ones, where plenty
of food excuses the Cock from feeding, and taking care of the
young Brood) whose Young needing Food in the Nest, the Cock
25 and Hen continue Mates, till the Young are able to use their
wing, and provide for themselves.

80. And herein I think lies the chief, if not the only reason,
why the Male and Female in Mankind are tyed to a longer conjunction
than other Creatures, *viz.* because the Female is capable of con-
ceiving, and *de facto* is commonly with Child again, and Brings
5 forth too a new Birth long before the former is out of a dependancy
for support on his Parents help, and able to shift for himself, and
has all the assistance is due to him from his Parents: whereby
the Father, who is bound to take care for those he hath begot, is
under an Obligation to continue in Conjugal Society with the
10 same Woman longer than other Creatures, whose Young being
able to subsist of themselves, before the time of Procreation
returns again, the Conjugal Bond dissolves of it self, and they are
at liberty, till *Hymen*, at his usual Anniversary Season, summons
them again to chuse new Mates. Wherein one cannot but admire the
15 Wisdom of the great Creatour, who having given to Man foresight
and an Ability to lay up for the future, as well as to supply the
present necessity, hath made it necessary, that *Society of Man and
Wife should be more lasting*, than of Male and Female amongst other
Creatures; that so their Industry might be encouraged, and their
20 Interest better united, to make Provision, and lay up Goods
for their common Issue, which uncertain mixture, or easie and
frequent Solutions of Conjugal Society would mightily disturb.

81. But though these are Ties upon *Mankind*, which make the *Conjugal Bonds* more firm and lasting in Man, than the other Species of Animals; yet it would give one reason to enquire, why this *Compact*, where Procreation and Education are secured, and Inheritance taken care for, may not be made determinable, either 5 by consent, or at a certain time, or upon certain Conditions, as well as any other voluntary Compacts, there being no necessity in the nature of the thing, nor to the ends of it, that it should always be for Life; I mean, to such as are under no Restraint of any positive Law, which ordains all such Contracts to be perpetual. 10

82. But the Husband and Wife, though they have but one common Concern, yet having different understandings, will unavoidably sometimes have different wills too; it therefore being necessary, that the last Determination, *i.e.* the Rule, should be placed somewhere, it naturally falls to the Man's share, as the 5 abler and the stronger. But this reaching but to the things of their common Interest and Property, leaves the Wife in the full and free possession of what by Contract is her peculiar Right, and gives the Husband no more power over her Life, than she has over his. The *Power of the Husband* being so far from that of 10 an absolute Monarch, that the *Wife* has, in many cases, a Liberty to *separate* from him; where natural Right, or their Contract allows it, whether that Contract be made by themselves in the State of Nature, or by the Customs or Laws of the Countrey they live in; and the Children upon such Separation fall to the Father 15 or Mother's Lot, as such Contract does determine.

83. For all the ends of *Marriage* being to be obtained under Politick Government, as well as in the State of Nature, the Civil Magistrate doth not abridge the Right, or Power of either naturally necessary to those ends, *viz.* Procreation and mutual Support

---

§ 81   5–7   This guarded hint at the justifiability of divorce was too much for the clerical Elrington, who says: 'To make the conjugal union determinable by consent, is to introduce a promiscuous concubinage.' Locke was prepared to go much further than this, as is seen in the notes in his diary for 1678, 1679, 1680 under the heading *Atlantis*. He suggests that 'He that is already married may marry another woman with his left hand.... The ties, duration and conditions of the left hand marriage shall be no other than what is expressed in the contract of marriage between the parties' (*Diary*, 1678, 199). On Locke's *Atlantis*, see de Marchi, 1955.
§ 82   5   Elrington says that this implies that the right of the husband arises solely from superior power, as indeed it does in Hobbes's *Leviathan*, chapter 20, which Locke's discussion resembles to some extent.

5 and Assistance whilst they are together; but only decides any
Controversie that may arise between Man and Wife about them.
If it were otherwise, and that absolute *Sovereignty* and Power of
Life and Death naturally belong'd to the Husband, and were
necessary to the Society between Man and Wife, there could be no
10 Matrimony in any of those Countries where the Husband is
allowed no such absolute Authority. But the ends of Matrimony
requiring no such Power in the Husband, the Condition of *Conjugal Society* put it not in him, it being not at all necessary to that
State. *Conjugal Society* could subsist and obtain its ends without it;
15 nay, Community of Goods, and the Power over them, mutual
Assistance, and Maintenance, and other things belonging to *Conjugal Society*, might be varied and regulated by that Contract, which
unites Man and Wife in that Society, as far as may consist with
Procreation and the bringing up of Children till they could shift
20 for themselves; nothing being necessary to any Society, that is
not necessary to the ends for which it is made.

84. The *Society betwixt Parents and Children*, and the distinct
Rights and Powers belonging respectively to them, I have treated
of so largely, in the foregoing Chapter, that I shall not here need
to say any thing of it. And I think it is plain, that it is far different
5 from a Politick Society.

85. *Master* and *Servant* are Names as old as History, but given
to those of far different condition; for a Free-man makes himself
a Servant to another, by selling him for a certain time, the Service
he undertakes to do, in exchange for Wages he is to receive:
5 And though this commonly puts him into the Family of his
Master, and under the ordinary Discipline thereof; yet it gives
the Master but a Temporary Power over him, and no greater,
than what is contained in the *Contract* between 'em. But there is
another sort of Servants, which by a peculiar Name we call *Slaves,*
10 who being Captives taken in a just War, are by the Right of
Nature subjected to the Absolute Dominion and Arbitrary Power

---

§ **83**   12–20   Passage rewritten for the 2nd edition: little difference of sense, except that
'Community of Goods' (line 15) is introduced.

§ **84**   3   'foregoing Chapter'—chapter VI; see note on II, § 77 (chapter VII).

§ **85**   8–16   On slavery compare II, § 24, 1–8 and references: here is added the
claim that slaves are outside civil society. 'Servants' in this paragraph, we must
not forget, covered many now classed as industrial or agricultural workers,
and that Locke and all his contemporaries looked upon them as under domestic
authority is significant of very different social assumptions; compare II, § 69, 6,
'*Apprentice*'.

of their Masters. These Men having, as I say, forfeited their
Lives, and with it their Liberties, and lost their Estates; and being
in the *State of Slavery*, not capable of any Property, cannot in that
State be considered as any part of *Civil Society*; the chief end 15
whereof is the preservation of Property.

86. Let us therefore consider a *Master of a Family* with all these
subordinate Relations of *Wife*, *Children*, *Servants* and *Slaves* united
under the Domestick Rule of a Family; which what resemblance
soever it may have in its Order, Offices, and Number too, with
a little Common-wealth, yet is very far from it, both in its Con- 5
stitution, Power and End: Or if it must be thought a Monarchy,
and the *Paterfamilias* the absolute Monarch in it, absolute Monarchy
will have but a very shattered and short Power, when 'tis plain,
by what has been said before, That the *Master of the Family* has
a very distinct and differently limited *Power*, both as to time and 10
extent, over those several Persons that are in it; for excepting
the Slave (and the Family is as much a Family, and his Power as
Paterfamilias as great, whether there be any Slaves in his Family
or no) he has no Legislative Power of Life and Death over any
of them, and none too but what a *Mistress of a Family* may have as 15
well as he. And he certainly can have no absolute Power over
the whole *Family*, who has but a very limited one over every
individual in it. But how a *Family*, or any other Society of
Men, differ from that, which is properly *Political Society*, we
shall best see, by considering wherein *Political Society* it self 20
consists.

87. Man being born, as has been proved, with a Title to perfect
Freedom, and an uncontrouled enjoyment of all the Rights and
Priviledges of the Law of Nature, equally with any other Man,
or Number of Men in the World, hath by Nature a Power, not
only to preserve his Property, that is, his Life, Liberty and Estate, 5
against the Injuries and Attempts of other Men; but to judge of,

---

§ **86** On this paragraph compare the *Third Letter for Toleration*, (*Works*, 1801, VI, 213). The
domestic unit being described is readily recognizable as that which prevailed in Locke's day
over the English-speaking world, see Laslett and Wall, 1972. It is not without interest that the
presence of a slave was regarded as not an unusual feature of such familial groups.
87 5 'that is, his Life, Liberty and Estate'—compare this extended definition of
property with I, § 9, 8–9; II §§ 57, 25; 59, 29–30; 85, 13; 123, 16–17; 131, 6; 135,
15; 137, 5; 171, 17; 173, 4–6; 209, 5–6; 221, 7; 222, 19–20; and see Introduction,
101. Contrast also, I, § 90, 13–18.

and punish the breaches of that Law in others, as he is perswaded the Offence deserves, even with Death it self, in Crimes where the heinousness of the Fact, in his Opinion, requires it. But because no *Political Society* can be, nor subsist without having in it self the Power to preserve the Property, and in order thereunto punish the Offences of all those of that Society; there, and there only is *Political Society*, where every one of the Members hath quitted this natural Power, resign'd it up into the hands of the Community in all cases that exclude him not from appealing for Protection to the Law established by it. And thus all private judgement of every particular Member being excluded, the Community comes to be Umpire, by settled standing Rules, indifferent, and the same to all Parties; and by Men having Authority from the Community, for the execution of those Rules, decides all the differences that may happen between any Members of that Society, concerning any matter of right; and punishes those Offences, which any Member hath committed against the Society, with such Penalties as the Law has established: Whereby it is easie to discern who are, and who are not, in *Political Society* together. Those who are united into one Body, and have a common establish'd Law and Judicature to appeal to, with Authority to decide Controversies between them, and punish Offenders, *are in Civil Society* one with another: but those who have no such common Appeal, I mean on Earth, are still in the state of Nature, each being, where there is no other, Judge for himself, and Executioner; which is, as I have before shew'd it, the perfect *state of Nature*.

88. And thus the Commonwealth comes by a Power to set down, what punishment shall belong to the several transgressions which they think worthy of it, committed amongst the Members of that Society, (which is the *power of making Laws*) as well as it has the power to punish any Injury done unto any of its Members, by any one that is not of it, (which is the *power of War and Peace*;) and all this for the preservation of the property of all the Members of that Society, as far as is possible. But though every Man who has enter'd into civil Society, and is become a member of any Commonwealth, has thereby quitted his power to punish Offences against the Law of Nature, in prosecution of his own private

---

18–21   Passage rewritten for 2nd edition.

§ 88   4 and 6   Marks of sovereignty again hinted at; see II, § 11, 6–8 and references.

Judgment; yet with the Judgment of Offences which he has given up to the Legislative in all Cases, where he can Appeal to the Magistrate, he has given a right to the Commonwealth to imploy his force, for the Execution of the Judgments of the Common- 15 wealth, whenever he shall be called to it; which indeed are his own Judgments, they being made by himself, or his Representative. And herein we have the original of the *Legislative* and *Executive Power* of Civil Society, which is to judge by standing Laws how far Offences are to be punished, when committed within 20 the Commonwealth; and also to determin, by occasional Judgments founded on the present Circumstances of the Fact, how far Injuries from without are to be vindicated, and in both these to imploy all the force of all the Members when there shall be need.

89. Where-ever therefore any number of Men are so united into one Society, as to quit every one his Executive Power of the Law of Nature, and to resign it to the publick, there and there only is a *Political, or Civil Society*. And this is done where-ever any number of Men, in the State of Nature, enter into Society to 5 make one People, one Body Politick under one Supreme Government, or else when any one joyns himself to, and incorporates with any Government already made. For hereby he authorizes the Society, or which is all one, the Legislative thereof to make Laws for him as the publick good of the Society shall require; 10 to the Execution whereof, his own assistance (as to his own Decrees) is due. And this *puts Men* out of a State of Nature *into* that of a *Commonwealth*, by setting up a Judge on Earth, with Authority to determine all the Controversies, and redress the Injuries, that may happen to any Member of the Commonwealth; which Judge 15 is the Legislative, or Magistrates appointed by it. And where-ever there are any number of Men, however associated, that have no such decisive power to appeal to, there they are still *in the state of Nature*.

---

12   Elrington (1798) castigates this as leaving it optional that men should resign up their power to political authority.

14–18   Used by Kendall to demonstrate Locke's 'collectivism', along with 11, § 120; see note there, and on 11, § 151, 19, 22 for 'representative'.

§ 89   1   'Men are so united'— in 1st ed. active mood, 'Men so unite'.

6   'People': first occurrence of this word, cf. Polin, 1960, 156.

13–19   Here Locke talks of the Legislative where the Judiciary might be expected; compare 11, § 88, 12–13, and Introduction, 118. The whole paragraph should be contrasted with Hobbes's *Leviathan*, chapter 18.

90. Hence it is evident, that *Absolute Monarchy*, which by some Men is counted the only Government in the World, is indeed *inconsistent with Civil Society*, and so can be no Form of Civil Government at all. For the *end of Civil Society*, being to avoid,
5 and remedy those inconveniencies of the State of Nature, which necessarily follow from every Man's being Judge in his own Case, by setting up a known Authority, to which every one of that Society may Appeal upon any Injury received, or Controversie that may arise, and which every one of the Society ought
10 to obey;† where-ever any persons are, who have not such an Authority to Appeal to, for the decision of any difference between them, there those persons are still *in the state of Nature*. And so is every *Absolute Prince* in respect of those who are under his *Dominion*.

91. For he being suppos'd to have all, both Legislative and Executive Power in himself alone, there is no Judge to be found, no Appeal lies open to any one, who may fairly, and indifferently, and with Authority decide, and from whose decision relief and
5 redress may be expected of any Injury or Inconveniency, that may be suffered from the Prince or by his Order: So that such a Man, however intitled, *Czar*, or *Grand Signior*, or how you please, is as much *in the state of Nature*, with all under his Dominion, as he is with the rest of Mankind. For where-ever any two Men are,
10 who have no standing Rule, and common Judge to Appeal to on Earth for the determination of Controversies of Right betwixt them, there they are still *in the state of Nature*, and under all the inconveniencies of it,‡ with only this woful difference to the

† *The publick Power of all Society is above every Soul contained in the same Society; and the principal use of that power is to give Laws unto all that are under it, which Laws in such Cases we must obey, unless there be reason shew'd which may necessarily inforce, that the Law of Reason, or of God, doth injoyn the contrary*, Hook. Eccl. Pol. l. 1. Sect. 16.

‡ *To take away all such mutual Grievances, Injuries and Wrongs*, i.e. such as attend Men in the State of Nature. *There was no way but only by growing into Composition and*

---

§ 90   1–2 'some Men', that is Filmer and his followers, certainly not Hobbes to whom monarchy was decidedly not the only form of government. See II, § 77 (chapter VII).

10   Reference sign for Hooker quotation inserted by editor; see note on II, § 74, 15. Passage on p. 353 of Keble's *Hooker*, 1836, 1, and Locke's 1676 edition 101–2, slightly modified in transcription here.

§ 91   13   Reference sign for Hooker quotation inserted by editor; see note on II, § 74, 15. See Keble's *Hooker*, 1836, 1, 302, Locke's 1676 edition, 86, slightly modified. Compare English treatise 1660, and Abrams' note: Polin, 1961, 105.

Subject, or rather Slave of an Absolute Prince: That whereas, in
the ordinary State of Nature, he has a liberty to judge of his Right, 15
and according to the best of his Power, to maintain it; now whenever his Property is invaded by the Will and Order of his Monarch,
he has not only no Appeal, as those in Society ought to have, but
as if he were degraded from the common state of Rational
Creatures, is denied a liberty to judge of, or to defend his Right, 20
and so is exposed to all the Misery and Inconveniencies that
a Man can fear from one, who being in the unrestrained state of
Nature, is yet corrupted with Flattery, and armed with Power.

92. For he that thinks *absolute Power purifies Mens Bloods*, and
corrects the baseness of Humane Nature, need read but the History
of this, or any other Age to be convinced of the contrary. He that
would have been insolent and injurious in the Woods of *America*,
would not probably be much better in a Throne; where perhaps 5
Learning and Religion shall be found out to justifie all, that he
shall do to his Subjects, and the Sword presently silence all those
that dare question it. For what the *Protection of Absolute Monarchy*
is, what kind of Fathers of their Countries it makes Princes to be,
and to what a degree of Happiness and Security it carries Civil 10
Society, where this sort of Government is grown to perfection,
he that will look into the late Relation of *Ceylon*, may easily see.

*Agreement amongst themselves, by ordaining some kind of Government publick, and by
yielding themselves subject thereunto, that unto whom they granted Authority to Rule and
Govern, by them the Peace, Tranquility, and happy Estate of the rest might be procured.
Men always knew that where Force and Injury was offered, they might be Defenders of them-
selves; they knew that however Men may seek their own Commodity; yet if this were done with
Injury unto others, it was not to be suffered, but by all Men, and all good Means to be withstood.
Finally, they knew that no Man might in reason take upon him to determine his own Right,
and according to his own Determination proceed in maintenance thereof, in as much as every
Man is towards himself, and them whom he greatly affects, partial; and therefore that Strifes
and Troubles would be endless, except they gave their common Consent, all to be ordered by
some, whom they should agree upon, without which Consent there would be no reason that one
Man should take upon him to be Lord or Judge over another. Hooker's Eccl. Pol. l. 1.
Sect. 10.*

§ 92　7　'presently'—immediately. This condemnation of absolute power is often
supposed to be directed against Hobbes (for example, *Leviathan*, chapter 18, 1904,
128), but it is as appropriate against Filmer and the phrase 'Fathers of their Countries'
in line 9 confirms that it was Filmer's absolute, patriarchal monarch which was in
Locke's mind.

12　'the late Relation of *Ceylon*'—*An Historical Relation of the Island of Ceylon*
by Robert Knox, 1680, bought by Locke on 29 August 1681; see Introduction, 55.

93. *In Absolute Monarchies* indeed, as well as other Governments of the World, the Subjects have an Appeal to the Law, and
Judges to decide any Controversies, and restrain any Violence
that may happen betwixt the Subjects themselves, one amongst
5 another. This every one thinks necessary, and believes he deserves
to be thought a declared Enemy to Society and Mankind, who
should go about to take it away. But whether this be from a true
Love of Mankind and Society, and such a Charity as we owe all
one to another, there is reason to doubt. For this is no more,
10 than what every Man who loves his own Power, Profit, or
Greatness, may, and naturally must do, keep those Animals from
hurting or destroying one another who labour and drudge only
for his Pleasure and Advantage, and so are taken care of, not out
of any Love the Master has for them, but Love of himself, and
15 the Profit they bring him. For if it be asked, what Security, *what
Fence* is there in such a State, *against the Violence and Oppression
of this Absolute Ruler?* The very Question can scarce be born.
They are ready to tell you, that it deserves Death only to ask after
Safety. Betwixt Subject and Subject, they will grant, there must
20 be Measures, Laws, and Judges, for their mutual Peace and
Security: But as for the *Ruler*, he ought to be *Absolute*, and is
above all such Circumstances: because he has Power to do more
hurt and wrong, 'tis right when he does it. To ask how you may
be guarded from harm, or injury on that side where the strongest
25 hand is to do it, is presently the Voice of Faction and Rebellion.
As if when Men quitting the State of Nature entered into Society,
they agreed that all of them but one, should be under the restraint
of Laws, but that he should still retain all the Liberty of the State
of Nature, increased with Power, and made licentious by Im-
30 punity. This is to think that Men are so foolish that they take care
to avoid what Mischiefs may be done them by *Pole-Cats*, or *Foxes*,
but are content, nay think it Safety, to be devoured by *Lions*.

---

§ 93 7–15 Compare 1, § 156 note and references.

32 This whole paragraph, and particularly this last statement (compare II, 1, 20–21), are
often quoted as Locke's judgment on Hobbes; see, for example, Gough, 1950, 36. This is
perhaps because of Hobbes's insistence that the claim that the sovereign was not under the
law led to the dissolution of civil society; see *Leviathan*, chapter 29. But it seems much more
likely to refer to Filmer, who repeatedly maintains that 'A King according to law makes no
kind of government', Laslett's edition, 304. Locke makes a generally similar statement
in his first *Essay on the Law of Nature*, Von Leyden, 1954, 118–19.

94. But whatever Flatterers may talk to amuze Peoples Under-
ſtandings, it hinders not Men, from feeling: and when they per-
ceive, that any Man, in what Station soever, is out of the Bounds
of the Civil Society which they are of; and that they have no
Appeal on Earth againſt any harm they may receive from him,   5
they are apt to think themselves in the ſtate of Nature, in respeƈt
of him, whom they find to be so; and to take care as soon as they
can, to have that *Safety and Security in Civil Society*, for which it
was firſt inſtituted, and for which only they entered into it. And
therefore, though perhaps at firſt, (as shall be shewed more at   10
large hereafter in the following part of this Discourse) some one
good and excellent Man, having got a Preheminency amongſt
the reſt, had this Deference paid to his Goodness and Vertue, as
to a kind of Natural Authority, that the chief Rule, with Arbitra-
tion of their differences, by a tacit Conſent devolved into his   15
hands, without any other caution, but the assurance they had of
his Uprightness and Wisdom: yet when time, giving Authority,
and (as some Men would perswade us) Sacredness to Cuſtoms,
which the negligent, and unforeseeing Innocence of the firſt Ages
began, had brought in Successors of another Stamp, the People   20
finding their Properties not secure under the Government, as
then it was, (whereas Government has no other end but the
preservation of Property) could never be safe nor at reſt, *nor think*
themselves in Civil Society, till the Legislature was placed in col-
leƈtive Bodies of Men, call them Senate, Parliament, or what you   25

---

§ 94   1–9   This is the first mention of revolutionism; compare II, §§ 168, 210.
   1   'amuze'＝mislead.
      11   Perhaps §§ 105 112 are meant (compare Seliger, 1968, 249), or even chapter xiv, 'Of
Prerogative'.
      22–3   This is Locke's strongest assertion of the preservation of property as the end
of government, though it could be a later insertion: see the discussion in Introduction, especially p. 102 and references. Tyrrell, characteristically, puts his similar point
in the context of previous discussion: 'I hope this great difficulty which hath puzled
some Divines, which is *prior in nature*, Propriety or civil Government is now cleared,
since it is apparent, Propriety, understood either as the application of natural things
to the uses of particular Men, or else as the general agreement of many men in the
division of a Territory, or Kingdom, must be before Government, one main end of
which is to maintain the Dominion or Property before agreed on' (1681, 2nd pagination, 116).
      24   'Legislature'—changed by Locke from 'Legislative'. It means the power of law-
making, not the law-making body; compare II, § 153, 16; § 154, 4.
      26   Reference sign for Hooker quotation inserted by editor; see note on II, § 74,
15: Keble's *Hooker*, 1836, i, 304–5; Locke's 1676 edition, 86–7, coming a little after
the passage given in the footnote to II, § 74. It is a remarkable fact that the same
passage appears again in the footnote to II, § 111, 8.

please.† By which means every single person became subject, equally with other the meanest Men, to those Laws, which he himself, as part of the Legislative had established: nor could any one, by his own Authority, avoid the force of the Law, when once
30 made, nor by any pretence of Superiority, plead exemption, thereby to License his own, or the Miscarriages of any of his Dependants. *No Man in Civil Society can be exempted from the Laws of it.*‡ For if any Man may do, what he thinks fit, and there be no Appeal on Earth, for Redress or Security against any harm he shall do;
35 I ask, Whether he be not perfectly still in the State of Nature, and so can be *no part or Member of that Civil Society*: unless any one will say, the State of Nature and Civil Society are one and the same thing, which I have never yet found any one so great a Patron of Anarchy as to affirm.

CHAP. VIII.

Of the Beginning of Political Societies.

95. MEN being, as has been said, by Nature, all free, equal and independent, no one can be put out of this Estate, and subjected to the Political Power of another, without his own *Consent*. The only way whereby any one devests himself of his

† *At the first, when some certain kind of Regiment was once appointed, it may be that nothing was then farther thought upon for the manner of governing, but all permitted unto their Wisdom and Discretion, which were to Rule, till by experience they found this for all parts very inconvenient, so as the thing which they had devised for a Remedy, did indeed but increase the Sore, which it should have cured. They saw, that to live by one Man's Will, became the cause of all Mens misery. This constrained them to come unto Laws wherein all Men might see their Duty beforehand, and know the Penalties of transgressing them.* Hooker's Eccl. Pol. I. 1. Sect. 10.

‡ *Civil Law being the Act of the whole Body Politick, doth therefore over-rule each several part of the same Body.* Hooker ibid.

32 Reference sign inserted as above: Keble, 314; 1676, 90, one slight variant. Elrington, 1798, contrasts this passage and Locke's appeal to it with II, § 12, 13–19, and complains that it leads too directly to government by the will of the people. It certainly implies that the 'meanest man' (l. 27) has property and so a political personality.

§ 95 *Chapter* VIII. This chapter clearly formed part of the original critique of Filmer, whose positions are cited and whose language is paraphrased; see notes on

Natural Liberty, and *puts on the bonds of Civil Society* is by agreeing 5
with other Men to joyn and unite into a Community, for their
comfortable, safe, and peaceable living one amongſt another, in
a secure Enjoyment of their Properties, and a greater Security
againſt any that are not of it. This any number of Men may do,
because it injures not the Freedom of the reſt; they are left as 10
they were in the Liberty of the State of Nature. When any number
of Men have so *consented to make one Community* or Government,
they are thereby presently incorporated, and make *one Body Politick*,
wherein the *Majority* have a Right to aɕt and conclude the reſt.

96. For when any number of Men have, by the consent of
every individual, made a *Community*, they have thereby made that
Community one Body, with a Power to Act as one Body, which
is only by the will and determination of the *majority*. For that
which aɕts any Community, being only the conſent of the indi- 5

---

§ 95, 9; § 98, 12–14; § 101, 23–5; § 103, 10–19; § 112, 8–12; § 114, 5–8; etc.; compare
note on 11, § 77, chapter VII. But it seems possible that §§ 100–22 were not written in
the original composition, but added a little later, after the composition of the *First
Treatise*, perhaps in the summer of 1681 when he seems to have added the quotations
from Hooker (see note on § 111, 8), or even after that. The evidence for this is
the fact that § 132 seems to follow on to § 99, and that chapter IX (§§ 123–31) is
a still later addition, perhaps of 1689; see note there. There is no evidence to show
that any part of this chapter VIII was written in 1689, though it is possible, of course,
that these discontinuities came about through a much more radical rearrangement of
the text in that year.

§ 95   2   'this Estate'—the third printing, not altered by Locke in the Christ's
master-copy, reads 'his Estate': corrected by editor with authority of later editions.

9   'any number of Men may do'—a contradiction of a very characteristic claim
of Sir Robert Filmer's (see Laslett, 1949, 65) and it is against Filmer that Locke's
arguments about majorities are formulated. Though it invites contrast with Hobbes's
famous paragraph on 'The Generation of a Commonwealth' (*Leviathan*, chapter 17,
1904, 118–19), Filmer, not Hobbes, was in Locke's mind. Elrington (1798) objects to
this that it is not a question of what men may do, but what they are 'under a direct
obligation', moral obligation, to do, and to Locke's statement about majorities
(line 15) that the numerical reasoning is fanciful; he makes power the foundation of
right.

11–14   For an exhaustive discussion of this passage, which he calls the most
concise of all statements of 'the faith of majority-rule democrats', see Kendall, 1941,
chapter VII.

§ 96   The general relationship between Locke's views and those of George Lawson
is well brought out by the similar content, but quite different demonstration, of their
attitude to the majority principle. In his *Examination of Hobbes*, 1657, Lawson says
that in all assemblies and societies, the major part concludes and determines the
whole, to avoid confusion and dissension, and to preserve order (p. 25). A common
source for both their views, and that of Tyrrell, could well have been the very well
known discussion by Grotius, *De Jure Belli*, Prolegomena (1712, p. x), and II, v, 17.

viduals of it, and it being necessary to that which is one body to move one way; it is necessary the Body should move that way whither the greater force carries it, which is the *consent of the majority*: or else it is impossible it should act or continue one
10 Body, *one Community*, which the consent of every individual that united into it, agreed that it should; and so every one is bound by that consent to be concluded by the *majority*. And therefore we see that in Assemblies impowered to act by positive Laws where no number is set by that positive Law which impowers
15 them, the *act of the Majority* passes for the act of the whole, and of course determines, as having by the Law of Nature and Reason, the power of the whole.

97. And thus every Man, by consenting with others to make one Body Politick under one Government, puts himself under an Obligation to every one of that Society, to submit to the determination of the *majority*, and to be concluded by it; or else this
5 *original Compact*, whereby he with others incorporates into *one Society*, would signifie nothing, and be no Compact, if he be left free, and under no other ties, than he was in before in the State of Nature. For what appearance would there be of any Compact? What new Engagement if he were no farther tied by any Decrees
10 of the Society, than he himself thought fit, and did actually consent to? This would be still as great a liberty, as he himself had before his Compact, or any one else in the State of Nature hath, who may submit himself and consent to any acts of it if he thinks fit.

98. For if *the consent of the majority* shall not in reason, be received, as *the act of the whole*, and conclude every individual; nothing but the consent of every individual can make any thing to be the act of the whole: But such a consent is next impossible
5 ever to be had, if we consider the Infirmities of Health, and Avocations of Business, which in a number, though much less than that of a Common-wealth, will necessarily keep many away from the publick Assembly. To which if we add the variety of

§ 97   The effect, if not the sense and phraseology, of this paragraph is very close to that of Hobbes, *Leviathan*, chapter 18, headed *No man can without injustice protest against the Institution of the Soveraigne declared by the major part* (1904, 122). See note on 11, § 98, 12-14.
§ 98   This paragraph was extensively modified by Locke in the Christ's copy, though not in such a way as to alter the sense.

Opinions, and contrariety of Interests, which unavoidably happen in all Collections of Men, the coming into Society upon such 10 terms, would be only like *Cato*'s coming into the Theatre, only to go out again. Such a Constitution as this would make the mighty *Leviathan* of a shorter duration, than the feeblest Creatures; and not let it outlast the day it was born in: which cannot be suppos'd, till we can think, that Rational Creatures should desire 15 and constitute Societies only to be dissolved. For where the *majority* cannot conclude the rest, there they cannot act as one Body, and consequently will be immediately dissolved again.

99. Whosoever therefore out of a State of Nature unite into a *Community*, must be understood to give up all the power, neces- sary to the ends for which they unite into Society, to the *majority* of the Community, unless they expressly agreed in any number greater than the majority. And this is done by barely agreeing 5 to *unite into one Political Society*, which is *all the Compact* that is, or needs be, between the Individuals, that enter into, or make up a *Common-wealth*. And thus that, which begins and actually con- *stitutes any Political Society*, is nothing but the consent of any number of Freemen capable of a majority to unite and incorporate into 10 such a Society. And this is that, and that only, which did, or could give *beginning* to any *lawful Government* in the World.

100. To this I find two Objections made.

First, *That there are no Instances to be found in Story of a Company of Men independent and equal one amongst another, that met together, and in this way began and set up a Government.*

---

11   Martial, *Epigrammaton*, 1, Praef.:
        'Cur in theatrum, Cato severe, venisti,
        An ideo tantum veneras, ut exires?'
A common anecdote about Cato of Utica; information from Mr E. J. Kenney.

12–14   A deliberate invocation of the language of Hobbes, clearly sarcastic and not intended as a critical comment on the theory of *Leviathan*, nor on any particular passage in it; see Introduction, 71. Locke and Hobbes were agreed on the necessity of the consent of the majority being taken for the act of the whole, and it was Filmer who denied it; see passages cited in note on II, § 95, 9. His defence of the majority principle against Filmer must be pronounced unsatisfactory, for he responded to the challenge to prove 'by some law of nature that the major part have the power to rule over the rest of the multitude' (Filmer, 82) by simply asserting that it is 'by the Law of Nature and Reason' (II, § 96, 16); compare Allen, 1928.

§ 100   It is possible that the paragraphs from this point to II, § 131, were added after the original composition, perhaps in 1681, for § 132 seems to follow on to § 99. See note on II, §§ 95 (ch. VIII); 101; 111, 18; 123 (ch. IX); 132 (ch. X).

5   Secondly, *'Tis impossible of right that Men should do so, because all Men being born under Government, they are to submit to that, and are not at liberty to begin a new one.*

101. To the first there is this to Answer. That it is not at all to be wonder'd, that *History* gives us but a very little account of Men, *that lived together in the State of Nature.* The inconveniencies of that condition, and the love, and want of Society no sooner
5 brought any number of them together, but they presently united and incorporated, if they designed to continue together. And if we may not suppose *Men* ever to have been *in the State of Nature,* because we hear not much of them in such a State, we may as well suppose the Armies of *Salmanasser,* or *Xerxes* were never
10 Children, because we hear little of them, till they were Men, and imbodied in Armies. Government is every where antecedent to Records, and Letters seldome come in amongst a People, till a long continuation of Civil Society has, by other more necessary Arts provided for their Safety, Ease, and Plenty. And then they
15 begin to look after the History of their *Founders,* and search into their *original,* when they have out-lived the memory of it. For 'tis with *Common-wealths* as with particular Persons, they are commonly *ignorant of their own Births* and *Infancies*: And if they know any thing of their *Original,* they are beholding, for it, to
20 the accidental Records, that others have kept of it. And those that we have, of the beginning of any Polities in the World, excepting that of the *Jews,* where God himself immediately interpos'd, and which favours not at all Paternal Dominion, are all either plain instances of such a beginning, as I have mentioned,
25 or at least have manifest footsteps of it.

102. He must shew a strange inclination to deny evident matter of fact, when it agrees not with his Hypothesis, who will

---

5–7   See II, § 112, 18–19. Both the obvious objections registered here occur in Filmer, for example, 81 and 232.
§ 101   This paragraph begins the fuller answer about the actual existence of a state of nature preceding the establishment of civil societies, hinted at in II, § 14, 1–3. It seems possible that in 1681 Locke decided to elaborate his argument on this point, and that this was why he extended his text here—see note on II, § 100 and references.
9   'Salmanasser'—the Assyrian conqueror (ninth century B.C.); 'Xerxes'—the Persian conqueror (defeated at Salamis 480 B.C.).
11–12   Compare I, § 144, 31–2 and I, § 145, 7.
23–5   These phrases show that Locke has Filmer in mind, and 'manifest footsteps' is Filmer's own expression (60) ridiculed in I, § 150.

not allow that the *beginning* of *Rome* and *Venice* were by the uniting together of several Men free and independent one of another, amongst whom there was no natural Superiority or Sub- 5 jection. And if *Josephus Acosta*'s word may be taken, he tells us, that in many parts of *America* there was no Government at all. *There are great and apparent Conjectures*, says he, *that these Men, speaking of those of Peru, for a long time had neither Kings nor Common-wealths, but lived in Troops, as they do this day in* Florida, 10 *the* Cheriquanas, *those of* Bresil, *and many other Nations, which have no certain Kings, but as occasion is offered in Peace or War, they choose their Captains as they please*, l. 1. c. 25. If it be said, that every Man there was born subject to his Father, or the head of his Family. That the subjection due from a Child to a Father, took not away 15 his freedom of uniting into what Political Society he thought fit, has been already proved. But be that as it will, these Men, 'tis evident, were actually *free*; and whatever superiority some Politicians now would place in any of them, they themselves claimed it not; but by consent were all *equal*, till by the same consent they 20 set Rulers over themselves. So that their *Politick Societies* all *began* from a voluntary Union, and the mutual agreement of Men freely acting in the choice of their Governours, and forms of Government.

103. And I hope those who went away from *Sparta* with *Palantus*, mentioned by *Justin l.* 3. *c.* 4 will be allowed to have been *Freemen independent* one of another, and to have set up a Government over themselves, by their own consent. Thus I have given several Examples out of History, of *People free and in the State of* 5 *Nature*, that being met together incorporated and *began a Commonwealth*. And if the want of such instances be an argument to prove

---

§ **102**   3   Locke is contradicting Filmer here, see 206 *et seq.*, 220 *et seq.*

6–13   A citation from Edward Grimestone's translation of Acosta, *The naturall and morall historie of the Indies*, 1604, a popular book with Locke, and by his side in 1681. The passage is found on 1, 72 of the 1880 reprint. The Cheriquanas are spelt with a 'g' in the original: 'a wild tribe in forests to the east of the Andes'.

14   A reminiscence of Filmer; see passage quoted in note to 11, § 114, 5–8.

§ **103**   2   Palantus was the leader of the Spartans who founded the city of Tarentum in Italy in the eighth century B.C. The account given by Trogus Pompeius is known only from the epitome of his universal history made by Justin in the second or third century A.D. The reference here is probably to the Paris edition of 1543.

that *Government* were not, nor could not be so *begun*, I suppose
the Contenders for Paternal Empire were better let it alone, than
10 urge it against natural Liberty. For if they can give so many
instances out of History, of *Governments begun* upon Paternal
Right, I think (though at best an Argument from what has been,
to what should of right be, has no great force) one might, without
15 any great danger, yield them the cause. But if I might advise
them in the Case, they would do well not to search too much into
the *Original of Governments*, as they have begun *de facto*, lest they
should find at the foundation of most of them, something very
little favourable to the design they promote, and such a power as
20 they contend for.

104. But to conclude, Reason being plain on our side, that
Men are naturally free, and the Examples of History shewing,
that the *Governments* of the World, that were begun in Peace,
had their beginning laid on that foundation, and were *made by*
5 *the Consent of the People*; There can be little room for doubt, either
where the Right is, or what has been the Opinion, or Practice of
Mankind, about the *first erecting of Governments*.

105. I will not deny, that if we look back as far as History will
direct us, towards the *Original of Common-wealths*, we shall generally
find them under the Government and Administration of one Man.
And I am also apt to believe, that where a Family was numerous
5 enough to subsist by it self, and continued entire together, without
mixing with others, as it often happens, where there is much Land
and few People, the Government commonly began in the Father.
For the Father having, by the Law of Nature, the same Power
with every Man else to punish, as he thought fit, any Offences
10 against that Law, might thereby punish his transgressing Children
even when they were Men, and out of their Pupilage; and they

10–19   A further reference to Filmer and his followers with their 'Paternal
Right'.
§ 104   3   On the limitation to governments begun in peace, see II, § 112, 140.
§ 105   With this paragraph begins a passage continuing to II, § 112 which repeats
and extends Locke's concessions to patriarchalism; compare II, § 74, 14–37 and note.
Again his argument is close to that of Tyrrell (for example, 1681, 83 on) and perhaps
even closer to Pufendorf—see *De Jure Naturae*, 1672, VII, i, entitled *De Causa
Impulsitiva Instituendae Civitatis*, especially § 5. He follows Edward Gee, Filmer's
first critic (1658, p. 150), in these comments on Filmer's patriarchalism.

were very likely to submit to his punishment, and all joyn with him against the Offender, in their turns, giving him thereby power to Execute his Sentence against any transgression, and so in effect make him the Law-maker, and Governour over all, that remained in Conjunction with his Family. He was fittest to be trusted; Paternal affection secured their Property, and Interest under his Care, and the Custom of obeying him, in their Childhood, made it easier to submit to him, rather than to any other. If therefore they must have one to rule them, as Government is hardly to be avoided amongst Men that live together; who so likely to be the Man, as he that was their common Father; unless Negligence, Cruelty, or any other defect of Mind, or Body made him unfit for it? But when either the Father died, and left his next Heir for want of Age, Wisdom, Courage, or any other Qualities, less fit for Rule: or where several Families met, and consented to continue together: There, 'tis not to be doubted, but they used their natural freedom, to set up him, whom they judged the ablest, and most likely, to Rule well over them. Conformable hereunto we find the People of *America*, who (living out of the reach of the Conquering Swords, and spreading domination of the two great Empires of *Peru* and *Mexico*) enjoy'd their own natural freedom, though, *cæteris paribus*, they commonly prefer the Heir of their deceased King; yet if they find him any way weak, or uncapable, they pass him by and set up the stoutest and bravest Man for their Ruler.

106. Thus, though looking back as far as Records give us any account of Peopling the World, and the History of Nations, we commonly find the *Government* to be in one hand, yet it destroys not that, which I affirm, (*viz.*) That the *beginning of Politick Society* depends upon the consent of the Individuals, to joyn into and make one Society; who, when they are thus incorporated, might set up what form of Government they thought fit. But this having given occasion to Men to mistake, and think, that by Nature Government was Monarchical, and belong'd to the Father, it may not be amiss here to consider, why People in the beginning generally pitch'd upon this form, which though

---

16   Elrington (1798) comments here that men had a *duty* to trust the heads of families and no arbitrary right to reject them, and on 11, § 106 that Locke does not maintain that men have an arbitrary right over their most important moral actions.

perhaps the Father's Preheminency might in the first institution of some Common-wealths, give a rise to, and place, in the beginning, the Power in one hand; Yet it is plain, that the reason, that continued the Form of *Government in a single Person*, was not any Regard, or Respect to Paternal Authority; since all petty Monarchies, that is, almost all *Monarchies*, near their Original, have been commonly, at least upon occasion, *Elective*.

107. First then, in the beginning of things, the Father's Government of the Childhood of those sprung from him, having accustomed them to the *Rule of one Man*, and taught them that where it was exercised with Care and Skill, with Affection and Love to those under it, it was sufficient to procure and preserve to Men all the Political Happiness they sought for, in Society. It was no wonder, that they should pitch upon, and naturally run into that Form of Government, which from their Infancy they had been all accustomed to; and which, by experience they had found both easie and safe. To which, if we add, that *Monarchy* being simple, and most obvious to Men, whom neither experience had instructed in Forms of Government, nor the Ambition or Insolence of Empire had taught to beware of the Encroachments of Prerogative, or the Inconveniencies of Absolute Power, which Monarchy, in Succession, was apt to lay claim to, and bring upon them, it was not at all strange, that they should not much trouble themselves to think of Methods of restraining any Exorbitances of those, to whom they had given the Authority over them, and of ballancing the Power of Government, by placing several parts of it in different hands. They had neither felt the Oppression of Tyrannical Dominion, nor did the Fashion of the Age, nor their Possessions, or way of living (which afforded little matter for Covetousness or Ambition) give them any reason to apprehend or provide against it: and therefore 'tis no wonder they put themselves into such a *Frame of Government*, as was not only as I said,

---

§ **106** 16–18 Compare II, § 132, 10–12. In his journal under 25 March 1679 (compare Introduction, 34) and under the heading *Politia*, Locke quotes from Sagard's *Canada* (1636: compare II, § 58 note) on the elective kingship of that region, which nevertheless usually permits the son to succeed to the father's throne. 'Their kings are rather obliged by consent and persuasion than compulsion, the public good being the reason of their authority . . . and this seems to be the state of regal authority in its original in all that part of the world', he writes, and initials the note (B.M. Add. MSS. 15642).

most obvious and simple, but also best suited to their present State and Condition; which stood more in need of defence against foreign Invasions and Injuries, than of multiplicity of Laws. The equality of a simple poor way of liveing confineing their desires within the narrow bounds of each mans smal propertie made few 30 controversies and so no need of many laws to decide them: And there wanted not of Justice where there were but few Trespasses, and few Offenders. Since then those, who liked one another so well as to joyn into Society, cannot but be supposed to have some Acquaintance and Friendship together, and some Trust one in 35 another; they could not but have greater Apprehensions of others, than of one another: And therefore their first care and thought cannot but be supposed to be, how to secure themselves against foreign Force. 'Twas natural for them to put themselves under a *Frame of Government*, which might best serve to that end; and 40 chuse the wisest and bravest Man to conduct them in their Wars, and lead them out against their Enemies, and in this chiefly be their *Ruler*.

108. Thus we see, that the *Kings* of the *Indians* in *America*, which is still a Pattern of the first Ages in *Asia* and *Europe*, whilst the Inhabitants were too few for the Country, and want of People and Money gave Men no Temptation to enlarge their Possessions of Land, or contest for wider extent of Ground, are little more 5 than *Generals of their Armies*; and though they command absolutely

---

§ 107   28–32   Rewritten by Locke in the Christ's copy, but differences immaterial The text is considerably modified in minute detail in this area, almost entirely for punctuation.
§ 108   1–2   Compare II, § 49, 1.
   6   '*Generals of their Armies*'—Locke shared with Tyrrell the view that a frequent origin of kingship was in the military leader, and that the dominance of such a leader may be a transitional stage between the state of nature and of society. See Tyrrell, 1681, 85 (the early kings of the Goths, Vandals, and 'our Saxons') and 92–3, referring to the 'Caciques', of the Caribbean Islands and Brazil. Indeed Tyrrell actually made a note on the point in Locke's journal for 1680, about the King amongst the inhabitants of the Hudson Bay area, who was 'only captain of so many families'. Acosta and Lery were probably their other sources, but the most straightforward statement is to be found in the *Histoire naturelle et Morale des Iles Antilles* (H. and L. 2491a, probably by Rocheford, but also attributed to Du Tertre and De Poincy), Rotterdam, 1658, which Locke possessed. The discussion in Grotius, 1625, I, iii, 8, may be compared and contrasted.
   The argument is repeated in the *Letters on Toleration*: 'There are nations in the *West Indies*, which have no other end of their society but their mutual defence against their common enemies. In these their captain, or prince, is sovereign commander in time

in War, yet at home and in time of Peace they exercise very little Dominion, and have but a very moderate Sovereignty, the Resolutions of Peace and War, being ordinarily either in the People, or
10 in a Council. Though the War it self, which admits not of Plurality of Governours, naturally devolves the Command into the *King's sole Authority*.

109. And thus in *Israel* it self, the *chief Business of their Judges, and first Kings* seems to have been *to be Captains in War*, and Leaders of their Armies; which, (besides what is signified by *going out and in before the People*, which was, to march forth to War, and
5 home again in the Heads of their Forces) appears plainly in the Story of *Jephtha*. The *Ammonites* making War upon *Israel*, the *Gileadites*, in fear send to *Jephtha*, a Bastard of their Family, whom they had cast off, and article with him, if he will assist them against the *Ammonites*, to make him their Ruler; which they do
10 in these words, *And the People made him head and captain over them*, Judg. 11. 11. which was, as it seems, all one as to be *Judge. And he judged Israel*, Judg. 12. 7. that is, was their *Captain-General, six Years*. So when *Jotham* upbraids the *Shechemites* with the Obligation they had to *Gideon*, who had been their *Judge* and
15 Ruler, he tells them, *He fought for you, and adventured his life far, and delivered you out of the hands of Midian*, Judg. 9. 17. Nothing mentioned of him, but what he did as a *General*, and indeed that

of war; but in time of peace, neither he nor any body else has any authority over any of the society' (*Second Letter*, 1690, *Works*, 1801, VI, 121). 'Let me ask you, Whether it be not possible that men, to whom the rivers and woods afforded the spontaneous provisions of life, and so with no private possessions of land, had no inlarged desires after riches or power, should live in one society, make one people of one language under one Chieftain, who shall have no other power to command them in time of common war against their common enemies, without any municipal laws, judges, or any person with superiority established amongst them, but ended all their private differences, if any arose, by the extemporary determination of their neighbours, or of arbitrators chosen by the parties. I ask you, whether in such a commonwealth, the Chieftain, who was the only man of authority amongst them, had any power to use the force of the commonwealth to any other end but the defence of it against an enemy, though other benefits were attainable by it?' (*Third Letter*, 1692, *Works*, 1801, VI, 223). This second passage, written in vindication of the first, is a most interesting exposition of Locke's views on the state of nature, or of such a state mixed with a state of society. Compare Seliger, 1968, p. 870.
§ 109 This assimilation of biblical history with the history of primitive peoples is characteristically Lockeian; compare I, § 158, 5–7, and see II, § 36, 9–25 and references.
3–4 '*going out and in before the People*'—a common Old Testament phrase for leading the Israelites to war; see, for example, Numbers xxvii. 17.
6–16 'the Story of *Jephtha*'—see II, § 21, 17, with note and references.

is all is found in his History, or in any of the rest of the Judges.
And *Abimelech* particularly is called *King*, though at most he was
but their *General*. And when, being weary of the ill Conduct   20
of *Samuel*'s Sons, the Children of *Israel* desired a King, *like all
the nations to judge them, and to go out before them, and to fight their
battels*, 1 Sam. 8. 20. God granting their Desire, says to *Samuel,
I will send thee a Man, and thou shalt anoint him to be Captain over
my People Israel, that he may save my People out of the hands of the*   25
Philistines, c. 9. v. 16. As if the only *business of a King* had been to
lead out their Armies, and fight in their Defence; and accordingly
at his Inauguration, pouring a Vial of Oyl upon him, declares to
Saul, that *the Lord had anointed him to be Captain over his inheritance,*
c. 10. v. 1. And therefore those, who after *Saul*'s being solemnly   30
chosen and saluted *King* by the *Tribes* at *Mispah*, were unwilling
to have him their King, make no other Objection but this, *How
shall this Man save us?* v. 27. as if they should have said, This Man
is unfit to be our *King*, not having Skill and Conduct enough in
War, to be able to defend us. And when God resolved to transfer   35
the Government to *David*, it is in these Words, *But now thy
Kingdom shall not continue: The Lord hath sought him a Man after his
own heart, and the Lord hath commanded him to be Captain over his
People*, c. 13. v. 14. As if the whole *Kingly Authority* were nothing
else but to be their *General*: And therefore the *Tribes* who had   40
stuck to *Saul*'s Family, and opposed *David*'s Reign, when they
came to *Hebron* with terms of Submission to him, they tell him,
amongst other Arguments they had to submit to him as to their
King, That he was in effect their *King* in *Saul*'s time, and therefore
they had no reason but to receive him as their *King* now. *Also*   45
(say they) *in time past, when Saul was King over us, thou wast he that
leddest out and broughtest in Israel, and the Lord said unto thee, thou shalt
feed my People Israel, and thou shalt be a Captain over Israel.*

110. Thus, whether *a Family* by degrees *grew up into a Commonwealth*, and the Fatherly Authority being continued on to the
elder Son, every one in his turn growing up under it, tacitly
submitted to it, and the easiness and equality of it not offending
any one, every one acquiesced, till time seemed to have confirmed   5
it, and settled a right of Succession by Prescription: or whether
several Families, or the Descendants of several Families, whom

---

45-8   II Sam. v. 2.

Chance, Neighbourhood, or Business brought together, uniting
into Society, the need of a General, whose Conduct might defend
10 them against their Enemies in War, and the great confidence the
Innocence and Sincerity of that poor but vertuous Age (such as
are almost all those which begin Governments, that ever come to
last in the World) gave Men one of another, made the first
Beginners of Common-wealths generally put the Rule into one
15 Man's hand, without any other express Limitation or Restraint,
but what the Nature of the thing, and the End of Government
required: which ever of these it was, that at first put the rule into
the hands of a single person, certain it is that no body was ever
intrusted with it but for the publick Good and Safety, and to those
20 Ends in the Infancies of Commonwealths those who had it,
commonly used it: And unless they had done so, young Societies
could not have subsisted: without such nursing Fathers tender
and carefull of the publick weale, all Governments would have
sunk under the Weakness and Infirmities of their Infancy; and
25 the Prince and the People had soon perished together.

111. But though the *Golden Age* (before vain Ambition, and
amor sceleratus habendi, evil Concupiscence, had corrupted Mens
minds into a Mistake of true Power and Honour) had more
Virtue, and consequently better Governours, as well as less
5 vicious Subjects; and there was then *no stretching Prerogative* on

---

§ 110   17–23   Modified and partially rewritten in the Christ's copy. On 'nursing Fathers'
and his other quasi-patriarchal statements compare II, § 105, note and references.

19–20   For Locke's doctrine of trust, see Introduction, 113 on, and compare in this
passage in particular the early words of his *Essay Concerning Toleration* of 1667: 'The
whole trust, power and authority of the magistrate is vested in him for no other
purpose, but to be made use of for the good, preservation, and peace of men in that
society over which he is set, and therefore this ought to be the standard and measure,
according to which he ought to square and proportion his laws, model and frame his
government' (Fox Bourne, 1876, I, 174).

§ 111   2   The Latin tag is from Ovid, *Metamorphoses*, I, 131. This hint of a golden
age is a highly traditional element, and is usually assumed to be a description of
Locke's state of nature; see Leslie Stephen, 1876 (1902), II, 137, followed, for example,
by Strauss, 1953, 216. If this is the intention it is in sharp contrast with the Hobbesian
view of the state of nature, though, as Strauss points out, rather difficult to reconcile
with Locke's own account of the Fall, for example, I, §§ 44, 45. Lamprecht, 1918,
127, however, takes the view that it refers not to the state of nature but to the early,
virtuous years of established government. As always, Locke's language is inexact,
but a close and sympathetic reading of this paragraph and II, §§ 107, 110 seems to
confirm this as the correct view.

the one side to oppress the People; *nor* consequently on the other any *Dispute about Priviledge*, to lessen or reſtrain the Power of the Magiſtrate;† and so no conteſt betwixt Rulers and People about Governours or Government: Yet, when Ambition and Luxury, in future Ages would retain and increase the Power, without doing the Business, for which it was given, and aided by Flattery, taught Princes to have diſtinct and separate Intereſts from their People, Men found it necessary to examine more carefully *the Original* and Ri;hts of *Government*; and to find out ways to *reſtrain the Exorbitances*, and *prevent the Abuses* of that Power which they having intruſted in another's hands only for their own good, they found was made use of to hurt them.

112. Thus we may see how probable it is, that People that wcre naturally free, and by their own consent either submitted to the Government of their Father, or united together, out of different Families to make a Government, should generally put the *Rule into one Man's hands*, and chuse to be under the Conduct of a *single Person*, without so much as by express Conditions limiting or regulating his Power, which they thought safe enough in his Honeſty and Prudence. Though they ncver dream'd of Monarchy being *Jure Divino*, which we never heard of among Mankind, till it was revealed to us by the Divinity of this laſt Age; nor ever allowed Paternal Power to have a right to Dominion,

---

† *At firſt, when some certain kind of Regiment was once approved, it may be nothing was then further thought upon for the manner of governing, but all permitted unto their Wiſdom and Diſcretion which were to Rule, till by experience they found this for all parts very inconvenient, so as the thing which they had devised for a Remedy, did indeed but increase the Sore which it should have cured. They saw, that* to live by one Man's Will, became the cauſe of all Mens miſery. *This conſtrained them to come unto Laws wherein all Men might see their Duty before-hand, and know the Penalties of transgressing them.* Hooker's Eccl. Pol. L. 1. Sect. 10.

---

8   Reference sign for Hooker quotation inserted by editor; see note on II, § 74, 15. This quotation is also used to illustrate II, § 94, 26; see note there. Its reappearance here may be due to the fact that §§ 100–31 were added after the original composition (see note on II, § 95 (chapter VIII) and references), though it may indicate some confusion in Locke's manuscript, or some misunderstanding by the compositor of the 1st edition not subsequently corrected. The quotation is fairly appropriate in both places; it shows some variants from Hooker's text, including Locke's underlining of a critical phrase, and between the two printings of it.

§ 112   8–12 The 'Divinity of this last Age' was Filmer's patriarchal doctrine, publicly owned by the pulpit and made 'the *Currant Divinity of the Times*'; see the Preface, 32–3. It is possible that lines 8–17 here were an addition of 1689.

or to be the Foundation of all Government. And thus much may suffice to shew, that as far as we have any light from History, we have reason to conclude, that all peaceful beginnings of
15 *Government* have been *laid in the Consent of the People.* I say *peaceful,* because I shall have occasion in another place to speak of Conquest, which some esteem a way of beginning of Governments.

The other Objection I find urged against the beginning of Polities, in the way I have mentioned, is this, viz.

113. *That all Men being born under Government, some or other, it is impossible any of them should ever be free, and at liberty to unite together, and begin a new one, or ever be able to erect a lawful Government.*

If this Argument be good; I ask, how came so many lawful
5 Monarchies into the World? For if any body, upon this supposition, can shew me any one Man in any Age of the World *free* to begin a lawful Monarchy; I will be bound to shew him Ten other *free Men* at Liberty, at the same time to unite and begin a new Government under a Regal, or any other Form. It being
10 demonstration, that if any one, *born under the Dominion* of another, may be so *free* as to have a right to command others in a new and distinct Empire; every one that is *born under the Dominion* of another may be so *free* too, and may become a Ruler, or Subject, of a distinct separate Government. And so by this their own Principle, either
15 all Men, however *born*, are *free*, or else there is but one lawful Prince, one lawful Government in the World. And then they have nothing to do but barely to shew us, which that is. Which when they have done, I doubt not but all Mankind will easily agree to pay Obedience to him.

114. Though it be a sufficient Answer to their Objection to shew, that it involves them in the same difficulties that it doth those they use it against; yet I shall endeavour to discover the weakness of this Argument a little farther.
5 *All Men,* say they, *are born under Government, and therefore they*

14–15 Compare II § 104, 3.

15–17 The other place is Chapter XVI II §§ 175–198.

18–19 See II, § 100, 5–7: these two lines were obviously intended to stand out of the paragraph numeration, hence the odd beginning of § 113.

§ 113 1–5 Compare note on II, § 100. This objection is not found stated in such a general form by Filmer, but it is a position consistently implied by him; see especially his *Forms* (Laslett, 1949, 185–229).

§ 114 5–8 A paraphrase of Filmer (Laslett's edition, 232): 'Every man that is born, is so far from being free-born, that by his very birth he becomes a subject to

cannot be at liberty to begin a new one. Every one is born a Subject to his Father, or his Prince, and is therefore under the perpetual tye of Subjection and Allegiance. 'Tis plain Mankind never owned nor considered any such natural *subjection, that they were born in,* to one or to the other, that tied them, without their own Consents, to a Subjection to them and their Heirs.

115. For there are no Examples so frequent in History, both Sacred and Prophane, as those of Men withdrawing themselves, and their Obedience, from the Jurisdiction they were born under, and the Family or Community they were bred up in, and *setting up new Governments* in other places; from whence sprang all that number of petty Common-wealths in the beginning of Ages, and which always multiplyed, as long as there was room enough, till the stronger, or more fortunate swallowed the weaker; and those great ones again breaking to pieces, dissolved into lesser Dominions. All which are so many Testimonies against Paternal Sovereignty, and plainly prove, That it was not the natural right of the Father descending to his Heirs, that made Governments in the beginning, since it was impossible, upon that ground, there should have been so many little Kingdoms; all must have been but only one Universal Monarchy, if Men had not been *at liberty to separate* themselves from their Families, and the Government, be it what it will, that was set up in it, and go and make distinct Common-wealths and other Governments, as they thought fit.

116. This has been the practice of the World from its first beginning to this day: Nor is it now any more hindrance to the freedom of Mankind, that they are *born under constituted and ancient Polities,* that have established Laws and set Forms of Government, than if they were born in the Woods, amongst the unconfined Inhabitants that ran loose in them. For those who would perswade us, that *by being born under any Government, we are naturally Subjects to it,* and have no more any title or pretence to the freedom of the State of Nature, have no other reason (bating that of Paternal

---

him that begets him: under which subjection, he is always to live, unless by immediate appointment from God, or by the grant or death of his Father, he become possessed of that power to which he was subject', ridiculed in the *First Treatise*; compare II, § 102, 14.

§ 116 9–10 This parenthesis demonstrates that Locke is still arguing against Filmer (compare § 115, 10–11): 'already answer'd' seems to refer to the text immediately preceding, rather than to the *First Treatise*.

10 Power, which we have already answer'd) to produce for it, but
only because our Fathers or Progenitors passed away their natural
Liberty, and thereby bound up themselves and their Posterity
to a perpetual subjection to the Government, which they themselves submitted to. 'Tis true, that whatever Engagements or
15 Promises any one has made for himself, he is under the Obligation
of them, but *cannot* by any *Compact* whatsoever, bind *his Children*
or Posterity. For this Son, when a Man, being altogether as free
as the Father, any *act of the Father can no more give away the liberty
of the Son*, than it can of any body else: He may indeed annex such
20 Conditions to the Land, he enjoyed as a Subject of any Commonwealth, as may oblige his Son to be of that Community, if he will
enjoy those Possessions which were his Fathers; because that
Estate being his Fathers Property, he may dispose or settle it as
he pleases.

117. And this has generally given the occasion to mistake in
this matter; because Commonwealths not permitting any part of
their Dominions to be dismembred, nor to be enjoyed by any but
those of their Community, the Son cannot ordinarily enjoy the
5 Possessions of his Father, but under the same terms his Father
did; by becoming a Member of the Society: whereby he puts
himself presently under the Government, he finds there established,
as much as any other Subject of that Commonwealth. And thus
the Consent of Free-men, born under Government, which only *makes*
10 *them Members of it*, being given separately in their turns, as each
comes to be of Age, and not in a multitude together; People take
no notice of it, and thinking it not done at all, or not necessary,
conclude they are naturally Subjects as they are Men.

118. But, 'tis plain, *Governments* themselves understand it
otherwise; they *claim no Power over the Son, because of that they had
over the Father*; nor look on Children as being their Subjects, by
their Fathers being so. If a Subject of *England* have a Child by an
5 *English* Woman in *France*, whose Subject is he? Not the King of

§ 118 Leslie Stephen comments that this paragraph 'leads straight to anarchy',
1902, 11, 140. I am indebted to Mr Parry, of Downing College, Cambridge, in the
following notes.
  4–5 In Locke's day, as in our own, a child of British subjects born in France was
a British citizen, under the statute *De natis ultra mare* of 25 Edward III, and it was
decided by a case of 1627 that either father or mother would suffice.

England's; for he must have leave to be admitted to the Priviledges of it. Nor the King of *France*'s; For how then has his Father a liberty to bring him away, and breed him as he pleases? And who ever was judged as a *Traytor* or *Deserter*, if he left, or warr'd against a Country, for being barely born in it of Parents that were 10 Aliens there? 'Tis plain then, by the Practice of Governments themselves, as well as by the Law of right Reason, that *a Child is born a Subject of no Country or Government.* He is under his Fathers Tuition and Authority, till he come to Age of Discretion; and then he is a Free-man, at liberty what Government he will put 15 himself under; what Body Politick he will unite himself to. For if an *English-Man*'s Son, born in *France*, be at liberty, and may do so, 'tis evident there is no Tye upon him by his Father being a Subject of this Kingdom; nor is he bound up, by any Compact of his Ancestors. And why then hath not his Son, by the same 20 reason, the same liberty, though he be born any where else? Since the Power that a Father hath naturally over his Children, is the same, where-ever they be born; and the Tyes of Natural Obligations, are not bounded by the positive Limits of Kingdoms and Common-wealths. 25

119. *Every Man* being, as has been shewed, *naturally free*, and nothing being able to put him into subjection to any Earthly Power, but only his own Consent; it is to be considered, what shall be understood to be *a sufficient Declaration of* a Mans *Consent, to make him subject* to the Laws of any Government. There is 5 a common distinction of an express and a tacit consent, which will concern our present Case. No body doubts but an *express Consent*, of any Man, entring into any Society, makes him a perfect Member of that Society, a Subject of that Government. The difficulty is, what ought to be look'd upon as a *tacit Consent*, and 10 how far it binds, *i.e.* how far any one shall be looked on to have

---

7   This does not seem to have been a general rule, but there were cases of foreign-born children of British parents being formally naturalized in the seventeenth century; see Parry, 1954.

11–13   Pollock comments that this is an 'opinion which no modern lawyer will accept, least of all a continental one', 1904, 244. Since, however, there was no right to nationality in the law of Locke's day, he is not necessarily wrong in what he says. He was strongly in favour of the naturalization of aliens on social and economic grounds; see Laslett, 1957 (i), 393.

§ 119   7–9   The *Fundamental Constitutions of Carolina*, Articles 117–18, make provision for just such an express declaration, but Seliger, 1968, p. 276, denies the relevance of this.

consented, and thereby submitted to any Government, where he
has made no Expressions of it at all. And to this I say, that every
Man, that hath any Possession, or Enjoyment, of any part of the
15 Dominions of any Government, doth thereby give his *tacit Consent*, and is as far forth obliged to Obedience to the Laws of that
Government, during such Enjoyment, as any one under it;
whether this his Possession be of Land, to him and his Heirs for
ever, or a Lodging only for a Week; or whether it be barely
20 travelling freely on the Highway; and in Effect, it reaches as far
as the very being of any one within the Territories of that
Government.

120. To understand this the better, it is fit to consider, that
every Man, when he, at first, incorporates himself into any
Commonwealth, he, by his uniting himself thereunto, annexed
also, and submits to the Community those Possessions, which he
5 has, or shall acquire, that do not already belong to any other
Government. For it would be a direct Contradiction, for any one,
to enter into Society with others for the securing and regulating
of Property: And yet to suppose his Land, whose Property is to
be regulated by the Laws of the Society, should be exempt from
10 the Jurisdiction of that Government, to which he himself the
Proprietor of the Land, is a Subject. By the same Act therefore,
whereby any one unites his Person, which was before free, to any
Commonwealth; by the same he unites his Possessions, which
were before free, to it also; and they become, both of them,
15 Person and Possession, subject to the Government and Dominion
of that Commonwealth, as long as it hath a being. *Whoever* therefore, from thenceforth, by Inheritance, Purchase, Permission, or
otherways *enjoys any part of the Land*, so annext to, and under the
Government *of that Commonwealth, must take it with the Condition* it
20 is under; that is, *of submitting to the Government of the Commonwealth*,
under whose Jurisdiction it is, as far forth, as any Subject of it.

---

§120 Kendall infers from this passage that society vouchsafes property to the
individual. Compare 11, §139, 4–5 and statements in the works on toleration.
Locke's *1st Letter* of 1689 implies that the magistrate may 'change propriety among
fellow-subjects', and the *Essay* of 1667 says 'The magistrate having a power
to appoint ways of transferring proprieties from one man to another, may establish
any, so they be universal, equal and without violence and suited to the welfare
of that society' (quoted here from the Huntington MS. The words underlined
are omitted in that printed by Fox Bourne (1876, 1, 183)).

121. But since the Government has a direct Jurisdiction only over the Land, and reaches the Possessor of it, (before he has actually incorporated himself in the Society) only as he dwells upon, and enjoys that: *The Obligation* any one is under, by Virtue of such Enjoyment, *to submit to the Government, begins and ends with the Enjoyment*; so that whenever the Owner, who has given nothing but such a *tacit Consent* to the Government, will, by Donation, Sale, or otherwise, quit the said Possession, he is at liberty to go and incorporate himself into any other Commonwealth, or to agree with others to begin a new one, *in vacuis locis*, in any part of the World, they can find free and unpossessed: Whereas he, that has once, by actual Agreement, and any *express* Declaration, given his *Consent* to be of any Commonweal, is perpetually and indispensably obliged to be and remain unalterably a Subject to it, and can never be again in the liberty of the State of Nature; unless by any Calamity, the Government, he was under, comes to be dissolved; or else by some publick Act cuts him off from being any longer a Member of it.

122. But submitting to the Laws of any Country, living quietly, and enjoying Priviledges and Protection under them, *makes not a Man a Member of that Society*: This is only a local Protection and Homage due to, and from all those, who, not being in a State of War, come within the Territories belonging to any Government, to all parts whereof the force of its Law extends. But this no more *makes a Man a Member of that Society*, a perpetual Subject of that Commonwealth, than it would make a Man a Subject to another in whose Family he found it convenient to abide for some time; though, whilst he continued in it, he were obliged to comply with the Laws, and submit to the Government he found there. And thus we see, that *Foreigners*, by living all their Lives under another Government, and enjoying the Priviledges and Protection of it, though they are bound, even in Conscience, to submit to its Administration, as far forth as any Denison; yet do not thereby come to be *Subjects or Members of that Commonwealth*. Nothing can make any Man so, but his actually entering into it by positive Engagement, and express Promise and Compact. This is that, which I think, concerning the beginning of Political Societies, and that *Consent which makes any one a Member* of any Commonwealth.

---

§ 121   15–18   Dissolution of Government and state of nature, see II, § 219, note and references.

17–18   Final phrase added in 2nd edition, 1694.

CHAP. IX.

Of the Ends of Political Society and Government.

123. IF Man in the State of Nature be so free, as has been said;
      If he be absolute Lord of his own Person and Possessions,
equal to the greatest, and subject to no Body, why will he part
with his Freedom? Why will he give up this Empire, and subject
5 himself to the Dominion and Controul of any other Power?
To which 'tis obvious to Answer, that though in the State of
Nature he hath such a right, yet the Enjoyment of it is very
uncertain, and constantly exposed to the Invasion of others. For
all being Kings as much as he, every Man his Equal, and the
10 greater part no strict Observers of Equity and Justice, the enjoyment of the property he has in this State is very unsafe, very
unsecure. This makes him willing to quit this Condition, which
however free, is full of fears and continual dangers: And 'tis not
without reason, that he seeks out, and is willing to joyn in Society
15 with others who are already united, or have a mind to unite for
the mutual *Preservation* of their Lives, Liberties and Estates, which
I call by the general Name, *Property*.

124. The great and *chief end* therefore, of Mens uniting into
Commonwealths, and putting themselves under Government, *is*

---

§ 123 *Chapter* IX.   There is nothing in this short chapter to connect it with what
goes before, or what comes after, which seems to be a continuation of the original
text from § 99—see notes on II, § 95 (chapter VIII), II, § 100 and II, § 132 (chapter X).
There are no references to connect it with the critique of Filmer, though some
parallels (see § 124, 8–9; § 125, 1–4; § 129, 3–4) with other statements in the *Second
Treatise*. In form it is a short restatement of his whole position, in brief paragraphs,
all leading up to a judgment on James II—see § 131. It seems, therefore, like
chapter XV (see note on II, § 169) to be an insertion of 1689.
   2   Compare II, § 6, 2–3 and Strauss, 1953, 227.
   16–17 On the extended definition of property set out here, see II, § 87, 5 note and
references. The whole paragraph should be compared and contrasted with the first
paragraph of *Leviathan*, chapter 17, and with II, § 19, 1–5 and references.
§ 124 1–3 The *locus classicus* for Locke's view of property in relation to government. Viner (see Introduction, 102) insists that property must here be taken to mean
not simply material possessions, but property in the extended sense, the 'Lives,
Liberties and Estates' of II, § 123, 15–16. In the *Epistola de Tolerantia* Locke puts

the Preservation of their Property. To which in the State of Nature there are many things wanting.

First, There wants an *establish'd,* settled, known *Law,* received 5 and allowed by common consent to be the Standard of Right and Wrong, and the common measure to decide all Controversies between them. For though the Law of Nature be plain and intelligible to all rational Creatures; yet Men being biassed by their Interest, as well as ignorant for want of Study of it, are not 10 apt to allow of it as a Law binding to them in the application of it to their particular Cases.

125. *Secondly,* In the State of Nature there wants *a known and indifferent Judge,* with Authority to determine all differences according to the established Law. For every one in that State being both Judge and Executioner of the Law of Nature, Men being partial to themselves, Passion and Revenge is very apt to carry 5 them too far, and with too much heat, in their own Cases; as well as negligence, and unconcernedness, to make them too remiss, in other Mens.

126. *Thirdly,* In the State of Nature there often wants *Power* to back and support the Sentence when right, and to *give* it due *Execution.* They who by any Injustice offended, will seldom fail, where they are able, by force to make good their Injustice: such resistance many times makes the punishment dangerous, and fre- 5 quently destructive, to those who attempt it.

---

the same point somewhat differently, with material possessions more to the forefront: 'But the pravity of mankind being such that they had rather injuriously prey upon the fruits of another mans labours (alieno labore partis frui) than take pains to provide for themselves, the necessity of preserving men in the possession of what honest industry has already acquired, and also of preserving their liberty and strength, whereby they may acquire what they further want, obliges men to enter into society one with another (ideo homini parta, ut opes et facultates; vel ea quibus parantur, ut corporis libertatem et robur, tuendi gratia, ineunda est cum aliis societas) that by mutual assistance and joint force they may secure unto each other their properties, in the things that contribute to the comfort and happiness of this life (ut mutuo auxilio et junctis viribus harum rerum ad vitam utilium sua cuique privata et secura sit possessio)' (Klibansky and Gough, 1968, 124). Compare Macpherson, 1951, 551.

8–9   Compare II, § 12, 10–12, verbal parallel.
§ 125   1–3   Compare II, § 136, 8.
3–4   Compare II, § 7.
4–5   The mention of 'Passion' recalls Hobbes, *Leviathan,* chapter 17 (1904, 115, etc.), and the insistence on partiality recalls Hooker (1836, I, 305, compare II, §91 and *English Tract* of 1660, 10). It is not demonstrable that Locke had either writer in mind.

127. Thus Mankind, notwithstanding all the Priviledges of the State of Nature, being but in an ill condition, while they remain in it, are quickly driven into Society. Hence it comes to pass, that we seldom find any number of Men live any time together in this
5 State. The inconveniencies, that they are therein exposed to, by the irregular and uncertain exercise of the Power every Man has of punishing the transgressions of others, make them take Sanctuary under the establish'd Laws of Government, and therein seek *the preservation of their Property*. 'Tis this makes them so
10 willingly give up every one his single power of punishing to be exercised by such alone as shall be appointed to it amongst them; and by such Rules as the Community, or those authorised by them to that purpose, shall agree on. And in this we have the original *right and rise* of both *the Legislative and Executive Power*,
15 as well as of the Governments and Societies themselves.

128. For in the State of Nature, to omit the liberty he has of innocent Delights, a Man has two Powers.
The first is to do whatsoever he thinks fit for the preservation of himself and others within the permission of the *Law of Nature*: by
5 which Law common to them all, he and all the rest of *Mankind are one Community*, make up one Society distinct from all other Creatures. And were it not for the corruption, and vitiousness of degenerate Men, there would be no need of any other; no necessity that Men should separate from this great and natural Community, and by
10 positive agreements combine into smaller and divided associations.
The other power a Man has in the State of Nature, is the *power to punish·the Crimes* committed against that Law. Both these he gives up, when he joyns in a private, if I may so call it, or particular Political Society, and incorporates into any Common-
15 wealth, separate from the rest of Mankind.

129. The first *Power, viz. of doing whatsoever he thought fit for the Preservation of himself*, and the rest of Mankind, *he gives up* to be regulated by Laws made by the Society, so far forth as the preservation of himself, and the rest of that Society shall require;

---

§ 127   10   'Single'—i.e. 'individual', not 'only'; see Kendall, 1941, 103.
§ 129   3–4   This limitation is elaborated in II, § 149, especially lines 22–5.
  2, 5   Elrington, 1798, comments here that a man is bound to give up this power: he is compelled by the law of nature itself to quit the state of nature, and he can lose no liberty by it, since this would imply that civil law was distinct from natural law.

which Laws of the Society in many things confine the liberty he 5
had by the Law of Nature.

130. *Secondly*, the *Power of punishing* he wholly *gives up*, and
engages his natural force, (which he might before imploy in the
Execution of the Law of Nature, by his own single Authority, as
he thought fit) to assist the Executive Power of the Society, as the
Law thereof shall require. For being now in a new State, wherein 5
he is to enjoy many Conveniencies, from the labour, assistance, and
society of others in the same Community, as well as protection from
its whole strength; he is to part also with as much of his natural
liberty in providing for himself, as the good, prosperity, and safety
of the Society shall require: which is not only necessary, but 10
just; since the other Members of the Society do the like.

131. But though Men when they enter into Society, give up
the Equality, Liberty, and Executive Power they had in the State
of Nature, into the hands of the Society, to be so far disposed
of by the Legislative, as the good of the Society shall require;
yet it being only with an intention in every one the better to 5
preserve himself his Liberty and Property; (For no rational
Creature can be supposed to change his condition with an intention to be worse) the power of the Society, or *Legislative* constituted by them, *can never be suppos'd to extend farther than the
common good*; but is obliged to secure every ones Property by pro- 10
viding against those three defects above-mentioned, that made
the State of Nature so unsafe and uneasie. And so whoever has
the Legislative or Supream Power of any Common-wealth, is
bound to govern by establish'd *standing Laws*, promulgated and
known to the People, and not by Extemporary Decrees; by 15
indifferent and upright *Judges*, who are to decide Controversies by
those Laws; And to imploy the force of the Community at home,
only in the Execution of such Laws, or abroad to prevent or redress
Foreign Injuries, and secure the Community from Inroads and
Invasion. And all this to be directed to no other *end*, but the 20
Peace, Safety, and *publick good* of the People.

---

§ 131 12–21 These statements, especially lines 12–14, seem likely to be a reference
to the actions of James II and the view he took of his position, for they are less
appropriate than his other political judgments to the actions of Charles II. This may
mark this paragraph, and indeed the whole chapter, as an insertion of 1689; see
note on 11, § 123, chapter IX, and compare Abrams' note on *English Tract* of 1660, p. 19.

CHAP. X.

Of the Forms of a Common-wealth.

132. THE Majority having, as has been shew'd, upon Mens first uniting into Society, the whole power of the Community, naturally in them, may imploy all that power in making Laws for the Community from time to time, and Executing those
5 Laws by Officers of their own appointing; and then the *Form* of the Government is a perfect *Democracy*: Or else may put the power of making Laws into the hands of a few select Men, and their Heirs or Successors; and then it is an *Oligarchy*: Or else into the hands of one Man, and then it is a *Monarchy*: If to him and his
10 Heirs, it is an *Hereditary Monarchy*: If to him only for Life, but upon his Death the Power only of nominating a Successor to return to them; an *Elective Monarchy*. And so accordingly of these the Community may make compounded and mixed Forms of Government, as they think good. And if the Legislative Power
15 be at first given by the Majority to one or more Persons only for their Lives, or any limited time, and then the Supream Power to revert to them again; when it is so reverted, the Community may dispose of it again anew into what hands they please, and so constitute a new Form of Government. For the *Form of Govern-*
20 *ment depending upon the placing* the Supreme Power, which is the *Legislative*, it being impossible to conceive that an inferiour Power should prescribe to a Superiour, or any but the Supreme make Laws, according as the Power of making Laws is placed, such is *the Form of the Common-wealth.*

§ **132**   *Chapter* x   This can be dated before 1685 (see note on § 133, 10), and since it follows on from § 99, which can be concluded from the words of its first line, is presumably the continuation and completion of chapter VIII (see notes on §§ 77, 100), written as part of the original critique of Filmer.

10–12 Compare II, § 106, 16–18.

12–24 These statements are point-blank denials of what Filmer had said, and of what Hobbes had said also (*Leviathan*, chapter 19). They blandly ignore Filmer's acute critique of mixed government in his *Anarchy of a Limited or Mixed Monarchy* (Laslett's edition, 277–313), though Locke shared with Filmer the traditional analysis of sovereignty; compare note on I, § 129, 10–15 and references.

19–24 Compare II, § 150.

133. By *Common-wealth*, I must be understood all along to mean, not a Democracy, or any Form of Government, but *any Independent Community* which the *Latines* signified by the word *Civitas*, to which the word which best answers in our Language, is *Commonwealth*, and most properly expresses such a Society of Men, which 5 Community or Citty in *English* does not, for there may be Subordinate Communities in a Government; and City amongst us has a quite different notion from Commonwealth: And therefore to avoid ambiguity, I crave leave to use the word *Commonwealth* in that sense, in which I find it used by King *James the First*, and 10 I take it to be its genuine signification; which if any Body dislike, I consent with him to change it for a better.

Chap. XI.

Of the Extent of the Legislative Power.

134. THE great end of Mens entring into Society, being the enjoyment of their Properties in Peace and Safety, and the great instrument and means of that being the Laws establish'd in that Society; the *first and fundamental positive Law* of all Commonwealths, *is the establishing of the Legislative* Power; as the *first and* 5

§ 133   2–3   Compare 'that great LEVIATHAN called a COMMON-WEALTH OR STATE (in latine CIVITAS)' (1904, XVIII), perhaps a re-echo, perhaps a coincidence; see II, § 212 and note.
    10   'King *James the First*'—1st edition, 'by K. *James* himself', changed in 1694. This is a striking indication that he wrote this passage before the accession of James II in 1685, see Introduction, 54, compare a second instance in II, § 200, 3, and 'either of our Queens' in I, § 47, 25. Locke is probably referring to the speeches of 1603 and 1609 quoted in II, § 200, for 'Commonwealth' occurs in both (II, § 200, 5 and 31). He quotes a maxim of 'King James', i.e. James I, in a letter of 17 March 1684 (de Beer, 2, 612).
§ 134   *Chapter* XI   There is no obvious internal evidence to date the composition of this chapter. It is far less clearly connected with the polemic against Filmer than other parts of the text, but its statements are consistent with the attitude Locke takes up in that controversy and it is probably best regarded as part of the first form of the text, before 1681. There is nothing whatever to indicate that any part of it was an addition of 1689.
    1–11   Compare the very similar passage in Locke's *Epistola de Tolerantia*, 1689, translated thus by Popple in the *Letter concerning Toleration* (*Works*, 1801, VI, 43). 'This is the

fundamental natural Law, which is to govern even the Legislative it self, is *the preservation of the Society*, and (as far as will consist with the publick good) of every person in it. This *Legislative* is not only *the supream power* of the Common-wealth, but sacred and
10 unalterable in the hands where the Community have once placed it; nor can any Edict of any Body else, in what Form soever conceived, or by what Power soever backed, have the force and obligation of a *Law*, which has not its *Sanction from* that *Legislative*, which the publick has chosen and appointed. For without this
15 the Law could not have that, which is absolutely necessary to its being a *Law*, *the consent of the Society*, over whom no Body can have a power to make Laws, but by their own consent,† and by Authority received from them; and therefore all the *Obedience*, which by the most solemn Ties any one can be obliged to pay,
20 ultimately terminates in this *Supream Power*, and is directed by those Laws which it enacts: nor can any Oaths to any Foreign Power whatsoever, or any Domestick Subordinate Power, discharge any Member of the Society from his *Obedience to the Legislative*, acting pursuant to their trust, nor oblige him to any
25 Obedience contrary to the Laws so enacted, or farther than they

---

† *The lawful Power of making Laws to Command whole Politick Societies of Men belonging so properly unto the same intire Societies, that for any Prince or Potentate of what kind soever upon Earth, to exercise the same of himself, and not by express Commission immediately and personally received from God, or else by Authority derived at the first from their consent, upon whose persons they impose Laws, it is no better than meer Tyranny. Laws they are not therefore which publick Approbation hath not made so.* Hooker's Eccl. Pol. I. 1. Sect. 10. *Of this point therefore we are to note, that sith Men naturally have no full and perfect Power to Command whole Politick Multitudes of Men, therefore utterly without our Consent, we could in such sort be at no Mans Commandment living. And to be commanded we do consent when that Society, whereof we be a part, hath at any time before consented, without revoking the same after by the like universal agreement.*
   Laws therefore humane, of what kind soever, are available by consent. Ibid.

---

original, this is the use, and these are the bounds of the legislative, which is the supreme power in every commonwealth. I mean, that provision may be made for the security of each man's private possessions; for the peace, riches, and public commodities of the whole people; and, as much as possible, for the increase of their inward strength, against foreign enemies.' On the priority of the legislative, compare II, § 212, especially lines 16 and 17: in the Latin treatise on the civil magistrate (1661) Locke insists that the supreme power is always in the legislative, see page 12.

   17   Reference sign for Hooker quotations inserted by editor; see note on II, § 74, 15. Passages in Keble, 1836, II, 307–8, Locke's 1676 edition, 87–8, fairly exactly quoted. Molyneux (1698) cites the first part of this passage to exactly the same effect as Locke.

do allow; it being ridiculous to imagine one can be tied ultimately to *obey* any *Power* in the Society, which is not *the Supream.*

135. Though the *Legislative,* whether placed in one or more, whether it be always in being, or only by intervals, tho' it be the *Supream* Power in every Common-wealth; yet,

First, It is *not,* nor can possibly be absolutely *Arbitrary* over the Lives and Fortunes of the People. For it being but the joynt 5 power of every Member of the Society given up to that Person, or Assembly, which is Legislator, it can be no more than those persons had in a State of Nature before they enter'd into Society, and gave up to the Community. For no Body can transfer to another more power than he has in himself; and no Body has an 10 absolute Arbitrary Power over himself, or over any other, to destroy his own Life, or take away the Life or Property of another. A Man, as has been proved, cannot subject himself to the Arbitrary Power of another; and having in the State of Nature no Arbitrary Power over the Life, Liberty, or Possession of another, but only 15 so much as the Law of Nature gave him for the preservation of himself, and the rest of Mankind; this is all he doth, or can give up to the Common-wealth, and by it to the *Legislative Power,* so that the Legislative can have no more than this. Their Power in the utmost Bounds of it, is *limited to the publick good* of the Society. 20 It is a Power, that hath no other end but preservation, and therefore can never have a right to destroy, enslave, or designedly to impoverish the Subjects.† The Obligations of the Law of Nature,

† *Two Foundations there are which bear up publick Societies, the one a natural inclination, whereby all Men desire sociable Life and Fellowship; the other an Order, expressly or secretly agreed upon, touching the manner of their union in living together; the latter is that which we call the Law of a Common-weal, the very Soul of a Politick Body, the parts whereof are by Law animated, held together, and set on work in such actions as the common good requireth. Laws politick, ordain'd for external order and regiment amongst Men, are never framed as they should be, unless presuming the will of Man to be inwardly obstinate, rebellious, and averse from all Obedience to the sacred Laws of his Nature; in a word, unless presuming Man to be in regard of his depraved Mind, little better than a wild Beast, they do accordingly provide notwithstanding, so to frame his outward Actions, that they be no hindrance unto the common good, for which Societies are instituted. Unless they do this they are not perfect.* Hooker's Eccl. Pol. l. 1. Sect. 10.

§ 135   11–12   Compare II, § 6, 18–19: the two paragraphs are quite close in sentiment and expression.
    17–23   Compare *Third Letter on Toleration* (1692), (*Works,* 1801, VI, 214): 'The power that is in the civil sovereign is the force of all the subjects of the commonwealth, which supposing it sufficient for other ends, than the preserving the members of the

cease not in Society, but only in many Cases are drawn closer, and
25 have by Humane Laws known Penalties annexed to them, to
inforce their observation. Thus the Law of Nature ſtands as an
Eternal Rule to all Men, *Legislators* as well as others. The *Rules*
that they make for other Mens Actions, muſt, as well as their own
and other Mens Actions, be conformable to the Law of Nature,
30 *i.e.* to the Will of God, of which that is a Declaration, and the
fundamental Law of Nature being *the preservation of Mankind,* no
Humane Sanction can be good, or valid againſt it.

136. *Secondly,* The *Legislative,* or Supream Authority, cannot
assume to its self a power to Rule by extemporary Arbitrary
Decrees,† but *is bound to dispense Juſtice,* and decide the Rights of
the Subject *by promulgated ſtanding Laws, and known Authoris'd Judges.*
5 For the Law of Nature being unwritten, and so no where to be
found but in the minds of Men, they who through Passion or
Intereſt shall mis-cite, or misapply it, cannot so easily be convinced
of their miſtake where there is no eſtablish'd Judge: And so it

---

† *Humane Laws are measures in respect of Men, whose actions they muſt direct, howbeit
such measures they are as have also their higher Rules to be measured by, which Rules are two,
the Law of God, and the Law of Nature; so that Laws Humane muſt be made according to
the general Laws of Nature, and without contradiction to any positive Law of Scripture,
otherwise they are ill made.* Ibid. l. 3. Sect. 9.

To conſtrain Men to any thing inconvenient doth seem unreasonable. Ibid. l .1. Sect. 10.

---

commonwealth in peace from injury and violence: yet if those who gave him that
power, limited the application of it to that sole end, no opinion of any other benefits
attainable by it can authorize him to use it otherwise.'
§ 135   23   Reference sign for Hooker quotation inserted by editor; see note on II,
§ 74, 15. See Keble's *Hooker,* 1836, I, 299, Locke's 1676 edition, 85, coming just after
the passage quoted in II, § 15, 3–13, and fairly exactly transcribed.
    23–6   Compare II, § 12, 16–19, note and references.
§ 136   5–7   Compare II, § 124, 8–12.
    3   Reference sign for Hooker quotations inserted by editor; see note on II, § 74,
15. The first passage is found on vol. I, p. 483 of Keble's *Hooker* and p. 142 of Locke's
1676 edition. It is the only reference to any book of the *Ecclesiastical Polity* other than
the 1st and the Preface: it is one of the few indications in any Locke context which
shows that he ever got further than the 1st Book—see Introduction, 56. It is the
more remarkable, then, that the passage is acknowledged by Hooker to be a quotation
from Aquinas, *Summa Theologiae,* I, ii, 95, Conclusio (1624, 624 B) Quaest. 95 Art. 3,
where these words are found: 'Lex autem humana...est quaedam regula vel mensura
regulata vel mensurata quaedam superiori mensura; quae quidem est duplex,
scilicet divina lex, et lex naturae.' The second passage comes from Keble, I, 306, and
1676, 87: both are quoted with insignificant variations.
    8   Compare II, § 125, 1–3: Locke is here recapitulating what he had written
there.

serves not, as it ought, to determine the Rights, and fence the Properties of those that live under it, especially where every one 10 is Judge, Interpreter, and Executioner of it too, and that in his own Case: And he that has right on his side, having ordinarily but his own single strength, hath not force enough to defend himself from Injuries, or to punish Delinquents. To avoid these Inconveniencies which disorder Mens Properties in the state of 15 Nature, Men unite into Societies, that they may have the united strength of the whole Society to secure and defend their Properties, and may have *standing Rules* to bound it, by which every one may know what is his. To this end it is that Men give up all their Natural Power to the Society which they enter into, and the 20 Community put the Legislative Power into such hands as they think fit, with this trust, that they shall be govern'd by *declared Laws*, or else their Peace, Quiet, and Property will still be at the same uncertainty, as it was in the state of Nature.

137. Absolute Arbitrary Power, or Governing without *settled standing Laws*, can neither of them consist with the ends of Society and Government, which Men would not quit the freedom of the state of Nature for, and tie themselves up under, were it not to preserve their Lives, Liberties and Fortunes; and by *stated Rules* 5 of Right and Property to secure their Peace and Quiet. It cannot be supposed that they should intend, had they a power so to do, to give to any one, or more, an *absolute Arbitrary Power* over their Persons and Estates, and put a force into the Magistrates hand to execute his unlimited Will arbitrarily upon them: This were to 10 put themselves into a worse condition than the state of Nature, wherein they had a Liberty to defend their Right against the Injuries of others, and were upon equal terms of force to maintain it, whether invaded by a single Man, or many in Combination. Whereas by supposing they have given up themselves to the 15 *absolute Arbitrary Power* and will of a Legislator, they have disarmed themselves, and armed him, to make a prey of them when he pleases. He being in a much worse condition who is exposed to

---

§ 137   This argument is irrelevant to Filmer, since he had denied the possibility of a state of nature, though Locke consistently overlooks this position, one of the strong points of patriarchalism. It is, however, relevant to Hobbes, and even recalls Filmer's own criticisms of Hobbes, 239–50, though not exactly tied to any Hobbesian proposition. This is typical of the Hobbes/Locke relationship—see Introduction, 67–78.

the Arbitrary Power of one Man, who has the Command of
20 100000. than he that is expos'd to the Arbitrary Power of 100000.
single Men: no Body being secure, that his Will, who has such
a Command, is better, than that of other Men, though his Force
be 100000. times ſtronger. And therefore whatever Form the
Common-wealth is under, the Ruling Power ought to govern by
25 *declared* and *received Laws*, and not by extemporary Dictates and
undetermined Resolutions. For then Mankind will be in a far
worse condition, than in the State of Nature, if they shall have
armed one or a few Men with the joynt power of a Multitude, to
force them to obey at pleasure the exorbitant and unlimited
30 Decrees of their sudden thoughts, or unreſtrain'd, and till that
moment unknown Wills without having any measures set down
which may guide and juſtifie their actions. For all the power the
Government has, being only for the good of the Society, as it
ought not to be Arbitrary and at Pleasure, so it ought to be
35 exercised by *eſtablished and promulgated Laws*: that both the People
may know their Duty, and be safe and secure within the limits of
the Law, and the Rulers too kept within their due bounds, and
not to be tempted, by the Power they have in their hands, to
imploy it to such purposes, and by such measures, as they would
not have known, and own not willingly.

138. *Thirdly,* The *Supream Power cannot take* from any Man any
part of his *Property* without his own consent. For the preservation of Property being the end of Government, and that for which
Men enter into Society, it necessarily supposes and requires, that
5 the People should *have Property*, without which they muſt be
suppos'd to lose that by entring into Society, which was the end
for which they entered into it, too gross an absurdity for any
Man to own. *Men* therefore *in Society having Property*, they have
such a right to the goods, which by the Law of the Community
10 are theirs, that no Body hath a right to take their subſtance, or
any part of it from them, without their own consent; without
this, they have no *Property* at all. For I have truly no *Property* in

---

§ 138 1–2 Elrington, 1798, notes here the duty of each individual to pay taxes.
5–7 Compare *Jura Populi Anglicani*, 1701, 30: 'The supreme Power cannot
take from any man any part of his Property without his own consent . . . (as a Very
Learned and Ingenious Auther tells us)', with a footnote to 'The Author of two
Treatises of Government, pag. 277'. This is presumably a slip for p. 274 of the 1694

that, which another can by right take from me, when he pleases, against my consent. Hence it is a mistake to think, that the Supream or *Legislative Power* of any Commonwealth, can do what it will, and dispose of the Estates of the Subject *arbitrarily*, or take any part of them at pleasure. This is not much to be fear'd in Governments where the *Legislative* consists, wholly or in part, in Assemblies which are variable, whose Members upon the Dissolution of the Assembly, are Subjects under the common Laws of their Country, equally with the rest. But in Governments, where the *Legislative* is in one lasting Assembly always in being, or in one Man, as in Absolute Monarchies, there is danger still, that they will think themselves to have a distinct interest, from the rest of the Community; and so will be apt to increase their own Riches and Power, by taking, what they think fit, from the People. For a Man's *Property* is not at all secure, though there be good and equitable Laws to set the bounds of it, between him and his Fellow Subjects, if he who commands those Subjects, have Power to take from any private Man, what part he pleases of his *Property*, and use and dispose of it as he thinks good.

139. But *Government* into whatsoever hands it is put, being as I have before shew'd, intrusted with this condition, and *for this end*, that Men might have and secure *their Properties*, the Prince or Senate, however it may have power to make Laws for the regulating of *Property* between the Subjects one amongst another, yet can never have a Power to take to themselves the whole or any part of the Subjects *Property*, without their own consent. For this would be in effect to leave them no *Property* at all. And to let us see, that even *absolute Power*, where it is necessary, is *not Arbitrary* by being absolute, but is still limited by that reason, and confined to those ends, which required it in some Cases to be absolute, we need look no farther than the common practice of Martial

---

or 1698 printing, where this paragraph appears. The author of the tract is generally recognized as Lord Somers, Locke's close friend and patron; it is very Lockeian in tone, and even more forthright about property and consent, since Locke leaves it possible to suppose that consent is collective, not individual.

13–17   Contrast Hobbes: '*Mine*, and *Thine* and *His*; that is to say, in one word *Propriety*; . . . belongeth in all kinds of Common-wealth to the Soveraign Power', *Leviathan*, 1904, 176, compare 240.

17–21   The government of England is obviously meant; compare II, § 143.

21–5   Compare II, §§ 143, 6–14; 163, 13–17; 164, 15 16.

§ 139   4–5   Compare II, § 120, note and references on a government's regulation of property.

Discipline. For the Preservation of the Army, and in it of the whole Commonwealth, requires an *absolute Obedience* to the Com-
15 mand of every Superiour Officer, and it is justly Death to disobey or dispute the most dangerous or unreasonable of them: but yet we see, that neither the Serjeant, that could command a Souldier to march up to the mouth of a Cannon, or stand in a Breach, where he is almost sure to perish, can command that Soldier to give him
20 one penny of his Money; nor the *General*, that can condemn him to Death for deserting his Post, or for not obeying the most desperate Orders, can yet with all his absolute Power of Life and Death, dispose of one Farthing of that Soldiers Estate, or seize one jot of his Goods; whom yet he can command any thing, and
25 hang for the least Disobedience. Because such a blind Obedience is necessary to that end for which the Commander has his Power, *viz.* the preservation of the rest; but the disposing of his Goods has nothing to do with it.

140. 'Tis true, Governments cannot be supported without great Charge, and 'tis fit every one who enjoys his share of the Protection, should pay out of his Estate his proportion for the maintenance of it. But still it must be with his own Consent,
5 *i.e.* the Consent of the Majority, giving it either by themselves, or their Representatives chosen by them. For if any one shall claim a *Power to lay* and levy *Taxes* on the People, by his own Authority, and without such consent of the People, he thereby invades the *Fundamental Law of Property*, and subverts the end of
10 Government. For what property have I in that which another may by right take, when he pleases to himself?

141. *Fourthly*, The *Legislative cannot transfer the Power of Making Laws* to any other hands. For it being but a delegated Power from the People, they, who have it, cannot pass it over to others. The People alone can appoint the Form of the Commonwealth, which
5 is by Constituting the Legislative, and appointing in whose hands that shall be. And when the People have said, We will submit to rules, and be govern'd by *Laws* made by such Men, and in such

---

§ **140** 3–6 Here Locke's individual doctrine of property and his assumption about majorities and representation are joined with traditional English constitutionalism. Elrington, 1798, characteristically comments that 'only part of the citizens' should have a right to taxation by consent, so that 'the property of individuals may be more secure'. On representatives compare note on 11, § 158, 5.

Forms, no Body else can say other Men shall make *Laws* for them; nor can the people be bound by any *Laws* but such as are Enacted by those, whom they have Chosen, and Authorised to make *Laws* 10 for them. The power of the *Legislative* being derived from the People by a positive voluntary Grant and Institution, can be no other, than what that positive Grant conveyed, which being only to make *Laws*, and not to make *Legislators*, the *Legislative* can have no power to transfer their Authority of making Laws, and place 15 it in other hands.

142. These are the *Bounds* which the trust that is put in them by the Society, and the Law of God and Nature, have *set to the Legislative* Power of every Commonwealth, in all Forms of Government.

First, They are to govern by *promulgated establish'd Laws*, not to 5 be varied in particular Cases, but to have one Rule for Rich and Poor, for the Favourite at Court, and the Country Man at Plough.

Secondly, These *Laws* also ought to be designed *for* no other end ultimately but *the good of the People*.

Thirdly, they must *not raise Taxes* on the Property of the People, 10 *without the Consent of the People*, given by themselves, or their Deputies. And this properly concerns only such Governments where the *Legislative* is always in being, or at least where the People have not reserv'd any part of the Legislative to Deputies, to be from time to time chosen by themselves. 15

Fourthly, The *Legislative* neither must *nor can transfer the Power of making Laws* to any Body else, or place it any where but where the People have.

---

§ 141   11–16   Added in the 2nd printing, 1694: Locke altered words in the earlier part of the paragraph after 1698. Compare I, §§ 25, 2–4; 85, 18–19 on grants: Pareyson, 1948, comments that Locke's view recalls the medieval theory of *concessio*.

Chap. XII.

Of the Legislative, Executive, and Federative Power of the Commonwealth.

143. THE *Legislative* Power is that which has a right *to direct* how *the Force of the Commonwealth* shall be imploy'd for preserving the Community and the Members of it. But because those Laws which are constantly to be Executed, and whose force
5 is always to continue, may be made in a little time; therefore there is no need, that the *Legislative* should be always in being, not having always business to do. And because it may be too great a temptation to humane frailty apt to grasp at Power, for the same Persons who have the Power of making Laws, to have also in
10 their hands the power to execute them, whereby they may exempt themselves from Obedience to the Laws they make, and suit the Law, both in its making and execution, to their own private advantage, and thereby come to have a distinct interest from the rest of the Community, contrary to the end of Society and Govern-
15 ment: Therefore in well order'd Commonwealths, where the good of the whole is so considered, as it ought, the *Legislative* Power is put into the hands of divers Persons who duly Assembled, have by themselves, or jointly with others, a Power to make Laws, which
20 when they have done, being separated again, they are themselves subject to the Laws, they have made; which is a new and near tie upon them, to take care, that they make them for the publick good.

144. But because the Laws, that are at once, and in a short time made, have a constant and lasting force, and need a *perpetual*

---

§ **143** *Chapter* XII   Though, as in the case of chapter XI (see note on II, § 134) there is nothing in the text to date the composition of this chapter, it is probably best regarded as part of the original text, before 1681. The separation of powers is hinted at several times elsewhere, in II, § 91, in II, § 107 where it is part of the anti-patriarchal argument, and II, § 127: the logical position indicating the existence of a Federative Power is established in II, § 14. There is no indication of an insertion or revision in 1689, and so no textual grounds for supposing that it is historically related to William III's constitutional position in respect of foreign policy.

15–21   The constitutional arrangements of England are those of the 'well order'd Commonwealth' Locke has in mind; compare II, §§ 138, 17–21; 151; 167; 213.

Execution, or an attendance thereunto: Therefore 'tis necessary there should be a *Power always in being*, which should see to the *Execution* of the Laws that are made, and remain in force. And 5 thus the *Legislative* and *Executive Power* come often to be separated.

145. There is another *Power* in every Commonwealth, which one may call *natural*, because it is that which answers to the Power every Man naturally had before he entred into Society. For though in a Commonwealth the Members of it are distinct Persons still in reference to one another, and as such are governed by the 5 Laws of the Society; yet in reference to the rest of Mankind, they make one Body, which is, as every Member of it before was, still in the State of Nature with the rest of Mankind. Hence it is, that the Controversies that happen between any Man of the Society with those that are out of it, are managed by the publick; and an 10 injury done to a Member of their Body, engages the whole in the reparation of it. So that under this Consideration, the whole Community is one Body in the State of Nature, in respect of all other States or Persons out of its Community.

146. This therefore contains the Power of War and Peace, Leagues and Alliances, and all the Transactions, with all Persons and Communities without the Commonwealth, and may be called *Federative*, if any one pleases. So the thing be understood, I am indifferent as to the Name. 5

147. These two Powers, *Executive* and *Federative*, though they be really distinct in themselves, yet one comprehending the *Execution* of the Municipal Laws of the Society *within* its self, upon all that are parts of it; the other the management of the *security and interest of the publick without*, with all those that it may receive 5 benefit or damage from, yet they are always almost united. And though this *federative Power* in the well or ill management of it be

---

§ **144**   3–5   Compare II, § 153, 2–5.
§ **145**   6–8   Compare II, § 14; § 183, 7–8.
§ **146**   On the federative power, see Introduction, 119, note and references. Lawson, *Politica Sacra* (1660), 1689, 63, recognizes something of this nature and has been supposed to be Locke's source. But in general his doctrine of the separation of powers is quite different from Locke's, and rather more specific. He bases it on Scripture (*Examination of Hobbes*, 1657, 56), and recognizes the three powers now regarded as usual: legislative, judicial and executive; see 1689, 72, 93, 97, etc.; 1657, 8. He is interested, perhaps, more in the gradation and nature, than the independence of these powers, though like Locke and everyone else he insisted on the independence of the judiciary.

of great moment to the commonwealth, yet it is much less capable
to be directed by antecedent, standing, positive Laws, than the
10 *Executive*; and so must necessarily be left to the Prudence and
Wisdom of those whose hands it is in, to be managed for the
publick good. For the *Laws* that concern Subjects one amongst
another, being to direct their actions, may well enough *precede*
them. But what is to be done in reference to *Foreigners*, depending
15 much upon their actions, and the variation of designs and interests,
must be *left* in great part *to* the *Prudence* of those who have this
Power committed to them, to be managed by the best of their
Skill, for the advantage of the Commonwealth.

148. Though, as I said, the *Executive* and *Federative Power* of
every Community be really distinct in themselves, yet they are
hardly to be separated, and placed, at the same time, in the hands
of distinct Persons. For both of them requiring the force of the
5 Society for their exercise, it is almost impracticable to place the
Force of the Commonwealth in distinct, and not subordinate
hands; or that the *Executive* and *Federative Power* should be *placed*
in Persons that might act separately, whereby the Force of the
Publick would be under different Commands: which would be
10 apt sometime or other to cause disorder and ruine.

CHAP. XIII.

Of the Subordination of the Powers of the Commonwealth.

149. THough in a Constituted Commonwealth, standing upon
its own Basis, and acting according to its own Nature,
that is, acting for the preservation of the Community, there can
be but *one Supream Power*, which is *the Legislative*, to which all the

§ 149 *Chapter* XIII In the view of the editor, this chapter was part of the first
version, but belongs to 1680–1 rather than to 1679. It is relevant to the Filmer controversy, but rather more to the political programme and activities of Shaftesbury. It
is concerned with the election, summoning, prorogation and dissolution of parliament and ends with a plea for parliamentary reform, all subjects of great importance
to Shaftesbury and his Whigs, especially in 1680 and 1681; see notes on §§ 156, 157.
Some of the remarks may conceivably have been added in 1689 as a reference to

rest are and must be subordinate, yet the Legislative being only 5
a Fiduciary Power to act for certain ends, there remains still *in the
People a Supream Power* to remove or *alter the Legislative,* when
they find the *Legislative* act contrary to the trust reposed in them.
For all *Power given with trust* for the attaining an *end,* being limited
by that end, whenever that *end* is manifestly neglected, or opposed, 10
the *trust* must necessarily be *forfeited,* and the Power devolve into
the hands of those that gave it, who may place it anew where they
shall think best for their safety and security. And thus the *Community* perpetually *retains a Supream Power* of saving themselves
from the attempts and designs of any Body, even of their Legis- 15
lators, whenever they shall be so foolish, or so wicked, as to lay
and carry on designs against the Liberties and Properties of the
Subject. For no Man, or Society of Men, having a Power to
deliver up their *Preservation,* or consequently the means of it, to
the Absolute Will and arbitrary Dominion of another; whenever 20
any one shall go about to bring them into such a Slavish Condition, they will always have a right to preserve what they have
not a Power to part with; and to rid themselves of those who
invade this Fundamental, Sacred, and unalterable Law of *Self-
Preservation,* for which they enter'd into Society. And thus the 25
Community may be said in this respect to be *always the Supream
Power,* but not as considered under any Form of Government,
because this Power of the People can never take place till the
Government be dissolved.

150. In all Cases, whilst the Government subsists, the *Legislative
is the Supream Power.* For what can give Laws to another, must

James II, but in general it seems to be a call to constitutional, even revolutionary
change made in defiance of Charles II.
  3–5 The supremacy of the legislative is a characteristic of Locke's theory and
so typical of the body of thought which he represented that it seems unnecessary to
look for a source of this concept in Lawson (e.g. 1657, 30) as Maclean wishes to
do (1947, 70).
  5–8 These phrases, and the whole doctrine of the paragraph, provide a sharp
contrast with Hobbes, *Leviathan,* chapter 18, revealing a systematic difference. It is
difficult to believe that Locke had Hobbes in mind when he wrote it.
  7 The apparent contradiction between the '*Supream Power*' here and in line 4
is explained by Lamprecht, 1918, 145, saying that 'the supremacy of the legislative is
complete under one condition and disappears entirely under another condition'.
  23–5 Compare II, § 129, 3–4.
  28–9 See chapter XIX (§§ 211–43); compare II, § 132, note and references; § 157, 26.
§ 150 Compare II, § 132, 19–24, II, § 134; and on lines 1–2 compare II, § 153, 1–2
(taken by Bastide, 1907, 236, as typical of Locke's verbal inconsistencies).

needs be superiour to him: and since the Legislative is no otherwise Legislative of the Society, but by the right it has to make
5 Laws for all the parts and for every Member of the Society,
prescribing Rules to their actions, and giving power of Execution,
where they are transgressed, the *Legislative* must needs be the
Supream, and all other Powers in any Members or parts of the
Society, derived from and subordinate to it.

151. In some Commonwealths where the *Legislative* is not
always in being, and the *Executive* is vested in a single Person, who
has also a share in the Legislative; there that single Person in
a very tolerable sense may also be called *Supream*, not that he has
5 in himself all the Supream Power, which is that of Law-making:
But because he has in him the *Supream Execution*, from whom all
inferiour Magistrates derive all their several subordinate Powers,
or at least the greatest part of them: having also no Legislative
superiour to him, there being no Law to be made without his
10 consent, which cannot be expected should ever subject him to the
other part of the Legislative, *he is* properly enough in this sense
Supream. But yet it is to be observed, that though *Oaths of
Allegiance* and Fealty are taken to him, 'tis not to him as Supream
Legislator, but as *Supream Executor* of the Law, made by a joint
15 Power of him with others; *Allegiance* being nothing but an
Obedience according to Law, which when he violates, he has no right
to Obedience, nor can claim it otherwise than as the publick
Person vested with the Power of the Law, and so is to be consider'd as the Image, Phantom, or Representative of the Common-
20 wealth, acted by the will of the Society, declared in its Laws;
and thus he has no Will, no Power, but that of the Law. But when
he quits this Representation, this publick Will, and acts by his
own private Will, he degrades himself, and is but a single private
Person without Power, and without Will, that has any Right to
25 *Obedience*; the Members owing no *Obedience* but to the publick
Will of the Society.

152. The *Executive Power* placed any where but in a Person,
that has also a share in the Legislative, is visibly subordinate and
accountable to it, and may be at pleasure changed and displaced;

---

§ 151   19, 22   'Representative' and 'Representation' are used in the technical,
Hobbesian sense here—see Gierke, 1934, 82-3, though to antithetical purposes,
which is typical of the relationship between the two men. Once again, Locke is clearly talking
of the English monarchy, its rights and powers.

so that it is not the *supream Executive Power* that is exempt from *Subordination*, but the *Supream Executive Power* vested in one, who 5 having a share in the Legislative, has no distinct superiour Legislative to be subordinate and accountable to, farther than he himself shall joyn and consent: so that he is no more subordinate than he himself shall think fit, which one may certainly conclude will be but very little. Of other *Ministerial* and *subordinate Powers* 10 in a Commonwealth, we need not speak, they being so multiply'd with infinite variety, in the different Customs and Constitutions of distinct Commonwealths, that it is impossible to give a particular account of them all. Only thus much, which is necessary to our present purpose, we may take notice of concerning them, 15 that they have no manner of Authority any of them, beyond what is, by positive Grant, and Commission, delegated to them, and are all of them accountable to some other Power in the Commonwealth.

153. It is not necessary, no nor so much as convenient, that the *Legislative* should be *always in being*. But absolutely necessary that the *Executive Power* should, because there is not always need of new Laws to be made, but always need of Execution of the Laws that are made. When the *Legislative* hath put the *Execution* 5 of the Laws, they make, into other hands, they have a power still to resume it out of those hands, when they find cause, and to punish for any mall-administration against the Laws. The same holds also in regard of the *Federative* Power, that and the Executive being both *Ministerial and subordinate to the Legislative*, which as 10 has been shew'd in a Constituted Commonwealth, is the Supream. The *Legislative* also in this Case being suppos'd to consist of several Persons (for if it be a single Person, it cannot but be always in being, and so will as Supream, naturally have the Supream Executive Power, together with the Legislative) may 15 *assemble and exercise their Legislature*, at the times that either their original Constitution, or their own Adjournment appoints, or when they please; if neither of these hath appointed any time, or there be no other way prescribed to convoke them. For the supream Power being placed in them by the People, 'tis always 20

---

§ 153   1–3   Compare II, § 144, 2–4.
  16 '*Legislature*'—power of law-making: changed by Locke after 1698 from '*Legislative*'; compare II, § 94, 24 and references.

in them, and they may exercise it when they please, unless by their original Conſtitution they are limited to certain Seasons, or by an Aᶜt of their Supream Power they have Adjourned to a certain time, and when that time comes, they have a right to *Assemble*
25 and *aᶜt* again.

154. If the *Legiſlative*, or any part of it be made up of Representatives chosen for that time by the People, which afterwards return into the ordinary ſtate of Subjeᶜts, and have no share in the Legislature but upon a new choice, this power of chusing muſt
5 also be exercised by the People, either at certain appointed Seasons, or else when they are summon'd to it: and in this latter Case, the power of convoking the Legislative, is ordinarily placed in the Executive, and has one of these two limitations in respeᶜt of time: That either the Original Conſtitution requires their *assembling* and
10 *aᶜting* at certain intervals, and then the Executive Power does nothing but Miniſterially issue direᶜtions for their Eleᶜting and Assembling, according to due Forms: Or else it is left to his Prudence to call them by new Eleᶜtions, when the Occasions or Exigencies of the publick require the amendment of old, or making
15 of new Laws, or the redress or prevention of any inconveniencies, that lie on, or threaten the People.

155. It may be demanded here, What if the Executive Power being possessed of the Force of the Commonwealth, shall make use of that force to hinder the *meeting* and *aᶜting of the Legiſlative*, when the Original Conſtitution, or the publick Exigencies require
5 it? I say using Force upon the People without Authority, and contrary to the Truſt put in him, that does so, is a ſtate of War with the People, who have a right to *reinſtate* their *Legiſlative in the Exercise* of their Power. For having ereᶜted a Legislative, with an intent they should exercise the Power of making Laws, either
10 at certain set times, or when there is need of it; when they are hindr'd by any force from, what is so necessary to the Society, and wherein the Safety and preservation of the People consiſts, the People have a right to remove it by force. In all States and Conditions the true remedy of *Force* without Authority, is to

---

§ 155 3 Compare II, § 215, 1, verbal parallel; see note on II, § 156 and references.
4 'Original Constitution'—see II, § 154, 9; § 156, 32; § 218, 1; the only instances of the use of Constitution in our sense: elsewhere it means an overriding law.
6, 16 'state of War'—see chapter III of *Second Treatise*.

oppose *Force* to it. The use of *force* without Authority, always 15
puts him that uses it into a *state of War*, as the Aggressor, and
renders him liable to be treated accordingly.

156. The Power *of Assembling and dismissing the Legislative,*
placed in the Executive, gives not the Executive a superiority
over it, but is a Fiduciary Trust, placed in him, for the safety of
the People, in a Case where the uncertainty, and variableness of
humane affairs could not bear a steady fixed rule. For it not being 5
possible, that the first Framers of the Government should, by any
foresight, be so much Masters of future Events, as to be able to
prefix so just periods of return and duration to the *Assemblies of
the Legislative,* in all times to come, that might exactly answer all
the Exigencies of the Commonwealth; the best remedy could be 10
found for this defect, was to trust this to the prudence of one,
who was always to be present, and whose business it was to watch
over the publick good. Constant *frequent meetings of the Legislative,*
and long Continuations of their Assemblies, without necessary
occasion, could not but be burthensome to the People, and must 15
necessarily in time produce more dangerous inconveniences, and
yet the quick turn of affairs might be sometimes such as to need
their present help: Any delay of their *Convening* might endanger
the publick; and sometimes too their business might be so great,
that the limited time of their sitting might be too short for their 20
work, and rob the publick of that benefit, which could be had
only from their mature deliberation. What then could be done,
in this Case, to prevent the Community, from being exposed
sometime or other to eminent hazard, on one side, or the other,
by fixed intervals and periods, set to the *meeting and acting of the* 25
Legislative, but to intrust it to the prudence of some, who being
present, and acquainted with the state of publick affairs, might
make use of this Prerogative for the publick good? And where
else could this be so well placed as in his hands, who was intrusted
with the Execution of the Laws, for the same end? Thus sup- 30
posing the regulation of times for the *Assembling and Sitting of the*
Legislative, not settled by the original Constitution, it naturally

§ 156   §§ 154 and 155 deal with the election and dissolution, this paragraph with the
summoning and proroguing, of English parliaments. Locke seems to have in mind
the repeated postponements, cancellations, failures to summon characteristic of
Charles II and the first object of Shaftesbury's activities in opposition, especially
during the Exclusion Controversy—see notes on 11, §§ 167, 213, and Introduction, 55.

fell into the hands of the Executive, not as an Arbitrary Power depending on his good pleasure, but with this trust always to have
35 it exercised only for the publick Weal, as the Occurrences of times and change of affairs might require. Whether *settled periods of their Convening*, or a *liberty* left to the Prince *for Convoking the Legislative*, or perhaps a mixture of both, hath the least inconvenience attending it, 'tis not my business here to inquire, but only to shew,
40 that though the Executive Power may have the Prerogative of *Convoking* and *dissolving* such *Conventions of the Legislative*, yet it is not thereby superiour to it.

157. Things of this World are in so constant a Flux, that nothing remains long in the same State. Thus People, Riches, Trade, Power, change their Stations; flourishing mighty Cities come to ruine, and prove in time neglected desolate Corners,
5 whilst other unfrequented places grow into populous Countries, fill'd with Wealth and Inhabitants. But things not always changing equally, and private interest often keeping up Customs and Priviledges, when the reasons of them are ceased, it often comes to pass, that in Governments, where part of the Legislative consists
10 of *Representatives* chosen by the People, that in tract of time this *Representation* becomes very *unequal* and disproportionate to the reasons it was at first establish'd upon. To what gross absurdities the following of Custom, when Reason has left it, may lead, we may be satisfied when we see the bare Name of a Town, of which
15 there remains not so much as the ruines, where scarce so much Housing as a Sheep-coat; or more Inhabitants than a Shepherd is to be found, sends *as many Representatives* to the grand Assembly of Law-makers, as a whole County numerous in People, and powerful in riches. This Strangers stand amazed at, and every one
20 must confess needs a remedy. Though most think it hard to find

---

§ 157 The reform of the franchise and electoral districts was a part of the political programme of Shaftesbury and the Whigs under Charles II, who introduced a Bill on the subject in the first parliament which they controlled, that of March 1679; see Ogg, *Charles II*, 1955, II, 480–2. The scheme of reform attributed to Shaftesbury (*Somers Tracts*, 1812) included the disfranchisement of rotten boroughs like the one mentioned in lines 12–19. This was presumably Old Sarum, near Salisbury, well-known to Locke as the home of his friend David Thomas; see Introduction, 63. This paragraph, then, was most probably written as part of the original in 1679, though it could have been added in 1681. Sir James Fitzjames Stephen, 1892, 154–5, regards this as 'the oddest illustration of the fanciful character of the results to which Locke's abstract principles led him in relation to civil government'.

one, because the Constitution of the Legislative being the original and supream act of the Society, antecedent to all positive Laws in it, and depending wholly on the People, no inferiour Power can alter it. And therefore the *People*, when the *Legislative* is once Constituted, *having* in such a Government as we have been speaking of, *no Power* to act as long as the Government stands; this inconvenience is thought incapable of a remedy.

158. *Salus Populi Suprema Lex*, is certainly so just and fundamental a Rule, that he, who sincerely follows it, cannot dangerously err. If therefore the Executive, who has the power of Convoking the Legislative, observing rather the true proportion, than fashion of *Representation*, regulates, not by old custom, but true reason, the *number of Members*, in all places, that have a right to be distinctly represented, which no part of the People however incorporated can pretend to, but in proportion to the assistance, which it affords to the publick, it cannot be judg'd, to have set up a new Legislative, but to have restored the old and true one, and to have rectified the disorders, which succession of time had insensibly, as well as inevitably introduced. For it being the interest, as well as intention of the People, to have a fair and *equal Representative*; whoever brings it nearest to that, is an undoubted Friend, to, and Establisher of the Government, and cannot miss the Consent and Approbation of the Community. *Prerogative* being nothing, but a Power in the hands of the Prince to provide for the publick good, in such Cases, which depending upon unforeseen and uncertain Occurrences, certain and unalterable Laws could not safely direct, whatsoever shall be done manifestly for the good of the People, and the establishing the Government upon its true Foundations, is, and always will be just *Prerogative*. The Power of Erecting new Corporations, and therewith *new Representatives*, carries with it a supposition, that in time the

§ 158   1–12   Locke, in solving the difficulty about electoral reform in accordance with that supreme law, the good of the people (§§ 157, 20–5; 158, 1), is dealing with a problem of his own making. Seliger, 1968, p. 365, takes a different view.

5   '*Representation*'—here used in its non-Hobbesian sense; compare note on II, § 151, 19, 22. Elrington, 1798, comments that Locke 'had no idea that he would be interpreted as attributing that power to the multitude', that Locke would have excluded from the suffrage those without property, that his remarks about proportioning representatives to districts obviate universal suffrage. This sentence and § 140 are cited by those who believe that Locke intended a definite restriction of the franchise, e.g. Seliger, 1963 (i).   16–17   Compare chapter XIV.

25 *measures of representation* might vary, and those places have a just right to be represented which before had none; and by the same reason, those cease to have a right, and be too inconsiderable for such a Priviledge, which before had it. 'Tis not a change from the present State, which perhaps Corruption, or decay has introduced,
30 that makes an Inroad upon the Government, but the tendency of it to injure or oppress the People, and to set up one part, or Party, with a distinction from, and an unequal subjection of the rest. Whatsoever cannot but be acknowledged to be of advantage to the Society, and People in general, upon just and lasting measures,
35 will always, when done, justifie it self; and whenever the People shall chuse their *Representatives upon* just and undeniably *equal measures* suitable to the original Frame of the Government, it cannot be doubted to be the will and act of the Society, whoever permitted, or caused them so to do.

CHAP. XIV.

Of PREROGATIVE.

159. WHere the Legislative and Executive Power are in distinct hands, (as they are in all moderated Monarchies, and well-framed Governments) there the good of the Society requires, that several things should be left to the discretion of him, that has
5 the Executive Power. For the Legislators not being able to foresee, and provide, by Laws, for all, that may be useful to the Community, the Executor of the Laws, having the power in his hands, has by the common Law of Nature, a right to make use of it, for the good of the Society, in many Cases, where the
10 municipal Law has given no direction, till the Legislative can conveniently be Assembled to provide for it. Many things there are, which the Law can by no means provide for, and those must

---

§ **159** *Chapter* xiv. In the editor's judgment this chapter belongs to Locke's original composition of 1679; compare note on 11, § 149, chapter xiii. It may have been touched up in places in 1689, especially in the final paragraph, § 168, but Prof. K. H. D. Haley comments that Locke could hardly have written as he did of the discretionary power in § 161 after the controversy over James II's dispensations. This and the hints of Shaftesbury's quarrel with Charles II about the summoning of Parliament (see § 167) seem sufficient grounds for this dating.

necessarily be left to the discretion of him, that has the Executive Power in his hands, to be ordered by him, as the publick good and advantage shall require: nay, 'tis fit that the Laws themselves 15 should in some Cases give way to the Executive Power, or rather to this Fundamental Law of Nature and Government, *viz*. That as much as may be, *all* the Members of the Society are to be *preserved*. For since many accidents may happen, wherein a ſtrict and rigid observation of the Laws may do harm; (as not to pull 20 down an innocent Man's House to ſtop the Fire, when the next to it is burning) and a Man may come sometimes within the reach of the Law, which makes no diſtinction of Persons, by an action, that may deserve reward and pardon; 'tis fit, the Ruler should have a Power, in many Cases, to mitigate the severity of the Law, 25 and pardon some Offenders: For the *end of Government* being the *preservation of all*, as much as may be, even the guilty are to be spared, where it can prove no prejudice to the innocent.

160. This Power to act according to discretion, for the publick good, without the prescription of the Law, and sometimes even againſt it, *is* that which is called *Prerogative*. For since in some Governments the Law-making Power is not always in being, and is usually too numerous, and so too slow, for the dispatch requisite 5 to Execution: and because also it is impossible to foresee, and so by laws to provide for, all Accidents and Necessities, that may concern the publick; or to make such Laws, as will do no harm, if they are Executed with an inflexible rigour, on all occasions, and upon all Persons, that may come in their way, therefore there 10 is a latitude left to the Executive power, to do many things of choice, which the Laws do not prescribe.

161. This power whilſt imployed for the benefit of the Community, and suitably to the truſt and ends of the Government, *is undoubted Prerogative*, and never is queſtioned. For the People are very seldom, or never scrupulous, or nice in the point: they are far from examining *Prerogative*, whilſt it is in any tolerable degree im- 5 ploy'd for the use it was meant; that is, for the good of the People, and not manifeſtly againſt it. But if there comes to be a *queſtion* between the Executive Power and the People, *about* a thing claimed as a *Prerogative*; the tendency of the exercise of such *Prerogative* to the good or hurt of the People, will easily decide that Queſtion. 10

24–6 On a ruler's right to pardon, compare II, § 11, 6–8 and note.

162. It is easie to conceive, that in the Infancy of Governments, when Commonwealths differed little from Families in number of People, they differ'd from them too but little in number of Laws: And the Governours, being as the Fathers of them, watching over
5 them for their good, the Government was almost all *Prerogative*. A few establish'd Laws served the turn, and the discretion and care of the Ruler supply'd the rest. But when mistake, or flattery prevailed with weak Princes to make use of this Power, for private ends of their own, and not for the publick good, the
10 People were fain by express Laws to get Prerogative determin'd, in those points, wherein they found disadvantage from it: And thus declared *limitations of Prerogative* were by the People found necessary in Cases, which they and their Ancestors had left, in the utmost latitude, to the Wisdom of those Princes, who made
15 no other but a right use of it, that is, for the good of their People.

163. And therefore they have a very wrong Notion of Government, who say, that the People have *incroach'd upon the Prerogative*, when they have got any part of it to be defined by positive Laws. For in so doing, they have not pulled from the Prince any thing,
5 that of right belong'd to him, but only declared, that that Power which they indefinitely left in his, or his Ancestors, hands, to be exercised for their good, was not a thing, which they intended him, when he used it otherwise. For the end of government being the good of the Community, whatsoever alterations are
10 made in it, tending to that end, cannot be 'an *incroachment* upon any body: since no body in Government can have a right tending to any other end. And those only are *incroachments* which prejudice or hinder the publick good. Those who say otherwise, speak as if the Prince had a distinct and separate Interest from the good of
15 the Community, and was not made for it, the Root and Source, from which spring almost all those Evils, and Disorders, which happen in Kingly Governments. And indeed if that be so, the People under his Government are not a Society of Rational Creatures entred into a Community for their mutual good; they

§ 162   1–4   Compare references in note on 11, § 74, 14–37, Locke's concessions to patriarchalism. Pareyson compares Locke's discussion of prerogative with Filmer's (Laslett's edition, 105–6).
§ 163   19–23   Compare 1, § 156 note and references.

376

are not such as have set Rulers over themselves, to guard, and 20
promote that good; but are to be looked on as an Herd of inferiour
Creatures, under the Dominion of a Maſter, who keeps them, and
works them for his own Pleasure or Profit. If Men were so void
of Reason, and brutish, as to enter into Society upon such Terms,
Prerogative might indeed be, what some Men would have it, an 25
Arbitrary Power to do things hurtful to the People.

164. But since a Rational Creature cannot be supposed when
free, to put himself into Subje-tion to another, for his own harm:
(Though where he finds a good and wise Ruler, he may not
perhaps think it either necessary, or useful to set precise Bounds
to his Power in all things) *Prerogative* can be nothing, but the 5
Peoples permitting their Rulers, to do several things of their own
free choice, where the Law was silent, and sometimes too againſt
the direЄt Letter of the Law, for the publick good; and their
acquiescing in it when so done. For as a good Prince, who is
mindful of the truſt put into his hands, and careful of the good of 10
his People, cannot have too much *Prerogative*, that is, Power to
do good: So a weak and ill Prince, who would claim that Power,
which his Predecessors exercised without the direЄtion of the
Law, as a Prerogative belonging to him by Right of his Office,
which he may exercise at his pleasure, to make or promote an 15
Intereſt diſtinЄt from that of the publick, gives the People an
occasion, to claim their Right, and limit that Power, which, whilſt
it was exercised for their good, they were content should be
tacitly allowed.

165. And therefore he, that will look into the *Hiſtory of England*,
will find, that Prerogative was always *largeſt* in the hands of our
wiseſt and beſt Princes: because the People observing the whole
tendency of their AЄtions to be the publick good, conteſted not
what was done without Law to that end; or if any humane frailty 5
or miſtake (for Princes are but Men, made as others) appear'd
in some small declinations from that end; yet 'twas visible, the
main of their ConduЄt ténded to nothing but the care of the
publick. The People therefore finding reason to be satisfied with
these Princes, whenever they aЄted without or contrary to the 10
Letter of the Law, acquiesced in what they did, and, without the
leaſt complaint, let them inlarge their *Prerogative* as they pleased,
judging rightly, that they did nothing herein to the prejudice of

their Laws, since they acted conformable to the Foundation and
15 End of all Laws, the publick good.

166. Such God-like Princes indeed had some Title to Arbitrary
Power, by that Argument, that would prove Absolute Monarchy
the best Government, as that which God himself governs the
Universe by: because such Kings partake of his Wisdom and
5 Goodness. Upon this is founded that saying, That the Reigns
of good Princes have been always most dangerous to the Liberties
of their People. For when their Successors, managing the Government with different Thoughts, would draw the Actions of those
good Rulers into Precedent, and make them the Standard of their
10 *Prerogative*, as if what had been done only for the good of the
People, was a right in them to do, for the harm of the People, if
they so pleased; it has often occasioned Contest, and sometimes
publick Disorders, before the People could recover their original
Right, and get that to be declared not to be *Prerogative*, which
15 truly was never so: Since it is impossible, that any body in the
Society should ever have a right to do the People harm; though
it be very possible, and reasonable, that the People should not
go about to set any Bounds to the *Prerogative* of those Kings or
Rulers, who themselves transgressed not the Bounds of the
20 publick good. For *Prerogative is nothing but the Power of doing
publick good without a Rule.*

167. The Power of *calling Parliaments* in *England*, as to precise
time, place, and duration, is certainly a *Prerogative* of the King,
but still with this trust, that it shall be made use of for the good
of the Nation, as the Exigencies of the Times, and variety of
5 Occasions shall require. For it being impossible to forsee, which
should always be the fittest place for them to assemble in, and
what the best Season; the choice of these was left with the
Executive Power, as might be most subservient to the publick
good, and best suit the ends of Parliaments.

---

§ **166**   1   Compare note on 11, § 42, 21–8, verbal parallel.
§ **167**   This overt mention of the constitution of England, clearly in Locke's mind
throughout (compare 11, § 143, 15–21, note and references), especially in reference to
the summoning of Parliament (see note on 11, § 149, chapter xiii), conceivably refers
to the situation of late 1680–early 1681. Charles II then exercised his prerogative
right to call parliament where he wished (see line 1) and summoned it at Oxford as
a move against Shaftesbury and his Exclusionists: on Locke and the Oxford Parliament, see Introduction, 31.

168. The old Question will be asked in this matter of *Prerogative*, But *who shall be Judge* when this Power is made a right use of? I Answer: Between an Executive Power in being, with such a Prerogative, and a Legislative that depends upon his will for their convening, there can be no *Judge on Earth*: As there can be 5 none, between the Legislative, and the People, should either the Executive, or the Legislative, when they have got the Power in their hands, design, or go about to enslave, or destroy them. The People have no other remedy in this, as in all other cases where they have no Judge on Earth, but to *appeal to Heaven*. For the 10 Rulers, in such attempts, exercising a Power the People never put into their hands (who can never be supposed to consent, that any body should rule over them for their harm) do that, which they have not a right to do. And where the Body of the People, or any single Man, is deprived of their Right, or is under the 15 Exercise of a power without right, and have no Appeal on Earth, there they have a liberty to appeal to Heaven, whenever they judge the Cause of sufficient moment. And therefore, tho' the *People* cannot be *Judge*, so as to have by the Constitution of that Society any Superiour power, to determine and give effective 20

---

§ **168**   1–2   'The old Question . . . *who shall be Judge?*'—a question fundamental to the *Second Treatise*, see §§ 13, 19, 20, 89, 93, 125, 131, 136, 181, 240, 241, and compare the references to Jephthah in note on II, § 21, 17. The question is raised in a very similar form in the *Epistola de Tolerantia*: if the magistrate and the subjects disagree 'quis erit inter eos judex? Resp. solus Deus: qui inter legislatorem et populum nullus in terris est judex' (Klibansky and Gough, 1968, 128: in the translation 'legislatorem' becomes 'supreme magistrate').

McIlwain, 1935, suggests that Locke was recalling here the doctrine of Hunton's *Treatise of Monarchie*, 1643, for he also asks again and again 'Who shall be the judge of the excesses of the sovereign lord in monarchies of this composure?'. His conclusion is: 'There can be no judge legal and constituted within that frame of government . . . an Appeale must be made *ad conscientiam generis humani*. . . . The fundamentall Lawes of that Monarchy must judge and pronounce sentence in every man's conscience.' Hunton, it will be seen, was talking of a particular form of government, a mixed monarchy, whereas Locke seems to be talking of all possible forms of government. Hunton's appeal is to everyone's conscience, which Filmer triumphantly pronounced as plain anarchy, whilst Locke's final appeal is to God, though he does occasionally talk of conscience in this connection (see II, § 21, 23). He possessed Hunton's book (H. and L. 2013), and he may have been influenced by him. It seems much more likely, however, that it was Filmer's criticism of Hunton (see, for example, Laslett's edition, 294–5) which was in question and shows that the paragraph belongs to 1679. In II, § 240, Locke contradicts what is said here in line 5; see Polin, 1960, 225.

15   'any single Man'—Locke at his most anarchistic; see Kendall, 1941, 89, and Strauss, 1953, 237.

Sentence in the case; yet they have, by a Law antecedent and paramount to all positive Laws of men, reserv'd that ultimate Determination to themselves, which belongs to all Mankind, where there lies no Appeal on Earth, *viz.* to judge whether they
25 have just Cause to make their Appeal to Heaven. And this Judgment they cannot part with, it being out of a Man's power so to submit himself to another, as to give him a liberty to destroy him; God and Nature never allowing a Man so to abandon himself, as to neglect his own preservation: And since he cannot take away
30 his own Life, neither can he give another power to take it. Nor let any one think, this lays a perpetual foundation for Disorder: for this operates not, till the Inconvenience is so great, that the Majority feel it, and are weary of it, and find a necessity to have it amended. But this the Executive Power, or wise Princes,
35 never need come in the danger of: And 'tis the thing of all others, they have most need to avoid, as of all others the most perilous.

Chap. XV.

Of Paternal, Political, and Despotical Power, considered together.

169. THough I have had occasion to speak of these separately before, yet the great mistakes of late about Government, having, as I suppose, arisen from confounding these distinct Powers one with another, it may not, perhaps, be amiss, to con-
5 sider them here together.

§ **169** *Chapter* xv This chapter is very similar to chapter ix; see note on II, § 123. It is repetitive and recapitulatory, it uses the general argument to reflect upon James II (see note on II, § 172, 10–19), it recalls II, §§ 2, 3, the introductory paragraphs clearly written in 1689 (see for instance, § 169 and § 171, 1–5). It has every indication of having been written in 1689 and it is interesting to see Locke, especially in § 174, linking his controversy with Filmer and his theory of property, with the political situation immediately after the Revolution.

170. *First* then, *Paternal* or *Parental Power* is nothing but that, which Parents have over their Children, to govern them for the Childrens good, till they come to the use of Reason, or a State of Knowledge, wherein they may be supposed capable to understand that Rule, whether it be the Law of Nature, or the municipal   5
Law of their Country they are to govern themselves by: Capable, I say, to know it, as well as several others, who live, as Free-men, under that Law. The Affection and Tenderness, which God hath planted in the Breasts of Parents, towards their Children, makes it evident, that this is not intended to be a severe Arbitrary   10
Government, but only for the Help, Instruction, and Preservation of their Off-spring. But happen it as it will, there is, as I have proved, no reason, why it should be thought, to extend to Life and Death, at any time, over their Children, more than over any body else, neither can there be any pretence why this parental   15
power should keep the Child, when grown to a Man, in subjection to the Will of his Parents any farther, than the having received Life and Education from his Parents, obliges him to respect, Honour, Gratitude, Assistance, and Support all his Life to both Father and Mother. And thus, 'tis true, the *Paternal* is a natural   20
Government, but not at all extending it self to the Ends, and Jurisdictions of that which is Political. The *Power of the Father doth not reach* at all to the *Property* of the Child, which is only in his own disposing.

171. *Secondly, Political Power* is that Power which every Man, having in the State of Nature, has given up into the hands of the Society, and therein to the Governours, whom the Society hath set over it self, with this express or tacit Trust, That it shall be imployed for their good, and the preservation of their Property: 5
Now this *Power*, which every Man has *in the State of Nature*, and which he parts with to the Society, in all such cases, where the Society can secure him, is, to use such means for the preserving

---

§ 170   This paragraph was corrected in detail by Locke in the Christ's copy, see Collation in Second Edition (repr. 1988): in rewriting lines 15–17 he omits a statement about 'the perfect use of Reason' and the attainment of manhood.

1   See II, § 69, 1, note and references, and on this paragraph as a whole compare chapter VI of the *Second Treatise* (§§ 52–76).

18   'Education', etc.—see note on II, § 58.

23   '*Property* of the Child'—see note on II, § 65, 17–24.

§ 171   1–5   Compare II, § 3, note and references.

of his own Property, as he thinks good, and Nature allows him;
10 and to punish the Breach of the Law of Nature in others so, as
(according to the best of his Reason) may most conduce to the
preservation of himself, and the rest of Mankind. So that the
end and measure of this Power, when in every Man's hands in the
State of Nature, being the preservation of all of his Society, that is,
15 all Mankind in general, it can have no other *end or measure*, when
in the hands of the Magistrate, but to preserve the Members of
that Society in their Lives, Liberties, and Possessions; and so
cannot be an Absolute, Arbitrary Power over their Lives and
Fortunes, which are as much as possible to be preserved; but
20 a *Power to make Laws*, and annex such *Penalties* to them, as may
tend to the preservation of the whole, by cutting off those Parts,
and those only, which are so corrupt, that they threaten the
sound and healthy, without which no severity is lawful. And this
Power has its Original only from Compact and Agreement, and the
25 mutual Consent of those who make up the Community.

172. *Thirdly, Despotical Power* is an Absolute, Arbitrary Power
one Man has over another, to take away his Life, whenever he
pleases. This is a Power, which neither Nature gives, for it has
made no such distinction between one Man and another; nor
5 Compact can convey, for Man not having such an Arbitrary Power
over his own Life, cannot give another Man such a Power over
it; but it is *the effect only of Forfeiture*, which the Aggressor makes

---

17 Compare II, § 87, 5, note and references, and II, §§ 87–9 on the whole
paragraph.
§ 172 9–19 This passage was rewritten and extended in the margin of the
Christ's copy, printed in the editions of Locke's lifetime. The effect is to give greater
emphasis and to strengthen the implication that a despot, a king for instance who uses force
against his people, is a 'wild beast, or noxious brute': compare the ferocious quotation from
Livy added to the title page in the Christ's copy at the time these corrections were made.
Even in the original version, this seems to be a clear reference to James II and his
activities, in very hostile, even spiteful terms, which is one of the indications that
this paragraph and the whole chapter were an insertion of 1689; see note on II, § 169,
chapter xv. There are many similar statements throughout the *Second Treatise*:
compare § 10, 2–5; § 11, 24–6 (verbal parallel); § 16, 4–8 (verbal parallel); § 181, 16–20
(verbal parallel); § 182, 21; § 230, 35–7; and it is possible that some of these were likewise put in or touched up in 1689. But the sentiment is very close to the description
of the subjects of absolute monarchies as herds of animals (see I, § 156, note and
references) and both arise quite naturally from Locke's general theory; see Introduction, 95. Taken together they seem to express Locke's way of describing
despotism, emphasized and sharpened in 1689, and again here in the later 1690s.

of his own Life, when he puts himself into the State of War with
another. For having quitted Reason, which God hath given to
be the Rule betwixt Man and Man, and the common bond whereby 10
humane kind is united into one fellowship and societie; and having
renounced the way of peace, which that teaches, and made use
of the Force of War to compasse his unjuSt ends upon an other,
where he has no right, and so revolting from his own kind to
that of BeaSts by making Force which is theirs, to be his rule of 15
right, he renders himself liable to be deStroied by the injur'd
person and the reSt of mankind, that will joyn with him in the
execution of JuStice, as any other wild beaSt, or noxious brute
†with whom Mankind can have neither Society nor Security†. And
thus *Captives*, taken in a juSt and lawful War, and such only, are 20
subjeƈt to a Despotical Power, which as it arises not from Compaƈt,
so neither is it capable of any, but is the State of War continued.
For what Compaƈt can be made with a Man that is not MaSter of
his own Life? What Condition can he perform? And if he be
once allowed to be MaSter of his own Life, the *Despotical, Arbitrary* 25
Power of his MaSter ceases. He that is MaSter of himself, and his
own Life, has a right too to the means of preserving it, so that
as soon as Compaƈt enters, Slavery ceases, and he so far quits his
Absolute Power, and puts an end to the State of War, who enters
into Conditions with his Captive. 30

† that is destructive to their being.†

173. *Nature gives* the firSt of these, *viz. Paternal Power to Parents*
for the Benefit of their Children during their Minority, to supply
their want of Ability, and underStanding how to manage their
Property. (By *Property* I muSt be underStood here, as in other
places, to mean that Property which Men have in their Persons 5
as well as Goods.) *Voluntary Agreement gives* the second, *viz.*
Political Power to Governours for the Benefit of their Subjeƈts, to
secure them in the Possession and Use of their Properties. And

19 *Alternative Reading.* For its authenticity and status, see Collation: it was
apparently an afterthought of Locke's, who seems to have decided to revert to the
original reading, and is critical to the relationship of the two master copies and the
texts which follow them; see Editorial Note.

§ 173   4–6 Compare II, § 87, 5 note and references.   5 Compare II, § 27, 2.
8–10 Compare II, § 138 and Cicero, *ejus* (sc. of society) *autem vinculum est ratio et*
oratio.

Forfeiture gives the third, *Despotical power to Lords* for their own
10 Benefit, over those who are ſtripp'd of all property.

174. He, that shall conſider the diſtinƈt rise and extent, and
the different ends of these several powers, will plainly see, that
paternal Power comes as far short of that of the *Magiſtrate*, as
Despotical exceeds it; and that *Absolute Dominion*, however placed,
5 is so far from being one kind of Civil Society, that it is as in-
conſiſtent with it, as Slavery is with Property. *Paternal Power* is
only where Minority makes the Child incapable to manage his
property; *Political* where Men have Property in their own disposal; and *Despotical* over such as have no property at all.

Снар. XVI.

Of CONQUEST.

175. THough Governments can originally have no other Rise
than that before mentioned, nor *Polities* be *founded* on
any thing but *the Consent of the People*; yet such has been the Disorders Ambition has fill'd the World with, that in the noise of
5 War, which makes so great a part of the Hiſtory of Mankind,

§ **175** *Chapter* xvi This chapter cannot be dated with any certainty, nevertheless
in the editor's opinion it belongs to the early stages of composition and was probably
written in 1681 or 1682; compare Martyn Thompson, 1976. Though it is connected with the
rest of the text (see the cross-reference in II, § 112, 15–17) the relationship is with the assumed
1681 addition (§§ 100–23; see note on § 100 and on § 95, chapter viii). Like chapters ix and xv
it is recapitulatory, and like them it leads to a reflection on the origin, rights and powers of a
monarchy which can only be English. It may then be pronounced an insertion, but there is
some doubt whether it was an insertion of 1681 or of 1689. Goldie, 1977, demonstrates that
the conquest argument was used on the traditionalist side in 1688–90. But there was an earlier
exchange over the Norman Conquest in 1681 and 1682; see Pocock, 1957, chapter vii, 'The
Brady Controversy'. This chapter, then, may be regarded as Locke's comment on this
conquest controversy in terms of his political theory, perhaps extended and amended in 1689,
though in ways not now recovered.
  6–8 It is not quite clear who were the many who reckoned 'Conquest as one of

this *Consent* is little taken notice of: And therefore many have miſtaken the force of Arms, for the consent of the People; and reckon Conqueſt as one of the Originals of Government. But *Conqueſt* is as far from setting up any Government, as demolishing an House is from building a new one in the place. Indeed it often 10 makes way for a new Frame of a Common-wealth, by deſtroying the former; but, without the Consent of the people, can never erect a new one.

176. That the *Aggreſſor*, who puts himself into the ſtate of War with another, and *unjuſtly invades* another Man's right, *can*, by such an unjuſt War, *never* come to *have a right over the Conquered*, will be easily agreed by all Men, who will not think, that Robbers and Pyrates have a Right of Empire over whomsoever 5 they have Force enough to maſter; or that Men are bound by promises, which unlawful Force extorts from them. Should a Robber break into my House, and with a Dagger at my Throat, make me seal Deeds to convey my Eſtate to him, would this give him any Title? Juſt such a Title by his Sword, has an *unjuſt* 10 *Conquerour*, who forces me into Submission. The Injury and the Crime is equal, whether committed by the wearer of a Crown, or some petty Villain. The Title of the Offender, and the Number of

---

the Originals of Government'. As Pocock has pointed out (1957, see especially 53–4, 148–50; compare Zagorin, 1954, 67–70), the English populist writers of the seventeenth century, including Milton, Locke and Sidney, all wrote as if the defenders of kingship and absolutism had argued from conquest, but in fact they did not. Filmer never used the argument, in anything like the form in which Locke attacked it, though his defender against Sidney, Edmund Bohun, finally approved of the justification of William III as a conqueror in 1688 as a way of settling Tory doubts (Bohun, *Diary*, 1853, 67, 101–13). Grotius is the only one of the great natural lawyers who even approached the position which Locke demolishes (*De Jure Belli*, III, viii, 8). There remains Hobbes, who assimilates patriarchal and despotic government as both based on force and presumably in some cases conquest as Locke discusses it, and sets it up as an alternative to his 'Commonwealth by Institution' (*Leviathan*, chapters 19, 20): he also talks of William I as a conqueror and of his successors exercising his right by conquest, in his *Dialogue of the Common Laws* and *Behemoth*. Goldie, 1977, makes it clear that Grotius was used by the conquest theorists in 1688–9, and it is possible, though not likely, that Locke had their case exclusively in mind.
§ 176   7–10   Compare II, § 186, 15–21, where the dagger becomes a 'Pistol at my breast'. Molyneux, 1698, in paraphrasing this passage seems to have conflated the two contexts (1720, 16). Hobbes believed that 'Covenants extorted by feare are valide' (1904, 94), but here and in this chapter Locke may be re-echoing Pufendorf (see especially 1672, VII, vii, 3), who in turn comments on Grotius, 1625, II, 3, 4.

his Followers make no difference in the Offence, unless it be to
15 aggravate it. The only difference is, Great Robbers punish little
ones, to keep them in their Obedience, but the great ones are
rewarded with Laurels and Triumphs, because they are too big
for the weak hands of Justice in this World, and have the power
in their own possession, which should punish Offenders. What is
20 my Remedy against a Robber, that so broke into my House?
Appeal to the Law for Justice. But perhaps Justice is denied, or
I am crippled and cannot stir, robbed and have not the means to
do it. If God has taken away all means of seeking remedy, there
is nothing left but patience. But my Son, when able, may seek
25 the Relief of the Law, which I am denied: He or his Son may
renew his *Appeal*, till he recover his Right. But the Conquered,
or their Children, have no Court, no Arbitrator on Earth to appeal
to. Then they may *appeal*, as *Jephtha* did, *to Heaven*, and repeat
their *Appeal*, till they have recovered the native Right of their
30 Ancestors, which was to have such a Legislative over them, as
the Majority should approve, and freely acquiesce in. If it be
objected, this would cause endless trouble; I answer, No more
than Justice does, where she lies open to all that appeal to her.
He that troubles his Neighbour without a Cause, is punished for
35 it by the Justice of the Court he appeals to. And he that *appeals
to Heaven*, must be sure he has Right on his side; and a Right too
that is worth the Trouble and Cost of the Appeal, as he will answer
at a Tribunal, that cannot be deceived, and will be sure to retribute
to every one according to the Mischiefs he hath created to his
40 Fellow-Subjects; that is, any part of Mankind. From whence 'tis
plain, that he that *Conquers in an unjust War, can* thereby *have no
Title to the Subjection and Obedience of the Conquered.*

177. But supposing Victory favours the right side, let us consider a *Conquerour in a lawful War*, and see what power he gets, and
over whom.

First, 'Tis plain he *gets no Power* by his Conquest *over those that*
5 *Conquered with him*. They that fought on his side cannot suffer by

28 'Jephtha'—see note on II, § 21, 17 and references.
§ 177 Molyneux, 1698, summarizes this paragraph: he quotes verbatim from lines
4–7, and uses phrases from lines 23–6; 1720, 16.
1–11 Compare Tyrrell, 1681, 85: 'Though some Governments have begun by
Conquest', yet those who fought with the conquerors 'had no obligation to serve
them, but from their own agreements which included a share of the conquests'.

the Conquest, but must at least be as much Freemen as they were
before. And most commonly they serve upon Terms, and on
Condition to share with their Leader, and enjoy a part of the
Spoil, and other Advantages that attend the Conquering Sword:
or at least have a part of the subdued Country bestowed upon 10
them. And *the Conquering People are not*, I hope, to be *Slaves by
Conquest*, and wear their Laurels only to shew they are Sacrifices
to their Leaders Triumph. They that found Absolute Monarchy
upon the Title of the Sword, make their Heroes, who are the
Founders of such Monarchies, arrant *Draw-can-Sirs*, and forget 15
they had any Officers and Soldiers that fought on their side in
the Battles they won, or assisted them in the subduing, or shared
in possessing the Countries they Master'd. We are told by some,
that the *English* Monarchy is founded in the *Norman* Conquest,
and that our Princes have thereby a Title to absolute Dominion: 20
Which if it were true, (as by the History it appears otherwise)
and that *William* had a right to make War on this Island; yet his
Dominion by Conquest could reach no farther, than to the *Saxons*
and *Britains* that were then Inhabitants of this Country. The
Normans that came with him, and helped to Conquer, and all 25
descended from them are Freemen and no Subjects by Conquest;
let that give what Dominion it will. And if I, or any Body else,
shall claim freedom, as derived from them, it will be very hard
to prove the contrary: And 'tis plain, the Law that has made no
distinction between the one and the other, intends not there should 30
be any difference in their Freedom or Priviledges.

178. But supposing, which seldom happens, that the Conquerers and Conquered never incorporate into one People, under
the same Laws and Freedom. Let us see next *what Power a
lawful Conquerer has over the Subdued*; and that I say is purely
Despotical. He has an Absolute Power over the Lives of those, 5
who by an Unjust War have forfeited them; but not over the

---

15 '*Draw-can-Sirs*'—characters who kill off everybody on all sides, a proverbial
phrase from the Duke of Buckingham's play *The Rehearsal*, composed 1663/4,
performed 1671 and often afterwards.
    19–24 This is the only mention of the Norman Conquest—see note on II, § 175
(chapter XVI): the 'some' who made it the foundation of the English monarchy are
discussed in the note to II, § 175, 6–8.
§ 178 5–6 Compare II, § 23, 9–13, and note on II, § 24, 1–8—Locke on slavery.
Molyneux, 1698, paraphrases the two passages; 1720, 18

Lives or Fortunes of those, who ingaged not in the War, nor over the Possessions even of those, who were actually engaged in it.

179. *Secondly*, I say then the *Conquerour* gets no Power but only over those, who have actually assisted, concurr'd, or consented to that unjust force, that is used against him. For the People having given to their Governours no Power to do an unjust thing, such
5 as is to make an unjust War, (for they never had such a Power in themselves:) They ought not to be charged, as guilty of the Violence and Unjustice that is committed in an Unjust War, any farther, than they actually abet it; no more, than they are to be thought guilty of any Violence or Oppression their Governours
10 should use upon the People themselves, or any part of their Fellow Subjects, they having impowered them no more to the one, than to the other. Conquerours, 'tis true, seldom trouble themselves to make the distinction, but they willingly permit the confusion of War to sweep altogether; but yet this alters not the Right:
15 For the Conquerours Power over the Lives of the Conquered, being only because they have used force to do, or maintain an Injustice, he can have that power only over those, who have concurred in that force, all the rest are innocent; and he has no more Title over the People of that Country, who have done him
20 no Injury, and so have made no forfeiture of their Lives, than he has over any other, who, without any injuries or provocations, have lived upon fair terms with him.

180. *Thirdly*, The *power a Conquerour gets* over those he over-comes *in a Just War, is perfectly Despotical*: he has an absolute power over the Lives of those, who by putting themselves in a State of War, have forfeited them; but he has not thereby a Right and
5 Title to their Possessions. This I doubt not, but at first sight will seem a strange Doctrine, it being so quite contrary to the practice of the World; There being nothing more familiar in speaking of the Dominion of Countries, than to say, such an one Conquer'd it. As if Conquest, without any more ado, convey'd a right of
10 Possession. But when we consider, that the practice of the strong and powerful, how universal soever it may be, is seldom the rule of Right, however it be one part of the subjection of the Con-quered, not to argue against the Conditions, cut out to them by the Conquering Sword.

181. Though in all War there be usually a complication of force and damage, and the Aggressor seldom fails to harm the Estate, when he uses force against the Persons of those he makes War upon; yet 'tis the use of Force only, that puts a Man into the State of War. For whether by force he begins the injury, or else having quietly, and by fraud, done the injury, he refuses to make reparation, and by force maintains it, (which is the same thing as at first to have done it by force) 'tis the unjust use of force that makes the War. For he that breaks open my House, and violently turns me out of Doors; or having peaceably got in, by force keeps me out, does in effect the same thing; supposing we are in such a State, that we have no common Judge on Earth, whom I may appeal to, and to whom we are both obliged to submit: For of such I am now speaking. 'Tis the *unjust use of force* then, that *puts a Man into the state of War* with another, and thereby he, that is guilty of it, makes a forfeiture of his Life. For quitting reason, which is the rule given between Man and Man, and using force the way of Beasts, he becomes liable to be destroyed by him he uses force against, as any savage ravenous Beast, that is dangerous to his being.

182. But because the miscarriages of the Father are no faults of the Children, and they may be rational and peaceable, notwithstanding the brutishness and injustice of the Father; the Father, by his miscarriages and violence, can forfeit but his own Life, but involves not his Children in his guilt or destruction. His goods, which Nature, that willeth the preservation of all Mankind as much as is possible, hath made to belong to the Children to keep them from perishing, do still continue to belong to his Children. For supposing them not to have joyn'd in the War, either through Infancy, absence, or choice, they have done nothing

---

§ 181   The French version (1691, etc., see Introduction, 12) differs more widely from the English in this paragraph than elsewhere, though the variations, which may have had Locke's approval, do not alter the sense.

12   'no common Judge on Earth'—compare note on II, § 168, 1–2 and references.

16–20   See note on II, § 172, 10–19 and references. Molyneux, 1698, after copying a phrase from II, § 178, 5, paraphrases this paragraph to this point, then reproduces these final phrases almost exactly; 1720, 18–19.

§ 182   1–9   See I, § 89 on, and II, § 72 on, for Locke's general account of children's rights in the property of their fathers and compare Molyneux (1698), 1720, 19 and 21.

to forfeit them: *nor has the Conqueror any right* to take them away, by the bare title of having subdued him, that by force attempted his deſtruction; though perhaps he may have some right to them, to repair the damages he has suſtained by the War, and the defence of his own right, which how far it reaches to the possessions of the Conquered, we shall see by and by. So that he that *by Conqueſt has a right over a Man's Person* to deſtroy him if he pleases, has *not* thereby a right *over his Eſtate* to possess and enjoy it. For it is the brutal force the Aggressor has used, that gives his Adversary a right to take away his Life, and deſtroy him if he pleases, as a noxious Creature; but 'tis damage suſtain'd that alone gives him Title to another Mans Goods: For though I may kill a Thief that sets on me in the Highway, yet I may not (which seems less) take away his Money and let him go; this would be Robbery on my side. His force, and the ſtate of War he put himself in, made him forfeit his Life, but gave me no Title to his Goods. The *right* then *of Conqueſt extends only to the Lives* of those who joyn'd in the War, *not to their Eſtates*, but only in order to make reparation for the damages received, and the Charges of the War, and that too with reservation of the right of the innocent Wife and Children.

183. Let the *Conqueror* have as much Juſtice on his side, as could be supposed, he *has* no *right* to seize more than the vanquished could forfeit; his Life is at the Victors Mercy, and his Service and Goods he may appropriate to make himself reparation; but he cannot take the Goods of his Wife and Children; they too had a Title to the Goods he enjoy'd, and their shares in the Eſtate he possessed. For Example, I in the ſtate of Nature (and all Commonwealths are in the ſtate of Nature one with another) have injured another Man, and refusing to give satisfaction, it comes to a ſtate of War, wherein my defending by force, what I had gotten unjuſtly, makes me the Aggressor. I am Conquered: My Life, 'tis true, as forfeit, is at mercy, but not my Wives and Childrens. They made not the War, nor assiſted in it. I could not forfeit their Lives, they were not mine to forfeit. My wife had a share in my Eſtate, that neither could I forfeit. And my Children also, being born of me, had a right to be maintained out of my

---

21   See II, § 172, 10–19, note and references.
22–7 See II, §§ 18; 19; 176, 7–10 and note.
§ 183 7–8 See II, § 141, 8, notes and references.

labour or Subﬅance. Here then is the Case; The Conqueror
has a Title to Reparation for Damages received, and the Children
have a Title to their Father's Eﬅate for their Subsiﬅence. For as
to the Wife's share, whether her own Labour or Compaﬅ gave 20
her a Title to it, 'tis plain, Her Husband could not forfeit what
was hers. What muﬅ be done in the case? I answer; The Fundamental Law of Nature being, that all, as much as may be, should
be preserved, it follows, that if there be not enough fully to *satisfy*
both, *viz.* for the *Conqueror's Losses*, and Childrens Maintenance, 25
he that hath, and to spare, muﬅ remit something of his full Satis-
faﬅion, and give way to the pressing and preferable Title of those,
who are in danger to perish without it.

184. But supposing the *Charge* and *Damages of the War* are to
be made up to the Conqueror, to the utmoﬅ Farthing, and that
the Children of the vanquished, spoiled of all their Father's
Goods, are to be left to ﬅarve and perish: yet the satisfying of
what shall on this score, be due to the Conqueror, will scarce 5
give him a *Title to any Countrey he shall Conquer*. For the Damages
of War can scarce amount to the value of any considerable *Traﬅ
of Land*, in any part of the World, where all the Land is possessed,
and none lies waﬅe. And if I have not taken away the Conqueror's
Land, which, being vanquished, it is impossible I should; scarce 10
any other spoil I have done him, can amount to the value of mine,
supposing it equally cultivated and of an extent any way coming
near, what I had over run of his. The deﬅruﬅion of a Years
Produﬅ or two, (for it seldom reaches four or five) is the utmoﬅ
spoil, that usually can be done. For as to Money, and such Riches 15
and Treasure taken away, these are none of Natures Goods, they
have but a Phantaﬅical imaginary value: Nature has put no such
upon them: They are of no more account by her ﬅandard, than
the Wampompeke of the *Americans* to an *European* Prince, or the
Silver Money of *Europe* would have been formerly to an *American*. 20
And five years Produﬅ is not worth the perpetual Inheritance
of *Land*, where all is possessed, and none remains waﬅe to be
taken up by him, that is disseiz'd: Which will be easily granted,
if one do but take away the imaginary value of Money, the dis-

---

§ 184   15–18   Compare II, § 46, 5–7, note and references.
    19   'Wampompeke'—wampum; vocal equivalent of 'wampumpeag', bead
money of the Algonkin Indians.

25 proportion being more, than between five and five hundred. Though, at the same time, half a years produ&t is more worth than the Inheritance, where there being more *Land*, than the Inhabitants possess, and make use of, any one has liberty to make use of the wa&te: But there Conquerers take little care to possess

30 themselves of the *Lands of the Vanquished*. No damage therefore, that Men in the &tate of Nature (as all Princes and Governments are in reference to one another) suffer from one another, can give a Conqueror Power, to dispossess the Po&terity of the Vanquished, and turn them out of their Inheritance, which ought to be the Possession of them and their Descendants to all Genera-

35 tions. The Conquerour indeed will be apt to think himself Ma&ter: And 'tis the very condition of the subdued not to be able to dispute their Right. But if that be all, it gives no other Title than what bare Force gives to the &tronger over the weaker. And, by

40 this reason, he that is &tronge&t will have a right to whatever he pleases to seize on.

185. Over those then, that joined with him in the War, and over those of the subdued Countrey that opposed him not, and the Po&terity even of those that did, the Conqueror, even in a ju&t War, hath, *by* his *Conque&t, no right of Dominion*: They are free

5 from any subje&tion to him, and if their former Government be dissolved, they are at liberty to begin and ere&t another to themselves.

186. The Conquerour, 'tis true, usually, by the Force he has over them, compels them, with a Sword at their Brea&ts, to &toop to his Conditions, and submit to such a Government as he pleases to afford them; but the enquiry is, What right he has to do so?

5 If it be said, they submit by their own consent; then this allows their own *consent* to be *necessary to give the Conquerour a Title to rule* over them. It remains only to be considered, whether *Promises*, *extorted by Force*, without Right, can be thought Consent, and *how far they bind*. To which I shall say, they *bind not at all*; because

---

25 'five hundred'—'five thousand' in the 1st edition. The disproportion is between the value of five years product and the value of the land in perpetuity. Compare chapter v, especially § 40 on, and note on § 45, 20–2.

31–2 Compare ii, §§ 183, 7–8; 14, 3–8, note and references.

§ 186 Molyneux, 1698, reproduces this paragraph almost in full: he follows Locke's exact words in lines 2–8, 12–14, 17–19. See ii, § 176, 7–10 and references.

whatsoever another gets from me by force, I still retain the Right of, and he is obliged presently to restore. He that forces my Horse from me, ought presently to restore him, and I have still a right to retake him. By the same reason, he that *forced a Promise* from me, ought presently to restore it, *i.e.* quit me of the Obligation of it; or I may resume it my self, *i.e.* chuse whether I will perform it. For the Law of Nature laying an Obligation on me, only by the Rules she prescribes, cannot oblige me by the violation of her Rules: Such is the extorting any thing from me by force. Nor does it at all alter the case, to say I *gave my Promise*, no more than it excuses the force, and passes the Rig t, when I put my Hand in my Pocket, and deliver my Purse my self to a Thief, who demands it with a Pistol at my Breast.

187. From all which it follows, that the *Government of a Conquerour*, imposed, by force, on the Subdued, against whom he had no right of War, or who joyned not in the War against him, where he had right, *has no Obligation* upon them.

188. But let us suppose that all the Men of that Community being all Members of the same Body Politick, may be taken to have joyn'd in that unjust War, wherein they are subdued, and so their Lives are at the Mercy of the Conquerour.

189. I say, this concerns not their Children, who are in their Minority. For since a Father hath not, in himself, a Power over the Life or Liberty of his Child; no act of his can possibly forfeit it: So that the Children, whatever may have happened to the Fathers, are Free-men, and the Absolute Power of the *Conquerour* reaches no farther than the Persons of the Men, that were subdued by him, and dies with them; and should he Govern them as Slaves, subjected to his Absolute, Arbitrary Power, he *has no* such *Right of Dominion over their Children*. He can have no Power over them, but by their own consent, whatever he may drive them to say, or do; and he has no lawful Authority, whilst Force, and not Choice, compels them to submission.

190. Every Man is born with a double Right: *First, A Right of Freedom to his Person*, which no other Man has a Power over, but

---

§§ 189, 190, 191   Here Locke returns to first principles; see i, § 88 on for inheritance, ii, § 4 for natural freedom, now coupled with inheritance, and ii, §§ 72, 73 and 116 for natural freedom from subjection to any government.

the free Disposal of it lies in himself. *Secondly, A Right*, before any other Man, to *inherit*, with his Brethren, his Fathers Goods.

191. By the first of these, a Man is *naturally free* from subjection to any Government, though he be born in a place under its Jurisdiction. But if he disclaim the lawful Government of the Country he was born in, he must also quit the Right that belong'd
5 to him by the Laws of it, and the Possessions there descending to him from his Ancestors, if it were a Government made by their consent.

192. By the second, the *Inhabitants* of any Countrey, who are descended, and derive a Title to their Estates from those, who are subdued, and had a Government forced upon them against their free consents, *retain a Right to the Possession of their Ancestors*,
5 though they consent not freely to the Government, whose hard Conditions were by force imposed on the Possessors of that Country. For the first *Conqueror never* having *had a Title to the Land* of that Country, the People who are the Descendants of, or claim under those, who were forced to submit to the Yoke of
10 a Government by constraint, have always a Right to shake it off, and free themselves from the Usurpation, or Tyranny, which the Sword hath brought in upon them, till their Rulers put them under such a Frame of Government, as they willingly, and of choice consent to. Who doubts but the Grecian Christians descendants
15 of the ancient possessors of that Country may justly cast off the Turkish yoke which they have so long groaned under when ever they have a power to do it? For no Government can have a right to obedience from a people who have not freely consented to it: which they can never be supposed to do, till either they are put
20 in a full state of Liberty to chuse their Government and Governors, or at least till they have such standing Laws, to which they have by themselves or their Representatives, given their free consent, and also till they are allowed their due property, which is so to be Proprietors of what they have, that no body can take away
25 any part of it without their own consent, without which, Men under any Government are not in the state of Free-men, but are direct Slaves under the Force of War.

§ 192   14–19   Locke modified this paragraph in the Christ's copy, inserting here the passage on the Grecian Christians which in the printed editions had come at the end. Rau, 1987, makes effective use of this passage in relation to late twentieth-century regimes.

193. But granting that the *Conqueror* in a juſt War has a Right to the Eſtates, as well as Power over the Persons of the Conquered; which, 'tis plain, he *hath* not: Nothing of *Absolute Power* will follow from hence, in the continuance of the Government. Because the Descendants of these being all Free-men, if he grants 5 them Eſtates and Possessions to inhabit his Country (without which it would be worth nothing) whatsoever he grants them, they have, so far as it is granted, *property* in. The nature whereof is, that *without a Man's own consent* it *cannot be taken from him*.

194. Their *Persons* are *free* by a Native Right, and their *properties*, be they more or less, are *their own, and at their own dispose*, and not at his; or else it is no property. Supposing the Conqueror gives to one Man a Thousand Acres, to him and his Heirs for ever; to another he lets a Thousand Acres for his Life, under the 5 Rent of 50 *l*. or 500. *l. per Ann*. Has not the one of these a Right to his Thousand Acres for ever, and the other, during his Life, paying the said Rent? And hath not the Tenant for Life a *property* in all that he gets over and above his Rent, by his Labour and Induſtry during the said term, supposing it be double the Rent? 10 Can any one say, The King, or Conqueror, after his Grant, may by his Power of Conqueror, take away all, or part of the Land from the Heirs of one, or from the other, during his Life, he paying the Rent? Or can he take away from either, the Goods or Money they have got upon the said Land, at his pleasure? If he 15 can, then all free and voluntary *Contracts* cease, and are void, in the World; there needs nothing to dissolve them at any time but Power enough: And all the *Grants* and Promises *of Men in power*, are but Mockery and Collusion. For can there be any thing more ridiculous than to say, I give you and yours this for ever; and 20 that in the sureſt and moſt solemn way of conveyance can be devised: And yet it is to be underſtood, that I have Right, if I please, to take it away from you again to Morrow?

195. I will not dispute now whether Princes are exempt from the Laws of their Countrey; but this I am sure, they owe subjeċtion to the Laws of God and Nature. No Body, no Power can exempt

---

§ 194 In this paragraph Locke is, typically, using the land-law of his time and country to illustrate what was, to him, a universal principle. He is still slightly ambiguous on the point of an individual having to consent as an individual to each act of alienation, cf. 11, § 139, 5–7 and note.

them from the Obligations of that Eternal Law. Those are so
5 great, and so strong, in the case of *Promises*, that Omnipotency
it self can be tyed by them. *Grants, Promises* and *Oaths* are
Bonds that *hold the Almighty*: Whatever some Flatterers say to
Princes of the World who all together, with all their People
joined to them, are in comparison of the great God, but as a
10 Drop of the Bucket, or a Dust on the Balance, inconsiderable
nothing!

196. The short of the *Case in Conquest* is this. The Conqueror,
if he have a just Cause, has a Despotical Right over the Persons
of all, that actually aided, and concurred in the War against him,
and a Right to make up his Damage and Cost out of their Labour
5 and Estates, so he injure not the Right of any other. Over the
rest of the People, if there were any that consented not to the
War, and over the Children of the Captives themselves, or the
Possessions of either he has no Power; and so can have, *by Virtue
of Conquest, no lawful Title* himself *to Dominion* over them, or derive
10 it to his Posterity; but is an Aggressor, if he attempts upon their
properties, and thereby puts himself in a state of War against them;
and has no better a Right of Principality, he, nor any of his Successors, than *Hingar*, or *Hubba* the *Danes* had here in *England*; or
Spartacus, had he Conquered *Italy* would have had; which is to
15 have their Yoke cast off, as soon as God shall give those under
their subjection Courage and Opportunity to do it. Thus, notwithstanding whatever Title the Kings of *Assyria* had over *Judah*, by
the Sword, God assisted *Hezekiah* to throw off the Dominion of
that Conquering Empire. *And the Lord was with Hezekiah, and*
20 *he prospered; wherefore he went forth, and he rebelled against the King of*
Assyria, and served him not, 2. Kings XVIII. vij. Whence it is plain,
that shaking off a Power, which Force, and not Right hath set
over any one, though it hath the Name of *Rebellion*, yet is no

---

§ **195** 6–7 Compare 1, § 6, 6: Hobbes (1904, 93) denied that a covenant could be
made with God 'without speciall Revelation', though it was Filmer and his followers
whom Locke thought of as flatterers of Princes; see, for example, 1, § 3.
§ **196** 13 '*Hingar*' and '*Hubba*'—presumably the Ingware and Ubba named as
the original Danish leaders of the first invasion (as distinct from raids) of England
in the 860's by the Anglo-Saxon Chronicle; see Stenton, *Anglo-Saxon England*, 1943,
244.
14 '*Spartacus*'—the escaped gladiator who nearly conquered Italy in the eighth
decade B.C.

Offence before God, but is that, which he allows and countenances, though even Promises and Covenants, when obtain'd by force, 25 have intervened. For 'tis very probable to any one that reads the Story of *Ahaz*, and *Hezekiah* attentively, that the *Assyrians* subdued *Ahaz*, and deposed him, and made *Hezekiah* King in his Father's Life time; and that *Hezekiah* by agreement had done him Homage, and paid him Tribute all this time.   30

CHAP. XVII.

Of USURPATION.

197. AS Conquest may be called a Foreign Usurpation, so *Usurpation* is a kind of Domestick Conquest, with this difference, that an Usurper can never have Right on his side, it being no *Usurpation* but where one *is* got into *the Possession of what another has Right to*. This, so far as it is *Usurpation*, is a change 5 only of Persons, but not of the Forms and Rules of the Government: For if the Usurper extend his Power beyond, what of Right belonged to the lawful Princes, or Governours of the Commonwealth, 'tis *Tyranny* added to Usurpation.

198. In all lawful Governments the designation of the Persons, who are to bear Rule, is as natural and necessary a part, as the Form of the Government it self, and is that which had its Establishment originally from the People. Hence all Common

---

24–35 On Ahaz, Hezekiah and the Assyrians, see II Kings xvi, xviii, xix, and I Chron. xxviii, xxix, xxxii: Locke's alternative reading does not seem to be accepted by modern biblical historians.

§ **197** *Chapter* xvii This chapter is obviously an addendum to chapter xvi and its probable date therefore is 1681 or 1682—see note on II, § 175. It is recapitulatory and parallels to its statements can be found in the *First Treatise*, §§ 71, 72, 78, 111, 119, 121, 122, but it does not seem to be the examination of Filmer's 'Title of Usurpers' promised in I, § 121, 9; see note there.

§ **198** 4–11 This passage is difficult to interpret: 'For the anarchy' in line 8 seems not to fit what comes before, though it does make sense with what follows. It may all be due to a printer's confusion not properly put right by Locke. Unfortunately

5 wealths with the Form of Government established, have Rules
also of appointing those, who are to have any share in the publick
Authority; and settled methods of conveying the right to them.
For the anarchy is much alike to have no forme of government
at all; or to agree that it shall be monarchical, but to appoint no
10 way to know or designe the person that shall have the power and
be the monarch. Whoever gets into the exercise of any part of
the Power, by other ways, than what the Laws of the Community
have prescribed, hath no Right to be obeyed, though the Form of
the Commonwealth be still preserved; since he is not the Person
15 the Laws have appointed, and consequently not the Person the
People have consented to. Nor can such an *Usurper*, or any
deriving from him, ever have a Title, till the People are both at
liberty to consent, and have actually consented to allow, and confirm in him, the Power he hath till then Usurped.

Chap. XVIII.

Of TYRANNY.

199. AS Usurpation is the exercise of Power, which another
hath a Right to; so *Tyranny* is *the exercise of Power beyond
Right*, which no Body can have a Right to. And this is making
use of the Power any one has in his hands; not for the good of

---

in the Christ's copy he failed to complete his correction. Having decided to move
the passage printed here in lines 7–11 from an earlier position, he failed to delete it,
with the result that the text in the 4th, 5th, 6th and Collected editions give it in both
positions, making the paragraph pretty well unintelligible.

§ **199** *Chapter* XVIII Up to the end of § 202 this chapter clearly belongs to the
series from chapter XVI, and was presumably written in 1681 or perhaps 1682 (see
notes on § 197, chapter XVII and § 175, chapter XVI), which is confirmed by the
reference to 'King James' in § 200, 3. But after § 202 the subject of tyranny is left
behind, and Locke discusses the related but much more interesting topic of resistance:
this whole passage to § 210 may well be a later insertion. In the editor's view it is
most unlikely to have been an insertion of 1689, for it all reads as if it were intended to
apply to resistance under contemplation, not to resistance which had taken place.
Moreover its statements are often quite inappropriate to the actions of James II: the
references to religion, for example, in § 209, 6–7 and § 210, 9–10—see Introduction,
54. But they do describe the actions of Charles II, at least as they were interpreted

those, who are under it, but for his own private separate Advan- 5
tage. When the Governour, however intituled, makes not the
Law, but his Will, the Rule; and his Commands and Actions are
not directed to the preservation of the Properties of his People,
but the satisfaction of his own Ambition, Revenge, Covetousness,
or any other irregular Passion.   10

200. If one can doubt this to be Truth, or Reason, because it
comes from the obscure hand of a Subject, I hope the Authority
of a King will make it pass with him. King *James* the first in his
Speech to the Parliament, 1603. tells them thus; *I will ever prefer*
the Weal of the Publick, and of the whole Commonwealth, in making 5
of good Laws and Constitutions to any particular and private Ends of
mine. Thinking ever the Wealth and Weal of the Commonwealth, to be
my greatest Weal, and worldly Felicity; *a Point wherein a lawful King*
doth directly differ from a Tyrant. For I do acknowledge, that the special
and greatest point of Difference that is between a rightful King, and an 10
usurping Tyrant, is this, That whereas the proud and ambitious Tyrant
doth think, his Kingdom and People are only ordained for satisfaction of
his Desires and unreasonable Appetites; *the righteous and just King doth*
by the contrary acknowledge himself to be ordained for the procuring of
the Wealth and Property of his People. And again in his Speech to 15
the Parliament, 1609. he hath these Words: *The KING binds*

---

by Shaftesbury and the Exclusion Whigs. There are sentences, and perhaps longer
passages, which may have been added in 1689, and § 205, 6–11 is an obvious example,
but in general it would seem that this part of the text was written before Locke's
departure for Holland in 1683, and may well be directly connected with the Whig
plans for overt resistance to Charles II in those years: compare Ashcraft, 1980, 198/

5–6   The point that a government must never have its 'own private separate
Advantage' is made repeatedly; see II, § 138, 24–5; § 143, 13–14; § 163, 14 ('distinct
and separate Interest'); § 164, 16.

§ 200   3   'King *James* the First'—'the First' added in errata to 3rd edition, 1698,
and inserted in the Christ's copy: compare II, § 133, 10, and see note and references
there.

4–31   See McIlwain, 1918 (an exact reproduction of King James's *Works*, 1616),
277, 278, 309–10, fairly exactly quoted, but with variations in spelling and punctuation and one interesting alteration: '*Property*' in line 15 reads 'prosperitie' in the
original. Filmer quotes King James extensively, mostly from his *Trew Law of Free*
Monarchies, and in *Patriarcha*, section 21, 103, he also uses the phrase about the tyrant
and the law in lines 25–6. Locke does not appear to have owned any work of
James I, but these speeches of 1603 and 1609 were used by others in the controversy
of the early 1680's, see, for example, *Vox Regis, or the difference betwixt a King ruling*
by Law and Tyrant by his own will...in two speeches of King James to the parliaments in
1603...1609...an Appendix to Vox Populi, London, 1681. This paragraph was obviously written 1679–81, see note on II, § 199, chapter XVIII; compare Polin, 1960, 216.

himself by a double Oath, to the observation of the Fundamental Laws
of his Kingdom. Tacitly, as by being a King, and so bound to protect as
well the People as the Laws of his Kingdom, and expressly by his Oath
20 *at his Coronation; so as every just King, in a setled Kingdom is bound to*
observe that Paction made to his People by his Laws in framing his
Government agreeable thereunto, according to that Paction which God
made with Noah, *after the Deluge. Hereafter, Seed-time and Harvest,*
and Cold and Heat, and Summer and Winter, and Day and Night shall
25 *not cease while the Earth remaineth. And therefore a King governing in*
a setled Kingdom, leaves to be a King, and degenerates into a Tyrant as
soon as he leaves off to rule according to his Laws. And a little after:
Therefore all Kings that are not Tyrants, or Perjured, will be glad to
bound themselves within the Limits of their Laws. And they that
30 *perswade them the contrary, are Vipers, and Pests both against them and*
the Commonwealth. Thus that Learned King who well understood
the Notions of things, makes the difference betwixt a *King* and
a *Tyrant* to consist only in this, That one makes the Laws the
Bounds of his Power, and the Good of the Publick, the end of
35 his Government; the other makes all give way to his own Will
and Appetite.

201. 'Tis a Mistake to think this Fault is proper only to
Monarchies; other Forms of Government are liable to it, as well
as that. For where-ever the Power that is put in any hands for
the Government of the People, and the Preservation of their
5 Properties, is applied to other ends, and made use of to impoverish, harass, or subdue them to the Arbitrary and Irregular
Commands of those that have it: There it presently becomes
Tyranny, whether those that thus use it are one or many. Thus we
read of the Thirty Tyrants at *Athens,* as well as one at *Syracuse;*
10 and the intolerable Dominion of the *Decemviri* at *Rome* was
nothing better.

202. *Where-ever Law ends, Tyranny begins,* if the Law be transgressed to another's harm. And whosoever in Authority exceeds
the Power given him by the Law, and makes use of the Force
he has under his Command, to compass that upon the Subject,
5 which the Law allows not, ceases in that to be a Magistrate, and

---

§ **201**   7–10   The Thirty Tyrants ruled in Athens 404–403 B.C., and the tyrants of
Syracuse were advised by Plato himself: the *Decemviri* were a board of ten who were
forced from the rulership of the Roman Republic in 449 B.C. for tyrannical behaviour.

acting without Authority, may be opposed, as any other Man, who by force invades the Right of another. This is acknowledged in subordinate Magistrates. He that hath Authority to seize my Person in the Street, may be opposed as a Thief and a Robber, if he indeavours to break into my House to Execute a Writ, notwithstanding that I know he has such a Warrant, and such a Legal Authority as will impower him to Arrest me abroad. And why this should not hold in the highest, as well as in the most Inferiour Magistrate, I would gladly be informed. Is it reasonable that the Eldest Brother, because he has the greatest part of his Father's Estate, should thereby have a Right to take away any of his younger Brothers Portions? Or that a Rich Man, who possessed a whole Country, should from thence have a Right to seize, when he pleased, the Cottage and Garden of his poor Neighbour? The being rightfully possessed of great Power and Riches exceedingly beyond the greatest part of the Sons of *Adam*, is so far from being an excuse, much less a reason, for Rapine, and Oppression, which the endamaging another without Authority is, that it is a great Aggravation of it. For the exceeding the Bounds of Authority is no more a Right in a great, than a petty Officer; no more justifiable in a King, than a Constable. But is so much the worse in him, in that he has more trust put in him, has already a much greater share than the rest of his brethren, and is supposed from the advantages of Education, imployment and Counsellors to be more knowing in the measures of right or wrong.

203. May the *Commands* then *of a Prince be opposed*? May he be resisted as often as any one shall find himself aggrieved, and but imagine he has not Right done him? This will unhinge and overturn all Polities, and instead of Government and Order, leave nothing but Anarchy and Confusion.

---

§ **202**   14–17   The greater rights of the eldest brother are discussed at length in the *First Treatise*; see, for example, §§ 114, 115.

17–20   Compare I, § 42, for the limitations on the powers of the rich man. The example given here, of the wealthy landowner and the cottager with his garden, comes straight out of the rural England of Locke's day.

26–31   This point is made again in II, § 231.

29–31   Locke rephrased this.

§ **203**   It is possible that the text from this point to the end of the chapter is an addition to the original, perhaps of 1681–2, perhaps even of 1689: see note to § 199 (chapter XVIII), where it is argued that it was written before 1683.

204. To this I Answer: That *Force* is to be *opposed* to nothing, but to unjuſt and unlawful *Force*; whoever makes any opposition in any other Case, draws on himself a juſt Condemnation both from God and Man; and so no such Danger or Confusion will
5 follow, as is often suggeſted. For,

205. *Firſt*, As in some Countries, the Person of the Prince by the Law is Sacred; and so whatever he commands, or does, his Person is ſtill free from all Queſtion or Violence, not liable to Force, or any Judicial Censure or Condemnation. But yet opposi-
5 tion may be made to the illegal Aɛts of any inferiour Officer, or other commissioned by him; unless he will by aɛtually putting himself into a State of War with his People, dissolve the Government, and leave them to that defence, which belongs to every one in the State of Nature. For of such things who can tell what
10 the end will be? And a Neighbour Kingdom has shewed the World an odd Example. In all other Cases the *Sacredness* of the person *exempts him from all Inconveniences* whereby he is secure, whilſt the Government ſtands, from all violence and harm whatsoever; Than which there cannot be a wiser Conſtitution. For the
15 harm he can do in his own Person, not being likely to happen often, nor to extend it self far; nor being able by his single ſtrength to subvert the Laws, nor oppress the Body of the People, should any Prince have so much Weakness and ill Nature as to be willing to do it, the Inconveniency of some particular mischiefs, that
20 may happen sometimes, when a heady Prince comes to the Throne, are well recompenced, by the peace of the Publick, and security of the Government, in the Person of the Chief Magiſtrate, thus set out of the reach of danger: It being safer for the Body, that some few private Men should be sometimes in danger to suffer,
25 than that the head of the Republick should be easily, and upon slight occasions exposed.

206. *Secondly*, But this Priviledge, belonging only to the King's Person, hinders not, but they may be queſtioned, opposed, and

---

§ 205   1   'Some Countries'—England is meant here; compare 1, § 90, 29–31.
  6–11   This passage seems to be an insertion of 1689 and a direct reference to
James II, here accused of having put himself into a state of war with his people and
dissolved the government. The 'Neighbour Kingdom' of line 10 is England again,
an even more indirect reference but typical of Locke: compare above note and see
Introduction, 78. It will be noted that dissolution of *government*, not *society*, here brings back
the state of nature: see Introduction, 114.

resisted, who use unjust force, though they pretend a Commission from him, which the Law authorizes not. As is plain in the Case of him, that has the King's Writ to Arrest a Man, which 5 is a full Commission from the King; and yet he that has it cannot break open a Man's House to do it, nor execute this Command of the King upon certain Days, nor in certain Places, though this Commission have no such exception in it, but they are the Limitations of the Law, which if any one transgress, the King's Com- 10 mission excuses him not. For the King's Authority being given him only by the Law, he cannot impower any one to act against the Law, or justifie him, by his Commission in so doing. The *Commission*, or *Command of any Magistrate, where he has no Authority*, being as *void* and insignificant, as that of any private Man. The 15 difference between the one and the other, being that the Magistrate has some Authority so far, and to such ends, and the private Man has none at all. For 'tis not the *Commission*, but the *Authority*, that gives the Right of acting; and *against the Laws there can be no Authority*. But, notwithstanding such Resistance, the King's 20 Person and Authority are still both secured, and so *no danger to Governor or Government*.

207. *Thirdly*, Supposing a Government wherein the Person of the Chief Magistrate is not thus Sacred; yet this *Doctrine* of the lawfulness of *resisting* all unlawful exercises of his Power, *will not* upon every slight occasion indanger him, or *imbroil the Government*. For where the injured Party may be relieved, and his 5 damages repaired by Appeal to the Law, there can be no pretence for Force, which is only to be used, where a Man is intercepted from appealing to the Law. For nothing is to be accounted Hostile Force, but where it leaves not the remedy of such an Appeal. And 'tis such *Force* alone, that *puts* him that uses it *into* 10 *a state of War*, and makes it lawful to resist him. A Man with a Sword in his Hand demands my Purse in the High-way, when perhaps I have not 12 *d*. in my Pocket; This Man I may lawfully kill. To another I deliver 100 *l*. to hold only whilst I alight, which he refuses to restore me, when I am got up again, but draws his 15 Sword to defend the possession of it by force, if I endeavour to retake it. The mischief this Man does me, is a hundred, or possibly a thousand times more, than the other perhaps intended me,

---

§ **207**   12–13   Compare II, § 18.

(whom I killed before he really did me any) and yet I might
20 lawfully kill the one, and cannot so much as hurt the other lawfully. The Reason whereof is plain; because the one using *force*,
which threatned my Life, I could not have *time to appeal* to the
Law to secure it: And when it was gone, 'twas too late to appeal.
The Law could not restore Life to my dead Carcass: The Loss
25 was irreparable; which to prevent, the Law of Nature gave me
a Right to *destroy* him, who had put himself into a State of War
with me, and threatned my destruction. But in the other case,
my Life not being in danger, I may have the *benefit of appealing*
to the Law, and have Reparation for my 100 *l.* that way.

208. *Fourthly*, But if the unlawful acts done by the Magistrate,
be maintained (by the Power he has got) and the remedy which
is due by Law, be by the same Power obstructed; yet the *Right of
resisting*, even in such manifest Acts of Tyranny, *will not* suddenly,
5 or on slight occasions, *disturb the Government*. For if it reach no
farther than some private Mens Cases, though they have a right
to defend themselves, and to recover by force, what by unlawful
force is taken from them; yet the Right to do so, will not easily
ingage them in a Contest, wherein they are sure to perish; it being
10 as impossible for one or a few oppressed Men to *disturb the
Government*, where the Body of the People do not think themselves
concerned in it, as for a raving mad Man, or heady Male-content
to overturn a well-settled State; the People being as little apt to
follow the one, as the other.

209. But if either these illegal Acts have extended to the
Majority of the People; or if the Mischief and Oppression has
light only on some few, but in such Cases, as the Precedent, and
Consequences seem to threaten all, and they are perswaded in
5 their Consciences, that their Laws, and with them their Estates,

---

§ **208**   Compare II, § 230, 1–10, and see Seliger, 1963 (ii), talking of *raison d'état*.

5–6   Elrington (1798) comments here that there are cases in which redress is
impossible, where it would injure innocent people, and that no one 'has a right to
overturn the peace of the Society he lives in and reduce his fellow-citizens to a State
of Nature, for the mere purpose of obtaining redress'.

§ **209**   The statements of this paragraph and § 210 are often taken to refer directly
to James II, and they seem more specific than the rest of the passage from § 203; see
note there. In the note on § 199 (chapter XVIII) and in the Introduction, 54 it is
argued that they are in fact more appropriate to the situation of the early 1680's than
of 1688–9, and it may be significant that the paragraph ends with the 'Father of a Family'
once again.

Liberties, and Lives are in danger, and perhaps their Religion too, how they will be hindered from resisting illegal force, used against them, I cannot tell. This is an *Inconvenience*, I confess, that *attends all Governments* whatsoever, when the Governours have brought it to this pass, to be generally suspected of their People; 10 the most dangerous State which they can possibly put themselves in: wherein they are the less to be pitied, because it is so easie to be avoided; It being as impossible for a Governor, if he really means the good of his People, and the preservation of them and their Laws together, not to make them see and feel it; as it is 15 for the Father of a Family, not to let his Children see he loves, and takes care of them.

210. But if all the World shall observe Pretences of one kind, and Actions of another; Arts used to elude the Law, and the Trust of Prerogative (which is an Arbitrary Power in some things left in the Prince's hand to do good, not harm to the People) employed contrary to the end, for which it was given: if the People shall 5 find the Ministers, and subordinate Magistrates chosen suitable to such ends, and favoured, or laid by proportionably, as they promote, or oppose them: If they see several Experiments made of Arbitrary Power, and that Religion underhand favoured (though publickly proclaimed against) which is readiest to intro- 10 duce it, and the Operators in it supported, as much as may be; and when that cannot be done, yet approved still, and liked the better: if a *long Train of Actings shew the Councils* all tending that way, how can a Man any more hinder himself from being per- swaded in his own Mind, which way things are going; or from 15 casting about how to save himself, than he could from believing the Captain of the Ship he was in, was carrying him, and the rest of the Company to *Algiers*, when he found him always steering that Course, though cross Winds, Leaks in his Ship, and want of Men and Provisions did often force him to turn his Course an- 20 other way for some time, which he steadily returned to again, as soon as the Wind, Weather, and other Circumstances would let him?

---

§ 210   2–4   'the Trust of Prerogative'—compare chapter xiv, especially §§ 163, 168; the definition of prerogative assumed here is the same, but the phrase is new. Compare ii, § 94, 1–9 on the sentiments of the first part of this paragraph.

13   '*long Train of Actings...*'—see note on ii, § 225, 5–6.

18   '*Algiers*'—the slave market for Christians captured by Moorish pirates.

C H A P. XIX.

Of the Dissolution of Government.

211. HE that will with any clearness speak of the *Dissolution of Government*, ought, in the first place to distinguish between the *Dissolution of the Society*, and the *Dissolution of the Government*. That which makes the Community, and brings Men
5 out of the loose State of Nature, into *one Politick Society*, is the Agreement which every one has with the rest to incorporate, and act as one Body, and so be one distinct Commonwealth. The usual, and almost only way whereby *this Union is dissolved*, is the Inroad of Foreign Force making a Conquest upon them. For in
10 that Case, (not being able to maintain and support themselves, as *one intire* and *independent Body*) the Union belonging to that Body which consisted therein, must necessarily cease, and so every one return to the State he was in before, with a liberty to

§ 211 *Chapter* XIX This chapter contains those statements of Locke's which associate his book most closely with the events of 1688-9. It is lacking in structure and obviously the result of successive correction and addition, but it seems to have belonged to Locke's original text, though perhaps not written before 1681 or 1682. The first part of the chapter, up to § 218, seems clearly to have been written well before 1688, especially § 218 itself which seems too hypothetical for a whig comment on the Revolution, even for Locke. Then come two paragraphs which were added in 1689 (§§ 219, 220), followed by a passage mainly belonging to the original text. The prolonged criticism of Barclay (§§ 232-9) seems to have been written in 1681 or 1682, certainly after he had added his material from Hooker. The final paragraphs seem to belong to the original, but were obviously modified and extended after the Revolution.

1-4 On the dissolution of government as opposed to the dissolution of society, and the community which survives the breakdown of government, see Introduction, 116. Maclean, 1947, points out an interesting parallel with the views of George Lawson here: compare *Politica Sacra* (1660), 1689, 24, 27, 59, 95, 217, etc., and his *Examination of Hobbes*, 1657, 15, etc. As in the case of the separation of powers (see note on II, § 146), Lawson is far more specific and rather different in his conceptions. He laid it down that when the government was dissolved, the counties maintained the community of England.

7-15 Compare II, § 175, 8-13, 11, § 185 and Hobbes's *Leviathan*, chapter 29: 'When in a warre (forraign or intestine,) the enemies get a finall Victory; so as...there is no farther protection of Subjects in their loyalty; then is the Common-wealth DISSOLVED, and every man at liberty to protect himselfe by such courses as his own discretion shall suggest to him' (1904, 242). In II, § 218, 12-14, Locke equates rebellion with foreign conquest in a similar way.

shift for himself, and provide for his own Safety as he thinks
fit in some other Society. Whenever the *Society is dissolved*, 'tis   15
certain the Government of that Society cannot remain. Thus
Conquerours Swords often cut up Governments by the Roots,
and mangle Societies to pieces, separating the subdued or scattered
Multitude from the Protection of, and Dependence on that Society
which ought to have preserved them from violence. The World   20
is too well instructed in, and too forward to allow of this way
of dissolving of Governments to need any more to be said of it:
and there wants not much Argument to prove, that where the
Society is dissolved, the Government cannot remain; that being as
impossible, as for the Frame of an House to subsist when the   25
Materials of it are scattered, and dissipated by a Whirl-wind, or
jumbled into a confused heap by an Earthquake.

212. Besides this over-turning from without, *Governments are
dissolved from within,*
    First, When the *Legislative* is *altered*. Civil Society being a State
of Peace, amongst those who are of it, from whom the State
of War is excluded by the Umpirage, which they have provided   5
in their Legislative, for the ending all Differences, that may arise
amongst any of them, 'tis in their *Legislative*, that the Members
of a Commonwealth are united, and combined together into one
coherent living Body. This *is the Soul that gives Form, Life, and
Unity* to the Commonwealth: From hence the several Members   10
have their mutual Influence, Sympathy, and Connexion: And
therefore when the *Legislative* is broken, or *dissolved*, Dissolution
and Death follows. For the *Essence and Union of the Society* consisting in having one Will, the Legislative, when once established
by the Majority, has the declaring, and as it were keeping of that   15
Will. The *Constitution of the Legislative* is the first and fundamental
Act of Society, whereby provision is made for the *Continuation
of their Union*, under the Direction of Persons, and Bonds of

§ 212   9-13   Compare Hobbes, *Leviathan*, chapter 29, continuation of passage
quoted in footnote to § 211: 'For the Sovereign is the publique Soule, giving Life
and Motion to the Common-wealth', and when it departs death follows. Locke
seems to be deliberately putting his legislative in the place of the sovereign, and
though there are very similar passages to this one in *Leviathan* about sovereignty
and the soul of a political society in Grotius (1625, II, ix, 1; 1712, 322) and Pufendorf
(1672, VII, iv, 1, 906) it may be that Locke had the words of Hobbes specifically in
mind here.
    16-17   Compare II, § 134, 4-5 and note, and chapter XI generally.

Laws made by persons authorized thereunto, by the Consent and
20 Appointment of the People, without which no one Man, or
number of Men, amongſt them, can have Authority of making
Laws, that shall be binding to the reſt. When any one, or more,
shall take upon them to make Laws, whom the People have not
appointed so to do, they make Laws without Authority, which
25 the People are not therefore bound to obey; by which means
they come again to be out of subjeⅽtion, and may conſtitute to
themselves a *new Legiſlative*, as they think beſt, being in full liberty
to resiſt the force of those, who without Authority would impose
any thing upon them. Every one is at the disposure of his own
30 Will, when those who had by the delegation of the Society, the
declaring of the publick Will, are excluded from it, and others
usurp the place who have no such Authority or Delegation.

213. This being usually brought about by such in the Commonwealth who misuse the Power they have: It is hard to consider
it aright, and know at whose door to lay it, without knowing
the Form of Government in which it happens. Let us suppose
5 then the Legislative placed in the Concurrence of three diſtinⅽt
Persons.

1. A single hereditary Person having the conſtant, supream,
executive Power, and with it the Power of Convoking and Dissolving the other two within certain Periods of Time.
10 2. An Assembly of Hereditary Nobility.

3. An Assembly of Representatives chosen *pro tempore*, by the
People: Such a Form of Government supposed, it is evident.

214. *Firſt*, That when such a single Person or Prince sets up
his own Arbitrary Will in place of the Laws, which are the Will
of the Society, declared by the Legislative, then the *Legiſlative
is changed*. For that being in effect the Legislative whose Rules and
5 Laws are put in execution, and required to be obeyed; when other
Laws are set up, and other Rules pretended, and inforced, than
what the Legislative, conſtituted by the Society, have enaⅽted,

---

§ 213 4-11 It is obviously the constitutional arrangements for the English
legislature that are being described; compare II, § 167, note and references, and
II, § 223.

9 'within certain Periods of Time'—Locke changes his ground here from the
earlier discussion of the summoning of parliament, which had left it at the discretion
of the executive—see, for example, § 156, especially 30-2; this may mark this
paragraph as having been written later. Seliger, 1968, 343, disagrees that Locke is shifting
here.

'tis plain, that the *Legislative is changed*. Whoever introduces new Laws, not being thereunto authorized by the fundamental Appointment of the Society, or subverts the old, disowns and overturns 10 the Power by which they were made, and so sets up a *new Legislative*.

215. *Secondly*, When the Prince hinders the Legislative from assembling in its due time, or from acting freely, pursuant to those ends, for which it was Constituted, the *Legislative is altered*. For 'tis not a certain number of Men, no, nor their meeting, unless they have also Freedom of debating, and Leisure of perfecting, 5 what is for the good of the Society wherein the Legislative consists: when these are taken away or altered, so as to deprive the Society of the due exercise of their Power, the *Legislative* is truly *altered*. For it is not Names, that Constitute Governments, but the use and exercise of those Powers that were intended to 10 accompany them; so that he who takes away the Freedom, or hinders the acting of the Legislative in its due seasons, in effect *takes away the Legislative*, and *puts an end to the Government*.

216. *Thirdly*, When by the Arbitrary Power of the Prince, the Electors, or ways of Election are altered, without the Consent, and contrary to the common Interest of the People, there also the *Legislative is altered*. For if others, than those whom the Society has authorized thereunto, do chuse, or in another way, 5 than what the Society hath prescribed, those chosen are not the Legislative appointed by the People.

217. *Fourthly*, The delivery also of the People into the subjection of a Foreign Power, either by the Prince, or by the Legislative, is certainly a *change of the Legislative*, and so a *Dissolution of the*

---

§ **215**   1–3   Compare II, § 155, 3.
§ **216**   This paragraph seems to refer to the attempt of both Charles II and James II to alter the parliamentary franchise by remodelling the charters of boroughs; see Thomson, *Constitutional History*, 1938, 452–3. Although the Bill of Rights of 1689 declared that James II had 'violated the freedom of election of members' and claimed that 'Election of Members of Parliament ought to be free', Locke's words and meaning here do not seem to be as close to that document as is so often assumed.
§ **217**   Compare II, § 239, 26–37 (added in 1694) and note ‡, Introduction, p. 45: Locke may have had in mind here the possibility of a Catholic king submitting his country to the Pope, which was provided against by the Bill of Rights. But there is no close parallel and it seems more likely that he was contemplating the sort of action condemned in a King even by William Barclay; see II, § 238.

Government. For the end why People entered into Society, being
to be preserved one intire, free, independent Society, to be
governed by its own Laws; this is lost, whenever they are given
up into the Power of another.

218. Why in such a Constitution as this, the *Dissolution of the
Government* in these Cases is to be imputed to the Prince, is
evident: because he having the Force, Treasure, and Offices of
the State to imploy, and often perswading himself, or being
flattered by others, that as Supream Magistrate he is uncapable
of controul; he alone is in a Condition to make great Advances
toward such Changes, under pretence of lawful Authority, and
has it in his hands to terrifie or suppress Opposers, as Factious,
Seditious, and Enemies to the Government: Whereas no other
part of the Legislative, or People is capable by themselves to
attempt any alteration of the Legislative, without open and visible
Rebellion, apt enough to be taken notice of; which when it
prevails, produces Effects very little different from Foreign Conquest. Besides the Prince in such a Form of Government, having
the Power of dissolving the other parts of the Legislative, and
thereby rendering them private Persons, they can never in
opposition to him, or without his Concurrence, alter the Legislative by a Law, his Consent being necessary to give any of their
Decrees that Sanction. But yet so far as the other parts of the
Legislative any way contribute to any attempt upon the Government, and do either promote, or not, what lies in them, hinder
such designs, they are guilty, and partake in this, which is
certainly the greatest Crime Men can be guilty of one towards
another.

219. There is one way more whereby such a Government may
be dissolved, and that is, when he who has the Supream Executive
Power, neglects and abandons that charge, so that the Laws

---

§ 218   It seems quite unlikely that even the cautious and devious Locke can have
written this paragraph after the events of 1688–9—see note on 11, § 211, chapter xix.
  1 'such a Constitution as this'—that is, the English Constitution; see note
on 11, § 213, 4–11, and for the use of the word 'constitution' in our sense, 11, § 155, 4.
  9–14   See 11, § 211, 7–15 and note.
  16   Compare 11, § 154, 2–3.
§ 219   This paragraph, and probably § 220, must have been written in 1689 to refer
to James II having 'abdicated the government...and withdrawn himself out of the
kingdom' so 'that the throne is thereby vacant', which were the words used in the
Parliamentary resolutions: compare note, ‡, Introduction, p. 45. The fact that these

already made can no longer be put in execution. This is demon-
ſtratively to reduce all to Anarchy, and so effectually to *diſſolve* 5
the Government. For Laws not being made for themselves, but
to be by their execution the Bonds of the Society, to keep every
part of the Body Politick in its due place and function, when that
totally ceases, the *Government* visibly *ceases*, and the People become
a confused Multitude, without Order or Connexion. Where there 10
is no longer the adminiſtration of Juſtice, for the securing of
Mens Rights, nor any remaining Power within the Community
to direct the Force, or provide for the Necessities of the publick,
there certainly is *no Government left*. Where the Laws cannot be
executed, it is all one as if there were no Laws, and a Government 15
without Laws, is, I suppose, a Myſtery in Politicks, unconceivable
to humane Capacity, and inconsiſtent with humane Society.

220. In these and the like Cases, *when the Government is diſſolved*,
the People are at liberty to provide for themselves, by erecting
a new Legislative, differing from the other, by the change of
Persons, or Form, or both as they shall find it moſt for their
safety and good. For the *Society* can never, by the fault of another, 5
lose the Native and Original Right it has to preserve it self, which
can only be done by a settled Legislative, and a fair and impartial
execution of the Laws made by it. But the ſtate of Mankind is
not so miserable that they are not capable of using this Remedy,
till it be too late to look for any. To tell *People* they *may provide* 10
for themselves, by erecting a new Legislative, when by Oppression,
Artifice, or being delivered over to a Foreign Power, their old
one is gone, is only to tell them they may expect Relief, when it
is too late, and the evil is paſt Cure. This is in effect no more
than to bid them firſt be Slaves, and then to take care of their 15
Liberty; and when their Chains are on, tell them, they may
act like Freemen. This, if barely so, is rather Mockery than
Relief; and Men can never be secure from Tyranny, if there be
no means to escape it, till they are perfectly under it: And
therefore it is, that they have not only a Right to get out of it 20
but to prevent it.

---

statements are difficult to reconcile with what Locke says elsewhere about the
dissolution of government as opposed to the dissolution of society (see Introduction,
114) may mark the passage as a subsequent insertion. But in II, § 121, 15–18, and in II, § 205,
6–11, he also seems to imply that dissolution of government puts the subject 'in the liberty of
the state of nature'.

221. There is therefore, secondly, another way whereby *Governments are dissolved*, and that is; when the Legislative, or the Prince, either of them act contrary to their Trust.

First, The *Legislative acts against the Trust* reposed in them, when
5 they endeavour to invade the Property of the Subject, and to make themselves, or any part of the Community, Masters, or Arbitrary Disposers of the Lives, Liberties, or Fortunes of the People.

222. The Reason why Men enter into Society, is the preservation of their Property; and the end why they chuse and authorize a Legislative, is, that there may be Laws made, and Rules set as Guards and Fences to the Properties of all the Members of the
5 Society, to limit the Power, and moderate the Dominion of every Part and Member of the Society. For since it can never be supposed to be the Will of the Society, that the Legislative should have a Power to destroy that, which every one designs to secure, by entering into Society, and for which the People submitted
10 themselves to the Legislators of their own making; whenever the *Legislators endeavour to take away, and destroy the Property of the People*, or to reduce them to Slavery under Arbitrary Power, they put themselves into a State of War with the People, who are thereupon absolved from any farther Obedience, and are left to
15 the common Refuge, which God hath provided for all Men, against Force and Violence. Whensoever therefore the *Legislative* shall transgress this fundamental Rule of Society; and either by Ambition, Fear, Folly or Corruption, *endeavour to grasp* themselves, *or put into the hands of any other an Absolute Power* over the Lives,
20 Liberties, and Estates of the People; By this breach of Trust they *forfeit the Power*, the People had put into their hands, for quite contrary ends, and it devolves to the People, who have a Right to resume their original Liberty, and, by the Establishment of a new Legislative (such as they shall think fit) provide for their

---

§ **221** 1 'secondly'—presumably follows on to the '*First*' in § 212, line 3, but the confusing numerations here may indicate successive recorrections to this whole area of the text: there is, e.g., no 'secondly' to the '*First*' of line 4 of this paragraph (though Hinton, 1974, suggests that the 'also' of § 222, 27 is to be taken for it).

§ **222** 1-16 Compare II, § 135.

1-2 Compare II, § 138, 3-4.

19-20 Compare II, § 87, 5, note and references.

20-2 Compare Lawson, *Politica Sacra* (1660), 1689, 62 (sovereignty may 'in some cases' be forfeit 'to the community'), and on trust generally (79, 217, etc.). See Maclean, 1947.

own Safety and Security, which is the end for which they are in 25
Society. What I have said here, concerning the Legislative, in
general, holds true also concerning the *supreame Executor*, who
having a double trust put in him, both to have a part in the Legislative, and the supreme Execution of the Law, Acts against both,
when he goes about to set up his own Arbitrary Will, as the Law 30
of the Society. He *acts* also *contrary to his Trust*, when he either
imploys the Force, Treasure, and Offices of the Society, to corrupt
the *Representatives*, and gain them to his purposes: or openly
pre-ingages the *Electors*, and prescribes to their choice, such,
whom he has by Sollicitations, Threats, Promises, or otherwise 35
won to his designs; and imploys them to bring in such, who have
promised before-hand, what to Vote, and what to Enact. Thus
to regulate Candidates and *Electors*, and new model the ways of
Election, what is it but to cut up the Government by the Roots,
and poison the very Fountain of publick Security? For the 40
People having reserved to themselves the Choice of their *Representatives*, as the Fence to their Properties, could do it for no other
end, but that they might always be freely chosen, and so chosen,
freely act and advise, as the necessity of the Commonwealth, and
the publick Good should, upon examination, and mature debate, 45
be judged to require. This, those who give their Votes before
they hear the Debate, and have weighed the Reasons on all sides,
are not capable of doing. To prepare such an Assembly as this,
and endeavour to set up the declared Abettors of his own Will,
for the true *Representatives* of the People, and the Law-makers 50
of the Society, is certainly as great a *breach of trust*, and as perfect
a Declaration of a design to subvert the Government, as is possible
to be met with. To which, if one shall add Rewards and Punishments visibly imploy'd to the same end, and all the Arts of per-
verted Law made use of, to take off and destroy all that stand in 55
the way of such a design, and will not comply and consent to
betray the Liberties of their Country, 'twill be past doubt what is
doing. What Power they ought to have in the Society, who thus
imploy it contrary to the trust that went along with it in its first

---

26–62   Probably an addition, or successive additions. Here Locke seems to have
James II's attempts to control the electorate specifically in mind (compare note on
11, § 216); see Burnet, 1724, 1, 719. The final lines can only refer to James II, and it
seems likely that the whole passage was added in 1689, making the paragraph the
longest in the book.

60 Inſtitution, is easie to determine; and one cannot but see, that
he, who has once attempted any such thing as this, cannot any
longer be truſted.

223. To this perhaps it will be said, that the People being
ignorant, and always discontented, to lay the Foundation of
Government in the unſteady Opinion, and uncertain Humour
of the People, is to expose it to certain ruine; And *no Government*
5 *will be able long to subsiſt,* if the People may set up a new Legislative,
whenever they take offence at the old one. To this, I Answer:
Quite the contrary. People are not so easily got out of their old
Forms, as some are apt to suggeſt. They are hardly to be prevailed
with to amend the acknowledg'd Faults, in the Frame they have
10 been accuſtom'd to. And if there be any Original defeĉts, or
adventitious ones introduced by time, or corruption; 'tis not an
easie thing to get them changed, even when all the World sees
there is an opportunity for it. This slowness and aversion in the
People to quit their old Conſtitutions, has, in the many Revolu-
15 tions which have been seen in this Kingdom, in this and former
Ages, ſtill kept us to, or, after some interval of fruitless attempts,
ſtill brought us back again to our old Legislative of King, Lords
and Commons: And whatever provocations have made the Crown
be taken from some of our Princes Heads, they never carried the
20 People so far, as to place it in another Line.

224. But 'twill be said, this *Hypothesis* lays a *ferment* for frequent
Rebellion. To which I Answer,
Firſt, No more than any other *Hypothesis.* For when the *People*
are made *miserable,* and find themselves *exposed to the ill usage of*
5 *Arbitrary Power,* cry up their Governours, as much as you will
for Sons of *Jupiter,* let them be Sacred and Divine, descended or
authoriz'd from Heaven; give them out for whom or what you

---

§ 223 4–6 Elrington, 1798, objects here that the right of changing government
depends not on the will of the people, but on their reason dictating the necessity of it.

9–10 'in the Frame they have been accustom'd to'—there is a parallel phrase,
perhaps accidental, in the *American Declaration of Independence,* ed. Becker, 1922, 10,
'the forms to which they are accustomed'.

15 'in this Kingdom'—here Locke again openly refers to England and her
Constitution; see II, § 213, 4–11, note and references.

16–20 This may be a reference to the events of 1688–9, and therefore a late addition, but it could perhaps as well refer to 1640–60 and the dynastic operations of the
fifteenth century.

please, the same will happen. *The People generally ill treated*, and contrary to right, will be ready upon any occasion to ease themselves of a burden that sits heavy upon them. They will wish and seek for the opportunity, which, in the change, weakness, and accidents of humane affairs, seldom delays long to offer it self. He must have lived but a little while in the World, who has not seen Examples of this in his time; and he must have read very little, who cannot produce Examples of it in all sorts of Governments in the World.

225. Secondly, I Answer, such *Revolutions happen* not upon every little mismanagement in publick affairs. *Great mistakes* in the ruling part, many wrong and inconvenient Laws, and all the *slips* of humane frailty will be *born by the People*, without mutiny or murmur. But if a long train of Abuses, Prevarications, and Artifices, all tending the same way, make the design visible to the People, and they cannot but feel, what they lie under, and see, whither they are going; 'tis not to be wonder'd, that they should then rouze themselves, and endeavour to put the rule into such hands, which may secure to them the ends for which Government was at first erected; and without which, ancient Names, and specious Forms, are so far from being better, that they are much worse, than the state of Nature, or pure Anarchy; the inconveniencies being all as great and as near, but the remedy farther off and more difficult.

226. Thirdly, I Answer, That *this Doctrine* of a Power in the People of providing for their safety a-new by a new Legislative, when their Legislators have acted contrary to their trust, by invading their Property, is *the best fence against Rebellion*, and the probablest means to hinder it. For Rebellion being an Opposition, not to Persons, but Authority, which is founded only in the Constitutions and Laws of the Government; those, whoever they be, who by force break through, and by force justifie their violation of them, are truly and properly *Rebels*. For when Men by entering into Society and Civil Government, have excluded force, and introduced Laws for the preservation of Property, Peace, and

---

§ **225**   5–6   Compare II, § 210, 13–14 (verbal parallel), and II, § 230, 10–15. The American Declaration of Independence has: 'But when a long train of abuses and usurpations pursuing invariably the same object...' (ed. Becker, 1922, 10).
   11–15   Compare II, § 137, 10–14.

Unity amongst themselves; those who set up force again in opposition to the Laws, do *Rebellare*, that is, bring back again the state
of War, and are properly Rebels: Which they who are in Power
15 (by the pretence they have to Authority, the temptation of force
they have in their hands, and the Flattery of those about them)
being likeliest to do; the properest way to prevent the evil, is to
shew them the danger and injustice of it, who are under the
greatest temptation to run into it.

227. In both the forementioned Cases, when either the Legislative is changed, or the Legislators act contrary to the end for
which they were constituted; those who are guilty are *guilty of
Rebellion*. For if any one by force takes away the establish'd
5 Legislative of any Society, and the Laws by them made pursuant
to their trust, he thereby takes away the Umpirage, which every
one had consented to, for a peaceable decision of all their Controversies, and a bar to the state of War amongst them. They,
who remove, or change the Legislative, take away this decisive
10 power, which no Body can have, but by the appointment and
consent of the People; and so destroying the Authority, which
the People did, and no Body else can set up, and introducing
a Power, which the People hath not authoriz'd, they actually
introduce a state of War, which is that of Force without Authority:
15 And thus by removing the Legislative establish'd by the Society
(in whose decisions the People acquiesced and united, as to that
of their own will) they unty the Knot, and *expose the People a new
to the state of War*. And if those, who by force take away the
Legislative, are *Rebels*, the *Legislators* themselves, as has been
20 shewn, can be no less esteemed so; when they, who were set up
for the protection, and preservation of the People, their Liberties
and Properties, shall by force invade, and indeavour to take them
away; and so they putting themselves into a state of War with
those, who made them the Protectors and Guardians of their
25 Peace, are properly, and with the greatest aggravation, *Rebellantes*
Rebels.

228. But if they, who say it *lays a foundation for Rebellion*, mean
that it may occasion Civil Wars, or Intestine Broils, to tell the
People they are absolved from Obedience, when illegal attempts
are made upon their Liberties or Properties, and may oppose the
5 unlawful violence of those, who were their Magistrates, when

they invade their Properties contrary to the trust put in them; and that therefore this Doctrine is not to be allow'd, being so destructive to the Peace of the World. They may as well say upon the same ground, that honest Men may not oppose Robbers or Pirates, because this may occasion disorder or bloodshed. If any mischief come in such Cases, it is not *to be charged* upon him, who defends his own right, but *on him*, that *invades* his Neighbours. If the innocent honest Man must quietly quit all he has for Peace sake, to him who will lay violent hands upon it, I desire it may be consider'd, what a kind of Peace there will be in the World, which consists only in Violence and Rapine; and which is to be maintain'd only for the benefit of Robbers and Oppressors. Who would not think it an admirable Peace betwixt the Mighty and the Mean, when the Lamb, without resistance, yielded his Throat to be torn by the imperious Wolf? *Polyphemus*'s Den gives us a perfect Pattern of such a Peace, and such a Government, wherein *Ulysses* and his Companions had nothing to do, but quietly to suffer themselves to be devour'd. And no doubt *Ulysses*, who was a prudent Man, preach'd up *Passive Obedience*, and exhorted them to a quiet Submission, by representing to them of what concernment Peace was to Mankind; and by shewing the inconveniencies might happen, if they should offer to resist *Polyphemus*, who had now the power over them.

229. The end of Government is the good of Mankind, and which is *best for Mankind*, that the People should be always expos'd to the boundless will of Tyranny, or that the Rulers should be sometimes liable to be oppos'd, when they grow exorbitant in the use of their Power, and imploy it for the destruction, and not the preservation of the Properties of their People?

230. Nor let any one say, that mischief can arise from hence, as often as it shall please a busie head, or turbulent spirit, to desire the alteration of the Government. 'Tis true, such Men may stir, whenever they please, but it will be only to their own just ruine and perdition. For till the mischief be grown general, and the ill designs of the Rulers become visible, or their attempts

---

§ **228**   20–8   See the *Odyssey*, Book IX.
§ **230**   1–10   Compare II, § 208.

sensible to the greater part, the People, who are more disposed to suffer, than right themselves by Resistance, are not apt to stir. The examples of particular Injustice, or Oppression of here and
10 there an unfortunate Man, moves them not. But if they universally have a perswasion, grounded upon manifest evidence, that designs are carrying on against their Liberties, and the general course and tendency of things cannot but give them strong suspicions of the evil intention of their Governors, who is to be
15 blamed for it? Who can help it, if they, who might avoid it, bring themselves into this suspicion? Are the People to be blamed, if they have the sence of rational Creatures, and can think of things no otherwise than as they find and feel them? And is it not rather *their fault*, who puts things in such a posture that they
20 would not have them thought, to be as they are? I grant, that the Pride, Ambition, and Turbulency of private Men have sometimes caused great Disorders in Commonwealths, and Factions have been fatal to States and Kingdoms. But whether the *mischief* hath *oftner* begun *in the Peoples Wantonness*, and a Desire to cast
25 off the lawful Authority of their Rulers; or *in the Rulers Insolence*, and Endeavours to get, and exercise an Arbitrary Power over their People; whether Oppression, or Disobedience gave the first rise to the Disorder, I leave it to impartial History to determine. This I am sure, whoever, either Ruler or Subject, by force goes
30 about to invade the Rights of either Prince or People, and lays the foundation for *overturning* the Constitution and Frame of *any Just Government*, is guilty of the greatest Crime, I think, a Man is capable of, being to answer for all those mischiefs of Blood, Rapine, and Desolation, which the breaking to pieces of Govern-
35 ments bring on a Countrey. And he who does it, is justly to be esteemed the common Enemy and Pest of Mankind; and is to be treated accordingly.

231. That *Subjects*, or *Foreigners* attempting by force on the Properties of any People, may be *resisted* with force, is agreed on

---

7–8   Parallel in the *American Declaration of Independence*, ed. Becker, 1922, 10: 'mankind are more disposed to suffer, while evils are sufferable, than to right themselves'.

32   'is guilty of the greatest Crime'. The 4th edition, 1713, the 1st Collected edition, 1714, and the 6th edition, 1764, all have 'is highly guilty of the greatest Crime', perhaps the reading of the hypothetical second master-copy—see Editorial Note.

36   See II, § 172, 10–19 note and references. The references here, however, may be to a person other than a monarch, and Hinton, 1974, suggests one or other of the ministers of Charles II, or even a subject of Charles I.

all hands. But that *Magiſtrates* doing the same thing, may be *resiſted*, hath of late been denied: As if those who had the greateſt Priviledges and Advantages by the Law, had thereby a Power 5 to break those Laws, by which alone they were set in a better place than their Brethren: Whereas their Offence is thereby the greater, both as being ungrateful for the greater share they have by the Law, and breaking also that Truſt, which is put into their hands by their Brethren. 10

232. Whosoever uses *force without Right*, as every one does in Society, who does it without Law, puts himself into a *ſtate of War* with those, againſt whom he so uses it, and in that ſtate all former Ties are cancelled, all other Rights cease, and every one has a *Right* to defend himself, and *to resiſt the Aggressor*. This is so 5 evident, that *Barclay* himself, that great Assertor of the Power and Sacredness of Kings, is forced to confess, 'That it is lawful for the people, in some Cases, to *resiſt* their King; and that too in a Chapter, wherein he pretends to shew that the Divine Law shuts up the people from all manner of Rebellion. Whereby it is 10 evident, even by his own Doctrine, that, since they may in some Cases *resiſt*, all resiſting of *Princes* is not Rebellion. His Words are these. *Quod siquis dicat, Ergone populus tyrannicæ crudelitati & furori jugulum semper præbebit? Ergone multitudo civitates suas famæ ferro, & flammâ vaſtari, seque, conjuges, & liberos fortunæ ludibrio* 15 *& tyranni libidini exponi, inque omnia vitæ pericula omnesque miſerias & moleſtias à Rege deduci patientur? Num illis quod omni animantium generi eſt à naturâ tributum, denegari debet, ut sc. vim vi repellant, seseq; ab injuriâ tueantur? Huic breviter responsum sit, Populo universo non negari defensionem, quæ juris naturalis eſt, neque ultionem quæ præter* 20 *naturam eſt adversus Regem concedi debere. Quapropter si Rex non in*

---

§ 231   7–10   Compare II, § 202, 26–31.
§ 232   5–7   On Locke's purpose in singling out Barclay for such detailed attention, see note on II, § 239, 16–17. He mentions Filmer's use of this author in I, § 4, 14 and § 67, 29 without comment, but he possessed William Barclay's two major works (*De Regno et Regali Poteſtati adversus Buchananum, Brutum, Boucherium et reliquos Monarchomachos*, 1600, and *De Potestatae Papae*, 1609, two of the most influential absolutist works, the first being directed in part against the *Vindiciae*) in an edition of 1612 in one volume (H. and L. 203). It was on his shelves in 1681, and on 15 July 1680 he bought a copy for the Earl of Shaftesbury. He noted the book in 1680 (II, § 236, 12 and note) and it seems likely that the passage from this paragraph down to 239 was written in 1681; see II, § 211, chapter XIX.
13–36   Passage on p. 375 of Locke's 1612 edition, inaccurately transcribed by him, with corrections in the errata of the 3rd edition, 1698.

singulares tantum personas aliquot privatum odium exerceat, sed corpus
etiam Reipublicæ, cujus ipse caput est, i.e. *totum populum, vel insignem*
aliquam ejus partem immani & intolerandâ sævitiâ seu tyrannide divexet;
25 *populo, quidem hoc casu resistendi ac tuendi se ab injuriâ potestas competit,*
sed tuendi se tantum, non enim in principem invadendi : & restituendæ
injuriæ illatæ, non recedendi à debitâ reverentiâ propter acceptam in-
juriam. Præsentem denique impetum propulsandi non vim præteritam
ulciscendi jus habet. Horum enim alterum à naturâ est, ut vitam scilicet
30 *corpusque tueamur. Alterum vero contra naturam, ut inferior de*
superiori supplicium sumat. Quod itaque populus malum, antequam
factum sit, impedire potest, ne fiat, id postquam factum est, in Regem
authorem sceleris vindicare non potest : Populus igitur hoc ampliùs quam
privatus quisquam habet : Quod huic, vel ipsis adversariis judicibus,
35 *excepto Buchanano, nullum nisi in patientia remedium superest. Cùm*
ille si intolerabilis tyrannis est (modicum enim ferre omnino debet) resistere
cum reverentiâ possit, Barclay *contra Monarchom.* l. 3. c. 8.

In *English* thus.

233. *But if any one should ask, Must the People then always lay them-*
selves open to the Cruelty and Rage of Tyranny? Must they see their
Cities pillaged, and laid in ashes, their Wives and Children exposed to
the Tyrant's Lust and Fury, and themselves and Families reduced by
5 *their King, to Ruine and all the Miseries of Want and Oppression, and*
yet sit still? Must Men alone be debarred the common Priviledge of
opposing force with force, which Nature allows so freely to all other
Creatures for their preservation from Injury? I Answer: Self-defence
is a part of the Law of Nature; nor can it be denied the Community, even
10 *against the King himself: But to revenge themselves upon him, must by*
no means be allowed them; it being not agreeable to that Law. Wherefore
if the King shall shew an hatred, not only to some particular Persons,
but sets himself against the Body of the Commonwealth, whereof he is the
Head, and shall, with intolerable ill usage, cruelly tyrannize over the
15 *whole, or a considerable part of the People; in this case the People have*
a right to resist and defend themselves from injury: But it must be with
this Caution, that they only defend themselves, but do not attack their
Prince: They may repair the Damages received, but must not for any
provocation exceed the bounds of due Reverence and Respect. They may
20 *repulse the present attempt, but must not revenge past violences. For it*
is natural for us to defend Life and Limb, but that an Inferiour should

*punish a Superiour, is against Nature. The mischief which is designed
them, the People may prevent before it be done, but when it is done, they
must not revenge it on the King, though Author of the Villany. This
therefore is the Priviledge of the People in general, above what any private* 25
*Person hath; That particular Men are allowed by our Adversaries them-
selves,* (Buchanan *only excepted) to have no other Remedy but Patience;
but the Body of the People may with Respect resist intolerable Tyranny;
for when it is but moderate, they ought to endure it.*

234. Thus far that great Advocate of Monarchical Power
allows of *Resistance*.

235. 'Tis true he has annexed two Limitations to it, to no
purpose:
First, He says, it must be with Reverence.
Secondly, It must be without Retribution, or Punishment;
and the Reason he gives, is, *Because an Inferiour cannot punish a* 5
Superiour.
First, How to *resist Force without striking again*, or how to *strike
with Reverence*, will need some Skill to make intelligible. He that
shall oppose an Assault only with a Shield to receive the Blows,
or in any more Respectful Posture, without a Sword in his hand, 10
to abate the Confidence and Force of the Assailant, will quickly
be at an end of his *Resistance*, and will find such a defence serve
only to draw on himself the worse usage. This is as ridiculous
a way of *resisting*, as *Juvenal* thought it of fighting; *ubi tu pulsas,
ego vapulo tantum.* And the Success of the Combat will be un- 15
avoidably the same he there describes it:

> ——*Libertas pauperis hæc est:*
> *Pulsatus rogat, & pugnis concisus, adorat,*
> *Ut liceat paucis cum dentibus inde reverti.*

This will always be the event of such an imaginary *Resistance*, 20
where Men may not strike again. He therefore *who may resist,
must be allowed to strike*. And then let our Author, or any Body else
joyn a Knock on the Head, or a Cut on the Face, with as much
Reverence and *Respect* as he thinks fit. He that can Reconcile Blows

---

§ 235   13–19   Juvenal, *Satires*, III, 289–90, 299–301: 'I writhe with the blows you
put upon me.... This is a poor man's freedom; the more he is beaten, the more he
implores, and he prostrates himself as he goes down in the struggle, so that he may
come back a little with his teeth.'

25 and Reverence, may, for ought I know, deserve for his pains, a Civil Respectful Cudgeling where-ever he can meet with it.

Secondly, As to his Second, *An Inferiour cannot punish a Superiour*; that's true, generally speaking, whilst he is his Superiour. But to resist Force with Force, being *the State of War* that *levels the Parties*, 30 cancels all former relation of Reverence, Respect, and *Superiority*: And then the odds that remains, is, That he, who opposes the unjust Aggressor, has this *Superiority* over him, that he has a Right, when he prevails, to punish the Offender, both for the Breach of the Peace, and all the Evils that followed upon it. *Barclay* there-35 fore, in another place, more coherently to himself, denies it to be lawful to *resist* a King in any Case. But he there assigns Two Cases, whereby a King may Un-king himself. His Words are,

Quid ergo nulline casus incidere possunt quibus populo sese erigere atque in Regem impotentius dominantem arma capere & invadere jure suo 40 *suâque authoritate liceat? Nulli certe quamdiu Rex manet. Semper enim ex divinis id obstat,* Regem honorificato; & qui potestati resistit, Dei ordinationi resistit: *Non aliàs igitur in eum populo potestas est quam si id committat propter quod ipso jure rex esse desinat. Tunc enim se ipse principatu exuit atque in privatis constituit liber:* 45 *Hoc modo populus & superior efficitur, reverso ad eum sc. jure illo quod ante regem inauguratum in interregno habuit. At sunt paucorum generum commissa ejusmodi quæ hunc effectum pariunt. At ego cum plurima animo perlustrem, duo tantum invenio, duos, inquam, casus quibus rex ipso facto ex Rege non regem se facit & omni honore & dignitate* 50 *regali atque in subditos potestate destituit; quorum etiam meminit* Winzerus. *Horum unus est, Si regnum [& rempublicam evertere conetur, hoc est, si id ei propositum, eaque intentio fuerit ut] disperdat, quemadmodum de Nerone fertur, quod is nempe senatum populumque* Romanum, *atque adeo urbem ipsam ferro flammaque vastare, ac novas sibi sedes* 55 *quærere decrevisset. Et de* Caligula, *quod palam denunciarit se neque civem neque principem senatui amplius fore, inque animo habuerit, interempto utrisque ordinis Electissimo quoque* Alexandriam *commigrare, ac ut populum uno ictu interimeret, unam ei cervicem optavit. Talia cum rex*

38–61 and § 236 Locke's 1612 edition, 440–1, badly transcribed and also amended in errata to 3rd edition: the words '*& rempublican . . . fuerit*' (51–52) omitted in the printed editions, though translated by Locke.

51 'Winzerus'—miscopy for Winzetus, that is, Ninian Winzet, Winget or Wingate, Scottish controversialist, who wrote against Knox and Buchanan. Locke had obviously never heard of him.

aliquis meditatur & molitur serio, omnem regnandi curam & animum
illico abjicit, ac proinde imperium in subditos amittit, ut dominus servi 60
pro derelicto habiti, dominium.

236. *Alter casus est, Si rex in alicujus clientelam se contulit, ac*
regnum quod liberum à majoribus & populo traditum accepit, alienæ
ditioni mancipavit. Nam tunc quamvis forte non eâ mente id agit populo
plane ut incommodet: Tamen quia quod præcipuum est regiæ dignitatis
amisit, ut summus scilicet in regno secundum Deum sit, & solo Deo 5
inferior, atque populum etiam totum ignorantem vel invitum, cujus liber-
tatem sartam & tectam conservare debuit, in alterius gentis ditionem
& potestatem dedidit; hâc velut quadam regni ab alienatione effecit, ut
nec quod ipse in regno imperium habuit retineat, nec in eum cui collatum
voluit, juris quicquam transferat; atque ita eo facto liberum jam & suæ 10
potestatis populum relinquit, cujus rei exemplum unum annales Scotici
suppeditant. Barclay contra Monarchom. Lib. 3. c. 16.

Which in *English* runs thus.

237. *What then, Can there no Case happen wherein the People may*
of right, and by their own Authority help themselves, take Arms, and
set upon their King, imperiously domineering over them? None at all,
whilst he remains a King. Honour the King, *and* he that resists the
Power, resists the Ordinance of God; *are Divine Oracles that will* 5
never permit it. The People therefore can never come by a Power over
him, unless he does something that makes him cease to be a King. For
then he divests himself of his Crown and Dignity, and returns to the state
of a private Man, and the People become free and superiour; the Power
which they had in the Interregnum, *before they Crown'd him King,* 10
devolving to them again. But there are but few miscarriages which bring
the matter to this state. After considering it well on all sides, I can find
but two. Two Cases there are, I say, whereby a King, ipso facto, *becomes*
no King; and loses all Power and Regal Authority over his People; which
are also taken notice of by Winzerus. 15

The first is, *If he endeavour to overturn the Government, that is, if he*
have a purpose and design to ruine the Kingdom and Commonwealth,

---

§ 236   12   This reference to Barclay appears on p. 73 of Locke's *Tablet* (MS. f. 28—
see note on II, § 22, 9 and references) thus:

80

Liberty
Barclay l 3 c 16

The 80 is certainly intended for 1680, and probably marks this passage as belonging to that year.

as it is recorded of Nero, *that he resolved to cut off the Senate and People of* Rome, *lay the City waste with Fire and Sword, and then remove to*
20 *some other place. And of* Caligula, *that he openly declar'd, that he would be no longer a Head to the People or Senate, and that he had it in his thoughts to cut off the worthiest Men of both Ranks, and then retire to* Alexandria: *And he wish'd that the People had but one Neck, that he might dispatch them all at a blow. Such designs as these, when any King*
25 *harbours in his thoughts and seriously promotes, he immediately gives up all care and thought of the Common-wealth; and consequently forfeits the Power of Governing his Subjects, as a Master does the Dominion over his Slaves whom he hath abandon'd.*

238. The other Case is, *When a King makes himself the dependent of another, and subjects his Kingdom which his Ancestors left him, and the People put free into his hands, to the Dominion of another. For however perhaps it may not be in his intention to prejudice the People; yet because*
5 *he has hereby lost the principal part of Regal Dignity,* viz. *to be next and immediately under God, Supream in his Kingdom; and also because he betray'd or forced his People, whose liberty he ought to have carefully preserved, into the Power and Dominion of a Foreign Nation. By this as it were alienation of his Kingdom, he himself loses the Power he had in*
10 *it before, without transferring any the least right to those on whom he would have bestowed it; and so by this act sets the People free, and leaves them at their own disposal. One Example of this is to be found in the* Scotch *Annals.*

239. In these Cases *Barclay* the great Champion of Absolute Monarchy, is forced to allow, That a King may be *resisted*, and *ceases to be a King.* That is in short, not to multiply Cases: In whatsoever he has *no Authority*, there he is no *King*, and may be
5 *resisted:* For *wheresoever the Authority ceases, the King ceases too*, and becomes like other Men who have no Authority. And these two Cases he instances in, differ little from those above mention'd, to be destructive to Governments, only that he has omitted the Principle from which his Doctrine flows; and that is, The breach
10 of trust, in not preserving the Form of Government agreed on, and in not intending the end of Government it self, which is the publick good and preservation of Property. When a King has Dethron'd himself, and put himself in a state of War with his

___

§ **239**   7   'those above mention'd'—presumably in §§ 212–24, especially § 217.

People, what shall hinder them from prosecuting him who is no King, as they would any other Man, who has put himself into 15 a State of War with them; *Barclay*, and those of his Opinion, would do well to tell us. This farther I desire may be taken notice of out of *Barclay*, that he says, *The mischief that is designed them, the People may prevent before it be done*, whereby he allows *resistance* when Tyranny is but in design. *Such Designs as these* (says he) *when any* 20 *King harbours in his thoughts and seriously promotes, he immediately gives up all care and thought of the Common-wealth*; so that according to him the neglect of the publick good is to be taken as an evidence of such a *design*, or at least for a sufficient cause of *resistance*. And the reason of all he gives in these words, *because he betray'd or forced* 25 *his People whose liberty he ought carefully to have preserved*. What he adds *into the Power and Dominion of a Foreign Nation*, signifies nothing, the fault and forfeiture lying in the loss of their *Liberty* which he *ought to have preserved*, and not in any distinction of the Persons to whose Dominion they were subjected. The People's 30 Right is equally invaded, and their Liberty lost, whether they are made Slaves to any of their own, or a *Foreign Nation*; and in this lies the injury, and against this only have they the Right of Defence. And there are instances to be found in all Countries, which shew that 'tis not the change of Nations in the Persons of 35 their Governours, but the change of Government, that gives the Offence. *Bilson*, a Bishop of our Church, and a great Stickler for the Power and Prerogative of Princes, does, if I mistake not, in his Treatise of *Christian Subjection*, acknowledge, That *Princes may*

16–17   Those of Barclay's opinion include Bilson and perhaps even Hooker (see below), and it is clear that Locke has picked out Barclay as typical of the whole absolutist school, insisting on his concessions to resistance. Grotius had done this as early as 1625 in his *De Jure Belli*, where (i, iv, 11) he cites the passage quoted in full by Locke in § 232. Mr Salmon shows (1959) that the example was followed by a considerable number of writers who insisted on Barclay's admissions as justifying action against despots, such men as Samuel Rutherford, William Prynne, John Canne, Richard Baxter, Pierre Jurieu and James Tyrrell (*Bibliotheca Politica*, 1691–2, 1718 ed., 106, printing the identical passage as in § 233, but differently translated). It is clear, then, that Locke was merely following a well-established convention, but he dealt more thoroughly with Barclay than anyone else. Although he was quoted in the political literature of 1689, Barclay's name is more typical of the period of Filmer, both in the 1640's and the early 1680's.

17–37   Passage inserted in 1694 and typical of the way Locke expanded his text, making it very difficult to distinguish original and addition. Compare II, § 217.

40 *forfeit their Power*, and their Title to the Obedience of their Subjects; and if there needed authority in a Case where reason is so
plain, I could send my Reader to *Bracton, Fortescue*, and the Author
of the Mirror, and others; Writers, who cannot be suspected to
be ignorant of our Government, or Enemies to it. But I thought
45 *Hooker* alone might be enough to satisfie those Men, who relying
on him for their Ecclesiastical Polity, are by strange fate carried to
deny those principles upon which he builds it. Whether they are
herein made the Tools of Cunninger Workmen, to pull down their
own Fabrick, they were best look. This I am sure, their Civil Policy
50 is so new, so dangerous, and so destructive to both Rulers and
People, that as former Ages never could bear the broaching of it;
so it may be hoped those to come, redeem'd from the Impositions
of those *Egyptian* Under-Taskmasters, will abhor the Memory of
such servile Flatterers, who whilst it seem'd to serve their turn,
55 resolv'd all Government into absolute Tyranny, and would have
all Men born to, what their mean Souls fitted them for, Slavery.

240. Here, 'tis like, the common Question will be made, *Who
shall be Judge* whether the Prince or Legislative act contrary to their

§ 239   37–9   Thomas Bilson (1547–1616, Warden of Winchester College, bishop
successively of Worcester and Winchester), *The True Difference between Christian
Subiection and Unchristian Rebellion*, 1585. This book was often quoted by the opponents
of absolutism, for exactly the same reason as Barclay was and frequently alongside
of him (by Prynne, for example)—because though an absolutist he admitted resistance in crucial cases. Locke does not seem to have possessed Bilson's book, and the
form of words here implies that he did not know it first-hand.
   42–3   '*Bracton*'—the judge (d. 1268) and author of *De Legibus et Consuetudinibus
Angliae*. '*Fortescue*'—Sir John Fortescue (1394?–1476?), Lord Chief Justice and
author of *De Laudibus Legum Angliae*. 'the Author of the Mirror', perhaps Andrew
Horne (d. 1328), author of a work very popular with constitutionalists in the
seventeenth century, but a highly suspect source, *The Booke called The Mirrour of
Justices*, printed in the 1640s. Compare note on II, § 13, 1–2. Locke recommended
Bracton and the Mirror in his *Thoughts on Reading and Study*, 1703, and his letter to
Rev. Richd. King, 170 (*Works*, 1801, III, 272; XI, 306): in his *Education* (*ibid*. IX, 177)
he requires a gentleman to 'take a view of our English constitution, in the ancient
books of the common law'. There is, however, no evidence that he ever possessed
or read any one of these books, a fact which bears on his indifference to constitutional history and constitutional development; see Introduction, 77 and note.
   45   '*Hooker*'—see note on II, § 5, 7–23: this sentence indicates that the paragraph
was written when, or not long after, Locke had decided to add the quotations from
Hooker, perhaps in 1681; see note on II, § 211, chapter XIX.
§ 240   1–2   '*Who shall be Judge*'—see II, § 168, 1–2, note and references. This
question occupies Locke until the end of the book, and the passage seems to have
been part of the original text, perhaps following on to § 231, but much modified and
extended in 1689—see note on II, § 211, chapter XIX.

Trust? This, perhaps, ill affected and factious Men may spread amongst the People, when the Prince only makes use of his due Prerogative. To this I reply, *The People shall be Judge*; for who shall 5 be *Judge* whether his Trustee or Deputy acts well, and according to the Trust reposed in him, but he who deputes him, and must, by having deputed him have still a Power to discard him, when he fails in his Trust? If this be reasonable in particular Cases of private Men, why should it be otherwise in that of the greatest 10 moment; where the Welfare of Millions is concerned, and also where the evil, if not prevented, is greater, and the Redress very difficult, dear, and dangerous?

241. But farther, this Question, (*Who shall be Judge?*) cannot mean, that there is no Judge at all. For where there is no Judicature on Earth, to decide Controversies amongst Men, *God* in Heaven is *Judge*: He alone, 'tis true, is Judge of the Right. But *every Man is Judge* for himself, as in all other Cases, so in this, 5 whether another hath put himself into a State of War with him, and whether he should appeal to the Supreme Judge, as *Jephtha* did.

242. If a Controversie arise betwixt a Prince and some of the People, in a matter where the Law is silent, or doubtful, and the thing be of great Consequence, I should think the proper *Umpire*, in such a Case, should be the Body of the *People*. For in Cases where the Prince hath a Trust reposed in him, and is dispensed 5 from the common ordinary Rules of the Law; there, if any Men find themselves aggrieved, and think the Prince acts contrary to, or beyond that Trust, who so proper to *Judge* as the Body of the *People*, (who, at first, lodg'd that Trust in him) how far they meant it should extend? But if the Prince, or whoever they be in the 10 Administration, decline that way of Determination, the Appeal then lies no where but to Heaven. Force between either Persons, who have no known Superiour on Earth, or which permits no Appeal to a Judge on Earth, being properly a State of War, wherein the Appeal lies only to Heaven, and in that State the *injured Party* 15 *must judge* for himself, when he will think fit to make use of that Appeal, and put himself upon it.

243. To conclude, The *Power that every individual gave the Society*, when he entered into it, can never revert to the Individuals

---

§ **241**   7   '*Jephtha*'—see note on II, § 21, 17 and references.

again, as long as the Society lasts, but will always remain in the
Community; because without this, there can be no Community,
5 no Common-wealth, which is contrary to the original Agreement:
So also when the Society hath placed the Legislative in any
Assembly of Men, to continue in them and their Successors, with
Direction and Authority for providing such Successors, *the Legislative can never revert to the People* whilst that Government lasts:
10 Because having provided a Legislative with Power to continue
for ever, they have given up their Political Power to the Legislative, and cannot resume it. But if they have set Limits to the
Duration of their Legislative, and made this Supreme Power in
any Person, or Assembly, only temporary: Or else when by the
15 Miscarriages of those in Authority, it is forfeited; upon the
Forfeiture of their Rulers, or at the Determination of the Time set,
it reverts to the Society, and the People have a Right to act as
Supreme, and continue the Legislative in themselves, or erect
a new Form, or under the old form place it in new hands, as
20 they think good.

FINIS.

---

§ 243   19–21   Modified slightly by Locke. The reference to 'new hands', and perhaps
much or even all of §§ 242, 243, seem to belong to 1689.

SUGGESTED READING

The following list of titles is intended to direct students to essential reading on Locke. It is therefore inevitably a selection. All works are published in London unless otherwise shown.

AARSLEFF, HANS, 1969. *The State of Nature and the Nature of Man in Locke. Locke.* In Yolton, 1969.

ABRAMS, P. 1967. *John Locke: Two Tracts on Government.* Cambridge.

APPLEBY, JOYCE O. 1976. Locke, Liberalism and the Natural Law of Money, *Past and Present*, LXXI.

ASHCRAFT, RICHARD, 1980. The Two Treatises and the Exclusion Crisis. In Pocock, J. G. A. and Ashcraft, R. eds., *John Locke*. Los Angeles.

ASHCRAFT, RICHARD, 1986. *Revolutionary Politics and Locke's Two Treatises of Government.* Princeton.

ASHCRAFT, RICHARD, 1987. *Locke's Two Treatises of Government.*

AXTELL, J. L. 1968. *The Educational Writings of John Locke.* Cambridge.

BATZ, WILLIAM G. 1974. The Historical Anthropology of John Locke, *Journal of the History of Ideas*, XXXV, 4.

BECKER, CARL, 1922. *The Declaration of Independence.* New York.

BLUHM, W. T., WINTFELD, N. and TEGER, S. 1980. Locke' Idea of God: Rational Truth or Political Myth?, *The Journal of Politics*, XLII, 2.

BRANDT, R., ed. 1981. *John Locke Symposium.* Wolfenbüttel.

BUTLER, M. A. 1978. Early Liberal Roots of Feminism: John Locke and the Attack on Patriarchy, *American Political Science Review*, LXXII, 1.

CLARK, J. C. D. 1985. *English Society 1688–1832.* Cambridge.

CLARK, J. C. D. 1986. *Revolution and Rebellion: State and Society in England in the Seventeenth and Eighteenth Centuries.* Cambridge.

COLIE, ROSALIE, 1966. John Locke and the Publication of the Private, *Philological Quarterly*, XLV.

COLMAN, JOHN, 1983. *John Locke's Moral Philosophy.* Edinburgh.

COX, RICHARD, H. 1960. *Locke on War and Peace.* Oxford.

CRANSTON, MAURICE, 1957. *John Locke, a Biography.*

DALY, JAMES, 1979. *Sir Robert Filmer and English Political Thought.* Toronto.

DE BEER, ESMOND, 1976–82. *The Correspondence of John Locke.* Oxford.

DICKINSON, H. T. 1977. *Liberty and Property: Political Ideology in Eighteenth Century Britain.*

DRURY, S. B. 1982. Locke and Nozick on property, *Political Studies*, XXX, 1.

DUNN, JOHN, 1967. Consent in the Political Theory of John Locke, *Historical Journal*, X, 3. Reprinted in Schochet, 1971.

DUNN, JOHN, 1969 (i). *The Political Thought of John Locke.* Cambridge.

DUNN, JOHN, 1969 (ii). The Politics of Locke in England and America in the Eighteenth Century. In Yolton, 1969.

DUNN, JOHN, 1984 (i). *John Locke*. Oxford.

DUNN, JOHN, 1984 (ii). The concept of trust in the politics of John Locke. In Rorty, R., *et al.*, ed., *Philosophy in History*, Cambridge.

FARR, J. and ROBERTS, C. 1985. John Locke on the Glorious Revolution, a rediscovered document, *Historical Journal*, XXVIII, 2.

FILMER, Sir ROBERT, 1949. Patriarcha *and the other political works*, ed. Laslett, P. Oxford.

FOX BOURNE, H. R. 1876. *The Life of John Locke*. 2 vols.

GOLDIE, MARK, 1977. Edmund Bohun and *ius gentium* in the revolution debate, 1689–93, *Historical Journal*, XX, 3.

GOLDIE, MARK, 1980. The Revolution of 1689 and the Structure of Political Argument, *Bulletin of Research in the Humanities*, 83.

GOLDIE, MARK, 1983. John Locke and Anglican Royalism, *Political Studies*, XXXI, 1.

GOLDWIN, R. A. 1963. John Locke. In Strauss, L. and Cropsey, J., eds., *History of Political Philosophy*. Chicago.

GOLDWIN, R. A. 1976. Locke's state of nature in political society, *The Western Political Quarterly*, XXIX, 1.

GOUGH, J. W. 1973 (1950). *John Locke's Political Philosophy, Eight Studies*. 2nd ed. Oxford.

GOUGH, J. W. 1976. James Tyrrell, Whig historian and friend of John Locke, *Historical Journal*, XIX, 3.

HALEY, K. H. D. 1968. *The First Earl of Shaftesbury*. Oxford.

HARRISON, JOHN and LASLETT, PETER, 1971 (1965). *The Library of John Locke*. 2nd ed. Oxford.

HOBBES, THOMAS, 1984 (1651). *De Cive*, ed. Warrender, H. Oxford.

HOOKER, RICHARD, 1836 (1632, etc.). *Works*, ed Keble, 3 vols. Oxford.

HUNDERT, E. J. 1972. The making of Homo faber: John Locke between ideology and history, *Journal of the History of Ideas*, XXXIII, 1.

HUNDERT, E. J. 1977. Market society and meaning in Locke's Political philosophy, *Journal of the History of Philosophy*, XV.

JOLLEY, N. 1975. Leibniz on Hobbes, Locke's *Two Treatises* and Sherlock's *Case of Allegiance*, *Historical Journal*, XVIII, 1.

KELLY, P. 1969. *The Economic Writings of John Locke*. Dissertation, University of Cambridge.

KELLY, P. 1977. Locke and Filmer: was Laslett so wrong after all? *The Locke Newsletter*, VIII.

KENDALL, WILLMOORE, 1941. John Locke and the doctrine of majority rule, *Illinois Studies in the Social Sciences*, XXVI, 2.

KENYON, J. P. 1977. *Revolution Principles: The Politics of Party, 1689–1720*. Cambridge.

LASLETT, PETER, 1956. The English Revolution and Locke's *Two Treatises of Government, Cambridge Historical Journal*, XII, 1.

LASLETT, PETER, 1969 (1957). John Locke, the Great Recoinage and the Board of Trade, 1695–1698. In Yolton, 1969.

LASLETT, PETER, 1964. Market Society and Political Theory—Review of Macpherson, 1962. *Historical Journal* VII.

LASLETT, PETER, 1965 (1983). *The World we have lost* . . . 3rd ed.

LASLETT, PETER, 1965. *See* Harrison, John.

LOCKE, JOHN.

An Essay concerning Human Understanding, 1690 (1975) ed. Nidditch, P. Oxford.

The Educational Writings, 1968, ed. Axtell, J. L. Cambridge.

The Economic Writings, see Kelly, P. 1969.

Epistola de Tolerantia, 1968, ed. Klibansky, R. and Gough, J. W. Oxford.

MACLEAN, A. H. 1947. George Lawson and John Locke, *Cambridge Historical Journal*, IX, 1.

MACPHERSON, C. B. 1962. *The Political Theory of Possessive Individualism.* Oxford.

MENAKE, G. T. 1981. Research note and query on the dating of Locke's *Two Treatises, Political Theory*, IX.

MENAKE, G. T. 1982 . . . a sequel, *Political Theory*, X.

MOLYNEUX, WILLIAM, 1698 (1720). *The Case of Ireland's being Bound by Acts of Parliament in England*. Dublin.

NOZICK, R. 1974. *Anarchy, State, and Utopia*. Oxford.

RAU, ZBIGNIEW, 1987. Some thoughts on civil society in Eastern Europe and the Lockean contractarian approach, *Political Studies*, XXXV.

SIDNEY, ALGERNON, 1698 (1772). *Discourses Concerning Government*. In *The Works of Algernon Sydney, a New Edition* [ed. by Joseph Robertson, publ. by Thomas Hollis], 1772.

SKINNER, QUENTIN, 1978 *The Foundations of Modern Political Thought*. 2 vols. Cambridge.

SNOW, VERNON, F. 1962. The Concept of Revolution in Seventeenth-century England, *Historical Journal*, V, 2.

STRAUSS, LEO, 1953. *Natural Right and History*. Chicago.

TARCOV, NATHAN, 1984. *Locke's Education for Liberty*. Chicago.

TARLTON, CHARLES D. 1978. Rope of sand: interpreting Locke's *First Treatise of Government, Historical Journal*, XXI, 1.

TARLTON, CHARLES, D. 1981. The Exclusion Controversy, Pamphleteering, and Locke's *Two Treatises, Historical Journal*, XXIV, 1.

THOMPSON, MARTYN P. 1976. The reception of Locke's *Two Treatises of Government, Political Studies*, XXIV, 2.

TUCK, RICHARD, 1979. *Natural Rights Theories: Their Origin and Development*. Cambridge.

TULLY, JAMES, 1980. *A Discourse on Property: John Locke and his Adversaries.* Cambridge.

TYRRELL, JAMES, 1681. *Patriarcha non Monarcha.*

VINER, JACOB, 1963. Possessive Individualism as Original Sin, *The Canadian Journal of Economics and Political Science* III.

VON LEYDEN, WOLFGANG, 1954. *John Locke, Essays on the Law of Nature.* Oxford.

WALDRON, JEREMY, 1984. Locke, Tully, and the Regulation of Property, *Political Studies*, XXXII, 1.

WARRENDER, J. 1957. *The Political Philosophy of Hobbes: His Theory of Obligation. Oxford.*

WESTERN, J. R. 1972. *Monarchy and Revolution: The English State in the 1680s.*

WOLIN, SHELDON, 1960. *Politics and Vision.* Boston, Mass.

WOOD, NEAL, 1983. *The Politics of Locke's Philosophy: A Social Study of An Essay Concerning Human Understanding.* California.

WOOD, NEAL, 1984. *John Locke and Agrarian Capitalism.* California.

YOLTON, J. W. 1956. *John Locke and the Way of Ideas.* Oxford.

YOLTON, J. W. 1969. *John Locke: Problems and Perspectives.* Cambridge.

BIBLIOGRAPHY

(All books published in London unless otherwise shown)

AARON, R. I. 1936. *An Early Draft of Locke's Essay, together with Excerpts from his Journals.* (With Gibb, J.) Oxford.

AARON, R. I. 1937. (2nd ed. 1955). *John Locke.* Oxford.

AARSLEFF, HANS, 1969. *The State of Nature and the Nature of Man in Locke.* In Yolton, 1969.

ABRAMS, P. 1961. *John Locke as a Conservative: An Edition of Locke's First Writings on Political Obligation.* Unpublished Dissertation in the Cambridge University Library. (Pagination of original Latin and English text retained in this version.)

ABRAMS, P. 1967. *John Locke: Two Tracts on Government.* Cambridge.

ACOSTA, JOSÉ DE, 1608 (1880). *The Naturall and Morall Historie of the East and West Indies* [tr. E. Grimstone]. (Ed. Markham, C. R., 2 vols. 1880.)

AINSWORTH, HENRY, 1622 (1639). *Annotations upon the Five Books of Moses.* . . .

ALBRITTON, R. R. 1976. The Politics of Locke's philosophy, *Political Studies*, XXIV, 3.

ALLEN, J. W. 1928. Sir Robert Filmer. In Hearnshaw, F. J. C., ed., *Social and Political Ideas of the Augustan Age.*

ALLEN, J. W. 1938. *English Political Thought 1603–1660*, vol. 1, 1603–44.

ANGLIM, JOHN, 1978. On Locke's State of Nature, *Political Studies*, XXVI, I.

APPLEBY, JOYCE O. 1976. Locke, Liberalism and the Natural Law of Money, *Past and Present*, LXXI.

APPLEBY, JOYCE O. 1978. *Economic Thought and Ideology in Seventeenth Century England.* Princeton.

AQUINAS, SAINT THOMAS, 1624. *Summa Theologica.* Lyons.

ARENILLA, L. 1961. The notion of Civil Disobedience According to Locke, *Diogenes*, XXXV.

ASHCRAFT, RICHARD, 1968. Locke's State of Nature, Historical Fact or Moral Fiction?, *American Political Science Review* LXII.

ASHCRAFT, RICHARD, 1969 (i). *Faith and Knowledge in Locke's Philosophy.* In Yolton, 1969.

ASHCRAFT, RICHARD, 1969 (ii). John Locke's Library: Portrait of an Intellectual, *Transactions of the Cambridge Bibliographical Society.*

ASHCRAFT, RICHARD, 1972. John Locke belimed: the case for political philosophy, *Political Studies*, XX, 2.

ASHCRAFT, RICHARD, 1980. The Two Treatises and the Exclusion Crisis, in Pocock, J. G. A. and Ashcraft, R. eds., *John Locke.* Los Angeles.

ASHCRAFT, RICHARD, 1986. *Revolutionary Politics and Locke's Two Treatises of Government*. Princeton.

ASHCRAFT, RICHARD, 1987. *Locke's Two Treatises of Government*.

ASHCRAFT, R. and GOLDSMITH, M. M. 1983. Locke, Revolution Principles and the Formation of Whig Ideology, *Historical Journal*, XXVI, 4.

AXTELL, J. L. 1968. *The Educational Writings of John Locke*. Cambridge.

BAGSHAW, EDWARD, junior, 1660. *The Great Question Concerning Things Indifferent in Religious Worship*.

BARBEYRAC, JEAN, 1734. *See* Pufendorf, Samuel von.

BARCLAY, WILLIAM, 1600 (1612). *De Regno et Regali Potestate*. Hanover.

BARCLAY, WILLIAM, 1609 (1612). *De Potestate Papae*. Hanover.

BARKER, Sir ERNEST, 1934. *See* Gierke, O. von.

BASNAGE DE BEAUVAL, HENRI, 1691. Review of Du Gouvernement Civil (*Histoire des Ouvrages des Sçavans*, 457).

BASTIDE, CH. 1907. *John Locke, ses Théories Politiques et leur Influence en Angleterre*. Paris.

BATZ, WILLIAM G. 1974. The Historical Anthropology of John Locke, *Journal of the History of Ideas*, XXXV, 4.

BAXTER, RICHARD, 1680. *The Second Part of the Nonconformist's Plea for Peace*.

BAYLE, PIERRE, 1725–7. *Œuvres Diverses*. 4 vols. The Hague.

BECKER, CARL, 1922. *The Declaration of Independence*. New York.

BERLIN, SIR ISAIAH, 1964. Hobbes, Locke and Professor Macpherson, *Political Quarterly*, XXXV.

BESUSSI, A. 1985. Studi Lockiani, *Teoria Politica*, I. 1.

BILSON, THOMAS, 1585. *The True Difference between Christian Subjection and Unchristian Rebellion*.

[BLACKBURNE, FRANCIS] 1780. *Memoirs of Thomas Hollis, Esq.*

BLUHM, W. T., WINTFELD, N. and TEGER, S. 1980. Locke's Idea of God: Rational Truth or Political Myth?, *The Journal of Politics*, XLII, 2.

BODIN, JEAN, 1566 (1945). *Methodus and Facilem Historiarum Cognitionem* [Method for the Easy Comprehension of History, tr. and ed. Reynolds, B.] New York.

BODIN, JEAN, 1576 (1606). *Les Six Livres de la République* [The Six bookes of a Commonweale, tr. Knolles, Richard].

BOHUN, EDWARD, 1684. *A Defence of Sir Robert Filmer, against Algernon Sidney*.

BOHUN, EDMUND, 1685. Edition of *Patriarcha*, *see* Filmer, Sir Robert.

BOHUN, EDMUND, 1853. *Diary and Autobiography*. Beccles.

BOWERS, FREDSON, 1953. *The Dramatic Works of Thomas Dekker*, vol. 1, Cambridge.

BOWERS, FREDSON, 1954. With Gerritsen and Laslett, *see* Laslett, 1954 (ii).

BRACTON, 1569, 1649, etc. *De Legibus ete Consuetudinibus Angliae.*

BRANDT, R., ed. 1981. *John Locke Symposium.* Wolfenbüttel.

BRENNAN, THERESA and PATEMAN, C. 1979. 'Mere auxiliaries to the Commonwealth'; Women and the origins of Liberalism, *Political Studies*, XVII, 2.

BROGAN, R. P. 1959. John Locke and Utilitarianism, *Ethics*, LXVIII, 1.

BROWN, L. F. 1933. *The First Earl of Shaftesbury.* New York.

BUCKINGHAM, GEORGE VILLIERS, 2nd Duke of, 1672. *The Rehearsal.*

BURNET, GILBERT, 1724, 1734. *History of His Own Time.* 2 vols.

BUTLER, M. A. 1978. Early Liberal Roots of Feminism: John Locke and the Attack on Patriarchy, *American Political Science Review*, LXXII, 1.

CARDAN, JEROME, 1640 (1663). Encomium Neronis. In: *Opera*, Leyden.

CARY, JOHN, 1698. *A Vindication of the Parliament of England in Answer to W. Molyneux.*

CASINELLI, W. 1959. The Consent of the Governed, *Western Political Quarterly*, XII.

CHAMBERLAYNE, EDWARD, 1700. *Anglia Notitia, or The Present State of England . . .* 19th ed.

CHERNO, M. 1957. Locke on Property, *Ethics.*

CHRISTIE, W. D. 1871. *A Life of . . . [the] First Earl of Shaftesbury.* 2 vols.

CHRISTOPHERSON, H. O. 1930. *A Bibliographical Introduction to John Locke*, Skrifter utgitt av der Norske Videnskaps-Akademi, Oslo. II, Hist. Filos. Klasse, 1930, No. 8, Oslo.

CLARENDON, EDWARD HYDE, 1st Earl of, 1676. *A Briefe View . . . Mr Hobbes Book Entitled* Leviathan. Oxford.

CLARK, J. C. D. 1985 *English Society 1688–1832.* Cambridge.

CLARK, J. C. D. 1986. *Revolution and Rebellion: State and Society in England in the Seventeenth and Eighteenth Centuries.* Cambridge.

CLARK, L. M. G. 1977. Woman and John Locke, or Who Owns the Apples in the Garden of Eden?, *Canadian Journal of Philosophy*, VII, 4.

CLEMENT, SIMON, 1698. *An Answer to Mr Molyneux, his Case of Ireland.*

COHEN, J. 1986. Structure, choice and Legitimacy: Locke's Theory of the State, *Philosophy and Public Affairs.*

COLELLA, E. P. 1984. The Commodity Form and Socialization in Locke's State of Nature, *International Studies in Philosophy*, XXVI.

COLIE, ROSALIE, 1955–6. Publication of Lady Masham's letter to Jean Le Clerc of 12 January 1705. *History of Ideas News Letter* (cyclostyled), vols. I and II, New York.

COLIE, ROSALIE, 1965. The Social Language of John Locke, *Journal of British Studies*, IV, 2.

COLIE, ROSALIE, 1966. John Locke and the Publication of the Private, *Philological Quarterly*, XLV.

COLMAN, JOHN, 1983. *John Locke's Moral Philosophy.* Edinburgh.

COSTA Y MARTINEZ, JOAQUIN, 1898. *Colectivismo Agrario en España*. Madrid.

COX, RICHARD H. 1960. *Locke on War and Peace*. Oxford.

CRANSTON, MAURICE, 1957. *John Locke, a Biography*.

CUMBERLAND, RICHARD, 1672. *De Legibus Naturae Disquisitio Philosophica*.

CVEK, P. P. 1984. Locke's Theory of Property: A Re-examination, *Auslegung*, XI.

CZAJOWSKI, C. J. 1941. *The Theory of Private property in Locke's Political Philosophy*. Notre Dame, Ind., U.S.A.

DALY, JAMES, 1979. *Sir Robert Filmer and English Political Thought*. Toronto.

DAY, J. P. 1966. Locke on Property, *Philosophical Quarterly*, XVI, 64. Reprinted in Schochet, 1971.

DE BEER, ESMOND, 1969. *Locke and English Liberalism: The Second Treatise of Government in its Contemporary Setting*. In Yolton, 1969.

DE BEER, ESMOND, 1976–82. *The Correspondence of John Locke*. Oxford.

DE MARCHI, E. 1953. Le origine dell'idea della toleranza religiosa nel Locke, *Occidente*, IX, 6.

DE MARCHI, E. 1955. Locke's Atlantis, *Political Studies*, III, 2.

DE ROCHEFORT, CESAR, 1658. *Histoire Naturelle et Morale des Isles Antilles*. Rotterdam. (Also attributed to de Poincy, L. and du Tertre, J. B.)

DEWHURST, KENNETH, 1963. *John Locke, Physician and Philosopher. A Medical Biography*.

DICKINSON, H. T. 1977. *Liberty and Property: Political Ideology in Eighteenth Century Britain*.

DRIVER, C. H. 1928. John Locke. In Hearnshaw, F. J. C. ed., *Social and Political Ideas of the Augustan Age*.

DRURY, S. B. 1980. Natural law and innate ideas, *Dialogue*, XIX, 4.

DRURY, S. B. 1982. Locke and Nozick on property, *Political Studies*, XXX, 1.

DUNN, JOHN, 1967 (i). Consent in the Political Theory of John Locke, *Historical Journal*, X, 3.

DUNN, JOHN, 1968. Justice and the Interpretation of Locke's Political Theory, *Political Studies*, XVI.

DUNN, JOHN, 1969 (i). *The Political Thought of John Locke*. Cambridge.

DUNN, JOHN, 1969 (ii). The Politics of Locke in England and America in the Eighteenth Century. In Yolton, 1969.

DUNN, JOHN, 1980. *Political Obligation in its Historical Context, Essays in Political Theory*, Cambridge.

DUNN, JOHN, 1981. Individuality and Clientage in the Formation of Locke's Social Imagination. In Brandt, 1981.

DUNN, JOHN, 1984 (i). *John Locke*. Oxford.

DUNN, JOHN, 1984 (ii). The concept of trust in the politics of John Locke. In Rorty, R., *et al.*, ed., *Philosophy in History*, Cambridge.

EDWARDS, STEWART, 1969. Political Philosophy belimed: the Case of Locke, *Political Studies*, XVII.

ELRINGTON, THOMAS, 1798. Annotated edition of *Second Treatise*.

ESSAY, 1705. [Anon.] *An Essay upon Government, wherein the Republican Schemes Revived by Mr Locke, Dr Blackal etc are Fully Considered and Refuted.*

EUCHNER, WALTER, 1962. Zum Streit un die Interpretation der politischen Philosophie John Lockes, *Politische Vierteljahrschrift*, III, 3. Cologne.

EUCHNER, WALTER, 1979. *Naturrecht und Politik bei John Locke.* Frankfurt.

EZELL, MARGARET, 1987. *The Patriarch's Wife.* Chapel Hill.

FAGIANI, F. 1983. *Nel crepuscolo della probabilità ragione ed esperienza nella filosofia sociale di John Locke.* Naples.

FARR, J. and ROBERTS, C., 1985. John Locke on the Glorious Revolution, a rediscovered document, *Historical Journal*, XXVIII, 2.

FERGUSON, ROBERT, 1681. *A Just and Modest Vindication of the Two Last Parliaments.*

FERGUSON, ROBERT, 1684. *An Enquiry into the Administration of Affairs in England.*

FERGUSON, ROBERT, 1688. *A Brief Justification of the Prince of Orange's Descent into England.*

FERGUSON, ROBERT, 1688. *A Representation of the Threatening Dangers.*

FILMER, SIR ROBERT

Advertisement

1653 (1679, 1680). *An Advertisement to the Jurymen of England touching Witches.*

Anarchy

1648 (1679, 1680, 1949). *The Anarchy of a Limited or Mixed Monarchy.*

Directions

1652 (1679, 1680, 1949). *Directions for Obedience to Governors.*

Forms

1652 (1679, 1680, 1949). *Observations upon Aristotles Politiques touching Forms of Government.*

Freeholder

1648 (1679, 1680, 1949). *The Freeholders Grand Inquest*

Necessity

1648 (1680, 1949). *The Necessity of the Absolute Power of All Kings.*

Original

1652 (1679, 1680, 1949). *Observations Concerning the Original Government upon Mr Hobs Leviathan, Mr Milton against Salmasius, H. Grotius De Jure Belli.*

Patriarcha
   1680. *Patriarcha, or the Natural Power of Kings.*
   1675 (1959). [Ed. Bohun, Edmund.]
Collected Editions
   1679. *The Freeholders Grand Inquest.*
   1680. *The Freeholders Grand Inquest.*
   1684. *The Freeholders Grand Inquest.*
   1696. *Observations Concerning the Original and Various Forms of Government* [reissue of 1684 ed.].
   1949. *See* Laslett, 1949.
   (*See* Laslett, 1949, 47–8. Concise Bibliography of the Works of Sir Robert Filmer).

FITZHUGH, GEORGE, 1960. *Cannibals All! or Slaves without Masters* (1857), ed. C. Vann Woodward, Harvard.

FORTESCUE, SIR JOHN, 1616, etc. *De Laudibus Legum Angliae.*

FOWLER, THOMAS, 1880. *Locke* (English Men of Letters).

FOX BOURNE, H. R. 1876. *The Life of John Locke.* 2 vols.

FRANKLIN, JULIAN, H. 1978. *John Locke and the Theory of Sovereignty.* Cambridge.

FURLEY, O. W. 1957. The Whig Exclusionists: Pamphlet Literature . . . 1679–81, *Cambridge Historical Journal*, XIII, 1.

FURLY, BENJAMIN, 1714. *Bibliotheca Furleiana . . . catalogus librorum B. Furly.* Rotterdam.

GARCILASO DE LA VEGA, 1633. *Le Commentaire Royale, ou L'Histoire des Yncas, Roys du Peru . . .* traduitte sur la version espagnolle par I. Baudoin. Paris.

GARCILASO DE LA VEGA, 1670. *Histoire de la Floride, ou Relation de ce qui s'est passé au Voyage Ferdinand de Soto.* Paris.

GAROTTI, L. R. 1961. *Locke e i suoi Problemi.* Urbino.

GEE, EDWARD, 1658. *Divine Right and Original of the Civil Magistrate.*

GERRITSEN, JOHAN, 1954. *See* Laslett, 1954 (ii).

GETTEL, R. R. 1970. *History of Political Thought*, ed. L. C. Wanlass.

GIERKE, OTTO VON, 1934. *Natural Law and the Theory of Society*, tr. and ed. Barker, Sir Ernest. 2 vols. Cambridge.

GOLDIE, MARK, 1977. Edmund Bohun and *ius gentium* in the revolution debate, 1689–93, *Historical Journal*, XX, 3.

GOLDIE, MARK, 1980. The Revolution of 1689 and the Structure of Political Argument, *Bulletin of Research in the Humanities*, 83.

GOLDIE, MARK, 1983. John Locke and Anglican Royalism, *Political Studies*, XXXI, 1.

GOLDWIN, R. A. 1963. John Locke. In Strauss and Cropsey, eds., *History of Political Philosophy*. Chicago.

GOUGH, J. W. 1950. *John Locke's Political Philosophy, Eight Studies.* Oxford.

GOUGH, J. W. 1976. James Tyrrell, 'Whig historian and friend of John Locke', *Historical Journal*, XIX, 3.

GREEN, T. H. 1895 (1931). *Lectures on the Principles of Political Obligation.*

GREENLEAF, W. H. 1966. Filmer's Patriarchal History, *Historical Journal*, IX, 2.

GROTIUS, HUGO, 1625 (1712). *De Jure Belli ac Pacis, Libri tres . . . Editio Novissima.* Amsterdam.

GWYN, W. B. 1965. The Meaning of the Separation of Powers. An Analysis of the Doctrine from its Origin to the Adoption of the United States Constitution, *Tulane Studies in Political Science*, IX.

HALEY, K. H. D. 1968. *The First Earl of Shaftesbury.* Oxford.

HALL, R. and WOOLHOUSE, R. 1983. *Eighty years of Locke Scholarship: A Bibliographical Guide.* Edinburgh.

HAMPSHIRE-MONK, I. 1978. *Resistance and Economy* in Dr. Anglim's Locke, *Political Studies*, XXVI.

HARRISON, JOHN and LASLETT, PETER, 1971. *The Library of John Locke.* Oxford. (Second edition of a work published in 1965 by the Oxford Bibliographical Society, New Series, Volume XIII. Oxford.)

HINTON, R. W. K. 1968. Husbands, Fathers and Conquerors. Patriarchalism in Hobbes and Locke, *Political Studies*, XVI, 1.

HINTON, R. W. K. 1974. A note on the dating of Locke's Second Treatise, *Political Studies*, XXII, 4.

HINTON, R. W. K. 1977. On recovering the Original of the Second Treatises, *The Locke Newsletter*, VIII.

HOBBES, THOMAS, 1651 (1904). *Leviathan.* [Facsimile reprint, ed. Waller, A. R., Cambridge, 1904.]

HOBBES, THOMAS, 1647 (1651). *De Cive.* In Molesworth, W., *English Works*, vol. II.

HOBBES, THOMAS, 1984 (1651). *De Cive*, ed. Warrender, H. Oxford.

HOTTS, THOMAS, *see* Blackburne, Francis.

HOOKER, RICHARD, 1632. *Of the Lawes of Ecclesiasticall Politie.*

HOOKER, RICHARD, 1666. *The Works of Mr R. Hooker.*

HOOKER, RICHARD, 1836. *Works*, a new edition by Keble, John. 3 vols. Oxford.

HUNDERT, E. J. 1972. The making of Homo faber: John Locke between ideology and history, *Journal of the History of Ideas*, XXXIII, 1.

HUNDERT, E. J. 1977. Market society and meaning in Locke's political philosophy, *Journal of the History of Philosophy*, XV.

HUNTON, PHILIP, 1643. *A Treatise of Monarchie.*

JAMES I. *see* McIlwain, C. H.

JENKINS, J. J. 1967. Locke and Natural Rights, *Philosophy*.

JOHNSON, MERVYN S. 1978. *Locke on Freedom, an Incisive Study of the Thought of John Locke.* Austin.

JOHNSTON, Mrs C. M. (*née* Ware), 1954. A Note on an Early Draft of Locke's *Essay, Mind*, no. 250.

JOHNSTON, Mrs C. M. (*née* Ware), 1956. Unpublished thesis for D.Phil., Bibliography of Locke's Philosophical Works, Bodleian Library, Oxford.

JOLLEY, N. 1972. Leibniz's critique of Locke. PhD dissertation, Cambridge.

JOLLEY, N. 1975. Leibniz on Hobbes, Locke's *Two Treatises* and Sherlock's *Case of Allegiance, Historical Journal*, XVIII, 1.

JOLLEY, N. 1984. *Leibniz and Locke: A Study of the New Essays on Human Understanding*. Oxford.

JONES, J. R. 1961. *The First Whigs: The Politics of the Exclusion Crisis, 1678–1683*.

JONES, J. R. 1978. *Country and Court: England 1658–1714.* Harvard.

JURIEU, PIERRE, 1689. *Lettres Pastorales, Adressées aux Fidèles de France qui Gémissent sous la Captivité de Babylone.* Amsterdam.

JUSTINUS, 1543. *Ex Trogi Pompei, historiis, libri* XXXIIII. Paris.

KELLY, P. 1969. The economic writings of John Locke. Dissertation, University of Cambridge.

KELLY, P. 1977. Locke and Filmer: was Laslett so wrong after all?, *The Locke Newsletter*, VIII.

KENDALL, WILLMOORE, 1941. John Locke and the doctrine of majority-rule, *Illinois Studies in the Social Sciences*, XXVI, 2, Urbana, Ill., U.S.A.

KENDALL, WILLMOORE, 1966. John Locke Revisited, *The Intercollegiate Review*, II, 4, pp. 217–34.

KENYON, J. P. 1974. The Revolution of 1688, resistance and contract. In McKendrick, N., ed., *Historical Perspectives, in Honour of J. H. Plumb*.

KENYON, J. P. 1977. *Revolution Principles: The Politics of Party 1689–1720.* Cambridge.

KING, PETER (7th Lord King), 1829 (1830). *The Life of John Locke, with Extracts from his Correspondence, Journals and Commonplace Books.* 1830 ed., 2 vols.

KLIBANSKY, R. and GOUGH, J. W. 1968. *John Locke, Epistola de Tolerantia.* Oxford.

KNOX, ROBERT, 1681. *An Historical Relation of the Island of Ceylon.*

LAMPRECHT, S.P. 1918. *The Moral and Political Philosophy of John Locke* (Archives of Philosophy, no. 11). New York.

LARKIN, P. 1930. *Property in the 18th Century, with Special Reference to England and Locke.* Cork.

LASLETT, PETER, 1948 (i). The Gentry of Kent in 1640, *Cambridge Historical Journal*, IX, 2.

LASLETT, PETER, 1948 (ii). Sir Robert Filmer, *William and Mary Quarterly*, 3rd Ser. V, 4, October.

LASLETT, PETER, 1949. Patriarcha *and other Political Works of Sir Robert Filmer* (Blackwell's Political Texts). Oxford.

LASLETT, PETER, 1952 (i). Locke and the first Earl of Shaftesbury, *Mind*, no. 241, January.

LASLETT, PETER, 1952 (ii). Letter in *Times Literary Supplement*, July.

LASLETT, PETER, 1952 (iii). Lord Masham's Library at Otes. Letter in *Times Literary Supplement*, August.

LASLETT, PETER, 1952 (iv). The 1690 Edition of Locke's *Two Treatises of Government, Transactions of the Cambridge Bibliographical Society*, 1, 4.

LASLETT, PETER, 1954 (i). Masham of Otes. In Quennell, P. ed., *Diversions of History.*[1]

LASLETT, PETER, 1954 (ii). Further Observations on Locke's *Two Treatises of Government*, 1690. With Bowers, Fredson, and Gerritsen, Johan, *Transactions of the Cambridge Bibliographical Society*, II, 1.

LASLETT, PETER, 1956. The English Revolution and Locke's *Two Treatises of Government, Cambridge Historical Journal*, XII, 1.

LASLETT, PETER, 1957 (i). John Locke, the Great Recoinage and the Board of Trade, 1695–1698, *William and Mary Quarterly*, 3rd. ser. XIV, 3, July. [*See* Laslett, 1969.]

LASLETT, PETER, 1957 (ii). The Library of John Locke. With Harrison, J. R. *Times Literary Supplement*, December.

LASLETT, PETER, 1964. *Market Society and Political Theory* Review of Macpherson, 1962. *Historical Journal* VII.

LASLETT, PETER, 1983. (1965). *The World we have lost, English Society before and after the Coming of Industry.*

LASLETT, PETER, 1965. *See* Harrison, John.

LASLETT, PETER, 1969. [Republication, with some corrections, of Laslett, 1957 (i). In Yolton, 1969.]

LASLETT, PETER, 1977. The conversation between the generations. In Laslett, P. and Fishkin, J. eds., *Philosophy, Politics and Society*, 5th Series.

LAWRENCE, WILLIAM, 1680, 1681. *Marriage by the Morall Law of God Vindicated*. [Published in two parts in these years (second entitled *The Right of Primogeniture in Succession to the Kingdoms of England and Scotland*), but one work.]

LAWSON, GEORGE, 1657. *An Examination of the Political Part of Mr Hobbs his* Leviathan.

LAWSON, GEORGE, 1660 (1689). *Politica Sacra et Civilis.*

LE CLERC, JEAN, 1686–   . [Editor] *La Bibliothèque Universelle*, Amsterdam, Wolfgang.

LE CLERC, JEAN, 1705. Eloge du Feu Mr Locke. *Bibliothèque Choisie*, VI, V.

[1] Reprinted from *History Today*, III, 8, August 1953.

LEITES, E. 1981. Locke's liberal Theory of Parenthood. In Brandt, 1981.

LERY, JEAN DE, 1578. *Histoire d'un Voyage fait en la Terre du Bresil.* La Rochelle.

[LESLIE, CHARLES,] 1698. *Considerations of Importance to Mr Molyneux's late Book.*

LETWIN, WILLIAM, 1963. *The Origins of Scientific Economics: English Economic Thought 1660–1776.*

LEWIS, H. D., 1940. Is there a Social Contract? *Philosophy.*

LOCKE, JOHN

   Collected Works

      1714. 3 vols., Fo. 1801. 10 vols., 8vo.

      1720. *A Collection of Several Pieces of Mr John Locke*, published by Mr Desmaiseaux under the direction of Anthony Collins.

   Individual Works, Separate Publications

      Essay (1690)

      1706. 5th edition, Fo.

      1894. (Ed. Fraser, A. C., 2 vols.) Oxford.

      1961. *Everyman* Edition, by Yolton, J. W.

      1975. (ed. Nidditch, P.) Oxford.

   Two Treatises (1690)

   Toleration

      Epistola de Tolerantia (1689) 1968 (ed. Klibansky, R. and Gough, J. W.) Oxford.

      Education (1693)

      1968. Critical edition, *see* Axtell, J. L.

   Economic Writings

      1969. Critical edition, *see* Kelly, P.

   All other published works cited from one of the collected editions. (*See* Aaron, Abrams, Rand, Von Leyden, for works published from manuscript.)

LONG, P. 1959. A Summary Catalogue of the Lovelace Collection of the Papers of John Locke in the Bodleian Library, *Oxford Bibliographical Society*, New Series, VIII.

LUTHER, MARTIN, 1520 (1888). Sermon von den guten Werken. In *Werke*, VI. Weimar.

MABBOTT, J. D., 1948. *The State and the Citizen.*

MACE, GEORGE. 1979. *Locke, Hobbes, and the Federalist Papers: An Essay on the Genesis of the American Political Heritage.* Illinois.

McILWAIN, C. H. 1918. *The Political Works of James I.* Cambridge, Mass., U.S.A.

McILWAIN, C. H. 1935 (1939). A Forgotten Worthy: Philip Hunton. Reprinted in *Constitutional and the Changing World*. Cambridge.

McKERROW, R. B. 1939. *Prolegomena for the Oxford Shakespeare: A Study in Editorial Method.* Oxford.

MACLEAN, A. H. 1947 (i). Unpublished Ph.D. dissertation on Locke as a political writer, Cambridge University Library.

MACLEAN, A. H. 1947 (ii). George Lawson and John Locke, *Cambridge Historical Journal*, IX, 1.

MACPHERSON, C. B. 1951. Locke on Capitalist Appropriation, *Western Political Quarterly*, IV, 4.

MACPHERSON, C. B., 1954. The Social Bearing of Locke's Political Theory, *Western Political Quarterly*, VII, 1.

MACPHERSON, C. B. 1962. *The Political Theory of Possessive Individualism*. Oxford.

MACPHERSON, C. B. 1967. Natural Rights in Hobbes and Locke. *Political Theory and the Rights of Man*, ed. Raphael, D. D.

MANWARING (OR MAYNWARING), ROGER, 1627. *Religion and Allegiance in Two Sermons*.

MARINI, F. 1969. John Locke and the Revision of Classical Liberalism, *Western Political Quarterly*, XXVII.

MARVELL, ANDREW, 1672. *The Rehearsal Transposed*.

MASHAM, DAMARIS, 1705 (1955–6). Letter to Jean le Clerc on Locke's life, University of Amsterdam MSS. J. 57a (*see* Colie, Rosalie, for publication).

MEDICK, H. 1973. *Naturzustand und Naturgeschichte der bürgerliche Gesellschaft. Die Ursprung der bürgerliche Sozialtheorie als Geschichtsphilosophie und Sozialwissenschaft bei Samuel Pufendorf, John Locke und Adam Smith*. Göttingen.

MENAKE, G. T. 1981. Research note and query on the dating of Locke's *Two Treatises, Political Theory*, IX.

MENAKE, G. T. 1982. . . . a sequel, *Political Theory*, X.

MILAM, MAX, 1967. The Epistemological Basis of Locke's Idea of Property, *Western Political Quarterly* XXI.

MIRROR, THE, 1642. *Mirroir des Justices* [? by Horne, Andrew].

MOLYNEUX, WILLIAM, 1698 (1720). *The Case of Ireland's being Bound by Acts of Parliament in England*. Dublin (1720 ed. London).

MONSON, C. H. 1958. Locke and his Interpreters, *Political Studies*, VI, 2.

MORE, Sir THOMAS, 1663. *Utopiae Libri Duo*. Oxford.

MOULDS, H. 1961. John Locke's Four Freedoms, *Ethics*, LXXI, 2.

MOULDS, H. 1965. John Locke and Rugged Individualism. *American Journal of Economics and Sociology*, XXIV.

MOYLE, WALTER, 1698 (1727). An Essay on the Lacedæmonian Government Addressed to Anthony Hammond, Esq. In *The Whole Works of Walter Moyle, Esq*. [edited by] Anthony Hammond, Esq. 1727. (*See* Robbins, 1968).

MURRAY, J. G. 1969. A Paradox in Locke's Theory of Natural Rights, *Dialogue*, VIII.

NELSON, J. 1978. Unlocking Locke's *Legacy*: a Comment, *Political Studies*.

NOZICK, R. 1974. *Anarchy, State and Utopia*. Oxford.

OGG, DAVID, 1934 (2nd ed. 1955). *England in the Reign of Charles II*. 2 vols. Oxford.

OLIVECRONA, KARL, 1974 (i). Locke on the origin of property, *Journal of the History of Ideas*, XXXV, 2.

OLIVECRONA, KARL, 1974 (ii). Locke's theory of appropriation, *Philosophical Quarterly*, XXIV and XCVI.

OLIVECRONA, KARL, 1975 (i). An insertion in para. 25 of the Second Treatise of Government?, *The Locke Newsletter*, VI.

OLIVECRONA, KARL, 1975 (ii). The term 'property' in Locke's Two Treatises of Government, *Archiv für Rechts-und Sozialphilosophie*, LXI.

OLIVECRONA, KARL, 1976. A note on Locke and Filmer, *The Locke Newsletter*, VII.

OSLER, SIR WILLIAM, 1914. [Editor of letter of Locke to Thomas Herbert, 8th Earl of Pembroke, with note on Locke's cure of the 1st Earl of Shaftesbury, *Oxford Magazine*, 1914, March.]

OXFORD UNIVERSITY, JUDGMENT OF, 1683 (1812). The Judgment of the University of Oxford . . . against Certain Pernicious Books and Damnable Doctrines. In *Somers Tracts*, 2nd edition by Walter Scott, VIII.

PAREYSON, L. 1948. [Critical edition of *Two Treatises* in Italian.]

PARKER, SAMUEL, 1670. *A Discourse of Ecclesiastical Politie*.

PARRY, CLIVE, 1954. British Nationality Law and the History of Naturalization. Milan. *Communicazione e Studi* of the Institute of International Law in the University of Milan.

PARRY, GERAINT, 1964. Individuality, Politics and the Critique of Paternalism in John Locke, *Political Studies*.

PARRY, GERAINT, 1978. *John Locke*.

PEMBROKE, THOMAS HERBERT, 8th Earl of, 1683. Letter to Locke of 3 December 1683. See Osler, Sir William.

PETTY, SIR WILLIAM, 1662. *A Treatise of Taxes and Contributions*.

PIETRANEA, GIULIO, 1957. Le teoria del valore di Locke e di Petty, *Societá*.

PITKIN, HANNA, 1965, 1966. Obligation and Consent, *American Political Science Review*.

PLAMENATZ, J. P. 1936. *Consent, Freedom and Political Obligation*, Oxford.

PLAMENATZ, J. P. 1963. *Man and Society*, Vol. I, Chap. 6.

POCOCK, J. G. A. 1957. *The Ancient Constitution and the Feudal Law*. Cambridge.

POCOCK, J. G. A. 1986. The Myth of John Locke and the Obsession with Liberalism. In Pocock, J. G. A. and Ashcraft, R., eds., *John Locke*. Los Angeles.

POLIN, RAYMOND, 1960. *La Politique Morale de John Locke*. Paris.

POLIN, RAYMOND, 1963. Justice in Locke's Philosophy. In Friedrich, C. H. and Chapman, J. W. eds. *Nomos VI Justice*, New York.

POLIN, RAYMOND, 1969. *John Locke's Conception of Freedom*. In Yolton, 1969.

POLLOCK, Sir FREDERICK, 1890, etc. *Introduction to the History of the Science of Politics*.

POLLOCK, Sir FREDERICK, 1904. Locke's Theory of the State, *Proceedings of the British Academy*, 1.

POOLE, ROSS. 1980. Locke and the Bourgeois State, *Political Studies*, XXVIII, 2.

POST, D. M. 1986. Jeffersonian Revisions of Locke; Education, Property-Rights, and Liberty, *Journal of the History of Ideas*.

PRIDEAUX, HUMPHREY, 1875. *Letters . . . to John Ellis*, ed. Thompson, E. M. (Camden Society).

Proposals humbly offered to the Lords and Commons in the Present Convention, *State Tracts*, 1693, Vol. II, pp. 455–7.

PUFENDORF, SAMUEL VON, 1660 (1672). *Elementa, Elementorum Jurisprudentiæ Universalis Libri Duo*. (1672 editio novissima, Cambridge.)

PUFENDORF, SAMUEL VON, 1672. *De Jure Naturae et Gentium Libri Octo*. Lund.

PUFENDORF, SAMUEL VON, 1688 (1934). *De Jure Naturale et Gentium Libri Octo*. Latin and English edition, 2 vols., tr. C. H. Oldfather and W. A. Oldfather. Oxford.

PUFENDORF, SAMUEL VON, 1706 (1734). *Le Droit de la Nature et des Gens . . .* , par le baron de Pufendorf, traduit du Latin avec des notes par Jean Barbeyrac (5th ed. 2 vols. Amsterdam).

RAND, BENJAMIN, 1927. *The Correspondence of John Locke and Edward Clarke*. Oxford.

RAND, BENJAMIN, 1931. *An Essay Concerning the Understanding, Knowledge, Opinion and Assent*. Cambridge, Mass., U.S.A. (Draft B of Locke's Essay.)

RAU, ZBIGNIEW, 1987. Some thoughts on civil society in Eastern Europe and the Lockean contractarian approach, *Political Studies*, XXXV.

RILEY, PATRICK, 1974. On finding an equilibrium between consent and natural law in Locke's political philosophy, *Political Studies*, XXII.

ROBBINS, CAROLINE, 1950. Thomas Hollis. *The William and Mary Quarterly*.

ROBBINS, CAROLINE, 1968. *Two English Republican Tracts*. [Nevile, Plato Redivivus; Moyle, Roman Government.] Cambridge.

RONALDS, FRANCIS, S. 1937. *The Attempted Whig Revolution of 1678–1681*. Illinois Studies in Social Studies.

RUSSELL, PAUL, 1986. Locke on Express and Tacit Consent: Misinterpretations and Inconsistencies, *Political Theory*, XIV, 2.

RYAN, ALAN, 1965. Locke and the Dictatorship of the Bourgeoisie, *Political Studies*.

SABINE, GEORGE, H. 1961. *A History of Political Theory*. New York.

SADLER, JOHN, 1649 (1682). *Rights of the Kingdom*.

SAGARD, GABRIEL, 1636. *Histoire du Canada*. Paris.

SAGARD, GABRIEL, 1632. *Le Grand Voyage du Pays des Hurons*. Paris.

SALMON, J. H. M. 1959. *The French Religious Wars in English Political Thought*. Oxford.

SALMON, J. H. M. 1982. An Alternative Theory of popular resistance: Buchanan, Rossaeus and Locke. In *Diritto es Potere nella Storia Europea*. Florence.

SANDERSON, ROBERT, 1660 (1696). *De Obligatione Conscientiae Praelectiones Decem*.

SCHLATTER, R. B. 1951. *Private Property: The History of an Idea*.

SCHLATTER, R. B. 1957. *Richard Baxter and Puritan Politics*. New Brunswick, N.J., U.S.A.

SCHOCHET, G. J. 1966. The Patriarchal Content of Stuart Political Thought. Unpublished Ph.D. dissertation, University of Minnesota.

SCHOCHET, G. J. 1969. *The Family and the Origins of the State in Locke's Political Philosophy*. In Yolton, 1969.

SCHOCHET, GORDON, J. ed. 1971. *Life, Liberty and Property: Essays on Locke's Political Ideas*. Belmont, California.

SCHOCHET, GORDON, J. 1975. *Patriarchalism in Political Thought*. Oxford.

SELDEN, JOHN, 1635 (1652). *Mare Clausum, Seu de Dominio Maris Libri Duo* (tr. Nedham, Marchamont, 1652).

SELIGER, M. 1963 (i). Locke's Theory of Revolutionary Action, *Western Political Quarterly*.

SELIGER, M. 1963 (ii). Locke's Natural Law, *Journal of the History of Ideas*.

SELIGER, M. 1968. *The Liberal Politics of John Locke*.

SELIGER, M. 1969. *Locke, Liberalism and Nationalism*. In Yolton, 1969.

SHAFTESBURY PAPERS, Public Record Office: old class-number, GD 24, present class-number, P.R.O. 30. (References are made to P.R.O. 30, bundle number in roman figures, item number in arabic figures.)

SHAFTESBURY, ANTHONY ASHLEY COOPER, 1st Earl of, 1689 (1812). Some Observations Concerning the Regulation of Elections for Parliament, found among the Earl of Shaftesbury's papers. In *Somers Tracts*, 2nd ed. by Walter Scott, 396–402. (No indication of Shaftesbury's authorship.)

SHAFTESBURY, ANTHONY ASHLEY COOPER, 3rd Earl of, 1705 (1851). Letter of February 1705, to Jean Le Clerc, *Notes and Queries*, 1st ser. 1851, 1.

SHANLEY, M. L. 1979. Marriage Contract and Social Contract in Seventeenth Century English Political Thought, *The Western Political Quarterly*, XXXII, 1.

SHIMOKAWA, KIYOSHI, 1986. A Critique of Laslett's treatment of the *Two Treatises*, *The Locke Newsletter*, XVI.

SIBTHORPE (or SYBTHORPE), ROBERT, 1627. *Apostolike Obedience Shewing the Duty of Subjects . . . Sermon.*

SIDNEY, ALGERNON, 1698 (1772). *Discourses Concerning Government.* In *The Works of Algernon Sydney, a New Edition* [ed. by Joseph Robertson, pub. by Thomas Hollis], 1772.

SIMON, W. M. 1951. John Locke, philosophy and political theory, *American Political Science Review*, XLV, 2, June.

SINGH, R. 1961. John Locke and the theory of natural law, *Political Studies*, IX, 2.

SKINNER, QUENTIN, 1965 (i). Hobbes on Sovereignty: An unknown discussion, *Political Studies*, XIII, 2.

SKINNER, QUENTIN, 1965 (ii). History and Ideology in the English Revolution, *Historical Journal*, VIII, 2.

SKINNER, QUENTIN, 1966 (i). The Ideological Context of Hobbes's Political Thought, *Historical Journal*, IX, 3.

SKINNER, QUENTIN, 1966 (ii). Thomas Hobbes and His Disciples in France and England, *Comparative Studies in Society and History*, VIII, 2.

SKINNER, QUENTIN, 1978. *The Foundations of Modern Political Thought*, 2 vols., Cambridge.

SMITH, CONSTANCE, J. 1963. Filmer and the Knolles Translation of Bodin, *Philosophical Quarterly*, XIII.

SMITH, JOHN, 1616. *Description of New England.*

SMYRNIADES, I., 1921. *Les Doctrines de Hobbes, Locke et Kant sur le Droit de l'Insurrection.* Paris.

SNOW, VERNON F. 1962. The Concept of Revolution in Seventeenth-century England. *Historical Journal*, V, 2.

SNYDER, D. C. 1986. Locke on Natural Law and Property Rights, *Canadian Journal of Philosophy*, XVI.

SOMERS, JOHN (Lord Somers), 1701. *Jura Populi Anglicani, or The Subject's Right of Petitioning.*

STATE TRACTS, 1692. *State Tracts, being a Farther Collection of Several Choice Treatises Relating to the Government 1660–1689.*

STEPHEN, Sir JAMES FITZJAMES, 1892. *Horae Sabbaticae*, 2nd Ser. (Reprint of articles from *The Saturday Review*).

STEPHEN, Sir LESLIE, 1876 (1902). *History of English Thought in the Eighteenth Century*, 2 vols. (3rd ed. 1902).

STILLINGFLEET, EDWARD, 1681. *The Unreasonableness of Separation.*

STRAKA, G. M. 1962. The Final Phase of Divine Right Theory in England, 1688–1702, *English Historical Review*, LXXVII.

STRAKA, G. M. 1962. *Anglican Reaction to the Revolution of 1688*. Madison.

STRAUSS, LEO, 1953. *Natural Right and History*. Chicago. (202–51 on Locke.)

STUBBE, HENRY, 1659. *An Essay in Defence of the Good Old Cause*.

STUBBE, HENRY, 1659. *A Light Shining Out of Darkness*.

TARCOV, NATHAN, 1984. *Locke's Education for Liberty*. Chicago.

TARLTON, CHARLES D. 1978. Rpe of sand: interpreting Locke's *First Treatise of Government, Historical Journal* , xxi, 1.

TARLTON, CHARLES D. 1981. The Exclusion Controversy, Pamphleteering, and Locke's *Two Treatises, Historical Journal*, xxiv, 1.

TARLTON, CHARLES D. 1985. The rulers now on earth: Locke's Two Treatises and the Revolution of 1688, *Historical Journal*, xxviii.

TEMPLE, SIR WILLIAM, 1680 (1757). *An Essay upon the Original and Nature of Government*. (Published in *Miscellanea*, 1680: in vol. 1 of *Works* (4 vols.), 1757.)

TENISON, THOMAS, 1670. *The Creed of Mr Hobbes Examined*.

TERRY, EDWARD, 1655. *A Voyage to East-India*.

THOMPSON, MARTYN P. 1976 (i). The reception of Locke's *Two Treatises of Government, Political Studies*, xxiv, 2.

THOMPSON, MARTYN P. 1976 (ii). On dating Chapter XVI of the Second Treatise of Government, *The Locke Newsletter*, vii.

THOMPSON, MARTYN P. 1979. Reception and influence: A reply to Nelson on Locke's *Two Treatises of Government, Political Studies*, xxvii.

THOMSON, M. A. 1938. *Constitutional History of England, 1642–1801*.

TUCK, RICHARD, 1979. *Natural Rights Theories: Their Origin and Development*. Cambridge.

TUCK, RICHARD, 1986. A New Date for Filmer's Patriarcha, *Historical Journal*, xxix, 1.

TUCKER, JOSIAH, 1781. *A Treatise Concerning Civil Government*.

TULLY, JAMES, 1980. *A Discourse on Property: John Locke and his Adversaries*. Cambridge.

TYNDALE, WILLIAM, 1528 (1848). The obedience of a Christian man. (In *Doctrinal Treatises*, Parker Society, Cambridge.)

TYRRELL, JAMES, 1681. *Patriarcha non Monarcha*.

TYRRELL, JAMES, 1691/2 (1718). *Bibliotheca Politica*.

TYRRELL, JAMES, 1692. *A Brief Disquisition of the Law of Nature, According to the Principle and Method laid down in Dr Cumberland . . . as also his confutation of Mr Hobs principles put into another method*.

VAUGHAN, C. E. 1925. *Studies in the History of Political Philosophy before and after Rousseau*. 2 vols. Manchester. (1, 130–204: *The Social Contract*, Locke.)

VAUGHAN, K. I. 1980. *John Locke. Economist and Social Scientist*. Chicago.

VIANO, C. A., 1960. *John Locke, dal Razionalismo all'Illuminismo*. Turin.

Vindiciae contra Tyrannos (by Brutus, pseud.), 1579. Edinburgh [Basel].

VINER, JACOB, 1963. Possessive Individualism as Original Sin, *The Canadian Journal of Economics and Political Science.*

VON LEYDEN, WOLFGANG, 1954. *John Locke, Essays on the Law of Nature.* Oxford.

VON LEYDEN, WOLFGANG, 1956. John Locke and Natural Law, *Philosophy*, XXXI, January.

VON LEYDEN, WOLFGANG, 1981. *Hobbes and Locke.*

VOX REGIS, 1681 (1808). [Anon.] *Vox Regis, or the Difference betwixt a King Ruling by Law and a Tyrant by His own Will . . . in Two Speeches of King James to the Parliaments in 1603 . . . 1609 . . . Appendix to Vox Populi.* (In Harleian Miscellany, vol. III.)

VOX POPULI, 1681 [Anon.] *Vox Populi, or the People's Claim to their Parliament's Sitting.*

WAINWRIGHT, ARTHUR. 1987. *John Locke, A Paraphrase and Notes on the Epistles of St Paul.* Oxford.

WALDMANN, M , 1959. A Note on John Locke's Theory of Consent, *Ethics*, LXVIII, 1.

WALDRON, JEREMY, 1984. Locke, Tully, and the Regulation of Property, *Political Studies*, XXXII, 1.

WALLACE, J. 1957. *The Political Philosophy of Hobbes: his theory of Obligation.* Oxford.

WALLACE, JOHN, M. 1980. The date of Sir Robert Filmer's *Patriarcha*, *Historical Journal*, XXIII, 1.

WARRENDER, J. 1957. *The Political Philosophy of Hobbes: His Theory of Obligation.* Oxford.

WESTERN, J. R. 1972. *Monarchy and Revolution: The English State in the 1680s.*

WESTON, C. C. and GREENBERG, J. R. 1981. *Subjects and Sovereigns: The Grand Controversy over Legal Sovereignty in Stuart England.* Cambridge.

WHITEHOUSE COLLECTION (papers of Locke in the possession of the late J. Howard Whitehouse, lately in care of Bembridge School, Isle of Wight, now in the Bodleian Library, Oxford, MS Locke b. 8).

WILLIS, RICHARD, 1697. [Anon.] *The Occasional Paper*, nos. 1–6.

WINDSTRUP, GEORGE, 1980. Locke on suicide, *Political Theory*, May.

WOLIN, SHELDON, 1960. *Politics and Vision.* Boston, Mass.

WOOD, NEAL, 1983. *The Politics of Locke's Philosophy: A Social Study of* An Essay Concerning Human Understanding. California.

WOOD, NEAL, 1984. *John Locke and Agarian Capitalism.* California.

WOODHOUSE, A. S. P. 1951 (1938). *Puritanism and Liberty, being the Army Debate* (1647–9).

WREN, MATTHEW, 1659. *Monarchy Asserted.*

YOLTON, J. W. 1955. Locke and the Seventeenth Century Logic of Ideas, *Journal of the History of Ideas*, XVI, 4, October.

YOLTON, J. W. 1956. *John Locke and the Way of Ideas.* Oxford.

YOLTON, J. W. 1958. Locke on the Law of Nature, *Philosophical Review*, October.

YOLTON, Y. W. 1961. *See* Locke, *Essay.*

YOLTON, J. W., ed. 1969. *John Locke: Problems and Perspectives.* Cambridge.

YOLTON, J. W. 1970. *Locke and the Compass of the Understanding.* Cambridge.

ZAGORIN, P. 1954. *A History of Political Thought in the English Revolution.*

INDEX

Cambridge Texts in the History of Political Thought

Titles published in the series thus far

Aristotle *The Politics and The Constitution of Athens* (edited by Stephen Everson)
  0 521 48400 6 paperback
Arnold *Culture and Anarchy and other writings* (edited by Stefan Collini)
  0 521 37796 X paperback
Astell *Political Writings* (edited by Patricia Springborg)
  0 521 42845 9 paperback
Augustine *The City of God against the Pagans* (edited by R.W. Dyson)
  0 521 46843 4 paperback
Austin *The Province of Jurisprudence Determined* (edited by Wilfrid E. Rumble)
  0 521 44756 9 paperback
Bacon *The History of the Reign of King Henry VII* (edited by Brian Vickers)
  0 521 58663 1 paperback
Bakunin *Statism and Anarchy* (edited by Marshall Shatz)
  0 521 36973 8 paperback
Baxter *Holy Commonwealth* (edited by William Lamont)
  0 521 40580 7 paperback
Bayle *Political Writings* (edited by Sally L. Jenkinson)
  0 521 47677 1 paperback
Beccaria *On Crimes and Punishments and other writings* (edited by Richard Bellamy)
  0 521 47982 7 paperback
Bentham *Fragment on Government* (introduction by Ross Harrison)
  0 521 35929 5 paperback
Bernstein *The Preconditions of Socialism* (edited by Henry Tudor)
  0 521 39808 8 paperback
Bodin *On Sovereignty* (edited by Julian H. Franklin)
  0 521 34992 3 paperback
Bolingbroke *Political Writings* (edited by David Armitage)
  0 521 78697 6 paperback
Bossuet *Politics Drawn from the Very Words of Holy Scripture*
(edited by Patrick Riley)
  0 521 36807 3 paperback
The British Idealists (edited by David Boucher)
  0 521 45951 6 paperback
Burke *Pre-Revolutionary Writings* (edited by Ian Harris)
  0 521 36800 6 paperback
Christine De Pizan *The Book of the Body Politic* (edited by Kate Langdon Forhan)
  0 521 42259 0 paperback
Cicero *On Duties* (edited by M. T. Griffin and E. M. Atkins)
  0 521 34835 8 paperback
Cicero *On the Commonwealth and On the Laws* (edited by James E. G. Zetzel)
  0 521 45959 1 paperback
Comte *Early Political Writings* (edited by H. S. Jones)
  0 521 46923 6 paperback

Conciliarism and Papalism (edited by J. H. Burns and Thomas M. Izbicki)
0 521 47674 7 paperback
Constant *Political Writings* (edited by Biancamaria Fontana)
0 521 31632 4 paperback
Dante *Monarchy* (edited by Prue Shaw)
0 521 56781 5 paperback
Diderot *Political Writings* (edited by John Hope Mason and Robert Wokler)
0 521 36911 8 paperback
The Dutch Revolt (edited by Martin van Gelderen)
0 521 39809 6 paperback
Early Greek Political Thought from Homer to the Sophists (edited by Michael
Gagarin and Paul Woodruff)
0 521 43768 7 paperback
The Early Political Writings of the German Romantics (edited by Frederick
C. Beiser)
0 521 44951 0 paperback
The English Levellers (edited by Andrew Sharp)
0 521 62511 4 paperback
Erasmus *The Education of a Christian Prince* (edited by Lisa Jardine)
0 521 58811 1 paperback
Fenelon *Telemachus* (edited by Patrick Riley)
0 521 45662 2 paperback
Ferguson *An Essay on the History of Civil Society* (edited by Fania Oz-Salzberger)
0 521 44736 4 paperback
Filmer *Patriarcha and Other Writings* (edited by Johann P. Sommerville)
0 521 39903 3 paperback
Fletcher *Political Works* (edited by John Robertson)
0 521 43994 9 paperback
Sir John Fortescue *On the Laws and Governance of England* (edited by Shelley
Lockwood)
0 521 58996 7 paperback
Fourier *The Theory of the Four Movements* (edited by Gareth Stedman Jones and
Ian Patterson)
0 521 35693 8 paperback
Gramsci *Pre-Prison Writings* (edited by Richard Bellamy)
0 521 42307 4 paperback
Guicciardini *Dialogue on the Government of Florence* (edited by Alison Brown)
0 521 45623 1 paperback
Harrington *The Commonwealth of Oceana* and *A System of Politics*
(edited by J. G. A. Pocock)
0 521 42329 5 paperback
Hegel *Elements of the Philosophy of Right* (edited by Allen W. Wood and
H. B. Nisbet)
0 521 34888 9 paperback
Hegel *Political Writings* (edited by Laurence Dickey and H. B. Nisbet)
0 521 45979 3 paperback

Marx *Later Political Writings* (edited by Terrell Carver)
0 521 36739 5 paperback
James Mill *Political Writings* (edited by Terence Ball)
0 521 38748 5 paperback
J. S. Mill *On Liberty*, with *The Subjection of Women* and *Chapters on Socialism*
(edited by Stefan Collini)
0 521 37917 2 paperback
Milton *Political Writings* (edited by Martin Dzelzainis)
0 521 34866 8 paperback
Montesquieu *The Spirit of the Laws* (edited by Anne M. Cohler, Basia Carolyn
Miller and Harold Samuel Stone)
0 521 36974 6 paperback
More *Utopia* (edited by George M. Logan and Robert M. Adams)
0 521 40318 9 paperback
Morris *News from Nowhere* (edited by Krishan Kumar)
0 521 42233 7 paperback
Nicholas of Cusa *The Catholic Concordance* (edited by Paul E. Sigmund)
0 521 56773 4 paperback
Nietzsche *On the Genealogy of Morality* (edited by Keith Ansell-Pearson)
0 521 40610 2 paperback
Paine *Political Writings* (edited by Bruce Kuklick)
0 521 66799 2 paperback
Plato *The Republic* (edited by G. R. F. Ferrari and Tom Griffith)
0 521 48443 X paperback
Plato *Statesman* (edited by Julia Annas and Robin Waterfield)
0 521 44778 X paperback
Price *Political Writings* (edited by D. O. Thomas)
0 521 40969 1 paperback
Priestley *Political Writings* (edited by Peter Miller)
0 521 42561 1 paperback
Proudhon *What is Property?* (edited by Donald R. Kelley and
Bonnie G. Smith)
0 521 40556 4 paperback
Pufendorf *On the Duty of Man and Citizen according to Natural Law*
(edited by James Tully)
0 521 35980 5 paperback
The Radical Reformation (edited by Michael G. Baylor)
0 521 37948 2 paperback
Rousseau *The Discourses and other early political writings* (edited by Victor
Gourevitch)
0 521 42445 3 paperback
Rousseau *The Social Contract and other later political writings* (edited by Victor
Gourevitch)
0 521 42446 1 paperback
Seneca *Moral and Political Essays* (edited by John Cooper and John Procope)
0 521 34818 8 paperback

Sidney *Court Maxims* (edited by Hans W. Blom, Eco Haitsma Mulier and Ronald Janse)

  0 521 46736 5 paperback

Sorel *Reflections on Violence* (edited by Jeremy Jennings)

  0 521 55910 3 paperback

Spencer *The Man versus the State* and *The Proper Sphere of Government* (edited by John Offer)

  0 521 43740 7 paperback

Stirner *The Ego and Its Own* (edited by David Leopold)

  0 521 45647 9 paperback

Thoreau *Political Writings* (edited by Nancy Rosenblum)

  0 521 47675 5 paperback

Utopias of the British Enlightenment (edited by Gregory Clacys)

  0 521 45590 1 paperback

Vitoria *Political Writings* (edited by Anthony Pagden and Jeremy Lawrance)

  0 521 36714 X paperback

Voltaire *Political Writings* (edited by David Williams)

  0 521 43727 X paperback

Weber *Political Writings* (edited by Peter Lassman and Ronald Speirs)

  0 521 39719 7 paperback

William of Ockham *A Short Discourse on Tyrannical Government* (edited by A. S. McGrade and John Kilcullen)

  0 521 35803 5 paperback

William of Ockham *A Letter to the Friars Minor and other writings* (edited by A. S. McGrade and John Kilcullen)

  0 521 35804 3 paperback

Wollstonecraft *A Vindication of the Rights of Men* and *A Vindication of the Rights of Woman* (edited by Sylvana Tomaselli)

  0 521 43633 8 paperback